A Bibliography of
American Sporting Books
1926-1985

A Bibliography of
American Sporting Books

1926-1985

By M. L. Biscotti

Foreword by
Gene Hill

Paintings by John Rice

Approved by
The Boone and Crockett Club

Meadow Run Press

MEADOW RUN PRESS INC.
P. O. BOX 370
FAR HILLS, NJ   07931

Foreword

There was a fine old shed on my farm near Princeton years ago that evolved into my office. Here was where I did my writing, surrounded by all my toys: shotguns, rifles, fly rods, all competing for corner space. The walls were almost solid book shelves with the odd painting by Ripley or print by Pleissner wedged in somehow. Books filled these shelves, were piled up by my big leather chair, were stacked on windowsills, and open floor space was becoming hard to find. Most visitors never said it out loud but I could see them thinking, "What do you need all this for?" Why indeed, dozens books on Africa when I'd been on several safaris; why a shelf on Atlantic salmon fishing when I'd fished most of the major rivers? Books on bears and birds and Yellowstone and elk were shuffled together like playing cards. Not a big collection, several hundred to a thousand perhaps, and I knew where every one was – almost.

I've always been a book person, not a collector really, but let's say a very eager and, most of the time, discriminate buyer. I believed in a sportsman having a broad representative collection of shooting and fishing books and a good selection of the necessary ancillary stuff: nature essays, travel, good fiction, memoirs – a little of everything.

My earliest outdoor interest was in the trapping columns of *Fur, Fish and Game*. My own trapping career began when I was about eight years old and lasted until I was in high school. My outdoor life seemed to languish from then through the army and college until the 1950's when I moved back to the country and tried to make up for lost time.

Outdoor books of general interest were still a relative novelty and along with acquiring all the new ones, there were the basics we had to have: Bergman's *Trout*, John Alden Knight's books on the woodcock and grouse, Queeny's *Prairie Wings* (which sold for fifteen dollars), Nash Buckingham's collections and the shooting how-to advice of Fred Etchen and Charley Askins. I thus acquired a good solid back-list of the earlier publications just as reference, or really, simply just to have. And if this sounds like a lot, you have to remember that most of these sold for around three dollars and could often be found for less.

The early outdoor writers, although well-educated for the most part, spent little effort on literary pretense. They were the self-styled experts and felt their job was mainly instructional. And I think they were right. Here we were, a whole generation of veterans or war workers who had been removed from the sporting life for a few critical years, a whole generation of young men who didn't know much about outdoor sports, but wanted to learn.

We read the books and dressed like the men in the photographs; neckties, high leather boots and a felt fedora were the choice for the bird field and about the same for the trout stream, changing the boots for ill-fitting and leaky waders. I also adopted pipe smoking, trying to add God-knows-what kind of charm to my slim and hollow image. But by dressing like "gentlemen" we added something to the outings that I think is lost today. Bird shooting and fly fishing were something special and we were going to honor it as best we could.

In the mid-1960's I was doing a lot of freelance outdoor writing myself with my main career as a copywriter in the advertising world. My time spent in the field trialing my Labrador retrievers and a modest amount of trapshooting added to my growing circle of friends, including a lot of the better known writers.

I lunched and week-ended with John Alden Knight, Larry Koller, Ed Zern, Lee Wulff among others. Oddly enough (though maybe not) they thought of themselves as primarily fishermen or shooters who wrote. With the exception of Jack O'Connor, who I saw whenever he came east, none of us ever discussed the craft of writing. Our chattering was exclusively about what we wrote about – dogs, game, guns, fishing and the like. The few almost pure storytellers like Col. Sheldon and Burton Spiller were very popular and influenced a coming surge of writing with the how-to woven into the narrative. Foster's wonderful *New England Grouse Shooting* comes to mind as one of the early ones, although there were others as well.

The general trend of outdoor writing overall, however, was toward the more and more technical. This was the era of new technology in rods, reels, fly-tying material as well as the increasing scientific study of the habits of the fish themselves. Almost overnight we went from bamboo and the classic rod makers to a brief flirtation with glass and then graphite – making the art of casting simpler and easier for all of us. The writing reflected this directly. We "matched the hatch" and we experimented with new flies and patterns. Our fly lines were another reason we could cast farther and fish faster and deeper water. We were literally in a new age.

Shooting and dogs were much the same, however. We had a blossoming of interest in field trials with both pointing dogs and retrievers and a few new books appeared as training techniques got modernized and adapted to the one- or two-dog owner. A few new shooting books came out, but with little to recommend them. The best shooting instructor still remains a box of shells. But the big game world was undergoing a change largely due to the writings of Jack O'Connor and Warren Page and the availability of superb big game hunts for very reasonable costs. In the early 1970's a first class two-week safari in Kenya, with about everything included, was well under six thousand dollars. Now and then a small volume on bird hunting made a showing, such as Havilah Babcock's work, and that of a few regional writers, though these were usually confined to the magazines. But this was the lull before the storm.

In the late 1970's outdoor writing made a subtle shift from the didactic to the more lyrical and literary. I suspect I was as responsible for this as anyone with the publication of a couple of books of outdoor essays that became quite popular. Other writers soon did the same and had equal success. No longer the shooter that wrote, we now had the writers that also shot.

As you might guess, the results were mixed, but shortly we were left with a dozen or so very distinguished writers – most of whom continue to delight us with their view of the fields, the waters and nature itself. Of this group we have a few serious writers who are top flight sportsmen and exceptional outdoor writers. Leading this little procession is Thomas McGuane and following behind are Jim Harrison, Russell Chatham, Guy de la Valdene and, most recently, Jeffrey Cardenas.

The emphasis has shifted from the technical means to success, to an acceptance of less of a "bag" and a far deeper appreciation of the little time we get to spend in the field. There is evolving a rejection of the ultra technical as the advantages in equipment and gadgetry we have now over less and less game seem overwhelming. Needless to say, today's odd political and social atmosphere has put both hunting and fishing under a certain critical scrutiny so now we see intellectual positions declared and defended.

In the end it will be the writers and the publishing world that will articulate a critical view of the field, advance necessary and immediate conservation issues, offer an acceptable and accountable ethos, and at the same time provide us, the readers, countless hours of enjoyment. I suspect that the small publishers will flourish, as they seem to be enterprises where a balance has been struck between pride and profit. They publish very fine and intelligent books for specific markets rather than mediocre books requiring mass sales. And just as an older generation of outdoor writers taught us returning servicemen the techniques of shooting and fishing, so will the outdoor writers of today show a younger generation how to deal with a rapidly changing environment – through books.

Gene Hill
May, 1997

Introduction

When the Boone and Crockett Club was formed by Theodore Roosevelt and several other sportsmen in 1887, one of its founding goals was to disseminate information, based on actual observation, about the wildlife and wilderness areas of America. Its members wrote about what they saw, and these publications were used as some of the source documents in shaping the early conservation efforts of America.

The last decade of the nineteenth century marked the beginning of a tremendous proliferation of books and periodicals aimed at the American sportsman. Some were fictionalized accounts, but many were actual observations written by authors who had a deep concern for preserving America's wilderness areas and wildlife. The twentieth century brought relative prosperity to many Americans, and they eagerly sought publications which would guide and inspire their leisure time activities.

By the end of the first quarter of the twentieth century, literally thousands of books, periodicals and pamphlets had been produced about hunting and conservation. John C. Phillips, naturalist, ornithologist and keen student of conservation believed a bibliography describing these works would be a useful tool for students of the subject, libraries and book collectors. After the early death of Charles Sheldon, Phillips obtained access to his extensive library and used it as the basis for his *American Game Mammals and Birds*, which was published in 1930. The importance of this book is immense, for Mr. Phillips recorded those early works that are now so scarce, that few have the opportunity to examine them except in private collections or in institutions.

Mr. Phillips' book listed titles published up to 1925. This date was at a time when the conservation movement in America had just begun. As President of the United States, Theodore Roosevelt spearheaded legislation that set aside huge tracts of American wilderness areas to preserve these resources for future generations. Other laws were enacted that would also help preserve game populations for future generations as well. In addition to the Boone and Crockett Club, other privately owned and funded conservation organizations like More Game Birds in America Foundation (later to become Ducks Unlimited) and the American Game Protective and Propagation Association (later to become the Wildlife Management Institute) were spreading the word about the subject to the American public.

From 1925 through the end of World War II, publications in this area appeared at a steady rate. Many of these are now regarded as important records of hunting and conservation at a time when game was abundant in areas of the country that were much less populated than at the present time. Books produced by commercial publishing firms in this period are now also becoming scarce; pamphlets and privately published works produced then, are even more scarce.

The real explosion in published material about conservation and hunting began after World War II, when returning servicemen enjoying economic prosperity, eagerly sought accounts of trips afield. Commercial publishers soon realized this demand and many produced dedicated series of books for the outdoorsman to enjoy. From 1950 to the present, thousands of items have been produced regarding conservation, hunting, angling and related matters.

The economic prosperity of the present has also enabled those so inclined to collect these books. Early out-of-print book dealers specializing in hunting and fishing books like Morris Heller, Ray Riling and Col. Henry Siegel began producing lists offering these books in the 1950's and 1960's. All of these men would also eventually produce important bibliographies recording those items in which they had a special interest. Two noted angling book collectors, Charles Wetzel and Henry Bruns wrote and published angling book bibliographies in this period as well. All of these are important books, but are relatively specific in their view.

Collectors in this area have become more discerning and have eagerly sought these bibliographies describing hunting, fishing and conservation books. There has not, however, been any book produced devoted to describing works on American game mammals and birds where John C. Phillips' book left off. This book attempts to fulfill that purpose.

It is the intention of this work to describe books and pamphlets published about American game mammals and birds between the years 1926 and 1985. Because the American hunter has provided such a huge contribution to conserving these animals, books about hunting are also listed and, indeed, make up a significant number of its entries.

The aim is to list all publications printed in the English language, regardless of the place of publication. Thus, a number of British, Canadian and even a few Australian entries are included, since all deal with the subject in North America. Books about firearms, particularly regarding their sporting use or regarding collecting various makes, are also included.

Bow hunting has become increasingly popular within the last fifty years, so archery works regarding hunting have also been included, but books about target archery have been omitted.

Books about hunting dogs have also been included, since the contribution these animals have made to the enjoyment of hunting and the outdoors has been immeasurable.

Foxhunting works have been included in this work (the subject expressed as a compound word is hunting for fox with the use of hounds and horses, without firearms). Ancillary to this are a number of histories of various American foxhunting clubs.

Those juvenile titles regarding the subject which are commonly encountered have also been listed, but certainly at least several hundred more children's books about various game animals were also produced in this time period that were not encountered.

General camping and woodcraft books were omitted, unless the author had a number of other titles appearing in the bibliography. Cookbooks about wild game also were omitted.

This edition of *A Bibliography of American Sporting Books* was produced as a tool for those wanting descriptions of books written on the subject. It should be used in conjunction with, and in addition to, several other bibliographies, including John C. Phillips' *American Game Mammals and Birds* (with later printings titled *A Bibliography of American Sporting Books*).

Descriptions provided here have had to be brief because of space limitations. Thus, relevant books published by The Derrydale Press have been listed, but much more detailed information can be obtained by reviewing the books written by Col. Henry Siegel or by Don Frazier.

Many of the authors listed in this work also wrote angling books, which are beyond the scope of this title. Annotations for authors who also had angling books published note that those angling titles can be found in another source.

Subject matter has been arranged alphabetically by author. Where obtainable, the year of the author's birth and death are also supplied. Beneath the author's name are listed the title or titles written. Following the title and subtitle, the following information is given for all books observed (titles without all of this information were not observed, but were recorded from reliable sources).

1)   Place of publication - A city is usually sufficient for identification (thus New York, Chicago, London, etc.) without listing a state as well. For smaller cities, the state is also listed.

2)   Year of publication of the first printing.

3)   Publisher - Publisher's names have been kept consistent throughout the book. These names appear here as they appear on the title pages of books they published. The same publisher, however, sometimes changed its name, and these name changes have been included. For example, Harper used the name Harper & Brothers for titles published prior to about 1960. After that time, their name became Harper & Row, Publishers, Inc.

4)   Number of pages and illustrations. The phrase "photographic plates" means black and white illustrations from photographs. Other illustrations are as noted.

5)   Size - Standard bibliographic sizes are given. If the book was issued with a dust jacket or slip case, this information follows the size. Books listed were cloth bound, unless otherwise noted.

6)   Deluxe, limited or large paper editions - This information is enclosed in box parentheses and includes the stated limitation.

7)   Printing history - Enclosed in standard parenthesis. This information might include additional printings by the same publisher or other publishers. It also includes information about prior editions, if any.

8)   Annotations - These have necessarily been kept brief.   If the book was published with a subtitle that was an accurate description of its contents, and the book was not noteworthy in other aspects, no annotation was given. Additional sources of information regarding particular titles or authors are also listed here. For example, the term, "See Phillips" refers to this author's books listed in the References Cited section in the rear of this book. The term "See **Smith, Albert**" refers to another author's work listed in the main body of text.

Annotations about relative scarcity are also given. These fall into two categories. "Scarce" means not commonly encountered, but available with a very diligent search that might consume several months, or even a year's time. "Rare" means practically unavailable - such a book might only be encountered once in a lifetime.

The relative scarcity of particular titles is a much-discussed and often misleading subject. Books in this subject area published by commercial firms prior to about 1965 generally had first printings of between two and three thousand copies. After that date, commercial firms had larger first print runs because of cost considerations. Most first editions produced by commercial firms in the subject after 1925 can be secured with a reasonable search, over a relatively short period of time.

Comments regarding scarcity of books that had a stated limitation are not given. A book produced with a stated limitation of 1000 copies will be more difficult to obtain than a title produced by a commercial firm that had no stated limitation, but is still obtainable with a diligent search. As the stated limitation decreases, relative scarcity obviously increases.   It goes without saying that a book produced with a stated limitation of 50 copies, for example, would be rare.

Many of the titles listed were privately printed. These works, almost without exception, are relatively more scarce than those produced by commercial houses.

Sources used in this compilation were numerous, including those listed in the References Cited section at the rear of the book.   The author also relied very heavily on the use of the United States Library of Congress to verify questions on particular titles or authors.

The author would like to thank the following people for supplying information used in this compilation: Richard G. Beagle of Arcadia, California; Jim and Judith Bowman of Bedford, New York; Ray Brazille of Coweta, Oklahoma; Ken Callahan of Peterborough, New Hampshire; Jim Casada of Rock Hill, South Carolina; Gary Estabrook of Vancouver, Washington; Harry Hodgdon of The Wildlife Society, Washington, D. C.; Bob Krause of Bay Village, Ohio; Laura

Rose of The National Sporting Library in Middleburg, Virginia; Ed Moxley of Vickery, Ohio; John Valle of West Hempstead, New York.

Much gratitude is extended to my wife Margo for her support and patience throughout the ordeal that produced this work.

In a compilation such as this, with a listing of some five thousand works recorded on nearly six hundred pages, omissions and errors are inevitable and, of course, are the sole responsibility of the author.

M. L. Biscotti
June, 1997

Abels, Robert

    Early American Firearms.   Cleveland, 1950, World Publishing Company.   60 pp., color and black and white illustrations. A title in World's American Arts Library.   12mo.

Abbett, Robert K.

    The Outdoor Paintings of Robert K. Abbett.   New York, 1976, Peacock Press / Bantam Books.   Unpaginated (approx. 50 pp.), illustrations by Abbett.   Introduction by Gene Hill.   Paper wrappers.

Abernathy, John R.

    Catch 'Em Alive Jack.   New York, 1936, Association Press.   224 pp., illustrations.   8vo; dust jacket.   A rare work that is the autobiography of this wolf hunter.

Abbott, Henry   1850-1943

    The Birch Bark Books of Henry Abbott.   Harrison, NY, 1980, Harbor Hill Books. 254 pp., photographic plates.   4to; dust jacket.   A facsimile reproduction of all 19 of the author's books.

    North Bay Brook.   New York, 1929, Privately printed. 56 pp., photographic plates.   18mo.

    Pine Brook.   New York, 1932, Privately printed.   48 pp., photographic plates.   18mo.

    Pioneering at Rowan-Wood.   New York, 1927, Privately printed. 54 pp., photographic plates.   18mo.

    Psychology of the Lost .   New York, 1930, Privately printed.   57 pp., photographic plates.   18mo.

    Raquette River.   New York, 1931, Privately printed.   54 pp., photographic plates.   18mo.

    Tirrell Pond.   New York, 1928, Privately printed.   42 pp., photographic plates.   18mo.

    Wildcat Mountain.   New York, 1926, Privately printed.   48 pp., photographic plates.   18mo.

    Mr. Abbott wrote and privately printed all of these titles about his yearly trips to the Adirondacks. All are about hunting, fishing or hiking and are interesting accounts of early sport in that region. It is generally believed that fewer than 100 copies of each title were printed and that he gave these away as Christmas gifts to his friends. All were bound in simulated birch bark paper over boards. The titles published prior to 1926 are: *The Anxious Seat*, 1914; *Lost Pond*, 1915; *Camping At Cherry Pond*, 1916; *Old Bare Back and Others*, 1917; *Camps and Trails*, 1918; *Fish Stories*, 1919; *The Chief Engineer*, 1920; *Cold River*, 1921; *Muskrat City,* 1922; *On the Bridge*, 1923; *Anthony Ponds*, 1924; *Fishing Brook*, 1925.

Acerrano, Anthony J.

    The Outdoorsman's Emergency Manual.   New York, 1976, Winchester Press.   337 pp., drawings, photographic plates.   8vo; dust jacket.

    The Practical Hunter's Handbook.   New York, 1978, Winchester Press. 246 pp., illustrations.   8vo; dust jacket.

Acerrano, Anthony J., continued
The Complete Woodsman's Guide. Tulsa, 1981, Winchester Press. 256 pp., drawings, photographic plates. 8vo; dust jacket.

Ackerman, Morris
Where to Hunt and Fish; the world's authority. Cleveland, Ohio, 1937-1938, Sportsman's Guide. The 22nd annual. 320 pp., illustrations, ads. 12mo. Paper wrappers. Presumably this was published yearly from about 1915. Scarce.

Ackerman, R. O.
Introduction to Muzzle Loading. Indiana, 1966. 20 pp., illustrations. 8vo. Paper wrappers.
Shooting the Percussion Rifle. Indiana, 1966. 20 pp., illustrations. 8vo. Paper wrappers.

Ackley, Parker O.   d. 1989
Handbook For Shooters and Reloaders. Volume I. Salt Lake City, 1962, Privately printed. 567 pp., photographic plates, drawings, charts. 8vo. (Reprinted many times; later printings in paper wrappers and some titled *Pocket Manual For Shooters and Reloaders*)
Handbook For Shooters and Reloaders. Volume II. Salt Lake City, 1969, Privately printed. 534 pp., photographic plates, drawings, charts. 8vo; dust jacket. (Reprinted many times; later printings in paper wrappers. Also a 1976 two volume set, Plaza Publishing)
Home Gun Care and Repair. Harrisburg, 1969, The Stackpole Company. 191 pp., illustrations. 12mo; dust jacket.

Acton, C. R.
The Modern Foxhound. New York, 1936, Windward House. 126 pp., plates. Printed in Great Britain. 12mo; dust jacket. (Simultaneously published, London, H. F. & G. Witherby)

Adams, Arthur W.
Furbearers of North Dakota. Bismarck, 1961. 102 pp., photographic plates, drawings. 8vo; dust jacket. Much on trapping of the various species.

Adams, Charles S.
Hunting Crows Year Round. New York, 1953, The Macmillan Company. 101 pp., photographic plates. 8vo; dust jacket.

Adams, Chuck

The Complete Book of Bowhunting. New York, 1978, Winchester Press. 298 pp., illustrations. 8vo; dust jacket.

The Complete Guide To Bowhunting Deer. Northfield, Illinois, 1984, DBI Books, Inc. 256 pp., illustrations. 4to. Paper wrappers.

Adams, L. H.

Mink Raising. Columbus, Ohio, 1935, A. R. Harding. 225 pp., photographic plates. 16mo. (Reprinted several times, same format and publisher)

Adams, P.

Arctic Island Hunter. London, 1961. 136 pp., photographic plates. 8vo; dust jacket.

Adams, Patricia and Winsome McIntosh

Alaska Journal - 1979. No place (Palm Beach), No date (ca. 1980), Privately printed. 80 pp., photographic plates, drawings, maps. 8vo. A scarce account of an Alaskan trip with some hunting and angling.

Addison, Ottelyn

Early Days in Algonquin Park. McGraw Hill Ryerson, 1974, Toronto. 144 pp., illustrations. 8vo. Paper wrappers. With much on hunting and fishing.

Addy, C. E.

Fall Migration of the Black Duck. Washington, D. C., No date (1953), United States Department of the Interior. 63 pp., plus 34 pp. of maps and charts. 4to. Paper wrappers.

Waterfowl Management on Small Areas. Washington, D. C., 1948, Wildlife Management Institute. 84 pp. , illustrations. 8vo. Paper wrappers. (Also a 1956 edition reported)

Adee, Captain Graham M.

Colored Plate and Sporting Books. New York, 1953, Parke-Bernet Galleries, Inc. 61 pp. 8vo. Paper wrappers. An auction catalog.

Adirondack Mountain Club

A. F. Tait: Artist in the Adirondacks, an exhibition of paintings and other works by the sporting and animal artist Arthur Fitzwilliam Tait (1819-1905). Blue Mountain Lake, New York, 1974, Adirondack Mountain Club, Inc. 74 pp., color reproductions. 8vo. Paper wrappers.

Ahlstrom, Mark E.
   The Whitetail. Minnesota, 1983, Crestwood House. 47 pp., illustrations.
A juvenile.

Aitken, Russell Burnett
   Great Game Animals of the World. New York, No date (ca. 1968), The
Macmillan Company. 192 pp., photographic plates in black and white and in
color. Folio; dust jacket. (Reprinted 1974, Winchester Press) Mostly on African
game, but some North American.

Akehurst, Richard
   Sporting Guns. New York, 1968, G. P. Putnam's Sons. 120 pp.,
photographic plates in black and white and in color. 8vo; dust jacket. (Also
reprinted, 1972, London) Mostly European shotguns.
   The World of Guns. London, 1972, Hamlyn. 127 pp., color and black
and white illustrations. 4to; dust jacket.

Akehurst, Richard, editor
   Random Shots; an anthology of shooting stories. London, 1974, Allen.
294 pp., illustrations. 8vo; dust jacket. Includes some North American hunting.

Akroyd, Charles H.
   A Veteran Sportsman's Diary. Inverness, 1926, Carruthers.
Frontispiece of the author. 4to. The memoirs of this sportsman with hunting and
angling around the world. A scarce work.

Alaska, State of
   Big Game of Alaska. Juneau, 1977, State of Alaska. 59 pp.,
photographic plates. 4to; dust jacket.

The Alaskan Sportsman
   The Alaska Book; story of our northern treasure-land, including
selections from Alaska, the 49th state, by E. Gruening and *The Alaskan
Sportsman.* Chicago, 1960, Furguson. 320 pp., photographic plates in black and
white and in color, drawings by Churchill Ettinger. Bound in full mission leather.
4to.
   Alaska Hunting and Fishing Tales. 1972, The Alaskan Sportsman
Magazine. 98 pp., photographic plates. 4to. Paper wrappers.

Albaugh, William A. III and Richard D. Steuart
   The Original Confederate Colt. New York, 1953, Greenberg: Publishers.
62 pp., photographic plates. A Gunroom Library Book. 8vo; dust jacket.

Albaugh, William A., III and Edward Simmons
  Confederate Arms. Harrisburg, 1957, The Stackpole Company. 278 pp., many illustrations. 8vo; dust jacket. (Reprinted, Bonanza)

Albaugh, William A., III, Hugh Benet, Jr. and Edward Simmons
  Confederate Handguns. 1963. 250 pp., illustrations. 8vo; dust jacket. (Reprinted, Bonanza)

Aldous, C. M. and H. L. Mendall
  The Status of Big Game and Fur Bearing Animals in Maine. Orono, Maine, 1941, University of Maine. 39 pp., maps. 4to. Paper wrappers.

Aldrich, John and Allen Duvall,
  Distribution of American Gallinaceous Game Birds. Washington, D. C., 1953, United States Fish & Wildlife Service. 30 pp., black and white and color illustrations from artwork by Bess MacMaugh and Bob Hines. 8vo. Paper wrappers. (Also a 1955 edition, same format and publisher)

Aldridge, James
  The Hunter. Boston, 1951, Little, Brown & Company. 277 pp. 8vo; dust jacket. A novel about a hunter in the Lake Huron region with some trapping.

Allan, Thomas B., editor
  Vanishing Wildlife of North America. Washington, D. C., 1974, National Geographic Society. 208 pp., color and black and white illustrations. 4to; dust jacket.

Alldredge, Eugene Perry
  Cowboys and Coyotes. Nashville, 1945, Privately printed. 184 pp., illustrations. 8vo; dust jacket. A scarce title describing ranch life in New Mexico in the early 1900's, with much hunting.

Allen, Arthur A.   1885-1964
  Dawn in a Duck Blind. Boston / Ithaca, New York, 1963, Houghton Mifflin Company / Cornell University Press. 28 pp., color and black and white illustrations. 8vo. Issued with a 33 1/3 RPM record. Spiral bound paper wrappers.
  The Golden Plover and Other Birds. Ithaca, New York, 1939, Comstock Books. 324 pp., color and black and white illustrations. 4to; dust jacket. Contains sections on some game birds.
  Stalking Birds With Color Camera. Washington, D. C., 1951, National Geographic Society. 329 pp., many color illustrations. 4to; dust jacket.

Allen, Bob
　　　Bob Allen's Shooter's Digest.　No place, 1956, Privately printed.　146 pp., photographic plates, drawings.　4to.　Spiral bound paper wrappers.　A general guide, plus a listing of shooting products.

Allen, Douglas
　　　Frederick Remington's Own Outdoors.　New York, 1964, Dial Press. 190 pp., text and illustrations by Remington.　4to; dust jacket.　Illustrations are mostly hunting scenes.

Allen, Durward L.　b. 1910
　　　The Farmer and Wildlife.　Washington, D. C., 1949, Wildlife Management Institute.　84 pp., photographic plates, drawings by Oscar Warbach. 8vo.　Paper wrappers.
　　　Michigan Fox Squirrel Management.　Lansing, 1942, Michigan Game Division, Department of Conservation.　404 pp., photographic plates, drawings by Oscar Warbach.　8vo.　Paper wrappers. (Reprinted 1943, cloth bound, same publisher) Scarce.
　　　Our Wildlife Legacy.　New York, 1954, Funk and Wagnalls Company. 422 pp., photographic plates.　8vo; dust jacket.
　　　Wolves of Minong; their vital role in a wildlife community.　Boston, 1979, Houghton Mifflin Company.　499 pp., illustrations, maps.　8vo; dust jacket.

Allen Durward L., editor
　　　Pheasants In North America.　Harrisburg, 1956, The Stackpole Company / Wildlife Management Institute.　490 pp., photographic plates, color frontispiece from a painting by Bob Hines. 8vo; dust jacket.

Allen, J. A. and W. McLure
　　　Theory and Practice of Fox Ranching.　Charlottetown, 1926, Irwin. 248 pp., photographic plates.　8vo.　An interesting and scarce item.

Allen, Joseph C.
　　　Tales and Travels of Martha's Vineyard.　Boston, 1938, Little, Brown & Company.　234 pp., illustrations. 8vo; dust jacket.

Allen, Ralph H. and Robert E. Waters
　　　Bobwhite Quail Management; facts and fiction.　No place, 1963, Alabama Department of Conservation.　40 pp., bibliography.　8vo.　Paper wrappers.　(Reprinted 1972, same format and publisher)

Allison, Benjamin R.
The Rockaway Hunting Club. Long Island, New York, 1952, Privately printed. 236 pp., photographic plates. 8vo; slipcased. A history of this sporting club.

Allison, Col., editor
The Trophy Hunters; action packed tales of big game trophies around the world, 1860 to today. Ultimo (Australia), 1979, Murray. 240 pp., color and black and white illustrations. 4to; dust jacket. An anthology of hunting stories by Weatherby, Gates, Selous, Baker and others.

Allsop, Kenneth
Adventure Lit Their Star. New York, 1964, Crown Publishers, Inc. 222 pp., drawings. 8vo; dust jacket. A fictionalized account of the life of a ringed plover.

Almirall, Leon V.   b. 1884
Canines and Coyotes. Caldwell, Idaho, 1941, The Caxton Printers, Ltd. 150 pp., illustrations. Foreword by Patrick Chalmers. 8vo; dust jacket.
Coyote Coursing. Denver, 1926, Privately printed. Unpaginated (approx. 64 pp.), illustrations by Henry J. Meloy and Arthur M. Heinemann. 4to. Both of these works are uncommon titles describing coyote hunting using various kinds of hounds.

Alsheimer, Charles J.
New York State Big Buck Club Record Book. New York, YFC Printers. 32 pp. (Also a second edition, same format and limited to 5000 copies)

Alsheimer, Charles J. and Larry C. Watkins
A Guide to Adirondack Deer Hunting. Dolgeville, New York, 1987, Beaver Creek Press. 221 pp., photographic plates, bibliography. 8vo. Paper wrappers.

Amber, John T.
Ten Rare Gun Catalogs - 1860 - 1899. New York, 1952, Greenberg: Publishers. Unpaginated (384 pp.), illustrations from old plates. 8vo; dust jacket. For many years Mr. Amber also edited *Gun Digest*, an annual firearms publication.

Ameigh, G. C., Jr. and Yule M. Chaffin
Alaska's Kodiak Island. Kodiak, Alaska, 1962. 163 pp., illustrations. 8vo. Paper wrappers. Containing much on fishing and hunting on the island.

American Art Dealers Association

Contemporary American Etchings. New York, 1930, Privately printed by American Art Dealers' Association. Unpaginated (approx. 100 pp.), frontispiece an original etching by Frank Benson, with other reproductions by Clark, Edward Hopper, Kirmse and others. 4to. A scarce work.

American Chesapeake Club

How To Train Your Retriever. No place, No date, American Chesapeake Club. Unpaginated (41 pp.), photographic plates. 4to. Paper wrappers.

American Foxhound Club

Breeding a Pack of Foxhounds. Millwood, Virginia, 1974, American Foxhound Club. 38 pp. 8vo. Paper wrappers.

Hunting the Fox. Millwood, Virginia, 1971, American Foxhound Club. 71 pp. 8vo. Paper wrappers.

The Huntsman in the Field. Millwood, Virginia, 1979, American Foxhound Club. 54 pp., illustrations. 8vo. Paper wrappers.

Organizing a Foxhunting Country. Millwood, Virginia, 1976, American Foxhound Club. 40 pp., illustrations. 8vo. Paper wrappers.

The Training and Hunting of Hounds in the Field. Millwood, Virginia, 1971, American Foxhound Club. 8 pp. 8vo. Paper wrappers. All of these pamphlets were regarding foxhunting.

American Wildlife Institute

The Story of Delta Waterfowl Research Station; a review of the purpose, history, objectives and achievements of a research project on the prairie provinces of Canada. Washington, D. C., 1950, American Wildlife Institute. 24 pp., photographic plates and drawings by Albert Hochbaum. 8vo. Paper wrappers.

Ames, Fisher

By Reef and Trail; Bob Leach's adventures in Florida. Boston, 1909, Little, Brown & Company. 312 pp., illustrations by Charles Livingston Bull. 8vo. An older juvenile with much hunting and fishing. Not in Phillips.

Ammann, G. A. "Andy"

A Guide To Capturing and Banding American Woodcock Using Pointing Dogs. Coraopolis, 1981, RGS. 32 pp., photographic plates. 8vo. Paper wrappers. Mr. Ammann was a pioneer in banding woodcock and in the scientific study of their migration patterns.

The Prairie Grouse of Michigan. Lansing, 1957, Michigan Department of Conservation. 200 pp., illustrations. 8vo. Paper wrappers.

Amory, Cleveland   b. 1917

Man Kind? New York, 1974, Harper & Row, Publishers, Inc. 372 pp., photographic plates. 8vo; dust jacket. A provocative anti-hunting work.

Ancker, "Rusty"

The Original Hunter's Guide and Almanac For 1939-1940. Chicago, 1939, Haywood. 199 pp., photographic plates, drawings. 8vo.

Anderson, Allen

A Critical Review of Literature on Puma (Felis concolor) No place, 1983, Colorado Division of Wildlife. 91 pp., bibliography. 4to. Paper wrappers.

Anderson, Harry G.

Food Habits of Migratory Ducks of Illinois. Urbana, Illinois, 1959, State of Illinois, Natural History Survey Division. 55pp., photographic plates, diagrams. 4to. Paper wrappers.

Anderson, Luther A.

How to Hunt Deer and Small Game. New York, 1959, The Ronald Press. 140 pp., photographic plates. 8vo; dust jacket.

How To Hunt Whitetail Deer. New York, 1968, Funk and Wagnalls Company. 116 pp., photographic plates. 8vo; dust jacket.

Hunting the American Game Field. Chicago, 1949, Ziff-Davis Publishing Company. 311 pp., photographic plates. 8vo; dust jacket.

Hunting, Fishing and Camping. New York, 1945, The Macmillan Company. 214 pp., photographic plates. 8vo; dust jacket. (Reprinted twice, same format and publisher)

Hunting the Uplands With Rifle and Shotgun. New York, 1977, Winchester Press. 214 pp., photographic plates. 8vo; dust jacket.

Hunting the Woodlands For Small and Big Game. San Diego, 1980, A. S. Barnes and Company, Inc. 205 pp., photographic plates. 8vo; dust jacket.

Anderson, Mabry I.

Outdoor Observations. Clarksdale, Mississippi, 1977, Privately printed by the author. 179 pp. Limited to 2000 copies. 8vo. A collection of outdoor essays with much hunting and fishing. More scarce than its limitation would suggest.

Anderson, Peter

In Search of the New England Coyote. Chester, Connecticut, 1982, Globe Pequot Press. 219 pp., illustrations, bibliography. 8vo. Paper wrappers.

Andrews, Clarence L.
The Eskimo and His Reindeer in Alaska. Caldwell, Idaho, 1939, The Caxton Printers, Ltd. 253 pp. photographic plates, maps. 8vo; dust jacket.
An account of the introduction of reindeer to the native Eskimos.

Andrews, Duncan
Tally Ho! 400 Years of Foxhunting. New York, 1975, The Grollier Club. 40 pp., with tipped in bookplate of the author. 16mo. Paper wrappers.
Including a bibliography of foxhunting books and prints with some American titles.

Andrews, Captain R. C.
From Tyro To Master; a manual on the fundamentals of the shooting game. Washington D. C., 1942, The National Rifle Association of America. 60 pp., photographic plates. 8vo. Paper wrappers.

Andrews, Lt. Col. R. C., et al.
Shooting the .22 Rifle. Washington D. C., The National Rifle Association of America. 58 pp. 8vo. Paper wrappers.

Andrews, Roy Chapman   1884-1960
An Explorer Comes Home. New York, 1947, Doubleday and Company. 276 pp. 8vo; dust jacket. Mr. Andrews was a renowned anthropologist, adventurer and explorer who had many books to his credit including *On The Trail Of Ancient Man*, first published by Putnam's in 1926.

Andrews, Roy Chapman, editor
My Favorite Stories of the Great Outdoors. New York, 1950, Greystone Press. 404 pp. Tall 8vo; dust jacket. Thirty-five stories, a few of which are on hunting

Angell, Tony
Owls. Seattle, 1974, Washington State University Press. 80 pp., illustrations. 4to; dust jacket. (Reprinted 1975, same format and publisher) [Also a deluxe first edition of 100 numbered and signed copies]

Angier, Bradford
Home in Your Pack. Harrisburg, 1967, The Stackpole Company. 192 pp. 12mo; dust jacket. (Reprinted 1967, same format and publisher)
How To Go Live in the Woods on $10 a Week. Harrisburg, 1959, The Stackpole Company. 269 pp., maps. Introduction by Lt. Col. Townsend Whelen. 8vo; dust jacket. (Reprinted several times, same format and publisher)
Contains some big game hunting.
How To Live in the Woods on Pennies a Day. Harrisburg, 1971, Stackpole Books. 192 pp., illustrations. 4to; dust jacket. (Reprinted, same format and publisher)

Angier, Bradford, continued

Living Off the Country; how to stay alive in the woods. Harrisburg, 1956, The Stackpole Company. 241 pp. drawings by Vena Angier. 8vo; dust jacket. (Reprinted many times, same format and publisher)

The Master Backwoodsman. Harrisburg, 1978, The Stackpole Company. 224 pp., illustrations. 8vo; dust jacket.

Skills For Taming the Wilds; a handbook of woodcraft wisdom. Harrisburg, 1967, The Stackpole Company. 286 pp., drawings. 8vo; dust jacket. (Also a 1967 edition titled, *Taming the Wilds,* Galahad)

We Like It Wild. Harrisburg, 1963, The Stackpole Company. 213 pp. 8vo; dust jacket. The author's autobiographical account of life in the woods of British Columbia.

Wilderness Cookery. Harrisburg, 1970, The Stackpole Company. 256 pp., photographic plates, drawings. 8vo. Paper wrappers.

Mr. Angier wrote at least 25 books, all dealing with living self-sufficiently. Most of these had incidental mention of hunting or fishing. Listed here the titles most commonly encountered.

Angier, Bradford and Vena Angier

Wilderness Wife. Radnor, Pennsylvania, 1976, Chilton Book Co. 177 pp., photographic plates. 8vo; dust jacket.

Angier, Bradford

Also see **Whelen, Lt. Col. Townsend**

Also see **Colby, Carroll B.**

Angier, R. H.

Firearm Blueing and Browning. Onslow County, North Carolina, 1936, Small Arms Technical Publishing Company. 151 pp., frontispiece, drawings. 18mo; dust jacket. (Reprinted several times, same format and publisher. Also reprinted, The Stackpole Company)

Annabel, Russell   1905-1979

Alaskan Tales. New York, 1953, A. S. Barnes and Company, Inc. 137pp. 8vo; dust jacket. The author's scarcest book with hunting all of Alaska's major species except mountain sheep and musk ox.

Hunting and Fishing in Alaska. New York, 1948, Alfred A. Knopf, Inc. 341 pp., color frontispiece, photographic plates. A Borzoi Book For Sportsmen. 8vo; dust jacket.

Tales of a Big Game Guide. New York, 1938, The Derrydale Press. 198 pp., photographic plates. Limited to 950 numbered copies. Tall 8vo. (Reprinted 1985, Premier Press)

Mr. Annabel's writings appear from the early 1930's when he had his first magazine article published, to the publication of *Alaskan Days, Mexican Nights* in 1987 by The Amwell Press. At this writing new anthologies of his articles not previously published in book form are also going to press. His name will always be synonymous with big game hunting in Alaska.

Annixter, Paul (*pseud.* of **Howard Sturtzel**) **b. 1894**
Brought To Cover. New York, 1950, A. A. Wyn. 247 pp. 8vo; dust jacket. A collection of outdoor stories.
Swiftwater. New York, 1950, A. A. Wyn. 256 pp. 8vo; dust jacket. A novel of a North Maine Woods family.
Wilderness Ways. Philadelphia, 1930, Penn Publishing Company. 313 pp., black and white illustrations, drawings, color frontispiece and illustrated end-papers by Charles Livingston Bull. 8vo; dust jacket.

Anonymous
American Fisherman and Hunter's Annual. New York, 1945, Periodical Sales. 112 pp., front cover illustrations by F. L. Jaques, photographic plates. 8vo. Paper wrappers. (Also produced annually after this date for a number of years) With articles by Buckingham, Farrington and others.
Borrego Cimarron; Direccion General de la Fauna Silvestre. Mexico, 1976, Subsecretaria Forestal y de la Fauna. 231 pp., photographic plates, maps. Text in Spanish and English. 4to. Paper wrappers. Hunting desert bighorn sheep in Baja, California.
The Fox's Prophecy. New York, 1939, Sporting Gallery and Bookshop. 25 pp., illustrations from drawings by Robert Ball. Limited to 1000 copies. 12mo. (Originally published, 1871, Great Britain) Foxhunting.
Game Birds of North America. Harrisburg, 1953, The Stackpole Company. 30 pp., illustrations by T. M. Shortt and Luis Henderson. 4to. Paper wrappers.
Hell For Leather. New York, 1928, The Derrydale Press. 36 pp., three hand-colored plates from old engravings. Limited to 350 numbered copies. 8vo. Foxhunting.
Hunting at Stoney. No place, No date (ca. 1962), Privately printed. 62 pp., photographic plates. 12mo. Paper wrappers. Hunting deer and small game on this Lake Ontario island.
Hunting Log. Mt. Kisco, New York, 1954, Hunting Logs. Unpaginated, blank, ruled leaves. 8vo.
Jockey Hollow Field Trial Club; its history, aims and functions. Clinton, New Jersey, 1955, Privately printed. Unpaginated, photographic plates. 8vo. Paper wrappers. Includes articles by H. P. Davis and Evelyn Monte.
Rare and Beautiful Guns. New York, 1975, Galahad Books. 128 pp., color and black and white illustrations. Folio; dust jacket. (Originally published as *Guns and Gun Collecting*, Octopus Books, London)
Ruffed Grouse in Minnesota. Grand Rapids, Minnesota, 1965, Herald. 22pp., color illustrations. 8vo. Paper wrappers.
Selected Alaska Hunting and Fishing Tales. Anchorage, Various dates (1970's), Alaska Northwest Publishing Company. Four volumes of from 70 to 140 pp. All 4to. All paper wrappers.

Anonymous, continued

The Sportsman's Portfolio of American Field Sports. New York, 1929, Privately printed for Ernest R. Gee by The Derrydale Press. 43 pp., illustrated from old plates. Oblong 8vo. Limited to 400 copies. (A facsimile reproduction of the 1855 M. M. Ballou edition)

The Story of the Parmachenee Club. Parmachenee Lake, Maine, No date (ca. 1930), Privately printed by the club. Unpaginated (17 pp.), photographic plates, map. 4to. Paper wrappers. A rare history of this club with much on partridge and deer hunting.

Antunano, J. A. Sanchez

Practical Education of the Bird Dog. Chicago, 1934, American Field Publishing Company. 164 pp., photographic plates. 12mo. Paper wrappers. (Reprinted many times, same format and publisher)

Arizona Game and Fish Commission

Arizona Big Game Investigations, 1971-1978. No place, No date, Arizona Game and Fish Commission. Three volumes. Unpaginated (approx. 1000 pp.), photographic plates, charts, maps. 4to. Spiral bound paper wrappers.

The Sonoran Pronghorn. No place, 1981, Arizona Game and Fish Commission. Photographic plates, maps. 4to. Paper wrappers.

Wildlife Research in Arizona, 1980-81. Phoenix, 1981, Arizona Game and Fish Commission. 64 pp., photographic plates, drawings, maps. 4to. Paper wrappers. (Also a 1981-82 edition, same format and publisher)

Arizona Wildlife Federation

Arizona Wildlife Trophies. Phoenix, 1980, Arizona Wildlife Federation. Third edition. 190 pp., photographic plates. Limited to 1500 numbered copies. 8vo. A record of big game trophy animals harvested in the state.

Arkva, Mort

The Incipient Elk Hunter. Missoula, Montana, 1983, Mountain Press Publishing Company. 112 pp., illustrations.

Armstrong, Major, Nevill A. D.

After Big Game in the Upper Yukon. London, 1937, John Long, Ltd. 287 pp., photographic plates, maps. 8vo; dust jacket. (Reprinted 1937, same format and publisher) An uncommon and important book describing the big game in the Macmillan River area.

Armstrong, W. W.

The Economic Value of Hunting and Fishing in Arizona in 1956. Phoenix, 1958. 36 pp., illustrations. 8vo. Paper wrappers.

Arnow, Harriette
>*Hunter's Horn.*   New York, 1949, The Macmillan Company.   508 pp.
8vo; dust jacket.   A novel of Kentucky, with much foxhunting.

Arnold, Lee W.
>*The Golden Eagle;* and its economic status.   Washington, D. C., 1954,
United States Department of the Interior.   35 pp., photographic plates, black and
white reproduction of Fuertes paintings, bibliography.   8vo.   Paper wrappers.

Arnold, Lloyd
>*High on the Wild With Hemingway.*   Caldwell, Idaho, 1969, Caxton
Printers, Ltd.   343 pp. photographic plates.   8vo; dust jacket.   (Reprinted 1969,
same publisher and format.   Also reprinted, 1977, in paper wrappers, Grosset &
Dunlap) [Also a specially bound, limited first edition of 950 numbered copies
signed by John Hemingway; slipcased] The story of the Hemingways in Idaho from 1939
to 1961; contains much hunting.

Arnold, Richard
>*Automatic and Repeating Shotguns.*   New York, 1958, A. S. Barnes and
Company, Inc.   173 pp., photographic plates, drawings.   8vo; dust jacket.
(Reprinted, same publisher and format.   Also a 1958 British edition)
>*The Book of the .22.*   New York, 1964, A. S. Barnes and Company, Inc.
188 pp., illustrations.   8vo; dust jacket.   (Reprinted, same format and publisher)

Arsenault, Ricard P., editor
>*The Maine Antler and Skull Trophy Club 4th Annual Big Game Records
Publication*: 1982.   1982, Privately printed.   64 pp.   Presumably three earlier editions
were also produced.

Arthur, Robert
>*The   Shotgun   Stock;*   design,   construction   and   embellishment.
Cranbury, New Jersey, 1971, A. S. Barnes and Company, Inc.   175 pp.,
illustrations.   8vo; dust jacket.   An uncommon work much sought after by advanced
shooters and stock-makers.

Ashbrook, Frank G.
>*Fur Farming For Profit.*   New York, 1948.   429 pp., illustrations.
8vo; dust jacket.
>*Rabbits For Food and Fur.* New York, 1930, Orange Judd Publishing
Company.   176 pp., photographic plates.   8vo; dust jacket.   (Reprinted several
times, same format and publisher)
>Mr. Ashbrook also wrote several titles relating to game cooking.

Askins, Charles, Sr.   1860-1947

The American Shotgun. New York, 1930, The Macmillan Company. 321 pp., illustrations.   12mo; dust jacket. (Originally published, 1910, Outing Publishing Company.   Reprinted 1921, The Macmillan Company)

Game Bird Shooting. New York, 1931, The Macmillan Company. 312 pp., frontispiece in color, photographic plates. Edited by Edward Cave. Tall 8vo; dust jacket.

Modern Shotguns and Loads; together with a treatise on the art of wing shooting.   Marshallton, Delaware, 1929, Small Arms Technical Publishing Company. 416 pp., frontispiece, photographic plates. Tall 8vo; dust jacket.

Rifles and Rifle Shooting. New York, 1934, The Macmillan Company. 244 pp., illustrations.   12mo; dust jacket.   (Originally published, 1912, Outing Publishing Company)

Shooting Facts; for the novice and expert. Denver, 1928, Outdoor Life Books.   83 pp., frontispiece, illustrations. Book Number 8 of the Recreation Library.   16mo.   Paper wrappers. (Reprinted several times, same format and publisher)

Shotgun - Ology; a handbook of useful shotgun information. New York, 1926, United States Cartridge Company.   63 pp., drawings, tables.   Paper wrappers.

Super-X: A Discussion of Long Range Loads For 10, 12, 16, 20 and 410 Gauge Shotguns.   East Alton, Illinois, 1927, Western Cartridge Co.   36 pp. 12mo.   Paper wrappers.

Wing and Trap Shooting. New York, 1928, The Macmillan Company. 168 pp., illustrations.   12mo; dust jacket.   (Originally published, 1910, Outing Publishing Company.   Also published with the same title by Macmillan, written by **Charles Askins, Jr.,** which see)

Wing Shooting; for the novice and expert. Denver, 1928, Outdoor Life Books.   88pp., drawings.   Volume 6 in the Recreation Library Series.   16mo. Paper wrappers.   (Reprinted several times, same format and publisher)

Askins, Charles, Jr.   b. 1907

The Art of Handgun Shooting.   New York, 1941, A. S. Barnes and Company, Inc.   219 pp., photographic plates.   8vo; dust jacket. A title in Barnes' Sportsman's Library series. (Reprinted many times, same format and publisher)

Askins on Pistols and Revolvers.   Washington, D. C., 1980, The National Rifle Association of America.   144 pp., illustrations.   4to.   Paper wrappers.

Gunfighters. Washington, D. C., 1981, The National Rifle Association of America.   293 pp., illustrations.   8vo.

Hitting the Bullseye; Iver Johnson manual how to shoot.   Fitchburg, Massachusetts, 1936, Iver Johnson Company.   23 pp., illustrations.   Paper wrappers.

Askins, Charles, Jr., continued

The Pistol Shooter's Book; a modern encyclopedia. Harrisburg, 1953, The Stackpole Company. 347 pp., photographic plates. 8vo; dust jacket. (Reprinted and revised several times, various publishers)

The Shotgunner's Book; a modern encyclopedia. Harrisburg, 1958, The Stackpole Company. 365 pp., photographic plates. 8vo; dust jacket. (Reprinted, Bonanza)

Texas, Guns and History. New York, 1970, Winchester Press. 246 pp. 8vo; dust jacket. (Reprinted, Bonanza) Tales of Texas badmen as well as the author's experiences at gun-fighting.

Unrepentant Sinner; the autobiography of Col. Charles Askins. San Antonio, Texas, 1985, Tejano. 322 pp., photographic plates. 8vo; dust jacket. [Also a limited edition of 1000 numbered and signed copies, Amwell Press]

Wing and Trap Shooting. New York, 1948, The Macmillan Company. 205 pp., photographic plates, drawings. 12mo; dust jacket. (Reprinted several times, same format and publisher)

These father-son authors wrote extensively about firearms and hunting from 1910 to 1985. Many out-of-print book specialists use their names synonymously in error. They both had military titles, which adds to the confusion. Primarily, the Senior Askins wrote about shotguns and the Junior Askins wrote about handguns.

Askins, Charles, Jr.
Also see **Colt's Patent Fire Arms Manufacturing Company**

Atlantic Waterfowl Council

The Atlantic Flyway Waterfowl Management Guide. No place, 1964, Atlantic Waterfowl Council. 99 pp., illustrations. 8vo. Paper wrappers.

Maryland Waterfowl Identification Guide. No place, 1956, Atlantic Waterfowl Council. 56 pp., illustrations. 8vo. Paper wrappers.

New York Waterfowl Identification Guide. No place, 1956, Atlantic Waterfowl council. Illustrations. 8vo. Paper wrappers.

Audubon, John James and John Bachman

Audubon Game Animals; a selected treasury for sportsmen from the *Quadrupeds of North America.* Maplewood, New Jersey, 1968, Hammond. Edited by V. H. Cahalane. 172 pp., color illustrations. 4to.

Delineations of American Scenery and Character. New York, 1926, G. A. Baker & Company. 349 pp., illustrations. (Reprinted 1970, Arno) Contains Audubon's essay on deer hunting.

Auer, Harry A.

Campfires in the Yukon. New York, 1926, D. Appleton & Co. 204 pp., photographic plates, maps. 8vo; dust jacket. (Originally published, 1916, Stewart-Kidd, Inc.)

Austin, Oliver S.

Water and Marsh Birds of the World. New York, 1967, Golden Press. 223 pp., color illustrations by Arthur Singer. 8vo. Paper wrappers. Some North American game birds.

Austing, G. Ronald and J. B. Holt

The World of the Great Horned Owl. Philadelphia, 1966, J. B. Lippincott Co. 158 pp., photographic plates. A title in Lippincott's Living World series. 4to; dust jacket.

Austing, G. Ronald and J. B. Holt, continued

The World of the Red Tailed Hawk. Philadelphia, 1964, J. B. Lippincott Co. 128 pp., photographic plates. A title in Lippincott's Living World series. 4to; dust jacket.

Autenrieth, R. E. and E. Fichter

On the Behavior and Socialization of Pronghorn Fawns. Washington, D. C., 1975, The Wildlife Society. Monograph #42. 111 pp., photographic plates. 4to. Paper wrappers.

Averill, Gerald

Ridge Runner. Philadelphia, 1948, J. B. Lippincott Co. 217 pp. 12mo; dust jacket. (Reprinted, same format and publisher) Reminiscences of a Maine outdoorsman. Scarce.

Aymar, Gordon   b. 1893

Bird Flight. New York, 1938, Garden City Publishing Company. 234 pp., photographic plates. 4to; dust jacket. [Also a deluxe edition of an unspecified limitation]

B of V (Brotherhood of Venery)

Some Lessons. No place, no date (ca. 1939), Privately printed for the use of the Order. 91 pp., frontispiece and another plate by Richard Bishop. 8vo. A compilation of 12 lectures delivered annually from about 1926 to 1938 by the Brotherhood of Venery. Rare.

Some Lessons; volume II. No place, no date (ca. 1947), Privately printed for the use of the Order. 75 pp. 8vo. Another curious collection of essays produced by this organization, composed of naturalists, sportsmen and outdoor writers. This collection has several articles by Aldo Leopold and one by Col. H. P. Sheldon. Rare.

Babcock, Elizabeth S.

Betty Babcock's Illustrated Hunting Diary; recording the sport of the season for the followers of the Meadow Brook Hounds, 1935 - 1936. New York, 1936, National Press Company. Drawings by the author. Oblong 8vo. (Also a 1936 - 1937 edition, same format and publisher) Scarce journals of the American foxhunting scene in its Golden Age.

Babcock, Havilah   1898-1964

The Best of Babcock. New York, 1974, Holt, Rinehart & Winston. 275 pp., illustrations. Selected and with an introduction by Hugh Grey. 8vo; dust jacket.

The Best of Babcock, The Education of Pretty Boy, I Don't Want To Shoot an Elephant, and *Jaybirds Go To Hell on Friday.* Four volumes in a set of 1025 numbered copies. Auburn Hills, Michigan, 1985, Gunnerman Books. 8vo; slipcased together.

The Education of Pretty Boy. New York, 1960, Henry Holt and Company, Inc. 160 pp., drawings by Arthur Fuller. 8vo; dust jacket. A novel centered around a hunting dog.

I Don't Want To Shoot an Elephant. New York, 1958, Henry Holt and Company, Inc. 184 pp. 8vo; dust jacket. (Reprinted 1958, same format and publisher)

Jaybirds Go to Hell on Friday; and other stories. New York, 1965, Holt, Rinehart & Winston, Inc. 149 pp. 8vo; dust jacket. (Reprinted several times, same format and publisher)

My Health is Better in November; thirty five stories of hunting and fishing in the South. Columbia, South Carolina., 1947, University of South Carolina Press. 235 pp., line drawings. 8vo; dust jacket. (Reprinted many times, various publishers)

Tails of Quail 'N Such. New York, 1951, Greenberg: Publishers. 237 pp., line drawings by William Schaldach. 8vo; dust jacket. (Reprinted twice in 1951 and 1957, same format and publisher. Also reprinted, 1985, University of South Carolina) [Also a deluxe first edition, specially bound and limited to 299 numbered copies signed by the author; slipcased]

Havilah Babcock was an English professor at the University of South Carolina who wrote extensively about the Carolina low-country and its game bird hunting. His sporting stories remain as popular today as when they first appeared in print.

Babcock, Philip H.
   Falling Leaves. New York, 1937, The Derrydale Press. 201 pp., drawings by A. L. Ripley. Limited to 950 numbered copies. Tall 8vo. Hunting tales.

Babson, William Arthur
   Modern Wilderness. New York, 1940, Doubleday, Doran & Co., Inc. 261 pp., color and black and white illustrations. 8vo; dust jacket. Wildlife observations in Morris County, New Jersey, with some duck hunting.

Back, Joe
   Horses, Hitches and Rocky Trails. Chicago, 1959, Sage Books. 117 pp., drawings, diagrams. 8vo; dust jacket. (Reprinted several times, same format and publisher). A complete presentation of horse packing for hunting and camping.
   Mooching Moose and Mumbling Men. Boulder, Colorado, 1963, Johnson. 131 pp., drawings by the author. 8vo; dust jacket. Big country hunting tales from the pen of a professional guide. Uncommon.

Bacon, Bernard and Wilma Bacon, editors
   1975 Official National Pictorial of the Irish Setter Club of America, Inc. Providence, Rhode Island, No date (ca. 1976), Privately printed by the club. 852 pp., photographic plates. 4to; dust jacket.

Badcock, Lt. Colonel G. H.
   The Early Life and Training of a Gundog. Idle, 1931, Bradford. 111pp., photographic plates. 8vo.

Bady, Donald B.
   Colt Automatic Pistols. Alhambra, California, 1973, Borden. Revised edition. 354 pp., photographic plates, reproductions of ads. 8vo; dust jacket.

Baekeland, George
   Gunner's Guide. New York, 1948, The Macmillan Company. 115 pp., drawings, diagrams. 8vo; dust jacket.

Baer, Larry L.
   The Parker Gun; an immortal American classic. Los Angeles, 1974, Beinfeld Publishing Co. 94 pp., color and black and white illustrations. 4to. (Reprinted many times, same format and publisher. Also a 1983 revised edition, Gun Room Press)
   The Parker Gun; an immortal American classic, Volume II. Los Angeles, 1976, Beinfeld Publishing Co. 146 pp., color and black and white illustrations. 4to. Limited to about 525 numbered copies. [Also a limited edition of both volumes was produced in an edition of approximately 500 copies, Josten's]

Baer, Larry L., continued

Parker Brothers 1895 Catalog. 23 pp. Limited to 500 numbered and signed copies. 8vo. Paper wrappers. (A facsimile reproduction of the 1895 catalog)

Bagg, Aaron Clark and Samuel Atkins Eliot

Birds of the Connecticut Valley in Massachusetts. Northampton, Massachusetts, 1937, Hampshire Bookshop. 813 pp., color frontispiece by Fuertes, black and white plates by Roger Torey Peterson, photographic plates. 4to. Much on game birds of th region.

Bailey, Dewitt, et al.

Guns and Gun Collecting. London / New York, 1972, Octopus Books/ Crown Publishers, Inc. 128 pp., color and black and white illustrations. Folio; dust jacket.

Bailey, J. A., et al.

Readings in Wildlife Conservation. Washington, D. C., 1974, The Wildlife Society. 722 pp., photographic plates, drawings, bibliography. 8vo. Paper wrappers. A compilation of papers on large and small game animals by Leopold, Dasman, Craighead, Gabrielson and others.

Bailey, R. W. and K. T. Rinell

History and Management of the Wild Turkey in West Virginia. No place, 1968, West Virginia Department of Game and Fish. 59 pp., photographic plates, maps, bibliography. 8vo. Paper wrappers.

Bailey, Robert G.

River of No Return. Lewiston, Idaho, 1935, Privately printed. 515 pp., illustrations. Limited to 1400 numbered and signed copies. 8vo. (Also a 1947 revised edition, limited to 2000 numbered copies) With some hunting and fishing accounts.

Bailey, Robeson, editor

The Field and Stream Game Bag. New York, 1948, Doubleday & Co., Inc. 306 pp. 8vo; dust jacket. (Reprinted 1949, same format and publisher) An anthology of mostly small game stories by Rutledge, Babcock, Spiller and others.

Bailey, Vernon

Beaver Habits and Experiments in Beaver Culture. Washington, D. C., 1927, U. S. Department of Agriculture. 40 pp., photographic plates, drawings. 8vo. Paper wrappers.

Baillie, J. L.

    Ontario Grouse. Toronto, Ontario, 1956, ROM   19 pp., drawings by T. M. Shortt. 4to. Paper wrappers.

Baillie, William A.

    Sport in Art; an iconography of sport during 400 years, from the beginning of the 15th to the end of the 18th centuries.   New York, 1969, Blom. 422 pp., many photographic reproductions.   Folio. (Originally published, 1925) A discussion of the evolution of sport through paintings of the period.

Baird, John

    Hawken Rifles, The Mountain Man's Choice.   1976, Gun Room Press. 95 pp., photographic plates.   4to; dust jacket.   (Reprinted, same format and publisher)

Baker, Carlos

    Ernest Hemingway; a life story.   New York, 1969, Charles Scribner's Sons.   697 pp., photographic plates.   8vo; dust jacket.   (Reprinted several times, same format and publisher)

    Ernest Hemingway; selected letters. New York, 1981, Charles Scribner's Sons.   948 pp.   8vo; dust jacket. (Reprinted several times, same format and publisher) [Also a deluxe first edition, specially bound and limited to 500 numbered and signed copies; slipcased]   A selection of Hemingway's letters to such notables as F. Scott Fitzgerald, Arnold Gingrich and others, including his own family.

Baker, Clyde   1894-1943

    Modern Gunsmithing.   Marshallton, Delaware, 1928, Small Arms Technical Publishing Company.   530 pp., frontispiece, photographic plates, drawings. 8vo; dust jacket. (Also a 1933 second edition, same publisher. This second edition also reprinted, The Stackpole Company)

Baker, Ezekiel   1758-1836

    Baker's Remarks on the Rifle.   Huntington, West Virginia, 1946, Standard Publications, Inc. 269 pp. 8vo. (Originally published, 1835, London)

Baker, J. A.

    The Peregrine. New York, 1967, Harper & Row, Publishers, Inc. 191 pp.   8vo; dust jacket. (Reprinted 1967, same format and publisher) A detailed personal record of peregrine falcon observations, with some account of the species' impact on game.

Baker, Ron

    The American Hunting Myth.   New York, 1985, Vantage Press, Inc. 287 pp.   8vo.   A provocative indictment of hunting.

Balleisen, Charles E.

Principles of Firearms. New York, 1945, John Wiley & Sons. 146 pp., illustrated. Tall 8vo. Deals primarily with exterior ballistics and firearms design from a technical standpoint.

Ballou, R. M.

Nesting, Distribution and Mortality Studies of Canada Geese. No place, 1956, Wyoming Game and Fish Commission. 31 pp. Paper wrappers. (Also a 1957 revised edition, same format and publisher)

Banasiak, Chester F.

Deer in Maine. Augusta, 1961, Game Division of Maine. 159 pp., photographic plates, drawings. 8vo. Paper wrappers.

Bancroft, Griffith

Vanishing Wings; a tale of three birds of prey. New York, 1972, Franklin Watts, Inc. 149 pp., photographic plates, bibliography. 8vo; dust jacket. A novel based on factual life histories of an eagle, a falcon and an osprey.

Banfield, A. W. F.

The Barren Ground Caribou. Ottawa, 1951, Department of Resources and Development. 56 pp., photographic plates, maps. 4to. Paper wrappers.

A Revision of the Reindeer and Caribou Genus Rangifer. Ottawa, 1961, National Museum. 137 pp., photographic plates, maps, charts, bibliography. 8vo. Paper wrappers.

Bangor & Aroostook Railroad Company

In the Maine Woods. Bangor, Maine, 1926, Bangor & Aroostook Railroad Company. 160 pp., photographic plates, maps. 8vo. (First published in 1921, and reprinted yearly through most of the 1930's, same format and publisher) Much on hunting and fishing in the North Maine Woods.

Banko, Winston E.

The Trumpeter Swan; its history, habits and population in the United States. Washington, D. C., 1960, United States Department of the Interior. 214 pp., photographic plates, maps, bibliography. 8vo. Paper wrappers. (Reprinted 1963, same format and publisher. Also reprinted, 1980, University of Nebraska Press)

Barber, George and Larry Reader

Decoy Carving Techniques; for the intermediate carver. Exton, Pennsylvania, 1984, Schiffer Publishing Company. 56 pp., color and black and white illustrations. 4to. Paper wrappers.

Barber, Joel   1876-1952

Catalog of the Abercrombie & Fitch Exhibition of Wildfowl Decoys, 1931. New York, 1931, Abercrombie & Fitch, Inc.   4pp.   8vo.   Paper wrappers.

Catalog of an Exhibition of American Wild Fowl Decoys; The Joel Barber Collection of old decoys: modern decoys by Charles E. Wheeler.   New York, 1932, Abercrombie & Fitch, Inc.   10 pp.   8vo.   Paper wrappers.

'Long Shore.   New York, 1939, The Derrydale Press.   108 pp., illustrations from drawings by Arthur D. Fuller.   16mo.   Limited to 750 copies, numbered and signed by the author; two-piece box.   (Reprinted, ca. 1970, Potomac, Maryland)   Poetry of wildfowlers and wildfowl hunting along the Eastern seaboard.

Wild Fowl Decoys. New York, 1934, Windward House.   156 pp., black and white and color illustrations from photographs and paintings.   4to; dust jacket. (Reprinted 1937, Garden City Publishing Company.   Also reprinted with a few additional plates, 1954, Dover, in paper wrappers)

Wild Fowl Decoys. New York, 1934, The Derrydale Press.   156 pp., plates, drawings by the author.   Limited to 55 specially bound, numbered copies signed by the author.   4to; slipcased.

The writing of Mr. Barber was the first to call attention to waterfowl decoy carving as an art form. His books remain in great demand by both decoy collectors and waterfowl enthusiasts.

Barber, Lunette and William Hamnett

Our Wildlife Neighbors; important game mammals, fur-bearers, and upland game birds of North Carolina.   Raleigh, no date (ca. 1960), North Carolina Wildlife Commission.   44 pp., drawings.   8vo.   Paper wrappers.

Barbour, Thomas

John Charles Phillips.   Cambridge, Massachusetts, 1939, Privately printed.   Unpaginated   (9 pp.), frontispiece of John C. Phillips.   8vo.   Paper wrappers.   An obituary, tribute and biographical sketch of Mr. Phillips. Scarce.

Bare, Collen Stanley

Mule Deer.   New York, 1981, Dodd, Mead & Co.   56 pp., illustrations. A juvenile.

Barick, Frank B.

Hunting in North Carolina.   Raleigh, 1975, North Carolina Wildlife. 46 pp., photographic plates, maps.   8vo.   Paper wrappers.   (Reprinted 1976, same format and publisher)

Barkalow, F. S. and M. Shorten

The World of the Gray Squirrel.   Philadelphia, 1973, J. B. Lippincott Co. 160 pp., photographic plates.   A title in Lippincott's Living World series.   4to; dust jacket.

Barkalow, Frederick, Jr.
A Game Inventory of Alabama. No place, 1949, Alabama Department of Conservation. 140 pp., photographic plates. 8vo. Paper wrappers.

Barker, A. J.
Shotguns and Shooting. Boulder, Colorado, 1973, Paladin Press. 84 pp., illustrations. 8vo.

Barker, Edwin H.
The Quest of the Fountain of Youth. New York, 1925, Privately printed. 24 pp., frontispiece of J. M. Parker, in whose memory the book was written. Limited to 25 copies. 8vo. A rare work describing a Mexican mountain lion hunting trip with some turkey hunting and tarpon fishing.

Barker, Elliott S. 1886-1988
Beatty's Cabin; adventures in the Pecos high country. Albuquerque, 1953, University of New Mexico Press. 220 pp., photographic plates, maps. 8vo; dust jacket. (Reprinted 1970, Calvin Horn Publisher, Inc.) Big game hunting in the high country of the Southwest.
Eighty Years With Rod and Rifle. Santa Fe, New Mexico, 1976, Sunstone Press. 102 pp., photographic plates. Preface by Tony Hillerman. 8vo. Paper wrappers. The memories of a lifetime of hunting and fishing in the Southwest. Scarce.
Smokey Bear and the Great Wilderness. Santa Fe, New Mexico, 1982, Sunstone Press. 149 pp. Contains some hunting.
When the Dogs Barked "Treed;" a year on the trail of the longtails. Albuquerque, 1946, University of New Mexico Press. 209 pp., photographic frontispiece and plates. 8vo; dust jacket. (Reprinted, 1975) Hunting Mountain Lions.
Western Life and Adventures, 1889-1970. Albuquerque, New Mexico, 1970, Calvin Horn Publisher, Inc. 289 pp., photographic plates. 8vo; dust jacket. (Reprinted 1974, with the title *The Great Southwest*, by The Lowell Press) More of the author's reminiscences of a lifetime of hunting.

Barker, Fred C. and John S. Danforth
Hunting and Trapping on the Upper Magalloway River and Parmachenee Lake; a winter in the wilderness. Boston, 1929, Lothrop, Lea & Shepard. 238 pp., photographic plates, map. 12mo. (A reproduction of the 1881 first edition) An early account of this wilderness area of Maine.

Barnard, Charles N., editor
Best of True. New York, 1956. 397 pp. 4to. [Also published as *Treasury of True* in a deluxe type format with the same contents]

Barnard, Charles N., editor, continued
Anthology of True; silver anniversary. New York, 1962, Thomas Nelson Publishers. 411 pp. 8vo; dust jacket. Includes stories by Ted Trueblood, Edwin Ware Smith, Roy Chapman Andrews and others originally appearing in this popular men's magazine.

Barnard, Henry (1811-1900) and J. D. Butler
Armsmear; the home, the arms and the armory of Samuel Colt. No place, 1976, Beinfeld. 399 pp., illustrations. Introduction by R. L. Wilson. Limited to 1776 copies. 4to. (A facsimile reproduction of the 1866 edition)

Barnes, Duncan , et al.
The History of Winchester Firearms - 1866-1980. Piscataway, New Jersey, 1980, Winchester Press. 237 pp., illustrations. 4to; dust jacket. (Reprinted and revised several times, same format and publisher. This work, an expanded and revised edition of the same title originally published in 1966 by **George Watrous**, which see)

Barnett, David
The Upper Yukon; another look at wilderness hunting. Clinton, New Jersey, 1983, Amwell Press. 196 pp., photographic plates. Limited to 1000 numbered and signed copies. 8vo; slipcased.

Barr, Basil D.
Big Game Hunting in Alaska, Arizona and North Carolina. Elizabethton, Tennessee, 1982, Privately Printed. 150 pp., photographic plates. 8vo. Paper wrappers. An account of all the major species in these regions from 1930 to 1967. Scarce.

Barrett, Harry B.
Lore and Legend of Long Point. Don Mills, Ontario, 1977, Burns & MacEachern. 240 pp., photographic plates, maps. Square 8vo; dust jacket. Waterfowling and gunning clubs on this famous Lake Erie peninsula.

Barrett, Peter, editor
Great True Hunts. New Jersey, 1967, Prentice-Hall, Inc. 287 pp., color and black and white photographic plates. 8vo; dust jacket.

Barsness, John
Hunting the Great Plains. Missoula, Montana, 1979, Mountain Press Publishing Company. 163 pp., illustrations. 8vo. Paper wrappers.

Bartlett, Des and Jan Bartlett

The Flight of the Snow Geese. New York, 1975, Stein and Day, Publishers. 189 pp., photographic plates. Foreword by Sir Peter Scott. 8vo; dust jacket. A chronicle of the migration of this species from northern Canada to Mexico.

Bartlett, Ilo Henry

Michigan Deer. Lansing, 1950, Michigan Department of Conservation. 50 pp. Paper wrappers.

Whitetails: Presenting Michigan's Deer Problem. Lansing, 1938, Michigan Department of Conservation. 64 pp. Paper wrappers.

Bartlett, William W.

History, Tradition and Adventure in the Chippewa Valley. Wisconsin, 1929, The Chippewa Printery. 244 pp. Containing a section on deer hunting during the late 1800's.

Bartram, William

Travels of William Bartram. New York, 1955, Dover Publications, Inc. 414 pp. Containing a very early account of deer hunting, dated 1791.

Basala, Allen C., editor

Official North Carolina Records of the Dixie Deer Classic: Volume I. North Carolina, 1982, Wake County Wildlife Club, Inc. 52 pp.

Bashline, L. James and Dan Saults, editors.

America's Great Outdoors, the story of the eternal romance between man and nature. An anthology of 200 years of writing and collected illustrations. Chicago, 1976, Ferguson / Outdoor Writers Association of America. 367 pp., illustrations in black and white and in color. 4to; dust jacket. [Also a deluxe edition, specially bound of an unspecified limitation; boxed]

Bashline, L. James, editor

The Eastern Trail. Rockville Center, New York, 1972, Freshet Press. 320 pp., illustrations. 8vo; dust jacket. An anthology of hunting and angling stories of the eastern U. S.

Basile, Kenneth and Cynthia Doerzbach

American Decorative Bird Carving. Salisbury, Maryland, 1981, Ward Foundation. 64 pp., color and black and white illustrations. 8vo. Paper wrappers. Containing much on decoy carving.

Bass, Rick

The Deer Pasture. College Station, Texas, 1985, Texas A & M University Press. 123 pp., drawings 8vo; dust jacket. An interesting approach to deer hunting, stressing tradition and values.

Batchelor, Ronald F.

The Roosevelt Elk in Alaska; its ecology and management. Juneau, 1965, Alaska Department of Fish and Game. 35 pp., diagrams, maps, bibliography. 4to. Paper wrappers.

Bateman, Hugh

The Wood Duck in Louisiana. No place, 1977, Department of Wildlife and Fisheries. 31 pp., color and black and white illustrations. 8vo. Paper wrappers.

Bateman, James A.

Animal Traps and Trapping. Harrisburg, 1971, The Stackpole Company. 286 pp., photographic plates. 8vo; dust jacket. (Reprinted many times, same format and publisher)

Batten, John H., editor

The Best of Sheep Hunting. Clinton, New Jersey, 1980, Amwell Press. Two volumes of 312 pp. and 272 pp. respectively, frontispiece by Carl Rungius, black and white illustrations from photographs and from drawings by Gordon Allen. Limited to 1000 numbered and signed copies. 8vo; slipcased together. (Also a 1981 trade edition, two volumes in one, same publisher. This trade edition reprinted 1985, same format and publisher) An anthology of hunting experiences from the pens of Demidoff, Roosevelt, O'Connor, Adiar and others.

The Forest and the Plain. Clinton, New Jersey, 1984, Amwell Press. 243pp., illustrations by Peter Darro. Limited to 1000 numbered and signed copies. 8vo; slipcased. Hunting big game around the world.

The Formidable Game. Clinton, New Jersey, 1983, Amwell Press. 264 pp., color frontispiece, drawings by Peter Darro. Limited to 1000 numbered and signed copies. 8vo; slipcased. Hunting dangerous species of big game in India and Africa with some North American bear hunting.

Skyline Pursuits. Clinton, New Jersey, 1981, Amwell Press. 318 pp., drawings by Gordon Allen. Limited to 1000 numbered and signed copies. 8vo; slipcased. Sheep hunting around the world.

Bausch & Lomb Corporation

Facts About Telescopic Sights; a manual of technical and practical information on the design and construction of telescopic sights - their performance and dependability. Rochester, New York, 1956, Bausch & Lomb Corporation. 88 pp., photographic plates, drawings. 8vo. Paper wrappers.

Bauer, Erwin A.   b. 1919

Bears in Their World. New York, 1985, Outdoor Life Books. 254 pp., color and black and white illustrations. 4to; dust jacket.

Deer in Their World. Harrisburg / New York, 1983, Stackpole Books / Outdoor Life Books. 242 pp., black and white and color photographic plates. 4to; dust jacket. (Reprinted 1984, same format and publisher)

The Digest Book of Deer Hunting. Chicago, 1979, Follett Publishing Co. 96 pp., illustrations. Paper wrappers.

Hunter's Digest. Chicago, 1973, Digest Books. 320 pp., photographic plates. 4to. Paper wrappers.

Hunting With a Camera; a world guide to wildlife photography. New York, 1974, Winchester Press. 324 pp., color and black and white illustrations. 4to; dust jacket.

Outdoor Photography. New York, 1965, E. P. Dutton & Co., Inc. / Outdoor Life Books. 141 pp., photographic plates. 8vo; dust jacket. (Reprinted in paper wrappers, same publisher. Also a 1979 revised edition, cloth bound, same publisher)

Treasury of Big Game Animals. New York, 1972, Harper & Row, Publishers, Inc. / Outdoor Life Books. 398 pp., color and black and white illustrations. 4to; dust jacket. (Reprinted several times, same format and publisher) An overview of all the big game animals of the world.

Bauer, Erwin A.

Also see **Laycock, George**

Baxter, B. M.

See **Ginner, X. B.**

Baxter, D. V. and Benjamin Labaree

On and Off Alaskan Trails. No place, 1937, Privately printed. 184 pp., photographic plates, drawings by Carelton Angell. 8vo.

Bayless, Marguerite

Bolinvar. New York, 1937, The Derrydale Press. Two volumes of 217 pp. and 200 pp. respectively, illustrations from drawings by Robert Ball. Limited to 950 numbered copies. 8vo; slipcased together. (Also a 1944 edition in one volume, titled *The Bolinvars*, Henry Holt and Company, Inc. Also a 1944 "Armed Services" edition in paper wrappers) The saga of a Delaware river valley family with some firearms hunting, but mostly equestrian foxhunting.

Baynes, Ernest Harold

My Wild Animal Guests. New York, 1930, The Macmillan Company. 125 pp., photographic plates. 8vo; dust jacket. Containing a biographical story of a deer.

Wildlife in the Blue Mountain Forest. New York, 1931, The Macmillan Company. 140 pp., illustrations. 8vo; dust jacket. Containing much on deer and deer hunting in New Hampshire.

Beach, Rex   1877-1949

Confessions of a Sportsman. New York, 1927, Garden City Publishing Company. 281 pp., photographic plates. 8vo; dust jacket. (Originally published, 1922, with the title *Oh Shoot!*, Harper & Brothers)

Personal Exposures; his own story. New York, 1940, Harper & Brothers. 303 pp. 8vo; dust jacket. The autobiography of this novelist and sportsman.

Beach, William Nicholas   1895-1955

In The Shadow of Mt. McKinley. New York, 1931, The Derrydale Press. 289 pp., photographic plates, illustrations from paintings by Carl Rungius. Limited to 750 copies. Tall 8vo; dust jacket. Hunting sheep, bear and caribou in Alaska. An important work on big game hunting in the Denali region.

Beaman, Arthur S.

The Chesapeake Bay Retriever. Fairfax, Virginia, 1981, Denlinger's 95 pp., photographic plates. 4to.

Bean, Leon Leonwood

Hunting-Fishing-Camping. Freeport, Maine, 1942, L. L. Bean, Inc. 96 pp., photographic plates. 8vo. (Reprinted many times, same publisher and format) Mr. Bean founded L. L. Bean, Inc., the Maine outdoors merchandise company; he also wrote *My Story*; the autobiography of a Down-East merchant.

Bear, Fred

The Archer's Bible. New York, 1968, Doubleday & Co., Inc. 160 pp., photographic plates. 4to; dust jacket. (Also produced in paper wrappers, same publisher. Also a 1980 revised edition, same publisher)

Fred Bear's Field Notes. New York, 1976, Doubleday & Co., Inc. 288 pp., black and white illustrations from photographs. 8vo; dust jacket. (Reprinted several times, same format and publisher)

Fred Bear's World of Archery. New York, 1979, Doubleday & Co., Inc. 402 pp., photographic plates. 4to; dust jacket.

Mr. Bear did much to popularize the sport of bowhunting, and proved that with the proper equipment and hunting techniques, it was an effective and humane way to hunt big game.

Bear, Sun
> *At Home in the Wilderness.* Sparks, Nevada, 1968, Privately printed. 90 pp., drawings. 8vo. Paper wrappers. Mostly wilderness skills, but some hunting and stalking.

Beard, Daniel B., et al.
> *Fading Trails;* the story of endangered American wildlife. New York, 1942, The Macmillan Company. 279 pp., illustrations from paintings and drawings. 8vo; dust jacket. (Reprinted 1947, same format and publisher)

Bearse, Ray
> *Centerfire American Rifle Cartridges 1892-1963.* South Brunswick, New Jersey, 1964, A. S. Barnes and Company, Inc. 198 pp., photographic plates. 8vo; dust jacket. (Reprinted 1966, same format and publisher)
> *Sporting Arms of the World.* New York, 1976, Harper & Row, Publishers, Inc. / Outdoor Life Books. 461 pp., photographic plates. 4to; dust jacket.

Beasom, Samuel L. and Sheila F. Roberson, editors
> *Game Harvest Management.* 1985, Texas A & M University Press. 374 pp., illustrations. 8vo.

Beattie, Kirk H. and Bruce A. Moss, editors
> *Proceedings of the Midwest Bowhunting Conference.* 1983, Wisconsin Chapter of the Wildlife Society. 238 pp.

Beazley, John, et al.
> *Training Setters and Pointers for Trials.* New York, 1973, Arco. 91 pp., illustrations. 8vo; dust jacket. (Reprinted, same format and publisher. Originally published, Great Britain)

Beck, B. B. and C. M. Wemmer, editors
> *The Biology and Management of an Extinct Species: Pere David's Deer.* New Jersey, 1983, Noyes Publications. 193 pp.

Beck, Joseph Spear
> *For the Beginning Book Collector;* The Derrydales. Manchester, Vermont, No date, Museum of American Flyfishing. Unpaginated (8 pp.). 4to. Paper wrappers. An introduction to collecting books produced by this sporting book publisher.

Becker, A. C.

Game and Bird Calling. South Brunswick, New Jersey, 1972, A. S. Barnes and Company, Inc. 147 pp., photographic plates. 8vo; dust jacket.

Waterfowl in the Marshes. South Brunswick, New Jersey, 1969, A. S. Barnes and Company, Inc. 155 pp., photographic plates. 4to; dust jacket. (Reprinted 1976, same publisher and format. Also a British edition)

Becker, Robert, editor

Bob Becker's Dog Digest. Chicago, 1947, Paul, Richmond & Company. 130 pp., photographic plates. 4to; dust jacket.

Beckham, Stephen Dow, editor

Tall Tales From Rogue River; the yarns of Hathaway Jones. Bloomington, Indiana, 1974, Indiana University Press. 178 pp., drawings by Christina Romano. Tales from Oregon, including hunting and fishing.

Beckham, O. L.

Ozark Memories; a book of short stories. Pittsburgh, Kansas, No date (ca. 1960), Pittcraft. 111 pp. 8vo. Paper wrappers. Much of the contents are devoted to possum and raccoon hunting. Scarce.

Bednarik, K. E. et al.

Canada Goose Management Investigations. Columbus, 1970, Ohio Division of Wildlife. 48 pp. Paper wrappers.

Beebe, B. F.

American Lions and Cats. New York, 1963, David McKay Co. 177 pp., illustrations. 12mo; dust jacket. With sections on bobcat, lynx, jaguar, jaguarundi, ocelot and cougar. Scarce.

Beebe, B. F. and James R. Johnson

American Bears. New York, 1965, David McKay Co. 182 pp., illustrations. 8vo; dust jacket.

Beebe, Frank Lyman

A Falconry Manual. Blaine, Washington, 1984, Hancock House. 197 pp., illustrations. 8vo; dust jacket.

Hawks, Falcons and Falconry. Seattle, Washington, 1976, Hancock House. 320 pp., photographic plates. 4to; dust jacket.

Beebe, Frank Lyman and Harold M. Webster

North American Falconry and Hunting Hawks. Denver, 1964, North American Falconry and Hunting Hawks. 315 pp., illustrations by the author in color and in black and white. Limited to 2000 numbered copies signed by both authors. 4to; dust jacket. (Reprinted several times, same format and publisher)

Beebe, William   1877-1962

Pheasants: Their Lives and Homes. New York, 1926, Doubleday, Page & Co., Inc. Two volumes of 257 pp. and 309 pp. respectively, each with black and white and color illustrations by Fuertes, Thorburn and others. Tall 8vo; dust jackets. (Reprinted 1931, same publisher and format. Also reprinted, 1936, same publisher, two volumes in one. Also a 1937 British edition, in two volumes) [Also a deluxe first edition, specially bound and limited to 201 numbered and signed copies] An important monograph.

Beebe, William, editor

The Book of Naturalists. New York, 1944, Alfred A. Knopf, Inc. 499 pp., illustrations. 8vo; dust jacket. (Reprinted 1948, same format and publisher. Also a 1944 British edition) An anthology of essays by the world's greatest naturalists with annotations by the editor.

Mr. Beebe was certainly one of America's most important naturalists, most of whose work focused on tropical birds, animals and fish. He was a prolific author, having written or edited 24 books and over 800 articles. See Berra.

Behn, Jack

"45-70" Rifles. Harrisburg, 1956, The Stackpole Company. 137 pp., illustrations. 8vo; dust jacket. A general discussion of rifles chambered for this caliber, with much emphasis on single-shot rifles manufactured by Sharps and Winchester.

Bell, Arthur W.

Cape Cod Color. Boston, 1931, Houghton Mifflin Company. 171 pp., frontispiece. 12mo; dust jacket. Some angling, but also small game hunting of the region. Scarce.

Bell, Bob

The Digest Book of Upland Game Hunting. Northfield, Illinois, 1979, DBI Books. 96 pp., photographic plates. 4to. Paper wrappers.

Hunting the Long-Tailed Bird. Rockville Center, New York, 1975, Freshet Press. 212 pp., photographic plates. 4to; dust jacket. Pheasant hunting.

Pennsylvania Big Game Records, 1965 - 1976. Harrisburg, 1977, Pennsylvania Game Commission. 112 pp., photographic plates, drawings. 8vo. Paper wrappers.

Bell, Isaac

The Huntsman's Log Book.   New York, 1947, Charles Scribner's Sons. 249 pp., photographic plates.   8vo; dust jacket.   (Originally published, Great Britain)   Foxhunting with much on hounds and their breeding.

Bell, Vereen

Two of a Kind.   Boston, 1943, Little, Brown & Company.   291 pp., frontispiece.   8vo.   A story about an English pointer.

Swamp Water.   Boston, 1943, Little, Brown & Company.   263 pp., frontispiece.   8vo; dust jacket.   A novel about a boy, his dog and an outlaw, trapping in the Okefenokee Swamp.

Bellrose, Frank C.   b. 1916

Duck Food Plants of the Illinois River Valley.   Urbana, 1941, State of Illinois, Natural History Survey Division.   43 pp., photographic plates. 4to. Paper wrappers.

Ducks, Geese and Swans of North America.   Harrisburg / Washington D. C., 1976, The Stackpole Company / Wildlife Management Institute.   Second edition.   540 pp., many illustrations in black and white and in color. 4to; dust jacket. (Reprinted 1978, same format and publisher.   Also a 1980 third revised edition, same format and publisher)   A revised edition of the same title written by **Francis A. Kortwright** , which see.

Sex Ratio and Age Ratios in North American Ducks.   Urbana, 1961, State of Illinois, Natural History Survey Division.   83 pp., illustrations.   4to. Paper wrappers.

Waterfowl Migration Corridors East of the Rocky Mountains in the United States.   Urbana, 1968, State of Illinois, Natural History Survey Division. 24 pp., maps.   4to. Paper wrappers.

Waterfowl Hunting in Illinois; its status and problems.   Urbana, 1944, State of Illinois, Natural History Survey Division.   35 pp., photographic plates, charts, maps.   4to.   Paper wrappers.

Waterfowl Populations and the Changing Environment of the Illinois River Valley.   Urbana, 1979, State of Illinois, Natural History Survey Division.. 54 pp., photographic plates.   4to.   Paper wrappers.

Belmont, A. and Toni Reynolds

Retriever Field Trials, 1967 - 1972.   1973, Retriever Field Trial News. 301 pp., photographic plates.   8vo.

Retriever Field Trials, 1973 -1978.   1981, Retriever Field Trial News. 350 pp., photographic plates.   8vo.

Bender, Doc

Maker's Spring.   Viroqua, Wisconsin, 1979, Bristow Press.   172 pp., illustrations.   8vo.   Containing some deer hunting and angling.

Bendell, J. F. and P. W. Elliott
  Behavior and Regulation of Numbers of Blue Geese. Ottawa, 1967, Canadian Wildlife Service. 76 pp. 4to. Paper wrappers.

Bennett, Logan J.
  The Blue Winged Teal; its ecology and management. Ames, Iowa, 1938, Collegiate Press. 144 pp., photographic plates, color frontispiece from a painting by Sid Horn, maps. 8vo.
  Training Grouse and Woodcock Dogs. New York, 1948, G. P. Putnam's Sons. 146 pp., photographic plates, drawings. 8vo; dust jacket. An important work.

Benoit, Larry
  How To Bag the Biggest Buck of Your Life. Duxbury, Vermont, 1974, Whitetail Press. 158 pp., photographic plates. 8vo; dust jacket. (Reprinted 1975, same publisher and format)

Benson, D. and S. D. Browne
  Canada Goose Populations and Stocking Program in New York in 1965. Albany, 1966, New York State Division of Fish and Game. 15 pp. Paper wrappers.

Benson, D. and L. W. Degraff
  Canada Goose Stocking in New York. Albany, 1961, New York State Division of Fish and Game. 13 pp. Paper wrappers.

Benson, D. A. and D. G. Dodds
  The Deer of Nova Scotia. Halifax, 1977, Department of Lands and Forests. 92 pp., photographic plates, map in color, bibliography. 4to. Paper wrappers.

Benson, Frank W.   1862-1951
  American Etchers, Volume XII; Frank Benson, N. A. New York, 1931, The Crafton Collection. Unpaginated, 12 pp. text and a listing of Benson's etchings by Charles L. Morgan plus 12 tipped in reproductions of Benson's etchings. 4to; dust jacket. [Also a deluxe edition of 75 copies, with an original signed etching as a frontispiece; issued with dust jacket]
  Modern Masters of Etching. London, 1925, The Studio. 8 pp. text plus 13 tipped in reproduction of etchings. Introduction by M. C. Salaman. Folio.

Benson, Frank W.

Also see **American Art Dealers' Association**

Also see **Ordeman, John T.,** *Frank W. Benson*

Also see **Paff, Adam**

Also see **Heintzelman, Arthur William**

Benson, Ragnor

Survival Poaching. Boulder, Colorado, 1980, The Paladin Press. 256 pp., diagrams. 8vo; dust jacket. An advocacy of the practice of poaching as well as a general how-to on making explosives and creating other civil disturbances; certainly repugnant to the sportsman and conservationist.

Bent, Arthur Cleveland   1866-1954

Life Histories of North American Birds of Prey: Order Falconiformes. Part One. Washington, D. C., 1937, Government Printing Office. 409 pp., plates. # 10 of the series. 8vo. Paper wrappers.

Life Histories of North American Birds of Prey: Order Falconiformes and Strigiformes. Part Two. Washington, D. C., 1938, Government Printing Office. 482 pp., plates. # 11 of the series. 8vo. Paper wrappers.

Life Histories of North American Gallinaceous Birds: Order Galliformes and Columbiformes. Washington, D. C., 1932, Government Printing Office. 490 pp., plates. # 9 of the series. 8vo. Paper wrappers.

Life Histories of North American Marsh Birds: Orders Odontoglossae, Herodiones and Paludicolae. Washington, D. C., 1926, Government Printing Office. 490 pp., plates. # 6 of the series. 8vo. Paper wrappers.

Life Histories of North American Shore Birds: Order Limicolae. Part One. Washington, D. C., 1927, Government Printing Office. 420 pp., plates. # 7 of the series. 8vo. Paper wrappers.

Life Histories of North American Shore Birds: Order Limicolae. Part Two. Washington, D. C., 1929, Government Printing Office. Plates. # 8 of the series. 8vo. Paper wrappers.

Life Histories of North American Wild Fowl: Order Anseres. Part One. Washington, D. C., 1925, Government Printing Office. 250 pp., plates. #4 of the series. 8vo. Paper wrappers.

Life Histories of North American Wild Fowl: Order Anseres. Part Two. Washington, D. C., 1925, Government Printing Office. 376 pp., plates. # 5 of the series. 8vo. Paper wrappers. (Also a 1951 edition, two volumes in one, Dover Publications)

Mr. Bent wrote 20 volumes in this series on all of the North American birds and waterfowl. All were also reprinted by Dover Publications in 1962 and 1963.

Bere, Rennie

Antelopes. New York, 1970, Arco. 96 pp., color and black and white illustrations. 8vo; dust jacket. With a section on pronghorn antelope.

Berg, Ben
　　Ben Berg's Guide To Your Choice Hunting Grounds.　　Madison, Wisconsin, 1963, Privately printed.　　288 pp., photographic plates, maps.　　8vo. Paper wrappers.　A guide to the Northwestern U. S.

Berg, Vernon E.
　　Decoy Collecting; an historical interpretation of an American phenomenon.　　No place, No date (ca. 1965), Privately printed.　　6 pp.　　8vo. Paper wrappers.

Bergerud, Arthur T.
　　The Population Dynamics of Newfoundland Caribou.　　Washington, D. C., 1971, The Wildlife Society.　　Monograph #25.　　55 pp., photographic plates, bibliography.　　4to.　Paper wrappers.

Bergh, Peter
　　The Art of Ogden Pleissner. Boston, 1984, David R. Godine, Publishers, Inc..　111 pp., black and white and color illustrations by Pleissner.　　4to; dust jacket. [Also a specially bound, limited edition of 400 numbered and signed copies; slipcased. Issued with an extra suite of plates.　　Also a deluxe edition, specially bound and limited to 400 numbered copies; slipcased. The deluxe edition also issued with an extra suite of plates and with a full sized, previously unpublished print by Pleissner]　The definitive monograph of this popular sporting artist.

Berkey, Barry, Velma Berkey and Richard Berkey
　　Pioneer Decoy Carvers; a biography of Lemuel and Stephen Ward. Cambridge, Maryland, 1977, Tidewater Publishers.　　161 pp., black and white and color illustrations photographic plates.　　4to; dust jacket. [Also a deluxe edition, specially bound and limited to 500 numbered copies signed by Lemuel Ward]

Berkey, Barry and Velma Berkey
　　Chincoteauge Carvers and Their Decoys.　　Faifax, Virginia, 1981, Privately printed.　　102 pp., color and black and white illustrations.　　Limited to 2000 copies.　4to.

Berlinger, Barney
　　Danger Down the Sights. New York, 1964, Vantage Press. 202 pp., plus 8 pp. photographic plates.　8vo; dust jacket.　Containing big game hunting in Canada and Alaska.

Bernard, Art
　　Dog Days.　　Caldwell, Idaho, 1969, The Caxton Printers, Ltd.　　204 pp., illustrations.　Foreword by Erle Stanley Gardiner.　　8vo; dust jacket.　Hunting with bird dogs in Utah and Nevada.

Bernsen, Paul S.

The Bugle of the Elk. New York, 1977, David McKay Co. 82 pp., illustrations. 8vo; dust jacket. An older juvenile.

The North American Waterfowler. Seattle, 1972, Salisbury Press. 206 pp., color plates from paintings by Les Kouba, drawings, photographic plates. Tall 8vo; dust jacket. Issued with a 45 RPM record "The Art of Duck Calling" by Harry Dye. (Reprinted 1974, in paper wrappers, Ballantine Books) [Also a deluxe first edition, specially bound and limited to 500 numbered and signed copies; slipcased]

Berra, Tim M.   b. 1943

William Beebe; an annotated bibliography.   Hamden, Connecticut, 1977, The Shoestring Press. 157 pp., frontispiece. 8vo; dust jacket.

Berry, W. D.

Deneki; an Alaskan Moose.   New York, 1967, The Macmillan Company.   Unpaginated, color and black and white illustrations.   4to; dust jacket.

Bersing, Otis

Bow and Arrow Big Game Hunting in Wisconsin.   Madison, 1973, Wisconsin Department of Conservation.   24 pp. Paper wrappers.

A Century of Wisconsin Deer. Madison, 1956, Wisconsin Conservation Department.   184 pp., maps, bibliography. 8vo.

Fifteen Years of Bow and Arrow Deer Hunting in Wisconsin. Madison, No date (1950), Wisconsin Conservation Department.   24 pp., photographic plates. Paper wrappers.

Besadny, C. D.

An Evaluation of Pheasant Stocking Through the Day-Old Chick Program.   Madison, 1963, Wisconsin Conservation Department.   84 pp., illustrations. 8vo. Paper wrappers.

Beshears, W. Walter

Wood Ducks in Alabama.   No place, 1974, Alabama Department of conservation.   45 pp., photographic plates, maps, bibliography. 8vo. Paper wrappers.

Betten, H. L.   1873-1964

Upland Game Shooting. Philadelphia, 1940, Penn Publishing Company. 450 pp., color plates from paintings by Lynn Bogue Hunt. 8vo; dust jacket. (Reprinted twice, same publisher and format. Also reprinted by Alfred A. Knopf, Inc. several times, in a smaller format as a title in Knopf's Borzoi Books For Sportsmen series) [Also a deluxe first edition specially bound and limited to 124 numbered copies, signed by the author and artist; slipcased. Issued with an extra over-size suite of plates]   Covers all major North American upland bird species as well as rabbits; one chapter on recipes. A well written and handsome book in any edition.

Beverly-Gidings, A. R.

River of Rogues.   New York, 1948, William Morrow & Co., Inc.   378 pp.   8vo; dust jacket.   A novel with the Maryland eastern shore as a setting, with some duck hunting.

Beverly-Gidings, A. R., editor

Frank Forester on Upland Shooting. New York, 1951, William Morrow and Co., Inc.   276 pp., illustrations. 8vo; dust jacket.   An anthology of Forester's works.

Beville, Vernon

Game on Your Land; managing the eastern wild turkey in South Carolina.   Columbia, 1984, South Carolina Wildlife and Marine Commission. Reprint edition.   42 pp., drawings.   4to.   Paper wrappers.

Bianchi, John

Blue Steel and Gun Leather; a practical guide to holsters.   North Hollywood, California, 1978, Beinfeld Publishing Company. 214 pp., photographic plates.   8vo; dust jacket.   (Reprinted several times, same format and publisher)

Bianki, Vitali

How I Wanted To Pour Salt on a Rabbit's Tail and Other Stories.   New York, 1967, G. Braziller.   151 pp., illustrations.   8vo; dust jacket.   Humorous hunting tales.

Biddle, Brig. Gen. Nicholas

Personal Memoirs: an autobiography...and accounts of various cruises and hunting expeditions.   Philadelphia, 1975, Privately printed.   353 pp., illustrations.   8vo.

Bigelow, Horatio   b. 1877

Flying Feathers; a Yankee's hunting experiences in the south. Richmond, Virginia, 1937, Garrett and Massie. 95 pp., illustrations. Introduction by Archibald Rutledge. 8vo.

Gunnerman. New York, 1939, The Derrydale Press. 246 pp., plates. Limited to 950 numbered copies. Tall 8vo.

Gunnerman's Gold; memories of fifty years afield with a scattergun. Huntington, West Virginia, 1943, Standard Publication, Inc. 128 pp., plates. Limited to 1000 numbered copies. 4to; dust jacket. (Also a variant binding in full red leather)

Mr. Bigelow was an accomplished author who also wrote *Scattergun Sketches*, published in 1922 by William Hazelton. He was friends and shooting companion to three other noteworthy author-shooters - Archibald Rutledge, Nash Buckingham and Col. Harold P. Sheldon.

Bigelow, Dr. Wilfred Abram

Forceps, Fin & Feather. Altoona, Manitoba, 1969, Friesen & Sons, Ltd. 115 pp., photographic plates. 8vo; dust jacket. (Reprinted several times, same format and publisher) The memoirs of a Canadian surgeon with much on angling and wildfowling.

Binford, Laurence C.

Birds of Western North America; non-passerines. New York, 1974, The Macmillan Company. 223 pp., color illustrations by Carlson. Folio; dust jacket. With much on wildfowl and upland birds.

Bingham, Caleb

The Hunters: or Sufferings of Hugh and Francis in the Wilderness....A True Story. Hanover, New Hampshire, 1954, Dartmouth College. 45 pp., woodcut illustrations. 18mo. (A facsimile reproduction of the 1814 edition) A story of two Dartmouth students who became lost on a 1778 hunting excursion.

Bingham, Robert W.

Early Buffalo Gunsmiths. Buffalo, 1934, Buffalo Historical Society. 18 pp., frontispiece. Paper wrappers.

Bird, Brandon (*pseud.* of **George Bird Evans and Kay Evans**)

Hawk Watch. New York, 1954, Dodd, Mead & Co. 200 pp. 8vo; dust jacket. A murder mystery with a falconry theme.

Bish, Tommy L.

Home Gunsmithing Digest. Northfield, Illinois, 1970, Gun Digest Publishing Co. 319 pp., photographic plates, drawings. 4to. Paper wrappers.

Bishop, Joseph Bucklin

A. Barton Hepburn; his life and service to his time. New York, 1923, Charles Scribner's Sons. 421 pp., illustrations. 8vo; dust jacket. Mr. Hepburn was a philanthropist who endowed many public libraries. He was also a big game hunter of considerable repute; this volume devotes one chapter to his big game hunts across North America. Not in Phillips. Rare.

Bishop, Richard E.   1887-1975

Bishop's Birds; etchings of waterfowl and upland game birds. Philadelphia, 1936, J. B. Lippincott Co. Unpaginated, 73 reproductions of etchings. Foreword by Col. H. P. Sheldon. Limited to 1050 numbered copies. 4to; boxed. [Also a deluxe edition, specially bound and illustrated with an original signed etching and limited to 125 numbered and signed copies; boxed]

Bishop's Wildfowl; a collection of etchings and oil painting reproductions. St. Paul, 1948, Brown and Bigelow. 282 pp., fully illustrated in black and white and in color. Introduction by Nash Buckingham. A limited edition of unspecified number. Folio; boxed.

The Ways of Wildfowl; featuring the distinguished paintings and etchings of Richard Bishop. Text by Russ Williams. Edited by T. C. Jones. Chicago, 1971, Ferguson / Doubleday & Co., Inc.. 260 pp., illustrated in black and white and in color. Folio; dust jacket. [Also a specially bound deluxe edition of unspecified limitation; slipcased]

Mr. Bishop remains one of the most popular of the world's twentieth century wildfowl artists.

Bissell, Nicky

Pointing Dog Training, Especially the Continental Breeds. Sherwood, Oregon, No date (ca. 1970), B. B. Supplies. 48 pp. 8vo. Paper wrappers.

The Official Book of the Brittany Spaniel. No place, 1972, Brittany Spaniel Club. 376 pp., photographic plates. 8vo. With mention of all field champions of the breed.

Bivins, John

Longrifles of North Carolina. York, Pennsylvania, 1968, George Shumway. 200 pp., illustrations. 4to; dust jacket.

Black, Glenn G.

See **Old Kickapoo**

Blackmore, Howard L.

Guns and Rifles of the World. New York, 1965, Viking Press. 134 pp., color and black and white illustrations. 4to; dust jacket.

Hunting Weapons. New York, 1972, Walker and Company. 401 pp., photographic plates, bibliography. Tall 8vo; dust jacket. A thoroughly illustrated discussion of firearms, bows, crossbows, spears, etc.

Blair, Claude
  Pistols of the World. New York, 1968, Viking Press. 206 pp.,
photographic plates. 4to; dust jacket.

Blair, Gerry
  Predator Caller's Companion. Tulsa, 1981, Winchester Press. 267
pp., photographic plates. 8vo; dust jacket.

Blaine, Gilbert
  Falconry. London / New York, 1936, Phillip Allen / Charles
Scribner's Sons. 253 pp., illustrations. 12mo; dust jacket.

Blanchard, Thomas, editor
  The Sportsman's Annual. Greenwich, Connecticut, 1936. 146 pp.,
illustrations. 4to. Paper wrappers. (Also a 1937 second and a 1938 third
edition, same format and publisher)

Bland, Dwain
  Some Turkey Scratchings; a guide reminiscences about wild turkeys.
Delmont, Pennsylvania, 1983, Penn's Wood. 103 pp., photographic plates. 8vo.
Paper wrappers.
  Turkey Hunter's Digest. Northbrook, Illinois, 1986, Digest Books.
256 pp., photographic plates. 4to. Paper wrappers.

Block, George III
  Block's Buck Book. Pennsylvania, 1983, Rainbow Graphics. 100 pp.
Paper wrappers.

Blogg, Percy T.
  There Are No Dull Dark Days. Baltimore, 1944, H. G. Roebuck & Son.
92 pp., illustrations. 8vo; dust jacket. Hunting and fishing on the Chesapeake Bay.

Bloodgood, Lida Fleitman
  Hoofs in the Distance. New York, 1953, D. Van Nostrand Company,
Inc. 131 pp., line drawings. A Van Nostrand Sporting Book. Limited to 985
numbered copies, and signed by the author. 4to; slipcased. Reminiscences of
foxhunting in the U. S. and abroad.

Blossom, F. A., editor
  Told at the Explorers Club; true tales of modern exploration. New
York, 1931, Albert & Charles Boni. 425 pp. 8vo; dust jacket. (Reprinted several
times, same format and publisher) Tales by Prentiss Gray, John Holman and others.

Boardman, Edwin A.
Wings in the Blue. Boston, 1936, Christopher Publishing House. 75 pp., 5 reproductions of etchings by Frank Benson. 8vo; dust jacket. Poems on ducks, geese and upland game birds. Scarce.

Boddington, Craig
Campfires and Game Trails, North American Big Game. Piscataway, New Jersey, 1985, Winchester Press. 295 pp., photographic plates, maps. 8vo; dust jacket.

Boddington, Craig, editor
America; the men and their guns that made her great. Los Angeles, 1981, Peterson Publishing Company. 186 pp., photographic plates. 8vo; dust jackets. With profiles of such notable shooters as Samuel Colt, Annie Oakley, Sergeant York and others.

Bodie, Idella
A Hunt For Life's Extras; the story of Archibald Rutledge. Orangeburg, South Carolina, 1980, Sandlapper Press. 176 pp., frontispiece of Rutledge. 8vo; dust jacket. An older juvenile introducing the reader to Rutledge and his life.

Bodio, Stephen
A Rage For Falcons. New York, 1984, Nick Lyons / Schocken. 135 pp., drawings. 8vo; dust jacket.

Bodsworth, Fred
Last of the Curlews. New York, 1955, Dodd Mead & Co. 128 pp., drawings by T. M. Shortt. 8vo; dust jacket. (Also a 1967 British edition) An account of this migrating shorebird, which was nearly hunted to extinction.
The Strange One. New York, 1955, Dodd Mead & Co. 312 pp. 8vo; dust jacket. The story of a barnacle goose.
Mr. Bodsworth was a popular Canadian writer whose writing centered around conservation and native American issues.

Boker, George Henry
The Legend of the Hounds. New York, 1929, William Edwin Rudge. 31 pp., illustrations by Gordon Ross. 8vo. [Also a deluxe edition of 200 numbered copies with hand-colored illustrations, signed by Ross] Foxhunting.

Bolen, Eric and M. K. Rylander
Whistling Ducks; zoography, ecology and anatomy. Lubbock, 1983, Special Publications, Texas Tech University. 67 pp., maps, bibliography. 4to. Paper wrappers.

Boles, Gerald W.
    Organizing and Operating a Successful Hunting Club. Chenoa, Illinois, 1985, Flyway Publishing Co. 152 pp., illustrations. 8vo.

Bolz, J. Arnold
    Portage into the Past by Canoe Along the Minnesota-Ontario Boundary Waters. Minneapolis, 1960, University of Minnesota Press. 181 pp., illustrations from artwork by Francis Lee Jaques. 8vo; dust jacket.

Bond, James H.
    America's Number One Trophy. Portland, Oregon, 1950, Privately printed. 44 pp., photographic plates. 4to. Paper wrappers. (Revised and reprinted several times, same format and publisher) Hunting grizzly bear, moose, elk, mule deer, sheep and goats.
    Bend the Rod Double. Portland, No date (ca. 1963), Privately printed. 115 pp., illustrations. 4to. Paper wrappers.
    From Out of the Yukon. Portland, Oregon, 1948, Binsford & Mort. 220 pp., plates. 8vo; dust jacket. (Reprinted several times by the author in a larger format in paper wrappers.) Big game hunting in this fabulous wilderness area.
    The Happy Hunting Ground. Portland, Oregon, 1954, Privately printed. 56 pp., photographic plates. 8vo. Paper wrappers. Big game hunting in the Yukon.
    Hold That Tiger; and other tales. Portland, Oregon, 1958, Privately printed. 67 pp., photographic plates. 4to. Paper wrappers.
    The Mountain Lion. Portland, No date, Privately printed. 82 pp., photographic plates. 4to. Paper wrappers.
    The Mule Deer; in search of big heads. Portland, Oregon, No date (ca.1950), Privately printed. 103 pp., photographic plates. 4to. Paper wrappers. (Reprinted, same format and publisher)
    The Rifleman in Alaska. Portland, Oregon, 1953, Privately printed. 48 pp., photographic plates. 4to. Paper wrappers. (Reprinted 1954, same publisher and format)

Bonner, Paul Hyde   1893-1968
    Aged in the Woods. New York, 1958, Charles Scribner's Sons. 157 pp., line drawings. 8vo; dust jacket. (Reprinted 1967, Abercrombie & Fitch, Inc.)
    The Glorious Mornings. New York, 1954, Charles Scribner's Sons. 228 pp., line drawings. 8vo; dust jacket. (Reprinted 1967, Abercrombie & Fitch, Inc.) [Also a presentation edition of the first edition, limited to 100 numbered and signed copies] Hunting various species of upland game, wildfowl and deer hunting; some angling.
    With Both Eyes Open. New York, 1956, Charles Scribner's Sons. 117 pp. 8vo; dust jacket. A novel set in Scotland and South Carolina, with much grouse and quail shooting.

Bookhout, Theodore A.

Waterfowl and Wetlands; an integrated review. Madison, Wisconsin, 1979, Midwest Fish and Wildlife Conference. 148 pp., illustrations. 8vo. Paper wrappers.

Boone and Crockett Club

North American Game Competition. New York, No date (ca. 1947), Boone and Crockett Club. 31 pp. Paper wrappers. This was the first annual Awards Ceremonies publication.

North American Big Game Competition. No place, 1949, Boone and Crockett Club. Single leaf folded, opening to approximately 21" X 16." (Ten more Awards Ceremony competitions were marked with publications in this format - 1950, 1951-52, 1953, 1954-55, 1956-57, 1958-59, 1960, 1961, 1962, 1963)

North American Big Game Competition. No place, 1964-65, Boone and Crockett Club. 8pp. Paper wrappers.

North American Big Game Competition. No Place, 1966-67, Boone and Crockett Club. 32pp. 8vo. Paper wrappers (The next eight Awards Ceremonies were marked with publications of this format with page counts varying from 20 to 40 pp. - 1968-69-70, 1971-72-73, 1974-75-76, 1977-78-79, 1980-81-82, 1983-84-85, 1986-87-88, 1989-90-91. Awards Ceremonies after this date were presented as cloth bound books)

Officers, By-Laws, Treasurer's Report and List of members, 1937-1938. New York, 1938, Privately printed by the club. 48 pp. 8vo. Paper wrappers. A scarce Boone & Crockett item which also contains the obituaries of Madison Grant and George Bird Grinnell.

Report of the Game Preservation Committee. No place, 1911, Privately printed by the club. 32 pp. 8vo. Paper wrappers. Rare.

Boone and Crockett Club

Boone and Crockett Club Record Books
   See: **Ely, Alfred et al., editors**
          Gray, Prentiss Nathaniel, editor
          Nesbitt, William H., et al., editors
          Webb, Samuel, et al., editors
          Waters, Robert S., et al., editors

Boorer, Michael

Wild Cats. Feltham, 1969, Hamlyn. 159 pp., illustrations. 8vo; dust jacket. (Reprinted 1970, Grosset & Dunlap) A general overview of all species worldwide.

Boothroyd, Geoffrey

Guns Through the Ages. New York, 1962, Stirling. 192 pp., photographic plates, drawings. 12mo; dust jacket. (Reprinted, ca. 1978, Bonanza)

The Handgun. New York, 1970, Crown Publishers, Inc. 564 p. illustrations. 4to; dust jacket.

Borden, Courtney (Mrs. C. L. L. Borden)

Adventures in a Man's World. New York, 1933, The Macmillan Company. 246 pp., frontispiece. 8vo; dust jacket. Duck and upland game bird hunting, big game hunting and some angling.

The Cruise of the "Northern Light;" explorations and hunting in the Alaskan and Siberian arctic. New York, 1928, The Macmillan Company. 317 pp., photographic plates, maps. 8vo; dust jacket. Scarce.

Borland, Hal   1900-1978

The History of Wildlife in America. Washington, D. C., 1975, The National Wildlife Federation. 205 pp., color and black and white photographic plates, drawings. 4to; dust jacket.

Our Natural World; the land and wildlife of America as seen and described by writers since the country's discovery. Philadelphia, 1965, J. B. Lippincott Co. 849 pp., illustrations. Tall 8vo; dust jacket. (Reprinted 1969, same format and publisher) With essays by Ruark, Leopold, Roosevelt and many others.

Bossenmaier, Eugene F. and W. H. Marshall

Field Feeding By Waterfowl in Southwestern Manitoba. Washington, D. C., 1958, Wildlife Management Institute. 32 pp., maps, bibliography. 4to. Paper wrappers.

Bosworth, N.

A Treatise on the Rifle. Huntington, West Virginia, 1946, Standard Publications, Inc. 113 pp. 12mo. (A facsimile reproduction of this title originally published in Great Britain in 1846)

Boughan, Rolla B.

Shotgun Ballistics For Hunters. New York, 1956, A. S. Barnes and Company, Inc. 159 pp., photographic plates, drawings. 8vo; dust jacket. (Reprinted 1964 and 1965, same format and publisher)

Boulton, Rudyard

Traveling With the Birds; a book on bird migration. Chicago, 1960, M. A. Donahue & Company. 64 pp., black and white and color illustrations by Walter Weber. Folio. (Originally published, 1933)

Bourjaily, Vance   b. 1922

Country Matters; collected reports from the fields and streams of Iowa and other places.   New York, 1973, Dial Press.   417 pp.   8vo; dust jacket.
Mostly upland game bird hunting; also contains a chapter about Ernest Hemingway.

The Unnatural Enemy; essays on hunting. New York, 1963, Dial Press. 190 pp., drawings by David Levine.   8vo; dust jacket.   (Reprinted, 1984, University of Arizona Press)

Bovet, Louis A., Jr.

Moose Hunting in Alaska, Wyoming and Yukon Territory. Philadelphia, 1933, Dorrance Publishing Company.   143 pp., photographic plates, drawings, maps. 8vo; dust jacket. A scarce big game hunting title.

Bovey, Martin K.

The Saga of the Waterfowl. Washington, D. C., 1949, Wildlife Management Institute. Unpaginated, 69 photographic plates by the author. 4to; dust jacket. (Reprinted 1949, same format and publisher)

Whistling Wings. Garden City, New York, 1947, Doubleday & Co., Inc. 162 pp., photographic plates by the author, drawings by Francis Lee Jaques. 8vo; dust jacket.

Bowden, G. and P. H. Pearce

Non-Resident Big Game Hunting and the Guiding Industry in British Columbia; an economic study.   Vancouver, 1968, University of British Columbia.   69 pp., drawings. 8vo. Paper wrappers.

Bowlen, Bruce

The Orvis Wing Shooting Handbook. New York, 1985, Nick Lyons Books. 83 pp., photographic plates. 8vo. Paper wrappers. (Reprinted many times, same format and publisher)

Bowman, Hank

Antique Guns. Greenwich, Connecticut, 1953, Fawcett Books. 144 pp., illustrations. Edited by Lucian Cary. 8vo. Paper wrappers. (Reprinted several times, various formats)

Antique Guns From the Stagecoach Collection. New York, 1964. 112 pp., photographic plates.   8vo. Paper wrappers. (Reprinted several times, various formats)

Famous Guns From Famous Collections. New York, 1957.   143 pp., photographic plates.   8vo. Paper wrappers. (Reprinted several times, various formats)

Famous Guns From the Harold's Club Collection. New York, 1962. 144 pp., photographic plates.   8vo; dust jacket. (Also reprinted in paper wrappers)

Bowman, Hank, continued

    Famous Guns From the Smithsonian Collection. Greenwich, Connecticut, 1966, Fawcett Books. 112 pp., illustrations. 8vo. Paper wrappers. (Reprinted several times, various formats)

    Famous Guns From the Winchester Collection. Greenwich, Connecticut, 1958, Fawcett Books. 144 pp., illustrations. 8vo; dust jacket. (Reprinted several times, various formats)

Bowring, Dave

    Bowhunting For Whitetails; your best methods for taking America's favorite deer. Harrisburg, 1985, The Stackpole Company. 304 pp., photographic plates, drawings. 8vo; dust jacket.

    How To Hunt; a basic guide to hunting big game, small game, upland birds and waterfowl. New York, 1978, Winchester Press. 200 pp., photographic plates. 8vo; dust jacket.

Boyce, Mark S. and Larry D. Hayden-Wing

    North American Elk; ecology, behavior and management. Laramie, 1979, The University of Wyoming. 294 pp., illustrations. 4to.

Boyd, Bud

    Bud Boyd's Guide To Hunting and Fishing in California. San Francisco, 1960, The Chronicle Publishing Co. 96 pp., illustrations. 4to; dust jacket. (Also published in paper wrappers)

Boyd, James

    The Long Hunt. New York, 1930. 376 pp., illustrations. Limited to 250 numbered and signed copies. 8vo.

Boyer, Samuel P.

    A Nationwide Survey on the Wild Turkey. Johnstown, Pennsylvania, 1929, Wild Turkey Conservation Association. 24 pp. 12mo. Paper wrappers. (Also a 1984 edition titled, *The Wild Turkey;* a survey. Durham, North Carolina, limited to 470 copies, also in paper wrappers)

Boyle, Robert H.

    At The Top of Their Game. New York, 1983, Nick Lyons / Winchester Press. 204 pp. 8vo; dust jacket. (Reprinted in paper wrappers) Biographical sketches of various sportsman, including Zane Grey, Dick Wolters, Lefty Krey and others.

    Sport; mirror of American life. Boston, 1963, Little, Brown & Company. 293 pp. 8vo; dust jacket. An insight of how sport affects the lives of Americans. Much on traditional team sports, but some mention of hunting and fishing.

Boynton, Mary Fuertes

Louis Agassiz Fuertes; his life briefly told and his correspondence edited. New York, 1956, Oxford University Press. 317 pp., illustrations. 8vo; dust jacket. A biography of Fuertes by his daughter, with his correspondence to Courteney Brandreth, Allan Brooks and others.

Bradford, K. M.

Deer Hunter's Handbook; or how to win your way through a bull session. Orinda, California, 1953, Maynard P. Buehler. 33 pp. 16mo. Paper wrappers.

Still Hunter's Handbook; or how to sit, sneak and stalk. Orinda, California, 1954, Maynard P. Buehler. 30 pp. 16mo. Paper wrappers.

Bradley, Norm

Fox Trapping Maine Methods. Island Falls, 1979, Privately printed. 41 pp., photographic plates, drawings. 8vo. Paper wrappers.

Bradner, Enos

The Inside on the Outdoors; an outdoor editor's 26 year scrapbook. Seattle, 1971, Superior Publishing Company. 256 pp., black and white illustrations from drawings by Allan Pratt. 8vo; dust jacket.

Bradt, G. W.

Michigan Wildlife Sketches; the native mammals of Michigan's forests, fields and marshes. Lansing, 1972, Michigan Department of Natural Resources. 85 pp., drawings by Charles E. Schafer. 8vo. Paper wrappers.

Brady, James

Modern Turkey Hunting; a thorough guide to the habits, habitat and methods of hunting America's largest game bird.. New York, 1973, Crown Publishers, Inc. 160 pp., illustrations. 8vo; dust jacket. (Reprinted, same format and publisher)

Brady, Lillian

Saga of a Whitetail Deer. Los Angeles, California, 1981, Amber Crest Books. 119 pp. The story of a white tail deer in a Minnesota wildlife refuge that was created by the author and her husband.

Brakefield, Tom

Big Game Hunter's Digest. Northfield, Illinois, 1977, DBI Books. 288 pp., illustrations.

Hunting Big-Game Trophies; a North American guide. New York, 1976, E. P. Dutton & Co., Inc. / Outdoor Life Books. 446 pp., photographic plates. 8vo; dust jacket.

Brakefield, Tom, continued

Small Game Hunting. Philadelphia, 1978, J. B. Lippincott Co. 253 pp., photographic plates. 8vo; dust jacket.

The Sportsman's Complete Book of Trophy and Meat Care. Harrisburg, 1975, The Stackpole Company. 223 pp., photographic plates. 8vo; dust jacket.

Brakhage, G. K.

Canada Goose Nesting and Management Studies on Selected Areas in Missouri. No place, 1965, Missouri Conservation Commission. 11 pp. Paper wrappers.

Branch, E. Douglas

The Hunting of the Buffalo. New York, 1929, D. Appleton & Co. 239 pp., photographic plates. 8vo; dust jacket. (Reprinted 1962, University of Nebraska Press) A historical discussion of the near extermination of this game animal by native Americans, sport hunters and commercial hunters. The first edition is scarce.

Brandborg, Stewart M.

Life History and Management of the Mountain Goat in Idaho. Boise, 1955, Idaho Department of Fish and Game. 142 pp., photographic plates, drawings, bibliography. 8vo. Paper wrappers.

Brander, Michael

The Hunting Instinct; the development of field sports over the ages. Edinburgh, 1964, Oliver. 176 pp., photographic plates, bibliography. 8vo; dust jacket.

Hunting and Shooting; from earliest times to the present day. New York, 1971, G. P. Putnam's Sons. 225 pp., color and black and white photographic plates. Tall 8vo; dust jacket. A history of the sport with a significant amount of North American hunting.

The International Encyclopedia of Shooting. London, 1972, Peerage. 352 pp., color and black and white illustrations. 4to; dust jacket.

The Roughshooter's Dog. New York, 1975, St. Martin's Press. 198 pp., photographic plates. 8vo; dust jacket. (Originally published, London) Training and hunting with the all purpose hunting dog.

Brandon, C. Watt

On the Big Game Trail - Jackson Hole, September, 1936. Kemmerer, Wyoming, No date (ca. 1937), Privately printed. 18 pp., photographic plates. 12mo. Paper wrappers. Rare.

Brandreth, Paul (*pseud.* of **Paulina B. Brandreth**)

Trails of Enchantment. New York, 1930, G. Howard Watt. 318 pp., illustrations. Introduction by Roy Chapman Andrews. 8vo; dust jacket. An enchanting and elegant account of the woods and of deer hunting, written by a woman who was an experienced hunter and an accomplished author.

Brandt, Herbert

Alaska Bird Trails; adventures of an expedition by dog sled to the delta of the Yukon River at Hooper Bay. Cleveland, 1943, Bird Research Foundation. 464 pp., color and black and white illustrations by Brooks and Kalmbach, photographic plates. 4to; dust jacket.

Braun, Clait R. and G. E. Rogers

The Whitetailed Ptarmigan in Colorado. No place, 1971, Colorado Game and Fish Commission. 80 pp., photographic plates, bibliography. 8vo. Paper wrappers.

Braun, D. Lee

See **Campbell, Robert, editor**

Brearley, Joan

This is the Irish Setter. Neptune City, 1975, TFH Books. Illustrations. 8vo.

Breede, Adam

Adventuring; a story of a trip around the world with big game hunting in Africa and India New York, 1926, Privately printed by the Grafton Press. 322 pp., photographic plates. 8vo. With one chapter on bear hunting in Alaska.

Brentano, Frances, editor

Big Cats. Chicago, 1949, Ziff-Davis Publishing Company. 306 pp. 8vo; dust jacket. (Also a 1949 British edition) An anthology of wild cat stories; mostly African and Asian, but some North American.

Brewer, Larry W.

The Ruffed Grouse in Western Washington. No place, 1980, Washington Game Department. 101 pp., black and white and color illustrations from photographs. 8vo. Paper wrappers.

Brewster, William

Concord River; selections from the journals of William Brewster. Cambridge, Massachusetts, 1937, Harvard University Press. Edited by S. O. Dexter. 257 pp., black and white and color illustrations from paintings and etchings by Frank Benson. 8vo; dust jacket.

Brewster, William, continued

October Farm: from the Concord journals and diaries of William Brewster. Cambridge, Massachusetts, 1937, Harvard University Press. 285 pp., photographic plates. 12mo.

Mr. Brewster was an eminent ornithologist. These two works have much on the habits of game birds in the area.

Bridenhagen, Keith

Decoy Pattern Book. New York, 1984, Sterling. 127 pp., full size patterns. Folio. Paper wrappers.

Bridenhagen, Keith and P. Spielman

Realistic Decoys; carving, texturing, painting and finishing. New York, 1984, Sterling. 224 pp., photographic plates. 4to. Paper wrappers.

Bridges, Harry P.

The Woodmont Story; hunting and fishing and raising wild turkeys in a sportsman's paradise. New York, 1953, A. S. Barnes and Company, Inc. 209 pp., photographic plates. Folio; dust jacket. Much on turkey hunting at the Woodmont Club in Hancock, Maryland.

Bridgman, Elizabeth Klein and Mary Atkinson Mitchell, editors

A Fascinating Game. Minneapolis, Minnesota, 1940, Privately printed. 84 pp., illustrations. 8vo. With one chapter on hunting and fishing. Scarce.

Briggs, Edward A.

Hounds in the Hills. Brattleboro, Vermont, 1938, Stephen Daye Press. 203 pp., photographic plates. 8vo; dust jacket. Raccoon and fox hunting.

Briggs, Ellis O.

Shots Heard Round the World; an ambassador's hunting adventures of four continents. New York, 1957, Viking Press. 149 pp., color and black and white illustrations. 8vo; dust jacket. (Also a 1958 British edition) Duck and game bird shooting.

Briggs, Frank

You Can Be an Expert Rifleman. New York, 1963. 96 pp., drawings, photographic plates. 8vo.

Brimly, C. S.

Mammals of North Carolina. Elon College, North Carolina, 1946, Carolina Biological. Unpaginated (36pp.). 4to. (A revision of 18 articles appearing in *Carolina Tips*, 1944-1946)

Brings, Lawrence M., editor

Outdoor Horizons. Minneapolis, 1957, Denison & Company. 231 pp., illustrations. An anthology of stories about American wildlife authored by Jack O'Connor, Jimmy Robinson and others.

Brister, Bob

Field & Stream 1973 Guide To Trap And Skeet. New York, 1973, CBS Publications. 92 p. illustrations. 4to.

The Golden Crescent. Houston, Texas, 1969, Zephyr Press. 125 pp., color illustrations by Jack Cowan. A deluxe type book with no limitation, signed by the author and illustrator. Oblong 4to. (Reprinted 1969, same format and publisher) Hunting and fishing from Louisiana to Mexico. Apparently, nearly all the copies of the first edition of this work were destroyed at the bindery. The second printing is also scarce.

Moss, Mallards and Mules. New York, 1973, Winchester Press. 216 pp., black and white illustrations from drawings by Stanley Farnham. 8vo; dust jacket. (Reprinted in 1973 and 1974, same publisher and format) [Also a 1974 Amwell Press edition, limited to 1000 numbered and signed copies; slipcased]

Shotgunning; the art and the science. New York, 1976, Winchester Press. 321 pp., photographic plates. 8vo; dust jacket. (Reprinted several times, same format and publisher) A very useful guide.

Bronson, W. S.

Horns and Antlers. New York, 1942, Harcourt, Brace & Co., Inc. 143 pp., black and white and color illustrations from photographs. 8vo; dust jacket. (Reprinted, same format and publisher)

Brooks, Alfred Hulse

Blazing Alaska's Trails. No place, 1953, University of Alaska / Arctic Institute. 528 pp., photographic plates, maps. 8vo. An account of Alaska's history with much on hunting, trapping and fishing. Scarce.

Brooks, David

Fur Animals of Indiana. Indianapolis, 1959, Indiana Department of Conservation. 195 pp., photographic plates, drawings, maps. 8vo. Paper wrappers. A commentary about trapping in the state.

Broome, Harvey

Faces of the Wilderness. Missoula, Montana, 1972, Mountain Press. 271 pp., photographic plates. 8vo; dust jacket. A general discussion of wilderness areas.

Brophy, William S.

L. C. Smith Shotguns. No place, 1977, Beinfeld Publishing Company. 244 pp., black and white and color illustrations from photographs. 4to. (Reprinted several times, various publishers with one titled, *Plans and Specifications of the L. C. Smith Shotgun*)

The Springfield 1903 Rifles; the illustrated, documented story of the design, development and production of all models, appendages and accessories. Harrisburg, 1985, Stackpole Books. 616 pp., illustrations. 4to.

Brothers, Al and Murphy E. Ray

Producing Quality Whitetails. Texas, 1975, Fiesta Publishing. 245 pp., illustrations. Relating to deer herd management.

Brower, Charles

Fifty Years Below Zero. New York, 1942, Dodd, Mead and Co. 310 pp., photographic plates. 8vo; dust jacket. Mostly arctic exploration, but some hunting and whaling.

Brower, David, editor

Wilderness: America's Living Heritage. Los Angeles, 1961, Sierra Club. 204 pp., photographic plates. 8vo; dust jacket.

Brown, Alexander Crosby

Life With Grover; a Chesapeake Bay Retriever who thought he was a person. Cambridge, Maryland, 1962, Tidewater Publishers. 69 pp., drawings. Tall 8vo; dust jacket. A humorous look at living and hunting with a Chesapeake Bay Retriever.

Brown, Charles P. and Stacey B. Robeson

The Ring-Necked Pheasant in New York. Albany, 1959, New York Department of Conservation. 39 pp., drawings by Wayne Trimm, bibliography. 8vo. Paper wrappers.

Brown, David E.   b. 1938

Arizona Wetlands and Waterfowl. Tucson, 1985, University of Arizona Press. 169 pp., color and black and white illustrations, bibliography. 4to; dust jacket.

The Grizzly in the Southwest; documentary of an extinction. Norman, 1985, University of Oklahoma Press. 274 pp., photographic plates. 8vo; dust jacket. Included are first-hand accounts of the species when it was still in the region. An important lesson in wildlife conservation.

The Wolf in the Southwest; the making of an endangered species. Tucson, 1983, University of Arizona Press. 195 pp., photographic plates. 8vo. Paper wrappers.

Brown, David M.
The .36 Calibers of the Colt Single Action Army. No place, 1965, Privately printed. 223 pp., photographic plates, drawings. 4to. A scarce monograph.

Brown, Delores Cline
Yukon Trophy Trails. Sidney, British Columbia, 1971, Gray's. 213 pp. 8vo; dust jacket. Hunting tales from the wife of a professional guide.

Brown, Earle B.
Basic Optics for the Sportsman. New York, 1949, Stoeger Arms Corp. 259 pp., drawings, photographic plates. 8vo; dust jacket.

Brown, Lt. Col. Edwards
Rimfire Rifleman. Harrisburg, 1947, The Military Service Publishing Company. 320 pp., illustrations by the author and Virginia S. Brown. 8vo; dust jacket. A valuable reference work for the rimfire rifle enthusiast.

Brown, J. Hammond, editor
Outdoors Unlimited; a collection of stories and articles which reflect the current American scene of the recreational outdoors. New York, 1947, A. S. Barnes and Company, Inc. 343 pp., black and white illustrations from drawings. 8vo; dust jacket. (Also a Grosset & Dunlap edition titled, *Great Hunting and Fishing Stories*) With stories by Buckingham, Wulff, Sheldon and illustrations by Schaldach, Hines and others.

Brown, Joan Winer
Simon the Pointer. New York, 1966, Viking Press. Illustrated by Jared Taylor. 8vo; dust jacket. A juvenile story about a courageous pointer.

Brown, Kenneth
The Medchester Club. New York, 1932, The Derrydale Press. 224 pp., drawings by W. Smithson Broadhead. Limited to 950 numbered copies. 8vo. An entertaining collection of golf and foxhunting stories.

Brown, Leslie
Birds of Prey; their biology and ecology. New York, 1977, A & W. 256 pp., color and black and white illustrations, bibliography. Tall 8vo; dust jacket.
Eagles. New York / London, 1970, Arco / Barker. 96 pp., color and black and white illustrations. 8vo. A general discussion of all the world's species.

Brown, Leslie and Dean Amadon
   Eagles, Hawks and Falcons of the World. New York, 1968, McGraw-Hill Publishing Company.   Two volumes of 414 pp. and 531 pp. respectively, each with black and white and color illustrations, bibliography.   4to; slipcased.
A most thorough and attractive reference.

Brown, Louis P.
   Books: Property of the Estate of the Late Louis P. Brown, Glen Falls, New York and Others.   New York, 1967, Parke-Bernet Galleries, Inc.   48 pp. 8vo.   Paper wrappers.   An auction catalog with some sporting lots.

Brown, M. L.
   Firearms in Colonial America; the impact on history and technology, 1492-1792.   Washington, D. C., 1980, The Smithsonian Institute.   450 pp., illustrations, bibliography.   4to; dust jacket.

Brown, Paul   1893-1958
   The American Spaniel Club Year Book and the Cocker Spaniel Pictured. No place, 1946, American Spaniel Club.   264 pp., color plate by Dr. Edgar Burke, drawings by the author.   Limited to 750 copies. 8vo.   Mr. Brown wrote and/or illustrated over 50 books including juveniles, dog books and important equestrian titles.

Brown, Peter
   Guns and Hunting. New York, 1955, A. S. Barnes and Company, Inc. 224 pp., photographic plates.   16mo; dust jacket. (Reprinted several times, slightly larger format, same publisher)

Brown, Tom, Jr.
   The Tracker. Englewood Cliffs, New Jersey, 1978, Prentice-Hall, Inc. 190 pp., illustrations.   (Reprinted 1978, Berkeley Books)

Brown, Tom, Jr. and William Owen
   The Search: The Continuing Story of the Tracker. Englewood Cliffs, New Jersey, 1980, Prentice-Hall, Inc.   219 pp., illustrations.

Brown, Vinson
   Reading the Woods. Harrisburg, 1969, The Stackpole Company.   160 pp., photographic plates, drawings.   Tall 8vo; dust jacket. Mostly general nature, but some on game ecology.

Brown, William F.   1906-1990

Field Trials; history, management and judging standards . New York, 1934, A. S. Barnes and Company, Inc. 221 pp., photographic plates. 8vo; dust jacket. (Reprinted many times, same format and publisher; later printings in Barnes' Sportsmen's Library series)

The Field Trial Primer. Chicago, 1934, American Field Publishing Company. 80 pp., photographic plates. 12mo; dust jacket.

Albert Frederick Hochwalt; a biography. Dayton, Ohio, 1939, Privately printed. 346 pp., photographic plates. 8vo; dust jacket. [Also a deluxe edition, specially bound and limited to 100 numbered copies signed by the author]

How To Train Hunting Dogs; a successful system of training pointing dogs, sporting spaniels and non slip retrievers. New York, 1942, A. S. Barnes and Company, Inc. 228 pp., photographic plates. A title in Barnes' Sportsman's Library series.   8vo; dust jacket. (Reprinted many times, same format and publisher)

National Field Trial Champions 1956-1966. New York, 1966, A. S. Barnes and Company, Inc. 252 pp., photographic plates. 8vo; dust jacket.

Retriever Gun Dogs; history, breed standards and training. New York, 1939, A. S. Barnes and Company, Inc.   143 pp., line drawings by Edwin Megargee, photographic plates. (Reprinted many times, same format and publisher; later printings in Barnes' Sportsmen's Library series)   8vo; dust jacket.

Retriever Gun Dogs; history, breed standards and training. West Hartford, Vermont, 1945, The Countryman Press. 143 pp., line drawings by Edwin Megargee, photographic plates.   Limited to 5000 copies.   8vo; dust jacket.   (Simultaneously published, London, Thos. Yoseloff) [Also a deluxe edition, specially bound with color frontispiece by Edwin Megargee and limited to 375 numbered copies, signed by the author and artist; slipcased)

Mr. Brown was a popular hunting dog trainer and writer who also published *American Field*, a weekly journal devoted to the sporting dog.

Brown, William F. and Nash Buckingham

National Field Trial Champions; an authentic and detailed history of the National Field Trial Championship Association since inception.   Harrisburg, 1955, The Stackpole Company.   520 pp., photographic plates, frontispiece in color from a painting by Edmund Osthaus.   4to; dust jacket.   [Also a deluxe edition, specially bound and numbered but with an unspecified limitation]

Browne, Bellmore H.

Guns and Gunning. Seattle, 1975, Shorey Publishing Company.   106 pp., plus ads, photographic plates. Limited to 200 copies.   12mo.   Paper wrappers. (Originally published, 1908, Stevens Arms Company) This was intended by Stevens to be primarily a promotion for their firearms.

Brownell, F. R. "Bob," editor

    Encyclopedia of Modern Firearms: Parts and Assembly, Volume I, Montezuma, Iowa, Brownell and Son, Inc. 1059 pp., photographic plates. 4to. (Reprinted 1960, same publisher and format)

    Gunsmith Kinks. Montezuma, Iowa, 1969, Brownell and Son, Inc. 496 pp., photographic plates. 8vo; dust jacket. (Reprinted many times, same format and publisher)

    Gunsmith Kinks II. Montezuma, Iowa, 1984, Brownell and Son, Inc. 496 pp., photographic plates. 8vo; dust jacket. (Reprinted many times, same format and publisher)

Browning, John M. and M. S. Browning

    A History of Browning Guns From 1831. Ogden, Utah, 1942, Browning Arms Company. 60 pp., photographic plates. 8vo. (Also published in paper wrappers)

Browning, J. and C. Gentry

    John M. Browning, American Gunmaker. An illustrated biography of the man and his guns. Garden City, New York, 1964, Doubleday & Co., Inc. 323 pp., photographic plates, frontispiece in color. 8vo; dust jacket. (Reprinted many times, same format, various publishers)

Browning, Meshach

    Forty-Four Years in the Life of a Hunter; being reminiscences of Meshack Browning, a Maryland hunter, roughly written down by himself. Philadelphia, 1928, J. B. Lippincott Co. 400 pp., illustrations. 8vo; dust jacket. (Originally published, 1859, and reprinted several times, various publishers) Hunting bear, deer, wolf, etc. in early Maryland.

Bruce, Jay C.

    Cougar Killer. New York, 1943, Comet Press. 172 pp., photographic plates. 8vo; dust jacket. A vanity press book by a man who claimed to have killed 669 cougars. He also claimed to have caught 32,000 trout in the seasons of 1899 and 1900. A repulsive reminder of the little value placed on wildlife by some people of that era.

Bruemmer, Fred

    The Arctic. Montreal, 1975, Infocor. 224 pp., color and black and white illustrations, bibliography. Folio; dust jacket. (Reprinted 1975, same format and publisher) A well-illustrated discussion including native hunting activities.

Bruette, Dr. William A.   b. 1873

American Duck, Goose and Brant Shooting.   New York, 1929, G. Howard Watt. 415 pp., frontispiece and other illustrations in color from paintings by Clement B. Davis. 8vo; dust jacket.   (Reprinted 1947, Charles Scribner's Sons) An important work by a writer with much experience in the subject.

The Cocker Spaniel; breeding, breaking and handling. New York, 1937, Stackpole Sons. 216 pp., photographic plates. 8vo; dust jacket. A scarce work about training the cocker spaniel as a hunting dog.

Log Cabins and Camps; how to build and furnish them. New York, 1934, G. Howard Watt. 96 pp., illustrations from plans by Robert Gardner and William Wicks. 8vo. Paper wrappers. (Reprinted, Nessmuk Library)

Modern Breaking; a book about bird dogs. New York, 1936, Nessmuk Library. 169 pp., black and white illustrations from paintings and drawings by Edmund Osthaus and Edwin Megargee. 12mo. Cloth backed paper wrappers. (Originally published, 1906, by the author, and reprinted in several formats by several publishers between 1906 and 1936)

Modern Dogs; their standards, care, feeding, breeding, training and treatment.   New York, No date (ca. 1932), Grosset & Dunlap.   244 pp., photographic plates. 8vo; dust jacket.

Modern Guncraft; hitting vs. missing. New York, 1936, Nessmuk Library. 128 pp., illustrated. 12mo. Paper wrappers. (Reprinted 1940, same format and publisher)

Sportsman's Encyclopedia. New York, 1935, Nessmuk Library. 264 pp., drawings. Cloth backed paper wrappers. (Originally published, 1923 and 1926, Forest and Stream Publishing Company in two volumes)

Mr. Bruette was an associate editor of *Forest and Stream* magazine and wrote extensively about hunting, gun dogs and the outdoors. See Phillips.

Brunner, Josef

Tracks and Tracking. New York, 1934, The Macmillan Company. 217 pp., drawings. 12mo; dust jacket. (Reprinted several times, same format and publisher. Originally published, 1909, Outing Publishing Company)

Bruns, Henry P.

Angling Books of the Americas.   Atlanta, 1975, The Angler's Press. 543 pp., illustrations. Thick 4to. A thorough angling book bibliography.

Brusewitz, Gunnar

Hunting; hunters, game weapons and hunting methods from the remote past to the present day.   New York, 1969, Stein & Day, Inc.   251 pp., illustrations. 4to; dust jacket. A general overview with one chapter on falconry.

Bryant, Nelson

    Fresh Air, Bright Water; adventures in wood, field and stream. New York, 1971, American Heritage. 283 pp. 8vo; dust jacket. A collection of the author's columns on hunting and angling originally appearing in *The New York Times.*

Bryant, Nelson and Hanson Carroll

    The Wildfowler's World. New York, 1973, Winchester Press. 127 pp., black and white and color illustrations from photographs. 4to; dust jacket.

Buchanan-Jardine, Sir John

    Hounds of the World. New York, 1937, Charles Scribner's Sons. 233 pp., black and white and many color illustrations from paintings by T. Ivester Lloyd and Baron Karl Reille. 4to. (Originally published, Great Britain)

Buchele, William and George Shumway

    Recreating the American Longrifle. York, Pennsylvania, 1970, Privately printed. 194 pp., illustrations. 8vo. A guide to building a Kentucky rifle.

Bucher, Ruth, editor

    The Book of Hunting. New York, 1973, Paddington Press. 319 pp., black and white and color illustrations. 4to; dust jacket. (Originally published, 1973, Germany, titled *Das Buch Der Jagd*)

Buckingham, Nash   **1880-1971**

    Blood Lines; tales of shooting and fishing. New York, 1938, The Derrydale Press. 227 pp., photographic plates. Limited to 1250 numbered copies. Tall 8vo. (Reprinted 1947, smaller format, G. P. Putnam's Sons)

    THE BUCKINGHAM LIBRARY. *De Shootinest Gent'man, Mark Right!, Ole Miss', Blood Lines, Tattered Coat, Game Bag* and *Hallowed Years.* Indianola, Mississippi, 1980, Delta Arms. Seven volumes. Issued in a limited edition of 2500 sets. 8vo; dust jackets; slipcased.

    De Shootinest Gent'man; and other tales. New York, 1934, The Derrydale Press. 240 pp., plates. Limited to 950 numbered copies. Tall 8vo. (Reprinted 1984, Premier Press) A collection of Mr. Buckingham's hunting tales.

    De Shootinest Gent'man. New York, 1941, Charles Scribner's Sons. 24 pp., plus a 10 pp. reminiscence of Capt. Money by the author, drawings by Robert Ball. Introduction by Russell Annabel. 8vo; dust jacket. This edition only contains the title story.

    De Shootinest Gent'man; and other tales. New York, 1943, G. P. Putnam's Sons. 222 pp., illustrated. 8vo; dust jacket. (Reprinted several times, same format and publisher)

Buckingham, Nash, continued

De Shootinest Gent'man; and other tales. New York, 1961, Thomas Nelson & Sons, Inc. 246 pp., color frontispiece; black and white illustrations from drawings by Hamilton Greene. 4to; plastic dust jacket. [Also a specially bound, limited edition of 250 numbered copies signed by the author and artist; slipcased]

A Duck Hunter's Viewpoint; as to the supply and the 1935 duck hunting regulations. New York, 1936, National Association of Audubon Societies. 14 pp. 8vo. Paper wrappers. An unusual Buckingham item.

Game Bag. New York, 1945, G. P. Putnam's Sons. 186 pp., black and white illustrations from drawings by H.P.A.M. Hoecker. 8vo; dust jacket. [Also a specially bound, limited edition of 1250 numbered and signed copies, slightly larger format]

Hallowed Years. Harrisburg, 1953, The Stackpole Company. 209 pp., introduction by Col. Harold P. Sheldon. 8vo; dust jacket. This title was probably printed a second time by Stackpole, since it is seen with two different binding variants. As with many other titles, Stackpole often reprinted books without identifying them as such.

Mark Right! New York, 1936, The Derrydale Press. 250 pp., plates. Limited to 1250 numbered copies. Tall 8vo. (Reprinted 1944, smaller format, G. P. Putnam's Sons)

Ole Miss'. New York, 1937, The Derrydale Press. 242 pp., plates. Foreword by Capt. Paul Curtis. Limited to 1250 numbered copies. Tall 8vo. (Reprinted 1946, smaller format, G. P. Putnam's Sons)

Tattered Coat. New York, 1944, G. P. Putnam's Sons. 210 pp., line drawings by Arthur Fuller. 8vo; dust jacket. (Reprinted twice, same format and publisher) [Also a specially bound, limited first edition of 995 numbered and signed copies, slightly larger format]

Mr. Buckingham continues to be one of the most celebrated sporting writers of the twentieth century.

Buckingham, Nash

Also see **Brown, William F.**

Also see **Cooper, Page**

Also see **Evans, George Bird, editor**

Also see **McGuire, Harry**

Buckley, Peter

Ernest. New York, 1978. 178 pp., photographic plates. Folio; dust jacket. A photo-essay of the life of Ernest Hemingway.

Buckman, C. T. "Buck"

75 Years With a Shotgun; an expert hunter and trapshooter shares experiences of a lifetime. Fresno, California, 1974, Valley Publishing Company. 143 pp., illustrations. 8vo; dust jacket. [Also a deluxe edition, limited to 100 numbered and signed copies] An uncommon shooting title.

Buckmaster, Robert
Sporting Books; the Robert Buckmaster Collection. New York, 1983, Swann Galleries, Inc. Unpaginated. 8vo. Paper wrappers. The auction catalog of this sporting library containing many hunting and angling works.

Buckwalter, Harold R.
Susquehanna River Decoys. Dallastown, Pennsylvania, 1978, Privately printed. 162 pp., photographic plates, drawings. 4to; dust jacket.

Budgett, H. M.
Hunting By Scent. New York, No date (1933), Charles Scribner's Sons. 122 pp., photographic plates, illustrations from paintings by Lionel Edwards. 4to. (Originally published, Great Britain) An interesting account of the subject as it relates to dogs in sport.

Buechner, Helmut K.
The Bighorn Sheep in the United States, Its Past, Present and Future. Washington, D. C., 1960, The Wildlife Society. 174 pp., photographic plates, maps, bibliography. 4to. Paper wrappers.

Bueler, Lois E.
Wild Dogs of the World. New York, 1973, Stein & Day, Publishers. 274 pp., photographic plates, bibliography. 8vo; dust jacket.

Bufkin, J. Earl
Handling Your Hunting Dog. St. Louis, 1937, The Ralston Purina Company. 64 pp., illustrations. 16mo. (Reprinted many times, same format and publsiher) A promotional booklet.

Bump, Gardiner, et al.
The Ruffed Grouse; life history, propagation, management. New York, 1947, New York State Conservation Department. 915 pp., photographic plates, black and white illustrations from drawings by Clayton Seagears and Fred Everett, four color plates from paintings by Everett, bibliography, appendices. Thick 8vo. (Reprinted 1978, Ken Szabo.) Despite its age, this is still considered a standard reference work.
Progress Report of the Ruffed Grouse Investigation. Albany, 1932, State of New York. 19 pp., photographic plates. 8vo. Paper wrappers. (An off-print from the 21st Annual Report, 1931)
Wildlife Habitat Changes in the Connecticut Hill Game Management Area. Ithaca, New York, 1950, Cornell University Press. 75 pp., photographic plates, maps. 8vo. Paper wrappers.

Bump, Robert

Is Our Day Planned For Us? I Believe So. No place, 1977, Privately printed. 7 pp. Limited to 200 numbered copies. 8vo. Paper wrappers. A scarce work dedicated to Brooksby Gray, describing an Adirondack deer hunt

Bunch, F. Q.

Expert Fox and Coyote Trapping; sets for land, water and snow; improved and original methods, all the old time sets used by experts, baits and scents and scent making. Red Wing, Minnesota, 1934, S. N. Gibson & Son. 66 pp., illustrations. 12mo. Paper wrappers. (Reprinted, same format and publisher)

Burch, Monte   b. 1943

Calling and Rattling Whitetail Bucks. Missouri, 1985, Outdoor World Press, Inc. 32 pp. Paper wrappers.

Gun Care and Repair; technical procedures for customizing sporting rifles. New York, 1978, Winchester Press. 191 pp., photographic plates. 8vo; dust jacket.

The Outdoorsman's Workshop. New York, 1977, Winchester Press. 238 pp., photographic plates, drawings. 8vo; dust jacket. Do-it-yourself projects for the outdoorsman.

Shotgunner's Guide. Tulsa, Oklahoma, 1980, Winchester Press. 162 pp., photographic plates. 8vo; dust jacket.

Waterfowling; a sportsman's handbook. New York, 1978, Harper & Row, Publishers, Inc.. 225 pp., photographic plates, drawings. 8vo; dust jacket.

Burden, W. Douglas   1898-1978

Look To the Wilderness. Boston, 1960, Little Brown & Company. 251 pp., photographic plates. Foreword by Roy Chapman Andrews. 8vo; dust jacket. (Reprinted 1962, same format and publisher) Tales of the author's hunting experiences for big game around the world.

Mr. Burden was close friends with Roy Chapman Andrews and they and their wives traveled extensively around the world. Burden was also a long-time member of the Boone and Crockett Club and, in 1927, wrote the first title published with the club's "Approval," *The Dragon Lizards of Komodo.*

Burdick, Charles Baker

Fins and Feathers; holidays afield and afloat. LaGrange, Illinois, 1936, Privately printed. 209 pp. 8vo. The author's experiences of hunting and fishing.

Burford, Virgil

North To Danger. New York, 1954, The John Day Company. 254 pp. 8vo. Mostly commercial diving in Alaska, but some bear hunting.

Burger, George V.
Practical Wildlife Management. New York, 1973, Winchester Press. 218 pp., illustrations. 8vo; dust jacket. Intended primarily for the landowner.

Burget, Martin
The Wild Turkey in Colorado. No place, 1957, Privately printed. 68 pp., illustrations. 4to. Paper wrappers.

Burk, Bruce   b. 1917
Game Bird Carving. New York, 1972, Winchester Press. 290 pp., black and white and color illustrations from photographs. 4to; dust jacket. (Reprinted many times, same format and publisher. Also two revised editions, 1974 and 1982, same format and publisher)
Waterfowl Studies. New York, 1976, Winchester Press. 254 pp., black and white and color illustrations from photographs. 4to; dust jacket. (Reprinted several times, same format and publisher) [Also an Amwell Press limited first edition of 1000 numbered and signed copies; slipcased]
Complete Waterfowl Studies; Volume III - Geese and Swans. Exton, Pennsylvania, 1984, Schiffer Publishing Company. The third volume in a comprehensive photographic study of American waterfowl. 200 pp., color and black and white illustrations. 4to; dust jacket. Two volumes were published prior to this work. All presented waterfowl from the carver's viewpoint.

Burk, Dale A.
Montana Hunting. Stevensville, Montana, 1981, Privately printed. 131 pp., illustrations. 8vo. Paper wrappers.

Burk, Dale A., editor
The Black Bear in Modern North America. New York, 1979, Boone and Crockett Club / Campfire Club of America. 210 pp., photographic plates. 8vo. Paper wrappers. [Also a limited edition of 100 copies, cloth bound]

Burke, Patricia H. A.
Barnegat Bay Decoys and Gunning Clubs. Toms River, 1985, Ocean County Historical Society. 44 pp., photographic plates, fold-out map, bibliography. Limited to 1000 copies. 8vo. Paper wrappers.

Burke, Ronnie
Ruger Model 77 Bolt Action Rifles. Dallas, 1983, Taylor Publishing Co. 100 pp., color and black and white illustrations. Limited to 3000 numbered and signed copies. 4to.

Burlingame, Mark W.

Hodgman's Handy Book of Sportsman's Secrets. Framingham, Massachusetts, 1946, Hodgman's Sporting Goods. 168 pp., illustrations. 16mo.

Burnham, Maj. Frederick Russell

Scouting on Two Continents. Garden City, New York, 1926, Doubleday, Page & Co., Inc. 370 pp., photographic plates, drawings, maps. 8vo; dust jacket. (Reprinted 1928, same format and publisher. Also reprinted 1942, Haynes) Military scouting in Africa, the southern U. S. and Mexico, with some hunting.

Burnham, Murray with Russell Tinsley

Murray Burnham's Hunting Secrets. Piscataway, New Jersey, 1983, Winchester Press. 161 pp. 8vo; dust jacket.

Burns, Fox

The Roving Outdoorsman. Terre Haute, Indiana, 1966, J. C. Brown Publishing Co.. 162 pp., illustrations. 8vo; dust jacket. International big-game hunting with some North American hunts.

Burrard, Major Gerald

Guns and Shooting. New York, 1962, A. S. Barnes and Company, Inc. 147 pp. 12mo; dust jacket. (Reprinted 1964, same publisher and format)

The Identification of Firearms and Forensic Ballistics. New York, 1934, Charles Scribner's Sons. 220 pp., frontispiece, plates. 8vo. (Originally published, London, Herbert Jenkins. Reprinted and revised several times after 1951, various formats and publishers)

In the Gunroom. London / New York, 1951. Herbert Jenkins / Greenberg: Publishers. 147 pp. 12mo; dust jacket.

The Modern Shotgun. London and New York, 1931, 1932, Herbert Jenkins / Charles Scribner's Sons. Three volumes; Volume I, *The Gun*, 252 pp.; Volume II, *The Cartridge*, 314 pp.; Volume III, *The Gun and The Cartridge*, 523 pp., all with photographic plates, charts, tables. 8vo. (Also a 1947 second edition and a 1950 third edition, same format and publisher. Also reprinted in 1961 and in 1964, A. S. Barnes and Company, Inc., in two volumes; slipcased) An important work that is scarce in its first printing.

Burrows, Roger

Wild Fox. New York, 1968, Taplinger. 202 pp., photographic plates, bibliography. 8vo; dust jacket.

Burton, John A., editor

Owls of the World; their evolution, structure and ecology. New York, 1973, E. P. Dutton & Co., Inc. 216 pp., color and black and white illustrations, maps. 4to; dust jacket. (Also printed in paper wrappers)

Bush, Walter L.

    A Saga of Duck and Goose Hunting.   Minneapolis, 1978, American Wildlife. 223 pp., photographic plates, color illustrations from paintings by Les Kouba. 4to; dust jacket.

Buss, Irven O.

    Wisconsin Pheasant Populations; progress report of pheasant investigations conducted 1936-1943.   Madison, 1946, Wisconsin Conservation Department. 184 pp., photographic plates. 8vo. Paper wrappers.

Butcher, O. L.

    Professional Fox Trapping. Third printing.   No place, 1974, Privately printed. 38 pp., photographic plates. 8vo. Paper wrappers.

    Trapper's Guide. No place, No date (ca. 1935), Privately printed. 100 pp., illustrations. 8vo. Paper wrappers.

Butler, David F.   **b. 1928**

    The American Shotgun. New York, 1973, Winchester Press. 243 pp., photographic plates. 8vo; dust jacket. (Reprinted 1975, Galahad Books)

    The New Archery. New York, 1968, A. S. Barnes and Company, Inc. 128 pp., photographic plates, drawings. 8vo; dust jacket.

    United States Firearms: The First Century, 1776-1875. New York, 1971, Winchester Press.   249 pp., photographic plates, drawings.   4to; dust jacket.

    Winchester '73, '76; the first repeating centerfire rifles. New York, 1970, Winchester Press.   95 pp., illustrations. 8vo; dust jacket.

Butler, Ovid M.

    American Conservation in Picture and Story. Washington, D. C., 1935, American Forestry Association. 270 pp., illustrations. 8vo. (Reprinted 1941, same format and publisher)

Buxton, Henry

    Assignment Down East. Brattleboro, Vermont, 1938, Stephen Daye Press. 294 pp., black and white illustrations from drawings by Wayne Buxton, decorated end-papers by Andrew Wyeth. 8vo; dust jacket. With chapters on hunting, trapping and camping in Maine.

Buyukmihci, Hope Sawyer

    Hour of the Beaver. Chicago, 1971, Rand McNally & Company.   173 pp., photographic plates. 8vo; dust jacket. Observations of beaver, deer, ruffed grouse and other animals in southern New Jersey.

Buzzacott, Francis H.

The Complete American and Canadian Sportsman's Encyclopedia of Valuable Instruction. Revised edition. Chicago, 1929, M. A. Donohue & Co. 520 pp., illustrations. 8vo. (Originally published, 1905, Elgin, Illinois)

Byron, David

Gunmarks. New York, 1979, Crown Publishers, Inc. 185 pp., photographic plates. 8vo; dust jacket. A treatise on proof-marks used by various firearms manufacturers.

Cabell, Charles A., III and David St. Clair

Safari; Pan Am's guide to hunting with gun and camera around the world. New York, 1968, Pan- American Airlines. 319 pp., photographic plates. 8vo; dust jacket.

Cade, Tom

The Falcons of the World. Ithaca, New York, 1982, Cornell University Press. 188 pp., color illustrations from paintings by R. D. Cade, bibliography. Folio; dust jacket.

Cadieux, Charles L.   b. 1919

Coyotes; predators and survivors. Washington, D. C., 1983, Stone Wall Press. 233 pp., photographic plates.   8vo; dust jacket.

Goose Hunting. Boston, 1979, Stone Wall Press. 197 pp., photographic plates. 8vo; dust jacket. (Reprinted twice to 1983, same format and publisher)

These Are Endangered. Washington, D. C., 1981, Stone Wall Press. 223 pp., photographic plates, drawings by Bob Hines. 8vo; dust jacket. (Reprinted twice to 1984, same format and publisher)

Wildlife Management on Your Land. Harrisburg, 1985, Stackpole Books. 320 pp., photographic plates.   8vo; dust jacket.

Cadious, Yves and Alphonse Richard

Modern Firearms, Sporting Guns and Competition Weapons. New York, 1977, Grosset & Dunlap.   68 pp., illustrations.   8vo. Paper wrappers. (Originally published, France)   Containing information on firearms not usually found in the U. S.

Caesar, Gene

Mark of the Hunter   New York, 1953, William Sloane Associates, Inc. 250 pp. 8vo; dust jacket. A novel with much wolf and deer hunting in the Upper Peninsula of Michigan.

The Wild Hunters; the wolves, the bears and the big cats. New York, 1957, G. P. Putnam's Sons. 252 pp., illustrations, bibliography. 8vo; dust jacket.

Cahalane, Victor Harrison   b. 1901

A Biological Survey of Katmai National Monument. Washington, D. C., 1959, Smithsonian Institute.   246 pp., photographic plates, map.   8vo. Paper wrappers. This region of Alaska was devastated by a volcanic eruption in 1912. Much on bears.

Cahalane, Victor Harrison, editor

Alive in the Wild. Englewood Cliffs, New Jersey, 1970, Prentice-Hall, Inc. 244 pp., drawings by Robert Candy.   8vo; dust jacket. (Reprinted 1970, same format and publisher) Brief accounts of life histories of many game animals.

Cahalane, Victor Harrison, editor, continued

John James Audubon. A selected treasury for sportsmen: Audubon's game animals. Maplewood, New Jersey, 1968, Hammond. 172 pp., color and black and white illustrations. 4to.

Mammals of North America. New York, 1964. 682 pp., illustrations by Francis Lee Jaques. 8vo; dust jacket.

Caldwell, Elsie Noble

Alaska Trail Dogs. New York, 1950, Smith. 150 pp., photographic plates, map. 8vo. Sled dog travel with some hunting.

Caldwell, J. B.

Introducing Alaska. New York, 1947, G. P. Putnam's Sons. 202 pp., illustrations. 8vo; dust jacket. A general guide to the area with a significant amount on hunting and fishing.

Calef, George

Caribou and the Barren Lands. Ottawa, 1981, CARC/Firefly Books. 176 pp., illustrations in color and black and white, bibliography. 4to; dust jacket.

Calhoun, J. and F. Loomis

Prairie Whitetails. Springfield, Illinois, No date (ca. 1974), Privately printed. 49 pp., photographic plates. 8vo. Paper wrappers.

Calhoun, William Caldwell

History of the Forest Lake Club, 1882-1932. Lackawaxen Township, Pike County, Pennsylvania, 1932, Privately printed. 262 pp., photographic plates. 8vo. Containing much on the hunting and fishing of the area. Rare.

Calkins, Frank

Rocky Mountain Warden. New York, 1970, Alfred A. Knopf, Inc. 266 pp., photographic plates. 8vo; dust jacket. (Reprinted 1971, same format and publisher)

Call, Mayo W.

Nesting Habits and Surveying Techniques For Common Western Raptors. Denver, 1978, United States Department of Agriculture, Bureau of Land Management. 115 pp., photographic plates, drawings, bibliography. 4to. Paper wrappers.

Callison, I. P.

Wolf Predation in the North Country. No place, 1947, Privately printed. 89 pp., illustrations. 8vo. Paper wrappers.

Cameron, Angus and Peter Parnell.
The Night Watchers. New York, 1971, Four Winds. 111 pp., drawings by Peter Parnell. Folio; dust jacket. (Reprinted twice, same format and publisher)
A study of the North American owls with illustrations by Peter Parnell.
Mr. Cameron was a senior editor at both Little, Brown & Company and at Alfred A. Knopf, Inc. He worked with such notable outdoor writers as Elmer Keith, Larry Dobie, Jack O'Connor, Joseph Bates and Eric Leiser. In addition to being an avid fisherman, his life-long avocation has been the study of raptors.

Cameron, Jenks
The Bureau of Biological Survey; its history, activities and organization. Baltimore, 1929, The John Hopkins Press. 339 pp., illustrations. 8vo.

Camp, Doug
Turkey Hunting Spring and Fall. Nashville, 1983, Outdoor Skills. 165 pp., photographic plates, drawings. 8vo. Paper wrappers.

Camp, Raymond R.   1908-1962
All Seasons Afield; with rod and gun. New York, 1939, Whittlesey House. 252 pp., photographic plates. 8vo; dust jacket. (Reprinted, same format and publisher. Also a 1939 British edition)
Duck Boats: Blinds: Decoys; and eastern seaboard wildfowl. New York, 1952, Alfred A. Knopf, Inc. 240 pp., color and black and white plates from photographs and paintings. A Borzoi Book For Sportsmen. 8vo; dust jacket.
Game Cookery in America and Europe. New York, 1958, Coward, McCann, Inc. 252 pp. 8vo; dust jacket. (Also a 1983 revised edition, Wild Duck Publishers)
Ray Camp's Hunting Handbook. Greenwich, Connecticut, 1951, Privately printed. 144 pp., illustrations. 8vo. Paper wrappers.

Camp, Raymond R., editor
The Collier's Book of Hunting and Fishing. New York, 1954, A. S. Barnes and Company, Inc. 223 pp., drawings. 8vo; dust jacket.
The Hunter's Encyclopedia. Harrisburg and New York, 1948, Stackpole and Heck, Inc. 1152 pp., photographic plates, drawings and 17 color illustrations from paintings by T. M. Shortt and Luis Henderson. 4to; dust jacket. (Also a second edition, same format and publisher. In 1966 and after, a third revised edition titled, *The New Hunter's Encyclopedia.* This third edition was also revised as *The Standard Book of Hunting and Shooting,* edited by **Robert B. Stringfellow**, which see) The publisher also reprinted a series of books in paper wrappers called **The Sportsman's Bookshelf**, some of which were compiled from some of the chapters of this book.

Camp, Raymond R., editor, continued

Hunting Trails; a sportsman's treasury.   New York, 1961, D. Appleton-Century-Crofts, Inc.   502 pp., chapter heading illustrations.   Thick 8vo; dust jacket.   An anthology of hunting stories by Annabel, Holland, Babcock and others.

Let's Go Hunting! New York, 1951, Brevity.   30 pp., color illustrations. 8vo.   Paper wrappers.   An introductory pamphlet to the sport.

Mr. Camp was Outdoor Editor for *The New York Times.* He also wrote or edited several angling titles.   See Bruns.

Campbell, Charles A.

Traditions of Hartwood: a narrative which has to do with the region in the vicinity of Hartwood, Sullivan County, New York, with special references to the history of the Hartwood Club.   Winter Park, Florida, 1930, Privately printed. 155 pp., photographic plates.   8vo.

Campbell, Dennis, editor

Alabama Whitetail Records. 1989, Alabama Whitetail Records.   362 pp., illustrations.

Campbell, George R.

Taxidermy For the Amateur; a manual of instructions for mounting animals, birds, snakes, fish and other specimens.   New York, 1934, Schoepfer. 48 pp., photographic plates, drawings.   4to.   Paper wrappers.

Campbell, Robert, editor

Skeet Shooting With Lee Braun; a world champion shows how skeet can make you a better field shot.   New York, 1967,The Benjamin Company.   160 pp., photographic plates, fold-out chart.   8vo; dust jacket.   (Also reprinted in paper wrappers)

Trapshooting; with Lee Braun and the Remington pros.   New York, 1967, The Benjamin Company.   158 pp., photographic plates, fold-out chart. 8vo; dust jacket.   (Reprinted 1969, same format and publisher)

Campbell, Samuel A.

Moose Country; a boy naturalist in an ancient forest. Indianapolis, 1950, The Bobbs-Merrill Company. 235 pp., drawings.   A juvenile with much on moose and bear; set in the Canadian woods.

Canadian National Railways

Hunting, Fishing and Canoe Trips in Canada.   Montreal, 1946, Canadian National Railways.   128 pp., photographic plates, fold-out map.   8vo. Paper wrappers.

Canadian Travel Bureau

Canada's Game Fields; a brief description of Canada's big a⁻ᵈ small game resources.   Ottawa, 1935, Canadian Travel Bureau.   32 pp., photographic plates.   8vo.   Paper wrappers.   (Reprinted several times, same format and publisher)

Canadian Wildlife Service

The Canada Goose.   Ottawa, 1968, Canadian Wildlife Service.   6pp. Paper wrappers.

Caras, Roger A.   b. 1928

Coyote For a Day,   New York, 1977, E. P. Dutton & Co., Inc. / Windmill.   Unpaginated, drawings by Diane Paterson.   4to; dust jacket.   A juvenile.

The Custer Wolf; biography of an American renegade.   Boston, 1966, Little, Brown & Company.   175 pp., drawings.   8vo; dust jacket.   (Reprinted several times, various publishers)

Dangerous To Man; wild animals, a definitive study of their reputed dangers to man.   Philadelphia, 1964, Chilton Books.   8vo; dust jacket.   (Also a 1975 revised edition, Holt, Rinehart & Winston)

Death as a Way of Life.   Boston, 1970, Little, Brown & Company.   173 pp.   8vo; dust jacket.   A narrative of hunting philosophy from earliest times to the present as well as a discussion of the role of hunters in conservation.

Last Chance on Earth; a requiem for wildlife.   New York, 1966, Chilton Books.   207 pp., color frontispiece and black and white drawings by Charles Frace.   Oblong 4to; dust jacket.   (Reprinted several times, various publishers)

Monarch of Deadman Bay; the life and death of a Kodiak bear.   Boston, 1969, Little, Brown & Company.   185 pp., drawings by Charles Frace.   8vo; dust jacket.   (Reprinted several times, various publishers)

North American Mammals; fur-bearing animals of the United Sates and Canada.   New York, 1967, Meredith.   578 pp., color and black and white illustrations, maps.   Square 8vo; dust jacket.   (Reprinted 1974, Galahad)

Source of the Thunder: the biography of a California Condor.   Boston, 1970, Little, Brown & Company.   181 pp., illustrations.   8vo; dust jacket. (Reprinted, University of Nebraska Press)

Panther!   Boston, 1969, Little, Brown & Company.   185 pp., drawings. 8vo; dust jacket.   The life story of the Florida Everglades panther.

The Library of Congress lists no less than 80 entries for Mr. Caras, most of which are animal and nature books.

Carbyn, Ludwig N.

Wolves in Canada and Alaska; their status, biology and management. Ottawa, 1983, Canadian Wildlife Service.   134 pp., photographic plates, maps, bibliography.   4to. Paper wrappers.

Cardoza, James

The History and Status of the Black Bear in Massachusetts and Adjacent New England States. Westborough, 1976, Fisheries and Wildlife Commission. 113 pp., photographic plates, maps, bibliography. 8vo. Paper wrappers.

Cardwell, Lawrence

Mountain Medicine. Caldwell, Idaho, 1941, Caxton Printers, Ltd. 232 pp., illustrations. 8vo; dust jacket. The author left city life and retreated to a ranch in the Arizona mountains. Contains some cougar hunting and trout fishing. Not in Bruns. Scarce.

Carey, A. Merwyn

American Firearms Makers; where, when and what they made from the colonial period to the end of the nineteenth century. New York, 1953, Crowell Publishers, Inc. 154 pp., photographic plates. 8vo; dust jacket.

Carhart, Arthur H.   b. 1892

Hunting North American Deer. New York, 1946, The Macmillan Company. 232 pp., photographic plates. 8vo; dust jacket.

Hunting and Fishing is Big Business. 1947. 8 pp. Paper wrappers. (Originally appeared in the August, 1947 issue of *Sports Afield*)

Report of the Deer-Elk Survey 1939-1940. No place, 1940, Colorado Game and Fish commission. 79 pp., charts, maps. 4to. Paper wrappers.

Carhart, Arthur H. and Stanley P. Young

The Last Stand of the Pack. New York, 1929, J. H. Sears & Co. 295 pp., photographic plates. 8vo. An account of the killing of the last renegade wolf pack in Colorado by government hunters. Scarce.

Carlisle, Donald Thompson   1894-1956

The Belvidere Hounds. New York, 1935, The Derrydale Press. Unpaginated (approx. 100 pp.), cartoon drawings throughout. Foreword by Richard E. Danielson. Folio; printed glassine dust wrapper. A collection of cartoons of foxhunting hounds. Most originally appeared in *The Sportsman* magazine.

Carlisle, G. L. and Percy Stanbury

Shotgun Marksmanship. South Brunswick, New Jersey, 1962, A. S. Barnes and Company, Inc. 224 pp., illustrations. 8vo; dust jacket. (Reprinted 1969, same format and publisher. Originally published, Great Britain)

Carlton, H. W.

Spaniels; their breaking for sport and filed trails. Washington, D. C., 1945, Denlinger's. 122 pp., photographic plates. 8vo. Paper wrappers. (Originally published, 1915, London)

Carlton, L. A.

History of Hunting Trip in Sierra Madres, Northern Mexico, August 21, to October 1, 1922. No place, No date (ca. 1922), Privately printed. 60 pp. Square 8vo. A record of this hunting trip for deer, mountain lion, bear and wild turkey. Not in Phillips. Rare.

Carman, W. Y.

A History of Firearms From the Earliest Times To 1914. New York, 1955. 207 pp., illustrations. 8vo; dust jacket.

Carmichael, Jim

The Book of the Rifle. Harrisburg, 1985, Stackpole Books. 564 pp., photographic plates. 4to; dust jacket.

The Complete Just Jim. Prescott, Arizona, 1973. 117 pp., illustrations. 8vo. Paper wrappers.

Do-It-Yourself Gunsmithing. New York, 1977, Harper & Row, Publishers, Inc. / Outdoor Life Books. 372 pp., photographic plates. 8vo; dust jacket. (Reprinted, same format and publisher)

The Modern Rifle. New York, 1975, Winchester Press. 342 pp., photographic plates. 8vo; dust jacket.

The Woman's Guide To Handguns. Indianapolis, 1982, Bobbs-Merrill Company, Inc. 190 pp., illustrations. 8vo; dust jacket.

Carmony, Neil B. and David E. Stone, editors

Tales From Tiburon; an anthology of adventures in Seriland. Phoenix, 1983, South West Natural History Association. 146 pp., photographic plates, maps, bibliography. 8vo. Mostly travel and exploration of the Sonoran desert in the U. S. Southwest, but with a 65 pp. chapter "Hunting With the Seris, 1921-1922" by Charles Sheldon.

Carpenter, Robert Ruliph Morgan   b. 1877

Game Trails From Alaska To Africa. Philadelphia, 1938, Privately printed. 180 pp., photographic plates, fold-out map. Limited to 800 copies. 4to.

Game Trails In Idaho and Alaska. No place, 1940, Privately printed. 43 pp., photographic plates. Limited to 400 numbered copies. 8vo. Hunting elk, mule deer, grizzly bear and mountain sheep in Idaho and Alaska.

Carr, James R.

Savage Automatic Pistols. No place, No date (ca. 1968), Privately printed. 131 pp., illustrations. 8vo; dust jacket. Intended for the collector of Savage Arms Co. automatic pistols.

Carrighar, Sally

Home to the Wilderness. Boston, 1973, Houghton Mifflin Company. 330 pp., photographic plates. 8vo; dust jacket. (Reprinted 1973, same format and publisher) Ms. Carrighar's autobiography.

Icebound Summer. New York, 1953, Alfred A. Knopf, Inc. 262 pp., drawings by Kane. 8vo; dust jacket. (Reprinted, same format and publisher) Native Eskimo hunting.

Moonlight at Midday. New York, 1958, Alfred A. Knopf, Inc. 389 pp., photographic plates. 8vo; dust jacket. (Reprinted several times, same format and publisher) All about Alaska, its animals and people.

One Day on Beetle Rock. New York, 1944, Alfred A. Knopf, Inc. 196 pp., drawings by Kane. 8vo; dust jacket. (Reprinted many times, same format and publisher) Ecological study of animal life in the high Sierras.

One Day at Teton Marsh. New York, 1947, Alfred A. Knopf, Inc. 239 pp., illustrations. 8vo; dust jacket. (Reprinted several times, same format and publisher) Ecological study of wildlife on a marsh in Jackson Hole, Wyoming.

Wild Heritage. Boston, 1965, Houghton Mifflin Company. 276 pp., drawings. 8vo; dust jacket.

Wild Voice of the North. Garden City, New York, 1959, Doubleday & Co., Inc. 191 pp., illustrations. 8vo; dust jacket.

Ms. Carrighar wrote extensively about the Great North; all of her books had much on the ecology of the region.

Carson, Rachel L.   1907-1964

Chincoteauge; a National Wildlife Refuge. Washington, D. C., 1947, United States Government Printing Office. 19 pp., illustrations by S. A. Bridges and K. L. Howe. Number 1 of the Conservation in Action series. Tall 8vo. Paper wrappers. Much on wildfowl of the area.

Silent Spring. Boston, 1962, Houghton Mifflin Company. 368 pp., illustrations by Lois and Louis Darling. 8vo; dust jacket. (Reprinted several times, same format and publisher) The author points out how industry and government are polluting our world. Many believe this book was responsible for the birth of the environmental movement. Certainly a very important work.

Carter, Brian C.

The American Goldeneye in Central New Brunswick. Ottawa, 1958, Canadian Wildlife Service. 47 pp., charts, bibliography. 8vo. Paper wrappers.

Carter, W. Horace

Wild and Wonderful Santee Cooper Country. Tabor City, 1981, Atlantic. 391 pp., photographic plates, map. 8vo. Paper wrappers. An account of hunting and fishing opportunities in this area of South Carolina.

Carter, Winthrop L.

George Boyd; the shorebird decoy, an American folk art. Fayetteville, New York, 1978, Tenant House. 16 pp., color and black and white illustrations. Limited to 2000 copies. Oblong 8vo. Paper wrappers. A biography of this shore bird decoy carver.

Cartier, John O.

Getting The Most Out of Modern Wildfowling. New York, 1974, St. Martin's Press. 396 pp., photographic plates. 8vo; dust jacket. (Also a 1981 revised edition titled, *Hunting North American Waterfowl*, Outdoor Life Books)

The Modern Deer Hunter. New York, 1976, Funk & Wagnalls Outdoor Life Books. 310 pp., photographic plates. 8vo; dust jacket.

Cartier, John O., editor

20 Great Trophy Hunts; personal accounts of hunting North America's top big game animals. New York, 1980, David McKay Co. 269 pp., photographic plates. 8vo; dust jacket.

Cartwright, E. R.

A Late Summer; the memoirs of E. R. Cartwright. London, 1964, Caravel. 224 pp., photographic plates. 8vo; dust jacket. Contains some North American hunting for big game and waterfowl.

Cartwright, Bertram William (b. 1890) and Angus H. Shortt (b. 1908)

Treasury of Waterfowl. Englewood Cliffs, New Jersey, 1957, Prentice-Hall, Inc. 143 pp., drawings and paintings in black and white and color by the authors. 4to; dust jacket. (Originally published, 1948, with the title *Know Your Ducks and Geese*, Sports Afield Publishing Company) The paintings in this book originally appeared in 36 consecutive issues of *Sports Afield* magazine between 1946 and 1948.

Cary, Lucian   1886-1971

The Colt Gun Book. Greenwich, Connecticut, 1961, Fawcett Books. 144 pp., illustrations. 8vo. Paper wrappers.

Guns and Shooting. Greenwich, Connecticut, No date (ca. 1952), Fawcett Books. 142 pp., illustrations. 8vo; dust jacket. (Reprinted 1954 and 1960, Arco)

Lucian Cary on Guns. Greenwich, Connecticut, 1950, Fawcett Books. 143 pp., photographic plates. 8vo. Paper wrappers. (Reprinted several times)

The New Lucian Cary on Guns. New York, 1954. 140 pp., photographic plates. 4to; dust jacket. (Reprinted several times)

Casson, Paul W.

Decoy Collecting Primer. Middlebury, 1978, Erikson. 83 pp., photographic plates. 8vo. Paper wrappers.

Casson, Paul W., continued

Decoys Simplified. Rockville Centre, New York, 1972, Freshet Press. 95 pp., plans, color plates. 4to; dust jacket.

Castles, W. T. and V. F. Kimball

Firearms and Their Use. Brooklyn, New York, 1942, Chemical Publishing Company. 231 pp., photographic plates, large bibliography. Tall 8vo.

Castletown, Lord

EGO; random records of sport, service & travel in many lands. London, 1923, Murray. 245 pp. 8vo. Mostly European travel and sport, but with one section on big game hunting in the western U. S. in 1877 for buffalo, bear and sheep. Not in Phillips.

Catlin, Mrs. Randolph

The Derrydale Press: notes from an informal talk. Charlottsville, Virginia, 1951, Bibliographical Society of the University of Virginia. 8pp. 4to. Paper wrappers. An early bibliography of this important sporting book publisher.

Caton, John Dean   1812-1895

The Antelope and Deer of America. New York, 1974, Arno Press. 426 pp., plus ads, illustrations from old plates. 8vo. (Originally published, 1877 and reprinted several times thereafter)

Caulfield, Patricia

Everglades. New York, 1971, Ballantine Books / The Sierra Club. 143 pp., color photographs by the author. Text by Peter Matthiessen. 8vo. Paper wrappers.

Cavanaugh, James, editor

Bowhunting Manual. National Field Archery Association, 1962. Second edition. 176 pp., illustrations. Paper wrappers.

Cay, John Eugene, Jr.

Ducks, Dogs and Friends. Savannah, Georgia, 1979, Privately printed. 47 pp., map. Limited to 2000 copies. 8vo.

Ward Allen - Savannah River Market Hunter. Savannah, Georgia, 1958, Privately printed. 48 pp., photographic plates, drawings by Ray Dilley. 8vo. Limited to 350 numbered and signed copies. (Also a 1959 second printing of 200 copies, same format and publisher)

Central Flyway Council
   Waterfowl Identification Guide.   St. Paul, Minnesota, 1958, Central Flyway Council.   48 pp., drawings.   12mo.   Paper wrappers.   (Also a 1972 edition, same format and publisher)

Chace, Earl G.
   Wonders of the Pronghorn.   New York, 1977, Dodd Mead & Co.   64 pp., photographic plates.   8vo; dust jacket.   A natural history of the species.

Chadwick, Douglas
   The Beast the Color of Winter; the mountain goat observed.   San Francisco, 1983, The Sierra Club.   208 pp., photographic plates, maps, drawings. 8vo; dust jacket.   (Also reprinted, paper wrappers)

Chamberlain, E. B.
   Florida Waterfowl Populations, Habitats and Management.   No place, 1960, Florida Game and Fish Commission.   62 pp., photographic plates, maps, bibliography.   4to.   Paper wrappers.

Chandler, Roy F.
   Alaskan Hunter;   a book about big game hunting.   Deer Lake, Pennsylvania, 1977, Bacon & Freeman.   281 pp., photographic plates.   4to.   A scarce privately printed work.
   A History of Hunting in Perry County. Deer Lake, Pennsylvania, 1974, Bacon & Freeman.   200 pp., many illustrations.   Limited to 1000 numbered copies.   4to.   A history of this Pennsylvania county's hunting experiences.   More scarce than its limitation would suggest.
   Kentucky Rifle Patchboxes and Barrel Marks.   Deer Lake, Pennsylvania, 1971, Privately printed.   400 pp., photographic plates, drawings.   4to.

Chansler, Walter S.
   The River Trapper.   Columbus, Ohio, 1928, Hunter-Trader-Trapper.   214 pp., illustrations.   12mo.
   Successful Trapping Methods.   New York, 1955, D. Van Nostrand Company, Inc.   151 pp., line drawings.   8vo; dust jacket.   (Also a 1968 revised edition, same format and publisher)

Chapel, Charles Edward   1904-1967
   The Art of Shooting.   New York, No date (ca. 1950),   A. S. Barnes and Company, Inc.   424 pp., illustrations.   8vo; dust jacket.
   The Boy's Book of Rifles.   New York, 1948, Coward, McCann, Inc. 274 pp., bibliography, drawings by Dick Spencer.   8vo; dust jacket.

Chapel, Charles Edward, continued

The Complete Guide To Gunsmithing: Gun Care and Repair. New York, 1962, A. S. Barnes and Company, Inc. 479 pp., illustrations. 8vo; dust jacket.

Field, Skeet and Trap Shooting. New York, 1949, Coward, McCann, Inc. 288 pp., illustrated. 8vo; dust jacket. (Also a 1962 revised edition, A. S. Barnes and Company, Inc.)

Gun Care and Repair. New York, 1942, Coward, McCann, Inc. 454 pp., photographic plates. Tall 8vo; dust jacket. (Reprinted 1951, same format and publisher)

Gun Collecting. New York, 1939, Coward, McCann, Inc. 232 pp., photographic plates, bibliography. 8vo; dust jacket. (Reprinted, same format and publisher) A beginner's guide.

The Gun Collector's Handbook of Values. San Leandro, California, 1940, Privately printed. 220 pp., photographic plates. 8vo. Observed in both paper wrappers and in cloth. (Revised many times to 1977, Coward, McCann, Inc.)

Guns of the Old West. New York, 1961, Coward, McCann, Inc. 306 pp., photographic plates, bibliography. 4to; dust jacket.

Simplified Pistol and Revolver Shooting. New York, 1950, Coward, McCann, Inc. 248 pp., drawings. 8vo; dust jacket.

Simplified Rifle Shooting. New York, 1950, Coward, McCann, Inc. 240 pp., drawings, bibliography. Foreword by Gen. Julian S. Hatcher. 8vo; dust jacket.

United States Martial and Semi-Marshall Single Shot Pistols. New York, 1962. 386 pp., drawings. 8vo; dust jacket.

Chapman, Abel   1851-1929

Retrospect; reminiscences and impressions of a hunter-naturalist in three continents, 1851-1928. London, 1928, Gurney and Jackson. 353 pp., color and black and white illustrations. 8vo. Contains some North American hunting.

Chapman, Joseph A., et al.

The Status, Population and Harvest of the Dusky Canada Goose. Washington, D. C., 1969, The Wildlife Society. Monograph # 18. 48 pp., illustrations, bibliography. 4to. Paper wrappers.

Chapman, John Ratcliffe

Instructions To Young Marksmen; in all that relates to the general construction,.....as exhibited in the "Improved American Rifle." Manchester, Vermont, 1941, Clarke Press. Printed for Maj. Ned Roberts. 210 pp., illustrated. 8vo. Limited to 525 copies. (Originally published, 1848, D. Appleton & Co. This facsimile reprint also contains 50 addition pages of material. Also reprinted as the original, 1976, Beinfeld Publishing Co.)

Chapman, Wendell and Lucie Wendell

Wilderness Wanderers; adventures among wild animals in Rocky Mountain solitude. New York, 1937, Charles Scribner's Sons. 318 pp., photographic plates. Tall 8vo; dust jacket.

Charlesworth, W. M.

Golden Retrievers. New York, 1952, A. S. Barnes and Company, Inc. 96 pp., photographic plates. 12mo; dust jacket.

Chase, Will H.

Alaska's Mammoth Brown Bears. Kansas City, Missouri, 1947, Burton Publishing Company. 129 pp., frontispiece. 8vo; dust jacket. (Also a 1947 revised edition, same format and publisher)

The Sourdough Pot. Kansas City, Missouri, 1943, Burton Publishing Company. 206 pp., illustrations. 8vo; dust jacket. (Reprinted 1943, same format and publisher) Mostly about the Alaska gold rush with incidental mention of hunting.

Cheever, Byron

Mason Decoys. Heber City, Utah, 1974, Hillcrest Publications. 166 pp., illustrations in color and black and white from photographs. 4to; dust jacket. (Reprinted 1978 and 1985, same format and publisher)

Ward Bros. Heber City, Utah, No date, North American Decoys. 70 pp., color and black and white illustrations. 4to; dust jacket. A scarce work.

L. T. Ward and Bros.; wildfowl counterfeiters. Hillcrest Heights, Maryland, 1971, Privately printed. Unpaginated; 72 color and black and white plates. 4to; dust jacket

Cherr, Pat

The Bear in Fact and Fiction. New York, 1967, Crown Publishers, Inc. / Harlin Quist. 159 pp., illustrations. 8vo; dust jacket.

Childs, Arney R., editor

Rice Planter and Sportsman; the recollections of J. Motte Alston, 1821-1909. Columbia, 1953, University of South Carolina Press. 148 pp., illustrations. 8vo; dust jacket. Includes one chapter on hunting and much on the natural history of the area.

Chinn, George, Jr. and Hardin Bayless

Encyclopedia of American Hand-Arms; a book of fact about American short arms, detailing their birth and development and describing in minute detail models from early 18th century to present. Huntington, West Virginia, 1942, Standard Publications, Inc. 349 pp., illustrations. 4to; dust jacket.

Chowning, Larry S.

  Barcat Skipper; tales of a Tangier Island water-man.   Centreville, Maryland, 1983, Tidewater Publishers.   155 pp.   8vo; dust jacket.   Stories of this area of the Chesapeake Bay, with some hunting.

Christensen, Glen C.

  The Chukar Partridge in Nevada.   No place, 1954, Nevada Fish and Game Commission.   77 pp., illustrations, maps.   8vo.   Paper wrappers.   (Also a second edition that was reprinted several times, same format and publisher, titled *The Chukar Partridge;* its introduction, life history and management)

Christy, Bayard H., editor

  The Book of Huron Mountain; a collection of papers concerning the history of the Huron Mountain Club and the antiquities and the natural history of the region.   Chicago, 1929, Privately printed for the club by The Lakeside Press.   216 pp., illustrations, map.   8vo.   A history of this Michigan hunting and angling club. Scarce.

Church, Mrs. Charles

  Sale Catalog of Sporting Books.   New York, 1962, Parke-Bernet Galleries, Inc.   50 pp.   8vo.   Paper wrappers.   An auction catalog.

Churchill, Robert   1886-1958

  Churchill's Shotgun Book; a guide to the use of the smooth-bored game gun.   New York, 1955, Alfred A. Knopf, Inc.   277 pp., photographic plates. 8vo; dust jacket.   (Reprinted 1963, The Stackpole Company. Originally published in London by Michael Joseph titled, *Game Shooting.*   This title was also revised and reprinted, 1971, The Stackpole Company, titled *Churchill's Game Shooting,* by **MacDonald Hastings,** which see.)

Cisin, Catherine

  Especially Ocelots.   Amagansett, New York, 1967, Privately printed. 167 pp., photographic plates, drawings, bibliography.   8vo.   Paper wrappers.   A handbook for keeping these and other wild cats in captivity.

Claflin, Bert

  American Waterfowl; hunting ducks and geese.   New York, 1952, Alfred A. Knopf, Inc.   285 pp., plates from photographs and paintings, color frontispiece by Lynn Bogue Hunt.   A Borzoi Book For Sportsmen.   8vo; dust jacket

Claflin, William H., Jr.

Partridge Adventures. Cambridge, Massachusetts, 1951, Privately printed. 65 pp., photographic plates, 2 fold-out charts. 8vo; dust jacket. A scarce title that is reported to have had a limitation of only 100 copies.

Partridge Rambles; in which the author sets forth his reasons why he prefers to hunt that noble bird without the use of the dog. Together with some hints to those who might like to take up that fascinating sport. No place (New Hampshire), 1937, Privately printed. 32 pp., frontispiece. Limited to 250 copies. 12mo.

Clapham, Richard

The Book of the Fox. New York, 1931, The Derrydale Press. 104 pp., photographic plates, drawings by Lionel Edwards and Marguerite Kirmse. Limited to 750 copies. 8vo.

Foxes, Foxhounds and Foxhunting. New York, 1922, Charles Scribner's Sons. 318 pp., photographic plates. 8vo; dust jacket. (Simultaneously published in Great Britain)

Clark, Atwood

Gun Dogs and Their Training. New York, 1935, Charles Scribner's Sons. 253 pp., photographic plates. 12mo; dust jacket.

Clark, Bob

Long Beards, Long Spurs and Fanned Tails. Boiling Springs, Pennsylvania, 1981, Northwoods Publications. 107 pp., photographic plates. 8vo Paper wrappers. Turkey hunting.

Clark, Edward

Up, Bob, Seek; the story of a retriever. New York, 1966, Exposition Press. 60 pp., frontispiece by Marguerite Kirmse. 8vo; dust jacket.

Clark, Eldon R.

Woodcock Status Report, 1969. Washington, D. C., 1970, United States Fish and Wildlife Service. 35 pp., maps. 4to. Paper wrappers.

Clark, Gregory

Outdoors With Gregory Clark. Toronto, 1972, McClelland & Stewart, Ltd. 158 pp., photographic plates. 8vo; dust jacket.

Clark, Harold B.

We Are In Alaska Now; a doggerel diary. New York, 1937, Privately printed. 47 pp., drawings by J. M. Guerry. 8vo. A diary with much hunting and fishing.

Clark, James Lippitt   b. 1883

The Care of Your Hunting Trophies. New York, 1937, Privately printed. 39 pp., photographic plates, drawings.   8vo.   Paper wrappers.   A guide to field preparation and after care.

Good Hunting; fifty years of collecting and preparing habitat groups for the American Museum of Natural History.   Norman, 1966, University of Oklahoma Press.   242 pp., illustrations.   8vo; dust jacket.

The Great Arc of the Wild Sheep. Norman, 1964, University of Oklahoma Press.   247 pp., illustrations.   8vo; dust jacket. (Reprinted twice to 1970, same format and publisher. Also reprinted, 1978, same publisher in paper wrappers)   A definitive book of the world's wild sheep.

In the Steps of the Great American Museum Collector; Carl Ethan Akeley.   New York, 1968, Evans.   127 pp., illustrations.   8vo; dust jacket.

Scoring Big Game Trophies; a new system of measuring.   New York, 1945, Privately printed.   Unpaginated (approx. 28 pp.), drawings.   8vo. Paper wrappers.   Scarce.

Trails of the Hunted.   Boston, 1928, Little, Brown & Company. 309 pp., photographic plates. 8vo; dust jacket. (Reprinted several times, various publishers. Also a 1929 British edition)   Big game hunting around the world.

Mr. Clark did much collecting and taxidermy for the American Museum of Natural History. He also was a wildlife sculptor of considerable talent. His private studio issued catalogs (two observed, 1929, 1931) offering his taxidermy services as well as his bronze sculptures.

Clark, Leonard

Yucatan Adventure.   London, 1959, Hutchinson.   256 pp., photographic plates.   8vo; dust jacket.   Mostly travel and adventure but with some bird and crocodile hunting.

Clark, Marvin H.

Pinnell and Talifson: Last of the Great Brown Bear Men.   Spokane, Washington, 1980, Great Northwest.   224 pp., photographic plates.   8vo; dust jacket. (Reprinted several times, same format and publisher)

Track of the Kodiak.   Anchorage, 1984, Alaska Northwest Publishing Company.   224 pp., photographic plates.   8vo; dust jacket.

Clark, Richard J., et al.

Working Bibliography of the Owls of the World; with summaries of current taxonomy and distributional status.   Washington, D. C., 1978, Raptor Informational Center.   319 pp.   4to.   Paper wrappers.   A most comprehensive guide with over 6000 entries.

Clark, Roland   1874-1957

Roland Clark's Etchings.   New York, 1938, The Derrydale Press. Unpaginated, 69 plates of etchings plus a signed frontispiece etching.   Limited to 800 numbered copies.   Elephant folio; two-piece box.   [Also a deluxe edition specially bound with two signed etchings and limited to 50 numbered copies; two-piece box]   A collection of the author's etchings.

Gunner's Dawn.   New York, 1937, The Derrydale Press.   125 pp., frontispiece a signed etching, drawings, 5 plates in color from paintings by the author.   Limited to 950 numbered copies.   4to; two-piece box. [Also a large paper edition, specially bound with a signed and hand-colored frontispiece and limited to 50 numbered copies]   (The limited edition reprinted, 1983, Premier Press)   Tales of waterfowling.

Pot Luck.   West Hartford, Vermont, 1945, The Countryman Press.   101 pp., line drawings and six color plates from paintings by the author. Limited to 5000 copies.   8vo; slipcased.   (Reprinted, same format and publisher)   [Also a specially bound, limited first edition of 450 numbered copies, signed by the author; slipcased.   Also a deluxe first edition, specially bound with a signed etching as a frontispiece and limited to 150 numbered copies, signed by the author; slipcased]   Upland and waterfowl hunting in an attractive little book in any edition.

Stray Shots.   New York, 1931, The Derrydale Press.   124 pp., etchings by the author.   Limited to 500 copies.   Tall 8vo.   [Also a large paper edition, specially bound and illustrated and limited to 35 numbered copies]   An elegant, well written waterfowling book.

Stray Shots and Pot Luck.   Camden, South Carolina, 1984, Premier Press.   Two volumes in one.   215 pp., foreword by Ernie Hickock.   Limited to 3000 numbered copies.   8vo.

Mr. Clark was both a talented wildfowl artist and writer.   His art and all his books are important and valued highly by collectors.

Clark, Roland

Also see **Ordeman, John T.**

Clarke, James

Man is the Prey.   New York, 1969, Stein and Day, Publishers.   318 pp., illustrations.   8vo; dust jacket.   Instances of man-killing by various wild animals; mostly African and Asian, but some North American bear accounts.

Clarkson, Ewan

Wolf Country; a wilderness pilgrimage.   New York, 1975, E. P. Dutton & Co., Inc.   147 pp.   8vo; dust jacket.   The timber wolf in Minnesota; also much on deer, moose and other wildlife.

Clarkson, Peter and Linda Sutterlin

Bear Essentials; a source book and guide to planning bear education programs. Missoula, Montana, 1984, Privately printed. 67 pp., drawings. 8vo. Paper wrappers.

Clawson, George B.

Trapping and Tracking. New York, 1977, Winchester Press. 202 pp., illustrations. 8vo; dust jacket.

Clayton, J. D.

Ruger No. 1. Southport, Massachusetts, 1983, Blacksmith Corporation. 192 pp., color and black and white illustrations. Edited by John T. Amber. 8vo; dust jacket. A detailed treatise describing this model of rifle produced by The Ruger Arms Manufacturing Co.

Cleland, Robert Glass   1885-1957

This Reckless Breed of Men; the trappers and fur traders of the Southwest. New York, 1950, Alfred A. Knopf, Inc. 361 pp., color frontispiece, photographic plates, bibliography. 8vo; dust jacket. (Reprinted several times, various publishers) A scholarly and definitive work, based on extensive research of published and unpublished manuscripts.

Clement, Roland C.

The Living World of Audubon. New York, 1974, Ridge Press. 272 pp., illustrations in color from photographs and paintings. Folio; dust jacket. (Reprinted 1976, same format and publisher) Also contains illustrations from America's best wildlife photographers.

Clephan, Robert Coltman

The Earliest Hand Firearms. Huntington West Virginia, 1946, Standard Publications, Inc. 66 pp. 8vo. (A facsimile reproduction of the 1906 first edition)

Clepper, Henry, editor

Leaders of American Conservation. New York, 1971, The Ronald Press. 353 pp. 8vo.

Origins of American Conservation. New York, 1966, The Ronald Press. 193 pp., portraits. 8vo.

Cleveland, Grover   1837-1908

Fishing and Shooting Sketches. New York, 1966, Abercrombie & Fitch, Inc. 209 pp., drawings by Hy Watson. 12mo; dust jacket. (A facsimile reproduction of 1906 first edition)

Cleveland, H. W. S.
   Hints To Riflemen. Philadelphia, 1948, Ray Riling Arms Books. 262 pp., illustrations. 8vo. (A facsimile reproduction of the 1864 first edition)

Clifton, Violet
   The Book of Talbot. New York, 1933, Harcourt and Company. 439 pp., photographic plates, fold-out maps. 8vo; dust jacket. The biography of Talbot Clifton with much barren ground hunting for caribou and musk-oxen.

Cline, Walter M.   1873-1941
   The Muzzle Loading Rifle....then and now. Huntington, West Virginia, 1942, Standard Publications, Inc. 162 pp., photographic plates. 4to; dust jacket. (Reprinted 1943, same publisher and format)   An important monograph with much information on the early important gunsmiths.

Cobb, Bert
   Hunting Dogs.   New York, 1931, The Crafton Collection, Inc. Unpaginated, 12 black and white portraits of dogs, tipped in. Text by Freeman Lloyd. 4to; dust jacket. [Also a deluxe edition, with an original signed drypoint and limited to 100 numbered copies]
   Portraits of Dogs.   New York, 1931, The Crafton Collection, Inc. Unpaginated, 12 black and white portraits of dogs, tipped in. Text by Warren Hutty. 4to; dust jacket. [Also a deluxe edition, specially bound and illustrated]

Cochran, E. Winston
   Deer Tales and Pen Feathers.   San Antonio, 1975, The Naylor Company. 64 pp., illustrations. 8vo; dust jacket. Hunting in Texas as told through poetry.

Cochrane, Robert L. and R. H. Nicklaus
   Crippling Effects of Lead, Steel and Copper Shot on Experimental Mallards and Effects of Lead and Steel Shot on Shooting of Flighted Mallards. Washington, D. C., 1976, The Wildlife Society. Monograph # 51. 29 pp. 4to. Paper wrappers.

Coffey, Leora S.
   Wilds of Alaska Big Game Hunting.   New York, 1963, Vantage Press. 172 pp., illustrations by the author, photographic plates. 8vo; dust jacket. (Reprinted twice, various formats and publishers)

Cofield, Thomas R.
   Training the Hunting Retriever; Labrador, Chesapeake and Golden. Princeton, New Jersey, 1959, D. Van Nostrand Company, Inc.   138 pp., photographic plates.   A Van Nostrand Sporting Book.   8vo; dust jacket. (Reprinted in 1963 and 1967, same format and publisher)

Coggin, Joe and Perry C. Coggin
The Wild Turkey in Virginia. Richmond, Virginia, 1975, Game and Inland Fisheries Commission. 132 pp., illustrations, map. 4to. Paper wrappers.

Cogswell, Howard L.
Waterbirds of California. Berkeley, 1977, University of California Press. 399 pp., color and black and white illustrations. 8vo.

Colby, Carroll B.   1904-1977
Big Game: Animals of the Americas, Africa and Asia. New York, 1967, Coward, McCann, Inc. 48 pp., illustrations. 4to; dust jacket.
Firearms By Winchester; a part of United States History. New York, 1957. 48 pp., photographic plates. 4to; dust jacket.
Fur and Fury; the talented weasel family. New York, 1963, Duell, Sloan and Pearce, Inc. 127 pp., photographic plates, drawings. 8vo; dust jacket.
Small Game: Animals Of The Americas. New York, 1968, Coward, McCann, Inc. 48 pp., illustrations. 4to; dust jacket.
Six-Shooter. New York, 1956. 48 pp., photographic plates. 4to; dust jacket. A mixture of revolvers and automatic pistols from the past and present.
Wild Deer. New York, 1966, Duell, Sloan and Pearce, Inc. 126 pp., illustrations. 8vo; dust jacket.
Wild Dogs. New York, 1965, Duell, Sloan and Pearce, Inc. 128 pp., illustrations. 8vo; dust jacket.
Most of Mr. Colby's books were older juveniles.

Colby, Carroll B. and Bradford Angier
The Art and Science of Taking To the Woods. Harrisburg, 1970, The Stackpole Company. 288 pp., illustrations. 4to; dust jacket.

Colby, Francis Thompson
Francis Thompson Colby; a man of his time. No place (Boston), No date (ca. 1973), Museum of Science. 22 pp., photographic plates. 4to. Paper wrappers. Mr. Colby was a renowned big game hunter whose trophy room was reconstructed in the Boston Museum of Science.

Cole, D. B.
Canada Geese Nesting Sites on Islands in Southern Alberta. 1974, Alberta Department of Lands and Forests, Fish and Wildlife Division. 18 pp. Paper wrappers.

Cole, Glenn F.
The Pronghorn Antelope; its range use and food habits in Central Montana, with special reference to alfalfa. Bozeman, 1956, Montana State College. 63 pp., photographic plates, bibliography. 8vo. Paper wrappers.

Cole, Harold

I Think I'll Get One Hundred; thirty years of whitetail hunting with shotgun, rifle and bow. Connecticut, 1982, Privately printed. 217 pp.

Colehour, Frank E.

My Travelogue; as told to Thelma Shull. Rockford, Illinois, 1940, Privately printed. 91 pp., photographic plates. 8vo. A rare work with much on hunting bear, sheep, caribou and moose.

Coleman, John B.

Hunting Big Game in Jackson Hole, Wyoming - Fifty days in Uinta County with James S. Simpson. San Francisco, No date (ca. 1928), Privately printed. 61 pp. 4to. A rare big game title describing a hunting trip the author took with James S. Simpson, who was his guide.

Coles, Charles

Game Birds. London, 1981, Collins. 117 pp., color plates by Maurice Pledger, pencil sketches, bibliography. Elephant folio; dust jacket. (Also a 1983 U. S. edition, Dodd, Mead & Co., Inc.)

Colio, Quintina

American Decoys; ducks, eiders, scooters, geese, brant, swan, shorebirds from peeps to curlew, gulls, terns, owls, crows, blackbirds, herons, loons, fish and other unusual decoys from 1865 to 1920. Ephrata, Pennsylvania, 1972, Privately printed. 96 pp., black and white and color photographs. 4to. Paper wrappers. [Also a deluxe edition, specially bound and limited to 550 numbered and signed copies]

Colles, James   1828-1898

Journal of a Hunting Excursion to Louis Lake in 1851. Blue Mountain Lake, New York, 1961, Adirondack Museum. Unpaginated (73 pp.). Limited to 1000 copies. 4to. [Also a deluxe edition, specially bound and limited to 50 numbered and signed copies; slipcased] An uncommon title with a reproduction of the hand-written journal in facsimile as well as a type-set version.

Collier, Eric

Three Against the Wilderness. New York, 1959, E. P. Dutton & Co., Inc. 349 pp., illustrations by Joseph Cellini. 8vo; dust jacket. (Reprinted many times, same format and publisher) Pioneering in the wilderness of British Columbia.

Collins, John S.

My Experiences in the West. Chicago, 1970, R. R. Donnelley Company. 252 pp., photographic plates, map in color. 12mo. (Originally published, 1904, titled, *Across the Plains in '64*) Much hunting bear, sheep, mountain goat, deer, grouse, etc.

Colt, Samuel   1814-1862

Sam Colt's Own Record; Samuel Colt's own record of transactions with Captain Walker and Eli Whitney, Jr. in 1847.   Hartford, Connecticut, 1949, The Connecticut Historical Society.   157 pp., portraits.   Foreword and notes by John E. Parsons.   Limited to 1000 copies.   8vo.

Colt, Samuel

Also see **Edwards, William B.**
Also see **Keating, Bern**
Also see **Mitchell, James L.**
Also see **Rohan, Jack**
Also see **Rosa, Joseph C.**
Also see **Rywell, Martin**

Colt's Patent Fire Arms Manufacturing Company

A Century of Achievement.   Hartford, Connecticut, 1937, Colt's Patent Fire Arms Manufacturing Company.   96 pp., photographic plates.   Paper wrappers.   [Also a deluxe edition, specially bound]   More than a sales brochure, this work traces the history of the company and includes a chapter on handgun shooting by Charles Askins, Jr.

Colt's 100th Anniversary Fire Arms Manual.   Hartford, Connecticut, 1937, Colt's Patent Fire Arms Manufacturing Company.   96 pp., illustrations. 8vo.   Paper wrappers.

Comeau, Napoleon

Life and Sport on the North Shore; of the lower St. Lawrence and Gulf. Quebec, 1954, Daily Telegraph Printing House,   440 pp., photographic plates. 8vo. (Originally published, 1909, same format and publisher)   An important book on angling, trapping and hunting in the region.   See Phillips.

Conatser, Dean

Bowhunting the Whitetail Deer.   New York, 1977, Winchester Press. 171 pp., illustrations.   8vo; dust jacket.   (Also reprinted in paper wrappers)

Cone, Arthur L.

The Complete Guide To Hunting.   New York, 1970, The Macmillan Company.   335 pp., photographic plates.   8vo; dust jacket.   (Also a book club edition, same publisher.   Also reprinted, 1978, Stoeger Arms Co., in   paper wrappers)

Conger, Roger

Some Memorable Hunting Trips.   1970.   Big game hunting in the western states.   Rare.

Conibear, Kenneth

North Land Footprints; or lives on Little Bent Tree Lake. New York, 1937, Charles Scribner's Sons. 339 pp. 8vo; dust jacket. A fictional account of animal life and man's influence upon it around the lake.

Conklin, W. Gard

The Pymatuming; state game refuge and museum. Harrisburg, 1938, Pennsylvania Game Commission. 52 pp., black and white and color illustrations; maps. 8vo. Paper wrappers. (Reprinted several times, same format and publisher) This man-made lake on the northern portion of the Ohio and Pennsylvania border is still a significant wildfowl refuge and home to record-size muskellunge and other game fish.

Conley, Clare

The Field & Stream Guide To Upland Game Birds. New York, 1966, Holt, Rinehart & Winston. 127 pp. drawings, maps. 8vo. Paper wrappers.

Connell, Herbert S.

Moose Hunting in the Laurentians. New York, 1937, Privately printed. 108 pp., photographic plates plus frontispiece by Carl Rungius. Limited to 150 numbered copies. 4to. Copies of this work have also been observed lacking the limitation stamp, which might indicate that two printings were actually produced.

Connett, Eugene V., 3rd   1891-1969

Adventures in Cover Collecting. New York, 1955, D. Van Nostrand Company, Inc. 72 pp., photographic plates. 8vo. Paper wrappers. Connett was also an enthusiastic stamp collector. This philatelic work deals with collecting first day covers.

Duck Decoys: How To Make Them, How to Paint Them and How To Rig Them. New York, 1953, D. Van Nostrand Company, Inc. 116 pp., photographic plates; three color illustrations from paintings by Dr. Edgar Burke. A Van Nostrand Sporting Book. 8vo; dust jacket. (Reprinted many times, same format, various publishers) A straightforward, practical guide to the subject.

Feathered Game From a Sporting Journal. New York, 1929, The Derrydale Press. Unpaginated, 11 colored plates from paintings by Dr. Edgar Burke. Limited to 500 numbered copies. 4to. [Also a large paper edition, specially bound with a hand-colored frontispiece and limited to 50 numbered copies] An exquisite wing shooting book in either edition.

The Small Boat Skipper; and his problems. New York, 1952, W. W. Norton & Co., Inc. 213 pp., frontispiece, drawings. 8vo; dust jacket.

Wing Shooting and Angling. New York, 1922, Charles Scribner's Sons. 226 pp., illustrations by A. B. Frost and Oliver Kemp. 8vo; dust jacket.

Connett, Eugene V., 3rd, editor

American Sporting Dogs. New York, 1948, D. Van Nostrand Company, Inc. 549 pp., plates. A Van Nostrand Sporting Book. Tall 8vo; dust jacket.

A Decade of American Sporting Books and Prints. New York, 1937, The Derrydale Press. 71 pp., drawings. 8vo. Limited to 950 numbered copies. This was The Derrydale Press' own bibliography of their works produced to this date.

Duck Shooting Along the Atlantic Tidewater. New York, 1947, William Morrow and Co., Inc. 308 pp., color illustrations by Dr. Edgar Burke and Lynn Bogue Hunt, photographic plates. Large 4to; dust jacket. (Reprinted 1956, same format and publisher. Also reprinted several times, Bonanza) [Also a deluxe first edition, specially bound and limited to 100 numbered and signed copies; slipcased. Issued with an extra suite of plates]

Upland Game Bird Shooting in America. New York, 1930, The Derrydale Press. 249 pp., many illustrations from paintings and photographs. Limited to 850 copies. Folio; dust jacket. [Also a deluxe edition, specially bound with a signed William Schaldach etching as the frontispiece and limited to 75 copies] (Also reprinted, 1985, Premier Press)

Wildfowling in the Mississippi Flyway. New York, 1949, D. Van Nostrand Company, Inc. 387 pp., plates. A Van Nostrand Sporting Book. 4to; dust jacket. (Reprinted 1984, Premier Press)

Eugene V. Connett, 3rd had the single greatest influence on the production of the American sporting book in the twentieth century. He was not only a competent author, but the angling and hunting anthologies he edited are important records of sport in an era of abundant fish and game. In sporting book design, he was without peer, and his Derrydale Press and Van Nostrand Sporting Books will continue to be highly collected, not only for their excellence of design, but also for their content. See Bruns, for angling titles written or edited by him. See Siegel and Frazier for information on The Derrydale Press.

Conningham, Frederick A. b. 1890

Currier & Ives Prints. New York, 1949, Crown Publishers, Inc.. 300 pp., photographic plates. 8vo; dust jacket. (Also a 1970 revised edition, same format and publisher)

Currier & Ives Prints. Cleveland, 1950, World Publishing Company. 63 pp., color and black and white illustrations. Limited to 950 numbered copies. 12mo; slipcased.

Connolly, Louise

The Pheasants; a brief description of A. R. Kuser's gift of three groups of pheasants. Newark, New Jersey, 1927, Newark Museum. 37 pp., photographic plates; map. 12mo. Paper wrappers. With an essay on William Beebe.

Conoley, William N., Jr.

Waterfowl Heritage; North Carolina decoys and gunning lore. Wendell, North Carolina, 1982, Webfoot, Inc. 324 pp., illustrations in color and in black and white from photographs. 4to; dust jacket.

Conover, Boardman

A Study of the Torrent Ducks. Chicago, 1943, Field. 12 pp. 8vo. Paper wrappers.

Conrad, Howard Louis

Uncle Dick Wooten; the pioneer frontiersman of the Rocky Mountain region. Chicago, 1952, R. R. Donnelley Company. 465 pp., photographic plates, maps. 12mo. Contains much on big game hunting.

Cooch, F. G.

The Breeding Biology of the Northern Eider; in the Cape Dorset Area, Northwest Territories. Ottawa, 1965, Canadian Wildlife Service. 68 pp., photographic plates, maps, bibliography. 8vo. Paper wrappers.

Cook, Earnshaw

Hollica Snooze. Rindge, New Hampshire, 1957, R. R. Smith. 313 pp., illustrations from drawings by Bob Hines. 8vo; dust jacket. [Also a deluxe edition, specially bound and limited to 100 numbered and signed copies] Humorous episodes of duck and goose hunting on the Eastern shore.

Cooper, Courtney Ryley

High Country; the Rockies yesterday and to-day. Boston, 1926, Little, Brown & Company. 294 pp., illustrations. 8vo; dust jacket.

Cooper, Jeff

The Complete Book of Modern Handgunning. New York, 1961, Bramhall House. 262 pp., illustrations. Tall 8vo; dust jacket.

Cooper, John Irwin

The History of the Montreal Hunt. Montreal. 1953, The Montreal Hunt. Introduction by A. Henry Higginson. A numbered edition of unspecified limitation. 4to. A history of this foxhunting club.

Cooper, Page, editor

Famous Dog Stories. New York, 1949, Doubleday & Co., Inc. 336 pp., drawings by D. Thorne. 8vo; dust jacket. Containing one dog story written by Nash Buckingham.

Cooper River Joe (*pseud.* of **Charles Henry Remington**)

A Golden Cross on Trails From the Valdez Glacier. Los Angeles, 1939, White-Thompson Publishing Company. 200 pp., illustrations by N. G. Thompson. 8vo.

Cooper, T. T.

Travels of a Pioneer of Commerce. New York, 1967, Abercrombie & Fitch, Inc. 475 pp., plates from old engravings. 8vo; dust jacket. (A facsimile reproduction of the 1871 London edition) Some Western hunting.

Corbett, Lucy and Sydney Corbett

Pot Shots From a Grosse Ile Kitchen. New York, 1947, Harper & Brothers, Inc. 213 pp., illustrations. 8vo; dust jacket. Some recipes, but also hunting, and hunting dogs. Grosse Ile is an island on Lake Erie, just south of Detroit.

Corder, E. M.

Deer Hunter. New York, 1979, Jove Publications. 189 pp. An uncomplimentary look at the sport of deer hunting.

Cordier, A. H.

A Wyoming Big Game Hunt. Kansas City, Missouri, 1907, Privately printed. 56 pp., photographic plates. 12mo. Paper wrappers. Mostly elk hunting. Not in Phillips.

Cory, Charles B.

Hunting and Fishing In Florida. New York, 1970, Arno Press. 304 pp., drawings, photographic plates. 8vo. (A facsimile reproduction of the 1896 first edition)

Cory, Harper

The Bears of Jasper. London, 1946, Nelson. 119 pp., photographic plates. 8vo; dust jacket. An account of the bears of Jasper National Park.

Cory, Obe

Beartracker! An outfitter's guide to bear hunting with hounds. Idaho Falls, 1979, Privately printed. 211 pp., illustrations. 8vo; dust jacket. An uncommon and thorough work.

Costello, David F.

The World of the Prairie Dog. Philadelphia, 1970, J. B. Lippincott Co. 160 pp., photographic plates, bibliography. A title in Lippincott's Living World series. 4to; dust jacket. (Reprinted, same format and publisher)

Cottam, Clarence

Food Habits of North American Diving Ducks. Washington, D. C., 1939, United States Department of the Interior. 140 pp., color plates by Allan Brooks, photographic plates, bibliography. Paper wrappers.

Cottam, Clarence, and James B. Trefethen, editors
   Whitewings; the life history, status and management of the white-winged dove. Princeton, New Jersey, 1968, D. Van Nostrand and Company, Inc. 348 pp., drawings and color plates by Bob Hines. 8vo; dust jacket.

Cottar, Frank
   Cassiar Jingles.   1928.   Poetry and prose about big game hunting in the Glacier Lake area. Rare.

Coulter, Malcolm W. and William R. Miller
   Nesting Biology of Black Ducks and Mallards in Northern New England. Montpelier, 1968, Vermont Fish and Game Commission.   73 pp., photographic plates, bibliography. 8vo. Paper wrappers.

Cowardin, Lewis M., et al.
   Mallard Recruitment in the Agricultural Environment of North Dakota. Washington, D. C., 1985, The Wildlife Society. Monograph # 92.   37 pp., photographic plates, maps, bibliography. 4to. Paper wrappers.

Cowher, Lou, et al.
   How To Build a Muzzle Loading Rifle; Building a Muzzle Loading Target Pistol, Making a Powder Horn, The Manufacture of Gun Flints. Ohio, 1958, National Muzzle Loading Rifle Association. 107 pp., illustrations. 8vo; dust jacket. (Reprinted several times with similar titles, various places)

Cox, Alex
   Deer Hunting in Texas. A handbook for hunters. San Antonio, 1947, The Naylor Company. 105 pp., drawings by the author. 8vo. (Reprinted several times, same publisher)

Cox, Charles E., Jr.
   John Tobias, Sportsman. New York, 1937, The Derrydale Press. 204 pp., illustrations from drawings by A. L. Ripley. Limited to 950 numbered copies. Tall 8vo. Hunting upland birds and waterfowl with some angling.

Cox, James
   The Endangered Ones. New York, 1975, Crown Publishers, Inc. 224 pp., color and black and white illustrations. 4to; dust jacket. A description of more than 300 endangered species.

Coykendall, Ralf W., Jr.   b. 1929
   Chester; the story of a decoy. No place (Landgrove), 1984, Privately printed. Unpaginated (30 pp.), drawings (some hand-colored). Limited to 350 numbered copies. 8vo. Paper wrappers. A juvenile.

95

Coykendall, Ralf W., Jr., continued

Decoy Collecting. Londonderry, New Hampshire, 1985, Sporting Connection. 36 pp., photographic plates. Limited to 750 numbered and signed copies. 8vo. Paper wrappers.

Wildfowling At a Glance. Harrisburg, 1968, The Stackpole Company. 94 pp., illustrations. 12mo; dust jacket.

You and Your Retriever. New York, 1963, Doubleday & Co., Inc. 155 pp., illustrations. 8vo; dust jacket.

Coykendall, Ralf W., Jr., editor

Joel Barber's Americana. No place, 1983, Privately printed. Unpaginated (39 pp.), drawings. Limited to 250 numbered copies. 8vo. Paper wrappers. [Also a deluxe edition, specially bound; slipcased]

Modern Decoys. Londonderry, New Hampshire, 1985, Privately printed. 13 pp., photographic plates; drawings. Limited to 950 numbered and signed copies. 4to. Paper wrappers. [Also a deluxe edition, specially bound and limited to 50 numbered and signed copies; boxed. Issued with a hand-carved miniature decoy]

Coykendall, Ralf W., Sr.

Duck Decoys and How To Rig Them. New York, 1955, Henry Holt and Company, Inc.. 125 pp., photographic plates and drawings. Tall 8vo; dust jacket. (Reprinted several times, same format and publisher. Also a 1983 revised "Collector's Edition," Winchester Press, and edited by Ralf Coykendall, Jr.; slipcased)

Coyle, David Cushman

Conservation; an American story of conflict and accomplishment. New Brunswick, New Jersey, 1957.

Coziah, Calvin

Buck, Bows and Campfires; forty years of hunting trophy bucks. Soda Springs, Idaho, 1981, Privately printed. 159 pp., illustrated in black and white and in color from photographs and drawings. 8vo; dust jacket.

Cradock, Chris

A Manual of Clayshooting. New York, 1983, Hippocrane Books. 182 pp., illustrations. 8vo; dust jacket. (Originally published, Great Britain)

Craige, Capt. John Houston

The Practical Book of American Guns. Cleveland, 1950, The World Publishing Company. 352 pp., drawings, photographic plates. 8vo; dust jacket.

Craighead, Frank C.   b. 1916

   The Track of the Grizzly.   San Francisco, 1979, Sierra Club Books. 261 pp., photographic plates, bibliography.   8vo; dust jacket.   (Reprinted several times, same format and publisher)

Craighead, John J. (b. 1916), et al.

   A Definitive System For Analysis of Grizzly Bear Habitat and Other Wilderness Resources.   Missoula, 1982, University of Montana.   279 pp., illustrations.   4to.   Paper wrappers.

   Elk Migrations In and Near Yellowstone National Park.   Washington, D. C., 1972, United States Wildlife Service.   48 pp., photographic plates, maps. 4to.   Paper wrappers.

Craighead, Frank C. and John J. Craighead

   Grizzly Bear Pre-hibernation and Denning Activities as Determined by Radio-tracking.   Washington, D. C., 1972, United States Wildlife Service.   35 pp., photographic plates.   8vo.   Paper wrappers.

   Hawks in the Hand.   Boston, 1939, Houghton Mifflin Company   290 pp., photographic plates.   8vo; dust jacket.   Falconry and much on the habits of other raptors.

   Hawks, Owls and Wildlife.   Harrisburg, 1950, The Stackpole Company and the Wildlife Management Institute.   443 pp., photographic plates, color frontispiece from a painting by Walter A. Weber.   8vo; dust jacket.   (Reprinted 1969, paper wrappers, Dover)   A thorough study of the effects of raptors on small game.

Crammond, Michael

   A Bear Behind.   Vancouver, B. C., 1973, Mitchell.   209 pp., illustrations.   8vo; dust jacket.   Tall tales of the outdoors.

   Big Game Hunting in the West.   Vancouver, B. C., 1965, Mitchell. 166 pp., photographic plates, drawings.   8vo; dust jacket.

   Game Bird Hunting in the West.   Vancouver, British Columbia, 1967, Mitchell.   252 pp., photographic plates, drawings.   8vo; dust jacket.

   Hunting and Fishing in North America.   Norman, 1953, University of Oklahoma Press.   394 pp., photographic plates, drawings by Olaus J. Murie. 8vo; dust jacket.   (Reprinted, same format and publisher)

   Killer Bears.   New York, 1981, Charles Scribner's Sons / Outdoor Life Books.   313 pp.   8vo; dust jacket.   (Reprinted several times, same format and publisher)

Crane, Stephen

   Killing His Bear.   No place, 1949, Privately printed.   4 pp.   Limited to 100 copies.   8vo.   This account of the author's bear hunt was published for presentation purposes.   Scarce.

Craven, Scott R.
The Canada Goose - Branta canadensis; an annotated bibliography. Washington, D. C., 1981, United States Fish and Wildlife Service.   66 pp. 4to. Paper wrappers.

Crawford, Everett Lake
See **Hunter, Anole**

Crawford, Florence
Girl of the Desert; the life and writings of one of the most extraordinary women in America today. New York, 1961, Greenwich. 134 pp., photographic plates. 8vo; dust jacket. Hunting adventures over many years by this woman hunter.

Crawford, John S.
At Home With the High Ones; a portfolio of photographs and text. Anchorage, 1976, Alaska Northwest Publishing Company. A 32 pp. booklet of text and 32 full color photographs loosely inserted in a paper portfolio. An uncommon work on grizzly bear, goat, sheep and others.
Wolves, Bears and Bighorns. Anchorage, 1981, Alaska Northwest Publishing Company. 176 pp., illustrated in color and black and white from photographs. 4to; dust jacket. (Reprinted and revised several times, same format and publisher) Hunting big game in Alaska.

Crawford, Lewis F.
Rekindling Campfires; the exploits of Ben Arnold (Connor) (Wa-si-cu Tam-a-he-ca), an authentic narrative of sixty years in the old West as Indian fighter, gold miner, cowboy, hunter and Army scout. Bismarck, North Dakota, 1926, Capital. 324 pp., illustrations, maps. 8vo; dust jacket. An important Americana title containing some hunting.

Crisler, Lois
Arctic Wild. New York, 1958, Harper & Brothers. 301 pp., photographic plates. 8vo; dust jacket. (Reprinted 1973, same format and publisher) Photographing wildlife in Alaska's Brooks Range.
Captive Wild. New York, 1968, Harper & Row, Publishers, Inc. 238 pp., photographic plates. 8vo; dust jacket. The author shared her home with a wolf family.

Crispens, Charles G., Jr.
Quails and Partridges of North America; a bibliography. Seattle, 1960, University of Washington Press. 125 pp. 8vo. A scarce and thorough bibliography.

Crites, Arthur S.

A Hunter's Tale of the Great Outdoors. Los Angeles, 1952, Ward Richie Press. 229 pp., photographic plates, drawings. 8vo. Containing grizzly and brown bear and Rocky Mountain big horn sheep hunting.

Cromer, Ed

Fishing and Hunting Guide of North America. Ft. Worth, Texas, 1948. 180 pp., illustrations. 8vo. Paper wrappers.

Cronk, Oscar E.

They Called Him Wildcat; the life and legend of V. E. "Wildcat" Lynch. No place, No date (ca. 1975), Privately printed. 147 pp., photographic plates. Paper wrappers. Hunting and angling in Maine.

Crookston, Newell J.

The Story of Old Ephraim. North Logan, Utah, No date (ca. 1960), Privately printed. 22 pp., photographic plates, drawings. 8vo. Paper wrappers. The story of the hunting of the last grizzly bear in Idaho.

Crosby, Alexander L.

Canada Geese. Champaign, Illinois, 1966, Garrard. 64 pp., illustrations. A title in the Junior Science Book series. 8vo; dust jacket.

Crosby, Josef F.

The Destruction of the North American Wolf. No place, No date (ca. 1960), Privately printed. 25 pp., photographic plates, map. 12mo. Paper wrappers.

Cross, Gorham L.

See **G. Grouse**

Crossman, Captain Edward C.   1888-1939

Small - Bore Rifle Shooting. Marshallton, Delaware, 1927, Small Arms Technical Publishing Company. 359 pp., drawings, photographic plates.

The Book of the Springfield. Marines, Onslow County, North Carolina, 1932, Small Arms Technical Publishing Company. 451 pp., photographic plates, drawings. 8vo; dust jacket. (Also a second edition, 1951, co-authored by **Roy F. Dunlap,** same publisher. This second edition reprinted, The Stackpole Company) A most comprehensive work on the United States Springfield rifle.

Military and Sporting Rifle Shooting. Marines, Onslow County, North Carolina, 1932, Small Arms Technical Publishing Company. 499 pp., photographic plates, drawings. 8vo; dust jacket. A companion volume to *The Book of the Springfield.*

Crouse, Russel   b. 1893

Mr. Currier and Mr. Ives; a note on their lives and times.   New York, 1930, Doubleday, Doran & Co., Inc.   138 pp., color and black and white illustrations.   4to; dust jacket.   [Also a deluxe edition of 301 numbered and signed copies]

Crow, Rankin

Rankin Crow and the Oregon Country.   Ironside, 1970, Privately printed.   242 pp., photographic plates.   8vo; dust jacket. The author's memoirs of ranch life in eastern Oregon, with much hunting.   Uncommon.

Crowe, Philip Kingsland   1908-1976

Sport is Where You Find It.   New York, 1953, D. Van Nostrand Company, Inc. 189 pp., illustrations from drawings by Paul Brown. Limited to 1450 copies signed by the author.   A Van Nostrand Sporting Book. 8vo; dust jacket.

World Wildlife; the last stand.   New York, 1970, Charles Scribner's Sons. 308 pp., photographic plates. 8vo; dust jacket.

Cruickshank, Allan

Wings in the Wilderness.   New York, 1947, Oxford University Press. 125 pp., photographic plates. 8vo ; dust jacket.

Cruickshank, Allan, editor

Hunting With the Camera.   New York, 1957.   215 pp., color and black and white illustrations.   8vo; dust jacket.

Cruickshank, Helen Gere

A Paradise of Birds; when spring comes to Texas.   New York, 1968, Dodd Mead & Co. 398 pp., photographic plates. 8vo; dust jacket. With sections on wild turkey, wildfowl and shorebirds.

Cruickshank, Helen Gere, editor

John and William Bartram's America; selections from the writings of the Philadelphia naturalists. New York, 1957, The Devin-Adair Company. 418 pp., illustrations, some by F. L. Jaques. 8vo; dust jacket. Natural history of the southern U. S. in the late eighteenth century.

Crump, Irving

Out of the Woods; wild animal stories. New York, 1941, Dodd, Mead & Co. 269 pp., black and white illustrations from drawings by Enos Comstock. 8vo; dust jacket.

Cudahy, John

Mananaland; adventuring with camera and rifle through California and Mexico. New York, 1928, Duffield and Company. 250 pp., photographic plates, map. 8vo. Much on desert bighorn, antelope and cougar. Scarce.

Culbertson, Owen

Sporting Books From the Library of Owen Culbertson. New York, 1933, Anderson Art Association. 51 pp. 8vo. Paper wrappers. An auction catalog with 284 lots.

Culler, John, editor

Carolina's Hunting Heritage. Columbia, South Carolina, 1978, South Carolina Wildlife / Amwell Press. 207 pp., illustrations. Limited to 750 numbered and signed copies. 4to; slipcased.

Cummings, Charles S., 2nd.

Everyday Ballistics. Harrisburg, 1950, Stackpole and Heck, Inc. 138 pp., charts. 8vo; dust jacket. A practical discussion of the subject and how it relates to the average shooting sportsman.

Cunningham, Eugene   b. 1896

Triggernometry; a gallery of gunfighters, with technical notes on leather slapping as a fine art, gathered from many a loose holstered expert over the years. New York, 1934, The Press of the Pioneers. 441 pp., photographic plates. 8vo. (Reprinted 1941 and 1952, Caxton Printers, Ltd.) Biographic sketches of the famous gunfighters of the old west. A title sought by collectors of antique single action revolvers.

Cunningham, Marci

The Deerhunter's Guide to Success. Pennsylvania, 1985, Backwoods Books. 48 pp. Paper wrappers.

Currier, Paul J., et al.

Migratory Bird Habitat on the Platte Rivers in Nebraska. Grand Island, Nebraska, 1985, Platte River Whooping Crane Critical Habitat Maintenance Trust. 177 pp., photographic plates. 8vo. Paper wrappers.

Currier & Ives

Currier & Ives Print Portfolio Series; hunting and fishing. Maplewood, 1976, Hammond. 14 color plates plus two pp. text. Folio. Paper wrappers.

Currier & Ives

    Also see **Crouse, Russel**
    Also see **Peters, Fred J.**
    Also see **Peters, Harry T.**

Curry-Lindahl, Kai

Let Them Live; a world wide survey of animals threatened with extinction.   New York, 1972, William Morrow & Co., Inc.   394 pp., bibliography.   8vo; dust jacket.

Wildlife of Prairies and Plains. New York, 1981, Harry N. Abrams, Inc. 232 pp., color illustrations; photographic plates, maps.   8vo; dust jacket.

Curtis, Capt. Paul A.   1889-1943

American Game Shooting.   New York, 1927, E. P. Dutton & Co., Inc. 279 pp., photographic plates.   8vo; dust jacket.

Guns and Gunning.   Philadelphia, 1934, Penn Publishing Company. 384 pp., photographic plates, color frontispiece from a painting by Fred Everett. 8vo; dust jacket.   (Reprinted 1941, Outdoor Life Books.   Also reprinted three times, smaller format in 1943, 1945 and 1946, Alfred A. Knopf, Inc. as a title in Knopf's Borzoi Books For Sportsmen series)

Sportsmen All.   New York, 1938, The Derrydale Press.   160 pp., illustrations from drawings by Marguerite Kirmse.   Limited to 950 numbered copies.   Tall 8vo.   The author recounts his experiences with hunting dogs.

Curtiss, R.

An Account of the Natural History of New England and of Nova Scotia and Lower Canada.   New York, 1924, Privately printed.   104 pp.   Limited to 100 copies.   8vo.   A scarce account of the wildlife of the area.   Not in Phillips.

Cutright, Paul

Theodore Roosevelt, The Naturalist.   New York, 1956, Harper & Brothers.   297 pp., photographic plates.   8vo; dust jacket.

Dahlberg, Burton L. and Ralph C. Guettinger
   The White-Tailed Deer in Wisconsin.   Madison, Wisconsin, 1956, Technical Wildlife Bulletin No. 14.   292 pp., drawings, maps.   8vo.

Daigre, Ambrose P.
   Hunter's Guide To Waterfowl of Louisiana.   New Orleans, 1941, Louisiana Department of Conservation.   60 pp., color and black and white illustrations by Allan Brooks.   8vo.   Paper wrappers.

Dailey, E. J.
   Practical Muskrat Raising. Columbus, Ohio, 1927, A. R. Harding. 136 pp., drawings, photographic plates.   16mo.   (Reprinted several times, same format and publisher)
   Traplines and Trails. Columbus, Ohio, Various dates, Hunter-Trader-Trapper. 242 pp., photographic plates. 12mo. (Originally published, 1925, same format and publisher)   Much on trapping and other lore of the Adirondacks

Dalgety, C. T.
   Wildfowling.   New York, 1937, Charles Scribner's Sons.   254 pp., illustrations. 12mo; dust jacket.

Dalke, P. D. et al.
   The Ecology and Management of the Wild Turkey in Missouri.   No place, 1946, Missouri Conservation Commission.   Photographic plates, drawings. 8vo.   Paper wrappers.

Dalrymple, Byron W.   b. 1910
   The Complete Book of Deer Hunting.   New York, 1973, Winchester Press. 247 pp., photographic plates. 8vo; dust jacket. (Also a Tulsa, Oklahoma edition, same format and publisher)
   Complete Guide To Hunting Across North America.   New York, 1970, Harper & Row, Publishers, Inc. / Outdoor Life Books.   848 pp., photographic plates.   8vo; dust jacket.
   Deer Hunting With Dalrymple: a lifetime of lore on the whitetail and mule deer.   New York, 1978, David McKay Co. 248 pp., photographic plates. 8vo; dust jacket. (Reprinted, Arco)
   Doves and Dove Shooting.   New York, 1949, G. P. Putnam's Sons. 243 pp., photographic plates. Tall 8vo; dust jacket.
   How To Call Wildlife.   New York, 1975, Outdoor Life Books. 179 pp., photographic plates.   8vo. Paper wrappers. (Reprinted many times, same format and publisher)
   Hunting For the Pot, Fishing For the Pan.   Harrisburg, 1981, The Stackpole Company. 338 pp., photographic plates. 8vo; dust jacket.

Dalrymple, Byron W., continued

North American Big Game Hunting. New York, 1974, Winchester Press. 383 pp., photographic plates. 8vo; dust jacket. (Reprinted 1975, Stoeger Arms Corp.)

North American Game Animals. New York, 1978, Crown Publishers, Inc. / Outdoor Life Books. 516 pp., full page illustrations in color and others in black and white by Douglas Allen. 4to; dust jacket. (Reprinted 1985, Stackpole Books)

Survival in the Outdoors. New York, 1972, E. P. Dutton & Co., Inc. / Outdoor Life Books. 309 pp., illustrations. 8vo; dust jacket. (Reprinted, same format and publisher)

Mr. Dalrymple is probably one of the most-read outdoor writers of the twentieth century. His works were published in very large printing runs by Outdoor Life Books and others, and were sold inexpensively to sportsmen who wanted sound information at a reasonable price. He wrote several hunting titles after 1985 as well as many angling titles. See Bruns.

Dalrymple, Tom, editor

Bowhunting in Arizona; including records of game animals. Tucson, 1980, Arizona Bowhunters Record Book Committee. 150 pp., photographic plates, drawings, diagrams. Limited to 2000 numbered copies. 8vo; dust jacket.

Dam, Brian

New York State Big Buck Club Record Book. 1984, New York State Big Buck Club. 29 pp. (The third edition of this state's records) There were two earlier editions of this work, edited by **Charles J. Alsheimer**, which see.

Damon, G. E.

Gun Fun With Safety. Huntington, West Virginia, 1947, Standard Publications, Inc. 206 pp., photographic plates. Tall 8vo; dust jacket.

Daniel, Glenda and J. Sullivan

A Sierra Club Naturalist's Guide To the North Woods of Michigan, Wisconsin and Minnesota. San Francisco, 1981, The Sierra club. 408 pp., photographic plates, drawings, bibliography. 8vo. (Also produced in paper wrappers, 1981, same format and publisher)

Danielson, Richard E. **1886-1957**

Martha Doyle. New York, 1938, The Derrydale Press. 152 pp., drawings by Edwin Megargee. Limited to 1250 numbered copies. 4to. Mostly foxhunting.

Danziger, Jeff

The Illustrated Unofficial Hunting Rules. Shelbourne, Vermont, 1984, New England Press. Unpaginated (approx. 60 pp.), drawings. 8vo. Paper wrappers. (Reprinted, same format and publisher) A humorous look at hunting.

Darling, J. N., Harold P. Sheldon and Ira N. Gabrielson

Game Management on the Farm. Washington, D. C., 1936, United States Department of Agriculture. 22 pp., drawings. 8vo. Paper wrappers.

Darling, Louis

Greenhead. New York, 1954, William Morrow & Co., Inc. 95 pp., color frontispiece by the author. 8vo; dust jacket. A juvenile title by this popular wildlife illustrator.

Darner, Kirt

How to Find Giant Bucks. Marceline, Missouri, 1983, Walsworth Publishing Company. 283 pp., illustrations. 8vo. [Also a 1985 "Collector's Limited Edition" of 500 numbered and signed copies]

Dary, David A.

The Buffalo Book; the full saga of the American animal. Chicago, 1974, Swallow. 374 pp., photographic plates, drawings, bibliography. 8vo; dust jacket.

Dashwood, Richard Lewes

Chiploquorgan: or Life By the Camp Fire; in Dominion Canada and Newfoundland. Frederickton, New Brunswick, 1979, St. Anne's. 293 pp., plates. Limited to 500 numbered copies. 8vo. (A facsimile reproduction of the 1871 edition)

Dasmann, Raymond F.   b. 1919

Wildlife Biology. New York, 1964, John Wiley & Sons, Inc. 231 pp., photographic plates, charts. 8vo; dust jacket. A textbook with emphasis on western American species.

Dasmann, William

If Deer Are To Survive. Harrisburg / Washington D. C., 1971, The Stackpole Company / The Wildlife Management Institute. 128 pp., photographic plates. 8vo; dust jacket.

Deer Range: Management and Improvement. Jefferson, North Carolina, 1981, McFarland & Company, Inc. 168 pp., illustrations. 8vo.

Datig, Fred A.
 Cartridges For Collectors; Volume I - Centerfire.   Los Angeles, Borden. 176 pp., illustrations, bibliography. 8vo; dust jacket. (Reprinted 1963, same format and publisher)
 Cartridges For Collectors; Volume II - centerfire, rimfire, patent ignition.   Beverly Hills, California, 1958, Fadco.   176 pp., illustrations, plus ads.   8vo; dust jacket.

Daumier, Honore
 Hunting and Fishing.   New York, No date (ca. 1975), Pantheon Books, Inc.   24 loose black and white prints accompanied by a six page booklet of text, in paper folder.   Folio. (Also a 1975 French edition with English translations in a section of notes) Humorous hunting and angling scenes.

Dauphine, T. C.
 Biology of the Kaminuriak Population of Barren Ground Caribou; Part 4: Growth, Reproduction and Energy Reserves.   Ottawa, 1976, Canadian Wildlife Service.   71 pp., photographic plates, charts, bibliography.   Paper wrappers.

Davids, Richard and Dan Guravich
 Lords of the Arctic; a journey among the polar bears. New York, 1982, The Macmillan Company. 140 pp., photographic plates in color. 8vo; dust jacket. An in-depth study of the Polar bear.

Davidson. William R., editor
 Diseases and Parasites of White-Tailed Deer.   Athens, Georgia, 1981, University of Georgia.   458 pp., illustrations.   8vo.

Davies, Henry E.
 Ten Days on the Plains.   Dallas, 1985, Southern Methodist University Press.   178 pp., photographic plates.   Edited by Paul Andrew Hutton.   8vo. (A reprint of the scarce 1872 edition, with added material)   A description of the hunting expedition led by General Philip Sheridan and guided by William "Buffalo Bill" Cody.

Davies, Thurston W.
 California: The Angler's Atlas and Hunting Guide. Long Beach, 1948, Angler's Atlas Company. 101 pp., illustrations, maps. 4to. Paper wrappers. Contains much on out of the way hunting areas.

Davis, Chester
 Let's Go Fishing and Hunting in North Carolina.   Raleigh, 1963.   68 pp., photographic plates.   4to.   Paper wrappers.

Davis, Don, editor

Muzzle Loading Shooting and Winning With the Champions. No place, 1973, Powder, Patch and Ball Publications. 169 pp., illustrations. Paper wrappers.

Davis, Harry P.

A Forgotten Heritage; the story of a people and the early American rifle. Huntington, West Virginia, 1941, Standard Printing and Publishing Company. 199 pp., photographic plates. 8vo; dust jacket. Scarce.

Davis, Henry E.

The American Wild Turkey. Georgetown, South Carolina, 1949, Small Arms Technical Publishing Company. 319 pp., frontispiece in color from a painting by Walter A. Weber, drawings by E. Stanley Smith. 8vo; dust jacket. (Reprinted 1952, same format and publisher. Also reprinted, 1984, Old Masters)
A classic work with much on ecology of the species; presented in an entertaining manner.

Davis, Henry P.   1894-1970

The Modern Dog Encyclopedia. Harrisburg, 1948, The Stackpole Company. 626 pp., photographic plates, drawings. Thick 4to; dust jacket. (Reprinted twice, same format and publisher)

Training Your Own Bird Dog. New York, 1948, G. P. Putnam's Sons. 175 pp., photographic plates, drawings. 8vo; dust jacket. (Reprinted many times, same format and publisher)

Davis, James R.

Gray Squirrel Management in Alabama. No place, 1978, Alabama Department of Conservation. 29 pp., photographic plates, bibliography. 8vo. Paper wrappers.

Management For Alabama Wild Turkeys. Montgomery, Alabama, 1976, Alabama Department of Conservation. 53 pp., photographic plates, charts. 8vo. Paper wrappers.

Management For Mourning Doves in Alabama. No place, 1977, Alabama Department of Conservation. 28 pp., photographic plates, bibliography. 8vo. Paper wrappers.

The White-Tailed Deer in Alabama. No place, 1979, Alabama Department of Conservation. 60 pp., photographic plates, bibliography. 8vo. Paper wrappers.

Davis, James R. and Eugene J. Wilder

History of Wild Turkey Restocking in Alabama. No place, 1985, Alabama Department of Conservation. 27 pp., photographic plates, bibliography. 8vo. Paper wrappers.

Davis, Marcellus, Henry Davis and C. T. Davis
    The Stranger.   Philadelphia, 1938, J. B. Lippincott Co. 59 pp., drawings by Fred McCaleb. Foreword by Nash Buckingham Small 8vo; dust jacket.   [Also a deluxe edition, specially bound with a signed etching as a frontispiece and limited to 250 numbered copies signed by the authors; slipcased] Hunting fox with hounds and firearms.

Davis, William C.
    Handloading.   Washington, D. C., 1981, The National Rifle Association of America.   322 pp., photographic plates, drawings.   4to; dust jacket. A manual for reloading metallic rifle and pistol cartridges.

Davison, Paul
    Gone Away With the Fort Leavenworth Hunt. Fort Leavenworth, Kansas, 1940, Privately printed by the club.   228 pp., illustrations, map. Limited to 500 copies. 8vo. A history of this foxhunting club, 1926 - 1940.
    The Fort Leavenworth Hunt. Fort Leavenworth, Kansas, 1939, Privately printed.   255 pp., illustrations. 8vo. The text includes 54 blank leaves for a hunt diary. Scarce.

Davison, Verne E.
    Bobwhites on the Rise. New York, 1949, Charles Scribner's Sons. 150 pp., drawings by Wallace Hughes, bibliography. 8vo; dust jacket.

Davy, G. Burton
    Saga of the Rockies. Manchester, New Hampshire, No date (ca. 1945), Privately printed. 39 pp., photographic plates. 12mo. Describes a 1944 hunting trip in the Canadian Rockies with much sheep, grizzly and mule deer hunting. Rare.

Dawson, Jim
    Whitetail Hunting. Harrisburg, 1982, Stackpole Books.   224 pp., illustrations. A basic treatment of the subject.

Day, Albert M.
    North American Waterfowl. New York and Harrisburg, 1949, Stackpole and Heck, Inc.   329 pp., color frontispiece and other drawings by Bob Hines, bibliography. 8vo; dust jacket. (Also a 1959 second revised edition, slightly smaller format, same publisher) Mr. Day was very instrumental in early wildfowl conservation programs.

Day, Donald, editor
    The Hunting and Exploring Adventures of Theodore Roosevelt: told in his own words. New York, 1955, Dial Press, Inc. 431 pp. 8vo; dust jacket.

Day, J. Wentworth

Sporting Adventure.   New York, No date (ca. 1937), G. P. Putnam's Sons.   288 pp., photographic plates plus drawings by "Fishhawk."   4to; dust jacket.   Printed from British sheets; covers, woodcock, waterfowling, punt gunning, poaching.

Dean, Herman

Travel Notes.   Huntington, West Virginia, 1957, Standard Publications, Inc.   69 pp.   8vo.   Some travel to Alaska and northern provinces of Canada.

Mr. Dean was owner of Standard Publishing Company in Huntington, West Virginia. His firm published several dozen firearms and hunting titles in the 1940's and 1950's. This scarce work was the last title using this imprint and was produced by him for presentation purposes.

Deane, J.

Deane's Manual of Firearms.   Huntington, West Virginia, 1946, Standard Publications, Inc.   286 pp., pull-out diagrams.   8vo.   (A facsimile reproduction of 1858 first edition)

Deane, John J.

Camp Recollections.   No place, No date (ca. 1911), Privately printed. 24 pp., illustrations.   8vo.   A rare title of prose and poetry about an elk hunt.   Not in Phillips.

Deason, Wilborn J.

Nature's Silent Call.   Waukegan, Illinois, 1925, Bunting Publishing Company.   405 pp., photographic plates.   8vo.   Traveling, camping and big game hunting in the Klamath Valley and Yellowstone.   Not in Phillips.

Debutts, Mary Custis Lee and Rosalie Woodland, editors

Charlotte Haxall Noland, 1883 - 1969.   Middleburg, Virginia, 1971, Foxcroft School.   100 pp., illustrations.   8vo.   The biography of the founder of Foxcroft School with much foxhunting at the famous Middleburg Hunt and surrounding Virginia countryside.

Decker, Maurice H.

Hunting Small Game With Shotgun and Rifle.   St. Paul, Minnesota, 1936, Webb Book Publishing Company.   76 pp., illustrations.   Paper wrappers. (Also a 1946 revised edition, same format and publisher)

Practical Manual of Guns. Chicago, 1946, Paul, Richmond & Company. 192 pp., drawings.   16mo; dust jacket.

Deems, E. F. and Duane Pursley, editors

North American Furbearers; a contemporary reference. No place, 1983, International Association of Fish and Wildlife Agencies.   217 pp., photographic plates, maps, extensive bibliography.   8vo.   An account of 23 species in all U. S. states and Canada.

Deep River Jim (*pseud.* of **Clayton Holt Ernst**)

Deep River Jim's Wilderness Trail Book. Boston, 1935, Open Road. 320 pp. drawings. 16mo. Paper wrappers. (Reprinted many times, various publishers)

Second Trail Book. Boston, 1948, Open Road. 318 pp., drawings. 8vo. Paper wrappers. Designed for the woodsman, this is organized by months of the year.

DeFalco, Joe

The Complete Deer Hunt. Franklin Square, New York, 1969, Privately printed. 117 pp., illustrations. 8vo; dust jacket. (Reprinted 1970, Grosset & Dunlap)

DeGanahl, Charles Francis

The Life and Letters of Charles Francis DeGanahl; collected by his wife for his children. New York, 1949, Smith. Two volumes of 974 pp., photographic plates, map. Limited to 200 numbered copies, signed by Mrs. DeGanahl. 8vo. Containing some North American hunting. Mr. DeGanahl was involved in business in Africa, Mexico and the U. S. and hunted extensively throughout the world.

DeGarmo, W. R. and J. Gill

West Virginia Whitetails. Charleston, 1958, West Virginia Division of Game. 88 pp., photographic plates, drawings, maps. 8vo. Paper wrappers.

DeHaas, Frank

Bolt Action Rifles. Northfield, Illinois, 1971, Gun Digest Publishing Company. 320 pp., photographic plates. Edited by John Amber 4to. Paper wrappers. (Reprinted 1973, same format and publisher)

Single Shot Rifles and Actions. Chicago, 1969, Gun Digest Publishing Company. 342 pp., photographic plates, drawings. 4to. Paper wrappers. (Reprinted several times, various formats and publishers)

Delacour, Jean **1890-1985**

Pheasant Breeding and Care. Fon-Du-Lac, Wisconsin, 1959. 113 pp., drawings, two color plates. 8vo. (Reprinted twice, same format and publisher. Also revised editions in 1973 and 1978, TFH, in paper wrappers)

The Pheasants of the World. Salt Lake City, 1957. 351 pp., 32 plates, some in color from paintings by J. C. Harrison. 4to. (Reprinted several times, same format, London)

Delacour, Jean and Sir Peter Scott.

The Waterfowl of the World. London, 1954, 1956, 1959, 1964, Country Life, Ltd. Four volumes of 284 pp., 232 pp., 270 pp., and 364 pp. respectively. Text by Jean Delacour and illustrations in color and in black and white by Sir Peter Scott. 4to; dust jackets. (Reprinted several times, same publisher) A most thorough and important work.

de la Valdene, Guy

Making Game; an essay on woodcock. Oshkosh, Wisconsin, 1985, Willow Creek Press. 202 pp., color frontispiece, drawings by Russell Chatham. 8vo. An authoritative work on the natural history and hunting of woodcock by a talented writer.

Delman, Maury

Bowhunting. Chicago, No date (ca. 1958), National Research Bureau. 31 pp. 8vo. Paper wrappers.

Everybody's Archery Guide. Derby, Connecticut, 1965, Topical Magazines. 128 pp., illustrations. 4to. Paper wrappers.

Delph, John and Shirley Delph

Factory Decoys of Mason, Stevens, Dodge and Peterson. Exton, Pennsylvania, 1980, Schiffer Publishing Company. 168 pp., photographic plates. 4to; dust jacket.

New England Decoys. Exton, Pennsylvania, 1980, Schiffer Publishing Company. 159 pp., photographic plates. 4to; dust jacket.

Demeritt, D. B.

Maine Made Guns and Their Makers. No place, 1973, Plumer. 209 pp., photographic plates. Limited to 1500 copies. 4to.

Denis, Armand

Cats of the World. Boston, 1964, Houghton Mifflin Company. 144 pp., photographic plates, bibliography. 8vo; dust jacket.

Denlinger, Milo G. 1890-1953

The Complete Cocker Spaniel. Washington, D. C., 1946, Denlinger's. 272 pp., illustrations by Paul Brown. 8vo. (Revised and reprinted several times, same format and publisher)

The Complete Irish Setter. Washington, D. C., 1949, Denlinger's. 128 pp., illustrations. 8vo.

Denlinger, William, editor
> *The Complete Beagle.* Richmond, Virginia, 1956, Denlinger's, Inc. 303 pp., illustrations. 8vo.
> *The Complete Weimaraner.* Richmond, Virginia, 1954, Denlinger's. 128 pp., illustrations. 8vo. (Also a revised and expanded edition, same publisher)
>> The Denlingers specialized in dog books and published titles on many different breeds.

Dennett, Carl
> *That Reminds Me.* Boston, 1947, Privately printed. 220 pp., illustrations. 8vo. A memoir with hunting in Maine and South Carolina.

Denny, George H.
> *The Dread Fishwish;* and other tales. Rockville Center, New York, 1975, Freshet Press. 223 pp., drawings. 4to; dust jacket. Contains some upland game bird hunting.

Depperman, W. H.
> *Shooter's Choice.* Cleveland, 1952, World Publishing Company. 189 pp., photographic plates. Tall 8vo; dust jacket. Firearms collecting, ballistics, reloading, etc. Scarce.

DePoncins, Gontran
> *Kabloona.* No place, 1941, Reynal & Hitchcock. 339 pp., photographic plates, drawings, maps. 8vo. An account of living, hunting and fishing with the Eskimos.

DeSormo, Maitland C.
> *John Bird Burnham;* Klondiker, Adirondacker, eminent conservationist. Saranac Lake, New York, 1978, Adirondack Yesteryears, Inc. 272 pp., photographic plates. 4to; dust jacket. The biography of this early conservationist, who was a confidant of Teddy Roosevelt and who helped Roosevelt form many of his conservation policies. Mr. Burnham was essentially the author of the Migratory Bird Act.

DeSormo, Maitland C., editor
> *Told Around the Campfire;* by Henry van Hoevenbergh of Adirondack Lodge. Old Forge, 1967, North Country. 102 pp., photographic plates, map. 8vo; dust jacket.

Dewhurst, C. Kurt
> *Downriver and Thumb Area Michigan Waterfowling;* the folk arts of Nate Quillen and Otto Misch. No place, 1981, Michigan State University. 14 pp., photographic plates, drawings. 4to. Paper wrappers.

Dexter, F. Theodore

Thirty-Five Years Scrap Book of Antique Arms. Topeka, Kansas, 1947, Privately printed. Two volumes. Unpaginated (approx. 110 pp. and 150 pp.), many illustrations. Limited to 2000 numbered copies. Oblong 4to. Intended for the use of collectors, with photographs, descriptions, and prices.

Forty-Two Years Scrapbook of Rare and Ancient Firearms. Los Angeles, 1954, Privately printed. 320 pp., photographic plates. Limited to 2000 numbered and signed copies. 4to; dust jacket. Both of these works are much more scarce than their limitations would suggest.

Dickey, Charles   b. 1920

Backtrack. Clinton, New Jersey, 1977, Amwell Press. 150 pp., drawings by Donald Shoffstall. Limited to 1000 numbered and signed copies. 8vo; slipcased.

Bobwhite Quail Hunting. Birmingham, Alabama, 1974, Oxmoor House. 112 pp., photographic plates; drawings. 4to. Paper wrappers. (Also a 1975 second edition, smaller format, cloth bound, same publisher)

Deer Hunting. Birmingham, Alabama, 1977, Oxmoor House. 110 pp., illustrations. 4to. Paper wrappers.

Dove Hunting. New York, 1976, Galahad. 112pp., photographic plates, drawings. 4to; dust jacket.

Movin' Along With Charley Dickey. Piscataway, New Jersey, 1985, Winchester Press. 224 pp., drawings by Joe Fornelli. 8vo; dust jacket.

Opening Shots and Parting Lines. Clinton, New Jersey, 1983, Amwell Press. 208 pp., drawings. Limited to 1000 numbered and signed copies. 8vo; slipcased.. (Also a 1983 trade edition, Winchester Press, reprinted by them many times)

Dickson, James

Camping in the Muskoka Region; a story of Algonquin Park. Toronto, 1959, Ontario Department of Lands and Forests. 164 pp., photographic plates, map. 8vo; dust jacket. (A reproduction of the rare 1886 first edition) With much on small and big game hunting of the region.

Dieter, William

Hunter's Orange. New York, 1983, Atheneum Publishers. 241 pp. (Reprinted, same format and publisher) A novel of a contemporary buffalo hunt in southeastern Utah with an anti-hunting theme.

Dietz, Lew   b. 1906

The Allagash. New York, 1968, Holt, Rinehart and Winston. 264 pp., illustrations, maps. 8vo; dust jacket.

Dietz, Lew, continued

Jeff White; young trapper.　Boston, 1951, Little, Brown & Company. 191 pp., drawings by William Moyers.　(Reprinted several times, same format and publisher)　A novel of adventure in the Maine woods. Mr. Dietz wrote four other *Jeff White* adventure books; all were older juveniles with incidental mention of hunting, trapping, etc.

Touch of Wilderness; a Maine woods journal.　New York, 1970, Holt, Rinehart and Winston.　220 pp.　8vo; dust jacket.　A collection of essays about Maine, including its people, hunting, trapping, etc..

Digness, Tom

Fox Trapping Made Easy; simple, easy methods.　Zanesville, 1980, Franklin.　64 pp., photographic plates. 8vo. Paper wrappers.

Dill, Herbert H. and F. B. Lee

Home Grown Honkers.　Washington, D. C., 1970, United States Fish and Wildlife Service.　154 pp., photographic plates, drawings, bibliography. 4to.　Paper wrappers.　(Reprinted 1970 and 1973, same format, International Wild Waterfowl Association)　Breeding wild Giant Canada Geese.

Dillin, John G. W.

The Kentucky Rifle; a study of the origin and development of a purely American type of firearm, together with accurate historical data concerning early Colonial gunsmiths, and profusely illustrated with photographic reproductions of their finest work. Washington, D. C., 1944, The National Rifle Association of America. Second edition. 133 pp., photographic plates.　Folio.　(Originally published, 1924, The National Rifle Association of America.　Also reprinted several times after 1944, various publishers)　The second edition is generally regarded as the most comprehensive. An important work.

Dillon, Richard

The Legend of Grizzly Adams - California's Greatest Mountain Man. New York, 1966, Coward, McCann, Inc.　223 pp., photographic plates.　8vo; dust jacket.　With much on bears and bear hunting.

Dilts, Mark C., editor

Of Grouse and Things; the best of the *Drummer*, 1975-1984. Pennsylvania, 1985, The Ruffed Grouse Society.　152 pp., line drawings.　4to; dust jacket.　A selection of the best stories published in the Grouse Society's magazine.

Dimick, S. W.

Pistol Highlights of 1940.　Hartford, Connecticut, 1941, Colt's Patent Firearms Manufacturing Company. 42 pp., photographic plates. Paper wrappers.

Dimock, Anthony W. (1842-1918) and Julian A. Dimock (1873-1945)
   Florida Enchantments.   New York, 1926, Frederick A. Stokes.   318 pp., illustrations.   8vo.   (Originally published, 1908, Outing Publishing Company)   Mostly angling, but with some wildlife and ecology of the region.   Anthony Dimock wrote several other important angling titles.   See Bruns.

Dimock, Julian A.
   Outdoor Photography.   New York, 1929, The Book League.   131 pp., photographic plates.   12mo.   (Originally published, 1912, Outing Publishing Company)   Julian Dimock was a pioneer of outdoor action photography.   This work deals mostly with angling pursuits.

Dippie, Brian W., editor
   Nomad; George A. Custer in "Turf, Field and Farm."   Austin, 1980, University of Texas Press.   174 pp., photographic plates, map.   4to; dust jacket.   A reproduction of Gen. Custer's hunting contributions and notes on thoroughbred race horses to this periodical under the pen name "Nomad" during the 1860's and 70's.

Dixon, Joseph Scattergood
   A Study of the Life History and Food Habits of Mule Deer in California.   Sacramento, 1934, California Fish and Game Commission.   146 pp., illustrations.   (Originally published in *California Fish and Game* magazine, July and October, 1934)

Dixon, Paige
   Summer of the White Goat.   New York, 1977, Atheneum Publishers.   105 pp., drawings, bibliography.   8vo; slipcase.   An older juvenile about mountain goats in Glacier National Park.

Doane, Paul M.
   Gunology; a comprehensive course for professional gun salesmen.   No place, 1964, Winchester-Western Company.   62 pp., photographic plates.   4to.

Dobie, J. Frank   1888-1964
   The Ben Lilly Legend.   Boston, 1950, Little, Brown & Company.   237 pp., frontispiece in color of Ben Lilly (1856-1936), illustrations.   8vo; dust jacket.   (Reprinted many times, same format and publisher.   Also a 1952 British edition)   The biography of a self-proclaimed great bear hunter.
   Guide To Life and Literature of the Southwest.   Austin, 1943, University of Texas Press.   111 pp., illustrations.   8vo.   (Also a 1952 revised edition, Southern Methodist University Press)   Containing excellent sections on buffalo hunting, bear hunting, natural history and the personalities involved in these areas.

Dobie, J. Frank, continued
  The Voice of the Coyote.   Boston, 1949, Little Brown & Company. 386 pp., illustrated by Olaus Murie. 8vo; dust jacket. (Reprinted many times, same format and publisher. Also a 1950 British edition)
  Mr. Dobie wrote extensively about the Southwest and most of his works had at least some incidental mention of hunting.

Dobie, J. Frank
  Also see **Tinkle, Lon**
  Also see **McVicker, Mary Louise**

Dobson, Joseph A.
  The Dobson 14-day Method of Dog Training.   Tulsa, 1981, Winchester Press. 150 pp., photographic plates.   8vo; dust jacket.

Dodge, Geraldine R.
  The English Cocker Spaniel in America.   New York, 1942, English Cocker Spaniel Club of America.   250 pp., illustrations.   4to.

Donald, Garry
  Trophy Deer of Saskatchewan.   Saskatchewan, 1985, Privately printed. 304 pp., illustrations.

Donaldson, Harvey A., et al.
  The Ultimate in Rifle Precision; 1949 Yearbook of the Benchrest Shooters Association. Washington, D. C., 1949, The Sportsman's Press. 147 pp., illustrations. 8vo. (Also a 1950 second edition, same format and publisher)

Donovan, Robert E.
  Hunting Whitetail Deer. New York, 1978, Winchester Press.   228 pp., illustrations.   8vo; dust jacket.

Dougan, John C.
  Know Your Ruger Single Action Revolver, 1953 - 1963.   Southport, Massachusetts, 1981, Blacksmith Corporation.   191 pp., photographic plates, drawings.   Edited by John T. Amber.   8vo; dust jacket.

Doughty, John
  The Cabinet of Natural History and American Rural Sports.   Boston / Barre, Massachusetts, 1973, Imprint Society / Barre Publishing Co., Inc. 150 pp., illustrations. Edited by Gail Stewart.   Limited to 1950 copies.   4to; slipcased. (A facsimile reproduction of the 1830 first edition)

Doughty, John, continued

Some Early American Hunters. New York, 1928, The Derrydale Press. 41 pp. plus ads, frontispiece a hand colored engraving. Limited to 375 numbered copies. 8vo. (A facsimile reproduction that was originally written as part of the *Cabinet of Natural History and Rural Sports,* 1830)

Douglas, Dick, Jr.

A Boy Scout in the Grizzly Country. New York, G. P. Putnam's Sons. 181 pp., photographic plates, drawings by Albert Schaffenberg. 8vo; dust jacket. (Reprinted several times to 1929) "Alaska adventures with the biggest of bears." Not in Phillips or the Library of Congress.

Douglas, Gilean

Silence Is My Homeland; life on Teal River. Harrisburg, 1978, The Stackpole Company. 160 pp., drawings by S. S. Brown. 8vo; dust jacket.

Douglas, Leon

Camp Recollections. 1911. Includes a story of a successful hunt for big game in Wyoming. Not in Phillips. Rare.

Douglas, William O.   1898-1980

A Wilderness Bill of Rights. Boston, 1965, Little, Brown & Company. 192 pp., illustrations. 8vo; dust jacket.

My Wilderness; the Pacific Northwest. New York, 1960, Doubleday & Co., Inc. 206 pp., illustrations from drawings by Francis Lee Jaques, maps. 8vo; dust jacket.

My Wilderness; east to Katahdin. Garden City, New York, 1961, Doubleday & Co., Inc. 290 pp., illustrations by Francis Lee Jaques. 8vo; dust jacket. (Also reprinted in an Outdoor Life Book Club edition) U. S. Supreme Court Justice William O. Douglas was an ardent and outspoken conservationist.

Dow, Edson

Adventures in the Northwest. Wenatchee, Washington, 1964, Privately printed. 253 pp. 8vo. Big game hunting with bow and rifle in the Cascades for cougar, elk, bear, goat and deer. A scarce title also including much on trail packing with horses.

Driver, Peter M.

In Search of the Eider. London, 1974, Saturn. 172 pp., illustrations. Tall 8vo; dust jacket. British expeditions to northern Canada performing research on this species of wildfowl.

Duck, L. G. and J. B. Fletcher

A Survey of the Game and Fur Bearing Animals of Oklahoma. No date (1945), Game and Fish Commission. 144 pp., photographic plates, fold-out maps. Tall 8vo.

Ducks Unlimited

Cooperation Unlimited; a conservation manual for Ducks Unlimited Kee-men. Winnipeg, 1946, Ducks Unlimited, Inc. 50 pp., color plates by T. M. Shortt, photographic plates. 8vo. Paper wrappers.

Ducks Unlimited. No place, 1937, Ducks Unlimited, Inc. 32 pp., maps. Tall 8vo. Paper wrappers.

Ducks Unlimited Wing Watcher's Guide. Chicago, 1973, Ducks Unlimited, Inc. 30 pp., color illustrations by Angus Shortt. 8vo. Paper wrappers.

Our Winged Heritage. New York, No date, Ducks Unlimited, Inc. 42 pp., color and black and white illustrations by Richard Bishop. Limited to 1000 copies. Oblong 4to; slip case. Paper wrappers.

Waterfowl in Canada. Manitoba, 1967, Ducks Unlimited, Inc. 40 pp., illustrations. 8vo. Paper wrappers.

Ducks Unlimited

Also see **Leitch, W. G.**
Also see **More Game Birds in America Foundation**
Also see **Tennyson, Jon R.**

Duffey, David Michael

Bird Hunting Know How. Princeton, New Jersey, 1968, D. Van Nostrand Company, Inc. 192 pp., photographic plates. 8vo; dust jacket. (Also a 1978 edition titled, *Bird Hunting Tactics*, Willow Creek Press)

Dave Duffey Trains Gun Dogs. Croton-on-Hudson, New York, 1974, Dreenan Press. 245 pp., photographic plates. 8vo.

Expert Advice on Gun Dog Training. Piscataway, New Jersey, 1977, Winchester Press. 249 pp., photographic plates. 8vo; dust jacket. (Also a 1985 revised edition, same format and publisher)

Hunting Dog Know How. Princeton, New Jersey, 1965, D. Van Nostrand Company, Inc. 177 pp., photographic plates. A Van Nostrand Sporting Book. 8vo; dust jacket. (Reprinted many times, various publishers)

Hunting Hounds; the history, training and selection of America's trail, tree and sight hounds. New York, 1972, Winchester Press. 186 pp., photographic plates. 8vo; dust jacket. (Reprinted several times, same format and publisher)

Duffey, McFadden

Hunting and Fishing in Louisiana. New Orleans, 1969, Pelican. 131 pp., photographic plates. 8vo. Paper wrappers.

Dufresne, Frank

Alaska's Animals and Fishes. West Hartford, Vermont, 1946, The Countryman Press. 297 pp., plates in black and white and color from drawings and paintings by Bob Hines. Limited to 10,000 copies. 4to; dust jacket. (Also a 1955 second edition, Binsfort and Mort) [Also a deluxe first edition, specially bound and limited to 475 copies, numbered and signed by the author and artist; slipcased]

My Way Was North; an Alaskan autobiography. New York, 1966, Holt, Rinehart and Winston. 274 pp., illustrations by Rachel S. Horne. 8vo; dust jacket.

No Room For Bears. New York, 1965, Holt, Rinehart and Winston. 252 pp., illustrations by Rachel S. Horne. 8vo; dust jacket. (Reprinted several times, same format and publisher) An account of the author's experiences in Alaska while Game Commissioner of that state.

Dufresne, Frank

Also see **The Sportsman's Bookshelf**
Also see **Godfrey, Joe Jr.**

Dugmore, A. Radclyffe

The Workers in the Wilds; being an account of the life and work of the beaver. London, 1934, Herbert Jenkins. 192 pp., photographic plates. 12mo; dust jacket.

Dumke, Robert T.

Habitat Development For Bobwhite Quail On Private Lands in Wisconsin. Madison, 1982, Wisconsin Department of Natural Resources. 46 pp., photographic plates, map. 4to. Paper wrappers.

Dumke, Robert T., et al., editors

Wildlife Management of Private Lands. Milwaukee, Wisconsin, 1981, The Wisconsin Chapter of the Wildlife Society. 576 pp., illustrations. The compilation of a symposium held to discuss this important issue.

DuMont, John S.

American Engraved Powder Horns; the Golden Age, 1755-1783. Caanan, 1978, Phoenix   108 pp., color and black and white illustrations. Limited to 1500 numbered and signed copies.

Gun Collecting; Patterson and Walker Colts. No place, No date, Privately printed.   6 pp. Paper wrappers.

Dunbar, N. J., editor

Images of Early Sport in Canada.   Montreal, 1976, McGill University. 96 pp., color and black and white illustrations.   Square 4to; dust jacket.   A well illustrated overview with text in both French and English.

Duncan, Bob

Buffalo Country.   New York, 1959, E. P. Dutton & Co., Inc.   256 pp., illustrations.   8vo; dust jacket.   An account of the great American buffalo herds and the men who hunted them.

Dunham, Harvey   b. 1887

Adirondack French Louie: Early Life in the North Woods.   Utica, New York, 1952, Privately printed by the author.   199 pp., illustrations.   8vo; dust jacket.   (Also reprinted, 1970)

Dunlap, Jack

American, British and Continental Pepperbox Firearms.   Los Altos, 1964, Privately printed.   279 pp., photographic plates, drawings, old ads.   4to; dust jacket.

Dunlap, Roy F.   b. 1914

Gun Owner's Book of Care, Repair and Rifle Improvement.   New York, 1974, Harper & Row Publishers,   Inc. / Outdoor Life Books.   336 pp., illustrations   8vo; dust jacket.   (Reprinted several times, same format and publisher)

Gunsmithing.   Georgetown, South   Carolina, 1950, Small Arms Technical Publishing Company.   714 pp. frontispiece in color, other illustrations from photographs and drawings.   Thick 8vo; dust jacket.   (Reprinted 1952 and 1955, same format and publisher.   Also reprinted in 1959 and 1963, The Stackpole Company)

Dunlap, Roy F.

Also see **Crossman, Captain Edward C.,** *The Book of the Springfield.*

E. P. DuPont de Nemours & Co.

The Trapshooting Club Handbook; how to organize, equip and conduct clubs for trapshooters.   Wilmington, Delaware, No date (ca. 1935), E. P. DuPont de Nemours & Co.   54 pp., photographic plates, drawings.   8vo.   Paper wrappers.

Wild Game - Its Legal Status.   Wilmington, Delaware, No date (ca. 1940), E. P. DuPont de Nemours & Co.   50 pp.   8vo.   Paper wrappers.

Durant, Kenneth
> *Guide Boat Days and Ways.*   Blue Mountain Lake, New York, 1963, Adirondack Museum.   268 pp., maps, drawings.   8vo.   Paper wrappers. Concerning the region's guide boats with much hunting and fishing.

Dutro, Earl
> *Earl Dutro and His Beagles.*   Davenport, Iowa, 1926, Privately printed. 12 pp., photographic plates.   16mo.   Paper wrappers.   Lists the standards for the breed, plus a transcript of a talk given by the author.   Scarce.

Dutton, William S.
> *DuPont - One Hundred and Forty Years.*   New York, 1942, Charles Scribner's Sons.   396 pp., illustrations.   8vo; dust jacket.   A history of this firm as well as a history of gunpowder and explosives in the U.S.

Dyke, Samuel
> *The Pennsylvania Rifle.*   Lititz, Pennsylvania, 1974, Lancaster Historical Society.   61 pp., photographic plates, drawings.   8vo.   Paper wrappers.   A history of the Pennsylvania rifle with a listing of early gunsmiths.
> *Thoughts on the American Flintlock Pistol.*   York, Pennsylvania, 1974, George Shumway.   Second edition.   61 pp., photographic plates.   4to.   Paper wrappers.

Dymond, J. R.
> *Fish and Wildlife*; a memorial to W. J. K. Harkness.   Toronto, 1964. 214 pp., frontispiece.   8vo; dust jacket.   A tribute to this Ontario biologist and conservationist.

Earnest, Adele

> *The Art of the Decoy*; American bird carving. New York, 1965, Clarkson N. Potter. 208 pp., color and black and white photographic plates, line drawings by Lou Schifferl. 8vo; dust jacket. (Also a 1965 second edition, Bramhall House; this edition reprinted several times. Also reprinted, 1982, Schiffer) [Also a specially bound presentation edition of the first edition of unspecified number]

Eason, Al

> *The Best of Al Eason.* Overton, Texas, 1977, Privately printed. 172 pp., drawings by Mark Wingfield. 8vo. A collection of the author's best newspaper columns on hunting and fishing.

East, Ben   b. 1898

> *Bears*; a veteran outdoorsman's account of the most fascinating and dangerous animals in North America. New York, 1972, Crown Publishers, Inc. / Outdoor Life Books. 275 pp., illustrations. 8vo; dust jacket. (Reprinted many times, same format and publisher)
>
> *Danger!* New York, 1970, E. P. Dutton & Co., Inc. / Outdoor Life Books. 328 pp., drawings by Tom Beecham. 8vo; dust jacket. Hunting dangerous game around the world.
>
> *The Ben East Hunting Book.* New York, 1974, Harper & Row Publishers, Inc. / Outdoor Life Books. 360 pp., illustrated in black and white and in color. Tall 8vo; dust jacket.
>
> *The Last Eagle.* New York, 1974, Crown Publishers, Inc. 144 pp., illustrations. 8vo; dust jacket. The story of an American bald eagle in the Michigan wilderness.
>
> *Narrow Escapes and Wilderness Adventures.* New York, 1960, E. P. Dutton & Co. / Outdoor Life Books. 321 pp., drawings by Nick Eggenhofer. 8vo; dust jacket.

East, Ben, editor

> *Survival*; 23 true life sportsman's adventures. New York, 1967, E. P. Dutton & Co., Inc. / Outdoor Life Books. 369 pp., drawings by Tom Beecham. 8vo; dust jacket.

East, Ben

> Also see **Money, Anton**

Easton, Robert and MacKenzie Brown

> *Lord of Beasts*: the saga of Buffalo Jones. Tucson, 1961, University of Arizona. 287 pp., illustrations 8vo; dust jacket. (Also a 1964 British edition) Mr. Jones started as a buffalo hunter, but encountered many other animals in his colorful career.

Eaton, Louis Woodbury

Pork, Molasses and Timber; stories of bygone days in the logging camps of Maine.   New York, 1954, Exposition Press.   Photographic plates.   8vo; dust jacket.

Salt Water, Fresh Water and Fire Water.   New York, 1955, Blackmore. 92 pp., photographic plates.   8vo; dust jacket.   Both of these scarce works are primarily Maine woods lore with incidental mention of hunting and fishing.

Eaton, Randall L., editor

The Human / Animal Connection.   Nevada, 1985, Sierra Nevada Press. 90 pp.   A discussion of the philosophy of hunting.

Eberstadt, Lindley

American Sporting Books; selections from the library of Lindley Eberstadt.   New York, 1981, Sotheby & Co.   8vo.   Paper wrappers.   An auction catalog.

Echols, Lee E.

Dead Aim. New York, 1951, Greenberg: Publishers. 116 pp. 12mo; dust jacket.   Humorous account of the author's experiences at handgun shooting competitions.

Ecker, Dave (with **Bob Zwirz**)

"....and now Stainless:" The Charter Arms Story.   No place, 1981, Charter Arms Corporation.   165 pp., photographic plates.   8vo.   A history of this firearms manufacturer.

Eckert, Allan W.

The Owls of North America. New York, 1974, Doubleday & Co., Inc. 278 pp., color and black and white illustrations, maps, bibliography.   Folio; dust jacket.

The Silent Sky; the incredible extinction of the passenger pigeon. Boston, 1965, Little, Brown & Company.   243 pp., photographic frontispiece. 8vo; dust jacket.

Eddy, John W.

Hunting the Alaska Brown Bear; the story of a sportsman's adventure in an unknown valley after the largest carnivorous animal in the world.   New York, 1930, G. P. Putnam's Sons.   253 pp., photographic plates, maps.   8vo; dust jacket.   An important early account of bear hunting in this region.

Ederer, Bernard F.

Hunting the White-Tailed Deer.   Minneapolis, Minnesota, 1940, University of Minnesota Press.   78 pp., photographic plates, drawings 12mo. Paper wrappers.

Edey, Maitland A.

American Water Birds - Also Hawks, Owls and Game Birds. New York, 1941, Random House, Inc. 72 pp., color plates from paintings by L. A. Fuertes. 4to; dust jacket.

Edgerly, James H.

The Revolving-Cylinder Colt Pistol Story from 1839-1847. Topeka, Kansas, 1937, F. Theodore Dexter. 26 pp., photographic plates. 8vo. Paper wrappers. Rare.

Edminster, Frank C.   b. 1903

American Game Birds; of field and forest, their habits, ecology and management. New York, 1954, Charles Scribner's Sons. 490 pp., photographic plates, diagrams. 4to; dust jacket. (Reprinted 1954, Castle Books)

Hunting Whitetails. New York, 1954, William Morrow & Co., Inc. 192 pp., illustrations. 8vo; dust jacket.

The Ruffed Grouse; its life story, ecology and management. New York, 1947, The Macmillan Company. 385 pp., photographic plates, drawings. 8vo; dust jacket. Mr. Edminster was an authority on this subject, having written portions of *The Ruffed Grouse*, by **Gardiner Bump**, which see. The work here covers the entire range of the species.

Edwards, William B.

The Story of Colt's Revolver; the biography of Col. Samuel Colt. Harrisburg, 1953, The Stackpole Company.   470 pp., photographic plates, drawings. 4to; dust jacket.

Eggert, Richard

Fish and Hunt the Backcountry. Harrisburg, 1978, The Stackpole Company. 233 pp., illustrations. 8vo; dust jacket.

Ehrenfeld, David W.

Biological Conservation. New York, 1970, Oxford University Press. 360 pp., illustrations. 8vo; dust jacket. (Also a 1972 edition titled, *Conserving Life on Earth*, same format and publisher)   An overview of the subject with an analysis of how hunting and conservation work together.

Eifert, Virginia S.

Land of the Snowshoe Hare. New York, 1960, Dodd Mead & Co.   271 pp., photographic plates. 8vo; dust jacket. Animal life in the Northern woods.

Einarsen, Arthur S.   b. 1897

Black Brant; sea goose of the Pacific coast.   Seattle, 1965, University of Washington.   142 pp., illustrations, maps, bibliography.   8vo; dust jacket.

The Pronghorn Antelope; and its management.   Washington, D. C., 1948, Wildlife Management Institute.   238 pp., photographic plates, two color plates from paintings by Walter A. Weber.   8vo; dust jacket. (Reprinted 1948, same format and publisher)

Ekin, Craig

Howard Hill; the man and the legend.   Hamilton, Montana, 1982, Charger Productions.   231 pp., photographic plates.   8vo.   The biography of this famous archery hunter.

Eley, Howard Clifton

Ducks and Decoys.   Easton, Maryland, No date (ca. 1970), Easton Publishing Company.   Unpaginated (12 pp.), photographic plates, drawings.   Folio.   A useful discussion of wildfowl identification and of placing decoys in the field.

The Wonderful World of Gunning Waterfowl.   Easton, Maryland, No date (1971), Easton Publishing Company.   Unpaginated (approx. 100 pp.), photographic plates, cartoons.   Folio.   Paper wrappers.

Elgas, B., et al.

Keeping and Raising Wild Geese in Captivity.   Salt Lake City, No date (ca. 1972), International Wild Waterfowl Association.   69 pp.   Paper wrappers.

Ellarson, R. S.

Canada Goose Problems and Control on Farms.   Madison, 1969, University of Wisconsin Extension Service.   6 pp.   Paper wrappers.

Elliot, David D.

The Labrador Retriever.   East Islip, 1936, Privately printed.   Unpaginated (36 pp.), photographic plates.   Limited to 1000 copies.   Oblong 4to.

Training Gun Dogs To Retrieve.   New York, 1952, Henry Holt and Company, Inc.   128 pp., drawings by Ernest Hart.   12mo; dust jacket. (Reprinted several times, same format and publisher)   The author was a Scottish game keeper and dog trainer who worked at the famous Wingan Kennels on Long Island.

Elliot, Kay

The Care and Training of Your Bird Dog.   Dallas, 1939, Cockrell & Son.   77 pp., illustrations from etchings by D. F. Atchley.

Elliott, Charles   b. 1906

Care of Game Meat and Trophies. New York, 1975, Outdoor Life Books. 152 pp., illustrations.   8vo. Paper wrappers.   (Reprinted many times, same format and publisher)

Field Guide To Wild Turkey Hunting.   Delmont, 1984, Penn's Woods. 83 pp., drawings. 32mo. Paper wrappers.

Gone Huntin'. Harrisburg, 1954, The Stackpole Company. 270 pp., illustrations.   8vo; dust jacket.

Ichauway Plantation. No place, 1974, Privately printed.   106 pp., color illustrations.   8vo; slipcased.   A description of Robert Woodruff's Georgia plantation, with much quail and turkey hunting.   A scarce book.

Prince of Game Birds; the bobwhite quail.   Atlanta, 1974, Georgia Department of Natural Resources.   193 pp., photographic plates, drawings. Limited to 5000 copies. 8vo; dust jacket.

Turkey Hunting With Charlie Elliott; the old professor tells all about hunting America's big game bird.   New York, 1979, David McKay Co.   275 pp., photographic plates.   4to; dust jacket. (Reprinted several times, various publishers)

Elliott, Russ

Your Shotgun Vs. You.   Kansas City, 1955, Brown-Lowell-White Press. 116 pp., drawings by Lee Davis.   12mo; dust jacket.

Elliott, William   1788-1863

Carolina Sports by Land and Water. New York, 1967, Abercrombie & Fitch, Inc. 172 pp. 12mo; dust jacket. (A facsimile reproduction of the 1846 edition)

Ellis, Mel

Run, Rainey, Run. New York, 1967, Holt, Rinehart and Winston. 152 pp., drawings by Mel Kishner.   8vo; dust jacket. The story of a German shorthaired pointer.

Wild Goose, Brother Goose.   New York, 1969, Holt, Rinehart and Winston.   159 pp.   8vo; dust jacket. (Reprinted 1970, same format and publisher) A novel detailing the life of a Canada goose over a two year period.

Elman, Robert   b. 1930

The Atlantic Flyway.   New York, 1972, Winchester Press.   200 pp., color and black and white illustrations.   4to; dust jacket. (Also a 1980 second edition co-authored with W. Osborne, same publisher)

Fired in Anger; the personal handguns of American heroes and villains. Garden City, New York, 1968, Doubleday & Co., Inc.   480 pp., photographic plates.   4to; dust jacket.

Elman, Robert, continued

First in the Field; America's pioneering naturalists. New York, 1977, Van Nostrand Reinhold Co. Mason. 231 pp., plates. 8vo; dust jacket. (Also a 1977 edition, Mason. Also a 1982 edition titled, *America's Pioneering Naturalists,* Winchester Press) Biographical information on early conservationists.

The Hunter's Field Guide; to the game birds and animals of North America. New York, 1974, Alfred A. Knopf, Inc. / The Ridge Press. 655 pp., color photographs, drawings by Ned Smith. 12mo; dust jacket.

1,001 Hunting Tips. New York, 1978, Winchester Press. 511 pp., photographic plates. 8vo; dust jacket. (Reprinted 1978, with the title *Advanced Hunting*; tips and techniques, same format and publisher)

Elman, Robert, editor

All About Deer Hunting in America. New York, 1976, Winchester Press. 255 pp., illustrations. 8vo; dust jacket. With chapters by Elman, Bashline, Carmichael and others.

The Complete Book of Hunting. New York, 1980, Abbeville Press, Inc. 320 pp., photographic plates in black and white and in color. 4to; dust jacket. (Reprinted 1984, same format and publisher) [Also a deluxe first edition, specially bound and limited to 500 numbered and signed copies; slipcased] An anthology of big and small game hunting authors.

The Great American Shooting Prints. New York, 1972, Alfred A. Knopf, Inc. 72 plates in color with text. 4to; dust jacket. [Also a deluxe edition, specially bound and limited to 450 copies; slipcased. Issued with an extra suite of plates] A selection of sporting paintings by Frost, Hunt, Benson, Ripley, Pleissner, and others.

The Sportsman's Wilderness. Secaucus, New Jersey, 1974, Ridge Press. 253 pp., color and black and white illustrations. 4to. A selection of articles first appearing in *American Sportsman* magazine.

Elman, Robert and George Peper, editors

Hunting America's Game Animals and Birds. New York, 1973, Winchester Press. 368 pp., photographic plates. 8vo; dust jacket. (Reprinted 1975, same format and publisher) An anthology of hunting stories by Russell, O'Connor and others.

Elman, Robert and David Seybold, editors

Seasons of the Hunter. New York, 1985, Alfred A. Knopf, Inc. 233 pp., drawings by Joseph Fornelli. Foreword by Vance Bourjaily. 8vo; dust jacket. An anthology of African and North American hunting stories.

Ely, Alfred, et al., editors

North American Big Game. New York, 1939, Charles Scribner's Sons. 533 pp., photographic plates. Limited to 3000 copies. 8vo; dust jacket.. The second Boone and Crocket Club Record Book.

Emlen, John T. and B. Glading
Increasing Valley Quail in California. Berkeley, 1945, University of California Press. 56 pp., photographic plates, drawings, maps. 8vo. Paper wrappers.

Enders, John O.
A Fox Hunter's Scrapbook. Hartford, Connecticut, 1945, Privately printed. Illustrations. 8vo. Limited to 500 numbered copies. Gunning for fox with dogs.
Random Notes on Hunting. Hartford, 1955, Privately printed. 67 pp., photographic plates. Limited to 300 numbered copies. 8vo. The author's experiences hunting upland game in Connecticut and North Carolina.

Endicott, Wendell
Adventures in Alaska and Along the Trail. New York, 1928, Frederick A. Stokes Company. 344 pp., photographic plates. 8vo; dust jacket. (Reprinted 1929, same format and publisher) Containing sheep and goat hunting in the Canadian Rocky Mountains and Alaska, as well as some Atlantic salmon fishing.

Engberg, Robert, editor
John Muir Summering in the Sierra. Madison, Wisconsin, 1984, University of Wisconsin Press. 160 pp. Containing a description of one of the few hunts in which Muir participated (as an observer).

Engelhardt, Wolfgang
Survival of the Free; the last strongholds of wild animal life. New York, 1962, G. P. Putnam's Sons. 258 pp., many color and black and white photographs. 4to; dust jacket. (First published, 1956, Germany) A plea for conservation told through wildlife preserves on all continents.

Epping, C.
Old 721. Tacoma, Washington, 1983. 102 pp., photographic plates. Limited to 200 copies. 8vo. One man's quest for game with his favorite rifle

Erickson, Albert W.
The Black Bear in Alaska; its ecology and management. Juneau, 1965, Alaska Department of Fish and Game. 19 pp., bibliography. 4to. Paper wrappers.
The Brown-Grizzly Bear in Alaska; its ecology and management. Juneau, 1965, Alaska Department of Fish and Game. 42 pp., bibliography. 4to. Paper wrappers.

Erickson, Arnold, et al.
The White-Tailed Deer of Minnesota. No place, 1961, Minnesota Department of Conservation. 64 pp., illustrations. 4to. Paper wrappers.

Erickson, Mary

  A Jay Shoot In California. Berkeley, 1937, University of California Press. 5 pp. 8vo. Paper wrappers. (Originally appearing in Vol. 39 of *The Condor*) An account of the controversial practice of sportsmen's clubs in Calaveras County, California which organized hunts for jays, hawks, owls, etc. in order to improve quail populations.

Erno, Richard B.

  The Hunt. New York, 1959, Crown Publishers, Inc. 220 pp. 8vo; dust jacket. A mystery written against the backdrop of a northern Michigan deer hunt.

Ernst, Clayton Holt

  See **Deep River Jim**

Errington, Paul L.

  An Analysis of Mink Predation Upon Muskrats in North Central US. Ames, 1943, Iowa State University Press. 126 pp., photographic plates. 8vo. Paper wrappers.

  Muskrats and Marsh Management. Harrisburg / Washington D. C., 1961, The Stackpole Company / The Wildlife Management Institute. 183 pp., photographic plates. 8vo; dust jacket.

  Muskrat Populations. Ames, 1963, Iowa State University Press. 665 pp., frontispiece. 8vo; dust jacket.

  Of Men and Marshes. New York, 1957, The Macmillan Company. 150 pp., black and white illustrations by Albert Hochbaum. 8vo; dust jacket.

  Of Predation and Life. Ames, Iowa, 1967, Iowa State University Press. 277 pp., bibliography, black and white illustrations by Dycie Madson. 8vo; dust jacket.

  The Red Gods Call. Ames, 1973, Iowa State University Press. 171 pp., photographic plates. Tall 8vo; dust jacket. Mr. Errington's autobiography with much hunting and trapping in South Dakota and Canada.

  Some Contributions of a Fifteen Year Local Study of the Northern Bobwhite To a Knowledge of Population Phenomena. Ames, Iowa, 1945, Ecological Monographs. 34 pp. 4to. Paper wrappers.

Errington, Paul L. and F. N. Hamerstrom

  The Northern Bob-White's Winter Territory. Ames, 1936, Iowa State University. 443 pp., photographic plates, bibliography. 8vo. Paper wrappers.

Erskine, Anthony J.

  Buffleheads. Ottawa, 1971, Canadian Wildlife Service. 240 pp., photographic plates, maps, bibliography. 8vo. Paper wrappers.

Eschmeyer, R. W.

Al Alligator. Oxford, Ohio, 1953, Fisherman's Press. 49 pp., black and white illustrations by Roy K. Willis. 12mo; dust jacket. A Juvenile. In 1952 and 1953 the author also wrote the juveniles *Billy Bass, Bob White, Bobby Bluegill, Charlie Cottontail, Freddy Fox Squirrel, Mac Mallard, Tommy Trout, Willie Whitetail* and *Woody Woodcock*, same publisher and format.

Escritt, L. B.

Riflemen and Pistolmen. New York, 1963, Arco. Third printing. 156 pp., black and white illustrations from drawings and photographs. 8vo; dust jacket. (Originally published, 1955, Great Britain)

Esmonde, Thomas H. Grattan

More Hunting Memories. Dublin, 1930, Levins Press. 194 pp., photographic plates. 12mo. Much on Canada and a sequel to the author's *Hunting Memories of Many Lands*, 1920. See Phillips.

Estey, Paul C.

The Woodchuck Hunter. Onslow County, North Carolina, 1936, Small Arms Technical Publishing Company. 135 pp., photographic plates. 18mo; dust jacket.

Etchen, Fred

Commonsense Shotgun Shooting. Huntington, West Virginia, 1946, Standard Publications, Inc. 187 pp., photographic plates. 8vo; dust jacket.

How To Be an Expert at Shotgun Shooting. Greenwich, Connecticut, 1946, Fawcett Books. 144 pp., illustrations. 8vo. Paper wrappers.

Etherton, Lt. Col. P. T.

Adventures in Five Continents. London, No date (ca. 1928), Hutchinson. 320 pp., photographic plates. 8vo. Mostly adventure, but some big game hunting in British Columbia and the American Rocky Mountains.

Etulain, Richard W.

A Bibliographical Guide To the Study of Western American Literature. Lincoln, 1982, University of Nebraska Press. 317 pp. 8vo. With listings of many sporting book authors.

Evanoff, Vlad

Hunting Secrets of the Experts. New York, 1964, Doubleday & Co. Inc. 251 pp., photographic plates. 8vo; dust jacket.

Evans, George Bird   b. 1906

An Affair With Grouse. No place (Bruceton Mills, West Virginia), 1982, Old Hemlock. 213 pp., black and white illustrations by the author.   8vo; dust jacket.   [Also a 1982, Amwell Press limited edition of 1000 numbered and signed copies; slipcased]

Opus 10: Men Who Shot and Wrote About It.   No place (Bruceton Mills, West Virginia), 1983, Old Hemlock. 203 pp., photographic plates. Limited to 990 numbered and signed copies.   8vo; slipcased.   Biographical sketches of such notable authors as Forester, Hallock, Foster, Spiller, Ben Ames Williams and others.

Troubles With Bird Dogs; and what to do about them. New York, 1975, Winchester Press. 307 pp., photographic plates.   8vo; dust jacket.   [Also a specially bound, limited edition of 1500 numbered and signed copies; slipcased, 1985, Old Hemlock]

The Upland Shooting Life. New York, 1971, Alfred A. Knopf, Inc. 301 pp., photographic plates. 8vo; dust jacket. (Reprinted several times, same format and publisher)

Evans, George Bird, editor

The Best of Nash Buckingham. New York, 1973, Winchester Press. 320 pp., photographic plates.   8vo; dust jacket.   (Reprinted, same format and publisher)   An anthology of Mr. Buckingham's writings with accompanying text by Mr. Evans.

The Bird Dog Book. Clinton, New Jersey, 1979, Amwell Press.   305 pp., black and white and color illustrations by Edmund Osthaus. Limited to 1000 numbered and signed copies.   8vo; slipcased.   (Also a 1989 trade edition, same contents and publisher)   An anthology of hunting dog stories by Holland, Sheldon, Hochwalt and others.

Dear John: Nash Buckingham's Letters to John Bailey. No place (Bruceton Mills, West Virginia), 1984, Old Hemlock. 205 pp., photographic plates.   8vo; dust jacket.   [Also a specially bound, limited edition of 575 numbered and signed copies; slipcased]

Recollections of a Shooting Guest; including the unfinished manuscript of Dr. Charles C. Norris.   Clinton, New Jersey, 1978, Amwell Press.   186 pp., black and white illustrations by Gordon Allen. Foreword by Kay Evans. Limited to 1000 numbered and signed copies.   8vo; slipcased.   The Evans were close friends with Dr. Norris, author of *Eastern Upland Shooting.*   This work combines some of their correspondence with him and an unfinished manuscript Dr. Norris had intended to publish.

The Ruffed Grouse Book.   Clinton, New Jersey, 1977, Amwell Press. 258 pp., black and white illustrations by Shoffstall. Limited to 1000 Numbered and signed copies.   8vo; slipcased.   (Also a 1989 trade edition, same contents and publisher)   An anthology of ruffed grouse hunting stories by Forester, Seton, Mershon, Phillips, Sheldon, Schaldach and others.

Evans, George Bird, editor, continued

The Upland Gunner's Book; an anthology. Clinton, New Jersey, 1979, Amwell Press. 263 pp., black and white illustrations by Tom Hennessey. Foreword by William C. Steinkraus. Limited to 1000 numbered and signed copies. 8vo; slipcased. (Also a 1986 trade edition, same contents and publisher) An anthology of upland gunning stories by Pringle, Rutledge, Buckingham, Phillips, Babcock, Waterman, Hill and others.

The Woodcock Book. Clinton, New Jersey, 1977, Amwell Press. 286 pp., black and white illustrations by Donald Shoffstall. Limited to 1000 numbered and signed copies. 8vo; slipcased. (Also a 1989 trade edition, same contents and publisher) An anthology of woodcock stories by Hallock, Rutledge, Grinnell, Ben Ames Williams, Phillips, Holland and others.

George Bird Evans began his literary career co-authoring mystery novels with his wife, Kay in the early 1950's (see **Bird, Brandon**). An avid upland hunter and setter breeder all his life, he started writing about hunting as his second career. Additionally, his critical commentary adds much value to the various anthologies he edited. He wrote and published several other original upland titles after 1985, and at this writing he is working on another upland title to be published in 1997.

Evans, G. W. "Dub"

Slash Ranch Hounds. Albuquerque, 1951, University of New Mexico Press. 244 pp., photographic plates. 8vo; dust jacket. Cougar and bear hunting with hounds. Scarce.

Evans, Hubert

The Silent Call. New York, 1930, Dodd, Mead & Co. 248 pp., illustrations by H. E. M. Sellen. 8vo; dust jacket. A novel with much information on the migration of game animals and fish.

Evans, Humphrey

Falconry; an illustrated introduction. New York, 1974, Arco. 160 pp., illustrations. 4to. (Originally published, 1973, Great Britain)

Evans, Joe

Bear Stories. El Paso, Texas, No date, Privately printed. 48 pp., illustrations. Paper wrappers.

Evans, Keith

Characteristics and Habitat Requirements of the Greater Prairie Chicken and Sharp-Tailed Grouse - A Review of the Literature. Washington, D. C., 1968, United States Department of Agriculture. 32 pp., illustrations. 4to. Paper wrappers.

Everett, Michael

Birds of Prey. New York, No date (ca. 1975), G. P. Putnam's Sons. 128 pp., color illustrations, charts, maps. 8vo; dust jacket.

Everett, Fred   b. 1892
    Fun With Game Birds: bird hunting in words, paint and lines. Harrisburg, 1954, The Stackpole Company.   287 pp., black and white and color illustrations by the author. Foreword by Charlie Fox. Introduction by Gardiner Bump. 8vo. [Also a deluxe edition, specially bound and numbered, but with no stated limitation]

Everitt, Simon W.   b. 1858
    Tales of Wild Turkey Hunting.   Chicago, 1928, William Hazelton. Edited by William H. Ball. 127 pp., sepia photographs, frontispiece by Fuertes. 12mo. (Also reprinted, ca. 1984, Old Masters,)   An important, scarce and early work on turkey hunting.

Evers, Alf
    The Catskills; from wilderness to Woodstock.   Garden City, New York, 1972, Doubleday & Co., Inc.   821 pp., photographic plates.   8vo; dust jacket. A history of the region, including its fishing and hunting heritage.

Ewan, Joseph   b. 1909
    Rocky Mountain Naturalists; biographies of nine leading naturalists of the Rocky Mountain area, supplemented by a roster in biographical dictionary form of natural history collectors. Denver, 1950, University of Denver. 358 pp., portraits. 8vo; dust jacket.

Explorer's Club
    Through Hell and High Water. New York, 1941, National Travel Club. 385 pp., illustrations. Tall 8vo; dust jacket. With one chapter on Dall sheep hunting by R. R. M. Carpenter.
    Explorer's Club Tales; true stories of exploration, research and adventure as told at the Explorer's Club by men of daring and achievement. New York, 1936, Dodd Mead & Co. 301 pp., photographic plates. 8vo; dust jacket. (Also a 1940 second edition, Tudor) Hunting and angling around the world.

Explorer's Club
    Also see **Blossom, F. A., editor**

Fadala, Sam   b. 1939

Black Powder Hunting. Harrisburg, 1978, The Stackpole Company. 256 pp., photographic plates. 8vo; dust jacket.

Sam Fadala's Muzzleloading Handbook.   Piscataway, New Jersey, 1985, Winchester Press. 212 pp., photographic plates. 8vo; dust jacket.

Sam Fadala's Muzzleloading Notebook. New York, 1985, Winchester Press. 256 pp., photographic plates. 8vo; dust jacket.

Successful Deer Hunting.   Northfield, Illinois, 1983, DBI Books. 288 pp., photographic plates. Tall 8vo. Paper wrappers.

Falk, John R.

The Complete Guide to Bird Dog Training.   New York, 1976, Winchester Press. 247 pp., photographic plates. 8vo; dust jacket.

The Practical Hunter's Dog Book. New York, 1971, Winchester Press. 318 pp., photographic plates. 8vo; dust jacket. (Reprinted many times, same format and publisher)

Farley, G. M.

An Annotated Zane Grey Checklist.   Mattituck, New York, 1988, Ameron House.   120 pp., photographic plates.   8vo. (Reprinted several times, same format and publisher) An excellent bibliography of Grey's works.

Farnham, Albert B.   b. 1870

Home Manufacture of Furs and Skins. Columbus, Ohio, 1941, A. R. Harding.   285 pp., illustrations. 16mo. (Originally published, 1916, same format and publisher)

Home Tanning and Leather Making Guide. Columbus, Ohio, 1950, A. R. Harding.   176 pp., illustrations. 16mo. (Originally published, 1922, same format and publisher)

Home Taxidermy For Pleasure and Profit. Columbus, Ohio, 1944, A. R. Harding.   246 pp., illustrations. 16mo. (Originally published, 1916, same format and publisher)

Farquhar, Carley

The Sportsman's Almanac; a guide to hunting and fishing in the 50 American states and National Forests and their principal game - mammals, birds and fishes.   New York, 1965, Harper & Row, Publishers, Inc.   493 pp., illustrations. 8vo; dust jacket.

Farrington, Selwyn Kip, Jr.   1904-1983

The Ducks Came Back; the story of Ducks Unlimited. New York, 1945, Coward, McCann, Inc. 131 pp., illustrations by Lynn Bogue Hunt.   4to; dust jacket. (Also a 1947 British edition) An account of the early history of Ducks Unlimited, Inc.

Interesting Birds of Our Country. Garden City, 1945, Doubleday & Co., Inc. Unpaginated, black and white and color illustrations by Lynn Bogue Hunt. Oblong 4to; dust jacket. A juvenile.

The Labrador Retriever; friend and worker. New York, 1976, Hastings House. 175 pp., photographic plates. 8vo; dust jacket.

Mr. Farrington was an author especially noted for big game fishing books. He also wrote extensively about sailing, hockey and the railroads as well as several juveniles. See Bruns.

Farris, Allen, et al.

The Ring-Necked Pheasant in Iowa. Des Moines, 1977, Iowa Conservation Commission.   147 pp., color and black and white illustrations. 8vo.

Farrow, Peter

What Use Are Moose? A glee of mooserimes. Thorndike, Maine, 1983, Thorndike Press.   Unpaginated (approx. 45 pp.), cartoon drawings. 12mo.

Farrow, W. Milton

How I Became a Crack Shot; with hints to beginners. Prescott, Arizona, 1980, Wolfe Publishing Company.   204 pp., illustrations 16mo. (A facsimile reproduction of the 1882 first edition)

Faulkner, William   1897-1962

The Big Woods. New York, 1955, Random House, Inc.   198 pp., black and white illustrations by Edward Shenton. 8vo; dust jacket. (Reprinted several times, same format and publisher)   With deer and bear hunting in the South by this renowned American writer.

Fawcett, Roger

A Tiger Tale With Bear Behind; an account of a 1959 hunt in India and a 1960 hunt in Alaska.   No place, No date, Privately printed.   63 pp., color illustrations, cartoons.   8vo.   Spiral bound paper wrappers. Hunting polar and brown bear, moose and caribou in Alaska and British Columbia.

Fears, J. Wayne   b. 1938

On Target For Successful Turkey Hunting. Mequon, Wisconsin, 1983, Target Communications.   92 pp., illustrations.   8vo. Paper wrappers.

The Sportsman's Guide To Swamp Camping. New York, 1979, David McKay Co.   274 pp., photographic plates.   8vo; dust jacket. Contains some hunting.

Fears, J. Wayne, continued

The Wild Turkey Book; an anthology. Clinton, New Jersey, 1981, Amwell Press. 274 pp., black and white illustrations from drawings by Tom Hennessey. Limited to 1000 numbered and signed copies. 8vo; slipcased. (Also a 1982 trade edition, same contents and publisher)

Feather, Noel

Battling Bucks; antler rattling techniques that work. Mequon, Wisconsin, 1985, Target Communications. 124 pp., photographic plates. 8vo; dust jacket.

Fegely, Thomas D.

Wonders of Geese and Swans. New York, 1976, Dodd Mead & Co. 96 pp., photographic plates, drawings, maps. 8vo; dust jacket. A juvenile with emphasis on conservation.

Wonders of Wild Ducks. New York, 1975, Dodd Mead & Co. 80 pp., photographic plates, drawings, maps. 8vo; dust jacket. A juvenile with emphasis on conservation.

Felton, Harold W.

The World's Most Truthful Man; tall tales told by Ed Grant in Maine. New York, 1961, Dodd Mead & Co. 150 pp., illustrations. 8vo; dust jacket. The author was a guide and woodsman; this work is mostly Maine lore with some fishing and hunting.

Ferber, Steve, editor

All About Rifle Hunting and Shooting in America. New York, 1977, Winchester Press. 263 pp., photographic plates. 8vo; dust jacket.

Fergus, Charles

The Wingless Crow; essays from the "Thornapples" column. Harrisburg, 1984, Pennsylvania Game Commission. 188 pp. 8vo; dust jacket.

Ferguson, Chick

Mink, Mary and Me; the story of a wilderness trapline. No place, 1946, Privately printed. 248 pp., photographic plates. 8vo. Scarce.

Ferguson, Henry Lee   1884-1959

The English Springer Spaniel in America. New York, 1932, The Derrydale Press. 106 pp., photographic plates. Limited to 850 copies. Tall 8vo.

Ferris, Bill

Bill Ferris Writes From His Columns. Shippensburg, Pennsylvania, 1978, Privately printed. 35 pp., drawings. 8vo. Paper wrappers. A collection of the author's hunting and angling stories originally appearing in a local newspaper.

Ffolliott, Peter F. and Sonia Gallina, editors

Deer Biology, Habitat Requirements and Management in Western North America. Mexico, 1981, The Institute of Ecology. 238 pp. An excellent collection of papers dealing with the subject in Arizona, New Mexico and Mexico.

Field & Stream

How to Hunt Ducks, Geese, Turkeys, Grouse, Woodcock, Quail. New York, No date,, Field & Stream. 120 pp. 16mo. Paper wrappers.

The Field & Stream Reader; by a host of contributors from the magazine's beginning to the present. New York, 1946, Doubleday & Co., Inc. / Field & Stream. 434 pp. 8vo; dust jacket.

The Sportsman's World. New York, 1959, Henry Holt and Company, Inc. 272 pp., color and black and white photographic plates. Introduction by Robert Ruark. 4to; dust jacket.

Fiennes, Richard

The Order of Wolves. Indianapolis, 1976, The Bobbs-Merrill Company. 206 pp., black and white and color illustrations. 4to; dust jacket. A natural history of this predator.

Finlay, Eddie

Down the Creek. Columbia, South Carolina, 1967, Privately printed. 119 pp., photographic plates, cartoon drawings. 8vo. A collection of hunting and angling stories by this outdoor writer for the *Columbia Record.*

Finnerty, Edward   b. 1907

Trappers, Traps & Trapping. New York, 1976, A. S. Barnes and Company, Inc. 158 pp., black and white illustrations from drawings. 8vo; dust jacket.

Finton, Walter Lloyd   b. 1885

Alaskan Bear Adventures; the story of a sportsman-naturalist's hunt for the world's largest bear on the bleak Bering Sea shores of the Alaskan Peninsula. New York, 1937, Daniel Ryerson Inc. 167 pp., illustrations. Foreword by William T. Hornaday. 8vo; dust jacket. Uncommon.

Fischer, Gertrude

The Complete Golden Retriever. New York, 1974, Howell Book House. 288 pp., illustrations. 8vo. (Reprinted many times, same format and publisher)

Fischl, Josef and Leonard Lee Rue, III
After Your Deer is Down; the care and handling of big game. Tulsa, 1981, Winchester Press. 137 pp., photographic plates. 8vo. Paper wrappers.

Fish, Chet, editor
Deer Hunting Book. New York, 1974, Harper & Row, Publishers, Inc. / Outdoor Life Books. 275 pp., photographic plates. 8vo; dust jacket. An anthology of deer hunting stories by O'Connor, Rutledge, and others.
The Outdoor Life Bear Book. Harrisburg / New York, 1983, The Stackpole Company / Outdoor Life Books. 407 pp., black and white illustrations from drawings. 8vo; dust jacket. (Reprinted many times, same format and publisher) An anthology of bear stories originally appearing in *Outdoor Life* magazine.

Fisher, Billy Rae
Coon Catching Without Dogs and Traps. Greenville, 1982, Privately printed. 28 pp., illustrations. 8vo. Paper wrappers.

Fisher, James, et al.
Wildlife In Danger. New York, 1969, Viking Press. 368 pp., color illustrations. 4to; dust jacket. (Reprinted, same format and publisher) An account of vanishing species, including some game animals.

Fisher, Morris   1892-1968
Mastering the Pistol and the Revolver. New York, 1940, G. P. Putnam's Sons. 158 pp., photographic plates. 8vo; dust jacket. (Also reprinted 1940, same format and publisher)
Mastering the Rifle. New York, 1940, G. P. Putnam's Sons. 206 pp., photographic plates. 8vo; dust jacket. (Reprinted twice, same format and publisher)

Fisher, Ralph A.
The Guide To Javelina. San Antonio, 1957, The Naylor Company. 208 pp., photographic plates. 8vo; dust jacket.

Fitz, Grancel
How To Measure and Score Big Game Trophies; the official scoring method used by Boone and Crockett Club and Pope and Young Club. New York, 1963, Outdoor Life Books. 88 pp., illustrations, map. 4to. Paper wrappers. (Also a 1977 revised edition, edited by Betty S. Fitz, David McKay Co. This edition also reprinted, 1977, Blue-J Inc.)
North American Head Hunting. New York, 1957, Oxford University Press. 188 pp., photographic plates, color frontispiece. 8vo; dust jacket. Big game hunting in North America.

Fitzgerald, J. Henry

Colt's Police Revolver Hand Book. Hartford, Connecticut, 1926, Colt's Patent Fire Arms Manufacturing Company. 48 pp., photographic plates. 16mo. Paper wrappers. (Also several later editions, same publisher and format)

Shooting. Hartford, 1930, G. F. Book Co. 421 pp., photographic plates. 8vo. A detailed treatise on the use of handguns.

Flader, Susan L.

Thinking Like a Mountain; Aldo Leupold and the evolution of an ecological attitude toward deer, wolves, and forests. Columbia, 1974, University of Missouri Press. 284 pp. A presentation of Leopold's views of deer overpopulation and how these three factors inter-relate.

Fleckenstein, Henry A.

American Factory Decoys. Exton, Pennsylvania, 1981, Schiffer Publishing Company. 240 pp., color and black and white photographic plates. 4to; dust jacket.

Decoys of the Mid-Atlantic Region. Exton, Pennsylvania, 1979, Schiffer Publishing Company. 272 pp., color and black and white photographic plates, bibliography. 4to; dust jacket. [Also a deluxe edition, specially bound and illustrated and limited to 95 numbered and signed copies; slipcased]

New Jersey Decoys. Exton, Pennsylvania, 1983, Schiffer Publishing Company. 270 pp., color and black and white illustrations. 4to; dust jacket.

Shore Bird Decoys. Exton, Pennsylvania, 1980, Schiffer Publishing Company. 144 pp., color and black and white photographic plates. 4to; dust jacket. [Also a deluxe edition, specially illustrated and limited to 150 numbered and signed copies; slipcased]

Southern Decoys of Virginia and the Carolinas. Exton, Pennsylvania, 1983, Schiffer Publishing Company. 255 pp., color and black and white photographic plates. 4to; dust jacket.

Flemming, Tom

The Complete Book on Rattling Whitetails. Indiana, 1982, Blue-J., Inc. 96 pp., photographic plates. Paper wrappers.

Fletcher, John and R. G. Busnel

Effects of Noise on Wildlife. New York, 1978, Academic Press. 305 pp., illustrations. 8vo.

Flick, R. Jay

Sporting and Color Plate Books....the Important Library Collected by the Late R. Jay Flick, Lennox, Massachusetts. New York, 1946, Parke-Bernet Galleries, Inc. 140 pp. 8vo. Paper wrappers. An auction catalog with 584 lots, some of which were sporting titles.

Flint, Charles Ranlett   1850-1934

Memories of An Active Life; men and ships and sealing wax.   New York, 1923, G. P. Putnam's Sons.   349 pp., photographic plates.   8vo; dust jacket.   The author was the founder of the Grace Lines shipping company, and was an avid hunter and fisherman.   Not in Phillips.

Floing, William O.

The Out-of-Doors; as I knew it.   No place, 1936, Privately printed.   46 pp., drawings.   Limited to 36 numbered copies.   12mo.   Containing stories of angling and one story of moose hunting; this was published posthumously by the author's wife.

Flowers, Ralph

The Education of a Bear Hunter.   New York, 1975, Winchester Press. 277 pp., photographic plates.   8vo; dust jacket.

Fluck, John J.

Colt-Root Model; an illustrated monograph.   Topeka, Kansas, 1950, F. Theodore Dexter.   24 pp., illustrations.   4to.   Paper wrappers.

Folta, Richard C.

Of Bench and Bears; Alaska's bear hunting judge.   Anchorage, Alaska, 1946, Great Northwest Publishing Co.   206 pp., photographic plates.   8vo; dust jacket.   The biography of Judge George Folta, known by most criminals as the "hanging judge."   Judge Folta killed more than 200 bears in his hunting career of over 50 years.   This was written by his son and contains much on bear hunting.   Scarce.

Foote, John Taintor   1881-1950

Angler's All; the great fishing stories of John Taintor Foote.   New York, 1947, Appleton-Century-Crofts, Inc.   212 pp., drawings by Milton C. Weiler. 8vo; dust jacket.

Blister Jones.   Indianapolis, 1913, The Bobbs-Merrill Company.   324 pp., photographic plates. 12mo; dust jacket.   Thoroughbred horse racing and the author's first book.

Broadway Angler.   New York, 1937, D. Appleton-Century Co.   44 pp.   12mo; dust jacket.   Humorous fishing story.

Change of Idols.   New York, 1935, D. Appleton-Century Co.   52 pp. 12mo; dust jacket.   Humorous fishing story.

Daughter of Delilah.   New York, 1936, D. Appleton-Century Co.   51 pp.   12mo; dust jacket.   Humorous fishing story.

Dumb Bell of Brookfield.   New York, 1917, D. Appleton & Co.   262 pp., frontispiece.   12mo; dust jacket.   A pack of six dog stories; the title story is regarded by many as among the best dog stories ever written.

Foote, John Taintor, continued

Dumb Bell and Others; the great dog stories of John Taintor Foote. New York, 1946, D. Appleton-Century Company, Inc. 309 pp. 8vo; dust jacket. (Reprinted 1946, Grosset & Dunlap. Also a 1947 edition titled, *Great Dog Stories,* Garden City Publishing Company)

Fatal Gesture. New York, 1933, D. Appleton & Co. 68 pp. 12mo; dust jacket. Humorous angling stories and a sequel to *A Wedding Gift.*

Full Personality. New York, 1935, D. Appleton-Century Company, Inc. 148 pp. 12mo; dust jacket. A handsome middle-aged man meets a debutante. One of Foote's scarcer titles.

Hell Cat. New York, 1936, D. Appleton-Century Co. 78 pp. 12mo; dust jacket. A non-sporting title about a Broadway personality.

Hoofbeats. New York, 1950, D. Appleton-Century Company, Inc. 243 pp., illustrations by Milton C. Weiler. 8vo; dust jacket. (Reprinted, Grosset & Dunlap) An anthology of Foote's best horse stories.

Jing. New York, 1936, The Derrydale Press. 37 pp., drawings by A. L. Ripley. Limited to 950 numbered copies. 12mo. A story of a bird-dog.

The Look of Eagles. New York, 1916, D. Appleton & Co. 72 pp., frontispiece. 12mo; dust jacket. Thoroughbred horse racing.

The Lucky Seven. New York, 1918, D. Appleton & Co. 309 pp. 12mo; dust jacket. A collection of the author's short stories.

The Number One Boy. New York, 1926, D. Appleton & Co. 237 pp. 12mo; dust jacket. An adventure novel of a group of Americans in China during the Boxer rebellion. A scarce Foote title.

Pocono Shot; a dog story. New York, 1924, D. Appleton & Co. 142 pp. 12mo; dust jacket.

The Song of the Dragon. New York, 1923, D. Appleton & Co. 311 pp. 12mo; dust jacket. A collection of 7 stories, three of which are sporting.

Sporting Days. New York, 1937, D. Appleton-Century Company, Inc. 159 pp., black and white illustrations from drawings by Arthur Fuller. 8vo; dust jacket. An anthology of the author's sporting stories.

Trub's Diary. New York, 1928, D. Appleton & Co. 269 pp. 12mo; dust jacket. A diary as told by a bull terrier pup.

A Wedding Gift; a fishing story. New York, 1924, D. Appleton Co. 63 pp. 12mo; dust jacket. A humorous angling title, wherein the hero takes his wife fly fishing on their honeymoon.

Mr. Foote was a popular writer in the 1920's and 1930's. Nearly all his books were reprinted many times. In addition to the titles listed above, his short stories often appeared in the *Saturday Evening Post.* He was also an accomplished play-writer who had many of his works produced on and off Broadway and in the 1940's, he even did some script writing in Hollywood. All his works are listed here.

Foote, Leonard E.

The Vermont Deer Herd; a study in productivity. Montpelier, 1945, Vermont Fish and Game Service. 125 pp., photographic plates, maps, bibliography.

Foran, W. Robert

A Hunter's Saga. London, 1961, Hale. 192 pp., photographic plates. 8vo; dust jacket. Big game hunting around the world with considerable North American species.

Forbes, Allan 1874-1955

Sport in Norfolk County; with a chapter on polo by W. Cameron Forbes and a preface on hunting by Henry G. Vaughn. Boston, 1938, Houghton Mifflin Company. 274 pp., photographic plates. Limited to 665 numbered and signed copies. 8vo; slipcased. Mostly on the equestrian sports and golf, but containing some hunting with firearms.

Forbes, John Ripley

William Temple Hornaday; in the steps of the great American zoologist,. New York, 1966, M. Evans and Company. 128 pp., black and white illustrations. 8vo; dust jacket. Older juvenile biography of this eminent naturalist.

Forbes, Stanley, et al.

The White-Tailed Deer In Pennsylvania. Harrisburg, 1971, Pennsylvania Game Commission. Drawings by Nick Rosato. 8vo. Paper wrappers.

Forbes, Thomas

Guide to Better Archery. Harrisburg, 1955, The Stackpole Company. 307 pp., illustrations. 8vo; dust jacket. (Also a 1960 revised edition, titled *New Guide To Better Archery*, same format and publisher. This revised edition reprinted, 1962 and 1967, Collier)

Ford, Alice

Audubon's Animals; the quadrupeds of North America. New York, 1951, Thomas Y. Crowell Company / Outdoor Life Books. 222 pp., illustrations in black and white and in color from Audubon's paintings. 8vo; dust jacket.

John James Audubon. Norman, 1964, University of Oklahoma Press. 488 pp., color and black and white illustrations. 8vo; dust jacket. A most authoritative biography.

Ford, Barbara

Black Bear; the spirit of the wilderness. Boston, 1981, Houghton Mifflin Company. 182 pp., photographic plates. 8vo; dust jacket. A natural history of the species.

Ford, Corey   1902-1969

The Best of Cory Ford. New York, 1975, Holt, Rinehart and Winston. Edited by Jack Samson. 266 pp., drawings.   8vo; dust jacket.   An anthology of many of the Lower Forty stories.

Every Dog Should Have a Man; the care and feeding of dog's best friend. New York, 1952, Henry Holt and Company, Inc. 40 pp., illustrations. 8vo; dust jacket.

The Gazelle's Ears. New York, 1926, George H. Doran & Co. 306 pp., cartoon illustrations.   8vo; dust jacket.   A parody of hunting and fishing subjects with some non-sporting subjects as well..

Minutes of the Lower Forty. New York, 1962, Holt, Rinehart and Winston. 159 pp., illustrations. 8vo; dust jacket. Humorous hunting and angling tales.

Uncle Perk's Jug; the misadventures of the Lower Forty Shooting, Angling and Inside Straight Club. New York, 1964, Holt, Rinehart and Winston. 150 pp., drawings by Walter Dower.   8vo; dust jacket.   More humorous hunting and angling tales.

Where the Sea Breaks Its Back; the epic story of a pioneer naturalist and the discovery of Alaska.   Boston, 1966, Little, Brown & Company. 206 pp., bibliography.   Introduction by Frank Dufresne.   8vo; dust jacket.   (Reprinted 1966, same format and publisher. Also a 1967 British edition)   The story of George Wilhelm Stellar and his ocean voyage to Alaska with much on the wildlife of the area.   This title is said to be the author's favorite of all his works.

You Can Always Tell a Fisherman; but you can't tell him much.   The minutes of the Lower Forty Shooting, Angling and Inside Straight Club.   New York, 1958, Henry Holt and Company, Inc.   159 pp., drawings by Walter Dower.   8vo; dust jacket.   Humorous sporting stories that originally appeared in *Field & Stream* magazine.

Ford, Corey, editor

Cold Noses and Warm Hearts. Englewood Cliffs, New Jersey, 1958, Prentice-Hall, Inc. 269 pp., illustrations. 8vo; dust jacket. An anthology of dog stories.

Ford, Corey and Allastair McBain

A Man of His Own; and other dog stories. New York, 1949, Whittlesey House.   196 pp., drawings by Robert Candy. 8vo; dust jacket. A scarce Ford title with sporting content.

Mr. Ford wrote in four distinct genres - parody, humor, military history and strategy and sporting works. He had an extraordinary wit and humor which are exhibited to no small degree in his sporting works, but his parodies of life in New York and Hollywood and of contemporary American literature are accurate portrayals of issues and events occurring at the time. In addition to the works above which have sporting content, he also wrote the following:

And How Do We Feel This Morning?	1964, Prentice Hall, Inc.
Coconut Oil.	1931, Brewer, Warren & Putnam
The Day Nothing Happened..	1959, Doubleday & Co., Inc.
Daughter of the Gold Rush.	1958
Donovan of OSS.	1970, Little, Brown & Company
Corey Ford's Guide To Thimking.	1959, Doubleday & Co., Inc.

Has Anybody Seen Me Lately?	1958, Doubleday & Co., Inc.
The Horse of Another Color.	1946, Henry Holt and Company, Inc.
How To Guess Your Age.	1950, Doubleday & Co., Inc.
Never Say Diet.	1954, Henry Holt and Company, Inc.
The Office Party.	1951, Doubleday & Co., Inc.
A Peculiar Service.	1965, Little, Brown & Company
Salt Water Taffy.	1929, G. P. Putnam's Sons
Short Cut To Tokyo.	1943, Charles Scribner's Sons
Three Rousing Cheers For the Rollo Boys.	1925, George H. Doran & Co.
The Time of Laughter.	1967, Little, Brown & Company
War Below Zero.	1943
What Every Bachelor Knows.	1961, Doubleday & Co., Inc.
With Allastair McBain	
Cloak and Dagger.	1946, Random House, Inc.
From the Ground Up.	1943, Charles Scribner's Sons
The Last Time I Saw Them.	1946, Charles Scribner's Sons
Using the pseudonym, John Riddell	
The John Riddell Murder Case.	1930, Charles Scribner's Sons
In the Worst Possible Taste.	1932, Charles Scribner's Sons
Meaning No Offense.	1928, John Day

Forester, Frank (*pseud.* of Henry William Herbert) 1807-1858

THE SPORTING NOVELS OF FRANK FORESTER. The Hitchcock edition in four volumes. *The Warwick Woodlands, My Shooting Box, The Quorndon Hounds, The Deerstalkers.* New York, 1930, The Derrydale Press. 200, 187, 145 and 185 pp. respectively; all illustrated in facsimile from the original editions. Limited to 750 sets. Tall 8vo; slipcased together.

The Warwick Woodlands. New York, 1930, The Derrydale Press. 200 pp., plates from old engravings, hand-colored frontispiece by Robert Ball. Limited to 250 numbered copies. Tall 8vo.

My Shooting Box. New York, 1941, The Derrydale Press. 187 pp., plates from old engravings; hand-colored frontispiece by Robert Ball. Limited to 250 numbered copies. Tall 8vo.

Mr. Forester is generally regarded as the father of American sporting literature. See Phillips.

Forester, Frank

Also see **Beverly-Giddings, A. R., editor**
Also see **Hunt, William S.**
Also see **Seybolt, Paul S.**
Also see **Van Winkle, William M.**
Also see **White, Luke**

Fors, W. Barlow

Collector's Handbook U. S. Cartridge Revolvers, 1856 - 1899. No place, 1973, Privately printed. 91 pp. 8vo; dust jacket.

Forsman, Eric D., et al.

Distribution and Biology of the Spotted Owl in Oregon. Washington, D. C., 1984, The Wildlife Society. Monograph # 87. 64 pp., photographic plates, maps, bibliography. 4to. Paper wrappers.

Fosburg, Hugh   1916-1976

A Clearing in the Wilderness. Garden City, New York, 1969, Doubleday & Co., Inc. 134 pp., photographic plates. 8vo; dust jacket. An account of the Baker tract in the Adirondacks, with some hunting and trapping.

The Drowning Stone. New York, 1958, William Morrow & Co., Inc. 189 pp. 8vo; dust jacket. A novel about a game warden in the Adirondacks.

The Good Chance. New York, 1964, William Morrow & Co., Inc. 125 pp. A novel of logging and woodlore in the Adirondacks.

The Hunter. New York, 1950, Charles Scribner's Sons. 233 pp. 8vo; dust jacket. A novel with mountain lion hunting in New Mexico.

One Man's Pleasure; a journal of the wilderness world. New York, 1960, William Morrow & Co., Inc. 191 pp. 8vo; dust jacket. Containing some hunting in the Adirondacks.

The Sound of White Water. New York, 1955, Charles Scribner's Sons. 192 pp. 8vo; dust jacket. A novel of canoeing in the northern Adirondacks.

Foss, Joe   b. 1915

The Outdoorsman. New York, 1968, Robert Halmi. 96 pp., color and black and white illustrations. 4to. Hunting various types of game throughout the U. S. plus a chapter on outdoor photography by Robert Halmi.

Foster, Elizabeth

The Islanders. Boston, 1946, Houghton Mifflin Company. 348 pp., drawings by John O'Hara Cosgrove. 8vo; dust jacket. The account of four generations of a family who built a summer home on Rangeley Lake, Maine, with much hunting and fishing.

Foster, James

20th Century Dog Breeding with the American Pointer and His Family Tree. San Antonio, 1939, The Naylor Company. 301 pp., photographic plates. Introduction by Albert F. Hochwalt. 8vo; dust jacket. Uncommon.

Foster, Laura

Keer-loo; the true story of a young wood duck. Healdsburg, California, 1965, Naturegraph. 80 pp., drawings by the author. 8vo. Paper wrappers.

Foster, William Harnden   1886-1941

New England Grouse Shooting. New York, 1942, Charles Scribner's Sons.   193 pp. frontispiece in color and other drawings all by the author.   4to; dust jacket.   (Reprinted twice, 1947, 1970, same format and publisher.   Also reprinted, ca. 1983, Willow Creek Press)   Mr. Foster not only wrote this classic grouse book, but also produced the fine illustrations gracing its pages. A very popular work, especially in its first edition.

Fowler, Ann and D. L. Walters, editors

Charles Morgan on Retrievers. New York, 1968, Abercrombie & Fitch, Inc.   168 pp., photographic plates.   4to; dust jacket.   (Reprinted 1971, same format and publisher)   [Also a deluxe first edition, specially bound and limited to 100 numbered and signed copies]

Fox, Michael W.   b. 1937

Behavior of Wolves, Dogs and Related Canids.   New York, 1974, Harper & Row, Publishers, Inc.   220 pp., illustrations.   8vo; dust jacket. Focuses on behavior patterns of domesticated wild canids as well as the domestic dog.

The Soul of the Wolf.   Boston, 1980, Little, Brown & Company.   131 pp., illustrations.   8vo; dust jacket.

Fox, Michael W., editor

The Wild Canids; their systematics, behavioral ecology and evolution. New York, 1975, D. Van Nostrand Rinehold Co.   508 pp., photographic plates, bibliography.   8vo; dust jacket.   A collection of articles regarding the wild dog species of the world, including coyote and wolf.

Franck, Harry

The Lure of Alaska.   New York, 1939, Frederick A. Stokes Co. Photographic plates.   8vo; dust jacket.   Much on hunting, trapping, canoeing.

Frank, Charles W., Jr.

Anatomy of a Waterfowl; for carvers and painters.   Gretna, 1982, Pelican.   128 pp., fold-out illustrations. Oblong 4to; dust jacket.

Louisiana Duck Decoys.   New Orleans, 1975, Privately printed.   125 pp., color and black and white illustrations.   Oblong 4to.   Paper wrappers. (Reprinted 1979, cloth bound.   Also a 1985 revised and expanded edition, titled *Wetland Heritage - The Louisiana Duck Decoy*)

Frankenstein, Alfred

After the Hunt; William Harnett and other American still life painters, 1870-1900.   Berkeley, 1953, University of California Press.   189 pp., color and black and white illustrations.   4to; dust jacket. (Also a 1975 revised edition, same format and publisher)   Includes many paintings related to hunting.

Fraser, John, et al.
   The National Retriever Field Trial Club, 1941-1960. No place, No date (ca. 1960), Privately printed. 146 pp., photographic plates. 8vo.

Fratzke, Bob
   Taking Trophy Whitetails. Mequon, Wisconsin, 1983, Target Communications. 124 pp., photographic plates. 8vo. Paper wrappers.

Frazer, Perry D.   1866-1943
   Elementary Gunsmithing. Onslow County, North Carolina, 1938, Small Arms Technical Publishing Company. 208 pp., plates, drawings. 18mo; dust jacket. (Reprinted twice, same format and publisher. Also reprinted, The Stackpole Company)

Frazer, Maj. William D.   b. 1884
   American Pistol Shooting; a manual of instruction in modern pistol marksmanship. New York, 1929, E. P. Dutton & Co., Inc. 326 pp., illustrations. Tall 8vo; dust jacket.

Frazier, Don   b. 1924
   Recognizing Derrydale Press Books. No place, 1983, Privately printed. Unpaginated (106 pp.), photographic plates. Limited to 347 numbered copies. Oblong 4to. [Some copies issued with a slipcase and a portfolio of color photographs of each book published by Derrydale] A fine bibliography of the works produced by this important sporting book publisher.

Frederick, Karl T.
   Pistol Regulation. Washington, D. C., 1931, The National Rifle Association of America. 49 pp., illustrations. 8vo. Paper wrappers. (Reprinted from a series of articles in *The Rifleman* magazine)

Frederickson, Olive A. (with **Ben East**)
   The Silence of the North. The incredible story of a woman's fight for survival in the wilderness. New York, 1972, Crown Publishers, Inc. 209 pp., photographic plates. 8vo; dust jacket. Canadian wilderness living in the 1930's with much bear and moose hunting.

Free, James Lamb
   Training Your Retriever. New York, 1949, Coward, McCann, Inc. 326 pp., photographic plates. 8vo; dust jacket. (Revised and reprinted many times, same format and publisher)

Freeman, Edward A.
 How To Hunt Deer. Harrisburg, 1956, The Stackpole Company. 243 pp., black and white illustrations from drawings by Henry B. Kane. 8vo; dust jacket. (Reprinted several times, same format and publisher)

Freeman, Gage Earle
 Practical Falconry; to which is added "How I Became a Falconer." St. Louis, 1954, Hecht. 89 pp., drawings. 8vo. (Reprinted 1965, same publisher. Originally published, 1869, London)

Freeman, Lewis R.
 Many Rivers. New York, 1937, Dodd, Mead & Co. 368 pp., photographic plates. 8vo; dust jacket. Mostly travel and adventure on many of the world's great rivers, but with some grizzly hunting in the Yukon.

French, C. E., et al.
 Nutritional Requirements of White Tailed Deer For Growth And Antler Development. University Park, 1955, Pennsylvania State University. 50 pp., photographic plates, bibliography. 8vo. Paper wrappers.

French, Edwin M. C.
 Senator Vest: Champion of the Dog. Boston, 1930, Meador Publishing Company. 64 pp., frontispiece of Senator Vest. 8vo. A biography of Missouri State Senator George Graham Vest who was a member of the Boone and Crockett Club and is best remembered for his famous speech, "A Tribute to the Dog," given in behalf of a plaintiff who was demanding $200 in damages from a neighbor who had shot his dog.

Frick, Childs
 Horned Ruminants of North America. New York, 1937, American Museum of Natural History. 669 pp., illustrations. Tall 8vo. Paper wrappers. Much on the ancestors of our present antlered big game. An important and scarce work.

Friley, C. E., Jr.
 Food Habits of the Canada Geese in the Swan Creek Marsh. Lansing, 1961, Michigan Department of Conservation. 9 pp. Paper wrappers.

Fritts, Steven H.
 Wolf Depredation on Livestock in Minnesota. Washington, D. C., 1982, United States Fish and Wildlife Service. 11 pp., bibliography. 4to. Paper wrappers.

Frome, Michael
 Battle For the Wilderness. New York, 1975, Praeger. 246 pp. 8vo; dust jacket. An account of the struggle between conservationists and government over the use of wilderness areas.

149

Frost, A. B. 1851-1928

Shooting Pictures. New York, 1972, Winchester Press. 14 pp., portfolio of 12 shooting prints. Limited to 750 copies. Elephant folio. (Originally published, 1895-1896, Charles Scriber's Sons) After more than a century, Frost's popularity as a sporting artist has not diminished.

Frost, A. B.

Also see **Lanier, Henry W.**
Also see **Reed, Henry M.**

Fuelsch, Don J.

Southern Angler's and Hunter's Guide. Hot Springs, 1964, Fuelsch. 960 pp., many illustrations. 8vo. Paper wrappers. (Also a 1965 revised edition, same format and publisher)

Fuertes, Louis Agassiz 1874-1927

Thirteen Gamebird Lithographs. Washington, D. C., No date (ca. 1940), American Wildlife Institute. A portfolio of six upland game birds and seven waterfowl. Folio. A scarce work produced by the organization that was to become The Wildlife Management Institute.

Fuertes, Louis Agassiz

Also see **Boynton, Mary Fuertes**
Also see **Marcham, Frederick George**
Also see **Peck, Robert McCracken**
Also see **Sutton, George Miksch,** *To a Young Bird Artist*

Fuller, Claud E. b. 1877

The Breech-Loader in the Service. The development of one hundred and one years, 1816 to 1917. Topeka, Kansas, 1933, Arms Reference Club of America. 381 pp., illustrations. 4to. (Reprinted 1965, Flayderman)

The Rifled Musket. Harrisburg, 1958, The Stackpole Company. 302 pp., photographic plates, drawings. 4to; dust jacket. (Reprinted, Bonanza)

Springfield Muzzle-Loading Shoulder Arms. New York, 1931, Francis Bannerman Sons. 176 pp., photographic plates. 4to. The standard reference work on the subject.

The Whitney Firearms. Huntington, West Virginia, 1946, Standard Publications, Inc. 335 pp., photographic plates. Tall 8vo; dust jacket.

Fuller, Claud E. and Richard D. Steuart

Firearms of the Confederacy. Huntington, West Virginia, 1944, Standard Publications, Inc. 333 pp., photographic plates. Tall 8vo; dust jacket.

Fuller, R. W.
   Canada Goose Establishment and Management.   Montpelier, 1964,
Vermont Fish and Game Department.   7 pp.   Paper wrappers.

Fuller, William A.
   *The Biology and Management of the Bison of Wood Buffalo National
Park.*   Ottawa, 1966, Canadian Wildlife Service.   52 pp., map, bibliography.
8vo.
   Wolf Control Operations, Wood Buffalo National Park, 1951-1952.
Ottawa, 1955, Canadian Wildlife Service.   23 pp., photographic plates,
bibliography.   4to.   Paper wrappers.

Fuller, William A. and John C. Holmes
   The Life of the Far North.   New York, 1972, McGraw-Hill Publishing
Company.   232 pp., color and black and white illustrations.   4to; dust jacket.
The wildlife and ecology of the polar and sub-polar regions of North America.

Fullerton, Arthur Grey
   Sunset At Midnight; autobiography.   Portland, Oregon, 1969, Privately
printed.   112 pp.   Limited to 1000 numbered copies.   8vo.   The memoirs of this
rancher, Alaskan missionary and big-game hunter.   More scarce than its limitation suggests.

Gabrielson, Ira Noel   1889-1977

Report to the Idaho Fish and Game Commission.   Washington, D. C., 1953, Wildlife Management Institute.   63 pp., illustrations.   8vo.

Wildlife Conservation.   New York, 1941, The Macmillan Company. 250 pp., photographic plates, drawings, maps.   8vo; dust jacket.   (Revised editions in 1951 and 1959, same format and publisher.   These editions reprinted many times)

Wildlife Management.   New York, 1951, The Macmillan Company. 274 pp., photographic plates.   8vo; dust jacket.

Wildlife Observation. New York, 1946, The Macmillan Company.   250 pp., photographic plates, maps.   8vo; dust jacket.   (Reprinted 1947, same format and publisher)

Wildlife Refuges.   New York, 1943, The Macmillan Company. 257 pp., photographic plates, maps.   Tall 8vo; dust jacket.

Gaddy, Lockhart

Lockhart Gaddy With his Friends - The Wild Geese.   North Carolina, 1964.   64 pp.   Paper wrappers.   Mr. Gaddy was an avid hunter-conservationist.   This work describes his private wild goose sanctuary.

Gaida, H.

Trapper's Instructor.   No place, 1946, Privately printed.   69 pp., illustrations.   8vo.   Paper wrappers.

Galbreath, D. S. and R. Moreland

The Chukar Partridge in Washington.   Washington, 1953.   55 pp., photographic plates, map.   8vo.   Paper wrappers.

Gambrill, Richard V. N.   (1890-1952)   and James C. Mackenzie

Sporting Stables and Kennels.   New York, 1935, The Derrydale Press. 139 pp., photographic plates.   Limited to 950 numbered copies.   Folio.   (Also a British edition of 200 numbered copies, Eyre & Spottiswoode)

Gannon, Robert

How To Raise and Train an English Springer Spaniel.   Neptune City, 1961, TFH.   64 pp., illustrations.   8vo.   Paper wrappers.

How To Raise and Train an Irish Setter.   Neptune City, 1961, TFH.   64 pp., illustrations.   8vo.   Paper wrappers.

Gard, Robert E.

Wild Goose Country; Horicon Marsh to Horseshoe Island. Madison, Wisconsin, 1975, Wisconsin House. 146 pp., color and black and white illustrations. Folio; dust jacket.

Wild Goose Marsh; Horicon stopover. Madison, Wisconsin, 1972, Wisconsin House. 216 pp., photographic plates. 4to; dust jacket. (Reprinted, same format and publisher)

Gard, Wayne

The Great Buffalo Hunt. New York, 1959, Alfred A. Knopf, Inc. 324 pp., black and white illustrations from drawings by Nick Eggenhofer, bibliography. 8vo; dust jacket. (Reprinted 1960, same format and publisher. Also reprinted, 1971, University of Nebraska Press)

Gardner, Robert Edward

Arms Fabricators Ancient and Modern. Columbus, Ohio, 1936, R. G. Adams Company. 337 pp., frontispiece, bibliography. 8vo.

American Arms and Arms Makers. Columbus, Ohio, 1938, F. J. Heer Printing Company. 167 pp., drawings. 8vo.

Five Centuries of Gunsmiths, Swordsmiths and Armorers 1400 - 1900. Columbus, Ohio, 1948, Walter F. Heer, Publisher. 244 pp., photographic plates. 8vo; dust jacket.

Small Armsmakers; a directory of fabricators. New York, 1963, Crown Publishers, Inc. 378 pp., 4to; dust jacket. (Reprinted, Bonanza)

Garretson, Martin S.

The American Bison; the story of its extermination as a wild species and its restoration under federal protection. New York, 1938, New York Zoological Society. 254 pp., photographic plates. 8vo.

A Short History of the American Bison. No place, 1934, American Bison Society. 66 pp., illustrations. 8vo.

Garrett, George

Fifty Years With Fox Hounds. Midland, Georgia, 1938, Privately printed. 206 pp., illustrations. 8vo. A scarce American foxhunting memoir.

Garrett, Helen

Rufous Redtail. New York, 1947, Viking Press. 158 pp., illustrations by F. L. Jaques. 8vo; dust jacket. A juvenile about the life of a red-tailed hawk.

Garton, George

Colt's S.A.A. Post War Models. North Hollywood, California, 1979, Beinfeld Publishing Company. 166 pp., photographic plates. 4to; dust jacket.

Garwood, G. T.
    See **Thomas, Gough**

Garza, L. R. and Robert Rogers
    Legend of the Muy Grande. Corpus Christi, Texas, 1983, Whitetail Publications.   160 pp., color and black and white illustrations.   8vo.   A history of the world's greatest deer hunting contest from 1966 to 1983.

Gaskins, Tom
    Tom Tells Tall Turkey Tales.   Palmdale, 1965, Privately printed.   36 pp., drawings.   8vo.   Paper wrappers.
    We Talk Turkey.   Palmdale, 1983, Privately printed.   76 pp.   8vo. Paper wrappers.

Gasque, James S.   1903-1967
    Hunting and Fishing in the Great Smokies.   New York, 1948, Alfred A. Knopf, Inc.   211 pp., photographic plates, color frontispiece.   A Borzoi Book For Sportsmen.   8vo; dust jacket.

Gates, Clayton
    Back to the Trapline.   Richmond, Virginia, no date (1946), Privately printed by the author.   103 pp.   8vo.   Paper wrappers.   Mostly trapping techniques, but some turkey hunting as well.
    Whitetail Deer Hunting; an instructive treatise on deer hunting especially applicable to the whitetail deer.   Columbus, Ohio, 1941, Walter F. Heer, Publisher.   43 pp., photographic plates.   A title in the Outdoorsman Handbook series.   18mo. Paper wrappers.
    The Year-Around Trapper. Richmond, Virginia, 1945, Privately printed by the author.   47 pp.   8vo.   Paper wrappers.

Gavin, T. A., et al.
    Population Characteristics, Spatial Organization and Natural Mortality in the Columbian White Tailed Deer.   Washington, D. C., 1984, The Wildlife Society.   41 pp., photographic plates, bibliography.   4to.   Paper wrappers.

Gay, John
    Rural Sports; together with the "Birth of the Squire" and "The Hound and The Huntsman."   Mt. Vernon, New York, 1930, William Edwin Rudge.   37 pp., illustrations by Gordon Ross.   Limited to 1550 copies.   Folio; slipcased. [Also a deluxe edition, specially bound and illustrated and limited to 225 numbered copies; slipcased]   Foxhunting.

Geagan, Bill
>*The Good Trail.*   New York, 1954, Coward, McCann, Inc.   237 pp., drawings.   8vo; dust jacket.   Hunting and angling in Maine.

Geary, Steven M.
>*Fur Trapping in North America.*   Piscataway, New Jersey, 1984, Winchester Press.   154 pp., photographic plates.   8vo.   Paper wrappers.

Gee, Ernest Richard   b. 1878
>*Early American Sporting Books.* New York, 1928, The Derrydale Press. 61 pp., plus ads.   Limited to 400 copies.   Tall 8vo.   (Reprinted in 1971 and 1974, same format, Haskell)
>*Sporting Panoramas.*   New York, No date (ca. 1930), Ernest R. Gee. 19 pp., photographic plates.   8vo.   Paper wrappers.   A description of nine sporting panoramas in the possession of Alfred B. Maclay that were painted by Alken, Cruikshank and others. A rare booklet describing an even more rare form of sporting art.
>*The Sportsman's Library*; being a descriptive list of the most important books on sport.   New York, 1940, R. R. Bowker Co.   158 pp., photographic plates.   Limited to 600 copies.   Tall 8vo.
>Mr. Gee was a dealer in rare books whose specialty was books on sport.   He was a bibliophile of the keenest sort who helped such famous collectors as Maclay, Schwerdt, Widener and others amass their incredible sporting libraries.

Gee, Ernest R.
>Also see **Anonymous**, *The Sportsman's Portfolio of American Field Sports.*
>Also see **A Gentleman**
>Also see **Kester, Jess Y.**
>Also see **Meynell, Hugo**
>Also see **Milnor, William**

Geis, Aelred D.
>*Breeding and Wintering Areas of Mallards Harvested in Various States and Provinces.*   Washington, D. C., 1971, United States Fish and Wildlife Service.   4to.   Paper wrappers.

Geist, Valerius   b. 1938
>*Mountain Sheep and Man;* in the northern wilds.   Ithaca, New York, 1975, Cornell University Press.   248 pp., photographic plates.   8vo; dust jacket. A natural history of bighorn sheep in Canada.
>*Mountain Sheep;* a study in behavior and evolution.   Chicago, 1971, University of Chicago Press.   383 pp., photographic plates, drawings, bibliography.   8vo; dust jacket.   (Reprinted 1977, same publisher in paper wrappers)

Genevoix, Maurice

The Last Hunt. New York, 1940, Random House, Inc. 281 pp., illustrations by Lynd Ward. 8vo; dust jacket. A novel of deer hunting.

A Gentleman

The Sportsman's Companion; or an essay on shooting. New York, 1930, Privately printed for Ernest R. Gee by The Derrydale Press. 52 pp. 8vo. (Also a 1948 edition limited to 1500 copies, different format, Stackpole & Heck, Inc.) Both editions are reproductions of the first American book on shooting, published in 1783.

Gentry, Christine

When Dogs Run Wild. North Carolina, 1983, McFarland & Company, Inc. 195 pp. 8vo. A discussion of the effects of stray dogs on deer populations.

George, Evan

A Spaniel Training Primer for Amateurs. San Francisco, 1941, Rosemont Press. 64 pp., photographic plates. Limited to 500 copies. 12mo; dust jacket.

George, Jean Craighead

The Grizzly Bear With the Golden Ears. New York, 1982, Harper & Row, Publishers, Inc. Illustrations by Tom Catania. Oblong 12mo; dust jacket. A juvenile.

Georgeson, C. C.

Reindeer and Caribou. Seattle, 1967, Shorey Publishing Company. 22 pp., photographic plates. Limited to 200 copies. 8vo. Paper wrappers. (Originally published, 1903, Bureau of Animal Industry)

Gerrits, H. A.

Pheasants; including their care in the aviary. Salt Lake City, 1961, Allen. 144 pp., color and black and white illustrations. 8vo. (Originally published, 1959, The Netherlands)

Gerstacker, Friedrich   1816-1872

Wild Sports in the Far West; the narrative of a German wanderer beyond the Mississippi, 1837-1843. Durham, North Carolina, 1968, Duke University Press. 409 pp. (Originally published, 1844, Germany) Primarily dealing with deer hunting.

Gibson, Charles Dana

Shoot If You Must. New York, 1950, Privately printed. 46 pp., frontispiece. 8vo. Limited to 250 numbered copies. Waterfowling and upland gunning in the Adirondacks, Maryland and Virginia.

Gibson, Langhorne

Golden Bridge Hounds; season 1930.   New York, 1930, Privately printed.   66 pp.   8vo.   Paper wrappers.   A diary of the 1930 foxhunting season by one of the joint Masters of Hounds.

Gier, H. T.

Coyotes in Kansas.   Manhattan, 1957, Kansas State University Press. 97 pp., photographic plates, drawings, bibliography.   Paper wrappers.

Gilbert, A. C.

The Man Who Lives in Paradise; the autobiography of A. C. Gilbert. New York, 1954, Rinehart & Company.   374 pp., photographic plates.   8vo; dust jacket.   The autobiography of this former Olympic pole vaulter who later became a successful manufacturer and member of the Boone and Crockett Club. With much big game hunting in North America. Scarce.

Gilbert, Bill

In God's Country.   Lincoln, 1984, University of Nebraska Press.   203 pp.   Contains the chapter "The Rites of Autumn" dealing with the annual deer hunt in Potter County, Pennsylvania.

Gilbert, Kenneth

Bird Dog Bargain.   New York, 1947, Henry Holt & Company.   200 pp., drawings.   8vo.   A juvenile about hunting with a bird dog.

Gilchrist, Duncan

The Big Game Hunter's and Fisherman's Complete Guide To Field Care of Trophies.   Hamilton, Montana, 1985, Privately printed.   96 pp., photographic plates.   8vo.   Spiral bound paper wrappers.

Hunting the Rocky Mountain Goat. Missoula, Montana, 1983, Pictorial Histories. 140 pp., photographic plates, maps.   8vo.   Paper wrappers.

On Bears and Bear Hunting. Clinton, New Jersey, 1984, Amwell Press. 260 pp., photographic plates, maps. Limited to 1000 numbered and signed copies. 8vo; slipcased.   (Also a 1984 trade edition, same contents and publisher)

Trophy Rooms of the Brooks Range;   plus secrets of a sheep and mountain goat guide. No place, 1981, Privately printed.   164 pp., photographic plates. 8vo. Paper wrappers (Also a 1984 second edition)

Gilder, W. H.

Schwatka's Search.   New York, 1966, Abercrombie & Fitch, Inc. 316 pp., plates from old engravings.   (A facsimile reproduction of the 1881 first edition)   Mostly far North adventure, with some hunting.

Giles, Robert H.
  Wildlife Management Techniques. Washington, D. C., 1971, The Wildlife Society. 633 pp., photographic plates, large bibliography. 4to. Paper wrappers. (Reprinted at least twice, same format and publisher. Also reprinted, 1978, W. H. Freeman & Company)

Gill, Harold B. Jr.
  The Gunsmith in Colonial Virginia. Williamsburg, Virginia, 1974, Colonial Williamsburg Foundation. 139 pp., photographic plates, drawings. 8vo.

Gill, John D.
  Review of Deer Yard Management. Augusta, 1957, Maine Department of Inland Fish and Game. 61 pp., photographic plates, bibliography. 8vo. Paper wrappers.

Gillett, Frederick
  See **Lort-Phillips, Frederick**

Gillette, Bertha Chambers
  Homesteading With the Elk; a story of frontier life in Jackson Hole, Wyoming. Idaho Falls, Utah, 1968, Privately printed. 175 pp. 8vo; dust jacket. A novel dealing with the development of the elk refuge at Jackson Hole, Wyoming. Scarce.

Gilley, Wendell
  Bird Carving; a guide to a fascinating hobby. Princeton, New Jersey, 1961, D. Van Nostrand Company, Inc. 115 pp., photographic plates, drawings. A Van Nostrand Sporting Book. 8vo; dust jacket. (Reprinted, Bonanza. Also a 1972 revised edition, titled *The Art of Bird Carving*, Hillcrest)

Gillham, Charles Edward
  Beyond the Clapping Mountains. New York, 1943, The Macmillan Company. 134 pp. Square 8vo; dust jacket. Scarce.
  Raw North. New York, 1947, A. S. Barnes and Company, Inc. 275 pp., drawings by Bob Hines. 8vo; dust jacket. Scarce.
  Sled Dog and Other Poems of the North. Huntington, West Virginia, 1950, Standard Publications, Inc. 78 pp.; slipcased. Scarce.
  Mr. Gillham lived in Alaska many years. He wrote extensively in periodicals as well as these books regarding hunting and other outdoor activities in the great North West.

Gilmore, Jene C.

Art For Conservation; the federal duck stamps. Barre, Massachusetts, 1971, Barre Publishing Co., Inc. 94 pp., black and white plates of duck stamps. Oblong 4to; dust jacket. [Also a deluxe edition, specially bound with an original signed etching and limited to 300 numbered copies; slipcased] Illustrates all the stamps from 1934 Through 1972.

Gilmore Oil Company

Where to Hunt and Fish in California, Oregon and Washington. Los Angeles, 1931, Gilmore Oil Company. 96 pp., photographic plates, drawings. Tall 8vo. Paper wrappers.

Gilsvik, Bob

The Complete Book of Trapping. Radnor, Pennsylvania, 1976, Chilton Books. 172 pp., illustrations. 4to; dust jacket.

All Season Hunting; a guide to early season, late season and winter hunting in America. New York, 1976, Winchester Press. 209 pp., illustrations. 8vo; dust jacket.

A Guide To Good Cheap Hunting. New York, 1978, Stein & Day, Publishers. 206 pp., photographic plates, drawings by the author. 8vo; dust jacket.

A Modern Trapline; methods and materials. Radnor, Pennsylvania, 1980, Chilton Books. 197 pp., drawings by David Gilsvik. 4to; dust jacket.

Gingrich, Arnold, editor   1903-1976

Esquire's Second Sports Reader. New York, 1946, A. S. Barnes and Company, Inc. 427 pp. 8vo; dust jacket. An anthology of stories dealing with all types of sports, including some on hunting and fishing.

Ginner, X. B. (*pseud.* of **B. M. Baxter**)

For Beginners Only. Portsmouth, Ohio, 1943, National Muzzle Loading Rifle Association. 47 pp., illustrations from drawings by the author. 12mo. Paper wrappers. (Also a 1949 second edition, same publisher) Relating to the basics of firing muzzle-loading firearms.

Gipson, Fred

Hound Dog Man. New York, 1949, Harper & Brothers. 247 pp. 8vo; dust jacket. A novel with a raccoon hunter as the central figure.

Girnau, Frederick, editor

Hunting and Trapping Manual. Milwaukee, Wisconsin, 1947, Gittleman's Beer Co. 111 pp., illustrations. 8vo. Paper wrappers.

Gist, Brooks D.

High Sierra Adventure. Visalia, 1950, Privately printed. 108 pp., photographic plates, drawings. 8vo; dust jacket. (Also a 1955 revised edition)

Glasier, Phillip

As the Falcon Her Bells. New York, 1963, E. P. Dutton & Co., Inc. 223 pp., color frontispiece, photographic plates plus woodcuts. 8vo; dust jacket. Mostly hunting with the falcon but some bird shooting over dogs.

Falconry And Hawking. Newton Centre, Massachusetts, 1979, C. T. Branford Co. 312 pp., illustrations. 4to. (Originally published 1978, London)

Glass, Eugene

The Cocker Spaniel. Battle Creek, Michigan, No date. Third edition. 85 pp., illustrations. 12mo. Not in Jones.

Glogan, Joseph

Sportsman's Book of U. S. Records 1981 Edition. New York, 1981. 128 pp., illustrations. 12mo. paper wrappers. Includes angling and hunting trophies.

Glover, Ronnie

More Than Luck; a guide for hunting the trophy buck. Louisiana, 1980, A Big Buck Publication. 52 pp. Advice for hunting in Mississippi and Louisiana.

Gluckman, Col. Arcadi   b. 1896

Catalog of United States Martial Short Arms. Buffalo, 1939, Otto Ulbrich Company. 68 pp., photographic plates. 8vo; dust jacket.

United States Martial Pistols and Revolvers. Buffalo, 1939, Otto Ulbrich Company. 249 pp., bibliography, photographic plates. 8vo; dust jacket. (Reprinted 1944, same format and publisher. Also reprinted 1956, same format, by The Stackpole Company and by Bonanza)

United States Muskets, Rifles and Carbines. Buffalo, 1948, Otto Ulbrich Company. 447 pp., plus 56 pp. of appendices, index, bibliography, photographic plates. 8vo; dust jacket. (Reprinted 1959, same format, The Stackpole Company. Also a 1965 revised and enlarged edition titled, *Identifying Old U. S. Muskets, Rifles and Carbines*, The Stackpole Company)

Gluckman, Col. Arcadi and Leroy De Forest Saterlee

American Gun Makers. Buffalo, 1940, Otto Ulbrich Company. 246 pp., bibliography. 8vo; dust jacket. (Reprinted 1945, same format and publisher. Also a 1953 second edition, The Stackpole Company)

Godfrey, Joe Jr., editor

Popular Mechanics Guide to Good Hunting and Trapping. Chicago, 1952, Popular Mechanics. 156 pp., illustrations. 8vo; dust jacket.

Godfrey,   Joe Jr. and Frank Dufresne, editors
The Great Outdoors. Minneapolis, 1947, Brown and Bigelow. 376 pp., photographic plates in color and black and white. Foreword by Corey Ford. 4to; specially bound. (Reprinted 1949, Whittlesey House)

Lure of the Open. St. Paul, 1949, Brown & Bigelow. 449 pp., color and black and white illustrations. Tall 8vo. (Also a specially bound 1954 edition, Sportsmen's Club, Chicago)

Goerch, Carl
Ocracoke. Raleigh, North Carolina, 1956, Privately printed. 223 pp., drawings. 8vo; dust jacket. (Reprinted many times, various publishers) A history of the island, with one chapter on duck hunting.

Goerg, Alfred J.
Pacific and Northwest Hunting. New York, 1952, Pageant Press. 112 pp., illustrations. 8vo; dust jacket.

Pioneer Handgun Hunting. Port Angeles, 1965, Privately printed. 203 pp., photographic plates. 4to. Hunting North American big game with handguns.

Gohdes, Clarence, editor
Hunting in the Old South; original narratives of the hunters. Baton Rouge, 1967, Louisiana State University Press. 176 pp., illustrations from old plates. 4to; dust jacket.

Golden Retriever Club of America
The Golden Retriever. 1950, Golden Retriever Club of America. Illustrations. 8vo; dust jacket.

Gooch, Bob   b. 1919
Coveys and Singles; the handbook of quail shooting. New York, 1980, A. S. Barnes and Company, Inc. 196 pp., illustrations. 8vo; dust jacket. (Also seen with Barnes' San Diego imprint)

In Search of the Wild Turkey. Waukegan, Illinois, 1978, Great Lakes Living Press, Ltd. 182 pp., photographic plates, maps. 8vo; dust jacket.

Squirrels and Squirrel Hunting. Cambridge, Maryland, 1972, Tidewater Publishers. 152 pp., photographic plates. 8vo; dust jacket.

Gooch, Dennie, et al.
History of the League of Kentucky Sportsmen, 1935 - 1957. No place, 1957, Privately printed. 43 pp., illustrations. 8vo. Paper wrappers.

Goodall, Charles S.
> *The Complete English Springer Spaniel.*   Middleburg, Virginia, 1958, Denlinger's.   128pp., illustrations.   8vo.
> *How To Train Your Own Gun Dog.*   New York, 1978,   Howell Book House.   160 pp., illustrations.   8vo.   (Reprinted many times, same format and publisher)

Goodall, Charles S. and Julia Gasow
> *The New Complete English Springer Spaniel.*   New York, 1974, Howell Book House.   288 pp., illustrations.   8vo.   (Reprinted several times, same format and publisher)

Goodwin, Derek
> *Crows of the World.*   Ithaca, New York, 1976, Comstock Press.   354 pp., color plates by Robert Gillmor, maps.   4to; dust jacket.

Goodwin, Fred and S. Stanley Hawbaker
> *The Art of Deer and Bear Hunting.*   Pennsylvania, 1953, Privately printed.   19 pp.

Gordon, Caroline   1895-1981
> *Alec Maury, Sportsman;* a novel.   New York, 1934, Charles Scribner's Sons.   300 pp.   8vo; dust jacket.   (Reprinted several times, various dates and publishers)   A fictionalized account of the author's father, with much hunting and angling.   The first edition is scarce.

Gordon, Ester and Bernard Gordon
> *Once There Was A Passenger Pigeon.*   New York, 1976, Walck.   Unpaginated (26 pp.), illustrations.   4to; dust jacket.   A juvenile about the extinction of this species.

Goss, Richard J.
> *Deer Antlers;* regeneration, function and evolution.   New York, 1983, Academic Press.   316 pp., illustrations.   8vo; dust jacket.   A thorough, scholarly work.

Gould, Arthur Corbin   1850-1903
> *Modern American Pistols and Revolvers.*   Plantersville, South Carolina, 1946, Small Arms Technical Publishing Company.   222 pp., illustrations.   8vo; dust jacket.   (A facsimile reproduction of the 1888 first edition)
> *Modern American Rifles.*   Plantersville, South Carolina, 1946, Small Arms Technical Publishing Company.   333 pp., illustrations.   8vo; dust jacket.   (A facsimile reproduction of the 1891 first edition)

Gould, Howard
     The Sporting Library of Howard Gould.   New York, 1940, Parke-Bernet Galleries, Inc.   25 pp.   8vo.   Paper wrappers.   An auction catalog.

Gould, John
     The Fastest Hound Dog in the State of Maine.   New York, 1953, William Morrow & Co., Inc.   94 pp., drawings by F. Wenderoth Saunders. 12mo; dust jacket. (Reprinted at least twice, same format and publisher)   Maine humor with a tale of a rabbit hound.

Gowland, John
     Smoke Over Sikanaska.   No place, 1955, Werner Luarie.   224 pp., drawings by Spencer Roberts.   8vo; dust jacket.   The experiences of a forest ranger in the Canadian Rocky Mountains.

Grady, Joseph F.
     The Adirondacks, Fulton Chain - Big Moose Region; the story of the wilderness.   Little Falls, 1933, Privately printed.   320 pp., photographic plates. 8vo.   Primarily a guide to the area, but containing some hunting and angling.

Graham, Edward H.   b. 1902
     The Land and Wildlife.   New York, 1947, Oxford University Press. 232 pp., illustrations.   8vo; dust jacket.

Graham, Edward H. and W. R. Van Dersal
     Wildlife For America; the story of wildlife conservation.   New York, 1949, Oxford University Press.   110 pp., illustrations.   8vo.   (Reprinted 1958, H. Z. Walsk)

Graham, Ron, John Kopec and C. Kenneth Moore
     A Study of the Colt Single Action Army Revolver.   Dallas, 1976, Taylor Publishing Co.   523 pp., illustrations.   4to; dust jacket.   A highly sought-after title by Colt firearms enthusiasts.

Grancsay, Stephen V.   b. 1897
     Brooklyn Museum: Loan Exhibition of European Arms and Armor. Brooklyn, New York, 1933, Brooklyn Museum.   48 pp., many photographic plates. 8vo.   Paper wrappers.
     American Engraved Powder Horns.   A study based on the Grenville Gilbert Collection.   New York, 1945, The Metropolitan Museum of Art.   96 pp. plus 47 photographic plates, bibliography.   Limited to 500 copies.   Folio.
     Master French Gunsmith's Designs. New York, 1950, Greenberg: Publishers.   22 pp. of text plus plates.   Limited to 749 numbered copies; slipcased.   Oblong 4to.   [Also a special edition of 80 numbered presentation copies for the members of the Arms and Armor Club of New York; slipcased]

Grancsay, Stephen V., continued

   Master French Gunsmith's Designs of the XVII-XIX Centuries; reproduced in facsimile.   New York, 1970, Winchester Press.   208 pp., illustrations, bibliography.   Limited to 1000 numbered copies.   Folio.   Much more scarce than the limitation would suggest.

Grand, Gordon   1883-1950

   The Banshee Shadow Flies.   No place, No date, Privately printed by J. H. Craig.   Unpaginated (21 pp.).   8vo.   Paper wrappers.   This angling story originally appeared as one of the chapters in *Colonel Weatherford and His Friends;* it also appeared later in *The Millbeck Hounds.*

   Colonel Weatherford and His Friends.   New York, 1933, The Derrydale Press.   242 pp., drawings by J. A. Twachtman.   Limited to 1450 copies.   8vo.

   Colonel Weatherford's Young Entry.   New York, 1935, The Derrydale Press.   214 pp., drawings by Paul Brown.   Limited to 1350 copies.   8vo.

   A Horse For Christmas Morning; and other stories.   New York, 1970, Winchester Press.   115 pp., drawings.   Foreword by Gordon Grand, Jr.   Limited to 1450 numbered copies.   8vo; slipcased.   The four stories in this work were previously published by Grand as Christmas gifts for the family's friends.   His son, Gordon Grand Jr., was an enthusiastic sportsman who became an officer with Olin Corporation, the parent company of Winchester Press.   The younger Grand lent his enthusiastic support to the publication of this volume as well as all of Winchester's early publishing efforts.

   The Millbeck Hounds.   New York, 1947, Charles Scribner's Sons.   368 pp., illustrations by Eleanor Iselin Mason.   8vo; dust jacket.   Mostly foxhunting.

   Old Man; and Other Colonel Weatherford stories.   New York, 1934, The Derrydale Press.   239 pp., drawings by William J. Hays.   Limited to 1150 copies.   8vo.

   Redmond C. Stewart; foxhunter and gentleman of Maryland.   New York, 1938, Charles Scribner's Sons.   198 pp., color frontispiece, photographic plates.   Tall 8vo; slipcased.

   The Silver Horn; and other sporting tales of John Weatherford.   New York, 1932, The Derrydale Press.   229 pp., drawings by J. A. Twachtman. Limited to 950 copies.   8vo.   (Reprinted several times by Windward House and Garden City Publishing Company)

   The Southborough Fox; and other Colonel Weatherford stories.   New York, 1939, The Derrydale Press.   239 pp., drawings by Eleanor Iselin Mason. Limited to 1450 copies.   8vo.

   All of Grand's books centered around foxhunting and the equestrian arts.

Grange, Wallace B.   b. 1905

   Feeding Wildlife in Winter.   Washington, D. C., 1937, United States Department of Agriculture.   20 pp., photographic plates.   8vo.   Paper wrappers.

   Those of the Forest.   Babcock, Wisconsin, 1953, Flambeau Publishing Company.   314 pp., drawings by Olaus J. Murie. 8vo; dust jacket. (Reprinted in facsimile, 1967, Abercrombie & Fitch, Inc.)

Grange, Wallace B., continued

The Way To Game Abundance; with an explanation of game cycles. New York, 1949, Charles Scribner's Sons. 365 pp., photographic plates. 8vo; dust jacket. An important conservation work.

Wisconsin Grouse Problems. Madison, No date (1948), Wisconsin Conservation Department. 318 pp., photographic plates, bibliography. 8vo.

Grant, James J.

Boy's Single Shot Rifles. New York, 1967, William Morrow & Co., Inc. 597 pp., photographic plates. 8vo; dust jacket.

More Single Shot Rifles. New York, 1959, William Morrow & Co., Inc. 322 pp., photographic plates. 8vo; dust jacket.

Single-Shot Rifles. New York, 1947, William Morrow & Co., Inc. 385 pp., photographic plates. 8vo; dust jacket.

Still More Single Shot Rifles. Harriman, Tennessee, 1979, Pioneer Press. 211 pp., photographic plates. 8vo; dust jacket.

Grant, Madison

The Kentucky Rifle Hunting Pouch; its contents and accouterments. No place, 1977, Privately printed. 207 pp., photographic plates; bibliography.

Grant, Madison

See **The Major**

Grant, Norman B., Jr., editor

Records of Alaska Big Game. No place, 1971, Alaska Big Game Trophy Club. 111 pp., photographic plates. 4to; dust jacket.

Grant, William W.

A Quarter Century of the Arapahoe Hunt. No place (Colorado), 1954, Privately printed. 43 pp., fold-out map. 8vo. A history of this Denver area foxhunting club (although their quarry was coyote).

Grant, William W.

Also see **Phipps, Lawrence C.**

Grantz, Gerald J.

Home Book of Taxidermy and Tanning. Harrisburg, 1969, The Stackpole Company. 160 pp., illustrations. Tall 8vo; dust jacket. (Reprinted 1977, same format and publisher)

Graves, Jackson A.

California Memories, 1857-1930. Los Angeles, 1930, Privately printed by the Times-Mirror Press. 330 pp., photographic plates. 4to. [Also a deluxe edition, specially bound and limited to 350 numbered and signed copies]

My Seventy Years in California (1857-1927). Los Angeles, 1927, Privately printed by the Times-Mirror Press. 478 pp., photographic plates. 8vo. Both of these scarce titles contain several chapters on hunting and angling.

Graves, John Woodcock

John Peel; the famous Cumberland hunting song. New York, 1932, The Derrydale Press. Unpaginated (10pp.), drawings by Robert Ball. Limited to 990 copies. Folio. A foxhunting song.

Graves, Robert

Goodbye to a River. New York, 1961, Alfred A. Knopf, Inc. 306 pp., illustrations by Russell Waterhouse. 8vo; dust jacket. A canoe trip down the Brazos River in Texas, with some duck hunting.

Gray, Brooksby

See **Bump, Robert**

Gray Owl (Wa-Sha-Quon-Asin)

The Men of the Last Frontier. London, 1931, Country Life Press. 253 pp., photographic plates, drawings. 8vo; dust jacket.

Pilgrims of the Wild. London, 1935, Lovat. 282 pp., photographic plates, drawings by the author. 8vo; dust jacket. The account of the author's life in the Canadian wilds, with much on beaver conservation and culture.

Tales of an Empty Cabin. London, 1936, Lovat. 335 pp., photographic plates. 8vo; dust jacket. All three of these works contain much hunting, trapping and adventure in the Canadian wilds.

Gray, David   1870-1968

THE SPORTING WORKS OF DAVID GRAY The Hitchcock Edition in three volumes. *Gallups I, Gallups II* and *Mr. Carteret.* New York, 1929, The Derrydale Press. 181 pp., 208 pp., and 163 pp. respectively, all illustrated from drawings by Paul Brown. Limited to 750 sets, numbered and signed by the author. 8vo; slipcased together. (Originally published, 1898, 1903 and 1910, respectively, The Century Company) Delightful stories of foxhunting in late nineteenth century America.

Gray, Ed, editor

Gray's Journal; the first collection. South Hamilton, Massachusetts, 1982, Gray's Sporting Journal. 79 pp., drawings by Russell Buzzell. Limited to 1000 numbered copies. 8vo.

Gray, Ed, editor, continued

Gray's Journal; the second collection. South Hamilton, Massachusetts, 1984, Gray's Sporting Journal. 79 pp., drawings by Russell Buzzell. Limited to 2000 numbered copies. 8vo.

Tales From Gray's; selections from *Gray's Sporting Journal,* 1975 - 1985. South Hamilton, Massachusetts, 1986, Gray's Sporting Journal. 267 pp. 8vo; dust jacket.

Gray, Prentiss Nathaniel   1884-1935

Camera Adventures in New Brunswick. No place, 1925, Privately printed. Unpaginated (approx. 70 pp.), many full page photographic plates in sepia. Limited to 10 numbered copies. 4to. Mr. Gray went to New Brunswick to photograph moose and white tailed deer. He had this record produced for presentation purposes.

Records of North American Big Game. New York, 1932, The Derrydale Press. 178 pp., illustrations from photographs and paintings (16 by Carl Rungius). Limited to 500 copies. 4to. The first Boone and Crocket Club record book.

North American Big Game; official measurement records compiled by Prentiss N. Gray. New York, 1934, The Derrydale Press / Remington Arms Company. 38 pp. , plus blank leaves. Paper wrappers.

Mr. Gray was an important member of the Boone & Crockett Club. He was as much an explorer and early wildlife motion picture photographer, as a hunter. In 1994, the Boone & Crockett Club published *From the Peace To the Fraser;* newly discovered North American Hunting and exploration journals, 1900 to 1930; this work had not been previously published. In addition to recounting his exploration of the region, it contains a biography of Mr. Gray, written by Sherman Gray, his son.

Gray, Prentiss Nathaniel
Also see **Grinnell, George Bird**

Gray, Robert

Cougar; the natural life of a North American mountain lion. New York, 1972, W. W. Norton & Co., Inc. 150 pp., photographic plates. 8vo; dust jacket.

Gray, Robert S.

A Visit To Texas in 1831; being the journal of a traveler through those parts most interesting to American settlers with descriptions of scenery, etc. Houston, 1975, Cordovan. Third edition. 184 pp., old plates, color map. 8vo; dust jacket. (Originally published in 1834 and revised in 1836. This third edition combines the text from the second edition and the plates from the first edition) One of the earliest western Americana titles illustrated with hunting plates.

Gray, Thelma

The Popular Beagle. New York, 1963, Arco. 220 pp., photographic plates 8vo; dust jacket.

Grayson, Charles, editor
> *The Sportsman's Hornbook.* New York, 1933, Random House, Inc. 169 pp. Limited to 500 copies. Tall 8vo. A collection of poetry on all types of sports, including several on foxhunting.

Greenberg, David B.
> *Raising Game Birds in Captivity.* Princeton, New Jersey, 1949, D. Van Nostrand Company, Inc. 224 pp., photographic plates, drawings. 4to; dust jacket.

Greene, Stephen, et al., editors
> *A Treasury of Vermont Life.* Woodstock, Vermont, 1956, Countryman Press. 192 pp., color and black and white illustrations. 4to. Contains some hunting and an article about the Shelbourne Museum.

Greenway, James C. Jr. and A. Lasell Ripley
> *The Laurel Brook Club: 1902 - 1957.* No place, 1958, Privately printed. 63 pp., color frontispiece and other black and white illustrations by Ripley. Limited to 150 numbered copies signed by the author and artist. 4to. A history of this club with much upland bird hunting.

Gregg, James R.
> *The Sportsman's Eye;* how to make better use of your eyes in the outdoors. New York, 1971, Winchester Press. 210 pp., photographic plates. 8vo; dust jacket. With much on the use of telescopic sights and binoculars.

Gregg, Larry
> *Population Ecology of Woodcock in Wisconsin.* Madison, 1984. Wisconsin Department of Natural Resources. 54 pp., photographic plates, bibliography. 4to. Paper wrappers.

Gregory, Tappan   b. 1886
> *Deer at Night in the North Woods.* Baltimore, Maryland, 1930, Charles C. Thomas. 211 pp., photographic plates. Photographing deer in the Upper Peninsula of Michigan.
> *Eyes in the Night.* New York, 1939, Thomas Y. Crowell Company. 243 pp., photographic plates. Photographing deer, moose, bear, etc. at night.
> *Nature Photography at Night.* Denver, 1957, Denver Museum of Natural History. 64 pp., photographic plates.

Greiner, James
> *The Red Snow;* a story of the Alaska gray wolf. New York, 1980, St. Martin's Press. 227 pp. 8vo; dust jacket.

Grennell, Dean

The ABC's of Reloading. Northfield, Illinois, 1974, Digest Books. 320 pp., illustrations. 4to. Paper wrappers.

Gresham, Claude Hamilton "Grits"   b. 1922

The Complete Wildfowler. New York, 1973, Winchester Press. 294 pp., illustrations. 8vo; dust jacket. (Reprinted 1974, same format and publisher) [Also a deluxe first edition of 500 numbered and signed copies, Winchester Press / Amwell Press]

Grey, Hugh, editor

Field & Stream Treasury. New York, 1955, Henry Holt and Company, Inc. / Field & Stream. 351 pp., color and black and white illustrations. 8vo. (Reprinted several times, same publisher and format) A collection of hunting and angling stories originally appearing in *Field & Stream* magazine.

Grey, Loren

Zane Grey-A Photographic Odyssey. Dallas, 1985, Taylor Publishing Co. 213 pp., photographic plates. 4to; dust jacket. A compilation of photographs from the estate of Zane Grey, compiled by his brother, Loren.

Grey, Zane   1872-1939

The Deer Stalker. New York, 1949, Harper & Brothers. 243 pp. 8vo; dust jacket. Grey participated in an expedition to move a huge mule deer herd, numbering some 40,000 head, from the Kaibab plateau to lower elevations in order to insure their survival over the winter. Although the expedition failed, this fictionalized account portrayed its success.

Don; the story of a lion dog. New York, 1928, Harper & Brothers. 69 pp., illustrations by Kurt Wiese. 12mo; dust jacket. Fictionalized account of hunting mountain lion in the Grand Canyon

Roping Lions in the Grand Canyon. New York, 1924, Harper & Brothers. 191 pp. 8vo; dust jacket. (Reprinted, Grosset & Dunlap) An account of an expedition Grey undertook with Buffalo Jones. Not listed in Phillips.

Zane Grey; the man and his work, an autobiographical sketch, critical appreciations and bibliography. New York, 1928, Harper & Brothers. 56 pp., photographic plates. 12mo; dust jacket.

Zane Grey's action packed western novels nearly all contained incidental mentioning of hunting, and several of his books had much to say about the preservation of the wild horse in the west. He was a dedicated conservationist whose best known sporting works are angling titles; *Tales of Fishes,* 1919, *Tales of Southern Rivers,* 1924, *Tales of Fishing Virgin Seas,* 1925, *Tales of the Angler's Eldorado- New Zealand,* 1926, *Tales of Swordfish and Tuna,* 1927, are all important works. See Bruns.

Grey, Zane
>Also see **Farley, G. M.**
>Also see **Gruber, Frank**
>Also see **Karr, Jean**
>Also see **Reiger, George, editor**
>Also see **Schneider, Norris F.**

Grice, David and John P. Rogers
>*The Wood Duck in Massachusetts.* Westborough, 1965, Massachusetts Fish and Game Department. 96 pp., photographic plates, maps, bibliography. 8vo. Paper wrappers.

Grieb, Jack R.
>*The Shortgrass Prairie Canada Goose Population.* Louisville, Kentucky, 1970, Wildlife Society. 49 pp., photographic plates. 4to. Paper wrappers.

Griffen, Jeff
>*The Hunting Dogs of America.* New York, 1964, Doubleday & Co., Inc. 311 pp., photographic plates, drawings. 4to; dust jacket.

Griffiths, Gesna Felts
>*Happy Times Hunting in Alabama's Beautiful Woods.* No place, No date, Privately printed. 58 pp., photographic plates. 8vo. Paper wrappers.
>The memoirs of a lady deer and turkey hunter.

Grinnell, George Bird   1849-1938
>*Beyond the Old Frontier;* adventures of Indian-fighters, hunters and fur traders. Massachusetts, 1976, Corner House Publishers. 374 pp. An anthology of Grinnell's selected writings.
>*Summer Hunt;* the account of an 1872 buffalo surround. No place, 1971, The Pony Press. 19 pp., illustrations. Limited to 44 numbered copies signed by the printer, Maralyn Dettman. 8vo. Paper wrappers.

Grinnell, George Bird, et al., editors
>*Hunting and Conservation.* New York, 1970, Arno Press. Co-edited with Charles Sheldon. 548 pp., illustrations. The sixth Boone & Crocket Club book. Thick 8vo. (Originally published, 1925, Yale University Press)

Grinnell, George Bird, et al., continued

Hunting Trails on Three Continents. New York, 1933, The Derrydale Press. Co-edited with Kermit Roosevelt, W. Redmond Cross and Prentiss N. Gray. 302 pp., photographic plates. The seventh Boone & Crocket Club book. Limited to 250 numbered copies. 8vo; dust jacket. (Also concurrently published, same format and contents, but with no limitation, Windward House)

Mr. Grinnell is certainly one of the fathers of the modern conservation movement in America. He was an associate editor for *Forest and Stream* magazine, and together with Theodore Roosevelt and several others, founded The Boone & Crockett Club. His conservation writing was both prolific and authoritative. He also edited or co-edited the first five Boone & Crocket Club books. See Phillips.

Griswold, Frank Gray   1855-1937

After Thoughts; recollections of Frank Gray Griswold. New York, 1936, Harper & Brothers. 202 pp. 8vo; dust jacket. [Also a deluxe edition of 150 copies, specially illustrated by Gordon Stevenson, privately printed at the Plimpton Press] Mr. Griswold's autobiography with much on angling, some on foxhunting and a commentary on the New York scene. It also contains a listing of the author's books.

The Horse and Buggy Days. Norwood, Massachusetts, 1936, Privately printed. 160 pp., frontispiece. 8vo.

Horses and Hounds. New York, 1926, E. P. Dutton & Co. 275 pp., color frontispiece and other black and white illustrations. Limited to 300 copies. 12mo.

The Memoirs of Diana Grisdale - MFH. Norwood, Massachusetts, 1932, Privately printed. 140 pp., bibliography of books by the author. 12mo. The story of an English girl who grew up to be a lady of society.

Plantation Days. Norwood, Massachusetts, 1935, Privately printed. 116 pp. 12mo. Contains one chapter with hunting.

Sport on Land and Water. Volume I. Norwood, Massachusetts, 1913, Privately printed. 163 pp., illustrated. 8vo.

Sport on Land and Water. Volume II. Norwood, Massachusetts, 1915, Privately printed. 152 pp., illustrated. 8vo.

Sport on Land and Water. Volume III. Norwood, Massachusetts, 1916, Privately printed. 143 pp., illustrated. 8vo.

Sport on Land and Water. Volume IV. Norwood, Massachusetts, 1917, Privately printed. 132 pp., illustrated. 8vo.

Sport on Land and Water. Volume V. Norwood, Massachusetts, 1920, Privately printed. 174 pp., illustrated. 8vo.

Sport on Land and Water. Volume VI. Norwood, Massachusetts, 1923, Privately printed. 182 pp., illustrated. 8vo.

Griswold, Frank Gray, continued

Sport on Land and Water. Volume VII. Norwood, Massachusetts, 1931, Privately printed. 143 pp., illustrated. 8vo. These seven volumes cover many aspects of sport, including, polo, steeplechasing, foxhunting and much on angling.

Mr. Griswold was a man of diverse interests who was financially able to cultivate the activities he enjoyed. His primary interests in sport were in horses and angling; his works on salmon fishing are important. See Bruns. He also wrote the following non-sporting books:

Clipper Ships and Yachts.	1927, E. P. Dutton & Co.
El Greco.	1929, The Derrydale Press
El Greco.	1930, Privately printed
Fra Filippo Lippi.	1934, Privately printed by E. P. Dutton & Co.
French Wines and Havana Cigars.	1929, Privately printed by E. P. Dutton & Co.
General Lewis Cass.	1916
The Gourmet.	1933, Privately printed by E. P. Dutton & Co.
The House Flags of the Merchants of New York.	1926, Privately printed.
The International Polo Cup.	1928, Privately printed by E. P. Dutton & Co.
The Kittens.	1916
Old Madeiras.	1929, Privately printed by E. P. Dutton & Co.
Race Horses and Racing.	1925, Privately printed.
Stolen Kisses.	1914

Grogan, Hiram J.

Modern Bow Hunting. Harrisburg, 1958, The Stackpole Company. 183 pp., photographic plates. 8vo; dust jacket.

Grollier Club

Six Hundred Years of Sport. New York, 1940, The Grollier Club. 37 pp. Foreword by Robert Henderson. Limited to 500 copies. 12mo. Paper wrappers. A catalog of an exhibition of sporting books displayed by this prestigious book collecting organization.

Grooms, Steve

Modern Pheasant Hunting. Harrisburg, 1982, The Stackpole Company. 222 pp., photographic plates. 8vo; dust jacket. (Reprinted 1984, in paper wrappers, same publisher)

Gross, Alfred O.

The Heath Hen. Boston, 1928, Natural History Society. 98 pp., frontispiece in color by L. A. Fuertes, bibliography. Folio. Paper wrappers.

Grossman, Mary Louise and John Hamlet

Birds of Prey of the World. New York, 1964, C. N. Potter. 496 pp., color and black and white illustrations, bibliography. Folio; dust jacket.

Groth, John

John Groth's World of Sport. New York, 1970, Winchester Press. 152 pp., color and black and white illustrations by Groth. Foreword by Arnold Gingrich. Text by Pat Smith. Oblong folio; dust jacket. Groth was a popular illustrator of the period.

Grouse, G. (*pseud.* of **Gorham L. Cross**)

Partride Shortnin;' being an instructive and irreverent sketch, commentary on the psychology, foibles and footwork of partridge hunters. Wellesley Hills, Massachusetts, 1949, Privately printed. Unpaginated (approx. 200 pp.), photographic plates. Limited to 100 copies. 8vo. Recounting tales of grouse, duck and woodcock hunting, and with some salmon and muskie fishing in the St. Lawrence river.

Groves, Earl

Talking Tomfoolery; with expert commentary by Ben Rogers Lee. No place, 1977, Privately printed. 101 pp., photographic plates. 8vo. Paper wrappers. Turkey hunting.

Groves, Lemuel R.

Northern Lights; sketches and songs of the huntsman's paradise. Boston, 1949, John W. Luce Co. 91 pp., illustrations. 8vo; dust jacket. Tales of Maine with much hunting and fishing.

Grubar, Francis S.

William Ranney; painter of the early West. New York, 1962, C. N. Potter. 65 pp. text plus an unpaginated (approx. 65 pp.) section of illustrations; color frontispiece. 8vo; dust jacket. Mr. Ranney was a popular western and sporting artist of the mid-twentieth century.

Gruber, Frank

Zane Grey. Roslyn, New York, 1969, Walter J. Black. 284 pp., photographic plates. 12mo. (Reprinted 1975, same format and publisher. Also reprinted 1970, Belmont Tower Books) A bibliography of Grey's work.

Gulliver, Joe

Gulliver Travels Again. No date (ca. 1978), Privately printed. 61 pp. Limited to 100 copies. 8vo. The author's reminiscences with much fishing and some duck hunting.

Grusendorf, W. F.

Fifty Years of White-Tailed Deer Hunting in Texas. New York, 1961, Vantage Press. 79 pp., photographic plates. 8vo; dust jacket. Scarce.

Grzimek, Bernhard

Wild Animals, White Man; some wildlife in Europe, Soviet Russia and North America. New York, 1966, Hill and Wang. 360 pp., color and black and white illustrations. 8vo; dust jacket. (Also a 1966 British edition) A report on the scarcer game animals of these regions.

Guggisberg, C. A. W.

Early Wildlife Photographers. New York, 1977, Taplinger Publishing Company. 128 pp., photographic plates and drawings. 8vo; dust jacket.

Wild Cats of the World. New York, 1975, Taplinger Publishing Company. 328 pp., photographic plates and drawings. 8vo; dust jacket. (Also a 1975 British edition)

Gullion, Gordon

Improving Your Forested Lands For Ruffed Grouse. Rochester, 1972, Ruffed Grouse Society. 34 pp., photographic plates. 4to. Paper wrappers.

Gullion, Gordon and Tom Martinson

Grouse of the North Shore. Oshkosh, Wisconsin, 1984, Willow Creek Press. 144 pp., photographs in color, bibliography. 4to. A natural history of the species in Minnesota.

Gunther, Jack Disborn and Charles O. Disborn

The Identification of Firearms. New York, 1935, John Wiley & Son. 342 pp., illustrations. 8vo; dust jacket.

Guyette, Dale and Gary Guyette

Decoys of Maritime Canada. Exton, Pennsylvania, 1983, Schiffer Publishing Company. 204 pp., black and white and color photographs. 4to; dust jacket.

Hacker, Rick

The Muzzleloading Hunter; being a complete guide for the black powder sportsman. Tulsa, 1981, Winchester Press. 282 pp., photographic plates, drawings. 8vo; dust jacket.

Hadwen, S. and L. J. Palmer

Reindeer in Alaska. Seattle, 1967, Shorey Publishing Company. 70 pp., photographic plates. Limited to 100 copies. 8vo. (A facsimile reproduction of the 1922 edition) A study of the introduction of domesticated reindeer into Alaska.

Hagel, Bob

Game Loads and Practical Ballistics For the American Hunter. New York, 1978, Alfred A. Knopf, Inc. 315 pp., illustrations. 8vo; dust jacket. (Reprinted, same format and publisher)

Hagerbaumer, David and Sam Lehman

Selected American Game Birds. Caxton, Idaho, 1972, Caxton Printers, Ltd.. 26 color plates, each with an accompanying page of text. Square 4to; dust jacket. (Reprinted, 1973 and 1980, same format and publisher) [Also a specially bound, limited first edition of 190 copies, signed and remarqued by both artists; slipcased] A most attractive book.

Hagie, Clarence Edwin   b. 1886

The American Rifle; for hunting and target shooting. New York, 1944, The Macmillan Company. 174 pp., illustrations. 8vo; dust jacket. (Reprinted several times, same format and publisher)

How To Hunt North American Big Game. New York, 1946, The Macmillan Company. 195 pp., photographic plates, drawings. Tall 8vo; dust jacket.

Haid, D.

Decoys of the Mississippi Flyway. Exton, Pennsylvania, 1981, Schiffer Publishing Company. 272 pp., color illustrations. 4to; dust jacket.

Haig-Brown, Roderick   1908-1976

Allison's Fishing Birds. Vancouver, 1980, Colophon. 35 pp., illustrations. 8vo; dust jacket. [Also a deluxe edition, specially bound and illustrated and limited to 25 numbered copies] This title was published posthumously by Valerie Haig-Brown, the author's daughter.

Ki-Yu; a story of a panther. Boston, 1934, Houghton Mifflin Company. 214 pp., drawings by Kurt Weise. 8vo; dust jacket. (Also a 1946 edition titled, *Panther*)

Haig-Brown, Roderick, continued

The Living Land; an account of the natural resources of British Columbia. Toronto, 1961, The Macmillan Company. 269 pp., color and black and white illustrations by Tommy Brayshaw and K. C. Smith, photographic plates, fold-out map. 8vo; dust jacket. [Also a deluxe edition, specially bound and limited to 1250 numbered copies signed by the author]

Measure of the Year. New York, 1950, William Morrow & Co., Inc. 260 pp. 8vo; dust jacket. (Also a 1950 Canadian edition) A collection of Haig-Brown's essays.

Mounted Police Patrol. New York, 1954, William Morrow & Co., Inc. 248 pp. 8vo; dust jacket. A juvenile.

The Salmon. Ottawa. 1974, Environment Canada, Fisheries and Marine Service. 79 pp., illustrations in color, maps. Folio.

Saltwater Summer. New York, 1948, William Morrow & Co., Inc. 256 pp., frontispiece in color. 8vo; dust jacket. A juvenile.

Starbuck Valley Winter. New York, 1943, William Morrow & Co., Inc. 310 pp. 8vo; dust jacket. (Reprinted several times, same format and publisher. Also a 1944 British edition) A juvenile novel of two young boys' hunting, fishing and trapping experiences.

The Whale People. London, 1962, Collins. 184 pp., drawings by Mary Weiler. 8vo; dust jacket. (Also a 1963 U. S. edition, William Morrow & Co., Inc.) A juvenile novel of a Nootka Indian boy growing up in the traditional way of his people.

Woods and River Tales; from the world of Roderick Haig-Brown. Toronto, 1981, McClelland & Stewart. 202 pp. Edited by Valerie Haig-Brown. 8vo; dust jacket. An anthology of Haig-Brown's works, most of which were previously unpublished.

Writings and Reflections; from the world of Roderick Haig-Brown. Toronto, 1982, McClelland & Stewart. 222 pp. Edited by Valerie Haig-Brown. 8vo; dust jacket. (Also printed, 1982, University of Washington Press)

A native of British Columbia, Mr. Haig-Brown was an outspoken conservationist who wrote extensively about many aspects of the subject. His notoriety as an author however, is mostly due to his angling books. His fly-fishing books are all important works, especially *The Western Angler*, originally published by The Derrydale Press in 1939. See Bruns for the author's angling works. He also wrote three novels and three histories for young readers with incidental mention of hunting or fishing:

Pool and Rapid	1932, A. & C. Black
The Tall Trees Fall (later printed as *Timber*)	1943, Collins
On the Highest Hill	1949, William Morrow & Co., Inc.
Captain of the Discovery	1956, The Macmillan Company
The Farthest Shores	1960, Longman's, Green
Fur and Gold	1962, Longman's, Green

Haig-Brown, Roderick

Also see **Robertson, Anthony**

Haight, Austin D.
The Biography of a Sportsman. New York, 1939, Thomas Y. Crowell Company. 209 pp., illustrations by Arthur D. Fuller. 8vo; slipcase. Much on upland hunting.

Haines, Donal Hamilton   b. 1886
Luck in All Weathers; personal adventures in hunting and fishing. New York, 1941, Farrar & Rinehart, Inc. 290 pp., illustrations by Ralph Boyer. 8vo; dust jacket. Much on upland game birds and waterfowl.
Sporting Chance. New York, 1935, Farrar, Straus and Company, Inc. 290 pp., drawings by Ralph Boyer. 8vo; dust jacket. A scarce novel with much fishing and hunting.

Haines, John
Of Traps and Snares. No place, 1981, Privately printed by the author. 46 pp. 8vo. Paper wrappers. The author recounts his trapping experiences in Alaska.

Haines, Francis
The Buffalo. New York, 1970, Thomas Y. Crowell Company. 242 pp., illustrations. 8vo; dust jacket. An account of the American Bison from prehistoric times to the present.

Hall, E. Raymond
American Weasels. Lawrence, 1951, University of Kansas Press. 458 pp., photographic plates, maps, bibliography. 8vo. Paper wrappers.

Hall, G. Harper
Great Moments in Action; the story of the Sun Life falcons. Montreal, 1955, Mercury Press. 36 pp., illustrations. 12mo. Paper wrappers. The story of nesting peregrine falcons atop the Sun Life Building in Montreal.

Hall, Maj. George
Sometime Again. Seattle, 1945, Superior Publishing Company. 218 pp., drawings. 8vo; dust jacket. The author relates his experiences while he was stationed in Alaska; with two chapters on sheep hunting.

Hall, Henry Marion   b. 1877
A Gathering of Shorebirds. New York, 1960, The Devin-Adair Company. 242 pp., drawings by J. H. Dick, bibliography. 4to; dust jacket. (Reprinted, same format, Bramhall) Covering all species of North and South American shore birds.
The Ruffed Grouse. New York, 1946, Oxford University Press. 91 pp., color and black and white illustrations by Ralph Ray. 4to; dust jacket.
Woodcock Ways. New York, 1946, Oxford University Press. 84 pp., color and black and white illustrations by Ralph Ray. 4to; dust jacket.

Hall, (Frederick) Leonard   b. 1899
  A Journal of the Seasons on an Ozark Farm.   Columbia, 1980, University of Missouri Press.   208 pp., illustrations.   8vo; dust jacket.   Containing a wistful account of a deer hunting camp in the Ozarks.   This was probably a revised edition of *Possum Trot Farm*, by the same author.
  Possum Trot Farm; an Ozark journal.   St. Louis, 1949, The Caledonia Press.   166 pp., illustrations by George Conrey.   Limited to 2500 copies.   8vo; dust jacket.   Containing hunting and fishing.
  Stars Upstream; life along an Ozark river.   Chicago, 1958, University of Chicago Press.   252 pp., photographic plates.   Foreword by Ira Gabrielson.   8vo; dust jacket.   A discussion of the Current River, with considerable mention of game animals.

Hall, Roberta A. and Henry S. Sharp, editors
  Wolf and Man; evolution in parallel.   New York, 1978, Academic Press.   210 pp., photographic plates, drawings.   8vo; dust jacket.

Hallock, Ken
  Hallock's .45 Automatic Handbook.   Oklahoma City, 1981, Privately printed.   Second printing.   178 pp., photographic plates.   8vo.   Paper wrappers.

Hallowell, Christopher
  People of the Bayou; Cajun life in lost America.   New York, 1979, E. P. Dutton & Co., Inc.   141 pp., drawings.   8vo; dust jacket.   Hunting, fishing and trapping in the delta area of Louisiana.

Halls, Lowell K., editor
  White Tailed Deer; ecology and management.   Harrisburg / Washington, D. C., 1984, The Stackpole Company / Wildlife Management Institute.   870 pp., color and black and white illustrations.   4to; dust jacket.   A most thorough reference.

Halmi, Robert
  In the Wilds of North America.   New York, 1971, Four Winds Publishing Company.   127 pp., photographic plates.   8vo; dust jacket.   Primarily containing descriptions of game animals.

Halpin, Warren T.
  Hoofbeats; drawings and comments.   Philadelphia, 1938, J. B. Lippincott Co.   Unpaginated (approx. 300 pp.), drawings by the author.   Limited to 1500 copies.   4to; boxed.   [Also a deluxe edition, specially bound and illustrated and limited to 150 numbered and signed copies; boxed]   A book of equestrian sport - polo, steeplechasing and foxhunting.

Halsted, Homer
> *How To Live in the Woods*.   Boston, 1948, Little, Brown & Company. 249 pp., illustrations.   12mo; dust jacket.

Hambleton, Jack
> *Hunter's Holidays*.   Toronto, 1947, Longmans, Green & Co.   207 pp., illustrations.   8vo; dust jacket.   Hunting small and big game in Ontario, with a chapter on archery.

Hamerstrom, Frances
> *Strictly For the Chickens*.   Ames, 1980, Iowa State University.   174 pp., photographic plates, drawings by Elva Hamerstrom Paulson.   8vo; dust jacket.   The author and her husband were wildlife biologists that devoted their careers to studying the prairie chicken of central Wisconsin

Hamilton, C. V.
> *Center Fire Metallic Rifle Cartridges; 1860-1960*.   Celina, Ohio, No date (1962), Privately printed.   26 pp. 4to.   Paper wrappers.

Hamilton, William J.
> *Life Histories and Economic Relations of the Opossum in New York State*.   Ithaca, New York, 1958, Cornell University Press.   48 pp., photographic plates, bibliography.   8vo.   Paper wrappers.

Hamlin, Benjamin Nason   b. 1870
> *Drifting Along;* with tales of past and present happenings.   Norwood, Massachusetts, 1939, Privately printed.   127 pp. 8vo.   With some foxhunting in New England.
> *In Sunshine and Shade;* stories of various entertaining incidents. Dedham, Massachusetts, 1946, Privately printed.   162 pp. 8vo.   Contains some duck and turkey hunting and some angling.
> *Such Jolly Years*.   Dedham, Massachusetts, 1937, Privately printed. 279 pp.   8vo.   With some foxhunting in New England, duck and turkey hunting in South Carolina.
> *Yarns of Today and Yesteryear*.   Milton, 1950, Privately printed.   100 pp. 8vo.   Paper wrappers.   Contains one chapter on foxhunting in New England.

Hamlin, Helen
> *Nine Mile Bridge;* three years in the Maine woods.   New York, 1945, W. W. Norton & Co., Inc.   233 pp., illustrations.   8vo; dust jacket.   The story of a game warden's wife in the Allagash region of Maine.
> *Pine, Potatoes and People;* the story of Aroostook.   New York, 1948, W. W. Norton & Co., Inc.   238 pp., illustrations.   8vo; dust jacket.   A collection of sketches of the people and geography of Aroostook County, Maine, with incidental mention of hunting.

Hammond, Ralph B. and Robert Hammond
  Training and Hunting the Brittany Spaniel. New York, 1971, A. S. Barnes and Company, Inc. 166 pp., photographic plates. 8vo; dust jacket. (Reprinted and revised several times, same format and publisher)

Hammond, Samuel H.   1809-1878
  Wild Northern Scenes. New York, 1967, Abercrombie & Fitch, Inc. 341 pp., plates form old engravings. 12mo; dust jacket. (A facsimile reproduction of the 1857 Derby and Jackson edition)

Hammond, Stephen Tillinghast   b. 1831
  My Friend the Partridge. Auburn Hills, Michigan, 1985, Gunnerman Books. 148 pp., illustrations. 16mo. (Originally published, 1908, Forest & Stream Publishing Company)

Hancock, Ralph, et al.
  Baja California; hunting, fishing and travel in lower California, Mexico. Los Angeles, 1953, Academy Publishers. 179 pp., illustrations. 8vo; dust jacket. (Reprinted 1954, same format and publisher)

Handley, Charles O.
  Wild Mammals of Virginia. Richmond, 1947, Commonwealth of Virginia Game and Fish Commission. 220 pp., photographic plates, maps, bibliography. 8vo.

Hanenkrat, William Frank
  The Education of a Turkey Hunter. New York, 1974, Winchester Press. 216 pp., illustrations by J. M. Roever. 8vo; dust jacket.

Hanenkrat, William Frank
  Also see **Pullum, Bill**

Hanger, George
  To All Sportsmen and Particularly To Farmers and Gamekeepers, etc. Richmond, Virginia, 1971, Richmond Publishing Company. 226 pp. 8vo. (A reproduction of the 1814 edition) Covers hunting various species of game, training horses, care of dogs, etc.

Hankwitz, Reed
  Your English Springer Spaniel. Fairfax, Virginia, 1973, Denlinger's. 160 pp., illustrations. 8vo.

Hanley, Wayne

    Natural History in America; from Mark Catesby to Rachel Carson. New York, 1977, Quadrangle Books. 339 pp., color and black and white illustrations. 8vo; dust jacket. With much biographical information on all of the most noted American conservationists.

Hanlon, J. E.

    Memorable Hunting Episodes. No place, 1966, Privately printed. 64 pp., drawings. Limited to 100 numbered and signed copies. 8vo. Cloth backed paper wrappers. A scarce grouse hunting title.

Hanna, Warren L.

    The Grizzlies of Glacier. Missoula, Montana, 1978, Mountain Press. 154 pp., photographic plates, bibliography. 8vo. Paper wrappers.

Hanrahan, Gene Z., editor

    The Wild Years: Ernest Hemingway. New York, 1972, Dell Paperbacks. 288 pp., frontispiece, including 7 pp. of sources. 16mo. Paper wrappers. A scarce bit of Hemingway biography that is a compilation of articles appearing in the *Toronto Star* between 1920-1924.

Hanson, Charles E., Jr.

    The Plains Rifle. Harrisburg, 1960, The Stackpole Company. 171 pp., photographic plates, drawings. Tall 8vo; dust jacket.

Hanson, Harold C.   b. 1917

    The Giant Canada Goose. Carbondale, Illinois, 1965, Southern Illinois University Press. 226 pp., photographic plates. 4to; dust jacket. Prior to the time of this publication, this sub-species was thought to have become extinct. This work describes its re-discovery in Rochester, Minnesota. It is interesting that this sub-species has now reproduced to such an extent that it has become a nuisance in much of the eastern and mid-western U. S.

Hanson, Harold C. and Robert L. Jones

    The Biochemistry of Blue, Snow and Ross' Geese. Carbondale, Illinois, 1976, Southern Illinois University Press. 281 pp., photographic plates, maps, bibliography. 4to; dust jacket.

Hanson, Harold C. and Charles W. Kossack

    The Mourning Dove in Illinois. Carbondale, Illinois, 1963, Illinois Department of Conservation. 133 pp., photographic plates in color and black and white, maps, bibliography. 4to. Paper wrappers.

Hanson, Harold C. and Robert H. Smith

    Canada Geese of the Mississippi Flyway; with special reference to an Illinois flock. Urbana, Illinois, 1950, Illinois Natural History Survey Bulletin. 210 pp., illustrations. 4to. Paper wrappers. (Also published as Volume 25, Article 3 of the survey in an edition of 146 pp.)

Hanson, Henry A., et al.

    The Trumpeter Swan in Alaska. Washington, D. C., 1971, The Wildlife Society. 83 pp., photographic plates. 4to. Paper wrappers.

Hanson, James A. and Kathryn J. Wilson.

    The Mountain Man's Sketch Book, Volume I. Chadron, 1980, Fur Press. 48 pp., drawings. 8vo. Paper wrappers.

    The Mountain Man's Sketch Book, Volume II. Chadron, 1982, Fur Press. 48 pp., drawings. 8vo. Paper wrappers. Each of these works provide illustrations regarding equipment, traps, firearms, etc. Unusual.

Hanson, Maurice F. b. 1907

    Pierpont the Foxhound. New York, 1939, Charles Scribner's Sons. Unpaginated (40 pp.), illustrations by D. T. Carlisle. 4to; dust jacket. A cartoon story of a foxhound.

Hanson, W. C.

    A Columbia River Canada Goose Population, 1950-1970. Washington, D. C., 1971, The Wildlife Society. 61 pp., illustrations. 4to. Paper wrappers.

Harben, Frank P.

    Hunting Wild Turkey in the Everglades. Safety Harbor, Florida, 1982, Harben Publishing Co. 341 pp., photographic plates. 8vo. Paper wrappers.

Harbour, Lt. Col. Dave

    Advanced Wild Turkey Hunting and World Records. Piscataway, New Jersey, 1983, Winchester Press. 284 pp., photographic plates. 4to; dust jacket.

    The Flying Sportsman. New York, 1952, A. S. Barnes and Company, Inc. 122 pp., photographic plates. A title in The Sportsman's Library series. 8vo; dust jacket.

    Hunting the American Wild Turkey. Harrisburg, 1975, The Stackpole Company. 256 pp., photographic plates, diagrams. 8vo; dust jacket.

    Modern ABC's of Bird Hunting. Harrisburg, 1966, The Stackpole Company. 191 pp. 8vo; dust jacket.

Harding, Arthur Robert, editor   b. 1871

Deadfalls and Snares. Columbus, Ohio, 1935, A. R. Harding.   218 pp., photographic plates, drawings.   16mo.   (Originally published, 1902, same format and publisher)

Fox Trapping. Columbus, Ohio, 1934, A. R. Harding.   179 pp., photographic plates, drawings.   16mo.   (Originally published, 1906, same format and publisher)

Fur Farming.   Columbus, Ohio, 1936, A. R. Harding.   278 pp., photographic plates, drawings.   16mo.   (Originally published, 1909, same format and publisher)

Mink Trapping. Columbus, Ohio, 1934, A. R. Harding.   171 pp., photographic plates, drawings.   16mo.   (Originally published, 1906, same format and publisher)

Steel Traps. Columbus, Ohio, 1935, A. R. Harding.   333 pp., photographic plates, drawings.   16mo.   (Originally published, 1907, same format and publisher)

3001 Questions and Answers. Columbus, Ohio, 1941, A. R. Harding. 395 pp., photographic plates, drawings.   16mo.   (Originally published, 1913, same format and publisher)

The Trapper's Companion.   Columbus, Ohio, Various dates, A. R. Harding.   157 pp., photographic plates, drawings.   16mo. Paper wrappers. (Originally published, 1919, same format and publisher)

Wolf and Coyote Trapping.   Columbus, Ohio, 1937, A. R. Harding. 252 pp., photographic plates, drawings.   16mo.   (Originally published, 1909, same format and publisher)

These little books produced by Harding were cloth bound (unless noted otherwise) and were probably reprinted later, but were not identified as such. The entire series produced by Harding were inexpensive, informative outdoor guides.

Hardy, J. W. and C. A. McConnell

Bobwhite Quail Propagation, Conditioning, and Habitat Management. No place, 1967, Tennessee Game and Fish Commission.   54 pp., illustrations. Oblong 8vo.   Spiral bound paper wrappers.

Harlow, Richard F.

An Evaluation of White Tailed Deer Habitat in Florida.   No place, 1959, Florida Game and Fresh Water Fish Commission.   64 pp., photographic plates, bibliography.   4to.   Paper wrappers.

Harper, Francis   b. 1886

The Barren Ground Caribou of Keewatin. Lawrence, 1955, University of Kansas Press.   163 pp., photographic plates.   8vo.   Paper wrappers.

The Birds of the Ungava Peninsula.   Lawrence, 1958, University of Kansas Press.   171 pp., photographic plates, maps.   4to.   Paper wrappers. Some discussion of game birds of this northern Labrador region.

Harper, Francis, continued

Caribou Eskimos of the Upper Kazan River, Keewatin. Lawrence, 1964, University of Kansas Press. 74 pp., photographic plates, bibliography. 8vo. Paper wrappers. Mostly a study of the people of this region, but some of their hunting activities are discussed.

The Friendly Montagnais and Their Neighbors in the Ungava Peninsula. Lawrence, 1964, University of Kansas Press. 121 pp., photographic plates, bibliography. 8vo. Paper wrappers. Mostly a study of the people of this Labrador region, but some of their hunting activities are discussed.

Land and Fresh Water Mammals of the Ungava Peninsula. Lawrence, 1961, University of Kansas Press. 178 pp., photographic plates, maps, bibliography. 8vo. Paper wrappers. Including three species of bear, moose, etc.

The Mammals of Keewatin. Lawrence, 1956, University of Kansas Press. 94 pp., photographic plates. 8vo. Paper wrappers.

Harper, Jack

Bird Dogs and Field Trials; the story of a hall of fame breeder, handler and writer. Stigler, Oklahoma, 1983, Cass Hill, Inc., Publishers. 280 pp., photographic plates. Introduction by William F. Brown. 8vo. A privately printed work by this native of Benton, Mississippi.

Harper, James

Ecological Study Of Roosevelt Elk; progress report, January 1, 1963-May 30, 1966. Portland, 1966, Research Division, Oregon State Game Commission. 4to. Paper wrappers.

The Ecology of the Roosevelt Elk. Portland, 1971, Oregon State Game Commission. 44 pp., illustrations. 4to. Paper wrappers.

Harper, James A., et al.

The Status and Ecology of the Roosevelt Elk in California. Washington, D. C., 1967, The Wildlife Society. Monograph # 16. 49 pp., illustrated. 8vo. Paper wrappers.

Harriman, Gladys F.

B. C. in A. D. 1938. No place, No date (1938), Privately printed. 74 pp., photographic plates. 8vo. Describes a Canadian hunting expedition for goat, sheep, caribou, etc. Scarce.

A Journey of Adventure. Mexico - January, February, 1938. No place, No date (1938), Privately printed. 60 pp., photographic plates. 8vo. Paper wrappers. Mainly travel, but with some deer hunting and photographing wild sheep of the area. Scarce.

Mulligan. No place, No date (ca. 1940), Privately printed. 49 pp. 8vo. A rare work with bear, mountain goat and sheep hunting in North America.

Harrington, C. Richard

Denning Habits of the Polar Bear. Ottawa, 1968, Canadian Wildlife Service. 30 pp., photographic plates, maps. 4to. Paper wrappers.

Harrignton & Richardson Arms Co.

Fifty Prize Hunting Stories; a collection of true experiences with a shotgun. Worcester, Massachusetts, 1911, Harrington & Richardson Arms Co. 114 pp., illustrations. 12mo. Paper wrappers. (Reprinted 1929, cloth backed boards, same publisher) Containing an early Archibald Rutledge story, "Now Boy, Be a Good Sportsman." Not in Phillips.

Harris, Albert W.

Bring Your Dog. Chicago, 1954, Privately printed by Rand McNally & Company. 166 pp., photographic plates. 8vo. Hunting turkey, ducks, raccoon and mountain lion with dogs. Scarce

The Chesapeake Bay Retriever. Chicago, 1946, Privately printed. 84 pp., photographic plates. Tall 8vo. Paper wrappers (cover a color illustration by Edwin Megargee). A non-technical discussion of the breed. Scarce.

The Yellow Dog. Chicago, 1939, Privately printed. 136 pp., illustrations. 8vo. Contains some turkey hunting in the Ozarks.

Harris, R. P.

The Foxes. Boston, 1936, Houghton Mifflin Company. 240 pp. 8vo; dust jacket. A novel of foxhunting.

Harry, Bryan and Willard E. Dilley

Wildlife of Yellowstone and Grand Teton Parks. Salt Lake City, 1964, Wheelright. 56 pp., color illustrations. 8vo. Paper wrappers.

Harshman, "Blue Tick Bill"

Big N' Blue. Missouri, 1946, Privately printed. 147 pp., illustrations. 8vo. Paper wrappers. (Reprinted 1960, Full Cry Walker Publishing Co.) Hunting for raccoon, mountain lion and bear with blue tick hounds.

Hart, Dennis and T. R. Mitchell

Quail and Pheasant Propagation. Washington, D. C., 1947, Wildlife Management Institute. 72 pp., illustrations. 8vo. Paper wrappers.

Hart, Ernest H.

This is the Weimaraner. Jersey City, New Jersey, 1965, TFH Publishers. 256 pp., photographic plates, bibliography. 8vo.

Hart, Scott

The Moon is Waning. New York, 1939, The Derrydale Press. 134 pp., illustrations from drawings by Edwin Megargee. Limited to 950 numbered copies. Tall 8vo. A novel with opossum hunting in Virginia.

Hart, Thomas

Some Early Philadelphia Sportsmen; or a few names to conjure with among old time Philadelphia worthies. Philadelphia, 1936, Privately printed. 16 pp., photographic plates. 8vo. Paper wrappers. Biographical sketches of noted anglers and foxhunters.

Hartley, Oliver

Hunting Dogs. Columbus, Ohio, 1937, A. R. Harding. 251 pp., photographic plates. Paper wrappers. 16mo. (Originally published, 1909, same format and publisher)

Hartman, Barney

Hartman on Skeet. Princeton, New Jersey, 1967, D. Van Nostrand Company, Inc. 143 pp., photographic plates. 8vo; dust jacket. (Reprinted 1973, A. S. Barnes and Company, Inc. Also a 1973 Canadian edition)

Hartman, Carl G.

Possums. Austin, 1952, University of Texas Press. 174 pp., photographic plates, drawings, bibliography. 4to; dust jacket. Covers ecology, habits and hunting.

Hartzler, Daniel

Arms Makers of Maryland. York, Pennsylvania, 1977, George Shumway. 312 pp. photographic plates. Folio; dust jacket.

Haskell, William S.

The American Game Protective and Propagation Association; a history. New York, 1937, The American Game Protective and Propagation Association. 67 pp., portraits. 8vo. A history of this conservation organization which was founded in 1911, and was the progenitor of the Wildlife Management Institute. A scarce work.

Hastings, Howard L. b. 1887

Animal Life in the Wilderness. New York, 1936, Cupples & Leon Company. 314 pp., color and black and white illustrations. Tall 8vo. An older juvenile with some North American big game discussed.

Hastings, MacDonald

Churchill's Game Shooting; the standard textbook of successful use of the shotgun. Harrisburg, 1967, The Stackpole Company. 252 pp., illustrations. 8vo; dust jacket. (Also a 1971 revised edition, same format and publisher. Both of these are essentially revisions of **Robert Churchill's**, *Churchill's Shotgun Book*, which see)

Game Book; sporting round the world. London, 1979, Michael Joseph. 173 pp., photographic plates. 8vo; dust jacket. Contains some North American hunting.

How To Shoot Straight. South Brunswick, New Jersey, 1970, A. S. Barnes and Company, Inc. 133 pp., photographic plates. 8vo; dust jacket. (Also a British edition)

The Other Mr. Churchill; a lifetime of shooting and murder. New York, 1963, Dodd, Mead & Co. 336 pp., photographic plates. 8vo; dust jacket. (Reprinted 1965, same format and publisher) The biography of Robert Churchill, shotgun manufacturer, shooting instructor and forensic arms expert.

Shooting-Why We Miss; questions and answers on the successful use of the shotgun. New York, 1977, David McKay Co. 78 pp., drawings. 8vo; dust jacket.

Mr. Hastings was a popular writer on both sides of the Atlantic, having written many mystery novels as well as sporting works. Mr. Hastings is also an expert on military history with both books and television broadcasting to his credit.

Hatch, Alden   1898-1975

Remington Arms; in American history. New York, 1956, Rinehart & Company, Inc. 359 pp., illustrations. 8vo; dust jacket. (Also a 1972 revised edition, Remington Arms Company)

Hatch, Alden and Foxhall Keene

Full Tilt; the sporting memoirs of Foxhall Keene. New York, 1938, The Derrydale Press. 170 pp., photographic plates, frontispiece in color. Limited to 950 numbered copies. 4to.

Hatcher, Maj. Julian Sommerville   1888-1963

The Book of the Garand. Washington, D. C., 1948, Infantry Journal Press. 292 pp., many illustrations, frontispiece of John C. Garand. 8vo; dust jacket. A detailed treatise on this military rifle.

Hatcher's Notebook. Harrisburg, 1947, The Military Service Publishing Company. 488 pp., many illustrations, frontispiece of the author. 8vo; dust jacket. (Revised and reprinted several times, same publisher) A general discussion of firearms and ballistics.

Pistols and Revolvers and Their Use. Marshallton, Delaware, 1927, Small Arms Technical Publishing Company. 399 pp., photographic plates, drawings. Tall 8vo; dust jacket.

Hatcher, Maj. Julian Sommerville, continued

    Textbook of Firearms Investigation; Identification and Evidence. Together with *Textbook of Pistols and Revolvers.* Plantersville, South Carolina, 1935, Small Arms Technical Publishing Company. Two volumes in one of 342 pp. and 533 pp., both with photographic plates. Thick 8vo; dust jacket. (Reprinted four times up to 1946, same format and publisher. Also a 1957 revised edition was written by Maj. Hatcher, Frank Jury and Jack Weller, The Stackpole Company)

    Textbook of Pistols and Revolvers. Marines, Onslow County, North Carolina, 1935, Small Arms Technical Publishing Company. 533 pp., photographic plates. 8vo; dust jacket.

Hatcher, Julian Sommerville, et al.

    Handloading. Washington, D. C., 1950, The National Rifle Association of America. 107 pp., illustrations. Handbook No. 1 of the N. R. A. Tall 12mo. Paper wrappers.

Hatt, Robert T.

    The Red Squirrel; its life history and habits, with special reference to the Adirondacks of New York and the Harvard Forest. Syracuse, 1929, Roosevelt Wild Life Annals. 146 pp., photographic plates, bibliography. 4to. Paper wrappers.   A detailed monograph of the species.

Haugen, Arnold O. and Harlan G. Metcalf

    Field Archery and Bowhunting. New York, 1963, The Ronald Press. 213 pp., illustrations.

Hausman, Leon August

    Birds of Prey in Northeastern North America. New Brunswick, New Jersey, 1948, Rutgers University Press. 164 pp., illustrations from paintings by J. B. Abbot and George M. Sutton. 4to; dust jacket.

Haveless, David P.

    Derrydale Press Price Guide. Brooklyn, Connecticut, 1975, Privately printed. 18 pp. 8vo. Paper wrappers.   An early attempt at producing a price guide for this sporting book publisher's titles.

Haven, Charles Tower   1904-1954

    A Comprehensive Small Arms Manual. For state guards, regular police departments, auxiliary police departments, coast guards auxiliaries, plant guards and civilians. New York, 1943, William Morrow & Co., Inc. 159 pp., photographic plates, drawings. 12mo; dust jacket. (Reprinted, same format and publisher)

Haven, Charles Tower, continued

Shooting Muzzle Loading Handguns. Falmouth, Massachusetts, 1947, Guns Inc. 132 pp., photographic plates; frontispiece. Tall 8vo; dust jacket.

Haven, Charles Tower and Frank A. Belden

A History of the Colt Revolve; and other arms made by Colt's Patent Fire Arms Manufacturing Company from 1836 to 1940. New York, 1940, William Morrow & Co., Inc. 711 pp., many photographic plates. 4to; dust jacket. (Reprinted, Bonanza) The first comprehensive book on the subject.

Hawbaker, Stanley

How To Trap and Use Lure and Bait For Greater Profit. Fort Louden, 1951, Privately printed. 32 pp., illustrations. 18mo. Paper wrappers.

Professional Mink Trapping Methods; description, habits, food, equipment, lures, professional trapping methods. No place, 1953, Privately printed. 93 pp., photographic plates, drawings by Ned Smith. 12mo. Paper wrappers.

Red and Gray Foxes and How To Trap Them. No place, 1969, Privately printed. Second edition. 44 pp., photographic plates, drawings. 12mo. Paper wrappers.

Trapping North American Furbearers. Ft. Louden, 1944, Privately printed. 216 pp., illustrations. Soft fabric wrappers. (Reprinted several times, same format and publisher)

Trapping and Trailing. No place, 1938, Privately printed. 60 pp., illustrations. 8vo. Paper wrappers.

Hawes, Harry B.

Fish and Game; now or never, a challenge to American sportsmen on wild life restoration. New York, 1935, D. Appleton-Century Company, Inc. 332 pp., photographic plates. 8vo; dust jacket. An important early conservation title.

Hawkins, A. S., editor

Flyways; pioneering waterfowl management in North America. Washington, D. C., 1984, United Stated Department of the Interior. 517 pp., photographic plates, drawings by H. Albert Hochbaum. 4to. A history of waterfowl management in North America.

Hayes, Tom

Hunting Whitetail Deer. New York, 1960, A. S. Barnes and Company, Inc. 256 pp., illustrations. 8vo; dust jacket. (Also a 1966 revised edition, same format and publisher. Also a 1977 third revised edition, titled *How To Hunt the Whitetail Deer*)

Hayes, Tom, continued
    The Modern Hunting Rifle. New York, 1964, A. S. Barnes and Company, Inc. 304 pp., illustrations. 8vo; dust jacket. (Reprinted 1966, same format and publisher)

Haynes, Bessie D. and Edgar Haynes, editors
    The Grizzly Bear; portraits in life. Norman, 1966, University of Oklahoma Press. 386 pp., drawings by Mary Baker. 8vo; dust jacket. (Reprinted several times, same format and publisher) An anthology of stories written by Roosevelt, Seton, Dobie and others.

Haynes, William Barber
    Goose and Duck Shooting San Antonio, 1961, The Naylor Company. 67 pp., photographic plates. 8vo; dust jacket. The author also wrote a book with this same title in 1924. The 1961 edition differs substantially form the earlier work.

Hayward, J. F.
    The Art of the Gunmaker, Volume I, 1500 -1660. New York, 1962, St. Martin's Press. 303 pp., plus 64 pp. of color and black and white plates. 8vo.
    The Art of the Gunmaker, Volume II, 1620 -1830. New York, 1963, St. Martin's Press. 379 pp., plus 50 pp. of color and black and white plates. 8vo.

Hazelton, William Chester, editor   1868-1951
    Classic Hunting Stories; by America's premier writers. Chicago, 1940, William C. Hazleton. 154 pp., photographic plates. 12mo. Stories by Sheldon, Hazelton and others, illustrations include Simon Everitt in a turkey blind.
    Days Among the Ducks. Chicago, 1938, William C. Hazelton. 160 pp., photographic plates, frontispiece. 8vo.
    Duck Shooting and Hunting Sketches. Chicago, 1943, William C. Hazelton. 128 pp., photographic plates. Mostly waterfowl hunting, but also woodcock, deer and buffalo.
    Supreme Duck Shooting Stories; premier narratives from famous ducking waters. Chicago, 1934, William C. Hazelton. 160 pp., photographic plates, drawings. 8vo; dust jacket. (Also a 1936 second edition, and a 1944 third edition, same format and publisher) Stories by Brown, Buckingham, Kimble and others.
    Mr. Hazelton published other waterfowling works prior to 1925 - see Phillips. Many of these were edited or written by him, but he also published titles by Bigelow, Haynes and Everitt. All his authored or published works are scarce. Several sources list Mr. Hazelton's year of birth as 1870, but 1868 is the year Mr. Hazelton listed as on his printer's union membership card (reference Ed Moxley).

Heacox, Cecil E.
    The Education of an Outdoorsman. New York, 1976, Winchester Press. 191 pp., illustrations by Wayne Trimm. 8vo; dust jacket.

Heacox, Cecil E., continued

The Gallant Grouse; all about the hunting and natural history of old Ruff. New York, 1980, David McKay Co. 182 pp., illustrations in black and white and in color by Wayne Trimm. 8vo; dust jacket. (Reprinted several times, same format and publisher)

Headley, Joel T.

The Adirondack, or, life in the woods. Harrison, New York, 1982, Harbor Hill Books. 461 pp., illustrations. 8vo; dust jacket. (Originally published, 1849, Baker and Scribner) Describing early hunting, angling and camping in the region.

Heady, Ray

Hard Head I; and other outdoor stories. Kansas City, 1980, Lowell. 299 pp., illustrations. 8vo; dust jacket. Hunting and angling stories by this columnist for the *Kansas City Star.*

Heck, Lutz   b. 1892

Animals, My Adventure. London, 1954, Methuen. 170 pp., photographic plates. 8vo; dust jacket. The author was the director of the Berlin Zoo during World War II. With three chapters on hunting big game in North America.

Heilner, Van Campen   1899-1970

A Book on Duck Shooting. Philadelphia, 1939, Penn Publishing Company. 540 pp., photographic plates, color plates from paintings by Lynn Bogue Hunt. 8vo; dust jacket. (Reprinted several times, same format and publisher to 1940. Also reprinted several times to 1947, Alfred A. Knopf, Inc. as a title in Knopf's Borzoi Books For Sportsmen series. Also a 1951 British edition) [Also a deluxe first edition, specially bound and limited to 99 copies, numbered and signed by the author and artist, with an extra color plate; slipcased. Issued with an over-sized extra suite of plates] In 1992 and 1995 this title was also reprinted, a testament to its enduring qualities. A classic that stands beside Grinnell's *American Duck Shooting,* and Bruette's *American Duck, Goose and Brant Shooting.*

Our American Game Birds. New York, 1941, Doubleday & Co., Inc. 178 pp., drawings and color illustrations by Lynn Bogue Hunt. 4to; dust jacket. (Reprinted 1946, same format and publisher. Also reprinted 1949, G. C. Publishing Company)

Heinsohn, Lillian Britt   *Southern Plantation: The Story of "Labrah."* including some of its treasured recipes. New York, 1962, Hearthside Press. 286 pp., illustrations. 8vo; dust jacket. (Reprinted, Bonanza Books)

Heintz, William W.
   A Duck Hunter's Diary. Irvington, 1953, Sportsman's Press. Unpaginated (64 pp.), drawings, with blank leaves for entries. 8vo. Spiral bound paper wrappers.

Heintzelman, Arthur William
   Etchings and Drypoints of Frank W. Benson; Volume5. Boston, 1959, Houghton Mifflin Company. 98 pp., illustrations, signed original etching as a frontispiece. Foreword by Arthur William Heintzelman. Limited to 400 numbered copies. Folio; dust jacket. This, the last in a five volume set begun by **Adam Paff**, which see.

Heintzelman, Donald S.   b. 1938
   Autumn Hawk Flights; the migrations in eastern North America.. New Brunswick, 1975, Rutgers University Press. 398 pp., photographic plates, bibliography. 8vo; dust jacket. An authoritative account of all the species of North American migrating raptors.
   A Guide To Hawk Watching In North America. University Park, 1979, Pennsylvania State University Press. 284 pp., illustrations. 8vo.
   A Guide To Northeastern Hawk Watching. Lambertville, 1972, Privately printed. 64 pp., photographic plates, drawings, maps. 8vo. Paper wrappers.
   A Guide To Owl Watching In North America. Piscataway, New Jersey, 1984, Winchester Press. 193 pp., illustrations. 8vo; dust jacket.
   Hawks and Owls of North America; a complete guide to North American birds of prey. New York, 1979, Universe Books. 195 pp., color and black and white illustrations, bibliography. 4to; dust jacket.
   North American Ducks, Geese and Swans. New York, 1978, Winchester Press. 236 pp., black and white and color photographs. 4to; dust jacket. (Reprinted 1978, same format and publisher)

Held, John Jr.
   Danny Decoy. New York, 1942. Unpaginated, illustrations by the author. 8vo; dust jacket. A juvenile.
   John Held Jr.'s Dog Stories. New York, 1930, Vanguard Press. 124 pp., illustrations by the author. 8vo; dust jacket. Contains several hunting dog stories.

Held, Robert
   The Age of Firearms; a pictorial history. New York, 1957, Harper & Brothers. 192 pp., illustrations. Folio; dust jacket.

Held, Robert, editor
   Arms and Armor Annual, Volume I. Northfield, Illinois, 1973, Digest Books. 320 pp., illustrations. 4to. Paper wrappers.

Helgeland, Glenn, editor

Archery World's Complete Guide To Bowhunting. Englewood Cliffs, New Jersey, 1975, Prentice-Hall, Inc. 262 pp., illustrations. 8vo; dust jacket.

Heller, Eloise

A History of the Chesapeake Bay Retrievers. San Rafael, California, 1959, American Chesapeake Club. 107 pp., color and black and white photographic plates. Limited to 500 copies. 4to. (Also a 1967 edition, limited to 1000 copies, same format and publisher).

Retriever Trial Handbook. No place, 1961, Privately printed. 235 pp., illustrations by Mary Preston. 8vo. Paper wrappers.

Hellmayer, Charles and B. Conover

Catalog of Birds of America; Part 1, Number 4. Chicago, 1949, Field. 358 pp. 8vo. Paper wrappers. Covers among other species, hawks, falcons, eagles and vultures.

Catalog of Birds of America; Part 1, Number 2. Chicago, 1949, Field. 358 pp. 8vo. Paper wrappers. Covers among other species, ducks, geese and swans.

Catalog of Birds of America; Part 1, Number 3. Chicago, 1949, Field. 383 pp. 8vo. Paper wrappers. Covers among other species, snipe, woodcock and shorebirds.

Hellstrom, Carl R.

S & W, 100 Years of Gunmaking, 1852-1952. Springfield, Connecticut, 1952, Smith & Wesson, Inc. 32 pp., photographic plates. 8vo. Paper wrappers. (Reprinted 1952, Newcomen) A brief history of this firearms manufacturer.

Helmericks, Constance   1918-1987

Down The Wild River North. Boston, 1968, Little, Brown & Company. 501 pp., drawings. 8vo; dust jacket. An account of a canoe trip taken by the author and her two teen-age daughters down the Peace and Mackenzie rivers.

Hunting in North America. Harrisburg, 1956, The Stackpole Company. 298 pp., illustrations by Ned Smith. 8vo; dust jacket. (Reprinted 1959, same format and publisher)

Helmericks, Constance and Harmon Helmericks

The Flight of the Arctic Tern. Boston, 1952, Little Brown & Company. 321 pp., color frontispiece, photographic plates. 8vo; dust jacket. An account of the authors' travels by float plane through the arctic with much hunting of grizzly bear, caribou, moose, etc.

Our Alaskan Winter. Boston, 1949, Little, Brown & Company. 271 pp., illustrations. 8vo; dust jacket.

Our Summer With The Eskimos. Boston, 1948, Little, Brown & Company. 239 pp., color and black and white illustrations. 8vo; dust jacket.

Helmericks, Constance and Harmon Helmericks, continued
    We Live in Alaska.   New York, 1945.   266 pp., photographic plates.
8vo; dust jacket. (Also a 1945 British edition) Not listed in the Library of Congress.
    We Live in the Arctic. Boston, 1947, Little, Brown & Company. 329
pp., photographic plates. 8vo; dust jacket. A relatively scarce Helmericks title describing
this husband and wife team's hunting experiences, which were mostly from a subsistence viewpoint.

Helmericks, Harmon "Bud" b. 1917
    Arctic Bush Pilot. Boston, 1956, Little, Brown & Company. 180 pp.,
illustrations. 8vo; dust jacket.
    Arctic Hunter.   Boston, 1955, Little, Brown & Company. 142 pp.,
illustrations. 8vo; dust jacket.
    The Last of the Bush Pilots. New York, 1969, Alfred A. Knopf, Inc.
361 pp., photographic plates.   8vo; dust jacket. (Reprinted several times, same
format and publisher) The author was a bush pilot, guide and member of The Explorer's
Club.
    Oolak's Brother. Boston, 1953, Little, Brown & Company. 144 pp.,
illustrations by Henry Bugbee Kane. A novel of Eskimo life.

Helstrom, Henning
    *Henning's Fishing, Hunting and Vacation Guide To the Pacific
Northwest.* Portland, Oregon, 1969. 624 pp., illustrations, maps. 4to; dust
jacket. (Also reprinted in paper wrappers)

Hemingway, Ernest 1899-1961
    The Short Stories of Ernest Hemingway. New York, 1961, Charles
Scribner's Sons. 499 pp. 8vo; dust jacket.
    Many of this noted novelist's works had incidental mentioning of hunting and his *The
Green Hills of Africa* was an account of his African Safari. His Nick Adams stories had much on fly
fishing, and most regard his short story, "Big Two-Hearted River" among the best angling stories
ever written. See Bruns.

Hemingway, Ernest
    Also see **Hanrahan, Gene Z., editor**
    Also see **Hotchner, A. E.**
    Also see **Poore, Charles**
    Also see **Ross, Lillian**

Hemingway, Gregory H.
    Papa; a personal memoir. Boston, 1976, Houghton Mifflin Company.
119 pp., photographic plates. Preface by Norman Mailer. 12mo; dust jacket.
(Reprinted several times, same format and publisher)

Hemingway, Leicester

My Brother, Ernest Hemingway.   Cleveland, Ohio, 1962, World Publishing Company.   283 pp., photographic plates.   8vo; dust jacket. (Reprinted 1967, smaller format in paper wrappers, Fawcett Publications)

Hemingway, Mary Walsh

How It Was. New York, 1976, Alfred A. Knopf, Inc.   537 pp., photographic plates. 8vo; dust jacket.   A view of Hemingway's life from his wife.

Hendee, John C. and Clay Schoenfeld

Human   Dimensions   in   Wildlife   Programs; reports   of   recent investigations.   Washington, D. C., 1973, Wildlife Management Institute.   193 pp. 8vo . Paper wrappers.

Henderson, David H.

Covey Rises and Other Pleasures.   Clinton, New Jersey, 1983, Amwell Press.   155 pp., color frontispiece and other black and white illustrations by Shepard Foley.   8vo; dust jacket.   [Also a deluxe edition limited to 1000 numbered and signed copies; slipcased]

Henderson, Dion

Algonquin; the story of a great dog.   New York, 1953, Henry Holt & Company, Inc.   152 pp., illustrations by Edwin Schmidt.   8vo; dust jacket.   A novel about an English pointer, with much bird hunting.   Scarce.

Henderson, Elliott and Stewart C. Woodworth

Crows.   Cambridge, Massachusetts, 1960, Privately printed.   153 pp., photographic plates, drawings.   Limited to 200 numbered copies.   12mo.   Crow shooting in New England, written in 1924, but not published until 1960.

Henderson, Luis M.

The Outdoor Guide.   Harrisburg, 1950, Stackpole & Heck, Inc.   351 pp., illustrations.   Tall 8vo; dust jacket.

Henderson, Robert W.

Early American Sport; a chronological check-list of books published prior to 1860.   New York, 1937, The Grollier Club.   135 pp., illustrations. Limited to 400 copies.   4to.   (Also a 1953 second revised edition, A. S. Barnes and Company, Inc.   Also a 1977 third revised edition, Fairleigh Dickinson University Press)

Henry, Marguerite

Cinnabar, the one o'clock fox. Chicago, 1956, Rand McNally & Company.   154 pp., drawings by Wesley Dennis.   8vo; dust jacket.   A juvenile story with some foxhunting. Ms. Henry wrote many juveniles, mostly about horses.

Henry, Samuel J.

Foxhunting is Different. New York, 1938, The Derrydale Press. 170 pp., drawings by Paul Brown. Limited to 950 numbered copies. Tall 8vo.

The Old Days With Horse and Hound; being the story of the Chevy Chase Hunt, 1892-1916. 1960, Privately printed. 49 pp. Paper wrappers. A history of this Maryland foxhunting club.

Henschel, Stan

How To Raise and Train a Coonhound. Jersey City, New Jersey, 1964, TFH Publishers. 64 pp., illustrations. 8vo. Paper wrappers.

How To Raise and Train a Labrador Retriever. Jersey City, New Jersey, 1964, TFH Publishers. 64 pp., illustrations. 8vo. Paper wrappers.

Henson, Truman

Binoculars, Telescopes and Telescopic Sights. New York, 1955, Greenberg: Publishers. 515 pp. photographic plates, diagrams, charts. Thick 8vo; dust jacket.

Sporting Rifles and Scope Sights. New York, 1950, David McKay Co. 351 pp., illustrations. Tall 8vo; dust jacket.

Herbert, Henry William

See **Forester, Frank**

Hercules Powder Company

Skeet and Trapshooting. Wilmington, Delaware, 1934, Hercules Powder Company. 62 pp., illustrations. 8vo. Paper wrappers.

Herman, Steven G., et al.

A Beginners Manual of Falconry. Davis, California, 1965, California Hawking Club. Illustrations, glossary, bibliography. 4to. Paper wrappers.

Herrero, Stephen

Bear Attacks; their causes and deterrence. New York, 1985, Winchester Press / Nick Lyons Books. 288 pp. 8vo; dust jacket. (Reprinted many times, same format and publisher) A thorough study.

Herrick, Francis Hobart

The American Eagle; a study in natural history and civil history. New York, 1934, D. Appleton-Century Company, Inc. 267 pp., photographic plates. 8vo; dust jacket.

Hershberger, Mel

Professional System of Bobcat Trapping. No place, 1980, Privately printed. 42 pp., photographic plates. 8vo. Paper wrappers.

Hert, Carl

　　Tracking the Big Cats. Caldwell, Idaho, 1955, The Caxton Printers, Ltd. 380 pp., illustrations. 8vo; dust jacket. A scarce title with western U. S. hunting for mountain lion, wolf, bobcat, sheep and bear.

Herter, George Leonard

　　Complete Crow Calling Manual. Waseca, Minnesota, Herter's, Inc. 18 pp., drawings. 8vo Paper wrappers. (Reprinted many times, same format and publisher)

　　Herter's Complete Professional Duck and Goose Calling Manual. Waseca, Minnesota, 1948, Herter's, Inc. 26 pp., photographic plates and drawings. 8vo. Paper wrappers. (Revised and reprinted many times)

　　Herter's Guide To New and Used Gun Values. Waseca, Minnesota, 1969, Herter's, Inc. 224 pp. 8vo. Paper wrappers.

　　Professional Guide Condensed Information Booklet. Waseca, Minnesota, 1954, Herter's Inc. Fourth edition. 27 pp., illustrations. 8vo. Paper wrappers.

Herter, George Leonard and Berthe Herter

　　George the Housewife. Waseca, Minnesota, 1968, Herter's, Inc. Third revised edition. 606 pp., illustrations. 8vo. (Also a 1972 revised fourth edition, same format and publisher) A humorous look at the domestic life.

　　How To Get Out of the Rat Race and Live on $10 a Month. Waseca, Wisconsin, 1965, Herter's, Inc. 329 pp., photographic plates, plus a list of the Herter books. 8vo.

Herter, George Leonard and Jacques Herter

　　How To Reload Shotgun, Rifle and Pistol Shells. Waseca, Minnesota, 1966, Herter's, Inc. 107 pp., photographic plates. 8vo.

　　Professional Guide's Manual. Waseca, Minnesota, 1961, Herter's, Inc. 165 pp., illustrations. 8vo. (Reprinted many times, same format and publisher)

　　Professional Loading of Rifle, Pistol and Shotgun Cartridges and Reloading Data. Waseca, Minnesota, 1963, Herter's, Inc. 766 pp., illustrations. 8vo. Paper wrappers. (Reprinted many times, same format and publisher)

Herter, George Leonard and Myron E. Barrie

　　Herter's Professional Course in the Science of Modern Taxidermy. Waseca, Minnesota, 1967, Herter's, Inc. Revised, second edition. 382 pp., photographic plates, drawings. 8vo. (This revised edition reprinted many times)

Herter, George Leonard and Russell Hofmeister
Professional and Amateur Archery Tournament and Hunting Instructions and Encyclopedia. Waseca, Minnesota, 1963, Herter's, Inc. 227 pp., illustrations.
George Herter founded Herter's Inc., a mail-order firm specializing in hunting and fishing supplies. He wrote, and his firm published these works, others dealing in angling topics, and annual catalogs of their wares.

Hertzberg, Robert
The Modern Handgun. New York, 1965, Arco. 111 pp., illustrations. 8vo; dust jacket.

Hester, Bob
The Secrets of Decoying Ducks and Geese. Fairfield, 1982, Privately printed. 32 pp., color and black and white illustrations. 8vo. Paper wrappers.

Hester, F. E. and J. Dermid
The World of the Wood Duck. Philadelphia, 1973, J. B. Lippincott Co. 160 pp., photographic plates, bibliography. A title in Lippincott's Living World series. 4to; dust jacket.

Hetrick, Calvin
The Bedford County Rifle; and its makers. York, Pennsylvania, 1974, George Shumway. Second edition. 41 pp., photographic plates. 4to. Paper wrappers. (Originally published, 1959)

Heuser, Ken
The Whitetail Deer Guide. New York, 1972, Henry Holt and Company, Inc. 208 pp., drawings. 8vo; dust jacket.

Heusmann, H. W. and Robert Bellville
Wood Duck Research in Massachusetts, 1970-1980. Westborough, Massachusetts, 1982, Massachusetts Division of Fisheries and Wildlife. Bulletin 19. 67 pp., photographic plates, maps, charts. 8vo. Paper wrappers.

Hewitt, Edward Ringwood   1866-1957
Those Were the Days; tales of a long life. New York, 1943, Duell, Sloane & Pearce, Inc. 318 pp. 8vo; dust jacket. An autobiography containing some grouse hunting. Mr. Hewitt was a noted angling author, having written *Secrets of the Salmon* and other titles. See Bruns.

Hewitt, Oliver H., editor.
   The Wild Turkey and Its Management. Washington, D. C., 1967, The Wildlife Society. 589 pp., black and white and color illustrations from paintings by Fuertes, Sutton and others. Thick 8vo; dust jacket. A highly valued and most complete work.

Hibben, Frank C.   b. 1910
   Hunting American Bears. Philadelphia, 1950, J. B. Lippincott Co. 237 pp., drawings by Paul Bransom. 8vo; dust jacket.
   Hunting American Lions. New York, 1948, Thomas Y. Crowell Company. 225 pp., illustrations by Paul Bransom. 8vo; dust jacket. (Reprinted 1950, University of New Mexico Press)

Higginson, Alexander Henry   1876-1958
   An Old Sportsman's Memories, 1876 - 1951. Berryville, Virginia, 1951, Blue Ridge Press. 304 pp., illustrations. Foreword by J. Stanley Reeve. 8vo.
   British and American Sporting Authors; their writings and biographies. Berryville, Virginia, 1949, Blue Ridge Press. 443 pp., illustrated. With a bibliography by Sydney Smith. 4to; slipcased. (Reprinted 1951, New York and London, Hutchinson) Primarily regarding authors of foxhunting material, but some hunting and angling authors are included. An important work.
   Foxhunting; theory and practice. London / Berryville, Virginia, 1948, Collins / Blue Ridge Press. 256 pp., color frontispiece, photographic plates, bibliography. 8vo; dust jacket.
   A Fox That Walked On Water. London, 1939, Collins. 88 pp., color and black and white illustrations. 4to; dust jacket. U. S. and British foxhunting tales.
   Letters From an Old Sportsman To a Young One. Garden City, New York, 1929, Doubleday, Doran & Co., Inc. 249 pp., illustrations by Lionel Edwards. Limited to 1500 copies. 8vo; dust jacket. [Also a deluxe edition of 201 numbered and signed copies, with a signed Edwards print contained in an envelope on the rear end-panel]
   The Perfect Follower; a hunting tale of two continents. London, 1944, Collins. 94 pp. 8vo. With some North American foxhunting.
   Try Back; a huntsman's reminiscences. New York, 1931, Huntington Press. 227 pp., photographic plates; one color illustration. Limited to 401 numbered and signed copies. 4to; slipcased.
   Two Centuries of Foxhunting. London, 1946, Collins. 256 pp., photographic plates. 8vo. With much on the history of American foxhunting.

Higginson, Alexander Henry, editor
   As Hounds Ran; four centuries of foxhunting. New York, 1930, Huntington Press. 240 pp., drawings by Aldin and Edwards, color frontispiece. Limited to 990 numbered copies. 4to; slipcased. An anthology of foxhunting stories and poetry, mostly British, but some U. S.

Higginson, Alexander Henry and Julian Ingersol Chamberlain

The Hunts of The United States and Canada; their masters, hounds and histories. Boston, 1908, Frank L. Wiles. 197 pp., illustrations. 4to.

Hunting In the United States and Canada; being an illustrated history of each of the hunt clubs and individual packs on the North American continent and presenting first hand information of early colonial foxhunting, hitherto unpublished, as well as reproductions of portraits of early celebrities, the existence of which has not been known to hunting men. New York, 1928, Doubleday, Doran & Co., Inc. 369 pp., color frontispiece, photographic plates, five fold-out maps. Limited to 450 numbered copies signed by both authors. 4to.

Highsmith, Richard, Jr., et al.

Conservation in the United States. Chicago, 1962, Rand McNally & Company. 322 pp., illustrations. 4to; dust jacket. (Reprinted several times, same format and publisher) A college level text.

Hightower, John   b. 1901

Pheasant Hunting. New York, 1946, Alfred A. Knopf, Inc. 227 pp., photographic plates, color plates from paintings by Lynn Bogue Hunt. A title in the Borzoi Books For Sportsmen series. 8vo; dust jacket. [Also a large paper edition, specially bound and illustrated and limited to 350 numbered copies signed by the author and artist; slipcased]

Hill, F. Warner

Labradors. New York, 1966, Arco. 85 pp., illustrations. 8vo.

Hill, Gene   1928-1997

Hill Country. New York, 1978, E. P. Dutton & Co., Inc. 166 pp., illustrations by Tom Hennessey. 8vo; dust jacket. (Reprinted several times, same format and publisher) [Also a limited first edition co-published by E. P. Dutton & Co., Inc. and Amwell Press; specially bound and limited to 1000 numbered and signed copies; slipcased]

A Hunter's Fireside Book; tales of dogs, ducks, birds and guns. New York, 1972, Winchester Press. 162 pp., drawings by Milton C. Weiler. 8vo; dust jacket. (Reprinted many times, same format and publisher)

A Listening Walk; and other stories. Piscataway, New Jersey, 1985, Winchester Press. 208 pp., drawings by Tom Hennessey. 8vo; dust jacket. [Also a specially bound, Amwell Press limited edition of 1000 numbered copies signed by the author; slipcased]

Mostly Tailfeathers; stories about guns and dogs and birds and other odds and ends. New York, 1974, Winchester Press. 162 pp., illustrations by Gordon Allen. 8vo; dust jacket. (Reprinted 1975, same format and publisher) [Also a deluxe first edition limited to 475 numbered copies; slipcased]

Hill, Gene, continued

Tears and Laughter; a couple of dozen dog stories. Los Angeles, 1981, Peterson Publishing Company. 168 pp., drawings by Herb Strasser. 8vo; dust jacket.

For many years Mr. Hill wrote a monthly column in *Field & Stream* magazine called "Hill Country." He was also an associate editor at *Sports Afield* magazine, wrote several books after 1985 and made many other contributions to outdoor periodicals.

Hill, Gene and Steve Smith

Outdoor Yarns and Outright Lies; 50 or so stories by two good sports. Harrisburg, 1983, Stackpole Books. 183 pp., drawings. 8vo; dust jacket.

The Whispering Wings of Autumn. Clinton, New Jersey, 1981, Amwell Press. 168 pp., illustrations by William Schaldach. Limited to 1000 numbered copies signed by the authors; specially bound. 8vo; slipcased. (Also a 1982 trade edition, same format and publisher)

Hill, Gene

Also see **Maass, David**

Hill, Howard

Archery Adventures. No place, 1955, Trend Books #125. 128 pp., illustrations. 8vo. Paper wrappers. This is a reprint of portions of the author's *Hunting the Hard Way.*

Hunting the Hard Way. Chicago, 1953, Wilcox & Follet Company. 318 pp., photographic plates. 8vo; dust jacket. (Also a 1956 second printing, same format and publisher. Also a 1956 British edition, same content and format)
Describes the hunting exploits of this big game archery hunter.

My Way Of Shooting a Bow and Arrow. Los Angeles, No date (ca. 1952), Instinctors, Inc. 11 pp., photographic plates. Paper wrappers.

Wild Adventure. Harrisburg, 1954, The Stackpole Company. 228 pp., photographic plates. Foreword by Errol Flynn. 8vo; dust jacket. (Also two British editions in 1955 and 1959)

Hill, Howard

Also see **Ekin, Craig**.

Hill, Ralph Nading and Lillian Baker Carlisle

The Story of the Shelburne Museum. Shelburne, Vermont, 1955, Privately printed. 56 pp., photographic plates. 4to. (Also a 1960 second revised edition, same format and publisher) This museum features an extensive decoy collection.

Hillen, William

     Blackwater River; "Toa-Thai-Kas." New York, 1972, W. W. Norton & Co., Inc. 169 pp., illustrations. 8vo; dust jacket. Hunting and fishing in British Columbia.

Hillman, Anthony

     Painting Duck Decoys. New York, 1985, Dover. 24 plates in color, 6 pp. text. 4to. Paper wrappers.

     Miniature Duck Decoys For Woodcarvers. New York, 1985, Dover. 16 full size patterns, 4 pp. text. Folio. Paper wrappers.

Hillman, Conrad N. and W. W. Jackson

     The Sharp Tailed Grouse in South Dakota. Pierre, 1973, South Dakota Game and Fish commission. 62 pp., photographic plates, drawings, maps. 8vo. Paper wrappers.

Himmelwright, A. L. A.

     Pistol and Revolver Shooting. New York, 1928, The Macmillan Company. 482 pp., illustrations. 8vo; dust jacket. (Originally published, 1916, same format and publisher. Also reprinted several times after 1928)

Hind, Henry Youle

     Explorations in the Interior of the Labrador Peninsula. Millwood, 1973, Kraus. 655 pp., illustrations, fold-out map. 4to; dust jacket. (A reproduction of the 1863 edition, but with two volumes in one)

Hines, Bob

     Ducks at a Distance; a waterfowl identification guide. Washington, D. C., 1963, United States Fish and Wildlife Service. 23 pp., color and black and white illustrations by the author. 8vo. Paper wrappers. (Also an expanded 1978 edition, in a slightly smaller format, same publisher)

Hines, Ruth L., editor

     White-Tailed Deer Population Management in the North Central States. Madison, Wisconsin, 1980, The Graphic Printing Company. 116 pp.

Hines, Ruth L. and Clay Schoenfeld

     Canada Goose Management; current continental problems and programs. Madison, 1968, Dembar. 195 pp., photographic plates, maps, bibliography. 4to; dust jacket.

Hines, William

Black-Tailed Deer Populations and Douglas Fir Reforestation in the Tillamook Burn, Oregon. Corvalis, Oregon, 1973. 59 pp., photographic plates. 4to. Paper wrappers.

Hinman, Bob

The Duck Hunter's Handbook. New York, 1974, Winchester Press. 252 pp., illustrations. 8vo; dust jacket. (Reprinted many times, same format and publisher, with later printings titled, *The Duck Hunter's Bible.* Also an edition in paper wrappers published by Stoeger Arms. Also a 1985 revised edition, Winchester Press)

The Golden Age of Shotgunning. New York, 1971, Winchester Press. 175 pp., illustrations. 8vo. (Also reprinted 1982, Wolfe Publishing) Describes the development of shotguns and shotgun hunting during the last quarter of the nineteenth century.

Hird, Ralph C.

Colored Plate and Sporting Books. New York, 1935, Anderson Galleries, Inc. 112 pp. 8vo. Paper wrappers. An auction catalog.

Hirsch, Peter I.

The Last Man in Paradise. Garden City, 1961, Doubleday Doran & Co., Inc. 239 pp., photographic plates. 8vo; dust jacket. Contains some North American sheep, brown bear and polar bear hunting.

Hoagland, Edward

The Moose on the Wall; field notes from the Vermont wilderness. London, 1974, Barrie & Jenkins. 178 pp. 8vo; dust jacket.

Red Wolves and Black Bears. New York, 1976, Random House, Inc. 273 pp. 8vo; dust jacket. (Reprinted 1976, same format and publisher. Also reprinted, 1983, Penguin Books)

Hochbaum, H. Albert   b. 1911

The Canvasback on a Prairie Marsh. Washington D. C., 1944, The American Wildlife Institute. 201 pp., plates. 8vo; dust jacket. (Also a 1959 revised edition, same format and publisher) [Also a deluxe first edition of unspecified limitation, specially bound with an original watercolor by the author as a frontispiece]

To Ride The Wind. London and Toronto, 1973, Richard Bonnycastle Books. 120 pp., color illustrations from paintings by Sir Peter Scott. Elephant Folio. [Also a specially bound, limited edition of 500 numbered and signed copies; slipcased] This work describes the Delta Marsh in Manitoba, Canada and its wildfowl breeding programs.

Hochbaum, H. Albert, continued

Travels and Traditions of Waterfowl. Minneapolis, 1955, University of Minnesota Press. 310 pp., drawings by the author. 4to; dust jacket. (Reprinted several times, various formats and publishers)

Hochbaum, Peter Weller

The Delta Marsh. No place (Edmonton), No date (1971), Department of Mines, Resources and Environmental Management. 52 pp., drawings. 4to. Paper wrappers. The story of this Canadian wildlife station.

Hochwalt, Albert F.   1869-1938

Beagles and Beagling. Columbus, Ohio, 1935, Privately printed. 120 pp., plus ads. 8vo. Paper wrappers. (Originally published, 1923, Sportsman's Digest Publishing Company)

Makers of Bird Dog History: 1; the national champions. Dayton, Ohio, 1927, Albert F. Hockwalt Company. 128 pp., photographic plates. 12mo; dust jacket.

The Modern Setter; a companion volume to the 1923 edition with complete index to both volumes. Dayton, Ohio, 1935, Albert F. Hochwalt Company. 285 pp., photographic plates. 8vo; dust jacket. (Reprinted, same format and publisher)

Your Dog's Care. Dayton, Ohio, 1941, Outdoorsman. 60 pp.   Paper wrappers.

Most of Hochwalt's writing pre-dates 1925 (see Phillips). He is responsible for recording much of the early history of the pointer and setter breeds in America and was for many years very active in the National Field Trial Championships.

Hodgson, Robert G.

Practical Methods of Mink Breeding. Toronto, 1945, Fur Trade Journal of Canada.   151 pp., photographic plates.   8vo. [Also a specially bound author's presentation edition]

A Scrapbook of Mink Raising.   Toronto, 1931, Fur Trade Journal of Canada.   352 pp., photographic plates.   8vo.

Successful Muskrat Farming.   Toronto, Fur Trade Journal of Canada. 368 pp., photographic plates, drawings.   8vo.   (Reprinted many times, same format and publisher)

Hoff, Roy

Roy Hoff Tells It As It Was; forty years of archery and bow hunting. California, 1980, Privately printed.   186 pp.   Written by the founder of *Archery* magazine.

Hoff, Syd   b. 1912

Hunting Anyone?   Indianapolis, Indiana, 1963, The Bobbs-Merrill Company   183 pp., cartoon illustrations.   8vo; dust jacket.   A humorous look at hunting by the author of *Upstream, Downstream and Out of My Mind*, a humorous book about fishing.   The author also wrote and illustrated numerous juveniles, many of which had animal themes.

Hoffman, Donald M.

The Scaled Quail in Colorado; range, population status and harvest. No place, 1965, State of Colorado Fish and Game Commission.   47 pp., photographic plates, maps, charts.   8vo.   Paper wrappers.

The Wild Turkey in Eastern Colorado.   No place, 1962, State of Colorado Fish and Game Commission.   49 pp., photographic plates, drawings. 8vo.   Paper wrappers.

Hoffman, Philip

Harry Carry.   Santa Barbara, California, 1946, Privately printed.   38 pp., drawings by W. J. Goodacre.   Limited to 250 numbered copies.   8vo. Foxhunting in Virginia at the turn of the century.   Uncommon.

Hogg, Ian V.

The Complete Illustrated Encyclopedia of the World's Firearms.   New York, 1978, A. and W.   320 pp., color and black and white illustrations.   4to; dust jacket.

Guns and How They Work.   New York, 1978.   185 pp., color and black and white illustrations.   4to; dust jacket.

Hogg, Ian V. and John Batchelor

The Complete Handgun, 1300 to the Present.   New York, 1979, Exeter Books.   128 pp., color and black and white illustrations.   Folio; dust jacket.

Hogner, Dorothy C.

Conservation in America.   Philadelphia, 1958, J. B. Lippincott Co.   240 pp., illustrations.   8vo; dust jacket.

Water Over the Dam.   Philadelphia, 1960, J. B. Lippincott Co.   220 pp., illustrations by Nils Hogner.   8vo; dust jacket.   A history and commentary on how man has harnessed water power through dam building and what effects this has had upon wildlife and conservation.

Holder, T. H., editor

A Survey of Arkansas Game.   Little Rock, 1951, Game and Fish Department.   155 pp., photographic plates.   4to.

Holland, Bob and Dan and Ray Holland

Good Shot! A book of rod, gun and camera. New York, 1946, Alfred A. Knopf, Inc. 152 pp., photographic plates. A Borzoi Book For Sportsmen. 4to; dust jacket. [Also a specially bound, limited edition of 850 numbered copies signed by the authors; slipcased]

Holland, Dan

The Upland Game Hunter's Bible. New York, 1961, Doubleday & Company, Inc. 192 pp., photographic plates. 4to. Paper wrappers.

Holland, Raymond P., Sr.   1884-1973

Bird Dogs. New York, 1948, A. S. Barnes and Company, Inc. 204 pp., photographic plates, drawings and color illustrations by Fred McCaleb. A title in The Sportsman's Library series.   8vo; dust jacket. [Also a deluxe edition, specially bound and limited to 250 numbered copies, signed by the author and artist; slipcased]

Hunting and Fishing Handbook. Boston, 1944, National Sportsman Magazine. 109 pp., illustrated. 8vo. Paper wrappers.

The Master. New York, 1946, A. S. Barnes and Company, Inc. 86 pp., drawings. 8vo; dust jacket. This story of a boy and his hunting dog has appeal to the juvenile as well as adult reader.

My Dog Lemon. New York, 1945, A. S. Barnes and Company, Inc. 85 pp., drawings by Wesley Dennis. 8vo; dust jacket.

My Gun Dogs. Boston, 1929, Houghton Mifflin Company. 182 pp., drawings by A. L. Ripley. 8vo; dust jacket.

Nip and Tuck. Philadelphia, 1939, Penn Publishing Company. 150 pp., photographic plates, line drawings by Arthur D. Fuller. 8vo; dust jacket. (Also a 1946 revised and enlarged edition, Alfred A. Knopf, Inc.)   [Also a deluxe first edition, specially bound and limited to 74 numbered copies signed by the author and artist; slipcased]

Now Listen Warden. West Hartford, Vermont, 1946, The Countryman Press. 130 pp., drawings by Wesley Dennis. 8vo; dust jacket.   [Also a deluxe edition, specially bound and limited to 475 numbered copies signed by the author and artist; slipcased] Humorous hunting stories.

Scattergunning; a book on hunting the feathered game of North America, describing the habits of the different species during the gunning seasons, methods of hunting, and guns and ammunition used. New York, 1951, Alfred A. Knopf, Inc.   379 pp., photographic plates, color frontispiece by William J. Schaldach. A Borzoi Book For Sportsmen. 8vo; dust jacket.

Seven Grand Gun Dogs. New York, 1961, Thomas Nelson & Sons, Inc. 152 pp., drawings by Charles Leidl. 4to; dust jacket.   [Also a deluxe edition, specially bound and limited to 250 numbered copies signed by the author and artist; slipcased]

Holland, Raymond P., Sr., continued

Shotgunning in the Lowlands. West Hartford, Vermont, 1945, The Countryman Press. 213 pp., drawings and eight color illustrations from paintings by Lynn Bogue Hunt. Limited to 3500 copies. 4to; slipcased. (Reprinted 1946, same format and publisher) [Also a deluxe first edition, specially bound and limited to 350 numbered copies signed by the author and artist; slipcased]

Shotgunning in the Uplands. West Hartford, Vermont, 1944, The Countryman Press. 213 pp., drawings and eight color illustrations from paintings by Lynn Bogue Hunt. 4to; dust jacket. (Reprinted 1945, same format and publisher; slipcased) [Also a deluxe first edition, specially bound and limited to 250 numbered copies signed by the author and artist; slipcased]

Holland, Raymond P., Jr.   b. 1910

Jim Hunter, Sportsman.   Boston, 1937, Houghton Mifflin Company. 198 pp., illustrations.   8vo; dust jacket.   A novel for the young adult sportsman that recounts an eastern teenager's experiences in the West. Both of these works are often mistakenly identified as being written by the senior Holland.

The Physical Nature of Flight.   New York, 1951, W. W. Norton & Co., Inc.   287 pp., photographic plates.   8vo; dust jacket. Scarce.

Holliman, Jeannie

American Sports, 1785 - 1835.   Durham, North Carolina, 1931, The Seeman Press.   222 pp.   8vo.   Containing much on early hunting and angling. Scarce.

Holman, John P.   b. 1881

Sheep and Bear Trails. New York, 1933, Frank Walters.   211 pp., photographic plates. 8vo; dust jacket.   [Also a deluxe edition, specially bound and limited to 75 numbered copies signed by the author; slipcased] An important sheep and grizzly title with some mountain goat and moose hunting; approved by the Boone and Crockett Club.

Holmes, Kenneth L.

Ewing Young; master trapper. Portland, Oregon, 1967, Binsford & Mort. 180 pp., illustrations by Remington and Russell.   8vo; dust jacket..

Holmes, Lawrie

Mount Desert Deer Past and Present.   No place, 1944, Privately printed. Second edition.   30 pp., photographic plates.   8vo.   Paper wrappers.   This was originally intended to acquaint the citizens of Mt. Desert Island with deer herd management.

Holmes, William D.

A Square in the Arctic Circle; an Alaskan hunt.   Hamden, Connecticut, 1960, Privately printed by the Shoestring Press.   168 pp., photographic plates. 8vo; dust jacket. Hunting polar bear, wolf and seal. Scarce.

Holmgren, Virginia C.

  The War Lord.   Chicago, 1969, Follett Publishing Co.   128 pp.,
illustrations.   8vo; dust jacket.   A juvenile depicting the transplanting of ring-necked
pheasants from the Orient to Oregon in 1882.

Holt, Clarence

  One Life in Maine.   No place, 1940, Privately printed.   190 pp.,
illustrations.   A numbered copy of unspecified limitation.   8vo; dust jacket.
The author's memoirs about life in Ellsworth, Maine, with much hunting and fishing.

Holzworth, John M.   b. 1888

  The Twin Grizzlies of Admiralty Island.   Philadelphia, 1932, J. B.
Lippincott Co.   250 pp., photographic plates.   8vo; dust jacket.   (Reprinted
several times, same format and publisher)

  The Wild Grizzlies of Alaska; a story of the grizzly and brown bears of
Alaska, their habits, manners and characteristics, together with notes on mountain
sheep and caribou, collected by the author for the United States Biological
Survey.   New York, 1930, G. P. Putnam's Sons.   417 pp., color frontispiece,
photographic plates.   8vo; dust jacket.   (Reprinted, same format and publisher)
An important and thorough work.   Putnam produced several printings of this work, but all were
marked "First Edition."   The true first edition is identified as being bound in dark blue cloth and
having a frontispiece in color.   Other printings have been observed bound in light blue or orange
cloth and having a color or black and white frontispiece.

Hone, Elisabeth

  *The Present Status of the Muskox in Arctic North America and
Greenland;* with notes on distribution, extirpation, transplantation, protection,
habits and life history.   Cambridge, 1934, American Committee for International
Wild Life Protection.   87 pp., photographic plate, maps, bibliography.   Folio.
Paper wrappers.   One of the few references available on this game animal and, quite scarce.

Hoover, Helen

  The Gift of the Deer.   New York, 1968, Alfred A. Knopf, Inc.   210 pp.,
illustrations.   8vo; dust jacket.

  The Long-Shadowed Forest.   New York, 1963, W. W. Norton & Co.,
Inc.   272 pp., drawings by Adrian Hoover.   8vo; dust jacket.

  A Place in the Woods.   New York, 1969, Alfred A Knopf, Inc.   292 pp.,
drawings by Adrian Hoover.   8vo; dust jacket. (Also a 1970 British edition)   Life
in the northern wilderness of Minnesota.

  Ms. Hoover's works were reprinted many times.   She also wrote *Animals at My Doorstep*,
an older juvenile.

Hoover, Robert, et al.

  The Antelope of Colorado.   No place, 1959, State of Colorado Fish and
Game Commission.   110 pp., photographic plates, maps, charts.   8vo.   Paper
wrappers.

Horak, Gerald J.

Kansas Prairie Chickens. Pratt, Kansas, 1985, Kansas Fish and Game Commission. 65 pp., color and black and white illustrations. 4to. Paper wrappers.

Hornaday, William Temple 1854-1937

Campfires in the Canadian Rockies. New York, 1927, Charles Scribner's Sons. 353 pp., photographic plates. Tall 8vo; dust jacket. (A reprint of the 1906 first edition. Also reprinted, 1967, Abercrombie & Fitch, Inc.)

Campfires on Desert and Lava. New York, 1967, Abercrombie & Fitch, Inc. 356 pp., photographic plates. Tall 8vo; dust jacket. (A facsimile reproduction of the 1908 first edition published by Charles Scribner's Sons)

The Extermination of the American Bison; with a sketch of its discovery and life history. Seattle, 1971, Shorey Publishing Company. 176 pp., illustrations, fold-out map. Limited to 200 copies. 8vo. Paper wrappers. (A facsimile reproduction of the 1887 edition)

Thirty Years War For Wildlife; gains and losses in the thankless task. New York, 1931, Charles Scribner's Sons. 292 pp., illustrations. 8vo; dust jacket. (Also a 1931 edition, same format and contents, Permanent Wild Life Protection Fund. Also reprinted, 1970, New York) This is Hornady's plea for wildlife game laws.

Mr. Hornaday was one of America's conservation pioneers. Most of his writings appeared prior to 1925. See Phillips.

Hornaday, William T.

Also see **Forbes, John Ripley**

Hornocker, Maurice G.

An Analysis of Mountain Lion Predation Upon Mule Deer and Elk in the Idaho Primitive Area. Washington, 1970, The Wildlife Society. Monograph # 21. 39 pp., photographic plates, bibliography. 4to. Paper wrappers.

Hosely, N. W.

Selected References On Management of White Tailed Deer, 1910-1966. Washington, D. C., 1968, United States Department of the Interior. 46 pp. 4to. Paper wrappers. A bibliography.

Hosmer, Herbert Buttrick

Tales of the Old Trapper. Boston, 1963, Privately printed. 68 pp. 8vo. Paper wrappers. Hunting and angling reminiscences in New England.

Hotchner, A. E.

Papa Hemingway; a personal memoir. New York, 1966, Random House, Inc. 304 pp. 8vo; dust jacket. (Reprinted several times, same format and publisher) A well written Hemingway biography.

Hough, Henry B.
   The Heath Hen's Journey To Extinction, 1792-1933. Edgartown, No date (1933), Duke's County Historical Society. 31 pp., photographic plates, maps. 8vo. Paper wrappers.

Hougham, Paul C.
   The Encyclopedia of Archery. New York, 1958, A. S. Barnes and Company, Inc. 202 pp., illustrations, glossary. 8vo; dust jacket.

Houghland, Mason
   Gone Away. Berryville, Virginia, 1933, Blue Ridge Press. 145 pp., drawings by Olive Whitmore. A limited edition of unspecified number. 4to. Foxhunting in Virginia.

Houghtaling, David H.
   Shotgunning; some "do's" and "don'ts" and a few scraps of information. No place, 1964, Privately printed. 23 pp. Limited to 250 copies. Paper wrappers.

Housholder, Bob
   Diary of a Big Game Hunter. Privately printed, 1971. 63 pp., photographic plates. 8vo. Big game hunting for several species of North American big game. Rare.
   Hunting and Guiding For Desert Big Horn Sheep and Javelina. Phoenix, Arizona, No date (1973), Privately printed. 90 pp., illustrations. Introduction by Barry Goldwater. Limited to 500 numbered copies. 8vo.
   Hunting and Guiding For Desert Big Horn Sheep. Messilla, New Mexico, 1989, Wild Sheep and Goat International. 147 pp., photographic plates. Limited to 500 numbered and signed copies. Tall 8vo.
   Hunting the Desert Bighorn. Privately printed, 1969. 22 pp., photographic plates. 8vo. Paper wrappers. Rare.

Housholder, Bob, editor
   The Grand Slam of North American Wild Sheep. Phoenix, Arizona, 1974, North American Wild Sheep Hunter's Association. 220 pp., illustrations. 8vo. (Reprinted 1974, same format and publisher)

Houston, Douglas B.
   The Northern Yellowstone Elk; ecology and management. New York, 1982, The Macmillan Company. 474 pp., illustrations. 4to; dust jacket.

Howard, John E., editor
   North American Big Game Hunting in the 1800's. Clinton, New Jersey, 1982, Amwell Press. 498 pp., color frontispiece plus drawings by Irene Bowers. Limited to 1000 numbered and signed copies. 8vo; slipcased.

Howard, John E., editor, continued

Strayed Shots and Frayed Lines; being classics of American sporting humor. Clinton, New Jersey, 1982, Amwell Press. 407 pp., drawings by Anthony Hillman. 8vo. [Also a deluxe edition, specially bound and limited to 1000 numbered and signed copies; slipcased]

Howard, Ros

Dog Tales of Bench and Field. Illinois, 1963, Privately printed. 48 pp. Paper wrappers.

Howe, James Virgil

The Amateur Guncraftsman; a practical handbook for those who like guns. New York, 1938, Funk & Wagnalls Company. 310 pp., photographic plates, drawings. 8vo; dust jacket. (Reprinted several times, same format and publisher)

The Modern Gunsmith; a guide for the amateur and professional gunsmith in the design and construction of firearms, with practical suggestions for all who like guns. New York, 1934, Funk & Wagnalls Company. Two volumes of 424 pp. each, both with many illustrations. 4to; dust jacket. (A Supplement was also published containing 64 pp. with illustrations in 1941, same publisher. Reprinted several times, same format and publisher with later printings containing the supplement) [Also a deluxe first edition in two volumes, specially bound with no specified limitation] A masterful and thorough treatment of the subject by an expert (this was the Howe of Griffin & Howe, Inc., the famous custom rifle makers). The deluxe edition is rare.

Howe, Walter J.

Professional Gunsmithing. Plantersville, South Carolina, 1946, Small Arms Technical Publishing Company. 526 pp., color frontispiece by Gayle Hoskins, illustrations. Thick 8vo; dust jacket. (Reprinted 1952, same publisher and format. Also reprinted, The Stackpole Company)

Hrdlicka, Ales

Alaska Diary; 1926 to 1931. Washington, D. C., 1943, Smithsonian Institute. 414 pp., photographic plates. 4to.

Hubback, Theodore Rathbone

Ten Thousand Miles To Alaska For Moose and Sheep. Seattle, Washington, 1966, Shorey Publishing Company. 15 pp., photographic plates. Limited to 150 copies. 4to. Paper wrappers. (Originally published in *Outdoor Life* magazine in 1921)

Hubback, Theodore Rathbone, continued

To Far Western Alaska for Big Game; being an account of two journeys to Alaska in search of adventure. New York / London, 1929, Charles Scribner's Sons / Rowland Ward, Ltd. 232 pp., photographic plates. 8vo; dust jacket. An important North American big game book.

Hubbard, Lucius L.

Woods and Lakes of Maine; a trip from Moosehead Lake to New Brunswick in a birch bark canoe, to which are added some Indian place names and their meanings. Somersworth, New Hampshire, 1971, New Hampshire Publishing Company. 223 pp., photographic plates. 8vo; dust jacket. (Originally published, 1883)

Hubbard, W. B.

Notorious Grizzly Bears. Denver, Colorado, 1960, Sage Books. 205 pp., photographic plates. 8vo; dust jacket.

Hubbard, Wilbur

Organized Hunts of America. Baltimore, 1955, Masters of Foxhounds Association / The Sporting Press. 180 pp. 8vo. A survey of the organized foxhunting clubs of America.

Huggler, Thomas

Midwest Meanders. Au Train, 1984, Avery. 174 pp., photographic plates, drawings. 8vo. Paper wrappers. Hunting and angling in the mid-west.

Hughie, Roy D., editor

Fourth Eastern Black Bear Workshop. Orono, Maine, 1978, Maine Fish and Game Department. 409 pp., photographic plates. 4to. Spiral bound paper wrappers. A significant compilation of papers from U. S. and Canadian sources on the species' ecology and management.

Hull, Denison

Thoughts on American Foxhunting. New York, 1958, David McKay Co. 191 pp., color and black and white illustrations. Limited to 1500 copies. 8vo; dust jacket. Scarce.

Hull, Russell

Trophy Bowhunting; the supreme challenge. Hill City, 1984, G & R. 132 pp., color and black and white photographs. Paper wrappers.

Humber, George M. and Shepard Krech, editors

The Georgia-Florida Field Trial Club, 1916-1948; with observations on the sport of hunting with dog and gun and a dissertation on the organization and management of field trials. New York, 1948, Charles Scribner's Sons. 125 pp., color frontispiece by A. L. Ripley, photographic plates. Limited to 600 numbered copies. 8vo. (Also a second edition, *The Georgia-Florida Field Trial Club, 1916-1966,* Privately printed by the club)

Hunnicutt, Samuel

Twenty Years Hunting and Fishing in the Great Smoky Mountains. Maryville, Tennessee, 1951, Byron's Printers and Publishers. 188 pp., illustrations. 12mo. Paper wrappers. A scarce outdoors memoir.

Hunt, Harrison J. and Ruth Hunt Thompson

North To the Horizon. Camden, 1980, Down East Publishers. 117 pp., photographic plates. 4to; dust jacket. Harrison Hunt was the surgeon for an ill-fated expedition to Greenland in 1913-1917. An interesting arctic account with some hunting.

Hunt, John and A. Hopkins

An Evaluation of Artificial Mallard Propagation in Wisconsin. Madison, Wisconsin, 1953, Wisconsin Conservation Department. 79 pp. 8vo. Paper wrappers.

Hunt, Lynn Bogue   1878-1960

An Artist's Game Bag. New York, 1936, The Derrydale Press. Unpaginated, black and white and color illustrations from paintings and drawings by the author. Limited to 1225 numbered copies. 4to; dust jacket. [Also a deluxe edition, specially bound and illustrated and limited to 25 numbered copies]

Fishing in America; the Field & Stream portfolio - six paintings by Lynn Bogue Hunt. New York, 1946, Gunning and Fishing Prints. A paper portfolio of six paintings with an accompanying 16 pp. text by S. Kip Farrington and Ted Trueblood. Elephant folio. This portfolio is considerably scarcer than the *Game Birds of America* portfolio.

Game Birds of America. With explanatory text by Ray P. Holland. New York, 1944, Field and Stream Magazine. A paper folio of 12 loose color plates with an accompanying text of 19 pp. Elephant folio.

How To Draw and Paint Birds. Tustin, California, No date. 30 pp., color and black and white illustrations by the author and Walter T. Foster. Folio. Rare.

Mr. Hunt remains a popular wildlife illustrator. He also illustrated many sporting and juvenile books as well as many covers for sporting periodicals of the day.

Hunt, R. A. and L. R. Jahn
  Canada Goose Breeding Populations of Wisconsin. Madison, 1966, Wisconsin Conservation Department. 67 pp., photographic plates, maps, bibliography. 8vo. Paper wrappers.

Hunt, William S.
  Frank Forester (Henry William Herbert), A Tragedy in Exile. Newark, New Jersey, 1933, Carteret Book Club. 128 pp., illustrations. Limited to 200 copies. 8vo. A very good biography of Forester with an excellent bibliography of his works.

Hunter, Anole (*pseud.* of **Everett Lake Crawford**) **1880-1960**
  Let's Ride To Hounds. New York, 1929, The Derrydale Press. 92 pp., drawings by Edward King. Limited to 850 copies. Tall 8vo. [Also a large paper edition, specially bound and limited to 50 numbered copies signed by the author]

Hunter, Carl
  The Bobwhite Quail in Arkansas. Little Rock, 1948, Arkansas Game and Fish Commission. 24 pp., drawings. 16mo. Paper wrappers.

Hunter, Martin
  Canadian Wilds. Columbus, Ohio, 1935, A. R. Harding. 277 pp., photographic plates. 16mo. (Also reprinted, 1936, same format and publisher. Originally published, 1907, same format and publisher)

Hunter, Rodello
  Wyoming Wife. New York, 1969, Alfred A. Knopf, Inc. 330 pp., drawings by Tracy Sugarman. 8vo; dust jacket. The author recounts how she joined her husband's hunting and fishing activities.

Huntley, Forry, editor
  Official Bowhunter's Manual. Redlands, California, 1958, National Field Archery Association. 114 pp., illustrations. 8vo. Paper wrappers. (Also a 1962 second edition, edited by James Cavanaugh, same format and publisher)

Huster, H. Harrison and Doug Knight
  Floating Sculpture; the decoys of the Delaware River. Spanish Fork, Utah, 1982, Hillcrest Publications. 169 pp., color and black and white illustrations. 4to; dust jacket.

Hutchens, Paul
  We Killed a Bear! Grand Rapids, Michigan, 1953. 86 pp. 12mo. A juvenile story.

Hutton, Hubert

  Hunting Dogs; their training and care. Lexington, Kentucky, 1938, Privately printed. 88 pp., illustrations, plus ads. 8vo. A scarce book with a chapter on the American Water Spaniel by Howard Peterson and a chapter on German Shorthairs by Dr. C. R. Thornton.

Hyde, Charles Leavitt

  Pioneer Days; the story of an adventurous and active life. The autobiography of a man who was a western cowboy at 17; a cattleman with great herds and big ranches at 30. New York, 1939, G. P. Putnam's Sons. 286 pp., photographic plates. 8vo; dust jacket. With some small and big game hunting in the West.

Hyde, Dayton

  Raising Wild Ducks in Captivity. New York, 1974, E. P. Dutton & Co., Inc. 319 pp., photographic plates. 8vo; dust jacket.

Illingworth, F.
   Falcons and Falconry.   New York, 1964, London House and Maxwell.
126 pp., photographic plates.   8vo; dust jacket.   (Originally published, 1948,
Great Britain)

Ingalls, Fay
   About Dogs - And Me.   Hot Springs, Arkansas, 1939, Privately printed.
91 pp., frontispiece, drawings.   8vo.   Bird hunting dogs with much on quail and grouse
shooting in North Carolina and Virginia. Scarce.

Ingle, Charles T.
   Sporting Dogs - Hounds.   The breeds and standards as recognized by
The American Kennel Club.   New York, 1935, G. Howard Watt, Inc.   118 pp.,
illustrations.   8vo; dust jacket.

Innis, Pauline B.
   The Wild Swans Fly.   New York, 1964, David McKay Co.   149 pp.
8vo; dust jacket.   A fictionalized account of a pair of whistling swans.

Irving, Washington
   A Tour of the Prairies.   Norman, 1956, University of Oklahoma Press.
214 pp.   (Originally published, 1835, Carey, Lea and Blanchard)   With much early
nineteenth century hunting.

Ives, Marguerite
   Seventeen Famous Outdoorsmen; known to Marguerite Ives.   Chicago,
1929, Canterbury.   192 pp., line drawings.   Limited to 500 numbered and signed
copies.   8vo.   Interviews with and short biographies of LaBranche, Hewitt, Pinchot, Wetzel
and others.

Jackman, E. R. and R. A. Long

The Oregon Desert. Caldwell, Idaho, 1964, Caxton Printers, Ltd. 407 pp., photographic plates, drawings, color illustrations. 8vo; dust jacket. (Reprinted several times, same format and publisher) With much on history, ranch life, natural history and one chapter on mule deer hunting.

Jackson, Lowell, editor

Benjamin J. Schmidt: A Michigan Decoy Carver, 1884-1968. 3irmingham, Michigan, 1970, Privately printed. 23 pp., photographic plates. 4to. Paper wrappers.

Jacob, Bart and Ben Conger

The Grand Spring Hunt; for America's wild turkey gobbler. New York, 1985, Winchester Press. 194 pp., photographic plates. 8vo; dust jacket.

Jacobs, Charles R., editor   b. 1909

Gun Digest. New York, 1944. 162 pp., photographic plates, drawings. 4to. Paper wrappers. (Also reprinted annually to date with the same format) Mr. Jacobs edited the first several issues of *Gun Digest.* Later issues were edited by John T. Amber.

Official Gun Book. New York, 1950, Crown Publishers, Inc.. 178 pp., many illustrations. 4to; dust jacket. Bound in cloth as well as in paper wrappers. (Also three annual editions in 1951, 1952 and 1953, *The New Official Gun Book*, same format and publisher)

Official Hunting Book; how, when and where to hunt in North America. New York, 1950, Crown Publishers, Inc. 160 pp., photographic plates, drawings. 4to; dust jacket.

Jaeger, Ellsworth

Tracks and Trailcraft. New York, 1948, The Macmillan Company. 381 pp., illustrated. 8vo; dust jacket. (Reprinted many times, same format and publisher)

Wildwood Wisdom. New York, 1945, The Macmillan Company. 491 pp., illustrations. 8vo; dust jacket. (Reprinted many times, same format and publisher)

Woodsmoke. New York, 1953, The Macmillan Company. 228 pp., illustrations. 8vo; dust jacket. (Reprinted several times, same format and publisher)

Mr. Jaeger wrote several other nature and woodcraft books.

James, Edsall

The Golden Age of Single-Shot Rifles. Harriman, Tennessee, 1974, Pioneer Press. 33 pp., photographic plates. 8vo. Paper wrappers.

James, M. R.
    Bowhunting For Whitetail and Mule Deer.   New Jersey, 1976, Jolex Publishers, Inc.   224 pp., illustrations.   Paper wrappers.
    Successful Bowhunting.   New York, 1985, Outdoor Life Books.   239 pp., illustrations.   8vo; dust jacket   (Reprinted, same format and publisher. Also reprinted, Blue-J Publications)

Jameson, E. W., Jr. and Hans J. Peeters.
    An Introduction to Hawking.   Davis, California, 1971, Privately printed. 42 pp., illustrations, glossary, bibliography.   4to.   Paper wrappers.

Jamieson, Paul F., editor
    The Adirondack Reader; the best writing on the adventures and contemplative life in one of America's most loved regions.   New York, 1964, The Macmillan Company.   494 pp., illustrations.   8vo; dust jacket.   An anthology of stories with much hunting and fishing.

Jamison, Rick
    Calling Coyotes and Other Predators.   Prescott, Arizona, 1980, Track Press.   172 pp., photographic plates.   8vo.   Paper wrappers.

Janes, Edward C.
    A Boy and His Gun.   New York, 1951, A. S. Barnes and Company, Inc. 207 pp., photographic plates.   Foreword by Col. H. P. Sheldon.   A title in The Sportsman's Library series.   8vo; dust jacket.   (Reprinted several times, same format and publisher)
    Hunting Ducks and Geese.   Harrisburg, 1954, The Stackpole Company. 187 pp., black and white and color illustrations.   8vo; dust jacket.   [Also a specially bound and numbered deluxe edition of unspecified limitation]
    Ringneck! Pheasants and pheasant hunting.   New York, 1975, Crown Publishers, Inc.   145 pp., photographic plates.   8vo; dust jacket.

Janovy, John
    Yellowlegs. New York, 1980, St. Martin's Press.   192 pp., illustrations. 8vo; dust jacket.   [Also a deluxe edition limited to 250 numbered copies, with a pencil signed print laid in; slipcased]   North American shorebirds.

Jaques, Florence Page   1890-1972
    As Far as the Yukon.   New York, 1951, Harper & Brothers.   243 pp., illustrations by Francis Lee Jaques.   8vo; dust jacket.
    Birds Across the Sky.   New York, 1942, Harper & Brothers.   243pp., illustrations by Francis Lee Jaques.   8vo; dust jacket.   (Reprinted several times, same format and publisher)

Jaques, Florence Page, continued

Canadian Spring. New York, 1947, Harper & Brothers. 216 pp., paintings by Francis Lee Jaques. 8vo; dust jacket.

Canoe Country. Minneapolis, 1938, University of Minnesota Press. 78 pp., illustrations by Francis Lee Jacques. 8vo; dust jacket. (Reprinted many times, same format and publisher)

The Geese Fly High. Minneapolis, 1939, University of Minnesota Press. 102 pp., illustrations by Francis Lee Jacques. 4to; dust jacket. (Reprinted 1964, same format and publisher)

Francis Lee Jaques; artist of the wilderness world. Garden City, New York, 1973, Doubleday & Co., Inc. 370 pp., may color and black and white illustrations. Square 4to; slipcased. A beautiful volume showcasing Mr. Jaques' illustrations.

Snowshoe Country. Minneapolis, 1944, University of Minnesota Press. 110 pp., illustrations by Francis Lee Jacques. 4to; dust jacket. (Reprinted twice, same format and publisher)

Frances Lee Jaques was certainly one of this century's best wildlife illustrators. His bird illustrations are especially noteworthy.

Jaques, Francis Lee 1887-1969
See **Luce, Donald R. and Laura M. Andrews**
See **Outdoor Life Books,** *Outdoor Life's Gallery of North American Game*

Jaques, H. E.

How To Know The Land Birds. Dubuque, Iowa, 1947, Brown. 196 pp., drawings. 8vo. Key to identification with distribution maps.

How To Know the Water Birds. Dubuque, Iowa, 1960, Brown. 159 pp., drawings. 8vo. Key to identification with distribution maps.

Jeffett, Frank

This Love of Hunting. Dallas, 1972, Tejas Press. 272 pp., illustrations. 8vo; dust jacket. The memoirs of the author of a lifetime of hunting along the Mississippi river for turkey and wildfowl, big game hunting in Wyoming and deer hunting in Texas. Scarce.

Jenkins, Marie M.

Deer, Moose, Elk, and Their Family. New York, 1979, Holiday House. 128 pp., illustrations.

Jenkinson, Michael

Beasts Beyond the Fire. New York, 1980, E. P. Dutton & Co., Inc. 273 pp., illustrations, bibliography. 8vo; dust jacket. True encounters with dangerous game.

Jenks, Almet
> *The Huntsman at the Gate.*   Philadelphia, 1952, J. B. Lippincott Co.
115 pp., illustrations.   8vo; dust jacket.   A novel with a foxhunting theme.

Jennings, Mike
> *Instinct Shooting*; the amazing method of marksmanship as taught by
Lucky McDaniel.   New York, 1959, Dodd, Mead & Co.   157 pp., illustrations.
8vo; dust jacket.   (Also several revised editions, same format and publisher)

Jerk, Leonard C.
> *The Elusive Bighorn Ram.*   Jasper, Alberta, 1979, Privately printed.   37
pp., photographic plates.   8vo.   Paper wrappers.   (Reprinted 1983, same format
and publisher)   Scarce.
> *Female Grizzly Rights;* grizzly attack - seventeen-hour ordeal.   Jasper,
Alberta, 1982, Privately printed.   63 pp., illustrations.   8vo.   Paper wrappers.
Scarce.

Jinks, Roy G.
> *125 Years With Smith & Wesson.*   North Hollywood, California, 1977,
Beinfeld. 290 pp., photographic plates.   8vo; dust jacket.   (Also a 1977 edition
titled, *History of Smith & Wesson*, same contents and publisher.   This edition
reprinted several times)

Jobson, John
> *The Best of John Jobson;* a treasury of twenty years.   Edited and with a
foreword by Steven Schroeder.   Clinton, New Jersey, 1982, Amwell Press.   396
pp., photographic plates, drawings.   Limited to 1000 numbered and signed
copies. 8vo; slipcased.   An anthology of the author's big game hunting stories originally
appearing in *Sports Afield* magazine.

Johenning, Leon
> *The Turkey Hunter's Guide.*   No place (Lexington), No date (1962),
Privately printed.   72 pp., photographic plates.   8vo.   Paper wrappers.
(Reprinted several times, same format and publisher)

Johns, Rowland, editor
> *Our Friend the Cocker Spaniel*; with methods of training for sport and
show.   New York, 1932, E. P. Dutton & Co., Inc.   85 pp., illustrations.   8vo;
dust jacket.
> *Our Friend the Springer Spaniel.*   New York, 1933, E. P. Dutton & Co.,
Inc.   87 pp., frontispiece.   16mo; dust jacket.   (Reprinted, same format and
publisher)

Johnsgard, Paul A.   **b. 1931**

   Diving Birds of North America. Lincoln, 1987, University of Nebraska Press.   292 pp., color and black and white illustrations, bibliography, maps. 4to; dust jacket.

   Ducks, Geese and Swans of the World. Lincoln, 1978, University of Nebraska Press.   404 pp., black and white and color illustrations, maps, bibliography. Thick 4to; dust jacket. [Also a deluxe edition, specially bound and illustrated, limited to 24 numbered copies signed by the author] A comprehensive and attractive book.

   Grouse and Quails of North America.   Lincoln, 1973, University of Nebraska Press. 553 pp., color and black and white illustrations. Thick 4to; dust jacket. (Reprinted twice, same publisher and format)

   The Grouse of the World. Lincoln, 1983, University of Nebraska Press. 413 pp., color and black and white illustrations, bibliography.   4to; dust jacket. (Also a 1983 British edition)

   A Guide to North American Waterfowl. Bloomington, 1979, University of Indiana Press.   274 pp., color and black and white illustrations, bibliography. 8vo; dust jacket.

   Handbook of Waterfowl Behavior.   Ithaca, New York, 1965, Cornell University Press.   378 pp., illustrated, bibliography.   8vo; dust jacket. (Reprinted 1976, same format and publisher. Also a 1965 British edition)

   Hawks, Eagles and Falcons of North America; biology and natural history.   Washington, D. C., 1990, Smithsonian Institute.   403 pp., color illustrations by John Felsing, maps, drawings, bibliography.   4to; dust jacket.

   North American Game Birds of Upland and Shoreline.   Lincoln, 1975, University of Nebraska Press.   183 pp., color and black and white illustrations, maps, bibliography. 8vo; dust jacket.

   The Plovers, Sandpipers and Snipes of the World.   Lincoln, 1981, University of Nebraska Press.   493 pp., color and black and white illustrations, maps, bibliography.   4to; dust jacket.

   Song of the North Wind; a story of the snow goose.   New York, 1974, Doubleday & Co., Inc. / Anchor.   150 pp., photographic plates, drawings by P. Geraghty. 8vo; dust jacket.

   Teton Wildlife; observations by a naturalist. Boulder, 1982, Colorado Associated University.   128 pp., color and black and white illustrations, bibliography. 8vo; dust jacket.

   Waterfowl; their biology and natural history. Lincoln, 1968, University of Nebraska Press. 138 pp., color and black and white illustrations; foreword by Sir Peter Scott.   8vo; dust jacket.   (Reprinted several times, same format and publisher)

   Waterfowl of North America. Bloomington, 1975, Indiana University Press.   575 pp., color and black and white illustrations, maps, bibliography. 8vo; dust jacket [Also a deluxe edition of 100 numbered copies]

Johnsgard, Paul A., editor
  The Bird Decoy; an American art form.   Lincoln, 1976, University of Nebraska Press. 191 pp., color and black and white illustrations. Tall 8vo; dust jacket.
  Mr. Johnsgard also wrote *Cranes of The World* (1983) and *Those of the Gray Wind;* the Sandhill Cranes (1981).

Johnson, Arch
  The Favorite Sets of North American Trappers.   No place, 1946, Privately   printed.   109   pp.,   illustrations.   8vo.   Paper   wrappers.

Johnson, Carl
  10 Exciting Hunts With Dogs.   Traverse City, Michigan, No date (ca. 1970), Privately printed.   Unpaginated (approx. 44 pp.), photographic plates, drawings.   4to. Paper wrappers.   Includes hunting bear and bobcat in Michigan. Scarce.

Johnson, George Brooks
  Miramichi   Woodsman.   Richmond,   Virginia,   1945,   Whittet   & Shepperson.   102 pp., illustrations.   Limited to 150 copies.   8vo.   Incidental mentioning of hunting and fishing, but an interesting account of the life of Paul Kingston, a logger in the Miramichi woods at the turn of the twentieth century.

Johnson, James Ralph
  The Last Passenger. New York, 1956, The Macmillan Company.   116 pp., drawings by the author.   8vo; dust jacket.   A fictionalized life history of the last passenger pigeon. Mr. Johnson wrote many other juveniles with animal themes.

Johnson, Melvin M., Jr.   1909-1955
  Practical Marksmanship; the technique of field firing.   New York, 1945, William Morrow & Co., Inc. 183 pp., illustrations. Tall 8vo; dust jacket. Mostly from a military viewpoint, but much practical application for the shooting sports.
  Rifles and Machine Guns. New York, 1944, William Morrow & Co., Inc. 390 pp., photographic plates, drawings.   8vo; dust jacket.   Mostly military armament, with some mention of sporting applications.

Johnson, Melvin M., Jr. and Charles T. Haven
  Ammunition; its history, development and use, 1600-1943. New York, 1943, William Morrow & Co., Inc.   374 pp., many illustrations, folding charts. 8vo. A history of the subject with emphasis on contemporary ammunition.

Johnson, Morris
  Feathers on the Prairie; a short history of upland game birds. Bismarck, 1964, North Dakota Fish and Game Department. 240 pp., illustrations.   8vo. Paper wrappers.

Johnson, Olga

Bears in the Rockies.   Libby, 1960, Privately printed.   80 pp., illustrations.   8vo.   Spiral bound paper wrappers.   A rare title with many first hand accounts of bear hunting.

Johnson, Oliver

A Home in the Woods; reminiscences of early Marion County (Indiana). Indianapolis, 1951, Indiana Historical Society.   92 pp.   8vo.   Paper wrappers. With a chapter containing bear, deer and turkey hunting in early Indiana.

Johnson, Peter H.

Parker, America's Finest Shotgun.   Harrisburg, 1961, The Stackpole Company.   260 pp., photographic plates.   8vo; dust jacket.   (Reprinted several times, various publishers)

Johnson, W. T.

History of Game Strains.   Americus, Georgia, 1953, Privately printed. 73 pp.   Tall 8vo.   Paper wrappers.

Johnston, Charles H. L., editor

The South Branch of the Potomac; by those who love it.   Wheeling, 1931, Hubbard.   103 pp., photographic plates.   12mo.   With some hunting and angling in a rare book.

Jonas Brothers.

Game Trails: Memoirs of a Thousand Sportsmen.   Denver, 1939, Jonas Brothers Taxidermists.   Unpaginated, illustrations.   8vo.   Paper wrappers.   (Also a 1958 edition limited to 500 copies, slightly larger format)   Displays the work of the publishers as well as information on hunting, care of trophies, etc.

Jones, Adrienne

Wild Voyageur; story of a Canada goose.   Boston, 1966, Little, Brown & Company.   174 pp., drawings.   8vo; dust jacket.   A novel about the life of a Pacific flyway Canada goose.

Jones, B. S.

Stories of Old Traveler.   New Orleans, Louisiana, 1966, Privately printed.   137 pp., photographic plate.   8vo; dust jacket.   Stories of hunting bobcat with "Traveler," a hound, throughout the southern U. S.   Scarce.

Jones, E. Gwynne

A Bibliography of the Dog.   London, 1971, The Library Association. 431 pp.   8vo.   A most useful reference for books about all breeds of dogs published in English.   Unfortunately, it is scarce.

Jones, James Elwood, Jr.

The James Ellwood Jones, Jr. Arms Collection. Hyannis, Massachusetts, 1981, Bourne Auctions. Two volumes of approximately 450 pp. with color and black and white illustrations. 4to. An auction catalog of a most impressive arms collection.

Jones, James S., editor

A History of the Packs of Harriers, Beagles and Bassets of New Jersey. New Vernon, 1968, Privately printed. 53 pp., photographic plates. 8vo. Paper wrappers.

Jones, Maj. Roy D.

Burning Powder. Springfield, Massachusetts, 1926, Smith & Wesson, Inc. Fourth edition. 79 pp., illustrations. 18mo. Paper wrappers. (Originally published, 1921, same format and publisher) Handgun shooting. Scarce.

Jones, Robert F.

Food Habits of the American Coot With Notes on Distribution. Washington, D. C., 1940, United States Department of the Interior. 52 pp., color frontispiece, maps, photographic plates. 8vo. Paper wrappers.

Jones, Robert F.

Blood Sport; a journey up the Hassayampa. New York, 1974, Simon and Schuster. 225 pp. 8vo; dust jacket. A novel about a hunting and fishing trip on the Hassayampa stream in Arizona.

Slade's Glacier. New York, 1981, Simon and Schuster. 205 pp. 8vo; dust jacket. A novel about Alaska in the 1950's, with much on big game hunting.

Jones, Robert L. and Harold C. Hanson

Mineral Licks, Geography and Biochemistry of North American Ungulates. Ames, 1985, Iowa State University Press. 301 pp., photographic plates. A scholarly work discussing the relationship between mineral-rich soil types and animal development, particularly as it relates to antler size.

Jones, Russell Lee

Reminiscences of Bird Shooting Days. No place (Hartford, Connecticut), 1957, Privately printed. 126 pp., photographic plates. Limited to 12 numbered copies. 4to. A rare and important documentary about upland game bird shooting in the Connecticut Valley between about 1880-1940.

Jonkel, Charles J.

How To Live in Bear Country. Missoula, Montana, No date, Ursid Research Center. 33 pp., drawings. 8vo. Paper wrappers.

Jonkel, Charles J., et al.
   The Present Status of the Polar Bear in the James Bay and Belcher Island Area. Ottawa, 1976, Canadian Wildlife Service.   42 pp., maps.   8vo. Paper wrappers.

Jonkel, Charles J. and Ian Cowan
   The Black Bear in the Spruce-Fir Forest.   Washington, 1971, The Wildlife Society.   57 pp., photographic plates, bibliography.   4to.   Paper wrappers.

Jorgensen, Frederick E.   b. 1864
   Twenty-Five years a Game Warden.   Brattleboro, Vermont, 1937, Stephen Daye Press.   171 pp., illustrations.   8vo.   The author was a game warden in Maine.

Jorgensen, S. E. and L. David Mech, editors
   Proceedings of a Symposium on the Native Cats of North America; their status and management.   Fort Snelling, Minnesota, 1971, United States Department of the Interior.   139 pp., illustrations.   4to. Spiral bound paper wrappers.

Kabat, Cyril, et al.
> *Seasonal Variation in Stress Resistance in the Hen Pheasant.* Madison, 1956, Wisconsin Conservation Department. 48 pp. 8vo. Paper wrappers.

Kaczynski, C. F. and E. B. Chamberlain
> *Aerial Surveys of Canada Geese and Black Ducks in Eastern Canada.* Washington, D. C., 1968, United States Fish and Wildlife Service. 29 pp. Paper wrappers.

Kaiser, Harvey H.
> *Great Camps of the Adirondacks.* Boston, 1982, David R. Godine, Publishers, Inc. 240 pp., color and black and white illustrations. 4to; dust jacket.

Kaminski, R. M. and J. M. Parker
> *Investigations of Nesting Giant Canada Geese in Southeastern Lower Michigan.* Lansing, 1976, Michigan Department of Natural Resources. 21 pp. Paper wrappers.

Kangas, Gene and Linda Kangas
> *Decoys*; a North American survey. Spanish Fork, Utah, 1983, Hillcrest Publications. 332 pp., color and black and white illustrations. 4to; dust jacket.
> *National Directory of Decoy Collectors: 1978, 1979.* Painesville, Ohio, 1979, Privately printed. 144 pp., photographic plates. Oblong 8vo. Paper wrappers. (Also a *National Directory of Decoy Collectors: Book II*, 1981, same format and publisher)

Kantor, MacKinlay
> *The Voice of Bugle Ann.* New York, 1935, Coward, McCann, Inc. 128 pp. 8vo; dust jacket. (Reprinted several times, same format and publisher) [Also a limited first edition of 500 copies] The story of a hound dog.
> *The Daughter of Bugle Ann.* New York, 1953, Random House, Inc. 122 pp. 8vo; dust jacket. Southern foxhunting.

Kanuit, Larry, compiler
> *Alaskan Bear Tales.* Anchorage, 1983, Alaska Northwest Publishing Company. 318 pp., line drawings. 8vo; dust jacket. (Reprinted many times, same format and publisher)

Karas, Nicholas
> *The Crow Shooter's Handbook.* Easton, Maryland, 1963. 54 pp. 12mo. Paper wrappers.
> *The Hunter's Handbook.* New York, 1963, Koster. 24 pp., drawings. 12mo. Paper wrappers.

Karr, Charles Lee, Jr. and Carroll Robbins Karr
Remington Handguns. Harrisburg, 1947, The Military Service Publishing Company. 125 pp., illustrations including one folding plate. 8vo; dust jacket. (Revised and reprinted several times, various publishers)

Karr, Jean
Zane Grey; man of the West. New York, 1949, Greenberg: Publishers, Inc. 229 pp., photographic plates. 8vo; dust jacket. (Reprinted 1951, Kingswood, slightly smaller format)

Karras, A. L.
North To Kree Lake. New York, 1970, Trident. 256 pp., illustrations by Laszlo Kubinyi. 8vo; dust jacket. An account of trapping in Northern Saskatchewan in the 1930's.

Kauf, Russ
Elwood Goes Hog Wild and Other Stories of the Outdoors. Washington, New York, 1977, Vantage Press. 132 pp. 8vo; dust jacket.

Kaufman, Henry J.
Early American Gunsmiths, 1650-1850. Harrisburg, 1952, The Stackpole Company. 94 pp., illustrations. 4to; dust jacket. (Reprinted, same format and publisher. Also reprinted, Bonanza)
The Pennsylvania-Kentucky Rifle. Harrisburg, 1960, The Stackpole Company. 376 pp., illustrations. 4to; dust jacket. (Reprinted, Bonanza) [Also a deluxe first edition, specially bound, numbered and signed by the author, but with no specified limitation]

Kaufman, John and Heinz Meng
Falcons Return. New York, 1975, William Morrow & Co., Inc. 128 pp., photographic plates. 8vo; dust jacket. An account of breeding peregrine falcons in captivity for re-introduction to the wilds; also a chapter on falconry.

Kaupanger, Olin
A Primer on Conservation. No place, 1952, Federal Cartridge Company. 100 pp., illustrations, bibliography. 8vo. An introduction to land, soil, water and game conservation.

Kay, Alex
Hunting For All Seasons. New York, 1973, Galahad. 159 pp. 8vo; dust jacket.

Kean, Robert Winthrop
Fourscore Years: My First Twenty-Four. No place, 1974, Privately printed. 264 pp., illustrations. 8vo. Includes a chapter on hunting big game in Alaska in 1915. Scarce.

Keating, Bern
The Flamboyant Mr. Colt and His Deadly Six-Shooter. New York, 1978, Doubleday & Co, Inc. 233 pp., illustrations. 8vo; dust jacket. A biography.

Keefe, James F.
The World of the Opossum. Philadelphia, 1967, J. B. Lippincott Co. 144 pp., photographic plates, bibliography. A title in Lippincott's Living World series. 4to; dust jacket.

Keenlyne, Kent
The Trophy Bowhunter in South Dakota. No place, No date (ca. 1985), Privately printed. 87 pp., photographic plates, charts. 8vo. Paper wrappers.

Keim, Charles
Alaska Game Trails With a Master Guide. Anchorage, 1977, Alaska Northwest Publishing Company. 310 pp., illustrations. 8vo. Paper wrappers. (Reprinted 1984, same format and publisher)

Keith, Elmer   1899-1984
Big Game Rifles and Cartridges. Onslow County, North Carolina, 1936, Small Arms Technical Publishing Company. 161 pp., photographic plates, line drawings, plus ads. 16mo; dust jacket. (Reprinted many times, various publishers)

Guns and Ammo For Hunting Big Game. Los Angeles, 1965, Peterson Publishing Company. 384 pp., illustrations. 4to; dust jacket. [Also published in padded leather, 1965, same publisher, as a set with Whelen and Angier's *Mr. Rifleman,* which see]

Hell, I Was There! Los Angeles, 1979, Peterson Publishing Company. 408 pp., photographic plates. 4to; dust jacket. (Reprinted many times, several publishers) Mr. Keith was dissatisfied with Winchester's editing and revisions of his *Keith;* an autobiography. He turned to his friends at *Guns and Ammo* magazine, for whom he wrote a monthly column for many years, to publish his autobiography as he wanted it. Both versions are highly entertaining reading regarding this marksman, hunter and proponent of big-bore rifles and handguns who lived from cowboy days to the jet age.

Keith; an autobiography. New York, 1974, Winchester Press. 381 pp., photographic plates. 8vo; dust jacket. (Reprinted in a Book Club edition, slightly smaller format, same publisher)

Keith, Elmer, continued

Elmer Keith's Big Game Hunting.   Boston, 1948, Little, Brown & Company.   420 pp., color frontispiece, photographic plates, drawings by the author.   8vo; dust jacket.   (Reprinted 1954, same publisher and format) Despite being almost 50 years old, this work still imparts much useful information on the subject.

Keith's Rifles For Large Game.   Huntington, West Virginia, 1946, Standard Publications, Inc.   406 pp., drawings and photographic plates.   Tall 8vo; dust jacket.   Apparently only about 1000 copies of this were sold, the balance of the first printing having been damaged from water.   When Herman Dean, the owner of Standard, refused to reprint it, Keith found Angus Cameron, a senior editor at Little, Brown & Company amenable to publishing it with changes as *Elmer Keith's Big Game Hunting.*

Shotguns - By Keith.   Harrisburg, 1950, Stackpole and Heck, Inc.   307 pp., illustrations.   8vo; dust jacket.   (Reprinted and revised several times by Stackpole and Bonanza)

Sixgun Cartridges and Loads; a manual covering the selection, use and loading of the most suitable and popular revolver cartridges.   Onslow County, North Carolina, 1936, Small Arms Technical Publishing Company.   151 pp., photographic plates, line drawings, plus ads.   16mo; dust jacket. (Reprinted 1945, same format and publisher)

Sixguns by Keith; the standard reference.   Harrisburg, 1955, The Stackpole Company.   308 pp., color and black and white illustrations.   4to; dust jacket.   [Also a numbered deluxe edition, specially bound and signed but with no stated limitation]

Mr. Keith also wrote articles and monthly columns in many outdoor periodicals from the 1930's to the 1970's.   He also wrote, *Safari* (1968), published by Safari Publications, which described his African hunt.

Keith, Lloyd B.

A Study of Wildfowl Ecology On Small Impoundments in Southeastern Alberta.   Washington, D. C., 1961, The Wildlife Society.   Monograph # 6.   88 pp., photographic plates, bibliography.   4to.   Paper wrappers.

Keith, Lloyd B., et al.

Demography and Ecology of a Declining Snowshoe Hare Population. Washington, D. C., 1984, The Wildlife Society.   Monograph # 90.   43 pp., photographic plates, bibliography.   4to.   Paper wrappers.

Keith, Sam

One Man's Wilderness.   Anchorage, 1981, Alaska Northwest Publishing Company.   75 pp., color photographs.   Oblong 4to.

Keller, W. Phillip

Canada's Wild Glory.   London, 1961, Jarrolds Publishers, Ltd.   336 pp., color and black and white illustrations.   8vo; dust jacket.   An informal guide book of Canada emphasizing its hunting and angling prospects.

Kellog, Charles E.

Silver Fox Pup Values; in relation to date of birth, age of vixens and other factors. Washington, D. C., 1941, United States Department of the Interior. 15 pp. 8vo. Paper wrappers. Intended as a guide to pelt values.

Kellog, Robert L.

Happy Hunting Grounds. Caldwell, Idaho, 1955, Caxton Printers, Ltd. 175 pp., photographic plates. 8vo; dust jacket. Big game hunting in British Columbia and Alaska. Scarce.

Kelly, Luther S. "Yellowstone"
See **Quaiffe, M. M.**

Kelly, Robert F., editor

The Sportsman's Anthology. New York, 1944, Howell. 396 pp. 8vo; dust jacket. An anthology of foxhunting, shooting and angling stories by Grand, Buckingham, Farrington and others.

Kelly, Robert G. b. 1898

More Trails on Six Continents. Charleston, West Virginia, 1973, Privately printed. 214 pp., photographic plates. 8vo; dust jacket.

Trails, Trout and Tigers; outdoor reminiscences on six continents. Charleston, West Virginia, 1961, Privately printed. 158 pp. 8vo; dust jacket. Both of these works have some North American big game hunting experiences.

Kelly, Tom

Dealer's Choice. Spanish Fort, Alabama, 1983, Wingfeather Press. 100 pp. 8vo; dust jacket. Turkey hunting and some angling tales.

Tenth Legion. Monroe, Alabama, 1973, Spur Enterprises. 119 pp. 8vo; dust jacket. (Reprinted several times, same format, various publishers) Turkey hunting in Alabama.

Kelly, Tim K.

The Official Colorado-Wyoming Hunting and Fishing Guide. Denver, 1980, Recreation. Fifteenth edition. 320 pp., illustrations. Paper wrappers.

Kelsall, John P.

Continued Barren Ground Caribou Studies. Ottawa, 1957, Canadian Wildlife Service. 148 pp., photographic plates, maps. 8vo. Paper wrappers.

Co-Operative Studies of Barren Ground Caribou, 1957-1958. Ottawa, 1960, Canadian Wildlife Service. 145 pp., maps. 8vo. Paper wrappers.

Kelver, Gerald O.

Maj. Ned H. Roberts and the Schuetzen Rifle. Mentone, Indiana, 1951, Privately printed. 99 pp., photographic plates. 8vo; dust jacket. Scarce.

Respectfully Yours; H. M. Pope, the Pope story as told from the files of his correspondence. No place (Ft. Collins), 1976, Privately printed. 228 pp., illustrations. 4to. H. M. Pope was a pioneer in producing accurate rifle barrels. Scarce.

Schuetzen Rifles - History & Loading. Boulder, 1972, Privately printed. 121 pp., illustrations. A limited edition of unspecified number. 8vo. Paper wrappers.

Kendall, Dr. Arthur I.

Rifle Making in the Great Smoky Mountains. Washington, D. C., 1941, National Park Service. 34 pp., illustrations. 16mo. Paper wrappers.

Kennard, C. H.

What Sport? London, 1947, Frederick Muller, Ltd. 87 pp., photographic plates. 8vo. Upland and big game hunting and some angling in British Columbia.

Kennedy, Bess

The Lady and the Lions. New York, 1942, Whittlesey House. 221 pp., photographic plates. 8vo; dust jacket. The adventures of a woman government cougar hunter.

Kennedy, Dave and Ernie Lewis

In Search of the Canada Goose. Matteson, 1977, Greatlakes. 149 pp., photographic plates, bibliography. 4to. Paper wrappers. Goose hunting in the central flyway.

Kennedy, John Pendleton

The Blackwater Chronicle; a narrative of an expedition into the land of Canaan, in Randolph County, Virginia. A country flowing with wild animals, such as panthers, bears, wolves, elk, deer, otter, badger, etc. With innumerable trout, etc. Charleston, 1978, West Virginia Department of Natural Resources. 223 pp., illustrations. 8vo. (A facsimile reproduction of the 1853 first edition)

Kennedy, Monty

The Checkering and Carving of Gunstocks. Georgetown, South Carolina, 1952, Small Arms Technical Publishing Company. 252 pp., photographic plates, drawings, plus ads. 4to; dust jacket. (Reprinted 1953 and 1954, same format and publisher. Also a 1962 second revised edition, The Stackpole Company. This revised edition reprinted many times, same format and publisher) This was the fourth booklet in a series produced by Small Arms relating to stockmaking; the other three were written by **Alvin Linden**, which see.

Kent, Edwin C.
    The Isle of Long Ago; sporting days. New York, 1933, Charles Scribner's Sons. 194 pp., photographic frontispiece, etching by William Schaldach. Limited to 1000 numbered copies. 8vo. Tales of upland gunning along the eastern seaboard of the U. S., with one chapter on salmon fishing.

Kent, William
    Reminiscences of Outdoor Life. San Francisco, 1929, A. M. Robertson. 304 pp., photographic plates. Foreword by Stewart Edward White. 8vo. Hunting and angling in the Western U. S.

Keogh, S. Gerald
    Sam Colt's New Model Pocket Pistol; the story of the 1855 Root Model revolver. 1964, Privately printed. 31 pp., photographic plates. 4to. Paper wrappers.

Kephart, George S.
    Campfires Rekindled. Mation, 1977, Channing. 146 pp., photographic plates, drawings. 8vo. Paper wrappers. The reminiscences of a life in the Maine woods by the son of Horace Kephart, author of *Camping and Woodcraft.*

Kephart, Horace   **1862-1931**
    The Book of Camping and Woodcraft. New York, 1939, The Macmillan Company. 479 pp., illustrations. 8vo; dust jacket. (Originally published, 1906, Outing Publishing Company)
    Our Southern Highlanders. New York, 1933, The Macmillan Company. 469 pp., photographic plates. 8vo; dust jacket. (This, a revised and enlarged edition of the 1913 Outing Publishing Company edition. The 1933 edition was also reprinted twice in 1949 and 1967, same format and publisher) Mostly travel and adventure with an account of the people of the southern Appalachians. Includes some bear hunting.
    Sporting Firearms. New York, 1928, The Macmillan Company. 153 pp., illustrations. 12mo; dust jacket. (Originally published, 1912, Outing Publishing Company)

Kerr, Richard M.
    Mule Deer Habitat Guidelines. Denver, 1981, United States Department of Agriculture / Bureau of Land Management. Photographic plates, maps. 4to. Paper wrappers.

Kester, Jesse Y.
    The American Shooter's Manual. New York, 1928, Privately printed for Ernest R. Gee by the Derrydale Press. 157 pp., illustrations from old plates. Limited to 375 copies. 8vo. Originally published in 1827 in Philadelphia, this title is one of the earliest sporting books published in America.

Kesting, Ted, editor
Lowland Game Birds. New York, 1962, Thomas Nelson & Sons, Inc.
182 pp., photographic plates. A title in the Sports Afield Library. 8vo; dust
jacket.
The Outdoor Encyclopedia. New York, 1957, A. S. Barnes and
Company, Inc. 433 pp., illustrations. 4to; dust jacket. (Also an edition bound
in mission leather)
Upland Game Birds. New York, 1962, Thomas Nelson & Sons, Inc.
198 pp., photographic plates. A title in the Sports Afield Library. 8vo; dust
jacket.

Keys, Elwood
Moose on the Ottawa. Winchester, Indiana, 1936, Privately printed.
293 pp., photographic plates. 12mo. Paper wrappers. The author recounts many of
his hunting trips to the Upper Peninsula of Michigan, Pennsylvania and into Canada for moose and
deer. Rare.

Kidney, Dorothy Boone
Away From it All. South Brunswick, New Jersey, 1970, A. S. Barnes
and Company, Inc. 200 pp., photographic plates, map. 8vo; dust jacket. Life in
the Allagash region of Maine, with some hunting.

Kienbusch, Carl Otto Von and Stephen V. Grancsay.
The Bashford Dean Collection of Arms and Armor in the Metropolitan
Museum of Art. Portland, Maine, 1933, The Arms and Armor Club of New York
City. 270 pp., many photographic plates. 4to.

Kilgore, Clinard
Henry Hillman's Experience in Alaska as a Pioneer. No place, 1974,
Privately printed. 103 pp., illustrations. 8vo. Includes some bear hunting.

Kimball, David and Jim Kimball
The Market Hunter. Minneapolis, 1969, Dillon Press, Inc. 132 pp.,
drawings by J. Breckinridge. 8vo; dust jacket. (Reprinted 1975, same format
and publisher) An account of the indiscriminate slaughter of waterfowl for the market; also with
a section on the meaning of hunting in modern times and its interaction with conservation.

Kindig, Joe, Jr.
Thoughts on the Kentucky Rifle in Its Golden Age. York, Pennsylvania,
1960, George N. Hyatt. 561 pp., illustrations. Limited to 200 numbered and
signed copies. Thick 4to; slipcased. (Reprinted several times, George
Shumway)

King, Bart

How To Raise and Train a Gordon Setter. Jersey City, New Jersey, 1965, TFH Publishers. 64 pp., illustrations. 8vo. Paper wrappers.

King, Calvin L.

Reasons For the Decline of Game in the Bighorn Basin of Wyoming. New York, 1965, Vantage Press. 161 pp., photographic plates. 8vo; dust jacket.

King, Ralph T.

Ruffed Grouse Management. Syracuse, New York, 1943, Roosevelt Wildlife Forest Experiment Stations. 20 pp., photographic plates. 8vo. Paper wrappers.

King, Maj. W. Ross

The Sportsman and Naturalist in Canada; or notes on the natural history of the game, game birds, and fish of that country. Toronto, 1974, Coles Publishing Company. 334 pp., illustrations. A title in the Coles Canadian Collection. 8vo; dust jacket. (A reproduction of the 1866 first edition)

Kingston, Lyle H.

On Behalf of the Hunted. New York, 1955, D. Appleton-Century-Crofts, Inc. 139 pp., drawings. 8vo; dust jacket. (Also published by C. C. Nelson Publishing Company) Stories of Wisconsin hunting and angling.

Kinkhead, Eugene

Squirrel Book. New York, 1980, E. P. Dutton & Co., Inc. 147 pp., drawings. 8vo; dust jacket.

Kinton, Tony

The Beginning Bowhunter. Indiana, 1985, ICS Books, Inc. 119 pp.

Kirkland, Wallace W.

Shenshoo: The Story of a Moose. Chicago, 1930, Thomas S. Rockwell Company. 64 pp. A juvenile.

Kirmse, Marguerite   1866-1954

Dogs in the Field. New York, 1935, The Derrydale Press. Unpaginated, 24 full-page illustrations from drawings by the author. Issued with an extra suite of six of the plates appearing in the book. Limited to 685 numbered copies. Oblong 4to; boxed. A collection of the author's sporting dog illustrations.

Ms. Kirmse was a popular dog illustrator of the period whose artwork appeared on the pages of many non-sporting dog books as well. She also produced a general dog work, *Marguerite Kirmse's Dogs*, 1930, published by The Derrydale Press.

Kirschner, Bob

The Art and Appreciation of Trophy Bowhunting. McKeesport, Pennsylvania, 1981, Privately printed. 262 pp. 8vo. Paper wrappers.

Everything I Know About Bucks With a Bow; it's in the hunt not the kill. McKeesport, Pennsylvania, 1974, Privately printed. 104 pp., photographic plates. 8vo. Paper wrappers.

Kitchen, David W.

Social Behavior and Ecology of the Pronghorn. Washington, 1974, The Wildlife Society. Monograph # 38. 96 pp., photographs, drawings, map, bibliography. 4to. Paper wrappers.

Kites, Clifford

Reminiscences of an Old Sportsman. Springfield, Massachusetts, 1951, Springfield Printing Company. 108 pp., illustrations 8vo;dust jacket. An uncommon book about hunting and fishing in western Massachusetts.

Kitteredge, Doug

See **Wambold, H. R. "Dutch"**

Kjelgaard, James Arthur "Jim" 1910-1959

The Black Fawn. New York, 1965, Dodd, Mead & Co. 215 pp., illustrations. 8vo; dust jacket.

Big Red. New York, 1945, Holiday House. 231 pp., illustrations by Bob Kuhn. 8vo; dust jacket. A juvenile about an Irish setter.

Fawn in the Forest. New York, 1962, Dodd, Mead & Co. 168 pp., illustrations. 8vo; dust jacket.

Furious Moose of the Wilderness. New York, 1965, Dodd, Mead & Co. 149 pp., illustrations. 8vo; dust jacket.

Mr. Kjelgaard wrote many other older juveniles with animal themes.

Kjelgaard, James Arthur "Jim," editor

Hound Dogs and Others; a collection of stories by members of Western Writers of America. New York, 1958, Dodd, Mead & Co. 245 pp., drawings by Paul Brown. 8vo; dust jacket. (Reprinted 1980, Arno)

Klein, Tom

Loon Magic. Ashland, 1985, Paper Birch. 130 pp., color and black and white illustrations, maps, bibliography. Folio; dust jacket. (Reprinted 1985, same format and publisher) An excellent monograph of the loon.

Klepper, Dan

The 13th Month; an outdoorsman's notebook. San Antonio, Texas, 1973, Express. 255 pp. 8vo. Paper wrappers. Tales of the year's best hunting and fishing trips.

Kletzly, Robert

The American Woodcock in West Virginia. Charleston, 1976, West Virginia Department of Natural Resources. 46 pp., illustrations. Paper wrappers.

Klimstra, W. D. and John L. Roseberry

Nesting Ecology of the Bobwhite in Southern Illinois. Washington, D. C., 1975, The Wildlife Society. 37 pp., photographic plate, bibliography. 4to. Paper wrappers.

Kline, Carl G.

Raising Wild Turkeys. Freeport, 1978, Privately printed. 32 pp., photographic plates, drawings. 8vo. Paper wrappers

Kline, Lee, editor

Colorado Bowhunting Records of Big Game Animals. Colorado, 1973, Colorado Bowhunters Association, Inc. 215 pp. 8vo; dust jacket. (Also a 1982 edition, same format and publisher)

Klineburger, Bert and Vernon W. Hurst.

Big Game Hunting Around the World. New York, 1969, Exposition Press. 376 pp., color and black and white photographs. 8vo; dust jacket. With accounts of sheep, goat, bear and caribou hunting in North America.

Klinkenberg, Jeff

Bird Dog in the Smokehouse. St. Petersburg, Florida, 1983, St. Petersburg Times. 94 pp., color and black and white illustrations by Scott Hiestand. Folio. Paper wrappers. Hunting and fishing tales.

Knap, Jerome J., editor

All About Wildfowling in America. New York, 1976, Winchester Press. 305 pp., illustrations. 8vo; dust jacket.

The Complete Hunter's Almanac. Toronto, 1978, Pagurian Press, Ltd. 291 pp., photographic plates, drawings. 8vo; dust jacket.

The Digest Book of Hunting Dogs. Northfield, Illinois, 1979, DBI Books. 95 pp., illustrations. 4to. Paper wrappers.

The Digest Book of Hunting Tips. Northfield, Illinois, 1979, DBI Books. 94 pp., illustrations. 4to. Paper wrappers.

The Hunter's Handbook; a guide to hunting in North America. New York, 1973, Charles Scribner's Sons. 186 pp., photographic plates. 8vo; dust jacket. (Also a 1976 Canadian edition)

Where to Fish and Hunt in North America. Toronto, 1974, Pagurian Press, Ltd. 192 pp., photographic plates. 8vo; dust jacket.

Knap, Jerome J. and Alyson Knap

Training the Versatile Gun Dog; a complete guide to training versatile gun dogs for hunting in North America. New York, 1974, Charles Scribner's Sons. 183 pp., photographic plates. 8vo; dust jacket. (Reprinted several times, same format and publisher)

Knight, John Alden   1891-1966

Ol' Bill and Other Stories. New York, 1942, Charles Scribner's Sons. 138 pp., drawings by Milton C. Weiler. 8vo; dust jacket. [Also a limited edition of 1,929 numbered copies signed by the author and illustrator]

Ruffed Grouse. New York, 1947, Alfred A. Knopf, Inc. 271 pp., photographic plates, 5 color plates from paintings by Dr. Edgar Burke. A Borzoi Book For Sportsmen. 8vo; dust jacket. [Also a large paper edition, specially bound and limited to 210 numbered copies signed by the author; slipcased. Issued with an extra plate, laid in]

Woodcock. New York, 1944, Alfred A. Knopf, Inc. 161 pp., photographic plates, color plates from paintings by Dr. Edgar Burke. A Borzoi Book For Sportsmen. 8vo; dust jacket. (Reprinted 1946, same format and publisher) [Also a large paper first edition, specially bound and limited to 275 numbered copies signed by the author and artist; slipcased]

John Alden Knight was known primarily for his angling works and his Solunar Theory, which proposed that fish are more or less active depending on the position of the sun relative to the phase of the moon. See Bruns.

Knight, Richard Alden

Mastering the Shotgun. New York, 1967, E. P. Dutton & Co., Inc. 127 pp., illustrations. 8vo; dust jacket. (Reprinted 1967, same format and publisher. Also a 1975 revised edition, same format and publisher)

Knight, Richard R.

The Sun River Elk Herd. Washington, D. C., 1970, The Wildlife Society. Monograph # 23. 66 pp., frontispiece, maps, bibliography. 8vo. Paper wrappers. The summary of a five year study of this Montana elk herd.

Knipe, Theodore

The Javelina in Arizona. Phoenix, No date (ca. 1956), Arizona Game and Fish Department. 96 pp., photographic plates, maps, drawings. 8vo. Paper wrappers.

Knott, M. O'Malley with Page Cooper

Gone Away With O'Malley; seventy years with horses, hounds and people. Garden City, New York, 1944, Doubleday, Doran & Co. 280 pp., drawings by Paul Brown. 8vo; dust jacket. Much on foxhunting by this Irish-born veterinarian.

Kohn, Bruce E.

 Status and Mcnagement of Black Bears in Wisconsin. Madison, 1982, Wisconsin Department of Natural Resources. 31 pp., photographic plates, maps. 4to. Paper wrappers.

Koller, Larry 1912-1967

 The Complete Book of Guns. Indianapolis, 1954, The Bobbs-Merrill Company. 144 pp., illustrations. 4to; dust jacket. Paper wrappers. (Reprinted twice, 1954, 1955, in paper wrappers, Maco. Also a 1956 edition titled, *Larry Koller's Book of Guns,* Random House, Inc.)

 The Complete Book of Hunting. Indianapolis, 1954, The Bobbs-Merrill Company. 144 pp., illustrations. 8vo; dust jacket. (Reprinted 1954, paper wrappers, Maco)

 The Complete Guide To Handguns. New York, 1962, G. H. Levy. 128 pp., illustrations. 4to; dust jacket. (Reprinted 1963, Maco)

 Fireside Book of Guns. New York, 1959, The Ridge Press, Inc. 284 pp., photographic plates. 4to; dust jacket. (Reprinted, same format and content, Simon & Schuster)

 The Golden Guide To Guns. New York, 1961, Golden Press. 157 pp., color and black and white illustrations. 8vo; dust jacket. (Also a 1966 revised edition, same format and publisher)

 Handguns. New York, 1957, Random House, Inc. 136 pp., illustrations. 8vo; dust jacket.

 How To Shoot; a complete guide to the use of sporting firearms - rifles, shotguns and handguns on the range and in the field. Garden City, New York, 1964, Doubleday & Co., Inc. 241 pp., illustrations. 8vo; dust jacket. (Reprinted 1966, same format and publisher. Also a 1976 revised edition, same format and publisher)

 Larry Koller's Hunting Annual. New York, 1957, Random House, Inc. 128 pp., photographic plates. 8vo; dust jacket.

 Larry Koller's New Gun Annual. New York, 1959, Maco. 127 pp., photographic plates, drawings. 8vo. Paper wrappers.

 Larry Koller's New Hunting Annual. Indianapolis, Indiana, 1955, The Bobbs-Merrill Company. 128 pp., photographic plates, drawings. 8vo; dust jacket.

 Popular Handguns. New York, 1957, Maco. 136 pp., illustrations. 8vo.

 Shots At Whitetails. Boston, 1948, Little, Brown & Company. 362 pp., photographic plates, drawings, frontispiece in color from a painting by Bob Kuhn. 8vo; dust jacket. (Reprinted several times, same format and publisher. Also reprinted in 1970 and 1975, Alfred A. Knopf, Inc.) An important deer hunting book.

 Sportsman's Workshop. Indianapolis, 1955, The Bobbs-Merrill Company. 128 pp., illustrations. 8vo.

Koller, Larry, continued

    The Treasury of Hunting. New York, 1965, Odyssey Press / The Ridge Press, Inc. 251 pp., color and black and white illustrations. 4to; dust jacket. (Reprinted 1965, same format and publisher)

Kortright, Francis H.

    The Ducks, Geese and Swans of North America. Washington, D. C., 1942, The American Wildlife Institute. 476 pp., 38 full page color plates from paintings by T. M. Shortt. 8vo; dust jacket. (Reprinted many times to 1947, same format and publisher. Also reprinted many times from 1947 to 1967 by Stackpole and The Wildlife Management Institute) [Also a deluxe first edition, specially bound and limited to 1000 copies, numbered and signed by the author and artist. Also another deluxe edition, 1960, The Stackpole Company, specially bound, but with no stated limitation] An informative and popular guide to the waterfowl of North America, attested to by its many printings. The Stackpole Company and The Wildlife Management Institute published this same title in a second edition in a larger format by **Bellrose, Frank**, which see.

Kotsiopoulos, George, translator.

    The Art and Sport of Falconry. Chicago, 1969, Argonaut. 92 pp., bibliography. 8vo; dust jacket. A translation of an ancient work.

Kozicky, Edward

    Shooting Preserve Management; the Nilo system. East Alton, Illinois, 1966, Winchester-Western Press. 312 pp., illustrations. 8vo; dust jacket. An explanation of the game farm management system used at Nilo Farm, Olin's game reserve.

Kozicky, Edward et al.

    Winchester Hunter's Handbook 1972-1973. New York, 1973, Winchester Press. 192 pp., photographic plates. 8vo. Paper wrappers.

Krakel, Dean, II

    Season of the Elk. Kansas City, 1976, Lowell Press. 117 pp., photographic plates. Oblong 4to; dust jacket. (Reprinted 1977, same format and publisher)

Kramer, Theodore F.

    Fifty Years of Duck Hunting. No place, 1974, Privately printed. 63 pp. Paper wrappers. Louisiana wildfowl hunting.

Krausman, Paul R. and Ernest D. Ables

    Ecology of the Carmen Mountains White-Tailed Deer. Washington, D. C., 1981, United States Department of the Interior. 114 pp. Ecological study of deer in Big Bend National Park, Texas.

Krausman, Paul R. and Norman S. Smith
Deer in the Southwest; a workshop.   1984, Arizona Cooperative
Wildlife Research Unit.   131 pp.

Krausman, Paul R., et al.
Annotated Bibliography of Desert Bighorn Sheep Literature, 1897-1983.
Phoenix, 1984, South West Natural History Association.   205 pp., photographic
plates, drawings. 8vo.

Kreig, Lowell E.
The Private Ownership of Firearms in the United States.   New York,
No date (ca. 1963), Olin Public Relations.   Unpaginated (approx. 300 pp.),
issued with an 8 pp. pamphlet of the same title in a front inside cover pocket.
4to.   A compilation of articles regarding the subject.

Krenz, Bill, editor
Bowhunting Big Game Records of California.   1983, California Big
Game Club.   290 pp., illustrations.   8vo.   Paper wrappers.

Kreps, E.
Camp and Trail Methods.   Columbus, Ohio, Various dates, A. R.
Harding.   273 pp., photographic plates and drawings.   16mo.   (Originally
published, 1910, same format and publisher)
Science of Trapping.   Columbus, Ohio, 1944, A. R. Harding.   245 pp.,
illustrations.   Paper wrappers.   (Originally published, 1909, same format and
publisher)

Kress, Claude W.
The Point System of Wing Shooting.   No place, 1937, Privately printed.
Two volumes.   Volume I, 40 pp. text.   Volume II, illustrations only.   Spiral
bound paper wrappers; slipcased.   Rare.

Krider, E. F.
Krider's Sporting Anecdotes. New York, 1966, Abercrombie & Fitch,
Inc.   292 pp., plates from old engravings.   8vo.   (A facsimile reproduction of the
1853 edition)

Kroeber, Theodora
Ishi in Two Worlds;   a biography of the last wild Indian in North
America.   Berkeley, 1961, University of California Press.   255 pp., color and
black and white illustrations.   8vo; dust jacket.   (Reprinted, same format and
publisher) [Also a 1976 deluxe edition with added illustrations, same publisher]
The story of Ishi, the last Indian archer, with much deer hunting.
Ishi: Last of His Tribe.   New York, 1981, Bantam Books.   213 pp.

Kromer, Ray

Sixty Sporting Years; hunting and fishing from boyhood to senior citizen. Cleveland, Ohio, 1981, K-Y Publishers. 308 pp., photographic plates. Limited to 1250 numbered and signed copies. 8vo; slipcased.

Kuechler, O.

Practical Fur Ranching. Columbus, Ohio, 1927, Hunter-Trader-Trapper. 216 pp., illustrations. 12mo. (Originally published, 1924, same format and publisher)

Kuhlhoff, Pete

Kuhlhoff on Guns. New York, 1970, Winchester Press. 180 pp., illustrations. 8vo; dust jacket.

Kukla, Robert J.

Gun Control. Harrisburg, 1973, Stackpole Books. 448 pp., photographic plates. 8vo; dust jacket. A documentation of attempts to eliminate the private possession of firearms in the U. S.

Kulish, John

Bobcats Before Breakfast. Harrisburg, 1969, The Stackpole Company. 189 pp., drawings. 8vo; dust jacket. The story of a hunter-guide and his family in the wilds of New Hampshire with much on bobcat hunting. Scarce.

Kurant, Frank

Deer Hunting Illustrated. Florence, Vermont, 1949, Privately printed. 45 pp., illustrations. 12mo. Paper wrappers.

Kuykendall, Roy G.

Fur Harvesting and Predator Control. No place, 1975, Privately printed. 68 pp., color and black and white photographic plates. 8vo. Paper wrappers.

Kytle, Jack

Alabama Hunter. Montgomery, 1941, WPA / Alabama Department of Conservation. 42 pp., photographic plates, drawings. 12mo. Paper wrappers.

Labisky, Wallace R.

Waterfowl Shooting. New York, 1954, Greenberg: Publishers. 150 pp., illustrations from drawings by Charles Leidl. Tall 8vo; dust jacket. (Reprinted 1954, same format and publisher)

Labrador Retriever Club

National Retriever Field Trial Club. No place, 1955, National Retriever Field Trial Club. 120 pp., illustrations. 8vo. A history of this organization.

Labrador Retriever Club 25th Anniversary, 1931 - 1956. No place (New York), 1956, Labrador Retriever Club. 164 pp., cover illustration by Edwin Megargee. 8vo. The Labrador Retriever Club has also issued many yearbooks and supplemental yearbooks beginning in 1931.

Labrador Retriever Club

Also see **National Amateur Retriever Club**

LaBrie, Jean

The Amateur Taxidermist; how to stuff and mount birds, fish, furred animals. New York, 1972, Hart Publishers. 156 pp., photographic plates. 8vo; dust jacket.

Lack, David

Evolution Illustrated By Waterfowl. New York, 1974, Harper & Row, Publishers, Inc. 96 pp., drawings. 8vo; dust jacket.

LaDue, Harry

Guide For Trapping and Care of Raw Furs. No place, 1935, Privately printed. 69 pp., illustrations. 8vo.

Laing, Hamilton M.

Allan Brooks: Artist - Naturalist. Victoria, British Columbia, 1979, British Columbia Provincial Museum. 249 pp., color and black and white illustrations. 8vo; dust jacket. A biography illustrating the works of this popular artist.

Lake, Fred and Hal Wright

A Bibliography of Archery. Manchester, England, 1974, The Simon Archery Foundation. 501 pp. Tall 8vo; dust jacket. A useful reference for all books published on the subject in the English language.

Lamb, Dana

Enchanted Vagabonds; in collaboration with June Cleveland. New York, 1938, Harper & Brothers. 415 pp., photographic plates, maps. 8vo; dust jacket. The account of a husband and wife who traveled by canoe down the Pacific coast from San Diego to Panama. It contains many instances of hunting and angling. This is not the same Dana Lamb who authored many angling titles in the 1960's and 1970's.

Lammon, L. D.
   Outdoors With "Dad" Lammon.   Coleraine, Minnesota, 1936, Itasca
Iron News.   381 pp., illustrations.   8vo.

Lamont, Thomas W.
   Henry P. Davidson; the record of a useful life, by his friend and partner.
New York, 1933, Harper & Brothers.   373 pp., photographic plates.   8vo; dust
jacket.   A biography with some North American big game hunting.   Also containing Davidson's
32 pp. African hunting diary.

Lampman, Ben Hur   1886-1954
   How Could I Be Forgetting?   Portland, Oregon, 1926, Walter May.
139 pp., illustrations.   8vo.   (Reprinted twice, same format and publisher)
   The Wild Swan; and other sketches.   New York, 1947, Thomas y.
Crowell Company.   205 pp., drawings.   8vo; dust jacket.   A few of this outdoor
writer's stories in this anthology relate to angling and hunting.   Mr. Lampman published several
other angling books.   His *A Leaf From French Eddy;* a collection of essays on fish, anglers and
fishermen, is generally regarded as a modern classic of the genre.   See Bruns.

Landers, Gunnard
   The Hunting Shack.   New York, 1979, Arbor House.   218 pp.   8vo;
dust jacket.   A murder mystery against the backdrop of a hunting camp.

Landis, Charles S.   1886-1961
   Twenty-Two Caliber Varmint Rifles. Plantersville, South Carolina, 1947,
Small Arms Technical Publishing Company.   531 pp., illustrations.   Tall 8vo; dust
jacket. (Reprinted several times, various publishers)
   .22 Caliber Rifle Shooting.   Marines, Onslow County, North Carolina,
1932, Small Arms Technical Publishing Company.   419 pp., illustrations.   8vo;
dust jacket.   Mostly as relating to target shooting.
   Hunting With the Twenty-Two.   Georgetown, South Carolina, 1950,
Small Arms Technical Publishing Company.   429 pp., illustrations.   8vo; dust
jacket.   Much on squirrel and woodchuck hunting.
   The Shooter's Guide.   Wilmington, Delaware, 1925, Hercules Powder
Company.   51 pp., illustrations.   Folio.   Paper wrappers.
   Woodchucks and Woodchuck Rifles. New York, 1951, Greenberg:
Publishers. 402 pp., photographic plates.   Tall 8vo; dust jacket.

Lang, Lincoln A.   b. 1867
   Ranching With Roosevelt; by a companion rancher.   Philadelphia, 1926,
J. B. Lippincott Co.   367 pp., photographic plates.   8vo; dust jacket.   Contains
some hunting experiences with Roosevelt.

Langford, Cameron
The Winter of the Fisher. New York, 1971, W. W. Norton & Co. 222 pp. 8vo; dust jacket. (Reprinted, same format and publisher. Also a 1971 Canadian edition) A novel depicting a year in the life of this fur-bearer.

Lanier, Henry W.   1874-1958
A. B. Frost: The American Sportsman's Artist. New York, 1933, The Derrydale Press. 154 pp., plates from drawings and paintings by Frost. Limited to 950 copies. Folio. (Reprinted 1985, Premier Press)

Lanks, Herbert C.
Highway To Alaska. New York, 1944, D. Appleton-Century Company, Inc. 8vo; dust jacket. (Reprinted, same format and publisher) Mostly a travel guide, but some hunting, trapping and angling.

Lariar, Lawrence
Hunt and Be Damned. Englewood Cliffs, New Jersey, 1956, Prentice-Hall, Inc. Unpaginated. 4to; dust jacket. Humorous hunting cartoons.

Larkin, Sarah
The Old Master. New York, 1955, Privately printed. 44 pp. 12mo. The story of a Labrador retriever.
The Old Master and Other Tails. New York, 1968, Privately printed. 103 pp., illustrations. 8vo. Hunting and field trials with Labrador retrievers.

Larsen, Thor
The World of the Polar Bear. London, 1978, Hamlyn. 96 pp., color illustrations, bibliography. Foreword by Sir Peter Scott. Folio; dust jacket.

Lasquin, R.
Collection of Sporting Books, Reference Books and Books on Fine Arts From the Library of R. Lasquin. New York, 1933, Plaza Book Auction Co. 62 pp. 8vo. Paper wrappers. An auction catalog with 493 lots, many of which were sporting books.

Latham, Roger M.   1914-1979
The Complete Book of the Wild Turkey. Harrisburg, 1956, The Stackpole Company. 265 pp., drawings by Ned Smith. 8vo; dust jacket. (Also a 1976 revised edition, same publisher. This revised edition reprinted several times)
The Ecology and Economics of Predator Management. Harrisburg, 1951, Pennsylvania Game Commission. 96 pp., bibliography. 8vo. Paper wrappers.

Latham, Sid

Camera Afield. Harrisburg, 1976, The Stackpole Company. 224 pp., color and black and white photographs. 4to; dust jacket. A guide to outdoor photography.

Great Sporting Posters of the Golden Age Harrisburg, 1978, Stackpole Books. Unpaginated, full page color plates plus 3 pp. text. Elephant Folio. Paper wrappers. (Reprinted 1982, same format and publisher) A reproduction of classic sporting advertisements.

Latrobe, Ferdinand C.

Iron Men and Their Dogs. Baltimore, 1941, Drechsler. 225 pp., illustrations. Limited to 1000 copies. 8vo. A description of the Bartlett-Hayword ironworks and 'Canton' and 'Sailor,' two Chesapeake Bay Retrievers. With one chapter on hunting canvasbacks on the Chesapeake.

Lauber, George, editor

How To Build Your Own Flintlock Rifle or Pistol. Olson, New Jersey, 1976, Privately printed. 13 pp. text plus 29 plates (some fold-out). 8vo. Paper wrappers.

Laverack, Edward

The Setter; with notices of the most eminent breeds, now extant; instructions how to breed, rear and break; dog shows, field trials, general management, etc. Washington, D. C., 1945, Denlinger's, Inc. 62 pp., photographic plates. 8vo. (A reproduction of the scarce 1872 edition)

Lawing, Nellie Neal

Alaska Nellie. Seattle, 1940, Chieftain Press. 201 pp., photographic plates. 8vo. (Reprinted several times, various publishers) An interesting autobiographical account of a woman hunter and trapper in Alaska.

Lawler, Joseph C. and Oscar S. Bay

Hunting; a few memorable trips. Rockland, Massachusetts, 1983, Privately printed. 113 pp., color and black and white illustrations. 4to; dust jacket. Big game hunting around the world, with some North American experiences. Scarce.

Lawrence, R. D.

The Ghost Walker. New York, 1983, Holt, Rinehart & Winston. 242 pp. 8vo; dust jacket. An account of a year long study of puma in British Columbia.

Lawson, Larry E.

Trophy Bucks of Indiana. 1985, Privately printed. 189 pp., illustrations. Accounts of taking trophy whitetails with photographs of record heads.

Lay, Daniel W.

Quail Management Handbook For East Texas. Austin, 1965, Texas Fish and Game Commission. Fifth printing. 47 pp., photographic plates, drawings. 8vo Paper wrappers.

Laycock, George   b. 1921

The Alien Animals. New York, 1966, American Museum of Natural History. 240 pp., photographic plates, bibliography. 8vo; dust jacket. An account of introducing various animal species into areas different than their native habitats.

America's Endangered Wildlife. New York, 1969, W. W. Norton & Co., Inc. 226 pp., illustrations. 8vo; dust jacket. (Reprinted several times, various publishers)

Animal Movers; a collection of ecological surprises. New York, 1971, American Museum of Natural History. 107 pp., photographic plates. 8vo; dust jacket. Another account of introducing various animal species into areas different than their native habitats.

Autumn of the Eagle. New York, 1973, Charles Scribner's Sons. 239 pp., photographic plates, bibliography. 8vo; dust jacket. The history and decline of the American bald eagle.

Big Nick; the story of a remarkable black bear. New York, 1967, W. W. Norton & Co., Inc. 186 pp., illustrations. 8vo; dust jacket.

The Deer Hunter's Bible. New York, 1963, Doubleday & Co., Inc. 153 pp., illustrations. 4to. Paper wrappers. (Reprinted many times, same format and publisher)

The Sign of the Flying Goose; the story of our National Wildlife Refuges. Garden City, New York, 1965, Garden City Publishing Company. 299 pp., photographic plates, maps. (Reprinted and revised several times, various publishers)

The Shotgunner's Bible. New York, 1969, Doubleday & Co., Inc. 173 pp., photographic plates. 4to. Paper wrappers.

Squirrels. New York, 1975, Four Winds Press. 102 pp., illustrations. 8vo; dust jacket.

Whitetail; the story of a white-tailed deer. New York, 1966, W. W. Norton & Co., Inc. 110 pp., illustrations. 8vo; dust jacket. A fictionalized account.

Wild Hunters; North America's predators. New York, 1978, David McKay Co. 121 pp., illustrations. 8vo; dust jacket.

Wild Travelers; the story of animal migration. New York, 1974, Four Winds Press. 110 pp., illustrations. 8vo; dust jacket.

Laycock, George and Erwin Bauer

Hunting With the Bow and Arrow. New York, 1965, Arco. 111 pp., illustrations. 8vo; dust jacket.

Learn, C. R.
    Bowhunter's Digest. Chicago, 1974. 288 pp., photographic plates. 4to. Paper wrappers.

Leatherman, Carroll Seabrook
    The Old Man...and the Dog. Princeton, New Jersey, 1984, Nassau Press. 152 pp., drawings by Philip Crowe. 8vo; dust jacket. The story of 'Miss One Dot,' the 1979 Grand National bird dog champion and her handler.

Leavitt, Bud
    Twelve Months in Maine. Bangor, Maine, 1977, Bangor Publishing Company. 196 pp., drawings by Tom Hennessey. 8vo; dust jacket. An anthology of the author's stories originally appearing in the *Bangor Daily News.*

Leclerc, Maurice J.
    The Retriever Trainer's Manual. New York, 1962, The Ronald Press. 210 pp., photographic plates. Oblong 8vo; dust jacket.

LeCount, Albert
    Analysis of the Black Bear Harvest in Arizona, 1968-1978. Phoenix, 1981, Arizona Game and Fish Commission. 42 pp., photographic plates, drawings, maps. 4to. Paper wrappers.
    The First Western Black Bear Workshop. Tempe, Arizona, 1979. 339 pp., tables, graphs. 4to. Paper wrappers.

Lee, Ben
    The Turkey Hunting World of Ben Lee. Huntsville, Alabama, 1983, Resta Corporation. 166 pp., photographic plates, drawings by Gayle Lee. 8vo. Paper wrappers.

Lee, Forest B., et al.
    Rearing and Restoring Giant Canada Geese in the Dakotas. Bismarck, 1984, North Dakota Fish and Game Department. 79 pp., photographic plates, bibliography. 4to. Paper wrappers.
    Waterfowl in Minnesota. No place, 1964, Minnesota Department of Conservation. 210 pp., photographic plates, maps, drawings, bibliography. 8vo. Paper wrappers.

Lee, Kenneth Fuller   **1894-1938**
    Big Game Hunting and Marksmanship; a manual on the rifles, marksmanship and methods best adapted to the hunting of the big game of the eastern United States. Onslow County, North Carolina, 1941, Small Arms Technical Publishing Company. 217 pp., illustrations plus ads. 16mo; dust jacket. (Reprinted 1944, same format and publisher)

Lee, Wayne C.

Scotty Philip; the man who saved the buffalo.   Caldwell, Idaho, 1975, Caxton Printers, Ltd.   334 pp., photographic plates.   8vo; dust jacket.   Mr. Philip gathered the remnants of the wild bison herd to form one group of animals that was to become the nucleus of today's North American bison herd.

Leffingwell, W. Bruce

The Art of Wing Shooting. New York, 1967, Abercrombie & Fitch, Inc. 192 pp., plates from old engravings.   8vo; dust jacket.   (A facsimile reproduction originally published 1890, Rand McNally & Company)

Legare, Robert

The Coonhound.   Columbus, Ohio, Various dates, Hunter-Trader-Trapper. 152 pp., illustrations.   12mo.   (Originally published, 1924, same format and publisher)

Lehman, Valgene W.

Atwater's Prairie Chicken: Its Life History and Management. Washington, D. C., 1941, United States Department of the Interior.   65 pp., photographic plates, bibliography.   Paper wrappers.

Bobwhites; in the Rio Grande plain of Texas.   College Station, 1984, Texas A & M University Press.   371 pp., color and black and white illustrations, maps, bibliography.   4to; dust jacket.

Leidesdorf, Arthur D.

The Sporting Library of Arthur D. Leidesdorf.   New York, 1958, Parke-Bernet Galleries, Inc.   97 pp.   8vo.   Paper wrappers.   An auction catalog containing a significant number of hunting and firearms books.

Leitch, W. G.

Ducks and Men.   Winnipeg, 1978, Ducks Unlimited.   268 pp., color and black and white illustrations.   4to; dust jacket.   The history of Ducks Unlimited - Canada.

LeMaster, Richard

Decoys; the art of the wooden bird.   Chicago, 1982, Contemporary Books, Inc.   156 pp., color and black and white illustrations.   4to; dust jacket.

The Great Gallery of Ducks and Other Waterfowl.   Chicago, 1985, Contemporary Books, Inc.   340 pp., color illustrations.   Folio; dust jacket.

The LeMaster Method of Waterfowl Identification.   Oakfield, No date, Scotch Game Call Company.   75 pp., color illustrations.   12mo.   Spiral bound paper wrappers.

Waterfowl; the artist's guide to anatomy, attitude and color.   Chicago, 1983, Contemporary Books, Inc.   186 pp., color and black and white illustrations. 4to; dust jacket.

LeMaster, Richard, continued
Wildlife in Wood; a duck carver's handbook. Chicago, 1978, Contemporary Books, Inc. 244 pp., photographic plates. Oblong 4to; dust jacket.

Lempfert, O. C.
Paw Prints; how to identify rare and common animals by their tracks. New York, 1972, Exposition Press. 71 pp., color and black and white illustrations. 8vo; dust jacket.

Lemmon, Robert S.
Our Amazing Birds; the little known facts about their private lives. New York, 1952, Doubleday & Co., Inc. 239 pp., illustrations by Don Eckelberry. 8vo; dust jacket. Some information on upland game birds.

Lendt, David L.
Ding; The Life of Jay Norwood Darling. Ames, Iowa, 1979, Iowa State University Press. 202 pp., illustrations, bibliography. 8vo; dust jacket. (Reprinted 1989, in paper wrappers, same publisher) [Also a 1984 edition of 100 numbered copies, Darling Conservation Foundation] The biography of Ding Darling, conservationist and illustrator of the first federal duck stamp.

Leneve, Lans
Hello, Sportsmen. New York, 1954, Pageant Press. 213 pp. 8vo; dust jacket. A collection of fishing and hunting stories.

Lenk, Torsten
The Flintlock; its origin and development. New York, 1965, Bramhall House. Edited by J. F. Hayward. 188 pp., photographic plates, bibliography. 4to; dust jacket. (Originally published, 1939, Sweden)

Lenon, Herbert
The Secrets of Successful Trapping. Gulliver, 1944, Privately printed. 53 pp., photographic plates. 8vo. Paper wrappers.

Lenz, Ellis Christian   b. 1896
Muzzle Flashes; five centuries of firearms and men. Huntington, West Virginia, 1944, Standard Publications, Inc. 812 pp., drawings by the author, photographic plates. Tall 8vo; dust jacket. (Also a second edition, same format and publisher, but printed on lighter paper stock) An account of the development of firearms and their influence on man.
Rifleman's Progress. Huntington, West Virginia, 1946, Standard Publications, Inc. 162 pp., drawings by the author, photographic plates. 4to; dust jacket. Target shooting in the U. S. and African big game hunting.

Leonard, Dale R.

Hunting Colorado's Bighorn. No place, No date (ca. 1969), Privately printed. Unpaginated (approx. 350 pp.), many photographic plates. 4to. A compilation of articles by many prominent sheep hunters. Scarce.

Leopold, Aldo   1886-1948

The Distribution of Wisconsin's Hares. Madison, 1945.   14 pp., illustrations. 8vo. Paper wrappers.

Game Management. New York, 1933, Charles Scribner's Sons.   481 pp., color frontispiece by Allan Brooks, other illustrations, charts, bibliography. 8vo; dust jacket.   (Reprinted many times, same format and publisher) An important work by an eminent conservationist.

Report on a Game Survey of the North Central States. Madison, Wisconsin, 1931, Sporting Arms and ammunition Manufacturer's Institute.   299 pp., illustrations. 4to.

Round River; from the journals of Aldo Leopold.   New York, 1953, Oxford University Press. Edited by Luna Leopold. 173 pp., drawings by Charles Schwartz. 8vo; dust jacket.   (Reprinted 1972, same publisher and format)

A Sand County Almanac; and sketches here and there.   New York, 1949, Oxford University Press. 226 pp., drawings by Charles W. Schwartz. 8vo; dust jacket.   Also published in paper wrappers.   (Reprinted and revised several times, various publishers.   Also a 1966 revised edition titled, *A Sand County Almanac With Other Essays on Conservation From "Round River."*)

Leopold, Aldo

Also see **Flader, Susan L.**

Leopold, A. Starker   1913-1983

The California Quail.   Berkeley, 1977, University of California Press. 281 pp., illustrations. 8vo; dust jacket.

Game Birds and Mammals of California.   Berkeley, 1951, California Book Co.   125 pp., illustrations.   4to.

The Nature of Heritible Wildness in Turkeys.   Berkeley, 1944, The Condor.   64 pp., photographic plates, bibliography.   4to.   Paper wrappers. A discussion of the adverse effects of interbreeding wild and domestic turkeys in southern Missouri.   A scarce and important wild turkey management study.

Status of Mexican Big Game Herds.   Washington, D. C., 1947, Wildlife Management Institute.   11 pp., maps.   8vo.   Paper wrappers.

Wildlife of Mexico; the game birds and mammals. Berkeley, 1959, University of California Press.   568 pp., color and black and white illustrations. Tall 8vo; dust jacket.   (Reprinted 1972, same format and publisher)

Leopold, A. Starker and F. Fraser Darling

Wildlife in Alaska. New York, No date (ca.1953), The Ronald Press. 129 pp., illustrations. 8vo. (Reprinted 1972, Greenwood Press) In the authors' words, "This field study concerns the great horned animals of Alaska and their environment in one of the last frontier lands of the world." Scarce.

Leopold, A. Starker, et al.

North American Game Birds and Mammals. New York, 1981, Charles Scribner's Sons. 198 pp., drawings, bibliography. 4to; dust jacket. (Reprinted 1984, in paper wrappers, same publisher) A natural history of the various species.

Leslie, David M. and Charles L. Douglas

Desert Bighorn Sheep of the River Mountains, Nevada. Washington, D. C., 1979, The Wildlife Society. 56 pp., photographic plates, maps, bibliography. Paper wrappers.

Leslie, Lionel A. D.

Wilderness Trails in Three Continents; an account of travel, big game hunting and exploration in India, China, East Africa and Labrador. London, 1931, Heath Cranton Ltd. 223 pp., photographic plates. Foreword by Winston Churchill. 8vo. The section on Labrador has mention of caribou.

Lester, Louis

See **Minehart, Charles D.**

Letourneau, Gene L.

America's New "Wolf." Portland, Maine, 1985, Privately printed. 115 pp., photographic plates. 8vo. Paper wrappers. (Reprinted, same format and publisher) A commentary about the proliferation of the coyote.

Sportsmen Say. Augusta, Maine, 1975, Privately printed. 215 pp., illustrations. 8vo; dust jacket. (Reprinted 1976, same format and publisher) Hunting and fishing in Maine.

Levine, Ed

The Adventures of Red Perkins; remembrances of an Adirondack guide. Lakemont, 1976, North Country. 66 pp., photographic plates. 8vo. Paper wrappers.

Lewenhaupt, Count C. A. C.

Sport Across the World. New York, 1933, E. P. Dutton & Co., Inc. 288 pp., photographic plates. 8vo; dust jacket. With some hunting in America.

Lewis, E. J.
The American Sportsman. New York, 1967, Abercrombie & Fitch, Inc. 510 pp., plates from old engravings. 8vo; dust jacket. (A facsimile reproduction originally published 1863, J. B. Lippincott Co.)

Lewis, Gerald
My Big Buck; outdoor stories of Maine. Thorndike, Maine, 1978, The Thorndike Press. 211 pp. Introduction by Arthur MacDougall, Jr. 8vo. (Reprinted 1978, same publisher)

Lewis, J.
Hobby Gunsmithing. Northfield, Illinois, 1972, Digest Publishing Company. Edited by Ralph T. Walker. Photographic plates. 4to. Paper wrappers.

Lewis, Jack, editor
Black Powder Gun Digest. Northfield, Illinois, 1977, Digest Publishing Company. 288 pp., photographic plates, drawings. 4to. Paper wrappers.
Bow and Arrow Archer's Digest. Northfield, Illinois, 1971, Digest Publishing Company. 320 pp., photographic plates, drawings. 4to. Paper wrappers. (Also a 1977 second edition, same format and publisher)

Lewis, James C.
The World of the Wild Turkey. Philadelphia, 1973, J. B. Lippincott Co. 158 pp., photographic plates, bibliography. A title in Lippincott's Living World series. 4to; dust jacket.

Lewis, John Taylor, Jr.
Ole Marster's Cedar Grove; the story of a Virginia plantation. Richmond, Virginia, 1957, Privately printed. 70 pp., photographic plates. 8vo. A rare turkey hunting title.

Lewis, Peter, editor
A Fox-Hunter's Anthology. New York, 1935, The Macmillan Company. 385 pp., color and black and white illustrations. 8vo; dust jacket. Includes notes on the authors.

Leydet, Francois
The Coyote; defiant sundog of the West. San Francisco, 1977, Chronicle Books. 222 pp., illustrations. 8vo; dust jacket.

Leyson, Burr

The Modern Colt Guide. New York, 1953, Greenberg: Publishers. 128 pp., illustrations. 12mo. Paper wrappers.

The Modern Remington Firearms Guide. New York, 1953, Greenberg: Publishers. 128 pp., illustrations. Paper wrappers. 8vo.

Liebers, Arthur

How To Raise and Train a German Shorthaired Pointer. Jersey City, New Jersey, 1961, TFH Publishers. 64 pp., illustrations. 8vo. Paper wrappers.

Liebers, Arthur and Paul Jeffries

How To Raise and Train a Weimaraner. Jersey City, New Jersey, 1959, TFH Publishers. 64 pp., illustrations. 8vo. Paper wrappers.

Liedel, Charles

Hunting With Rifle and Pencil. Frederickton, New Brunswick, 1955, Brunswick Press. 186 pp., drawings by the author. 8vo; dust jacket.

Ligon, J. Stokley

History and Management of Merriam's Wild Turkey. Albuquerque, 1946, New Mexico Game and Fish Department. 84 pp., photographic plates, maps. 8vo. Paper wrappers.

Upland Game Bird Restoration Through Trapping and Transplanting. Albuquerque, 1946, New Mexico Game and Fish Department. 77 pp., photographic plates. 8vo. Paper wrappers.

Wild Life in New Mexico; its conservation and management. Albuquerque, 1927, New Mexico Game and Fish Department. 212 pp., photographic plates, maps. 8vo.

Limerick, E. Eugene, editor

Virginia Bowhunters; official field archery manual. Fredericksburg, Virginia, 1961, Colonial Press. 145 pp., photographic plates, drawings, maps. 8vo. Spiral bound paper wrappers.

Lincks, F. M. "Cherokee"

Memoirs of a Kentucky Boy. New York, 1960, Vantage Press. 196 pp., photographic plates. 8vo; dust jacket. Hunting big game around the world. Scarce.

Lincoln, Frederick Charles   b. 1892

Migration of North American Birds. Washington, D. C., 1935. 72 pp., photographic plates, maps. 8vo. Paper wrappers.

Migration of Birds. Washington, D. C., 1950, U. S. Fish and Wildlife Service. 102 pp., illustrations by Bob Hines. 8vo. Paper wrappers. (Also a 1952 revised edition, Doubleday & Co., Inc.)

Lind, Ernie

    The Complete Book of Trick and Fancy Shooting. New York, 1975, Winchester Press. 159 pp., illustrations. 8vo; dust jacket. (Reprinted 1977, Citadel)

Linden, Alvin   d. 1946

    The Finishing of Gunstocks and Notes on the Conversion of the 1917 Enfield Rifle. Plantersville, South Carolina, 1941, Small Arms Technical Publishing Company. 46 pp., illustrations, folding charts. 4to Paper wrappers. (Reprinted several times, same format and publisher)

    The Inletting of Gunstock Blanks As Applied to Modifications of the Springfield Rifle. Plantersville, South Carolina, 1941, Small Arms Technical Publishing Company. 38 pp., illustrations, folding charts. 4to Paper wrappers. (Reprinted several times, same format and publisher)

    The Shaping of Inletted Blanks. With some notes on some alterations to the Model 70 Winchester rifle. Plantersville, South Carolina, 1943, Small Arms Technical Publishing Company. 54 pp., illustrations, folding charts. 4to Paper wrappers. (Reprinted several times, same format and publisher)

        These three pamphlets were part of a four part set relating to gun stock making (the fourth being Monty Kennedy's *Carving and Checkering of Gunstocks*, which see) published by Small Arms. These three Linden pamphlets were also combined and published as one volume titled *Alvin Linden Tells All About Restocking a Rifle* in 1969 by Stackpole. See Smith, Brian.

Linder, R. L. and C. N. Hillman, editors

    Proceedings of the Black Footed Ferret and Prairie Dog Workshop; September 4-6, 1973, Rapid City, South Dakota. Brookings, 1973, South Dakota University Press. 208 pp., photographic plates, bibliography, maps. 4to. Paper wrappers.

Lindorp, Edmund and Joseph Jares

    White House Sportsmen. Boston, 1964, Houghton Mifflin Company. 172 pp., photographic plates, bibliography. 8vo; dust jacket. Brief sketches of U. S. Presidents that fished or hunted, including Cleveland, Roosevelt, Eisenhower, etc.

Lindsay, Merrill   1915-1985

    The Kentucky Rifle. Pennsylvania, 1972, Historical Society of York County. Unpaginated, many color plates. 8vo; dust jacket. (Also reprinted 1972, slightly larger format, Arma)

    The Lure of Antique Guns. New York, 1976, David McKay Co. 146 pp., illustrations. 8vo; dust jacket. (Also a 1978 edition in paper wrappers titled, *The Lure of Antique Arms*) A primer of antique gun collecting.

    Miniature Arms. New York, 1970, Winchester Press 110 pp., color and black and white illustrations. 8vo; dust jacket.

    The New England Gun; the first 200 Years. New York, 1975. 187 pp., illustrations. 4to.

Lindsay, Merrill, continued

One Hundred Great Guns; an illustrated history of firearms. New York, 1967, Walker. 379 pp., color and black and white illustrations, bibliography. Folio; dust jacket.

Lindsey, N. M.

The Tale of A Wilderness Trapper. Columbus, Ohio, 1944, A. R. Harding. 66 pp., illustrations. 12mo. Paper wrappers.

Linduska, Joseph

Waterfowl Tomorrow. Washington, D. C., 1964, United States Department of the Interior. 770 pp., photographic plates. 8vo.

Linsdale, Jean M.

Observations of Waterbirds in California. San Francisco, 1938, California Fish and Game Commission. 43 pp., photographic plates, maps, bibliography. 8vo. Paper wrappers.

Linsdale, Jean M. and P. Quinton Tomich

A Herd of Mule Deer. Berkeley, 1953, University of California Press. 567 pp., photographic plates, drawings, maps, bibliography. 8vo; dust jacket.

Linton, Ida Ward

The Story of Lem Ward; as told to Glenn Lawson. Exton, Pennsylvania, 1984, Schiffer Publishing Company. 128 pp., photographic plates, illustrations by Jack Schroeder. 4to; dust jacket. The biography of this famous decoy carver.

Linton, James M. and Calvin W. Moore

The Story of Wild Goose Jack. Toronto, 1984, CBC Enterprises. 208 pp. 8vo; dust jacket. The saga of Jack Miner, who went from relentless hunter to a conservationist; he also established a very successful wildfowl refuge.

Lipton, James

An Exaltation of Larks; or the venereal game. New York, 1968, Grossman Publishing. 118 pp., illustrations. 8vo; dust jacket. (Reprinted several times, same format and publisher) The author has compiled an entertaining list of phrases describing various groups of animals, people, etc., some from historical usage and some made on his own. For example, a "wince of dentists," a "piddle of puppies," an "exaltation of larks," etc. Many of these terms describe game animals and birds.

Lippincott, Bill and Nancy Lippincott

Arthur R. MacDougall,Jr., Maine Author; a bibliography. Farmington, Maine, 1983, University of Maine. 41 pp., illustrations. Limited to 250 numbered copies. 8vo. Paper wrappers.

Lippincott, Joseph Wharton   1887-1976

Animal Neighbors of the Countryside. Philadelphia, 1938, J. B. Lippincott Co.   272 pp., drawings by Lynn Bogue Hunt.   8vo; dust jacket.

Long Horn: Leader of the Deer. Philadelphia, 1928, J. B. Lippincott Co.   188 pp., photographic plates.   12mo; dust jacket.

The Wahoo Bobcat. Philadelphia, 1950, J. B. Lippincott Co.   207 pp., drawings by Paul Bransom.   8vo; dust jacket.   The story of bobcats in the Florida wilderness.

Wilderness Champion. Philadelphia, 1944, J. B. Lippincott Co.   195 pp., illustrations by Paul Bransom.   8vo; dust jacket.   The story of a great hound.
Mr. Lippincott wrote many juveniles with animal themes.

Liscinsky, Stephen A.

The American Woodcock in Pennsylvania. Harrisburg, 1965, Pennsylvania Game Commission.   32 pp., illustrations by Ned Smith.   8vo. Paper wrappers.

The Pennsylvania Woodcock Management Study. Harrisburg, 1972, Pennsylvania Game Commission.   95 pp., photographic plates, drawings by Ned Smith, tables, bibliography.   8vo.   Paper wrappers.   A more thorough study based on the previous work by the same author.

Lister, C. B.

Simplified Small Arms Ballistics. For the sportsman and soldier. Washington, D. C., 1944, The National Rifle Association of America.   67 pp., line drawings. Paper wrappers.   (Also a 1950 second edition, same publisher and format)

Lister, Ronald

Antique Firearms; their care, repair and restoration.   New York, 1964, Crown Publishers, Inc.   (Reprinted, Bonanza)

Liu, Allan

The American Sporting Collector's Handbook. New York, 1976, Winchester Press. 239 pp., illustrations. 8vo; dust jacket.   (Also a 1982 revised and enlarged edition, same format and publisher)   A basic overview of collecting guns, sporting prints, books, duck stamps, etc.

American Sporting Collector. Amawalk, No date (ca. 1975), American Sporting Collector.   48 pp., photographic plates.   8vo. Paper wrappers.   A price guide for original sporting art, stamps, books, firearms, etc.

Lloyd, Freeman

All Setters; their histories, rearing and training, bench and show points and characteristics.   New York, 1931, Privately printed.   125 pp., photographic plates.   8vo; dust jacket.   (Reprinted several times, same format and publisher)

Lloyd, Freeman, continued
    All Spaniels; their breeding, rearing and training, bench and show points and characteristics. New York, 1930, Privately printed. 72 pp., photographic plates. 8vo. (Reprinted several times, same format and publisher)
    Spaniels and Their Training. No place, 1930, Privately printed. 72 pp., photographic plates. 8vo; dust jacket. (Reprinted many times, same format and publisher)

Lloyd, Freeman
    Also see **Cobb, Bert**
    Also see **Megargee, Edwin.**

Lockhart, James
    Wild America. New York, 1979, Thomas Nelson & Sons, Inc. 152 pp., many color illustrations of game animals. Oblong folio; dust jacket.

Lofberg, Lila and David Malcolmson
    Sierra Outpost. New York, 1941, Duell, Slaon & Pearce. 253 pp. 8vo; dust jacket. (Reprinted, same format and publisher) An account of the authors' experiences with coyotes and other wildlife while living at a California utility company outpost.

Lofgren, Robert E.
    The Old Moose Hunter. Minnesota, No date, Privately printed. 199 pp., photographic plates. 8vo. Paper wrappers. Hunting reminiscences of the author.

Logan, Herschel C. b. 1901
    Cartridges; a pictorial digest of small arms ammunition. Huntington, West Virginia, 1948, Standard Publications, Inc. 199 pp., drawings by the author. 4to; dust jacket. (Reprinted 1952, same format and publisher. Also reprinted 1959, Bonanza)
    Hand Cannon To Automatic. Huntington, West Virginia, 1944, Standard Publications, Inc. 172 plates from drawings by the author. Oblong 8vo; dust jacket. A pictorial history of the development of handguns.
    Underhammer Guns. Harrisburg, 1960, The Stackpole Company. 249 pp., illustrations. Tall 8vo; dust jacket. (Also a 1960 edition titled, *The Pictorial History of the Underhammer Gun*, Castle Books) Mr. Logan was a commercial artist by profession and an antique arms collector by avocation.

Loiselle, Emery J.
    Doctor Your Own Compound Bow, A-Z; manual for target archers, bowhunters, compound owners, future owners. Burlington, Massachusetts, 1976, Privately printed. 132 pp., illustrations. 8vo. Paper wrappers.

Lombard, Laurence M.

Flight to Alaska - 1930: the journal of "Flit," an open cockpit biplane and two young men who flew her from Boston to Alaska and back again, for a holiday, in the early days of aviation. No place (Princeton, New Jersey), 1966, Privately printed. 139 pp., photographic plates, map. 8vo; dust jacket. (Reprinted, same format and publisher) A scarce title in either printing, with several chapters on grizzly hunting.

Long, Amelia Reynolds

Outdoor Reference Guide. Harrisburg, 1959, The Stackpole Company. 288 pp., photographic plates. 4to; dust jacket. An encyclopedia of names and terms relating to the outdoors, including the shooting sports.

Long, Jeff

Outlaw; the true story of Claude Dalls. New York, 1985, William Morrow & Co., Inc. 239 pp. 8vo; dust jacket. The chronicle of a poacher and the manhunt that brought him to justice.

Long, Joe E.

Papa Was A Fisherman. Barre, Massachusetts, 1969, Barre Publishing Co., Inc. 98 pp. 8vo; dust jacket. Mostly fishing, but some bird hunting.

Long, Paul

All The Answers To All Your Questions About Training Pointing Dogs. New York, 1978. 85 pp. 8vo. Paper wrappers. (Reprinted several times, various publishers)

Training Pointing Dogs; all the answers to your questions. New York, 1985, Nick Lyons Books. 98 pp., photographic plates. 8vo; dust jacket. (Reprinted several times, some later printings in paper wrappers)

Longhurst, William M., et al.

A Survey of California Deer Herds; their ranges and management problems. No place, 1952, California Department of Fish and Game. 136 pp., photographic plates, maps, bibliography. 8vo. Paper wrappers.

Longrigg, Roger

The History of Foxhunting. New York, 1975, Potter. 272 pp., color and black and white illustrations. 4to; dust jacket. A world survey.

Loomis, B. F.

Pictorial History of the Lassen Volcano. San Francisco, 1926, Privately printed. 142 pp., illustrations, with fold-out map. 8vo. Mostly angling on Hat Creek and Manzanita Lake (California) before the eruption of this volcano, but some hunting in the area is included.

Lopez, Barry Holstun
  Of Wolves and Men. New York, 1978, Charles Scribner's Sons. 309 pp., photographic plates, bibliography. 8vo; dust jacket. An interesting and provocative account of the natural history of the species and man's perceptions of it.

Lorant, Stefan
  The Life and Times of Theodore Roosevelt. New York, 1959, Doubleday & Co., Inc. 640 pp., photographic plates. 4to; dust jacket.

Lord, Beman
  Look at Guns. New York, 1963. 46 pp., illustrations. 8vo; dust jacket. An overview from the earliest to modern day firearms.

Lort-Phillips, Frederick (*pseud.* of **Frederick Gillett**)
  The Wander Years; hunting and travel in four continents. London, 1931, Nash & Grayson. 315 pp., photographic plates. 8vo. Includes sheep and goat hunting in the west as well as deer and moose hunting in eastern North America. A scarce book.

Lott, Milton
  The Last Hunt. Boston, 1954, Houghton Mifflin Company. 399 pp. 8vo; dust jacket. (Reprinted 1955, Outdoor Life Book Club) A fictional account of a buffalo hunter's life. This was also made into a motion picture by Metro-Goldwin-Meyer.

Louisiana Wildlife and Fisheries
  Mourning Dove in Louisiana. No place, No date (ca. 1965), Louisiana Wildlife and Fisheries. 12 pp., photographic plates, drawings. 8vo. Paper wrappers.

Lovaas, Allan L.
  People and the Gallatin Elk Herd. Helena, 1970, Montana Fish and Game Commission. 44 pp., photographic plates, bibliography. 4to. Paper wrappers.

Love, Albert J.
  Field Archery Technique. Corpus Christie, Texas, 1956, Buccaneer Archery Company. 121 pp., illustrations. 8vo.

Lowther, John E.
  Spring Gobblers. Parsons, West Virginia, 1980, McClain Printing Company. 225 pp., photographic plates. 8vo; dust jacket. An account of spring turkey hunting.

Luard, G. D.
        Fishing Adventures in Canada and U. S. A.   London, 1950, Faber & Faber.   157 pp., photographic plates.   8vo; dust jacket.   Also includes some deer and wapiti hunting.

Luce, Donald R. and Laura M. Andrews
        Francis Lee Jaques; artist-naturalist.   Minneapolis, 1982, University of Minnesota Press.   76 pp., color and black and white illustrations.   4to; dust jacket.   A biographical essay.

Luckey, Carl F.
        Collecting Antique Bird Decoys; an identification and value guide. Florence, 1983, Books Americana.   179 pp., photographic plates.   8vo.   Paper wrappers.

Ludlum, Stuart D., editor
        Great Shooting Stories. Garden City, 1947, Doubleday & Co., Inc. 303 pp., decorations by Ted Placek. 8vo; dust jacket.

Lumpkin, Courtney "Foots"
        100 Deer.   Glencoe, Alabama, 1980, Privately printed.   158 pp., photographic plates.   8vo; dust jacket.

Lund, Fred P.
        And That's the Way it Was.   North St. Paul, Minnesota, 1973, Privately printed.   159 pp.
        I Mind; memories of the old hunting camp days and some of the best of my father's true stories.   North St. Paul, Minnesota, 1969, Privately printed. 78 pp.
        Iron River; my home town.   North St. Paul, Minnesota, 1975, Privately printed.   129 pp.   All three of these books contain episodes of hunting.

Lund, Thomas A.
        American Wildlife Law.   Berkeley, 1980, University of California Press. 179 pp.   8vo; dust jacket.

Lunt, Dudley C.
        Taylor's Gut; in the Delaware state.   New York, 1968, Alfred A. Knopf, Inc.   303 pp., illustrations.   8vo; dust jacket.   A study of Delaware marshes and their wildfowl.
        Thousand Acre Marsh; a span of remembrance.   New York, 1959, The Macmillan Company.   173 pp., illustrated.   8vo; dust jacket.

Lunt, Dudley C., continued
 The Woods and the Sea. New York, 1965, Alfred A. Knopf, Inc.   305 pp., drawings.   8vo; dust jacket.   Mostly backwoods travel and adventure, but some game animals and fly fishing.

Luttringer, Leo A.
 Pennsylvania Bird Life. Harrisburg, 1948, Pennsylvania Game Commission   120 pp., color and black and white illustrations by Ned Smith. 8vo.   Paper wrappers.   (Revised and reprinted several times, same format and publisher)
 Pennsylvania Birds of Prey.   Harrsiburg, 1948, Pennsylvania Game Commission.   32 pp., color and black and white illustrations.   8vo.   Paper wrappers.

Luttringer, Leo A. and Richard Gerstell
 Pennsylvania Wildlife.   Harrisburg, 1938, Pennsylvania Game Commission.   48 pp., color illustrations by Fred Everett, photographic plates. 8vo.   Paper wrappers.

Lynch, V. E.
 Thrilling Adventures; guiding, trapping, big game hunting from the Rio Grande to the wilds of Maine.   Portland, Maine, 1928, Privately printed by the Southworth Press.   174 pp., illustrations.   8vo.   Much on hunting deer, bobcat and bear.
 Trails To Successful Trapping.   Columbus, Ohio, 1935, A. R. Harding. 170 pp., photographic plates.   16mo.   (Also reprinted in paper wrappers)

Lynde, Chuck and Toni Lynde
 Oregon's Bow Hunting Big Game Records.   Oregon, 1983, Privately printed.   146 pp., photographic plates.   Limited to 1000 numbered copies.   8vo. Paper wrappers.

Lyon, Robert
 Who Was Nessmuk?   Wellsboro, Pennsylvania, 1971, Wellsboro Chamber of Commerce.   28 pp., illustrations.   8vo.   Paper wrappers.   A biographical sketch of George Washington Sears (1821-1890), who wrote much on woodcraft and angling.   For additional information see **Nessmuk** (*pseud.* of **George Washington Sears**), *The Adirondack Letters of George Washington Sears.*

Lytle, Horace b. 1884
 Bird Dog Days.   New York, 1926, D. Appleton & Co.   191 pp., illustrations.   12mo; dust jacket.

Lytle, Horace, continued

Breaking a Bird Dog. New York, 1924, D. Appleton & Co. 167 pp., illustrations. 12mo; dust jacket. (Originally published, 1923, R. F. Fenno & Co. The 1924 edition reprinted many times, same format and publisher)

Gun Dogs Afield. New York, 1942, G. P. Putnam's Sons. 277 pp., illustrations by Lynn Bogue Hunt, color frontispiece. Introduction by Ray P. Holland. 8vo; dust jacket. [Also a deluxe edition limited to 100 numbered and signed copies with a signed etching titled "Wing Retrieve" by Hunt, laid in; slipcased]

How To Train Your Bird Dog. Dayton, 1929, A. F Hochwalt. 224 pp., photographic plates. 8vo; dust jacket. (Reprinted many times to 1956, same format and publisher)

How to Win Field Trials. New York, 1950, D. Van Nostrand Company, Inc. 229 pp., photographic plates. A Van Nostrand Sporting Book. 8vo; dust jacket.

No Hunting? A story of the hunting fields - and a vision of what the future holds for sport with dog and gun. Dayton, Ohio, 1928, Field Sports Publishing Company. 281 pp., illustrations. 12mo; dust jacket.

Point! A book about bird dogs. New York, 1941, The Derrydale Press. 197 pp., photographic plates. Limited to 950 numbered copies. Tall 8vo. (Also a revised and expanded 1954 edition, The Stackpole Company)

Sandy; the story of an Airedale. New York, 1926, D. Appleton & Co. 144 pp. 8vo; dust jacket. A scarce title with much duck hunting.

Sandy Oorang; and other stories of dogs and the wilderness. New York, 1922, R. F. Fenno & Co. 257 pp., illustrations. 12mo. Hunting dog and other hunting and trapping stories. A scarce title, not listed in Phillips.

Simple Secrets of Dog Discipline; directed towards the puppy owner. New York, 1946, G. P. Putnam's Sons. 63 pp. 8vo; dust jacket. (Reprinted 1946, same format and publisher)

The Story of Jack; a tale of the North and other fascinating dog stories. Dayton, Ohio, 1920, Pettibone. 164 pp., drawings. 8vo. Scarce.

Mr. Lytle was active in field trials for many years. He wrote several books preceding 1925. See Phillips.

Maas & Steffen

Furbearers. St. Louis, 1927, Maas & Steffen. 26 pp., color and black and white illustrations. 8vo. Paper wrappers. Natural history of 27 species described, but mostly from the fur buyer's point of view.

Maass, David and Gene Hill

A Gallery of Waterfowl and Upland Birds. Los Angeles, 1978, Peterson Publishing Company. 120 pp., color paintings by David Maass. Folio; dust jacket. (Reprinted 1983, same format and publisher) [Also a deluxe first edition, specially bound and limited to 1000 numbered copies signed by the author and artist; slipcased]

MacClintock, Dorcas

Squirrels of North America. Princeton, New Jersey, 1970, D. Van Nostrand Reinhold Publishing Company. 184 pp., drawings by Walter Ferguson, maps. 4to; dust jacket.

MacCrimmon, Hugh R.

Animals, Man and Change; alien and extinct wildlife of Ontario. Toronto, 1977, McClelland & Stewart, Ltd. 160 pp., drawings, bibliography. 8vo; dust jacket. An account of the species that have become extinct since the settlement of the province.

MacDougall, Arthur R.   1896-1983

Adventures in a Model T; and other Dud Dean stories. Thorndike, Maine, 1980, Thorndike Press. 94 pp., drawings by Paul Plumer. 8vo. Paper wrappers.

Doc Blakesley, Angler. Portland, Maine, 1949, Falmouth Publishing House. 110 pp., drawings by Stanley Green. 8vo; dust jacket. [Also a deluxe edition of 500 numbered and signed copies; slipcased] Six angling stories.

Dud Dean and the Enchanted. Manchester, Maine, 1954, Falmouth Publishing House. 166 pp., illustrations by Leon Tebbetts. 8vo; dust jacket. [Also a limited edition of 300 numbered and signed copies]

Dud Dean and His Country. New York, 1946, Coward, McCann, Inc. 171 pp., color frontispiece and other drawings by Milton C. Weiler. 8vo; dust jacket. (Also a 1974 edition titled, *Dud Dean, Maine Guide,* Bond Wheelright) [Also a deluxe first edition, specially bound and with an extra color frontispiece; limited to 450 numbered and signed copies] Mostly angling tales, but some hunting of upland game; all in Maine.

Dud Dean Yarns. Bingham, Maine, 1934, Privately printed by Bingham Press. 181 pp. A numbered, limited edition of 800 copies. 8vo; dust jacket.

MacDougall, Arthur R., continued

Far Enough For All The Years.   Harrison, New York, 1940, Privately printed.   31 pp.   Limited to 200 copies.   8vo.   Paper wrappers.   (Also a 1948 revised edition, cloth bound, Falmouth Publishing House) A book of poems, including several on the outdoors and angling.

I Want Him.   Bingham, Maine, 1928, privately printed.   8 pp., illustrations.   16mo.   Paper wrappers.   Lippincott reports about 500 copies of this pamphlet were printed.

If It Returns With Scars; Dud Dean and Dock Blakesley stories. Bingham, Maine, 1942, Privately printed.   240 pp., drawings by Stanley Greene. Limited to 750 numbered copies.   8vo; dust jacket.   (Reprinted 1981, in paper wrappers, Thorndike Press)

The Old Lake Road.   No place, 1977, Privately printed.   62 pp.   8vo. Paper wrappers.   A book of poetry.

The Sun Stood Still; and other Dud Dean stories.   Bingham, Maine, 1939, Privately printed.   179 pp.   Introduction by Ray Holland.   Produced as a limited, numbered and signed edition of unspecified limitation (generally accepted to be 1400 copies). 12mo; dust jacket.

Under a Willow Tree.   New York, 1946, Coward, McCann, Inc.   200 pp., drawings by Milton C. Weiler.   8vo; dust jacket.   Maine angling tales.

Where Flows the Kennebec; more tales about Dud Dean. New York, 1947, Coward, McCann, Inc.   181 pp., drawings by Milton C. Weiler.   8vo; dust jacket.

Mr. MacDougall was a minister and was an avid outdoorsman by avocation. He began writing these outdoor stories as an amusement, and his first works were privately printed for presentation purposes. His classic prose captured the spirit and values of the Maine sportsmen. Listed here are all his original works, even though several only have incidental mention of hunting. He also edited *The Trout Fisherman's Bedside Book,* 1963.

MacDougall, Arthur R.

Also see **Lippincott, Bill and Nancy**

MacFarlan, Allan A.

Modern Hunting With Indian Secrets.   Harrisburg, 1971, The Stackpole Company.   223 pp., illustrations.   8vo; dust jacket.   (Reprinted 1974, same format and publisher)

MacFarland, Harold E.

Gunsmithing Simplified.   Washington, D. C., 1950, Infantry Journal Press. 302 pp., plates, drawings.   8vo; dust jacket.   (Reprinted three times to 1966, A. S. Barnes and Company, Inc.)

Introduction To Modern Gunsmithing.   Harrisburg, 1965, The Stackpole Company.   320 pp., photographic plates.   8vo; dust jacket.

MacFie, Harry

    Wasa-Wasa; a tale of trails and treasure in the far North.   New York, 1951, W. W. Norton & Co., Inc. 288 pp. 8vo; dust jacket. Tales of the gold rush in Canada and Alaska with much hunting and fishing.

Machetanz, Sara

    Where Else But Alaska?   New York, 1954, Charles Scribner's Sons. 214 pp., lithographs by Fred Machetanz, photographic plates. 8vo; dust jacket. The experiences of this couple living in the Alaskan wilderness.

Mackay, John W.

    Good Shooting! New York, 1960, A. S. Barnes and Company, Inc. 138 pp., photographic plates; diagrams. 8vo; dust jacket. With much bird dog training.

    Mark! New York, 1956, Coward, McCann, Inc. 121 pp., photographic plates. 4to; dust jacket. Bird hunting in Great Britain and the U. S.

    Robins Island. Smithtown, 1984, Privately printed. 130 pp., color and black and white illustrations. Limited to 500 copies. 4to; dust jacket. A description of an island near Long Island, New York the author owned and managed as a game reserve.

Mackay-Smith, Alexander   b. 1903

    The American Foxhound; 1747 - 1967   Millwood, Virginia, 1968, American Foxhound Club.   420 pp., color and black and white photographic plates, map. Limited to 1000 numbered and signed copies. Folio. [Also a deluxe edition, specially bound with a supplemental index and illustrations to form pages 421-451, limited to 100 numbered and signed copies) A most thorough study of the equestrian foxhound.

    Foxhunting in North America; a comprehensive guide to organized foxhunting in the U.S. and Canada. Millwood, Virginia, 1985, American Foxhound Club. 263 pp., illustrations. 8vo. A contemporary survey.

    Masters of Foxhounds. Boston, 1980, Master of Foxhounds Association Publications Committee.   216 pp., color and black and white illustrations. Folio. A history of the MFH association with biographies of all the presidents.

    The Songs of Foxhunting.   Millwood, Virginia, 1974, American Foxhound Club. 186 pp.   Limited to 1500 numbered and signed copies. Folio.

Mackay-Smith, Alexander, editor

    American Foxhunting; an anthology. 79 classic stories, sketches, essays and poems. Millwood, Virginia, 1970, American Foxhound Club.   212 pp., photographic plates, drawings. Limited to 2500 numbered copies. Folio.

MacKenty, John G.

    Duck Hunting. New York, 1953, A. S. Barnes and Company, Inc. 206 pp., photographic plates. A title in The Sportsman's Library series. 8vo; dust jacket. (Reprinted several times, same format and publisher)

    Getting the Most Out of Your .22. Englewood Cliffs, New Jersey, 1957, Prentice-Hall, Inc. 218 pp., illustrations. 8vo; dust jacket.

Mackey, Donald

    Anticosti; the untamed island. Toronto, 1979, The Ryerson Press. 160 pp., photographic plates, maps. 4to; dust jacket. Mostly salmon fishing, but some hunting on this island at the mouth of the St. Lawrence River.

Mackey, William J., Jr.

    American Bird Decoys; with a chapter on American decoys as folk art by Quintina Colio. New York, 1965, E. P. Dutton & Co., Inc. 256 pp., color and black and white illustrations. 4to; dust jacket. (Reprinted, Bonanza. Also reprinted several times, Schiffer) [Also a deluxe first edition, specially bound and limited to 50 numbered and signed copies]

Mackie, Richard J.

    Range Ecology and Relations of Mule Deer, Elk and Cattle in the Missouri River Breaks, Montana. Washington, D. C., 1970, The Wildlife Society. Monograph # 20. 79 pp., photographic plates, maps. 4to. Paper wrappers.

Maclay, Alfred B.

    Five Centuries of Sport; hunting racing, shooting, falconry, riding, cock fighting, coursing, angling, rare American sporting periodicals, etc. New York, 1945, Parke-Bernet Galleries, Inc. 182 pp., photographic reproductions. 4to. Paper wrappers.

    Rare Seventeenth-Nineteenth Century Books on Horsemanship, Falconry and Hunting; including the first issue, first edition of Alken's *Natural Sports of Great Britain* in contemporary binding, collected by the late Alfred B. Maclay. New York, 1956, Parke-Bernet Galleries, Inc. 84 pp. 8vo. Paper wrappers. These were auction catalogs of a landmark sporting book collection. Mr. Maclay was a client of both Ernest R. Gee and of the famous book dealer, Dr. A. S. W. Rosenbach. He was also friends with C. F. G. R. Schwerdt and between them they amassed virtually every sporting book published in the world prior to 1920.

MacNab, Col. A. J., Jr.

    MacNab on Skeet. Wilmington, Delaware, 1934, E. P. DuPont de Nemours & Co. 24 pp., illustrations. 16mo. Paper wrappers. (Reprinted 1936, same format and publisher)

MacNab, Col. A. J., Jr., continued

Pistol and Revolver Training Course. Prepared for the use of police and civilian clubs and individuals. No place, 1926, Privately printed. 27 pp., photographic plates. 12mo. Paper wrappers. Rare.

MacQuarrie, Gordon

The Last Stories of the Old Duck Hunters. Oshkosh, Wisconsin, 1985, Willow Creek Press. 151 pp., illustrations. 8vo.

More Stories of the Old Duck Hunters. Oshkosh, Wisconsin, 1983, Willow Creek Press. 198 pp., illustrations. 8vo.

Stories of the Old Duck Hunters and Other Drivel. Harrisburg, 1967, The Stackpole Company. 223 pp. 8vo; dust jacket. (Reprinted several times, various publishers. Willow Creek Press also offered all three of these titles, slipcased in a set in 1985)

Mr. MacQuarrie was the outdoor editor for the *Milwaukee Journal*. His waterfowling stories contain a humorous nostalgia that appeal to outdoorsmen.

Madaus, H. Michael

The Warner Collector's Guide To American Longarms. No place, 1981, Warner. 255 pp., color illustrations. Paper wrappers.

Madis, George

Winchester; dates of manufacture, 1894-1984. Brownsboro, Texas, 1984, Privately printed. 59 pp. Limited to 1000 signed copies. 16mo.

The Winchester Book. Dallas, Texas, 1961, Privately printed. 378 pp., photographic plates. 4to. (Revised and reprinted several times, various dates and publishers)

The Winchester Era. Brownsboro, Texas, 1984, Privately printed. 167 pp., photographic plates. Limited to 1000 signed copies. 12mo.

The Winchester Handbook. Brownsboro, Texas, 1979, Art and Reference House. 287 pp., illustrations. Limited to 1000 signed copies. 8vo. (Reprinted several times, various dates and publishers)

The Winchester Model 12. Brownsboro, Texas, 1982, Art and Reference House. 174 pp., photographic plates. Limited to 1000 signed copies. 8vo.

Madsen, Charles with J. S. Douglas

Arctic Trader. New York, 1957, Dodd, Mead & Co. 273 pp., photographic plates. 8vo; dust jacket. Contains some polar bear and walrus hunting.

Madson, John

The Cottontail Rabbit. East Alton, Illinois, 1963, Winchester Western Press. 56 pp., photographic plates plus drawings by Maynard Reece. 8vo. Paper wrappers.

Madson, John, continued

    The Elk. East Alton, Illinois, 1966, Winchester Western Press.   125 pp., illustrations by Charles Schwartz, bibliography. 8vo. Paper wrappers.

    Gray and Fox Squirrels. East Alton, Illinois, 1964, Winchester Western Press. 112 pp., illustrations, bibliography. 8vo. Paper wrappers.

    Hunting Dogs. East Alton, Illinois, 1981, Winchester Western Press. 32 pp., illustrations. 8vo. Paper wrappers.

    John Madson: Out Home. New York, 1979, Winchester Press. 206 pp., illustrations. Edited by Michael McIntosh. 8vo; dust jacket. A collection of the author's hunting and fishing stories.

    The Mallard. East Alton, Illinois, 1960, Winchester Western Press. 80 pp., photographic plates, bibliography. 8vo. Paper wrappers.

    The Mourning Dove. East Alton, Illinois, 1978, Winchester Western Press. 114 pp., photographic plates, bibliography. 8vo. Paper wrappers.

    The Ring Necked Pheasant. East Alton, Illinois, 1962, Winchester Western Press. 104 pp., illustrations, bibliography. 8vo. Paper wrappers.

    Ruffed Grouse. East Alton, Illinois, 1962, Winchester Western Press. 103 pp., illustrations, bibliography. 8vo. Paper wrappers.

    Stories From Under The Sky. Ames, 1961, Iowa State University Press. 205 pp., illustrations by Dycie Madson. 8vo; dust jacket. Hunting and fishing stories.

    Up on the River. New York, 1985, Nick Lyons Books.   276 pp., drawings. 8vo; dust jacket. A collection of stories including some on hunting and fishing.

    Where the Sky Began; land of the tall grass prairie. Boston, 1982, Houghton Mifflin Company. 321 pp., illustrations. 8vo; dust jacket.

    The White Tailed Deer. East Alton, Illinois, 1962, Winchester Western Press.   108 pp., illustrations, bibliography. 8vo. Paper wrappers. All of the Winchester booklets were reprinted several times.

Madson, John and E. Kozickey

    Careers in Wildlife Conservation.   No place (East Alton, Illinois), 1967, Olin Matheson Corp.   36 pp.   8vo.   Paper wrappers.   (Also a revised edition, same format and publisher)

    For the Young Hunters. East Alton, Illinois, 1963, Winchester Western Press. 32 pp., drawings. 8vo. Paper wrappers.

    Game, Gunners and Biology; the scientific approach to wildlife management. New York, 1971, Winchester Western Press.   49 pp., drawings, bibliography. 8vo. Paper wrappers.

    Principles of Game Management. East Alton, Illinois, 1962, Winchester Western Press. 25 pp., drawings. 8vo. Paper wrappers.

Madson, John, et al., editors

    The Outdoor Life Deer Hunter's Encyclopedia. New York, 1985, Times Mirror Magazines / Stackpole Books. 788 pp., photographic plates. Deals mainly with equipment needed for the hunt.

Magee, D. F.

The So Called "Kentucky Rifle" As Made in Lancaster County. No place, 1926, Lancaster County (Pennsylvania) Historical Society. 15 pp., photographic plates. 8vo. Paper wrappers.

Magee, Harvey White

The Story of My Life. Albany, 1926, Privately printed. 137 pp., frontispiece. 12mo. With two chapters on hunting.

Mahan, William E.

Bobwhite Quail. Edgefield, 1984, International Quail Foundation. Unpaginated (22 pp.), drawings. 4to. Paper wrappers. Designed to assist the wildlife manager who wants to increase populations of this game bird.

Maine Development Commission

Maine; fishing, hunting, canoeing. Augusta, 1933, Maine Development Commission. 48 pp., photographic plates, maps. 8vo. Paper wrappers. (Reprinted several times, same format and publisher)

Maine, The Land of Remembered Vacations; fishing, hunting, canoeing. Augusta, No date (ca. 1935), Maine Development Commission. 40 pp., photographic plates, fold-out map. 8vo. (Reprinted, same format and publisher) Paper wrappers. Includes a guide to the best fishing and hunting areas.

Maine Publicity Bureau

Hunting in Maine. Portland, Various dates (1940-1950's), Maine Publicity Bureau. 33 pp., ads. 8vo. Paper wrappers.

Maire, Susan S.

How To Raise and Train an English Setter. Jersey City, New Jersey, 1964, TFH Publishers. 64 pp., illustrations. 8vo. Paper wrappers.

The Major (*pseud.* of **Madison Grant**) **1865-1937**

Hank; His Lies and His Yarns. New York, 1931, Privately printed. 114 pp. Limited to 150 copies. 8vo. (Also a 1937 edition reported, slightly different format) Tales of adventure in the west and Alaska by one of the early members of the Boone and Crockett Club.

Major, Charles 1856-1913

The Bears of Blue River. New York, 1926, The Macmillan Company. 277 pp., frontispiece by A. B. Frost, other illustrations. 12mo; dust jacket. (Originally published, 1901, Doubleday & McClure Co. Reprinted several times after 1926, various publishers)

Mallet, Capt. Thierry

Glimpses of Barren Lands. New York, 1930, Privately printed by Revillon Freres. 142 pp., plates. 8vo.

Igloo Life; a brief account of a primitive arctic tribe living near one of the most northern trading posts of Revillon Freres. New York, 1923, Privately printed. 63 pp., photographic plates, drawings. 8vo. Although not listed as the author, most attribute this book to Capt. Mallet. It is an early arctic work with excellent photographs by Robert Flaherty. Not in Phillips.

Plain Tales of the Far North. New York, 1925, Privately printed by Revillon Freres. 136 pp., plates. 8vo. All these books have some mention of hunting and much on life in the far north.

Manchester, Herbert

Four Centuries of Sport in America. New York, 1931, The Derrydale Press. 245 pp., many illustrations from old plates, photographic plates. Introduction by Harry Worcester Smith. Limited to 850 copies. Folio; dust jacket. (Reprinted 1968, B. Blom) A well illustrated work detailing sport from the time of the Inca to the present.

Manierre, "Franny"

The Story of the Clow Deer Hunt. No place, 1938, Privately printed. 22 pp., photographic plates. 8vo. Paper wrappers. Deer hunting in Wisconsin with much on Cy Young, the great baseball player who accompanied the author on a deer hunt.

Manly, William Lewis

Death Valley in '49; an important chapter of California pioneer history....from a humble home in the Green Mountains to the gold mines of California. New York, 1929, Hebbert. 524 pp., drawings, maps. 8vo. (Originally published, 1894, Pacific Tree and Vine Company) The account of the band of settlers who traveled across the country and eventually gave Death Valley its name. This important Americana title contains much hunting. See Phillips.

Mann, E. B., editor

The World of Guns. Skokie, Illinois, 1964, The Shooting Industry. 92 pp., illustrations. 8vo. Paper wrappers. A compilation of articles regarding firearms and their uses by various authors.

Mann, Franklin W.   1856-1916

The Bullet's Flight; from powder to target. Huntington, West Virginia, 1942, Standard Publications, Inc. 384 pp., plates. Tall 8vo; dust jacket. (Reprinted four times to 1952, same format and publisher. Also reprinted, 1965, Ray Riling Arms Books. Both of these editions were facsimile reproductions, with a new introduction, of this title originally published in 1909 by Munn) The earliest scientific study of exterior ballistics.

Mann, William M.
   Wild Animals In and Out of the Zoo.   Washington, D. C., 1930, Smithsonian Institute.   362 pp., color and black and white illustrations, one by Rungius.   8vo.

Manning, T. H.
   Age Determination in the Polar Bear, Ursus maritimus Phipps. Ottawa, 1964, Canadian Wildlife Service.   12 pp.   8vo.   Paper wrappers.
   Geographical Variation in the Polar Bear Ursus maritimus Phipps. Ottawa, 1971, Canadian Wildlife Service.   27 pp., photographic plates, drawings, map.   8vo.   Paper wrappers.
   The Relationship of the Peary and Barren Ground Caribou.   Montreal, 1960, Arctic Institute of North America.   52 pp., bibliography.   4to.   Paper wrappers.

Mannix, Daniel P.   b. 1911
   The Fox and the Hound.   New York, 1967, E. P. Dutton & Co., Inc. 255 pp., drawings.   8vo; dust jacket.   A novel and the winner of the 1967 Dutton Animal Book Award.
   The Killers.   New York, 1968, E. P. Dutton & Co., Inc.   255 pp., photographic plates, bibliography.   8vo; dust jacket.   The story of a Cooper's hawk.
   The Last Eagle.   New York, 1966, McGraw-Hill Publishing Company. 149 pp., drawings.   8vo; dust jacket.   Fictionalized account of an American bald eagle.
   A Sporting Chance; unusual methods of hunting.   New York, 1967, E. P. Dutton & Co., Inc.   254 pp., photographic plates, bibliography.   8vo; dust jacket. (Reprinted 1967, same format and publisher)   Some of the methods included are with falcons, bola, blowguns and boomerang.

Mansell, William and Gary Low
   North American Birds of Prey.   New York, 1980, William Morrow & Co., Inc.   176 pp., color plates by Gary Low.   Folio; dust jacket.
   North American Marsh Birds.   New York, 1983, Harper & Row, Publishers, Inc.   189 pp., color illustrations by Low.   Folio; dust jacket.

Marburger, Rodney G.
   The King of Deer.   Texas, 1983, Privately printed.   272 pp.

Marcham, Frederick George, editor
   Louis Agassiz Fuertes and the Singular Study of Birds; paintings, drawings and letters.   New York, 1971, Harper & Row, Publishers, Inc.   220 pp., color and black and white artwork by Fuertes.   Foreword by Dean Amadon. Introduction by Roger Tory Peterson.   Folio; dust jacket.

Marcon, John G.
The Brush Cop.   Wisconsin, Chronotype Publications.   269 pp.
The account of a Wisconsin Conservation Warden, 1940-1960.

Markland, A. B.   1678-1722
Pteryplegia: The Art of Shooting Flying. York, 1931, The Derrydale
Press.   29 pp., illustrations from drawings by Robert Ball.   4to.   Limited to 500
copies. [The first 200 copies were numbered in a large paper edition, specially
bound and illustrated and signed by the artist and publisher]   A reproduction of the
first book on wing shooting; originally published in London in the early eighteenth century.

Marsden, Halsey M., et al.
*Social Behavior in Confined Populations of the Cottontail and the
Swamp Rabbit.*   Washington, D. C., 1964, The Wildlife Society.   39 pp.,
frontispiece, bibliography.   4to.   Paper wrappers.

Marsh, George
Sled Trails and White Water.   Philadelphia, 1929, Penn Publishing
Company.   298 pp., illustrations by Frank E. Schoonover, including a color
frontispiece.   8vo; dust jacket.   Stories of the north, with some hunting and trapping.

Marsh, James B.
Four Years in the Rockies; or the adventures of Isaac P. Rose, as hunter
and trapper in that remote region.   Columbus, No date (ca. 1951), Longs.   262
pp.   Limited to 1000 copies.   8vo.   (A reproduction of the scarce 1884
edition)

Marshall, Edison   b. 1894
The Heart of the Hunter. New York, 1956, McGraw-Hill Publishing
Company. 328 pp., illustrations by R. M. Powers. 8vo; dust jacket.   Stories of big
game hunting around the world including some in North America.

Marshall, Robert E.
The Onza; the story of the search for the mysterious cat of the Mexican
highlands.   New York, 1961, Exposition Press.   202 pp., illustrations,
bibliography.   8vo; dust jacket.

Martin, A. C. and F. M. Uhler
Food of Game Ducks in the United States and Canada.   Washington,
D. C., 1939, U. S. Department of Agriculture.   157 pp., photographic plates, color
plate by Kalmbach, maps.   8vo.   Paper wrappers.   (Also a 1951 revised and
expanded edition, same format and publisher)

Martin, Calvin

    Keepers of the Game.   Berkeley, 1978, University of California Press. 226 pp.   8vo; dust jacket. A discussion of the relationship between the American Indian, game animals and the early fur trade.

Martin, Cy

    The Saga of the Buffalo.   New York, 1973, Hart Publishing Co.   191 pp., color and black and white illustrations.   4to; dust jacket.

Martin, Elwood M. and Samuel M. Carney

    Population Ecology of the Mallard; a review of duck hunting regulations, activity and success, with special reference to the mallard. Washington, D. C., 1977, United States Fish and Wildlife Service.   Drawings, maps. 4to. Paper wrappers.

Martin, F. W.

    Color Marking and Field Observation of Canada Geese To Determine Breeding Territorialism, Family Organization and Population Dynamics. 1957, Utah Division of Wildlife Resources.   16 pp.   Paper wrappers.

Martin, John Stewart

    Learning to Gun. Garden City, New York, 1963, Doubleday & Co., Inc. 113 pp., illustrations.   4to; dust jacket. (Reprinted, Bonanza) A primer of shotgunning methods and hunting.

Mason, George F.

    Animal Tracks. New York, 1943, William Morrow & Co., Inc. 95 pp., drawings. 8vo; dust jacket. (Reprinted 1945, same format and publisher) A guide to identifying North American animal tracks.

    The Moose Group. New York, 1968, Hasting House. 62 pp., drawings by the author. 8vo; dust jacket. A description of the specimens composing the moose diorama in the American Museum of Natural History.

Mason, Jerry, editor

    The American Sportsman Treasury. New York, 1971, The Ridge Press, Inc. / Alfred A. Knopf, Inc. 252 pp., color and black and white illustrations. 4to; dust jacket. An anthology of hunting and fishing stories, art and photography originally published in *The American Sportsman,* a quarterly magazine published from 1968 to 1970.

    Sports Illustrated Book of the Outdoors. New York, 1959.   323 pp., photographic plates.   4to. Includes some hunting and fishing.

Mason, Robert Lindsay

    The Lure of the Great Smokies. Boston, 1927, Houghton Mifflin Company. 320 pp., photographic plates, fold-out map. 8vo; dust jacket. With several sections on hunting and early Smoky Mountain riflemen. Scarce.

Massachusetts Division of Fisheries and Game

Guide To Wildlife Management Areas (of Massachusetts). Westborough, Massachusetts, 1964, Massachusetts Division of Fisheries and Game. 29 pp., maps. 8vo. Paper wrappers.

The Massachusetts Fish and Game Association

The Massachusetts Fish and Game Association: A Brief history, 1935. Cambridge, Massachusetts, 1935, Privately printed. 32 pp. 4to. Paper wrappers. Includes a membership list with such notables as John C. Phillips, A. L. Ripley, Frank Benson, Aldo Leopold and others. An historically important organization.

Massey, Jay

A Thousand Campfires. Girdwood, Alaska, 1985, Bear Paw Publications. 127 pp. With some deer hunting in the northwest.

Bowhunting Alaska's Wild Rivers. Girdwood, Alaska, 1983, Bear Paw Publications. 176 pp.

Masson, W. V. and R. U. Mace

Upland Game Birds. Portland, Oregon, 1962. 44 pp., photographic plates. 8vo. Paper wrappers.

Mast, James F.

Coyote, Wild Cat, Gray Fox Trapping. No place, 1943, Privately printed. 87 pp., photographic plates, drawings. 8vo. Paper wrappers. (Reprinted several times, same format)

Mather, Charles E.

Master of Radnor; diary of Charles E. Mather, M.F.H., 1887-1901. No place, 1947, Privately printed. 100 pp., photographic plates. Foreword by R. E. Strawbridge. Limited to 750 numbered copies. 8vo. A season to season account of this Pennsylvania foxhunting club.

Mathias, Fred S.

The Amazing Bob Davis; his last vagabond journey. New York, 1944, Longman's, Green & Co. 362 pp., drawings. 8vo; dust jacket. A biographical account of this newspaper columnist with much hunting and angling.

Matson, J. R.

The Adaptable Black Bear. Philadelphia, 1967, Dorrance Publishing Company. 147 pp., photographic plates. 8vo; dust jacket.

Mattern, J. R.
Handloading Ammunition; a handbook covering all phases of the loading of metallic ammunition for revolvers, pistols and rifles. Marshallton, Delaware, 1926, Small Arms Technical Publishing Company. 380 pp., illustrations. 8vo. The first book published under this imprint owned by Thomas Samworth.

Matthews, John Joseph
Talking to the Moon. Norman, 1981, University of Oklahoma Press. 243 pp. With a chapter on deer hunting.

Matthiessen, Peter   b. 1927
Oomingmak; the expedition to the Musk Ox Island in the Bearing Sea. New York, 1967, Hastings House. 85 pp., photographic plates. 8vo; dust jacket.
The Wind Birds. New York, 1973, Viking Press. 160 pp., drawings, bibliography. 4to; dust jacket. Essentially a revised and expanded version of *The Shorebirds of North America.*
Wildlife in America. New York, 1959, Viking Press. 304 pp., drawings by Bob Hines. 8vo. (Reprinted several times, various formats and publishers) An account of how man and population pressures have affected wildlife.
Mr. Matthiessen writes insightful accounts about the influence of man on wildlife.

Matthiessen, Peter
Also see **Stout, Gardner D.,** *The Shorebirds of North America*
Also see **Caulfield, Patricia**

Mattis, George
Whitetail; fundamentals and fine points for the hunter. New York, 1969, Outdoor Life Books / World Publishing Company. 273 pp., drawings by William Reusswig. Tall 8vo; dust jacket. (Also a 1980 revised edition, Van Nostrand Reinhold Company)

Matunas, Edward
American Ammunition and Ballistics. Tulsa, 1979, Winchester Press. 220 pp., photographic plates, charts. Tall 8vo; dust jacket.
Deer Hunter's Guide to Guns, Ammo and Equipment. New York, 1983, Outdoor Life Books. 338 pp., photographic plates.
Handbook of Metallic Cartridge Reloading. Tulsa, Oklahoma, 1980, Winchester Press. 257 pp., photographic plates, charts. 8vo.

Maughmer, G. F., et al.
    Colt on the Trail; fascinating stories of actual experiences in the great outdoors, in all of which the Colt has played an important part. Hartford, Connecticut, 1931, Colt's Patent Fire Arms Manufacturing Company. 59 pp., line drawings. Preface by Col. Townsend Whelen. Paper wrappers. (Also a 1934 second edition, same format and publisher) True stories of the use of Colt's firearms, including bear, deer, mountain lion hunting, etc.

Maurice, Charlotte
    Jekyl Island, Some Historic Notes and Some Legends and a Brief Outline of the Early Days of the Jekyl Island Club by Charles Maurice. No place, 1923, Privately printed by the club. 23 pp. 8vo. A history of this Georgia hunting and fishing club. Not in Phillips.

Maurice, J. B.
    Training Pointers and Setters. New York, 1975, A. S. Barnes and Company, Inc. 116 pp., illustrations. 8vo; dust jacket.

Mavrogordato, Jack
    A Hawk in the Bush; a treatise on the training of the sparrow hawk and other short-winged hawks. New York, 1973, Clarkson Potter. 206 pp., illustrations. 8vo; dust jacket.

Maxwell, A. F. and Ivar Ruud
    The Year Long Day. Philadelphia, 1976, J. B. Lippincott Co. 240 pp., photographic plates. 8vo; dust jacket. The authors spent a winter in the Arctic trapping and hunting.

Maxwell, C. Bede
    The New German Shorthaired Pointer. New York, 1963, Howell Book House. 272 pp., illustrations. 8vo. (Reprinted and revised several times, same format and publisher)
    The Truth About Sporting Dogs. New York, 1972, Howell Book House. 336 pp., photographic plates, bibliography. 8vo.

Maxwell, Samuel L.
    Lever Action Magazine Rifles; derived from the patents of Andrew Burgess. No place, 1976, Privately printed by the author. 368 pp., illustrations. 4to.

May, John Birchard
    Edward Howe Forbush; a biographical sketch, with a list of the writings of Edward Howe Forbush by Rev. Robert F. Cheney. Boston, 1928, Boston Society of Natural history. 43 pp., photographic plates. 8vo. Paper wrappers.

May, John Birchard, continued

The Hawks of North America; their field identification and feeding habits. New York, 1935, National Association of Audubon Societies. 140 pp., color and black and white illustrations by Allan Brooks and Roger Tory Peterson, bibliography. 4to.

Maycock, William P.

Shoot 'em Again. Cody, Wyoming, 1980, Privately printed. 94 pp., photographic plates, drawings by the author. 8vo. Deer and antelope hunting in the West with much bow hunting for big game. Scarce.

Mayer, F. H. and C. B. Roth

The Buffalo Harvest. Denver, 1958, Sage Books. 96 pp., illustrations. 8vo; dust jacket.

Maynard, Roger

Advanced Bowhunting Guide. New Jersey, 1984, Stoeger Publishing Company. 222 pp., illustrations. 4to. Paper wrappers.

Mazzone, S. N.

A Big Game Hunter's Guide to the Colorado Rockies. Boulder, Colorado, 1980, High Rockies Enterprise. 134 pp.. photographic plates, maps. 8vo.

McAdams, Laura

Marias Temps Clair; an idyll picturing a man and a marsh, as seen through the eyes of a wife, against a background of some of the man's own words. St. Louis, 1944, Privately printed. 82 pp., photographic plates. 8vo. An account of a family camp on the Mississippi River, with much duck hunting and a biographical tribute to Clark McAdams, the author's husband. Scarce.

McAleenan, Joseph

Leaves From a Wyoming Diary. No place, 1924, Privately printed. 51 pp. printed on recto only. Limited to 30 copies. 4to. A description of hunting trips taken in the Wind River area of Wyoming between 1895 - 1910. Heller also lists Mr. McAleenan as the probable author of *Old Friends, Old Scenes, Old Thoughts*, 1925

McAtee, W. L., editor   1883-1962

Local Names of Migratory Game Birds. Washington, D. C., 1934, United States Department of Agriculture. 95 pp., drawings. 8vo. Paper wrappers.

Propagation of Aquatic Game Birds. Washington, D. C., 1930, United States Department of Agriculture. 40 pp., photographic plates, drawings. 8vo. Paper wrappers.

McAtee, W. L., editor, continued

Propagation of Upland Game Birds. Washington, D. C., 1930, United States Department of Agriculture. 60 pp., photographic plates, drawings. 8vo. Paper wrappers.

The Ring-Necked Pheasant and Its Management in North America. Washington, D. C., 1945, The American Wildlife Institute. 320 pp., plates, two color illustrations from paintings by T. Heaton Cooper. 8vo; dust jacket.

Wildfowl Food Plants; their value, propagation and management. Ames, Iowa, 1939, Collegiate Press. 141 pp., photographic plates, drawings. 8vo.

Wildlife of the Atlantic Coast Salt Marshes. Washington, D. C., 1941, United States Department of the Interior. 32 pp., illustrations. 8vo. Paper wrappers.

McBride, David P.

The Federal Duck Stamps; a complete guide. New York, 1982, Winchester Press. 206 pp., illustrations, bibliography. 4to; dust jacket. (Reprinted many times, same format and publisher)

McCabe, R. A. and A. S. Hawkins

The Hungarian Partridge of Wisconsin. South Bend, Indiana, 1946 Notre Dame University Press. 75 pp., photographic plates, maps, bibliography. 8vo. Paper wrappers.

McCarty, Diane, editor

German Shorthaired Pointers. Neptune City, New Jersey, 1980, TFH Books. 125 pp., illustrations. 12mo.

Labrador Retrievers. Neptune City, New Jersey, 1979, TFH Books. Illustrations. 8vo.

McCawley, E. S.

Shotguns and Shooting. New York, 1965, D. Van Nostrand Company, Inc. 146 pp., photographic plates. A Van Nostrand Sporting Book. 8vo; dust jacket.

McClellan, Edwin

A Hunting Log; covering his last trip, in the Cassiar Mountains, Northern British Columbia, August-October, 1923. Somerville, New Jersey, 1929, American Historical Society. 85 pp., photographic plates. 4to. Paper wrappers.
A rare posthumous hunting diary previously published in *Americana* magazine.

McClintock, Gray
> *The Wolves at Cooking Lake;* and other stories.   Albany, New York,
1932, J. B. Lyon Company.   224 pp., photographic plates.   12mo. An anthology
of stories originally broadcast on the radio and containing much hunting and fishing.

McClung, Robert M.
> *Samson: Last of the California Grizzlies.*   New York, 1973, William
Morrow & Co., Inc.   95 pp., illustrations by Bob Hines.   8vo; dust jacket.   An
older juvenile.
> Mr. McClung wrote many juveniles with animal themes, including, *The Mighty Bears,
Spike;* the story of a whitetail deer, *Honker;* the story of a wild goose, and others.

McConnell, Duncan
> *Gran'pappy's Pistol;* or, the hell with gun collecting.   New York, 1956,
Coward, McCann, Inc. 152 pp., illustrations.   12mo; dust jacket.   A humorous look
at gun collecting.

McCorrison, A. L.
> *Letters From Fraternity;* with an introduction by Ben Ames Williams.
New York, 1931, E. P. Dutton & Co., Inc.   251 pp.   8vo; dust jacket.   The
correspondence from Ben McCorrison to Ben Ames Williams, much of which helped Williams in
formulating his fictitious Fraternity Village.   With many hunting and angling reminiscences.

McCowan, Dan
> *Animals of the Canadian Rockies.*   New York, 1936, Dodd Mead & Co.
302 pp., frontispiece by Carl Rungius.   8vo; dust jacket.   (Reprinted several
times, various publishers)
> *A Naturalist in Canada.*   Toronto, 1941, The Macmillan Company.   294
pp., illustrations, frontispiece by Carl Rungius.   8vo; dust jacket. (Reprinted
1946, New York, The Macmillan Company)

McCoy, Sue, editor
> *Yarns of Wisconsin.*   Wisconsin, 1978, Tamarack Press.   224 pp.
With one chapter on deer camps.

McCracken, Harold   b. 1894
> *Alaska Bear Trails.*   Garden City, New York, 1931, Doubleday, Doran
& Co.   260 pp., photographic plates by the author. 8vo; dust jacket.
> *The Beast That Walks Like Man;* the story of the grizzly bear.   New
York, 1955, Hanover House.   319 pp., photographic plates.   8vo; dust jacket.
(Also published, 1957, London) An important work covering many aspects of the grizzly
bear.
> *The Biggest Bear on Earth.*   Philadelphia, 1943, Frederick A. Stokes.
114 pp., color and black and white illustrations by Paul Bransom.   4to; dust
jacket. A study of Alaska's bears.

McCracken, Harold, continued

Caribou Traveler. Philadelphia, 1949, J. B. Lippincott Co. 204 pp., drawings by Rod Ruth. 8vo; dust jacket. The story of the barren land caribou.

God's Frozen Children. Garden City, New York, 1930, Doubleday, Doran & Co., Inc. 291 pp., photographic plates. 8vo; dust jacket. An account of the author's expedition searching for remains of prehistoric man, but also containing much on Kodiak bears.

The Great White Buffalo. Philadelphia, 1946, J. B. Lippincott Co. 268 pp., illustrations. 8vo; dust jacket.

Hoofs, Claws and Antlers; the story of American big game animals. Garden City, New York, 1958, Garden City Books. 56 pp., color and black and white illustrations by Lee J. Ames. Folio; dust jacket. A scarce juvenile.

Hunters of the Stormy Sea. Garden City, New York, 1957, Doubleday & Co., Inc. 312 pp. 8vo; dust jacket. (Also a 1957 British edition) A history of the sea otter hunters in Alaska.

Iglaome; the lone hunter. New York, 1930, The Century Company. 248 pp., illustrations. 8vo.

Roughnecks and Gentlemen; memoirs of a maverick. Garden City, New York, 1968, Doubleday & Co., Inc. 441 pp., photographic plates. 8vo; dust jacket. Mr. McCracken's autobiography.

Sentinel of the Snow Peaks; a story of the Alaskan wilderness. Philadelphia, 1945, L. B. Lippincott Co. 151 pp., drawings by Enos Comstock. 8vo; dust jacket. (Reprinted 1945, same format and publisher) A novel about big horn sheep and a gold prospector.

Son of the Walrus King. Philadelphia, 1944, J. B. Lippincott Co. 129 pp., color frontispiece and drawings by Lynn Bogue Hunt. 8vo; dust jacket. A juvenile.

McCracken, Harold and Harry Van Cleve

Trapping; the craft and science of catching fur-bearing animals. New York, 1947, A. S. Barnes and Company, Inc. 196 pp., drawings by Howard L. Hastings. 8vo; dust jacket. (Reprinted several times, same format and publisher)

McCreight, M. I.

Buffalo Bone Days. Sykesville, Pennsylvania, 1939, Nupp Printing Co. 40 pp., portraits. 12mo. An account of the slaughter of the buffalo.

Theodore Roosevelt and Conservation Why; a 34 year moratorium on unpublished records. No place, No date (ca. 1949), Privately printed. 26 pp. 8vo. Paper wrappers. Correspondence between the author, Gifford Pinchot, Roosevelt and others. Rare.

McCrory, R. H.

Make Muzzle Loader Accessories. No place, 1971, Privately printed. 46 pp., illustrations. 8vo. Paper wrappers. How to make powder horns, shooting bags, etc.

The Modern Kentucky Rifle. No place, 1966, Privately printed. 99 pp., illustrations, fold-out drawings. 12mo. Paper wrappers.

McCullough, Dale R.

The George Reserve Deer Herd; population ecology of a k-selected species. Ann Arbor, 1979, University of Michigan. 271 pp., bibliography 8vo; dust jacket.

The Tule Elk; its history, behavior and ecology. Berkeley, 1969, University of California Press. 191 pp., illustrations, bibliography. 4to. (Reprinted 1971, same format and publisher)

McCurdy, Robert

Life of the Greatest Guide; hound stories and others of Dale Lee. Phoenix, 1979, Privately printed. 237 pp., photographic plates. Stories of Mr. Lee, who hunted with hounds throughout the Americas.

McDaniel, John M.

The Turkey Hunter's Book. Clinton, New Jersey, 1980, Amwell Press. 147 pp., illustrations. Limited to 1000 numbered and signed copies. 8vo; slipcased. (Also a 1980 edition in paper wrappers, same publisher. Also a 1981 trade edition, same publisher)

McDearmon, Kay

Rocky Mountain Bighorns. New York, 1980, Dodd, Mead & Co. 47 pp., photographic plates. 8vo; dust jacket. In addition, the author also wrote other juveniles like *Cougar* and *Polar Bear.*

McDonald, Jerry N.

North American Bison; their classification and evolution. Berkeley, 1981, University of California Press. 316 pp., illustrations. 4to; dust jacket.

McDonald, Ralph

A Down Home Gallery of American Wildlife. Cottonwood, Tennessee, 1980, Countryside Studio. 101 pp., color plates from the author's paintings. Limited to 1000 numbered copies. Oblong 4to; slipcased. Containing hunting and fishing scenes from the southern U. S.

McDowell, R. B.

Evolution of the Winchester. Tacoma, Washington, 1985, Armory Publications. 206 pp., illustrations. 4to; dust jacket. A discussion of the development and history of Winchester firearms.

McElroy, Harry
　　Desert Hawking. College Station, Texas, 1971, Peregrine Press. 113 pp., illustrations, glossary. 4to. Paper wrappers. (Reprinted 1974, Cactus Press)

McFall, Waddy F.
　　Taxidermy Step By Step. New York, 1975, Winchester Press. 230 pp., illustrations. 8vo; dust jacket.

McGee, Richard C.
　　The Original Tree Stand Handbook. Florida, 1982, Sportsman's Studios. 152 pp. A general discussion of tree stands used for deer hunting.

McGillen, Pete
　　Outdoors. Toronto, 1955. 177 pp., illustrations. 8vo; dust jacket. Hunting and angling stories by one of Canada's most popular outdoor writers.

McGinn, O. T.
　　American Big Game and How to Hunt Them; moose, elk, deer and caribou, also chapters on bears, beavers, wolves, big game rifles, etc. Grand Rapids, Michigan, 1931, Privately printed. 59 pp., photographic plates. 8vo. A scarce big game title written by a Catholic priest from Grand Rapids whose avocation was hunting.

McGivern, Ed
　　Ed McGivern's Book on Fast and Fancy Revolver Shooting and Police Training. Springfield, Massachusetts, 1938, King Richardson Company. 484 pp., photographic plates. 8vo. (Reprinted several times, various publishers) [Also a deluxe first edition, specially bound, but with no specified limitation]

McGrail, Joie and Bill
　　The Catch and the Feast. New York, 1969, Weybright. 196 pp., black and white and color photographic plates. 4to. Some hunting but mostly a cookbook.

McGraw, L. R. "Mac"
　　Hunter's Attract Flies....Fishermen Do Too! Colorado, 1985, Privately printed. 149 pp.

McGuane, Thomas 　 b. 1939
　　An Outside Chance; essays on sport. New York, 1980, Farrar, Straus & Giroux, Inc. 243 pp. 8vo; dust jacket.
　　The Sporting Club. New York, 1968, Simon & Schuster. 220 pp. 8vo; dust jacket. (Reprinted several times, same format, Farrar, Straus and Giroux) A novel with a hunting and fishing club backdrop.

McGuire, Bob

Advanced Whitetail Hunting Techniques. Johnson City, Tennessee, 1983, Bowhunting Productions. 124 pp., illustrations. 8vo. Paper wrappers.

Black Bears; a technical and hunting guide book Blountville, Tennessee, 1983, Bowhunting Productions. 183 pp., photographic plates. 8vo. With much on the life history of the species and hunting techniques for the bow hunter.

McGuire, Harry, editor

Tales of Rod and Gun; a collection of the best American hunting and fishing stories. New York, 1931, The Macmillan Company. 218 pp., photographic plates, frontispiece by Richard Bishop. 8vo; dust jacket. With the first appearance of Nash Buckingham's "De Shootinest Gent'man" in a cloth-bound book.

McHenry, Armond G., Jr.

The American Woodcock in Louisiana. Washington, D. C., 1983, United States Fish and Wildlife Service. 98 pp., illustrations. Paper wrappers.

McHenry, Robert and Charles Van Doren, editors

A Documentary History of Conservation in America. New York, 1972, Praeger. 422 pp., bibliography. Tall 8vo; dust jacket.

McHenry, Roy C. and Walter Roper

Smith & Wesson Handguns. Huntington, West Virginia, 1945, Standard Publications, Inc. 233 pp., photographic plates. 4to; dust jacket. (Reprinted 1947, same format and publisher)

McHugh, Tom

The Time of the Buffalo. New York, 1972, Alfred A. Knopf, Inc. 339 pp., illustrations, maps, bibliography. 8vo; dust jacket. Much on the natural history of the American bison and its relationship to native Americans.

McIlvaine, Jane

To Win the Hunt. Barre, Massachusetts, 1966, Barre Publishing Co., Inc. 100 pp., illustrations by Nelson McClary. 8vo; dust jacket; slipcased.

McIntosh, J. Rieman

A History of the Elk Ridge Foxhunting Club, The Elk Ridge Hounds, The Elk Ridge-Hartford Club, 1878 - 1978. Monkton, Maryland, 1978, Privately printed by the club. 121 pp., illustrations. 8vo. Paper wrappers. A history of one of America's oldest organized foxhunting clubs.

McIntosh, Michael   b. 1945

The Best Shotguns Ever Made In America. New York, 1981, Charles Scribner's Sons. 185 pp., photographic plates. 8vo; dust jacket. An illustrated history of the best of these kinds of firearms and their manufacturers.

McIntosh, Michael, editor

Classics of American Sporting Fiction. Clinton, New Jersey, 1984, Amwell Press. 275 pp., illustrations. 8vo. [Also a deluxe edition, specially bound and limited to 1000 numbered and signed copies; slipcased] An anthology of stories by Rutledge, Spiller, Sheldon and others.

McIntyre, Thomas

Days Afield; journeys and discoveries in hunting and fishing. New York, 1984, E. P. Dutton & Co., Inc. 205 pp., illustrations. 8vo; dust jacket. Chapters on hunting many species of small and big game, mostly in North America; also some angling.

McKenney, John

Tackroom Tattles. New York, 1934, Charles Scribner's Sons. 230 pp., drawings by Paul Brown. 8vo; dust jacket. Stories and verse of foxhunting.

McKenney, Lewis T.

Memories of Maine. Boston, 1934, Meador Publishing Co. 210 pp., illustrations. 8vo. With nearly half of the text devoted to hunting and fishing.

The North Woods. Boston, 1936, Meador Publishing Co. 232 pp., illustrations. 8vo. Also with much big and small game hunting in the North Maine Woods.

McKinney, J. Evans

Decoys of the Susquehanna Flats and Their Makers. Hockessin, Delaware, 1978, Holly Press. 96 pp., color and black and white illustrations. Limited to 1000 copies. 4to; dust jacket. (Also printed in paper wrappers, same date)

McLaughlin, Charles

Food Habits of the Ring-Necked Pheasant in the Connecticut River Valley, Massachusetts. Boston, 1942, Massachusetts Department of Conservation. 56 pp. 8vo. Paper wrappers.

McLean, Donald D.

The Quail of California. Sacramento, 1930, California Fish and Game Department. 47 pp., illustrations, fold-out maps. 8vo. Paper wrappers.

Upland Game of California. Sacramento, 1956. 39 pp., illustrations. 12mo. Paper wrappers.

McMahon, C. A.

Retriever Theory. Ann Arbor, Michigan, 1970, Privately printed. 865 pp., photographic plates, drawings, charts. Limited to 1000 numbered and signed copies. 8vo. A thorough work on dog training that is more scarce than its limitation would suggest.

McManus, Patrick F.   b. 1933

A Fine and Pleasant Misery. New York, 1978, Holt, Rinehart and Winston.   209 pp.   8vo; dust jacket.

The Grasshopper Trap.   New York, 1985, Holt, Rinehart and Winston. 214 pp.   8vo; dust jacket.

Kid Camping From Aaaaliii! To Zip.   New York, 1979, Lathrop, Lea and Shepard.   125 pp., illustrations.   8vo; dust jacket.

Never Sniff a Gift Fish.   New York, 1983, Holt, Rinehart and Winston. 217 pp.   8vo; dust jacket.

They Shoot Canoes, Don't They? New York, 1981, Holt, Rinehart and Winston.   218 pp.   8vo; dust jacket.

All of these titles by McManus contain humorous hunting, angling or outdoor tales; all were reprinted many times.

McMath, Neil

Continuing the Story of Turtle Lake.   Michigan, no date, Privately printed.   16 pp.   Paper wrappers.   A description of the Turtle Lake Deer Hunting Club in Michigan. Also see, **New, Harry S.**, for another title regarding this subject.

McMillan, Ian

Man and the California Condor; the embattled history and uncertain future of North America's largest free living bird.   New York, 1968, E. P. Dutton & Co., Inc.   191 pp., photographic plates.   8vo; dust jacket.

McMullen, J. A.

Old Pro and Four Other Stories.   San Antonio, 1955, The Naylor Company.   95 pp.   8vo; dust jacket.   Hunting dog tales.

McMullen, James P.

Cry of the Panther; quest of a species.   Englewood, Florida, 1984, Pineapple Press.   391 pp.   8vo; dust jacket.   The account of one man's mission to save the Florida panther.

McNally, Tom

Hunting For Boys.   Chicago, 1962, Follett Publishing Company.   96 pp., photographic plates.   12mo.   Paper wrappers.

McNamee, Thomas

The Grizzly Bear.   New York, 1984, Alfred A. Knopf, Inc.   308 pp., illustrations by Gordon Allen.   8vo; dust jacket.

McVicker, Mary Louise

The Writings Of J. Frank Dobie; a bibliography. Lawton, Oklahoma, 1968, Museum of the Great Plains.   258 pp., illustrations.

Meader, Stephen W.
    Trap Lines North; a true story of the Canadian woods. New York, 1936, Dodd, Mead & Co. 268 pp., photographic plates. 8vo; dust jacket. (Reprinted several times, same format and publisher)

Meager, Margaret Mary
    The Bison of Yellowstone National Park. Washington, D. C., 1973, National Park Service. 161 pp., photographic plates, fold-out map, bibliography. 8vo. Paper wrappers.

Meanly, Brooke
    Birds and Marshes of the Chesapeake Bay Country. Cambridge, Maryland, 1975, Tidewater Publishers. 157 pp., illustrations, fold-out map, bibliography. 8vo. Paper wrappers.
    Blackwater. Cambridge, Maryland, 1978, Tidewater Publishers. 148 pp., photographic plates, bibliography. 4to. Paper wrappers. A discussion of the wildlife of this Chesapeake Bay wildlife refuge.
    The Marsh Hen; a natural history of the Clapper Rail of the Atlantic Coast Salt Marsh. Centreville, Maryland, 1985, Tidewater Publishers. 123 pp., photographic plates, map, bibliography, drawings by John Taylor. 8vo. Paper wrappers.
    Natural History of the King Rail. Washington, D. C., 1969, United States Department of the Interior. 108 pp., photographic plates, bibliography. 8vo. Paper wrappers. With one chapter on hunting.
    Waterfowl of the Chesapeake Bay Country. Centreville, Maryland, 1982, Tidewater Publishers. 210 pp., illustrations. 4to; dust jacket.

Means, William Gordon
    My Bird Dogs and Hounds. Boston, 1953, Bruce Humphries, Inc. 154 pp., illustrations. 8vo; dust jacket.
    My Guns. Dedham, Massachusetts, 1941, Privately printed. 178 pp., illustrations from drawings by Oliver R. Shattuck. 8vo. Stories of hunting lion, deer, bear and wildfowl. Scarce.

Mech, L. David
    The Wolf; the ecology and behavior of an endangered species. New York, 1970, The American Museum of Natural History. 384 pp., illustrations. 8vo. (Reprinted many times, same format, various publishers)
    The Wolves of Isle Royale. Washington, D. C., 1966, United States Department of the Interior. 210 pp., illustrations, maps. 8vo. Paper wrappers. An account of the species on this remote Michigan island in Lake Superior.

Medlin, Faith

Centuries of Owls; in art and literature.   Norwalk, Connecticut, 1967, Silvermine Publishers.   84 pp., illustrations.   4to; dust jacket.   An account of owls in literature and art.

Mednick, Murray

The Deer Kill.   New York, 1972, Bobbs-Merrill Company, Inc.   96 pp.   A novel.

Megargee, Edwin   d. 1958

Dogs.   New York, 1942, Harper & Brothers.   96 pp., color and black and white paintings by the author.   Folio; dust jacket.   A scarce title with many illustrations of sporting dogs.

The Dog Dictionary.   Cleveland, 1954, World Publishing Company. 104 pp., illustrations by the author.   4to; dust jacket.   A scarce Megargee work that includes a fold-out family tree of dogs.

Gun Dogs at Work; six paintings.   New York, 1946, The Field & Stream Portfolio.   A portfolio of six, loose hunting dog prints accompanied by a 16 pp. Text volume written by Freeman Lloyd; both items in a paper folder.   Folio.

Mr. Megargee was an accomplished animal artist whose works were featured as illustrations in many sporting books and periodicals.   See Siegel.

Megargee, Harry

Scaup; sheerside Barnegat sneak box.   New York, 1942, Field & Stream.   Single folded sheet opening to 16" X 20" showing plans to built this duck boat-sneak box designed by Ed Broome.

Mendall, Howard L.

The Ring Necked Duck in the Northeast.   Orono, Maine, 1958, University Press (Maine).   317 pp., illustrations; maps, bibliography.   8vo. Paper wrappers.

Mendall, Howard L. and C. M. Aldous

The Ecology and Management of the American Woodcock.   Orono, Maine, 1943, Maine Co-Operative Wildlife Unit.   201 pp., illustrations, maps, bibliography.   8vo. Paper wrappers.   (Reprinted 1984, in facsimile but cloth bound and limited to 1025 copies, Gunnerman Press)

Merkt, Dixon MacD.

Shang; a biography of Charles E. Wheeler.   Clinton, New Jersey / Spanish Fork, Utah, 1984, Amwell Press / Hillcrest Publications.   199 pp., photographic plates.   Limited to 550 numbered and signed copies.   4to.   The biography of this Connecticut decoy carver.

Mermon, Dick
>*Crow Shooting Secrets.* New York, 1970, Winchester Press. 153 pp., illustrations. 8vo; dust jacket.

Merne, Oscar J.
>*Ducks, Geese and Swans.* New York, 1974, St. Martin's Press. 160 pp., color illustrations. 8vo; dust jacket.

Merrick, Elliot
>*True North.* New York, 1933, Charles Scribner's Sons. 353 pp., photographic plates. 8vo; dust jacket. Hunting, fishing and trapping in Labrador.

Merrill, Lawrence "Pete"
>*Deer Trails and Camp Tales.* Menominee, Michigan, 1983, Privately printed. 94 pp. Spiral bound paper wrappers. Hunting white-tailed deer in the Upper Peninsula of Michigan. Scarce.

Merrill, W. K.
>*The Hunter's Bible;* how to bag upland birds, ducks and geese and hunting small and big game. New York, 1968, Doubleday & Co., Inc. 182 pp., illustrations. 4to. Paper wrappers. (Reprinted many times, same format and publisher)

Merritt, J. I.
>*Baronets and Buffalo;* the British sportsman in the American West 1833-1881. Missoula, Montana, 1985, Mountain Press Publishing Company. 217 pp., illustrations. 8vo.

Mersfelder, L. C.
>*Cowboy, Fisherman, Hunter;* true stories of the great Southwest. Kansas City, 1941, Brown-White-Lowell Press. 246 pp., illustrations, fold-out map. 8vo; dust jacket. (Also a 1951 revised and enlarged edition, same format and publisher)

Messiter, Charles A.
>*Sport and Adventure Among the North American Indians.* New York, 1966, Abercrombie & Fitch, Inc. 368 pp., illustrations from drawings by Charles Whymper. 8vo. (A facsimile reproduction originally published in London, 1890)

Meyer, Jerry
>*Bear Hunting.* Harrisburg, 1983, The Stackpole Company. 159 pp., photographic plates. 8vo; dust jacket.

Meynell, Hugo

The Meynellian Science. New York, 1926, Privately printed for Ernest R. Gee. 24 pp., frontispiece by Gordon Ross. 12mo. [Also a large paper edition, specially bound with limitation not stated but generally accepted to be 21 copies] (Originally published in Great Britain, 18th century) An early dissertation on foxhunting theory developed by Hugo Meynell. The limitation on the regular edition is not stated and has been reported to be 100 copies or less. In fact, in a 1927 Gee catalog, the limitation is stated as 320 copies.

Michener, James A.   b. 1907

The Watermen. New York, 1979, Random House, Inc. 193 pp., illustrations. 8vo; dust jacket. Excerpted portions from the author's *Chesapeake* that have some market hunting exploits. Fiction.

Michmerhuizen, Lewey

Grandpa Recalls Deer Hunting Stories. Michigan, 1964, Lew Publishers. Unpaginated.

Migdalski, Edward C.

Clay Target Games. New York, 1978, Winchester Press. 258 pp., illustrations. 8vo; dust jacket.

Milbank, Jerimiah and G. F. Perry

Turkey Hill Plantation. No place, 1966, Privately printed. 128 pp., photographic plates. 4to; slipcased. Contains some turkey, quail and duck hunting.

Milbank, Kitty

The Flighty Prince. New York, 1963, Privately printed. 66 pp., frontispiece. Tall 8vo; slipcased. An uncommon work on turkey hunting in South Carolina.

Miscellanea. New York, 1963, Privately printed. 30 pp., frontispiece and drawings. 12mo. Contains one chapter on turkey hunting. Rare.

Millais, J. G.

Newfoundland and Its Untrodden Ways. New York, 1967, Abercrombie & Fitch, Inc. 340 pp., plates. 4to; dust jacket. (A facsimile reproduction originally published in 1907, Longman's Green and Co.)

Miller, Evelyn

How To Raise and Train A Cocker Spaniel. Jersey City, New jersey, 1955, TFH Publishers. 32 pp., illustrations. 8vo. Paper wrappers.

How To Raise and Train a Golden Retriever. New York, 1960, Sterling. 64 pp., photographic plates. 8vo; dust jacket. (Reprinted several times, same format and publisher)

Miller, Frank L.

Biology of the Kaminuriak Population of Barren Ground Caribou, Part II. Ottawa, 1974, Canadian Wildlife Service. 88 pp., illustrations, bibliography. 4to. Paper wrappers.

Miller, Frank L and A. Gunn

Response of Peary Caribou and Muskoxen to Turbo-Helicopter Harassment, Prince of Whales Island, Northwest Territories, 1976-1977. Ottawa, 1979, Canadian Wildlife Service. 90 pp., maps, bibliography. 4to. Paper wrappers.

Miller, Frank L., et al.

Distribution, Movements and Numbers of Peary Caribou and Muskoxen on Western Queen Elizabeth Islands, Northwest Territories. Ottawa, 1977, Canadian Wildlife Service. 54 pp., photographic plates, maps, bibliography. 4to. Paper wrappers.

Miller, Hack

Looking Back With Hack. Salt Lake City, Utah, 1981. 154 pp. 8vo; dust jacket. A collection of the author's hunting and fishing stories originally appearing in the Salt Lake City *Desert News*.

Miller, Harry

Gallery of American Dogs. New York, 1950, McGraw-Hill Publishing Company. 262 pp., photographic plates, drawings by Paul Brown. 8vo; dust jacket. A general work, with a large section on gun dogs.

Miller, Joaquin

True Bear Stories. Chicago, 1927, Rand McNally & Company. 229 pp., illustrations. Introduction by David Starr Jordan. 8vo. (A reproduction of the 1900 first edition)

Miller, Max

The Great Trek. Garden City, New York, 1935, Doubleday, Doran & Co., Inc. 224 pp., photographic plates. 8vo; dust jacket. An account of a five year drive of reindeer through Alaska and Northwest Canada.

Miller, Robert L., editor

Proceedings of the 1972 Black Bear Conference. Delmar, 1972, New York Department of Environmental Conservation. 56 pp., illustrations. 4to. Paper wrappers.

Miller, Warren H.   b. 1876

The Boys' Book Of Hunting And Fishing. New York, 1926, D. Appleton and Co.   291 pp., plates.   8vo; dust jacket.   (Originally published, 1916, George H. Doran Company)

The American Hunting Dog; modern strains of bird dogs and hounds and their training.   New York, 1926, D. Appleton & Co.   252 pp., photographic plates. 8vo; dust jacket.

Rifles and Shotguns; the art of rifle and shotgun shooting for big game and feathered game with special chapters on military rifle shooting.   New York, 1930, D. Appleton & Co.   233 pp., illustrations.   8vo; dust jacket.   (Originally published, 1917, George H. Doran & Co.)

The White Buffalo.   New York, 1926, D. Appleton and Co.   272 pp., illustrations. 8vo; dust jacket.

Miller, William R.

Vermont Waterfowl Identification Guide.   No place, 1955, Vermont Fish and Game Commission. 44pp., drawings by Alan Munro. 8vo. Paper wrappers.

Milliken, Henry

Hunting in Maine.   Freeport, Maine, 1947, L. L. Bean, Inc.   186 pp., illustrations.   Introduction by L. L. Bean.   8vo.   Hunting large and small game throughout the state.

Milling, Chapman J.

Buckshot and Hounds.   Cranbury, New Jersey, 1967, A. S. Barnes and Company, Inc.   132 pp.   8vo; dust jacket.   Deer hunting with shotguns and dogs; also duck, turkey and boar hunting.

Milne, Lorus and Margery J. Milne

The Mating Instinct.   Boston, 1954, Little, Brown & Company.   243 pp., drawings by Olaus J. Murie.   8vo; dust jacket.   With much on North American game animals and birds.

Milner, Robert

Retriever Training For the Duck Hunter.   Princeton, New Jersey, 1983, Nassau Press.   150 pp., photographs and drawings by Philip Crowe.   8vo; dust jacket.

Milnor, William

Memoirs of the Gloucester Foxhunting Club.   New York, 1927, Privately printed for Ernest R. Gee by The Derrydale Press.   47 pp., illustrations from old prints.   Limited to 375 numbered copies.   Tall 8vo.

Minehart, Charles D. (as told to **Louis Lester**)
Meat on the Pole; a story of the Orrstown Hunting Club. West Chester, Pennsylvania, 1948, Privately printed by the club. 25 pp., plus a 1 pp. poem by Lionel Wiggam. Limited to 100 numbered copies. 8vo. Paper wrappers.
A history of this Pennsylvania deer hunting club.

Miner, Jack   b. 1865
Jack Miner on Current Topics. Toronto, 1929, The Ryerson Press. 111 pp., photographic plates. 8vo. Much on the author's studies of Canada Geese plus a discussion on the Canada-U. S. bird treaty.

Minnesota Conservation Department
A Minnesota Guide To Raising and Releasing Canada Geese. No place, 1968, Minnesota Conservation Department. 11 pp.

Minor, Will C.
Footprints in the Trail. Chicago, 1950, Erle Press. 232 pp., illustrations by Rosemary Emerson. 8vo; dust jacket. Wildlife observations in the Rocky Mountains by sheep herders.

Miracle, Leonard
The Cougar is a Puma. New York, 1966, G. P. Putnam's Sons. 125 pp., photographic plates. 8vo; dust jacket.

Missildine, Fred and Nick Karas
Score Better at Skeet. New York, 1972, Winchester Press. 162 pp., illustrations. 8vo; dust jacket.
Score Better at Trap. New York, 1971, Winchester Press. 159 pp., photographic plates. 8vo; dust jacket.
Score Better at Trap and Skeet. South Hackensack, New Jersey, 1977, Stoeger Publishing Company. 162 pp., illustrations. 8vo. Paper wrappers.

Mississippi Flyway Council
Michigan Waterfowl Identification Guide. Burlington, Vermont, 1958, Mississippi Flyway Council. 48 pp., illustrations by Alan R. Munro. 12mo. Paper wrappers.

Mitchell, Horace   1903-1965
Game Farming; a text book for the more efficient and economical propagation of pheasants, quail, wild ducks and ornamental birds. Portsmouth, New Hampshire, 1930, Haley. 162 pp., photographic plates. 8vo.
Raising Game Birds. Philadelphia, 1936, Penn Publishing Company. 315 pp., line drawings and 8 color plates by R. V. Shutts. 8vo; dust jacket. (Reprinted three times by Alfred A. Knopf, Inc., smaller format, as a title in Knopf's Borzoi Books For Sportsmen series)

Mitchell, James L.
  Colt: A Collection of Letters and Photographs. Harrisburg, 1959, The Stackpole Company. 269 pp., illustrations. 4to; dust jacket. Scarce.

Mitchell, John G.
  The Hunt. New York, 1980, Alfred A. Knopf, Inc. 243 pp. 8vo; dust jacket. (Reprinted several times, various formats) A thought-provoking work comparing the views of American hunters determined to keep the legacy of hunting alive, with the views of those Americans determined to outlaw the shooting sports.

Mitchell, Margaret H.
  The Passenger Pigeon in Ontario. Ontario, 1935, R. O. M. 181 pp., color and black and white illustrations, bibliography. 4to. Paper wrappers.

Mochi, Ugo and T. Donald Carter
  Hoofed Animals of the World. New York, 1953, Charles Scribner's Sons. Unpaginated, with 40 full-page illustrations of game mammals plus descriptive text. Folio. (Reprinted 1971, smaller format) A scarce and informative work.

Moen, Aaron
  Agriculture And Wildlife Management. Lansing, New York, 1983, Corner Brook Press. 367 pp., illustrations. 4to.
  The Biology and Management of Wild Ruminants. Lansing, New York, 1980-1982, Corner Brook Press. Seven volumes. 4to.
  Deer Management at the Crane Memorial Reservation and Wildlife Refuge. New York, 1984, Corner Brook Press. 89 pp. 4to.
  Wildlife Ecology; an analytical approach. San Francisco, 1973, W. H. Freeman and Company. 458 pp. Primarily dealing with white tail deer.

Moen, Aaron and Ronald A. Moen.
  Deer Management at the Bernheim Foundation Properties, Clermont, Kentucky. New York, 1985, Corner Brook Press. 52 pp. 4to.

Moffit, Ella B.
  The Cocker Spaniel; companion, shooting dog and show dog; complete information on history, development, characteristics, standards for field and bench, with some practical advice on training, raising and handling. New York, 1935, Orange Judd Publishing Company. 232 pp., illustrations. 8vo; dust jacket. (Reprinted many times, same format and publisher)
  Elias Vail Trains Hunting Dogs; covering the pointing breeds, the spaniels and non-slip retrievers. New York, 1937, Orange Judd Publishing Company. 219 pp., illustrations. 8vo; dust jacket. (Reprinted several times, same format and publisher. Also reprinted, 1964, Howell Book House)

Moisan, Gaston

The Green Winged Teal; its distribution, migration and population dynamics. Washington, D. C., 1967, United States Department of the Interior. 248 pp., maps, bibliography. 4to. Paper wrappers.

Money, Anton (with **Ben East**)

This Was the North. New York, 1975, Crown Publishers, Inc. 244 pp., photographic plates. 8vo; dust jacket. (Reprinted 1975, same format and publisher. Also a 1975 Canadian edition) The account of an Englishman's stay in Alaska in 1923, with much hunting and trapping.

Monson, Gale and Lowell Sumner, editors

The Desert Bighorn; its life history, ecology and management. Tucson, 1980, University of Arizona Press. 370 pp., illustrations; maps. 8vo; paper wrappers in dust jacket. (Reprinted several times, same publisher)

Monson, Keith

Remember, the Deer Do. No place, 1985, Privately printed. 135 pp., photographic plates. 8vo. Paper wrappers. Deals with the technique of hunting deer by driving.

Montague, Andrew (with **S. V. Beckwith**)

Successful Shotgun Shooting. New York, 1971, Winchester Press. 160 pp., illustrations. 8vo; dust jacket. (Reprinted several times, same format and publisher)

Monte, Evelyn

Pet Brittany Spaniel. Fon-du-lac, Wisconsin, 1956, All-Pets, Inc. 64 pp., illustrations. Paper wrappers. A general discussion of the breed.

Montgomery, Rutherford G. b. 1896

High Country. New York, 1938, The Derrydale Press. 248 pp., photographic plates. Limited to 950 numbered copies. 8vo. A fictionalized account of hunting in the Rockies for mule deer, cougar, etc.

The Living Wilderness. New York, 1964, Dodd, Mead & Co. 294 pp., illustrations. 8vo; dust jacket.

Timberline Tales. Philadelphia, 1939, David McKay Co. 264 pp., color and black and white illustrations. 8vo; dust jacket. Contains some grizzly, wolf and cougar hunting.

The Trail of the Buffalo. Boston, 1939, Houghton Mifflin Company. 217 pp. illustrations. 8vo; dust jacket.

Yellow Eyes. Caldwell, 1937, Caxton Printers, Ltd. 243 pp., illustrations by L. B. Cram. 8vo; dust jacket. (Reprinted many times, same format and publisher) Cougar hunting fiction.

Mr. Montgomery was a prolific writer; the Library of Congress lists over two dozen entries for him, including many "Ken Barstow" adventure stories and other juveniles dealing with animals or the American west.

Moore, George and Allen Pearson

The Mourning Dove in Alabama. No place, 1941, Alabama Department of Conservation. 36 pp., illustrations. 8vo. Paper wrappers.

Moore, Phil H.

The Castle Buck; hunting and fishing adventures with a Nova Scotia guide. 300 pp., drawings. 8vo. New York and Toronto, 1945, Longman's, Green & Co. 8vo; dust jacket. (Reprinted 1946, same format and publisher)

Moore, Tera

A Pack of Labs; drawings and paintings by Tara More. Champaign, Illinois, 1982, Garrard Publishing Company. Unpaginated (62 pp.), color and black and white illustrations. 4to; dust jackets. Artwork of Labrador retrievers.

Moore, Warren

Guns; the development of firearms, air guns and cartridges. New York, 1963. 104 pp., illustrations. 4to; dust jacket. (Reprinted 1963, Grosset & Dunlap)

More Game Birds in America Foundation

More Game Birds By Controlling Their Natural Enemies; a practical manual for those who are propagating game birds. New York, No date (ca. 1930), More Game Birds in America Foundation. 63 pp., drawings. 8vo. Paper wrappers. (Also a 1936 revised edition, same format and publisher)

More Waterfowl By Assisting Nature. New York, 1931, More Game Birds in America Foundation. 109 pp., maps 12mo. Paper wrappers. (Reprinted 1932, same format and publisher)

The 1935 International Wild Duck Census. New York, 1935, More Game Birds in America Foundation. 79 pp., illustrations, fold-out map. 8vo. Paper wrappers.

Pheasant Breeding Manual. New York, No date (ca. 1930), More Game Birds in America Foundation. 61 pp., photographic plates. 8vo. Paper wrappers.

Quail Breeding Manual. New York, No date (ca. 1930), More Game Birds in America Foundation. 55 pp., photographic plates 8vo. Paper wrappers. (Also a 1935 revised edition, same format and publisher)

More Game Birds in America Foundation, continued

Small Refuges For Waterfowl. New York, 1933, More Game Birds in America Foundation. 64 pp., photographic plates, drawings. 8vo. Paper wrappers.

This foundation was the progenitor of Ducks Unlimited, which became a highly successful conservation organization, operated and funded without government assistance.

Morenus, Richard

Alaska Sourdough; the story of Slim Williams. New York, 1956, Rand McNally & Company. 278 pp. 8vo; dust jacket. Mostly biographical, but some hunting and fishing.

Moreton, Dave, editor

Gun Talk. New York, 1973, Winchester Press. 250 pp., illustrations. 8vo; dust jacket. An anthology of firearms opinions by Askins, Page, O'Connor, et al.

Morgan, Alma

The Elk Walker. New York, 1976. 47 pp. 8vo; dust jacket. Hunting elk in Washington state. Rare.

Morgan, Dale L.

Jedediah Smith and the Opening of the West. Indianapolis, 1953, The Bobbs-Merrill Company. 458 pp., illustrations, maps. 8vo; dust jacket. An important work with an account of the fur trade in America as well as Smith's biography.

Morgan, Lewis

The American Beaver and His Works. No place, 1970, Burt Franklin. 330 pp., illustrations. 8vo. (A reproduction of the 1867 edition)

Morris, Edmund

The Rise of Theodore Roosevelt. New York, 1979, Coward, McCann & Geoghegan, Inc. 886 pp., photographic plates. 8vo; dust jacket. An insightful biography of Roosevelt up to the time he became President. Containing some detail on his western American hunting.

Morrison, John A. and James C. Lewis, editors

Proceedings of the First National Bobwhite Quail Symposium: 23-26 April, 1972. Stillwater, Oklahoma, 1972, Oklahoma State University Press. 390 pp. maps, charts, bibliography. 8vo. Cloth backed paper wrappers.

Morrow, Beatrix T.

Kerry. New York, 1959, William Morrow & Co., Inc. 80 pp., illustrations. 8vo; dust jacket.

Swim For It, Bridget. New York, 1958, William Morrow & Co., Inc. 80 pp., illustrations. 8vo; dust jacket. Both of these works are older juvenile stories of an Irish water spaniel.

Mosby, Henry S. and Charles O. Handley
    The Wild Turkey in Virginia; its status, life history and management. Richmond, Virginia, 1943, Virginia Game Commission. 281 pp., color frontispiece and other illustrations by Fred Everett. Limited to 2000 copies. 8vo. (Also reprinted, 1943, in paper wrappers, Pittman-Robertson)

Mosby, Henry S. and Oliver H. Hewitt
    Wildlife Investigation Techniques. Washington, D. C., The Wildlife Society. Photographic plates, drawings, bibliography. 4to. (Also a 1965 revised edition, same format and publisher)

Moser, C. A. and C. Hjelte
    The Bighorn Sheep of Colorado. No place, 1962, Colorado Department of Fish and Game. 49 pp., photographic plates. 8vo. Paper wrappers.

Moser, J.
    Breeding Ecology of Canada Geese. 1972, West Virginia Division of Game and Fish. 10 pp. Paper wrappers.

Mosher, John
    The Shooter's Workbench. New York, 1977, Winchester Press. 229 pp., photographic plates, drawings. 8vo; dust jacket. A guide to building bench rests, racks, cleaning rods, etc.

Moulton, Forest Ray
    New Methods in Exterior Ballistics. Chicago, 1927, The University of Chicago Press. 268 pp., illustrated with figures. 8vo.

Mowat, Farley   b. 1921
    Never Cry Wolf. Boston, 1963, Little, Brown & Company. 247 pp. 8vo; dust jacket. (Reprinted many times, various formats and publishers) An account of the author's observations of the wolves of the Keewatin Barrens.
    People of the Deer. New York, 1951, The Jove Press. 303 pp. (Reprinted 1952, Little, Brown & Company) Much on caribou hunting with the Eskimos.
    Tundra; selections from the great accounts of arctic land voyages. Toronto, 1973, McClelland & Stewart. 415 pp., photographic plates, maps. 8vo; dust jacket. Mostly exploration, but many accounts of caribou hunting.

Moyen, Aaron N.
    Wildlife Ecology; an analytical approach. San Francisco, Freeman. 458 pp., photographic plates, drawings, bibliography. 4to. (Reprinted 1973, same format and publisher) Studies centered around white tailed deer populations.

Moyer, John W.
> *Trophy Heads.* New York, 1962, The Ronald Press. 258 pp., photographic plates. 8vo; dust jacket; slipcased. Includes habits and habitat of the big game animals of the five major continents. Scarce.

Moyle, John, editor
> *Ducks and Land Use in Minnesota.* No place, 1964, Minnesota Department of Conservation. 140 pp., illustrations, maps. 8vo. Paper wrappers.
> *The Mule Deer of Wyoming.* 1985, Wyoming Game and Fish Department. 154 pp.

Muller, Heinrich
> *Guns, Pistols and Revolvers.* New York, 1980, St. Martin's Press. 224 pp., illustrations. 8vo; dust jacket. With a concentration on hand-arms from the 14ᵗʰ to 19ᵗʰ centuries.

Mullin, John
> *Game Bird Propagation: The Wildlife Harvest System.* Goose Lake, Iowa, 1978. 194 pp., photographic plates. 8vo. Paper wrappers.

Mumey, Nolie
> *The Black Ram of Dinwoody Creek;* the story of Rocky Mountain Bighorn Sheep. Denver, 1951, Range Press. 192 pp., illustrations. Limited to 325 numbered and signed copies. 8vo.
> *Rocky Mountain Dick: (Richard W. Rock);* stories of his adventures in capturing wild animals. Denver, 1953, Privately printed. 86 pp., photographic plates, folding map. Limited to 500 numbered copies. Tall 8vo.

Munsterhjelm, Erik
> *The Wind and the Caribou;* hunting and trapping in northern Canada. London, 1953, George Allen & Unwin, Ltd. 234 pp., map. 8vo; dust jacket. (Also printed, Toronto, The Macmillan Company) Trapping fox, mink, muskrat and hunting caribou and bear in the lake Athabaska region during the 1930's.

Murie, Adolph   b. 1899
> *A Naturalist in Alaska.* New York, 1961, The Devin-Adair Company. 302 pp., illustrations. 8vo; dust jacket. (Also reprinted, 1963, paper wrappers) Relating Mr. Murie's experience in Alaska with grizzly bear, sheep, moose, etc.
> *The Ecology of the Coyote in Yellowstone.* Washington, D. C., 1940, United States Department of the Interior. 206 pp., photographic plates. 8vo. Paper wrappers.
> *Following Fox Trials.* Ann Arbor, 1936, University of Michigan Press, 45 pp., illustrations. 4to.

Murie, Adolph, continued

The Grizzlies of Mt. McKinley. Washington, D. C., 1981, United States Department of the Interior. 251 pp., illustrations. 8vo. (Reprinted 1985, University of Washington Press)

Mammals of Mount McKinley National Park, Alaska. No place, 1962, Mt. McKinley Natural History Association. 56 pp., drawings by Olaus Murie. 8vo. Paper wrappers.

The Moose of Isle Royale. Ann Arbor, 1934, University of Michigan Press. 44 pp., illustrations. 4to. Paper wrappers.

The Wolves of Mt. McKinley. Washington, D. C., 1944, United States Department of the Interior. 238 pp., illustrations. 8vo. Paper wrappers. (Reprinted several times, same format, various publishers)

Murie, J. O. and G. R. Michener, editors

The Biology of Ground-Dwelling Squirrels; Annual Cycles, Behavioral Ecology and Sociality. Lincoln, 1984, University of Nebraska Press. 459 pp., illustrations. 8vo; dust jacket.

Murie, Margaret

The Alaskan Bird Sketches of Olaus Murie; with excerpts from his field notes. Anchorage, 1979, Alaska Northwest Publishing Company. 58 pp., color illustrations. 4to. Paper wrappers.

Two in the Far North. New York, 1962, Alfred A. Knopf, Inc. 438 pp., illustrations by Olaus J. Murie. 8vo; dust jacket. (Reprinted several times, same format, various publishers)

Murie, Margaret and Olaus J. Murie

Wapiti Wilderness. New York, 1966, Alfred A. Knopf, Inc. 302 pp., illustrations. 8vo; dust jacket. (Reprinted 1985, Colorado Associated University Press)

Murie, Olaus J.   1889 - 1963

Alaska-Yukon Caribou. Washington, D. C., 1935, United States Department of Agriculture. 93 pp., illustrations, maps, bibliography. 8vo. Paper wrappers. (Reprinted 1954, same format and publisher. Also reprinted, 1981, Shorey Publishing Company)

The Elk of North America. Harrisburg, 1951, The Stackpole Company and The Wildlife Management Institute. 376 pp., photographic plates, color frontispiece from a painting by Walter A. Weber. 8vo; dust jacket. (Reprinted twice, same format and publishers. Also reprinted, 1979, Teton Bookshop) Despite being written nearly half a century ago, this remains an authoritative and useful work.

Murie, Olaus J., continued

Fauna of the Aleutian Islands and Alaskan Peninsula; Including *Invertebrates and Fishes Collected in the Aleutians, 1936-1938* by V. B. Sheffer. Washington, D. C., 1959, United States Department of the Interior.   406 pp., photographic plates, maps, large bibliography. 8vo. Paper wrappers. Scarce.

A Field Guide To Animal Tracks.   Boston, 1954, Houghton Mifflin Company.   375 pp., drawings by the author.   12mo; dust jacket. (Reprinted several times, same format and publisher)

Journeys To the Far North.   Palo Alto, California, 1973, The Wilderness Society / American West Publishing Company.   255 pp., drawings by the author. 8vo; dust jacket.

Murphey, Eugene Edmund

Wings at Dusk; and other poems.   New York, 1939, Longman's, Green & Co.   58 pp., drawings by Roger Tory Peterson. 8vo; dust jacket. Poems about shorebirds, waterfowl and other birds. Scarce.

Murphy, Charles F.

Working Plans For Working Decoys.   Tulsa, 1979, Winchester Press. 16 pp. text plus six full-sized plans. Paper wrappers; boxed.

Working Decoy Plans: Kit I.   Piscataway, New Jersey, 1984, New Century Publishers.   16 pp., color and black and white illustrations; accompanied by 6 fold-out plans. 4to; boxed.

Working Decoy Plans: Kit II.   Piscataway, New Jersey, 1986, New Century Publishers.   17 pp., color and black and white illustrations, accompanied by 6 fold-out plans. 4to; boxed.

Murphy, Jack

Abe and Me.   San Diego, 1977, Joyce Press.   192 pp., drawings by Chuck Beebe. 8vo; dust jacket.   The story of a Labrador retriever.

Murphy, Robert William   b. 1902

The Golden Eagle. New York, 1965, E. P. Dutton & Co., Inc.   157 pp., drawings. 8vo; dust jacket.

The Peregrine Falcon.   Boston, 1963, Houghton Mifflin Company. 157 pp., illustrations. 8vo; dust jacket.   (Reprinted several times, various publishers)

The Mountain Lion. New York, 1969, E. P. Dutton & Co., Inc.   129 pp., drawings. 8vo; dust jacket.

The Phantom Setter; and other stories.   New York, 1966, E. P. Dutton & Co., Inc. 256 pp., illustrations by John Schoenherr. 8vo; dust jacket.

The Stream. New York, 1971, Farrar, Straus and Giroux, Inc.   205 pp., illustrations by Bob Hines. 8vo; dust jacket.   A novel with considerable hunting and fishing.

Murphy, Robert William, continued

Wild Sanctuaries; our national wildlife refuges - a heritage restored. New York, 1969, E. P. Dutton & Co., Inc. 288 pp., color and black and white illustrations, maps. 4to; dust jacket.

Murphy, Stanley

Martha's Vineyard Decoys. Boston, 1978, David R. Godine, Publishers, Inc. 165 pp., color and black and white illustrations. 4to; dust jacket. [Also a deluxe edition, specially bound and limited to 55 numbered and signed copies; slipcased]

Murray, Douglas

The Ninety-Nine; a history of the Savage Model 99 rifle. No place, Privately printed. Unpaginated. Paper wrappers. (Also a revised edition, 1980)

Murray, Robert and O. E. Frye, Jr.

The Bobwhite Quail and Its Management in Florida. Tallahassee, 1957, Florida Fish and Game Commission. 56 pp., illustrations. 8vo. Paper wrappers.

Murray, William H. H.

Adventures in the Wilderness; or camp life in the Adirondacks. Syracuse, 1970, Adirondack. 236 pp. plus 95 pp. introduction, illustrations. 8vo; dust jacket. (A reproduction of the 1869 first edition, with a few added illustrations)

Musgrove, Bill and Blair and Gerry Musgrove

Fur Trapping. New York, 1979, Winchester Press. 246 pp., photographic plates. 8vo; dust jacket.

Musgrove, Jack W.

Waterfowl in Iowa. Des Moines, 1943, Iowa Conservation Commission. 113 pp., illustrated in color and black and white by Maynard Reese. 8vo. (Reprinted several times, same format and publisher)

Muskrat, Johnny and his Trapper Friends

Tips To Trappers, 1930-31. Philadelphia, 1930, Sears, Roebuck and Company. 32 pp., illustrations; fur shipping labels bound in. 8vo. Paper wrappers.

Mussehl, Thomas and F. W. Howell, editors

Game Management in Montana. Helena, 1971, Montana Fish and Game Department. 238 pp., illustrations, maps. 8vo. Paper wrappers.

Myatt, Maj. Frederick
    The Illustrated Encyclopedia of Pistols and Revolvers.   New York, 1980, Crescent Books.   208 pp., color illustrations.   Folio; dust jacket.

Myers, Charles E.
    Memoirs of a Hunter; covering a period of 58 years in the Pacific Northwest.   Davenport, Washington, 1948, Privately printed.   309 pp., photographic plates.   8vo; dust jacket. Mostly hunting big game in the far west, with some fishing. Scarce.

Myers, Edward and Judith Myers.
    A Bibliographical Check List of the Writings of Zane Grey. Collinsville, Connecticut, No date, Country Lane Books.   20 pp., illustrations. 8vo.   Paper wrappers.   (Reprinted and revised several times, same format and publisher)

Myers, James E.
    Jones. Springfield, Illinois, 1982, Lincoln-Heindon.   200 pp.   8vo. A novel centered around bird dog field trials.

Myrick, Jim
    Life Behind the Chase.   Licking, 1964, Derrickson.   109 pp., photographic plates. 12mo. Red and gray foxhunting; also Texas red wolf hunting; breeding of hounds.

Myrus, Don
    Collector's Guns.   New York, 1962.   128 pp., photographic plates, drawings.   8vo; dust jacket.

Nagler, Forrest

The Bow and Arrow For Big Game. No place (Albany, Oregon), No date (1940), Frank Taylor & Son. 70 pp., illustrations. 12mo. (Also published in paper wrappers. Also reprinted with *Archery, An Engineering View*, another of the author's works, two books in one)

Narramore, Earl

Handloader's Manual; a treatise on modern cartridge components and their assembly by the individual shooter into accurate ammunition to best suit his purposes. Onslow County, North Carolina, 1937, Small Arms Technical Publishing Company. 369 pp., plus ads, illustrations. 12mo;dust jacket. (Reprinted 1943, same format and publisher)

Principles and Practices of Loading Ammunition. Georgetown, South Carolina, 1954, Small Arms Technical Publishing Company. 952 pp., illustrations, tables, charts. Tall 8vo; dust jacket. (Reprinted twice, same format, The Stackpole Company)

National Amateur Retriever Club

The Handbook of Amateur Retriever Trials, Ten Year Edition, 1951 - 1961. No place, No date (ca. 1961), National Amateur Retriever Club. 197 pp. 8vo.

The National Rifle Association of America

The ABC of Practical Pistol Instruction. Washington, D. C., ca. 1942, The National Rifle Association of America. 28 pp., photographic plates, drawings. 8vo. Paper wrappers.

Deer Hunter's Guide. Washington, D. C., 1978, The National Rifle Association of America. 160 pp., illustrations. Paper wrappers.

Deer Hunting. Washington, D. C., No date (ca. 1965), The National Rifle Association of America. 36 pp. Reprints of articles originally appearing in The American Rifleman magazine.

Duck Hunting. Washington, D. C., No date (ca. 1965), The National Rifle Association of America. 24 pp., illustrations. 4to. Paper wrappers.

Illustrated Firearms Assembly Handbook. Washington, D. C., No date, The National Rifle Association of America. Two volumes with a total of 336 pp., illustrations. 4to. Paper wrappers.

The National Rifle Association Guide To Firearms Assembly; rifles and shotguns, pistols and revolvers. Washington, D. C., 1980, The National Rifle Association of America. 510 pp., photographic plates, drawings, ads. 4to. Paper wrappers.

This organization printed several dozen pamphlets promoting the shooting sports over the years. Nearly all were published in paper wrappers.

The National Rifle Association of America

Also see **Serven, James Edsall and James B. Trefethen**

National Shooting Preserve Directory
    Where and How To Hunt and Shoot.   New York, 1964, National Shooting Preserve Directory.   31 pp., illustrations.   8vo.   Paper wrappers.

National Sportsman
    Sportsman's Yearbook.   Boston, 1940, National Sportsman.   204 pp., photographic plates.   8vo.   Paper wrappers.   A collection of articles appearing in *Hunting and Fishing* magazine.

Naylor, Leonard
    Labradors. New York, 1952, A. S. Barnes and Company, Inc.   96 pp., photographic plates.   8vo; dust jacket.

Neasham, V. Aubrey, editor
    Wild Legacy; California hunting and fishing tales.   Berkeley, California, 1973, Howell-North Books.   178 pp., photographic plates.   8vo; dust jacket. An anthology.

Neely, W. W. and V. E. Davison
    Wild Ducks in Farmlands of the South.   14 pp., photographic plates. 8vo.   Paper wrappers.

Nelson, H. K.
    Recent Approaches to Canada Goose Management.   Washington, D. C., 1962, United States Fish and Wildlife Service.   25 pp.   Paper wrappers.

Nelson, Kendall L.
    Status and Habits of the American Buffalo (Bison bison) in the Henry Mountain Area of Utah.   No place, 1965, Utah State Department of Fish and Game.   142 pp., photographic plates, map, bibliography.   4to.   Paper wrappers.

Nelson, Noland
    Waterfowl Hunting in Utah.   No place, 1966, Utah State Department of Fish and Game.   100 pp., photographic plates, charts, maps.   8vo.   Paper wrappers.

Nelson, Norm
    Hunting the Whitetail Deer; how to bring home North America's No. 1 big game animal.   New York, 1980, David McKay Co. 206 pp., photographic plates.   8vo;dust jacket.

Nelson, Ray
    The Rod and Gun Club of the Air Scrap Book.   New York, 1953, Greenberg: Publishers.   64 pp.   8vo.   Paper wrappers.   A compilation of some frequently asked questions on the radio program "The Rod and Gun Club of the Air."

Nelson, Richard K.

Hunters of the Northern Forest; designs for survival among the Alaskan Kutchin. Chicago, 1973, University of Chicago. 339 pp., photographic plates, drawings, bibliography. 8vo; dust jacket. (Also reprinted in paper wrappers)

Hunters of the Northern Ice. Chicago, 1969, University of Chicago Press. 429 pp., photographic plates. 8vo;dust jacket. (Reprinted 1978, same format and publisher. Also reprinted in paper wrappers) Hunting techniques of the Eskimos.

Nero, Robert W.

The Great Gray Owl; phantom of the northern forest. Washington, D. C., 1980, Smithsonian Institute. 167 pp., color and black and white illustrations, bibliography. 4to; dust jacket.

Nesbit, William   b. 1876

How to Hunt With the Camera; a complete guide to all forms of outdoor photography. New York, 1926, E. P. Dutton & Co., Inc. 337 pp., photographic plates by Akely, Chapman, Hornaday, Johnson, Phillips, and others. 4to; dust jacket.

Nesbitt, William H. and Jack S. Parker, editors

North American Big Game. Washington, D. C., 1977, Boone and Crockett Club / The National Rifle Association of America. 367 pp., photographic plates. 8vo; dust jacket. (Reprinted 1978, same format and publisher) The seventh Boone and Crockett Club Records Book.

Nesbitt, William H. and P. L. Wright, editors

Measuring and Scoring North American Big Game Trophies; the Boone and Crockett Club official scoring system with tips for field evaluation of trophies. Alexandria, Virginia, 1985, Boone and Crockett Club. 176 pp., photographic plates. 4to. Paper wrappers.

Records of North American Big Game. Alexandria, Virginia, 1981, Boone and Crockett Club. 409 pp., color and black and white illustrations. 8vo; dust jacket. (Reprinted, same format and publisher) [Also a deluxe first edition, specially bound and limited to 750 numbered copies] The eighth Boone and Crockett Club Records Book.

Ness, Fred C.   1896-1967

The ABC of Reloading. Washington, D. C., 1941, The National Rifle Association of America. 32 pp., illustrations. 8vo. Paper wrappers.

American Sighting Scopes. Washington, D. C., 1940, The National Rifle Association of America. 47 pp., illustrations. 8vo. Paper wrappers.

Ness, Fred C., continued

    Practical Dope on the Big Bores.   Harrisburg, 1948, Stackpole and Heck, Inc. 436 pp., photographic plates. 8vo;dust jacket. (Reprinted 1952, same format and publisher. Also a 1984 edition, Wolfe Publishing Company in an edition limited to 1500 copies)

    Practical Dope on the .22.   Harrisburg, 1947, Military Service Publishing Company. 313 pp., photographic plates, some in color. 8vo; dust jacket. (Reprinted twice, 1948, 1950, same format, Stackpole & Heck, Inc.) An important work relating to center-fire rifles of this caliber.

Ness, Fred C., et al.

    Remodeling Military Rifles.   Washington, D. C., 1940, The National Rifle Association of America. 48 pp., illustrations. 8vo. Paper wrappers. Details of remodeling the 1917 Enfield rifle for porting use; contributors include Ellis Christian Lenz, Lt. Col. Townsend Whelen and Alvin Linden.

Nessmuk (*pseud.* of **George Washington Sears**)   **1821-1890**

    The Adirondack Letters of George Washington Sears; whose name was "Nessmuk." Blue Mountain Lake, New York, 1962, Adirondack Museum. 177 pp., photographic plates, brief biographical sketch by Dan Brenan. 8vo; dust jacket.

Nevada Department of Fish and Game

    The Desert Bighorn Sheep of Nevada.   Reno, 1978, Nevada Department of Fish and Game. 81 pp., illustrations, maps, bibliography. 4to. Paper wrappers.

New, Harry S.

    The Story of Turtle Lake.   Michigan, 1923, Privately printed. 36 pp. The story of the origin of the Turtle Lake Deer Hunting Club. Not in Phillips. Also see **McMath, Neil,** for another title regarding this subject.

New Brunswick Travel Bureau

    Outdoors - New Brunswick; anglers and hunters paradise. Frederickton, No date (ca. 1954), New Brunswick Travel Bureau. Unpaginated (approx. 26 pp.), color and black and white illustrations. 8vo. Paper wrappers.

New Hampshire Fish and Game Department

    Hunting and Fishing.   Concord, 1939, New Hampshire Fish and Game Department. 11 pp., photographic plates, maps. 8vo. Paper wrappers.

    The Ring-Necked Pheasant in New Hampshire.   Concord, 1949, New Hampshire Fish and Game Commission. 82 pp., illustrations. 8vo. Paper wrappers.

New York Field Archers

What About Bowhunting in New York? No place (Leeds, New York), No date (1954), William W. Rice. 36 pp., illustrations. 8vo. Paper wrappers.

New York Zoological Society

Gallery of Wild Animal Paintings in the Zoological Park. New York, 1930, New York Zoological Society. Unpaginated, with 29 full page black and white plates, mostly of paintings by Carl Rungius, but a few by Fuertes, Horsfall, Knight and others. 4to. Paper wrappers. Scarce.

Newell, A. Donald

Gunstock Finishing & Care; a textbook, covering the various means and methods by which modern protective and decorative coatings may be applied in the correct and suitable finishing of gun and rifle stocks. Georgetown, South Carolina, 1949, Small Arms Technical Publishing Company. 444 pp., illustrations, glossary. 8vo; dust jacket. (Reprinted 1954, same publisher and format. Also reprinted, 1975, The Stackpole Company)

Newell, David M.   b. 1898

Cougars and Cowboys. New York, 1927, The Century Company. 222 pp., illustrations. Foreword by Kermit Roosevelt. 8vo. A scarce cougar and bear hunting title.

The Fishing and Hunting Answer Book. New York, 1948, Doubleday & Co., Inc. 285 pp., illustrations, some by Lynn Bogue Hunt. 8vo;dust jacket. (Reprinted twice, 1949, 1950, same format and publisher)

If Nothin' Don't Happen. New York, 1974, Alfred A. Knopf, Inc. 242pp., illustrations. 8vo; dust jacket.

The Trouble of It Is. New York, 1978, Alfred A. Knopf, Inc. 272 pp., drawings by Mark Livingston. 8vo; dust jacket. A humorous and sometimes poignant continuation of the trials and tribulations of the Driggerses and the Eppses families of north Florida, begun in Newell's *If Nothin' Don't Happen.* With much hunting and fishing.

David Newell was an editor at *Field and Stream* magazine during the 1940's and 1950's.

Newkirk, Newton

Back To Nature. Boston, 1927, National Sportsman. 172 pp., drawings. 12mo. Paper wrappers. (Originally published, National Sportsman)

Doc an' Jim an' Me; tales of camp life. Boston, 1927, National Sportsman. 71 pp., drawings. 8vo. (Originally published, 1906)

Newsome, William Moneypeny

White-Tailed Deer. New York, 1926, Charles Scriber's Sons. 288 pp., illustrated. 8vo;dust jacket. An important work.

Newton, Lord

Lord Landsdown; a biography.   London, 1929, Macmillan and Company.   536 pp., illustrations.   8vo; dust jacket.   The biography of this renowned statesman-sportsman, including some hunting and angling in Canada.

Nicholas, Anna Katherine

The Book of the Labrador Retriever.   Neptune City, New Jersey, 1983, TFH Publications.   478 pp., photographic plates.   4to.

Nichols, Robert M. "Bob"

Gun Blasts and How To Avoid Them.   New York, no date (ca. 1950), Field and Stream.   4pp.   4to.   Paper wrappers.

The Secrets of Double Action Shooting.   New York, 1950, G. P. Putnam's Sons.   152 pp., illustrations.   12mo;dust jacket.   (Reprinted 1950, same format and publisher)

The Shotgunner.   New York, 1949, G. P. Putnam's Sons.   373 pp., frontispiece.   8vo; dust jacket.   (Reprinted 1949, same format and publisher)

Skeet and How to Shoot It.   New York, 1939, Greenberg: Publisher. 177 pp., photographic plates.   8vo; dust jacket.   (Reprinted 1940, same format and publisher. Also reprinted, 1947, G. P. Putnam's Sons)

Nichols, Robert M. and Edward Cave

How to Hit 'Em.   East Alton, Illinois, 1935, Western Cartridge Company. 14 pp., illustrations, ads.   8vo.   Paper wrappers.

Niehuis, Charley

Trapping the Silver Beaver.   New York, 1956, Dodd, Mead & Co., Inc. 208 pp., drawings by Chris Kenyon.   8vo; dust jacket.   A novel about a boy trapper and the Department of Fish and Game.

Nile, Leroy

Kennebago Summer.   Farmington, Maine, 1947, Knowleton.   111 pp., text decorations.   12mo; dust jacket.   Much on the Rangely region of Maine with fly fishing and one chapter on Cornelia Crosby, the first woman to shoot a caribou in the state.

Nish, Darrell H.

The Effects of Water Development Upon Populations of Gambel's Quail in Southwestern Utah.   No place, 1964, United States Department of Fish and Game / Utah Department of Fish and Game.   135 pp., photographic plates, bibliography.   4to.   Paper wrappers.

Guidelines On Managing the Habitat of Meriam's Wild Turkey.   No place, 1973, Utah Department of Natural Resources. 26 pp., bibliography.   4to. Cloth backed paper wrappers.

Nixon, C. M., et al.

Squirrel Hunting in Illinois. Springfield, 1978, Illinois Department of Conservation. 37 pp., photographic plates. 8vo. Paper wrappers.

Nolting, Carl H.

The Wild Turkey in Virginia; its habits and management. Richmond, 1942, Game and Inland Fisheries Commission. 44 pp., photographic plates, map. 8vo. Paper wrappers.

Nonte, George C.

Basic Handloading. New York, 1978, Outdoor Life Books. 185 pp., illustrations. 8vo. Paper wrappers.

The Black Powder Guide. New York, 1981, Stoeger Arms Corp. 255 pp., illustrations. 4to. Paper wrappers.

Cartridge Conversions. Harrisburg, 1961, The Stackpole Company. 340 pp., illustrations. 8vo; dust jacket. (Also a 1967 revised edition titled, *The Home Guide To Cartridge Conversions*, same publisher) Describes the conversion of a metallic cartridge of one caliber to that of another, usually called a "wildcat."

Complete Book of the Air Gun. Harrisburg, 1970, The Stackpole Company. 288 pp., photographic plates. 8vo; dust jacket. (Reprinted 1973, same format and publisher)

Firearms Encyclopedia. New York, 1973, Harper & Row, Publishers, Inc. 341 pp., illustrations. 4to; dust jacket. (Reprinted many times, same format and publisher)

Handgun Competition; a comprehensive source-book covering all aspects of modern competitive pistol and revolver shooting. New York, 1978, Winchester Press. 367 pp., photographic plates, drawings. 8vo; dust jacket.

Handloading For Handgunners. Northfield, Illinois, 1978, DBI Books. 288 pp., illustrations. 4to. Paper wrappers.

Home Guide To Muzzle Loaders. Harrisburg, 1974, The Stackpole Company. 219 pp., photographic plates. 4to. Paper wrappers.

Modern Handloading. New York, 1972, Winchester Press. 410 pp., illustrations, charts, bibliography. 8vo; dust jacket. (Reprinted many times, same format and publisher)

Pistolsmithing. Harrisburg, 1974, Stackpole Books. 560 pp., illustrations. 8vo; dust jacket. (Reprinted many times, same format and publisher)

The Revolver Guide; an illustrated guide to selecting, shooting and caring for. New York, 1980, Stoeger Arms Corp.. 288 pp., illustrations. 4to. Paper wrappers.

Shooter's Bible Pistol & Revolver Guide. South Hackensack, New Jersey, 1967, Stoeger Arms Corp. 192 pp., illustrations. 4to. Paper wrappers. (Revised and reprinted several times, same format and publisher)

Mr. Nonte also wrote, and Stoeger published, several other non-hunting handgun and self-defense titles.

Nonte, George C. and L. E. Jurras
    Handgun Hunting. New York, 1975, Winchester Press. 245 pp., photographic plates. 8vo; dust jacket. (Reprinted 1976, in paper wrappers, Stoeger Arms Corp.)

Norman, Geoffrey
    The Orvis Book of Upland Shooting. New York, 1985, Nick Lyons Books / Winchester Press. 160 pp., illustrations. 8vo; dust jacket.

Norris, Dr. Charles C.   1876-1961
    Eastern Upland Shooting; with special reference to bird dogs and their handling. Philadelphia, 1946, J. B. Lippincott Co. 408 pp., photographic plates, frontispiece in color, bibliography. 8vo;dust jacket. An important upland shooting title with special emphasis on the author's considerable experiences with gun dogs.

Norris, Dr. Charles C.
    Also see **Evans, George Bird,** *Recollections of a Shooting Guest.*

Norris, Ralph S.
    Science of Hunting the Whitetail Deer. North Leeds, Maine, 1972, Privately printed. 116 pp., photographic plates. 8vo. Paper wrappers.

North, Dick
    The Saga of the Mad Trapper of Rat River. Yukon Territory, No date (ca. 1960), Privately printed. 33 pp. Paper wrappers.

North, A. and I. V. Hogg
    The Book of Guns and Gunsmiths. New Burlington, 1977. 255 pp., color and black and white illustrations. 4to;dust jacket.

Nova Scotia Bureau of Information
    Haunts of Fish and Game - Nova Scotia. Halifax, No date (ca. 1937), Nova Scotia Bureau of Information. Unpaginated, photographic plates. 8vo. Paper wrappers. A guide to the region.

Novak, Milan
    The Beaver in Ontario. Ontario, 1976, Ministry of Natural Resources. 21 pp., illustrations. 8vo. Paper wrappers.

Nunnery, Gene
    The Old Pro Turkey Hunter. Meridian, Mississippi, 1980, Privately printed. 144 pp., drawings by Norman Miller. 8vo; dust jacket.

Nutter, Waldo

Manhattan Firearms.   Harrisburg, 1958, The Stackpole Company.   250 pp., illustrations.   4to; dust jacket.   A history of this firearms manufacturer.

Oakley, Wiley

    Roamin;' with the roamin' man of the Smoky Mountains. Gatlinburg, Tennessee, 1940, Privately printed. 64 pp., photographic plates, drawings by the author. Limited to 750 copies. 8vo; dust jacket. Paper wrappers. (Also a 1941 second printing, limited to 500 copies, same format and publisher. Also reported, a third printing, 1944, The Mountain Press) The author's account of his life of hunting and fishing in the Smoky Mountains.

    Restin;' with the roamin' man of the Smoky Mountains. Gatlinburg, Tennessee, 1947, Privately printed. 62 pp., photographic plates. 8vo. Paper wrappers. More grouse and turkey hunting by the author of *Roamin.'*

Oates, D. W., et al.

    A Guide to Time of Death in Selected Wildlife Species. Lincoln, 1984, Nebraska Game and Parks. 72 pp., color illustrations. 4to. Spiral bound paper wrappers. Methods of determining time of death in various game species.

Oberfell, G. G. and Charles E. Thompson

    The Mysteries of Shotgun Patterns. Stillwater, 1957, Oklahoma State University Press. 164 pp., illustrations. Paper wrappers. (Reprinted several times, various formats, same publisher) A most thorough and useful guide.

Oberrecht, Kenn

    The Outdoor Photographer's Handbook. New York, 1979, Winchester Press. 270 pp., photographic plates, charts. 4to; dust jacket.

O'Brien, G. Patrick

    A Study of the Mexican Duck (Anas diazi) in Southeastern Arizona. Phoenix, 1975, Arizona Fish and Game Commission. 50 pp., photographic plates, bibliography. 8vo. Paper wrappers.

O'Connor, John Wolf "Jack" 1902 - 1978

    The Art of Hunting Big Game in North America. New York, 1947, Outdoor Life Books. 404 pp., photographic plates, drawings by Doug Allen. 8vo; dust jacket. (Reprinted and revised several times, same format and publisher)

    The Best of Jack O'Connor. Clinton, New Jersey, 1977, Amwell Press. 192 pp., illustrations. Limited to 1000 numbered and signed copies. 8vo; slipcased. (Also a 1984 trade edition, same format and publisher)

    The Big Game Rifle. New York, 1952, Alfred A. Knopf, Inc. 371 pp., photographic plates. A Borzoi Book For Sportsmen. 8vo; dust jacket.

    Boomtown; a novel of the southwestern silver boom. New York, 1938, Alfred A. Knopf, Inc. 331 pp. 8vo; dust jacket.

O'Connor, John Wolf "Jack," continued

Complete Book of Rifles and Shotguns; with a seven-lesson rifle shooting course. New York, 1961, Harper & Row, Publishers, Inc. / Outdoor Life Books. 477 pp., illustrations. 8vo; dust jacket. (Reprinted many times, same format and publisher)

Conquest; a novel of the old Southwest. New York, 1930, Harper & Brothers. 293 pp. 12mo; dust jacket. (Reprinted, Grosset & Dunlap) The author's first book. Scarce.

Game in the Desert. New York, 1939, The Derrydale Press. 298 pp., photographic plates, frontispiece in color by T. J. Harter. Limited to 950 numbered copies. 4to; boxed. Hunting various species of game in the southwestern U. S.

Game in the Desert Revisited. Clinton, New Jersey, 1977, Amwell Press. 306 pp., illustrations. Limited to 1000 numbered and signed copies. 8vo; slipcased. (Also a 1984 trade edition, same format and publisher. This trade edition also reprinted. Also reprinted as an Outdoor Life Book Club edition) Includes the entire text from *Game in the Desert*, plus two additional chapters.

Horse and Buggy West; a boyhood on the last frontier. New York, 1969, Alfred A. Knopf, Inc. 302 pp., drawings. 8vo; dust jacket. (Reprinted 1969, same format and publisher) Mr. O'Connor's autobiography.

The Hunter's Shooting Guide. New York, 1978, Outdoor Life Books. 170 pp., photographic plates. 8vo. Paper wrappers. (Reprinted, same format and publisher)

Hunting in the Rockies. New York, 1947, Alfred A. Knopf, Inc. 297 pp., color and black and white photographic plates. A Borzoi Book for Sportsmen. 8vo; dust jacket. Big game hunting in the Rocky Mountains with much on sheep hunting.

Hunting in the Southwest. New York, 1945, Alfred A. Knopf, Inc. 277 pp., photographic plates, color frontispiece. A Borzoi Book for Sportsmen. 8vo; dust jacket. This is with a few minor changes, a reprint of *Game in the Desert.*

Hunting on Three Continents With Jack O'Connor. Long Beach California, 1987, Safari Press. 303 pp., photographic plates. 8vo; dust jacket. [Also a deluxe edition, limited to 500 numbered copies, signed by the author's son]

The Hunting Rifle. New York, 1970. Winchester Press. 314 pp., photographic plates. 8vo; dust jacket. (Reprinted, same format and publisher)

Hunting With a Binocular. Rochester, New York, 1949, Bausch & Lomb Optical Co. 22 pp., photographic plates. 24mo. Paper wrappers. A promotional pamphlet written for Bausch & Lomb with some discussion of sheep hunting.

Jack O'Connor's Big Game Hunts. New York, 1963, E. P. Dutton & Co., Inc. / Outdoor Life Books. 415 pp., illustrations. 8vo; dust jacket.

Jack O'Connor: The Last Book; confessions of a gun editor. Clinton, New Jersey, 1984, Amwell Press. 247 pp., illustrations. 8vo; slipcased. (Reprinted 1985, same format and publisher) [Also a deluxe first edition, limited to 1000 numbered and signed copies; slipcased]

O'Connor, John Wolf "Jack," continued

Outdoor Life Shooting Book. New York, 1957, Outdoor Life Books. 80 pp., illustrations. 4to. Paper wrappers. (Reprinted many times, same format and publisher. Also a revised and expanded edition titled, *The Hunter's Shooting Guide*)

The Rifle Book. New York, 1949, Alfred A. Knopf, Inc. 332 pp., photographic plates. A Borzoi Book For Sportsmen. 8vo; dust jacket. (Reprinted and revised several times, same format and publisher)

Rifle and Shotgun Shooting Basics. New York, no date (ca. 1970). 41 pp., illustrations. 8vo. Paper wrappers. (Reprinted several times)

7-Lesson Rifle Shooting Course. New York, Outdoor Life Books. 37 pp., illustrations. 8vo. Paper wrappers. (Reprinted many times, same format and publisher)

Sheep and Sheep Hunting. New York, 1974, Winchester Press. 308 pp., photographic plates. 8vo; dust jacket. (Reprinted several times, same format and publisher) An important work.

The Shotgun Book. New York, 1965, Alfred A. Knopf, Inc. 332 pp., illustrations. 8vo; dust jacket. (Reprinted several times, same format and publisher)

Sporting Guns: How to Choose and How to Use. New York, 1947, Franklin Watts. 94 pp., illustrations. 4to. Paper wrappers.

Sportsman's Arms and Ammunition Manual. New York, 1952, Outdoor Life Books. 252 pp., photographic plates. 8vo; dust jacket. (Also reprinted in paper wrappers, same publisher)

O'Connor, John Wolf "Jack," et al.

Complete Book of Shooting; rifles, shotguns, handguns, with Roy Dunlap, Alex Kerr and Jeff Cooper. New York, 1965, Harper & Row, Publishers, Inc. / Outdoor Life Books. 385 pp., illustrated. 8vo; dust jacket. (Also a 1982 second revised edition, The Stackpole Company)

Outdoor Life's Sportsman's Encyclopedia. New York, 1947, Outdoor Life Books. 311 pp., illustrations. 8vo. (Reprinted 1949, same format and publisher. Also a 1956 revised edition, same format and publisher)

Two Thousand Ideas For Sportsmen. New York, 1947, Outdoor Life Books. 248 pp., illustrations. 8vo; dust jacket.

O'Connor, John Wolf "Jack" and George C. Goodwin

The Big Game Animals of North America. New York, 1961, E. P. Dutton & Co., Inc. / Outdoor Life Books. 264 pp., color and black and white illustrations. Folio; dust jacket. (Reprinted 1977, same format and publisher)

O'Connor, John Wolf "Jack" and Warren Page and Jim Carmichael

The Rifle Omnibus. Clinton, New Jersey, 1975, The Amwell Press. Three volumes in one, all previously published. *The Modern Rifle* by Carmichael, *The Hunting Rifle* by O'Connor and *The Accurate Rifle* by Page. 342 pp., 314 pp., and 215 pp. respectively, all with photographic plates. Limited to 750 numbered copies signed by all three authors. Tall 8vo; slipcased.

Oelgart, Isaac J.

The Borzoi Books For Sportsmen; a checklist and price guide. Litchfield, Connecticut, 1982, American Sporting Book Price Guides. 12 pp. Limited to 1000 copies, the first 75 of which were numbered, signed and hand-sewn. Narrow 8vo. Paper wrappers.

The 1982 Derrydale Price Guide. Litchfield, Connecticut, 1982, American Sporting Book Price Guides. 20 pp. Limited to 1500 copies. Narrow 8vo. Paper wrappers. (Also a revised 1984 edition, same format and publisher, limited to 400 copies)

Falconry and Hawking Treatises, 1575 - 1975; a checklist of primary sources with a list of related books of interest to falconers. Newburryport, Massachusetts, 1976, New Mews Press. 36 pp., illustrations. Limited to 400 numbered copies, the first 25 of which were specially bound. 12mo. Paper wrappers.

The Van Nostrand Sporting Books; a checklist and price guide. Arlington, Vermont, 1983, American Sporting Book Price Guides. 12 pp. Limited to 777 copies, the first 70 of which were numbered, signed and hand-sewn. Narrow 8vo. Paper wrappers.

Oelgart, Isaac J., editor

William Harnden Foster: Bird Dogs in New England. No place, 1984, Privately printed. Unpaginated (20 pp.) Limited to 1000 numbered copies. 8vo. Paper wrappers. This originally appeared in the June, 1920 issue of Massachusetts Fish and Game Association *Game Report.*

H. D. Thoreau On Partridges; selections from his journal, 1851-1860. No place, 1984, Privately printed. Unpaginated (20 pp.) Limited to 660 numbered copies, the first 60 of which were hand-sewn and contained marbled end-papers. 8vo. Paper wrappers. Both of these little pamphlets are examples of very fine printing produced on hand-made paper.

Oelgart, Isaac J.,

Also see **Siegel, Col. Henry A., et al.**

Ogilvie, Malcomb A.

Wild Geese. Vermillion, South Dakota, 1978, Buteo Books. 350 pp., color plates by Carol Ogilvie. 8vo; dust jacket. Covers all species of the world.

Ogren, Herman A.
     Barbary Sheep. Santa Fe, 1965, New Mexico Department of Game and Fish. 117 pp., photographic plates. 8vo. Paper wrappers. The account of this introduced species into New Mexico, with its ecology and management.

Ohye, Kay
     You and the Target; an all new trapshooting handbook to better scores. No place, 1978, Privately printed. 83 pp., photographic plates, diagrams. Numbered copies of an unspecified limitation. 8vo.

Oklahoma Department of Conservation
     Deer Hunter's Handbook. Oklahoma City, 1982, Oklahoma Department of Conservation. 24 pp. Paper wrappers.

Old Kickapoo (*pseud.* of **Glen G. Black**)
     American Beagling. New York, 1949, G. P. Putnam's Sons. 292 pp., photographic plates. 8vo; dust jacket.
     Your Field Trial Beagle. Bradford, Pennsylvania, No date (ca. 1959), Privately printed. 84 pp., illustrations. 8vo. Paper wrappers.

Oleberg, Carl
     Guide to Deer Hunting in the Catskill Mountains. New York, 1968, Outdoor Publications. 40 pp. Paper wrappers.

Olendorff, Richard R. and Sharon E. Olendorf
     An Extensive Bibliography of Falconry, Eagles, Hawks, Falcons, and Other Diurnal Birds of Prey. Fort Collins, Colorado, 1968, Privately printed. Three volumes paginated sequentially to 244 pp., some illustrations. Limited to 1000 numbered copies. 4to. Paper wrappers.

Olendorff, Richard R.
     Golden Eagle Country. New York, 1975, Alfred A. Knopf, Inc. 202 pp., illustrations. Folio; dust jacket. A discussion of a two year-long study of the species in the Rocky Mountains.

Olendorff, Richard R., et al.
     Raptor Management - The State of the Art in 1980. Denver, 1980, United States Department of Agriculture. 56 pp., bibliography. 4to. Paper wrappers.

Olsen, Jack   **b. 1925**
     Night of the Grizzlies. New York, 1969, G. P. Putnam's Sons. 245 pp. 8vo; dust jacket. Much information on the species with a focus on the 1967 grizzly attacks at Glacier National Park.

Olsen, Jack, continued

Slaughter the Animals, Poison the Earth. New York, 1971, Simon & Schuster. 287 pp., illustrations. 8vo; dust jacket. An examination of animal population controls, centralizing around the extermination of the coyote. Historically interesting in light of the recent proliferation of the coyote.

Olsen, Orange A.

Elk Below! No place, 1945, Privately printed. 104 pp., illustrations. 8vo; dust jacket. Information on elk, mule deer and bear. Mr. Olsen spent many years in conservation service obtaining animal counts by flying over animal herds in the west. He was killed in a flying accident making these counts and this book was produced as a tribute to his life work.

Olson, B. G. and Mike Miller

Blood on the Snow; and 17 other true tales of far north adventure from the *Alaska Sportsman.* Seattle, 1956, Superior Publishing Co. 279 pp., illustrations. 8vo; dust jacket. Contains some bear hunting.

Olson, John

John Olson's Book of the Rifle. Chicago, 1974, O'Hara Publications, Inc. 255 pp., illustrations, charts. 4to; dust jacket.

John Olson's Book of the Shotgun. Chicago, 1975, O'Hara Publications, Inc. 247 pp., illustrations. 4to; dust jacket.

Olson's Encyclopedia of Small Arms. Piscataway, New Jersey, 1985, Winchester Press. 262 pp., illustrations. 4to; dust jacket.

Olson, Ludwig

Mauser Bolt Rifles. Aberdeen, 1950, 1951, Privately printed. Two volumes of 68 and 107 pp. respectively, illustrations. 8vo. Paper wrappers. (Also a 1957 revised and enlarged edition, Fadco)

Olson, Sigurd F. **1899-1982**

The Hidden Forest. New York, 1969, Viking Press. 127 pp., color illustrations. 4to; dust jacket.

Listening Point. New York, 1958, Alfred A. Knopf, Inc. 243 pp., illustrations by Francis Lee Jaques. 8vo; dust jacket. (Reprinted 1960, same format and publisher) A story of the Quentico-Superior region of Minnesota.

The Lonely Land. New York, 1961, Alfred A. Knopf, Inc. 273 pp., illustrations by Francis Lee Jaques. 8vo; dust jacket. (Reprinted many times, same format and publisher. Also a 1972 Canadian edition)

Sigurd F. Olson's Wilderness Days. New York, 1972, Alfred A. Knopf, Inc. 233 pp., illustrations. 4to; dust jacket.

Of Time and Place. New York, 1982, Alfred A. Knopf, Inc. 172 pp., illustrations. 8vo; dust jacket.

Olson, Sigurd F., continued

Open Horizons. New York, 1969, Alfred A. Knopf, Inc. 229 pp., drawings by Les Kouba. 8vo; dust jacket. (Reprinted many times, same format and publisher) The autobiography of the author.

Reflections From the North Country. New York, 1976, Alfred A. Knopf, Inc. 172 pp., illustrations by Les Kouba. 8vo; dust jacket. (Reprinted several times, same format and publisher)

Runes of the North. New York, 1963, Alfred A. Knopf, Inc. 256 pp., illustrations by Bob Hines. 8vo. (Reprinted many times, same format and publisher)

The Singing Wilderness. New York, 1956, Alfred A. Knopf, Inc. 245 pp., illustrations by Francis Lee Jaques. 8vo; dust jacket. (Reprinted many times, same format and publisher)

Wilderness Ways. New York, 1972, Alfred A. Knopf, Inc. 233 pp., color and black and white illustrations. 4to; dust jacket. (Reprinted many times, same format and publisher)

Mr. Olson's beautiful prose about the north country of Minnesota helped pique an interest in conservation in an entire generation of Americans.

Olson, Sigurd F. and W. H. Marshall

The Common Loon in Minnesota. Minneapolis, 1952, University of Minnesota Press. 77 pp., photographic plates, maps, drawings, bibliography. 8vo. Paper wrappers.

O'Meara, Walter

The Savage Country. Boston, 1960, Houghton Mifflin Company. 308 pp., illustrations by Philip B. Parsons. 8vo; dust jacket. A history of the British fur trappers and traders of the North West Company of Canada.

Ondrack, Jack

Big Game Hunting in Alberta. Edmonton, 1985, Wildlife. 346 pp., photographic plates, drawings. 8vo; dust jacket.

O'Neil, Ted

The Muskrat in the Louisiana Coastal Marshes. New Orleans, 1949, Louisiana Wildlife and Fisheries Commission. 152 pp., photographic plates, fold-out maps, map in color in rear pocket, bibliography. 4to; dust jacket.

Onreat, Anthony

Sixty Below. New York, 1948, Didier. 192 pp., drawings by Eugene Beinert. Introduction by Dr. Thomas Wood. 8vo; dust jacket. A scarce collection of stories about hunting, fishing and trapping in the Canadian north.

Ontario Bowhunters Association

Bowhunting Notes. 1980, Ontario Bowhunters Association. 209 pp.

Ordeman, John T.   b. 1930

Frank W. Benson;   master of the sporting print.   Brooklandville, Maryland, 1983, Privately printed.   95 pp., color and black and white illustrations, bibliography, appendices.   Limited to 1000 numbered and signed copies.   4to; dust jacket.   [The first 50 copies were specially bound, numbered and signed; slipcased]   Lists some works not described in Paff with a commentary regarding the artist.   An important work.

To Keep a Tryst With the Dawn; an appreciation of Roland Clark. Henderson, North Carolina, 1989, Privately printed.   118 pp., many illustrations in black and white and color.   Introduction by Elizabeth Clark LaFleche.   Limited to 1100 numbered and signed copies.   4to; dust jacket. [The first 100 copies were specially bound, numbered and signed; slipcased]

William J. Schaldach; artist, author, sportsman.   St. Petersburg, Florida, 1988, Privately printed.   120 pp., color and black and white illustrations.   Limited to 1150 numbered and signed copies.   4to; dust jacket. [The first 150 copies were specially bound, numbered and signed; slipcased]

Ormond, Clyde   1906-1985

Bear! Black, grizzly, brown, polar.   Harrisburg, 1961, The Stackpole Company.   291 pp., illustrations.   8vo; dust jacket.

Complete Book of Hunting. New York, 1962, Harper & Row Publishers, Inc. / Outdoor Life Books.   467 pp., illustrations.   8vo; dust jacket. (Reprinted many times, same format and publisher)

Complete Book of Outdoor Lore. New York, 1964, Outdoor Life Books. 498 pp., illustrations.   8vo; dust jacket.   (Reprinted and revised several times. Later editions were titled *Complete Book of Outdoor Lore and Woodcraft*)

How To Track and Find Game.   New York, 1975, Funk & Wagnalls / Outdoor Life Books.   152 pp., illustrations.   8vo.   Paper wrappers. (Reprinted many times, same format and publisher. Also a 1977 edition titled, *How To Find and Track Outdoor Game,* same publisher)

Hunting in the Northwest.   New York, 1948, Alfred A. Knopf, Inc. 274 pp., photographic plates, color frontispiece.   A Borzoi Book For Sportsmen. 8vo; dust jacket.

Hunting Our Biggest Game. Harrisburg, 1956, The Stackpole Company. 197 pp., illustrations.   8vo; dust jacket.

Hunting Our Medium Size Game.   Harrisburg, 1958, The Stackpole Company. 219 pp., illustrations.   8vo; dust jacket.

The Outdoorsman's Handbook. New York, 1970, Outdoor Life Books. 336 pp., illustrations.   8vo; dust jacket. (Reprinted several times, same format and publisher)

Small Game Hunting.   New York, 1967, E. P. Dutton & Co., Inc. / Outdoor Life Books.   126 pp., photographic plates, drawings by Doug Allen. 8vo; dust jacket. (Reprinted several times, various formats)

Ornamental Pheasant Society of America
    First Publication of the Society. Wallingford, Connecticut, 1936, Privately printed.   41 pp., 12 full page plates, plus ads.   Foreword by William Beebe.   8vo.   Paper wrappers.

Orr, Robert T.
    The Rabbits of California.   San Francisco, 1940, Academy of Sciences. 207 pp., illustrations.   4to.   Paper wrappers.   The life histories of all seven species.

Ortega Y Gasset, Jose   1883-1955
    Meditations on Hunting.   New York, 1972, Charles Scribner's Sons. 152 pp., drawings by L. S. Brown.   Tall 8vo; dust jacket.   (Reprinted 1985, paper wrappers, same publisher.   Originally published, 1942, Spain)   The author presents his philosophy of the sport.   An important and articulate presentation of why men hunt.

Osborn, Chase
    Northwoods Sketches.   Lansing, 1949, Historical Society of Michigan. 127 pp.   8vo.   Stories of hunting and trapping by this former governor of Michigan.   Scarce.

Osborn, Robert Chesley   b. 1904
    How to Shoot Ducks.   New York, 1941, Coward, McCann, Inc. Unpaginated, 15 full page drawings. 12mo; dust jacket. (Reprinted many times, same format and publisher)
    How to Shoot Pheasant.   New York, 1955, Coward, McCann, Inc. Unpaginated, 30 full page drawings. 12mo; dust jacket.
    How to Shoot Quail.   New York, 1941, Coward, McCann, Inc. Unpaginated, 16 full page drawings. 12mo; dust jacket. (Reprinted 1941, same format and publisher)   All three of these works are humorous cartoon books.

Osborne, Owen
    Duck Hunters are Nuts.   Lewiston, Maine, 1971, Privately printed. 136 pp., illustrations by Tom Hennessey.   8vo.   (Reprinted 1972, same format and publisher)   Humorous stories of wildfowling.

Otteson, Stuart
    The Bolt Action; a design analysis.   New York, 1976, Winchester Press. 288 pp., photographic plates, drawings.   8vo; dust jacket.

Outdoor Life Books
    Fishing, Hunting and Camping Guide. New York, 1946, Outdoor Life Books.   238 pp., illustrations.   4to.   Paper wrappers.   (Reprinted 1947, same format and publisher)

Outdoor Life Books, continued

Four-In-One Adventure Book. New York, 1954, Outdoor Life Books. 384 pp., color and black and white illustrations by Bob Kuhn and Francis Lee Jaques. 8vo; dust jacket. (Also a 1955 second edition titled, *Second Four-In-One Adventure Book*, and a 1956 third edition titled, *Third Four-In-One Adventure Book*) Stories by Corbett, O'Connor, Snyder, Hemingway and others.

Great Outdoor Adventures; 24 of the greatest true action stories ever to appear in *Outdoor Life* magazine. New York, 1961, Outdoor Life Books. 319 pp., illustrations. 8vo; dust jacket.

Outdoor Life Cyclopedia; a complete guide for sportsmen. New York, 1942, Outdoor Life Books. 334 pp., illustrations. 8vo; dust jacket. (Reprinted several times, same format and publisher).

Outdoor Life Deer Hunter's Yearbook 1983. New York, 1982, Outdoor Life Books. 184 pp., color and black and white illustrations. 4to. Paper wrappers. (Also produced annually to at least 1991, same format and publisher)

Outdoor Life's Anthology of Hunting Adventures; the world's best stories of hunting adventures. New York, 1946, Grosset & Dunlap / Outdoor Life Books. 256 pp., illustrations. 8vo; dust jacket. A collection of stories originally published in *Outdoor Life* magazine

Outdoor Life's Deer Hunting Book. Harrisburg / New York, 1972, The Stackpole Company / Outdoor Life Books 275 pp., illustrations. 8vo; dust jacket. (Reprinted several times, same format and publisher)

Outdoor Life's Gallery of North American Game; a brilliant collection of paintings by Francis Lee Jaques, foremost artist of the outdoors, with descriptive text by distinguished authorities on wildlife. New York, 1946, Outdoor Life Books. 142 pp., color plates. Folio; dust jacket. (Reprinted many times, same format and publisher)

Outdoor Life's Shooting and Hunting Annual. New York, 1953, Outdoor Life Books. 256 pp., illustrations. 8vo. Paper wrappers.

The Story of American Hunting and Firearms. New York, 1959, McGraw-Hill Publishing Company / Outdoor Life Books. 172 pp., color and black and white photographic plates. Folio; slipcased. (Also a revised 1976 edition, same format and publisher)

Outdoor Writers Association of America

Outdoor Writers Instruction Manual. No place, 1966, Outdoor Writers Association of America. 192 pp., photographic plates. 8vo. Paper wrappers. A manual for aspiring outdoor writers.

Ovenden, Lou

Ducks and Spaghetti. New York, 1972, Vantage Press. 186 pp., color and black and white illustrations. 8vo; dust jacket. The author was Washington State Game Commissioner. Here, he presents an unusual waterfowling book.

Ovington, Ray

    Birds of Prey. St. Petersburg, Florida, 1975, Outdoors Publishing Company. 64 pp., illustrations. 8vo.

    THE COMPACT OUTDOORSMAN'S LIBRARY. New York, 1965, J. L. Pratt. Four volumes titled, *Upland Game Birds, Waterfowl and Lowland Game Birds, Small Game and Varmints* and *Big Game Animals.* Each 64 pp., illustrations. 16mo. Paper wrappers.

    The Young Sportsman's Guide To Game Animals. New York, 1962, Thomas Nelson & Sons, Inc. 91 pp., drawings by F. W. Davis. 8vo; dust jacket.

    The Young Sportsman's Guide To Game Birds. New York, 1962, Thomas Nelson & Sons, Inc. 96 pp., illustrations. 8vo; dust jacket.

    Mr. Ovington also produced many angling works. See Bruns.

Owen, Myrfyn

    Wild Geese of the World; their life history and ecology. London, 1980, Batsford. 236 pp., drawings and color plates by Joe Blossom. Foreword by Sir Peter Scott. 4to; dust jacket.

Ozark Ripley

    See **Ripley, Ozark**

Paca, Lillian Grace

The Royal Birds. New York, 1963, St. Martin's Press. 164 pp., drawings by the author. 8vo; dust jacket. A description of the 10 varieties of swans.

Packard, Ralph G.

Rifles That I Have Used and Designed. No place, 1939, Privately printed. 108 pp., illustrations. Introduction by Col. Townsend Whelen. Numbered copies of an unspecified limitation. 8vo. A scarce and curious firearms work.

Paff, Adam E. M.   b. 1896

Etchings and Drypoints of Frank W. Benson. Boston, Houghton Mifflin Company. Volume I, 1917; Volume II, 1919; Volume III, 1923 (Limited to 525 numbered copies); Volume IV, 1929, (Limited to 600 numbered copies); each with original pencil signed etchings by Benson as frontispieces. Folio. Not listed in Phillips. A fifth volume was produced in 1959, see **Heintzelman, Arthur W.** The comprehensive work on this important artist.

Page, Harry S.

Between the Flags. the recollections of a gentleman rider. New York, 1929, The Derrydale Press. 313 pp., plates, illustrations from drawings by Edward Voss. Limited to 850 copies. Tall 8vo.

Over the Open. New York, 1925, Charles Scribner's Sons. 155 pp., illustrations by Edward Voss. Limited to 1000 numbered copies. 8vo; slipcased. Both of these works contain the author's reminiscences of steeplechasing and foxhunting.

Page, Warren   1910-1977

The Accurate Rifle. New York, 1973, Winchester Press. 238 pp., photographic plates. 8vo; dust jacket. (Reprinted several times, various publishers)

The Field & Stream Guide To Deer Hunting. New York, 1966, Holt, Rinehart and Winston. 127 pp., illustrations. 8vo. Paper wrappers.

One Man's Wilderness. New York, 1973, Holt, Rinehart & Winston. 256 pp., illustrations. 8vo; dust jacket.

Paine, Philbrook

Squarely Behind the Beavers. New York, 1963, W. W. Norton & Co., Inc. 188 pp., drawings. 8vo; dust jacket. Well written, humorous stories about life in rural New Hampshire, including some hunting for deer, ducks and grouse.

Painter, Anna, editor

Dear Boys; letters about hunting in Texas by Theophilus S. Painter. Austin, Texas, 1973, San Felipe Press. 60 pp., illustrations. 8vo. Paper wrappers. Hunting deer and antelope in Texas.

Palmer, E. Lawrence

Are They Vermin? Ithaca, New York, 1937, Cornell University Press. 32 pp., illustrations. 8vo. Paper wrappers. A defense of hawks, owls and other birds of prey as they relate to sportsmen and farmers.

Palmer, J. Frederick

Grizzly Bear in the Canadian Rockies. Waukesha, Wisconsin, 1936, Privately printed. 39 pp., photographic plates. 12mo. Paper wrappers.

Kodiak Bear Hunt; stalking the giant bears of Alaska. New York, 1958, Exposition Press. 79 pp. 8vo; dust jacket.

Park, Ed

The World of the Bison. Philadelphia, 1969, J. B. Lippincott Co. 161 pp., photographic plates, bibliography. A title in Lippincott's Living World series. 4to; dust jacket. (Reprinted several times, same format and publisher)

The World of the Otter. Philadelphia, 1971, J. B. Lippincott Co. 161 pp., photographic plates, bibliography. A title in Lippincott's Living World series. 4to; dust jacket. (Reprinted 1971, same format and publisher)

Park, Francis E., Jr.

Deer Hunting. New York, 1954, A. S. Barnes and Company, Inc. 96 pp., photographic plates. 8vo; dust jacket. (Also reprinted, 1954, The Ronald Press)

Parker, Clement C.

Compendium of Works on Archery. Philadelphia, 1950, McMannus. 74 pp., illustrations. Limited to 300 copies. 8vo.

Parker, Eric

Colonel Hawker's Shooting Diaries. New York, 1931, The Derrydale Press. 300 pp., plates. 8vo; dust jacket. (Originally published in Great Britain in the nineteenth century)

Parker, Gerald R.

The Diets of Muskoxen and Peary Caribou on Some Islands in the Canadian Arctic. Sackville, 1978, Canadian Wildlife Service. 19 pp., illustrations. 8vo. Paper wrappers.

Distribution of Barren Ground Caribou Harvest in North Central Canada From Ear Tag Returns. Ottawa, 1972, Canadian Wildlife Service. 20 pp., illustrations. 8vo. Paper wrappers.

Trends in the Population of Barren Ground Caribou of Mainland Canada Over the Last Two Decades; a re-evaluation of the evidence. Ottawa, 1972, Canadian Wildlife Service. 12 pp., illustrations. 8vo. Paper wrappers.

Parker, Willie J.

Game Warden: Chesapeake Assignment. Centerville, Maryland, 1983, Tidewater Publishers. 275 pp., illustrations. 8vo; dust jacket.

Halt! I'm A Federal Game Warden; the amazing career of the toughest game warden of them all. New York, 1977, David McKay Co. 210 pp., photographic plates. 8vo; dust jacket.

Parkman, Francis   1823-1893

The Oregon Trail. New York, 1950, Times Mirror. 286 pp. (Originally published, 1849) With much on buffalo hunting. Mr. Parkman wrote extensively about the West and conservation in the mid-nineteenth century. See Phillips.

Parmalee, Claude

How to Be a Crack Shot With Rifle and Shotgun. New York, 1950, Greenberg: Publishers. 78 pp., photographic plates. 4to; dust jacket. (Second edition, paper wrappers, same publisher)

Parmalee, Paul W. and Forrest D. Loomis

Decoys and Decoy Carvers of Illinois. Dekalb, 1969, Northern Illinois University Press. 506 pp., many black and white and color illustrations. Square 8vo. (Reprinted 1979, in paper wrappers)

Parnell, Peter

The Daywatchers. New York, 1984, The Macmillan Company. 127 pp., drawings by the author. Folio; dust jacket. Birds of prey. The companion volume to *The Nightwatchers,* by **Cameron and Parnell,** which see.

Parrish, J. C.

Whitetails; written by a deer hunter, about deer hunting, for deer hunters. Detroit, Michigan, 1978, Harlo Press. 152 pp., illustrations. 8vo. Scarce.

Parry, Gareth and Rory Putman

Birds of Prey. New York, 1979, Simon & Schuster. 120 pp., color and black and white illustrations by Parry, maps. Folio; dust jacket.

Parsons, John E.

Catalogue of a Loan Exhibition of Percussion Colt Revolvers and Conversions, 1836-1873. New York, 1942, The Metropolitan Museum of Art. 41 pp., photographic plates. Preface by Stephen V. Grancsay. Limited to 1000 copies. 8vo. Paper wrappers.

Henry Derringer's Pocket Pistol. New York, 1952, William Morrow & Co., Inc. 255 pp., illustrations. 8vo; dust jacket.

Parsons, John E., continued

The First Winchester; the story of the 1866 repeating rifle. New York, 1955, William Morrow & Co., Inc. 207 pp., photographic plates, drawings. 8vo; dust jacket. (Also a 1960 revised edition, same format and publisher)

The Peacemaker and Its Rivals; an account of the single action Colt. New York, 1950, William Morrow & Co., Inc. 184 pp., photographic plates, drawings. 8vo; dust jacket. (Reprinted several times, same format and publisher)

Parsons, John E.

Also see **Colt, Samuel**

Partch, Virgil F.

The Dead Game Sportsmen. New York, 1954, Duell, Sloan & Pearce, Inc. Unpaginated, cartoon illustrations. 8vo. A humorous look at hunting.

Patterson, Jerry

Antiquities of Sport. New York, 1975, Crown Publishers, Inc. 150 pp., illustrations. 8vo; dust jacket. Much on artifacts of all types of sports, including angling and hunting.

Patterson, R. M.

The Buffalo Head. New York, 1961, William Sloane Associates, Inc. 273 pp., illustrations. 8vo; dust jacket. One man's adventures in the Canadian Rockies; autobiographical

Dangerous River. New York, 1954, William Sloane Associates, Inc. 314 pp., illustrations. 8vo; dust jacket. (Also a 1969 Canadian edition) Some trapping and much big game hunting along the Nahanni river in Canada's Northwest Territories.

Findlay's River. New York, 1968, William Morrow & Co., Inc. 315 pp., photographic plates, bibliography. 8vo; dust jacket. Adventures of a canoe trip down this British Columbia river with some big game hunting.

Mr. Patterson wrote several other books about travel and adventure in Canada's wilderness. All of his books had at least some incidental mention of hunting.

Patterson, Robert L.

The Sage Grouse in Wyoming. Denver, 1952, Sage Books / Wyoming Fish and Game Commission. 341 pp., illustrations by Charles W. Schwartz, bibliography. 8vo; dust jacket. Scarce.

Paulsen, Gary

Tracker. New York, 1984, Puffin Books. 90 pp. A deer hunting story for the juvenile

Paust, Gil

  Gun Book. New York, 1956, Lion. 192 pp., illustrations. 12mo. Paper wrappers.

  The Young Sportsman's Guide To Hunting. New York, 1961, Thomas Nelson & Sons, Inc. 96 pp., illustrations. 8vo; dust jacket.

Peach, Arthur Wallace

  The Country Rod and Gun Book. Weston, Vermont, 1938, The Countryman Press / Farrar & Rinehart, Inc. 224 pp., illustrations from drawings by Francis Toolman. 12mo; dust jacket.

Pearce, Eleanor

  Florida's Vanishing Era; from the journals of a young girl and her father, 1887 - 1910. (Also a 1949 second edition, with added illustrations, Privately printed) A rare bit of Americana with some mention of hunting in the area.

Pearson, Arthur M.

  The Northern Interior Grizzly Bear, Ursus arctos (Linneaus). Ottawa, 1975, Canadian Wildlife Service. 86 pp., illustrations, maps, bibliography. 4to. Paper wrappers.

Peattie, Donald C.

  Sportsman's Country. Boston, 1952, Houghton Mifflin Company. 180 pp., illustrations by Henry B. Kane. 8vo; dust jacket.

Peattie, Donald C., editor

  Audubon's America; the narrative and experiences of John James Audubon. Boston, 1940, Houghton Mifflin Company. 329 pp., color illustrations. 4to; dust jacket [Also a limited edition of 3025 signed copies, specially bound; boxed]

Peck, Robert McCracken

  A Celebration of Birds; the life and art of Louis Agassiz Fuertes. New York, 1982, Walker and Company. 178 pp., color and black and white illustrations of Fuertes' work, bibliography. 4to; dust jacket. (Reprinted, same format and publisher)

Pedersen, Larry "Slim"

  Predator Trapping Problems and Solutions. No place, No date, Privately printed. 54 pp., photographic plates. 8vo. Paper wrappers.

Peek, J. M.

Moose Habitat Selection and Relationships To Forest Management in Northeastern Minnesota. Minneapolis, 1976, Wildlife Society. 65 pp. 8vo. Paper wrappers.

Peery, Charles and Joe Coggin

Virginia's White-Tailed Deer. No place, 1978, Virginia Game Commission. 159 pp., color and black and white illustrations. 4to. Paper wrappers.

Peeters, Hans J. and E. W. Jameson, Jr.

American Hawking; a general account of falconry in the New World. Davis, California, 1970, Privately printed. 150 pp., color plates, glossary, bibliography. 4to.

Pell, Stuyvesant Morris

Scribblings of an Outdoor Boy; being reminiscences of S. M. Pell, up to the year 1943, when having reached the age of 38 years, he came to have a great adventure with life. Princeton, New Jersey, 1945, Privately printed. 75 pp., illustrations by the author, folding map. 8vo. Observations of bird and animal life with some snipe shooting on Long Island. A scarce work published posthumously by the author's wife at the Princeton University Press.

Pelton, Frank Curtis

Eel Rack; an epic narrative of the Delaware. 235 pp., frontispiece. Limited to 300 numbered and signed copies. 8vo. Containing much hunting with an excellent narrative about the early history of this river.

Pennsylvania Game Commission

Pennsylvania Game News Treasury. Harrisburg, 1979, Pennsylvania Game Commission. 528 pp., photographic plates, drawings by Bob Hines. 8vo; dust jacket. An anthology of stories originally appearing in *Pennsylvania Game News* from 1929 to 1979.

Peper, Eric and Jim Rikhoff, editors

Hunting Moments of Truth. New York, 1973, Winchester Press. 208 pp., drawings by Milton Weiler. 8vo; dust jacket. (Reprinted, same format and publisher. Also issued with these editors' *Fishing Moments of Truth* as part of a two volume set, 1973, limited to 750 numbered copies, Winchester Press / Amwell Press) An anthology of unusual hunting stories by Roosevelt, Evans, Page, O'Connor and others.

Perkins, Jim

American Boy's Rifles. No place, 1976, Privately printed. 245 pp., illustrations. 4to; dust jacket.

Perkins, George F., Sr.

   Journeys to the Adirondacks; for the years 1879-1882-1885.   No place, No date (ca. 1956), Privately printed.   20 pp.   16mo.   Paper wrappers.   The diaries of the author with much hunting and fishing.

Perkins, Marlin

   Animal Tracks; the standard guide for identification and characteristics. Harrisburg, 1954, The Stackpole Company.   64 pp., drawings by Luis Henderson. 4to.   Paper wrappers.   (Also a 1958 edition titled, *Pocket Field Guide To Animal Tracks*, smaller format, same publisher)

Perkins, Prescott D.

   Fins and Feathers.   No place, 1966, Privately printed.   30 pp.   4to. Paper wrappers.   Hunting and fishing reminiscences in New York and Delaware.

Perry, Clay

   A Gunroom Story of Sporting Arms; from Major Hugh Smiley. Henniker, New Hampshire, 1947, Privately printed.   20 pp., plates. 8vo. Paper wrappers.

Perry, Richard

   Bears.   New York, 1970, Arco.   96 pp., color and black and white illustrations.   8vo; dust jacket.   Natural history of the species and its inter-relationship with man.
   The World of the Polar Bear.   Seattle, 1966, University of Washington Press.   195 pp., photographic plates, map, bibliography.   8vo; dust jacket.

Perry, Walter

   Bucks and Bows.   Harrisburg, 1953, The Stackpole Company.   223 pp., illustrations.   8vo; dust jacket.   (Reprinted 1954, same format and publisher) Archery hunting for deer.

Peters, Fred J.   b. 1882

   Sporting Prints by Currier & Ives; being a practical checklist and collation with many intimate facts regarding the prints. New York, 1930, Antique Bulletin Publishing Company.   205 pp., black and white and color illustrations. Limited to 750 numbered copies.   4to; dust jacket

Peters, Harry T.   1881-1948

   Currier & Ives; printmakers to the American people.   Garden City, New York, 1929, 1931, Doubleday, Doran & Co., Inc.   Two volumes with many plates and accompanying text.   Folio; dust jacket.   (Reprinted, two volumes in one, 1942, same publisher.   In 1931, The New York Public Library published a 19 pp. work with this tile as well)   A general work on Currier & Ives.

Peters, Harry T., continued
> *Just Hunting.* New York, 1935, Charles Scribner's Sons. 247 pp., illustrations from drawings by Betty Babcock. 8vo; dust jacket. Essays on foxhunting with a section on the difference between American and British foxhunting by this MFH of the Meadow Brook Hounds.

Peters, Rogers
> *Dance of the Wolves.* New York, 1985, McGraw-Hill Publishing Company. 222 pp., photographic plates. 8vo; dust jacket. A general study of wolves.

Peters, W. Austin   b. 1900
> *Feathers Preferred;* a sportsman's soliloquy. Harrisburg, 1951, The Stackpole Company. 198 pp., illustrations. 8vo; dust jacket. Hunting wildfowl and upland birds.

Petersen, L. E. and Arthur H. Richardson
> *The Wild Turkey in the Black Hills.* Pierre, 1975, South Dakota Department of Game. 51 pp., photographic plates, charts. 8vo. Paper wrappers.

Peterson, Eugene T.
> *Hunter's Heritage;* a history of hunting in Michigan. Lansing, Michigan, 1979, Michigan United Conservation Clubs. 55 pp., photographic plates. 4to. Paper wrappers.

Peterson, Harold   b. 1939
> *The Last of the Mountain Men.* New York, 1969, Charles Scribner's Sons. 160 pp., photographic plates. Tall 8vo; dust jacket. (Reprinted 1969, in paper wrappers, same publisher) An account of Sylvan Hart's experiences in the Salmon River wilderness area of Idaho.

Peterson, Harold L.   b. 1922
> *Arms and Armor in Colonial America.* New York, 1956, Bramhall House. 350 pp., illustrations. 4to; dust jacket. (Reprinted, The Stackpole Company)
> *Encyclopedia of Firearms.* New York, 1964, E. P. Dutton & Co., Inc. 367 pp., color and black and white illustrations. Tall 8vo; dust jacket.
> *Pageant of the Gun;* a treasury of the stories of firearms. Garden City, New York, 1967, Doubleday & Co., Inc. 352 pp., illustrations. 8vo; dust jacket. (Reprinted, same format and publisher)
> *The Remington Historical Treasury of American Guns.* New York, 1966, Thomas Nelson & Sons, Inc. / The Ridge Press. 157 pp., color and black and white illustrations. 8vo; dust jacket. A history of Remington firearms with much information on the Browning brothers.

Peterson, Harold L., continued
The Treasury of the Gun. New York, 1962, Golden Press / Ridge Press. 252 pp., color and black and white illustrations. 4to; dust jacket.

Peterson, Harold L. and Robert Elman, editors
The Great Guns. New York, 1971, The Ridge Press, Inc. 252 pp., color and black and white illustrations. 8vo; dust jacket. (Reprinted 1978, same format and publisher) A pictorial history of some of the finest firearms ever produced.

Peterson, Peter Charles
Taking An Outlaw Grizzly. Denver, 1924, Outdoor Life Publishing Co. 12 pp. 12mo. Paper wrappers. Not in Phillips.

Peterson, Randolph L.
North American Moose. Toronto, 1955, University of Toronto Press. 280 pp., illustrations, bibliography. 8vo. Paper wrappers. (Reprinted twice, same format and publisher) An outstanding reference work.

Peterson, Rolf Olin
Wolf Ecology and Prey Relationships On Isle Royale. Washington, D. C., 1977, United States Department of the Interior. 210 pp., drawings, photographic plates, bibliography. 8vo. Paper wrappers.

Pettingill, Olin Sewall   b.1907
The American Woodcock; Philohela minor (Gmelin). Boston, 1936, Boston Society of Natural History. 391 pp., color frontispiece by George M. Sutton, photographic plates, bibliography. Folio. Paper wrappers. (Also a cloth bound edition reported) A scarce and important work.

Petty, Charles
High Standard Automatic Pistols, 1932 - 1950. North Carolina, 1976, Privately printed. 125 pp., illustrations. 8vo; dust jacket.

Petzal, David E., editor
The Expert's Book of Big Game Hunting in North America. New York, 1970, Simon & Schuster. 223 pp., illustrations. 8vo; dust jacket. (Reprinted 1976, same format and publisher) An anthology of stories by Carmichel, Brister and others.
The Expert's Book of the Shooting Sports; America's foremost shooting and hunting experts disclose the secrets of their specialties. New York, 1972, Simon & Schuster. 320 pp., photographic plates. 8vo; dust jacket.

Petzal, David E., editor, continued
The Expert's Book of Upland Game and Waterfowl Hunting. New York, 1973, Simon & Schuster. 315 pp., photographic plates. 8vo; dust jacket. (Reprinted 1975, same format and publisher) An anthology of stories by Evans, Dalrymple, Reiger and others.
The .22 Rifle. New York, 1973, Winchester Press. 149 pp., illustrations. 8vo; dust jacket.

Pfaffenberger, Clarence J.
Training Your Spaniel. New York, 1947, G. P. Putnam's Sons. 203 pp., photographic plates. 8vo; dust jacket. (Also a 1954 revised edition, same format and publisher)

Pferd, William, III
The Welsh Springer Spaniel; history, selection, training and care. New York, 1977, A. S. Barnes and Company, Inc. 8vo; dust jacket.

Phibbs, Harry C.
Hodge Podge. No place, 1940, Privately printed. 51 pp., photographic plates, drawings. 8vo. Published as a Christmas greeting, it contains short pieces on hunting and angling.

Philip, Hoffman
Wild Turkey Drive. Tucson, Arizona, 1943, Privately printed. Unpaginated (20 pp.), illustrations. 8vo. Limited to 200 numbered copies. Paper wrappers.

Phillips, Archie and Bubba Phillips
How To Mount Deer; for fun or profit. Harrisburg, 1980, Stackpole Books. 127 pp., photographic plates, diagrams. 8vo; dust jacket.

Phillips, David and Hugh Nash, editors
The Condor Question; captive or forever free? San Francisco, 1981, Friends of the Earth. 298 pp., photographic plates, bibliography. 8vo. Paper wrappers.

Phillips, Fred
Wild Turkey Investigations and Management Recommendations For the Bill Williams Mountain Area. Phoenix, 1982, Arizona Fish and Game Commission. 50 pp., color and black and white illustrations, bibliography. 4to. Paper wrappers.

Phillips, James H.

Undercover Wildlife Agent; the casebook of Federal Conservation Officer Robert O. Halstead. Tulsa, 1981, Winchester Press. 108 pp., illustrations. 8vo; dust jacket.

Phillips, John C.   1876-1938

American Game Mammals and Birds; a catalog of books 1582-1925, sport, natural history, and conservation, with the approval of the Boone & Crockett Club. Boston, 1930, Houghton Mifflin Company. 639 pp. Thick 8vo; dust jacket. (Reprinted 1978, Arno Press. Also a 1930 edition titled, *Bibliography of American Sporting Books*, same format and pagination, Edward Morrill and Son.) A bibliography of books and pamphlets published prior to 1925 about the subject; now regarded as a standard bibliographic reference for hunting and conservation works.

Bibliography of a Natural History of the Ducks. Cambridge, Massachusetts, 1926, Privately printed. 126 pp., color frontispiece. Limited to 75 numbered copies signed by the author. 4to. The bibliography section of Phillips' *A Natural History of the Ducks.*

Boy Journals 1887-1892. No place, 1915, Privately printed. 203 pp. 8vo. A rare Phillips item that was purportedly printed in an edition of 250 copies, of which 200 copies were destroyed. They are the author's journals from his boyhood.

Man's Influence of Ruffed Grouse Populations; suggestions for further investigations. Cambridge, Massachusetts, 1937, Privately printed. 24 pp. 8vo. Paper wrappers. (Also observed, cloth bound)

Migratory Bird Protection in North America; the history of control by the United States Government and a sketch of the treaty with Great Britain. No place, 1934, American Committee For International Wild Life Protection. 38 pp. 8vo.

A Natural History of the Ducks. Boston, 1922-1926, Houghton Mifflin Company. Four volumes of 264 pp., 409 pp., 383 pp., and 489 pp. respectively, extensively illustrated in color and black and white from paintings by Fuertes, Benson, and Brooks, distribution maps, extensive bibliography. Thick 4to; dust jackets. A monumental work describing all species of ducks encountered in the world, containing physical characteristics, synonymy, distribution, habits, etc.

The Sands of Muskeget; a Christmas holiday. Cambridge, Massachusetts, 1931, Privately printed. 46 pp., illustrated with two unsigned reproduction of etchings. Limited to 250 copies. 12mo. A Christmas keepsake produced by Phillips recounting a brant shooting party.

Shooting Stands of Eastern Massachusetts. Cambridge, Massachusetts, 1929, Privately printed. 158 pp., frontispiece by A. L. Ripley. Limited to 200 copies. 8vo.

A Sportsman's Scrapbook. Boston, 1928, Houghton Mifflin Company. 212 pp., illustrations by A. L. Ripley. 8vo; dust jacket. (Reprinted 1928, same format and publisher)

Phillips, John C., continued

A Sportsman's Second Scrapbook. Boston, 1933, Houghton Mifflin Company. 197 pp., color and black and white illustrations by A. L. Ripley. 8vo; dust jacket.

Wenham Great Pond. Salem, Massachusetts, 1938, Privately printed. 109 pp., illustrations. Limited to 400 copies. 8vo. (Also produced in another printing limited to 100 copies, same year and publisher)

Wenham Lake Shooting Record and the "Farm Bag," 1897-1925. Cambridge, Massachusetts, 1926, Privately printed. 299 pp. Limited to 100 copies. 8vo. A detailed shooting record.

Wenham Lake Shooting Record and the "Farm Bag," 1926-1935. Cambridge, Massachusetts, 1936, Privately printed at the Cosmos Press. 171 pp. Limited to 100 copies. 8vo. A sequel to the previous work.

Wild Birds Introduced or Transplanted in North America. Washington, D. C., 1928, United States Department of Agriculture. 63 pp. 8vo. Paper wrappers. A detailed account of the introduction of such species as doves, grouse, pheasants, and other game birds. A scarce and relatively important work.

Phillips, John C., editor

A Handbook of Conservation With Special Reference To the Landscape Features of Essex County. 1936, Privately printed by the Society For Preservation of the Landscape Features of Essex County, Massachusetts, etc.. 84 pp., frontispiece. Foreword and an article by John C. Phillips. 8vo. A scarce Phillips item.

New England Game Conference; held under the auspices of the Massachusetts Fish and Game Association. Cambridge, Massachusetts, 1930, Privately printed at the Cosmos Press. 71 pp. 8vo. Paper wrappers. Mr. Phillips was president of the association at this time and led the conference. This transcript contains a talk by Phillips, "Wanted - A Long Term Wild Life Policy," and among other talks, a reading of "Bird Dogs in New England" by William Harnden Foster. A scarce and historic New England conservation piece.

William Herbert Rollins - Journal of the Last Years, 1918 - 1929; with personal recollections by John C. Phillips. Cambridge, Massachusetts, 1933, Privately printed. 171 pp. Limited to 75 copies. 8vo. Paper wrappers (Also observed, cloth bound).

John Rowe; an eighteenth century Boston angler. Cambridge, Massachusetts, 1929, Privately printed. 32 pp. Limited to 150 copies. 8vo.

The Shooting Journal of George Henry Mackay 1865-1922. Cambridge, Massachusetts, 1929, Privately printed. 373 pp., frontispiece. Limited to 300 copies. 8vo.

George Washington, Sportsman; from his own journals. Cambridge, Massachusetts, 1928, Privately printed. 47 pp. Limited to 100 copies. 8vo.

Phillips, John C. and T. D. Cabot
Quick Water and Smooth; a canoeist's guide to New England rivers. Brattleboro, Vermont, 1935, Stephen Daye. 239 pp., fold-out map. 8vo. Canoeing in New England.

Phillips, John C. and Frederick C. Lincoln
American Waterfowl; their present situation and the outlook for their future. Boston, 1930, Houghton Mifflin Company. 312 pp., illustrations from drawings and paintings by Ripley, Brooks and others. 8vo; dust jacket. An early wildfowl conservation work.

Phillips, John C. and Lewis Webb Hill, editors
Classics of the American Shooting Field; a mixed bag for the kindly sportsman, 1783-1926. Boston, 1930, Houghton Mifflin Company. 214 pp., color and black and white illustrations from paintings by Benson, Fuertes and others. 8vo; dust jacket. [Also a deluxe edition, limited to 150 numbered copies, signed by both authors and Benson; slipcased] An anthology of outstanding hunting stories.

Phillips, John C.
Also see **Barbour, Thomas**
Also see **The Massachusetts Fish and Game Association**

Phillips, Philip R. and Robert Lawrence Wilson
Paterson Colt Pistol Variations. Dallas, 1979, Jackson Arms. 232 pp., color and black and white illustrations. 4to.

Phillips, W. Enos
The True Pointer and His Ancient Heritage. No place, 1970, Privately printed. 118 pp., color frontispiece, photographic plates, bibliography. 8vo.

Phillips, W. E.
The Conservation of the California Tule Elk. Edmonton, 1976, The University of Alberta Press. 120 pp.

Phipps, Lawrence C. and William W. Grant
Forty Years of the Arapahoe Hunt with *A Quarter Century of the Arapahoe Hunt.* No place, No date (ca. 1971), Privately printed by the club. 112 pp., map in rear pocket. A numbered edition of unspecified limitation. 8vo. First organized in 1907, this hunt used the Highlands Ranch as its headquarters, near Littleton, Colorado. Coyotes were hunted there with horses and hounds.

Pickering, Harold G.   b. 1888

Merry Xmas Mr. Williams, 20 Pine Street, N.Y.   New York, 1940, The Derrydale Press.   34 pp., drawings by Harry L. Timmons.   Limited to 267 numbered copies, signed by the author.   8vo.

Neighbors Have My Ducks.   New York, 1937, The Derrydale Press.   47 pp., drawings by Harry L. Timmons.   Limited to 227 numbered copies, signed by the author.   8vo.

Mr. Pickering commissioned The Derrydale Press to print both of these humorous wildfowling tales as well as three angling titles.   See Siegel.   Also see Frazier.

Pidcock, Jane Rainaud

Wings, Water and Dogs.   Savannah, 1962, Privately printed by the Pigeonhole Press.   64 pp., illustrations.   8vo; dust jacket.   Scarce.   Prose and poetry on wildfowl and Labrador retrievers.

Pierce, W. H.

13 years of Travels and Exploration in Alaska, 1877-1889.   Anchorage, 1977, Alaska Northwest Publishing Company.   105 pp., illustrations.   8vo. Paper wrappers.   (An abridged and edited reprint of the scarce 1890 first edition)

Pierce, Skip

Blackalope; antelope hunting with the salt of the earth in company with the scum of the earth.   New York, 1973, Vantage Press.   100 pp., color and black and white illustrations.   8vo; dust jacket.

Pigot, R.

Twenty Five Years Big Game Hunting.   London, 1928, Chatto and Windus.   307 pp., photographic plates.   8vo.   Big game hunting around the world, with one chapter on caribou hunting in Newfoundland.

Pike, Warburton   1861-1915

The Barren Ground of Northern Canada.   New York, 1967, Abercrombie & Fitch, Inc.   300 pp., maps.   8vo; dust jacket.   (A facsimile reproduction of the 1892 edition.   The title is also sometimes given as *Journeys To the Barren Ground of Northern Canada in Search of Musk-Ox*)

Through the Subarctic Forest; a record of a canoe journey from Fort Wrangel to the Pelly Lakes and down the Yukon River to the Bearing Sea.   New York, 1967, Abercrombie & Fitch, Inc.   295 pp., plates from old engravings, maps.   8vo; dust jacket.   (A reproduction of the 1896 edition)

Pimlott, Shannon et al.

The Ecology of the Timber Wolf In Algonquin Provincial Park.   Ontario, 1969, Ministry of Natural Resources.   92 pp., photographic plates, maps, bibliography.   Tall 8vo.   Paper wrappers.   (Reprinted several times, same format and publisher)

Pinchot, Gifford   1865-1946
Breaking New Ground.   New York, 1947, Harcourt, Brace & Company. 522 pp., photographic plates, drawings.   8vo; dust jacket.   The autobiography of this pioneer conservationist.
Mr. Pinchot helped formulate Theodore Roosevelt's conservation policies, particularly as relating to U. S. Forest reserves.   He went on to become governor of Pennsylvania.   An ardent and life-long sportsman, Pinchot also wrote several angling titles.   See Bruns.

Pinchot, Gifford
Also see **Pinkett, Harold T.**

Pinkerton, Katherine
Wilderness Wife.   New York, 1939, Carrick.   327 pp., photographic plates.   8vo; dust jacket.   An account of this woman's decision to give up city life to be with her husband in the woods.

Pinkett, Harold T.
Gifford Pinchot; private and public forester.   Urbana, Illinois, 1970, University of Illinois Press.   167 pp., photographic plates. 8vo; dust jacket.

Pirnie, Miles D.
Michigan   Waterfowl   Management.   Lansing,   1935,   Michigan Department of Conservation.   328 pp., photographic plates, charts, maps.   8vo.

Pisano, Beverly, editor
Brittany Spaniels.   New Jersey, 1983.   125 pp., illustrations.   8vo.
English Setters.   New Jersey, 1983.   125 pp., illustrations.   8vo.

Pleissner, Ogden   1905-1983
See **Bergh, Peter**

Plum, Dorothy A., editor
Adirondack Bibliography.   Gabriels, New York, 1958, Adirondack Mountain Club, Inc.   354 pp.   8vo.   (Also a 1973 supplement issued for titles published between 1956-1965, Adirondack Museum.   Also a 1994 supplement issued for titles published between 1966 and 1992, North Country Books)   All are excellent references for all literature pertaining to the region.

Plummer, A. P., et al.
Restoring Big Game Range in Utah.   Salt Lake City, 1968, Utah Division of Fish and Game.   183 pp., photographic plates, bibliography.   8vo. Paper wrappers.

Pochin, W. F.
   Angling and Hunting in British Columbia. Vancouver, British Columbia, 1946, Sun Directories, Ltd. 240 pp., illustrations. 8vo; dust jacket.

Podeschi, John B.
   Books on the Horse and Horsemanship; riding, hunting, breeding and racing, 1400-1941. New Haven, Connecticut, 1981, The Tate Gallery For the Yale Center For British Art. 427 pp., color and black and white illustrations. Thick 4to; dust jacket. A useful bibliography with the most important foxhunting books listed as well as periodicals on the subject. It was compiled from the Paul Mellon collection as one of four volumes describing that collection's books, drawings, paintings and ephemera.

Poelker, Richard J. and Harry D. Hartwell
   Black Bear of Washington; its biology, natural history and relationship to forest regeneration. Olympia, 1973, Washington State Game Department. 180 pp., color and black and white illustrations, maps, bibliography. 4to. Paper wrappers.

Pollard, Hugh B. C.   b. 1888
   Game Birds; rearing, preservation and shooting. London, 1929, Eyre & Spottiswoode. 185 pp., color and black and white illustrations by Philip Rickman. 4to; dust jacket. [Also a large paper edition, specially bound and limited to 99 numbered copies signed by the author and artist] Also published by Scribner's in America.
   Game Birds and Game Bird Shooting. London / Boston, 1936, Eyre & Spottiswoode / Houghton Mifflin Company. 284 pp., frontispiece, photographic plates, five color illustrations from paintings by Philip Rickman. 8vo; dust jacket.
   The Gun Room Guide. London / Boston, 1930, Eyre & Spottiswoode / Houghton Mifflin Company. 183 pp., frontispiece and 11 color illustrations by Philip Rickman and H. Frank Wallace. 4to; dust jacket. [Also a deluxe edition, specially bound and limited to 75 copies for sale in America]
   Hard Up on Pegasus. Boston, 1931, Houghton Mifflin Company. 208 pp., illustrations. 4to; dust jacket. A British foxhunting work co-published by Houghton Mifflin in America.
   A History of Firearms. London / Boston, No date (ca. 1926), Geoffrey Bles / Houghton Mifflin Company. 320 pp., halftone and colotype plates. 4to; dust jacket. (Reprinted 1973, same format, Burt Franklin)
   Pollard's History of Firearms. New York, 1983, The Macmillan Company. 559 pp., illustrations. 4to; dust jacket.
   Wildfowl and Waders; nature and sport in the Coastlands. London, 1928, Country Life. 83 pp., plus color and black and white plates. Limited to 950 numbered copies. Folio.

Pollard, Hugh B. C. and Phyllis Barclay-Smith

British and American Game Birds. London / New York, 1939, Eyre & Spottiswoode / Charles Scribner's Sons. 48 pp., color illustrations from paintings by Philip Rickman. Folio; dust jacket. (Reprinted 1945, Eyre & Spottiswoode. The Derrydale Press also produced two editions, specially bound. One was limited to 125 numbered and remarqued copies; slipcased. The other was limited to 10 numbered copies signed by the artist, and contained an original watercolor by Rickman and was boxed) A magnificent book in any edition.

Poole, J. Lawrence.

History of the Hollenbeck Club, 1900-1978. Kent, 1978, Privately printed. 43 pp., illustrations. Limited to 120 copies. 8vo. Paper wrappers. A history of this Connecticut hunting and fishing club.

Poore, Charles, editor

The Hemingway Reader. New York, 1953, Charles Scribner's Sons. 652 pp. 8vo; dust jacket. An anthology of Hemingway's writing, some with sporting content.

Pope, Dudley

Guns; from the invention of gunpowder to the twentieth century. New York, 1965, Delacorte Press. 256 pp., many illustrations in color and black and white. Square 4to; dust jacket. (Also a 1971 British edition)

Pope, Saxton T. 1875-1926

Hunting With the Bow and Arrow. New York, 1974, Popular Library. 232 pp., illustrations. (Originally published, 1923, James H. Barry Company. Also several printings by G. P. Putnam's Sons between 1923 and 1947)

A Study of Bows and Arrows. Berkeley, California / Cambridge, England, 1930, University of California Press / Cambridge University Press. 102 pp., illustrations. 4to; dust jacket. (First published in 1923, as a part of the *University of California Publication in Archeology and Ethnology*)
Saxton Pope is generally regarded as the father of American bowhunting.

Pope and Young Club

Bowhunting Big Game Records of North America. Boulder, Colorado, 1975, Johnson Publishing Company. 307 pp., photographic plates. 8vo; dust jacket. (Also a 1981 second edition, same format and publisher)

Popham, Arthur, Jr.

Stalking Game; from desert to tundra. Clinton, New Jersey, 1985, Amwell Press. 159 pp., photographic plates. Limited to 1000 numbered and signed copies. 8vo; slipcased. Includes hunting the major North American big game species.

Popowski, Bert   b. 1904

Calling All Game. Harrisburg, 1952, The Stackpole Company. 306 pp., illustrations. 8vo; dust jacket.

Calling All Varmints. Harrisburg, 1952, The Stackpole Company. 308 pp., illustrations. 8vo; dust jacket.

Crow Shooting. New York, 1946, A. S. Barnes and Company, Inc. 216 pp., photographic plates, drawings by Gordon Elliott. A title in The Sportsman's Library series. 8vo; dust jacket. (Reprinted many times, same format and publisher)

Hunting the Pronghorn Antelope. Harrisburg, 1959, The Stackpole Company. 225 pp., photographic plates, maps. 8vo; dust jacket.

Hunting Small Game. New York, 1948, The Macmillan Company. 225 pp., photographic plates; line drawings. 8vo; dust jacket.

Olt's Hunting Handbook. Pekin, Illinois, 1948, Privately printed by Olt. 167 pp., illustrations. 12mo; dust jacket.

The Redbook of Big Game Hunting. Illinois, 1961, Publisher's Development Corporation. 34 pp. Paper wrappers. Mostly a how-to guide on setting up the trip, picking guides, cost, etc.

The Varmint and Crow Hunter's Bible. New York, 1962, Doubleday & Co., Inc. 185 pp., illustrations. 8vo. Paper wrappers.

Popowski, Bert and Wilf E. Pyle

The Hunter's Book of the Pronghorn Antelope. Tulsa, 1982, Winchester Press. 356 pp., photographic plates. 8vo; dust jacket.

Popular Mechanics Press

Outdoor Sports the Year Round. Chicago, 1930. Popular Mechanics Press. 336 pp., many illustrations, diagrams. 8vo. Much on hunting, fishing and camping.

Porter, Clyde and Mae Reed

Ruxton of the Rockies. Norman, 1950, University of Oklahoma Press. 325 pp., illustrations. 8vo; dust jacket. The biography of an extraordinary man, George Ruxton, a British native who traveled and hunted extensively in the Rocky Mountains.

Potter, Dale R. et al.

Human Behavior Aspects of Fish and Wildlife Conservation; an annotated bibliography. Portland, Oregon, 1973, Pacific Northwest Forest and Range Experiment Station. 288 pp. 4to.

Powell, Dod H.

And So We Shall A-Hunting Go. New York, 1966, Vantage Press. 158 pp. 8vo; dust jacket. Hunting for bear, deer and elk in the Rockies.

Powell, E. Baden
 Killing Power; supplemented by tables and charts. Washington, D. C., 1944, The National Rifle Association of America. 46 pp., folding chart, tables. 8vo. Paper wrappers. A discussion of the relative killing power of various rifle calibers.

Powell, Michael
 A Waiting Game. New York, 1975, St. Martin's Press. 175 pp. A murder mystery centered around deer hunting.

Powell, Roger A.
 The Fisher; life history, ecology and behavior. Minneapolis, 1982, University of Minnesota. 217 pp., photographic plates, drawings, maps, bibliography. 8vo.

Powers, Alfred
 Animals of the Arctic; in action and adventure. New York, 1965, David McKay Co. 272 pp., drawings. 8vo; dust jacket. Accounts of present day as well as extinct game animals of the region.

Prante, Henry E.
 Henry E. Prante's Great Hunting Adventures. Vancouver, 1985, Special Interest Publications, Inc. 136 pp.

Pratt, Jerome J.
 White Flags of Apacheland. New York, 1966, Vantage Press. 126 pp. A study of the Coues deer.

Pray, Leon L.
 Taxidermy. New York, 1943, The Macmillan Company. 91 pp., illustrations. 8vo; dust jacket. (Reprinted many times, same format and publisher)
 The Whitetail Deer Head Book For the Taxidermist. New York, 1944, Modern Taxidermist Magazine. 40 pp.

Prenice, H. W., et al.
 The Beagle in America and England. Marceline, Missouri, 1955, Privately printed. 95 pp., photographic plates. Abridged and edited by A. D. Holcombe. 8vo. Paper wrappers. (An abridged edition of the 1920 first edition) An important work on beagles, the first edition being very comprehensive. See Phillips.

Prescott, Marjorie Wiggin
 Tales of A Sportsman's Wife. Boston, 1936, Privately printed for the author by Daniel Updike at the Merrymount Press. 18 pp., two original pencil signed etchings by the author. Limited to 150 copies. 8vo. Contains some moose hunting in Nova Scotia.

Prescott, Marjorie Wiggin, continued

Tales of a Sportsman's Wife: Shooting. Boston, 1939, Privately printed for the author by Daniel Updike at the Merrymount Press. 79 pp., two original etchings pencil signed by the author. Limited to 150 copies. 8vo. The author also wrote *Tales of a Sportsman's Wife: Fishing,* in 1937. All were bound alike and printed by Updike in editions of 150 copies.

Prickett, Tommy

Louisiana Bobwhite Basics. Baton Rouge, 1981, Louisiana Department of Wildlife. 37 pp., drawings. 8vo. Paper wrappers.

Proctor, Frank

Foxhunting in Canada; and some men who made it. Toronto, 1929, The Macmillan Company. 373 pp., illustrations. The author also wrote *Under Six Sovereigns;* foxhunting in Canada.

Prudhomme, E. C.

Gun Engraving Review. Shreveport, Louisiana, 1961, Gun Engraving Review Publishing Co. 168 pp., color and black and white illustrations. 4to. [The first 300 copies were numbered and signed by the author] Examples of fine firearms engraving with brief biographies of the engravers.

Master Gun Engraver. Los Angeles, 1973, R. W. Norton Gallery. 32 pp., illustrations. Paper wrappers. A booklet promoting Prudomme's work as an engraver.

Pruitt, William O.

Behavior of the Barren Ground Caribou. 1960, University of Alaska. 44 pp., drawings, bibliography. 8vo. Paper wrappers.

Pruyn, Francis Lansing

Duck Shooting. New York, 1945, Privately printed. 30 pp., illustrations by Benson, Bishop and others. 8vo. Paper wrappers. A scarce account of Eastern shore wildfowling.

Pryce, Dick

Safe Hunting! An introduction to hunting, guns and gun safety. New York, 1974, David McKay Co. 178 pp., photographic plates. 8vo; dust jacket.

Puckett, Riley

Advanced Bowhunting For the Modern Archer. Virginia, 1983, Privately printed. 75 pp.

Pugh, David

The Habits of Small Animals and Successful Methods of Trapping Them. Lawrence, Kansas, No date (ca. 1930), Privately printed. 33 pp. Paper wrappers.

Pulling, Pierre

Game and the Gunner; observations on game management and sport hunting. New York, 1973, Winchester Press. 233 pp., drawings. 8vo; dust jacket. (Reprinted several times, same format and publisher)

Pullum, Bill and William Frank Hanenkrat

Position Rifle Shooting; a how-to text for shooters and coaches. New York, 1973, Winchester Press. 272 pp., illustrations. Tall 8vo; dust jacket

Successful Shooting. Washington, D. C., 1981, The National Rifle Association of America. 213 pp., photographic plates, diagrams. 8vo; dust jacket.

Purdey, T. D. S. and Captain J. A. Purdey

The Shot Gun. New York, 1937, Charles Scribner's Sons. 237 pp., illustrations. 12mo; dust jacket. (Printed from British sheets)

Putnam, David Binney

David Goes To Greenland. New York, 1926, G. P. Putnam's Sons. 167 pp., drawings, photographic plates. 8vo; dust jacket. (Reprinted 1926, same format and publisher) An account of the Putnam-American Museum Greenland Expedition written by a 13 year-old. Includes hunting polar bear, walrus, etc. A scarce work.

Pryde, Duncan

Nunaga; ten years of Eskimo life. New York, 1971, Walker. 285 pp., color illustrations. 8vo; dust jacket. Much on hunting polar and sub-polar big game.

Pyle, Wilf E.

Hunting Predators For Hides and Profit. South Hackensack, New Jersey, 1985, Stoeger Arms Company. 256 pp., photographic plates. 4to. Paper wrappers.

Quaiffe, M. M., editor

Yellowstone Kelly; the memoirs of Luther S. Kelly.   New Haven / London, 1926, Yale University Press / Oxford University Press.   268 pp., illustrations.   8vo; dust jacket. An entertaining biography of this Indian scout and Western personality with much hunting in Wyoming and Montana. Scarce.

Quay, Thomas L.

Mourning Dove Populations in North Carolina.   Raleigh, 1954, North Carolina Game Division.   47 pp., photographic plates, maps, bibliography.   8vo. Paper wrappers.

Quee, Ethel M., editor

Transactions of the Twelfth North American Wildlife Conference. Washington, D. C., 1947, Wildlife Management Institute.   632 pp., photographic plates, diagrams 8vo. Paper wrappers.

Transactions of the Thirteenth North American Wildlife Conference. Washington, D. C., 1948, Wildlife Management Institute.   650 pp., photographic plates, diagrams 8vo. Paper wrappers.

Queeny, Edgar M.   b. 1897

Cheechako; the story of an Alaskan bear hunt. New York, 1941, Charles Scribner's Sons.   133 pp., color frontispiece plus other photographic plates. Introduction by Nash Buckingham.   Limited to 1200 copies   8vo; slipcased.

Prairie Wings; pen and camera flight studies. New York, 1946, Ducks Unlimited.   255 pp., frontispiece in color, sketches by Richard E. Bishop, many photographic plates by the author.   4to; dust jacket. (Reprinted 1947, J. B. Lippincott Co., same format and contents. Also reprinted, 1962, Alhambra, California; limited to 2000 copies. Also reprinted, 1979, Schiffer Publishing Company) [Also a deluxe first edition, specially bound and limited to 225 numbered copies, signed by the author and artist; slipcased.]

Quinlan, S. B., et al.

A Guide To Wildlife Viewing in Alaska.   No place, 1983, Alaska Department of Fish and Game.   170 pp., illustrations.   4to. Paper wrappers.

Quinn, Tom

The Working Retrievers; the training, care and handling of retrievers for hunting and field trials.   New York, 1983, E. P. Dutton & Co., Inc.   257 pp., color and black and white illustrations.   4to; dust jacket.

Radcliffe, T.
Spaniels For Sport.   New York and London, 1969, Faber and Faber. 136 pp., photographic plates.   8vo; dust jacket.   (Reprinted, 1978)   A discussion of the Carlton method of training hunting spaniels.

Radclyffe, Major C. E.
Round the Smoking Room Fire; a collection of sporting adventures and yarns.   London, 1933, John Murray.   230 pp., photographic plates.   8vo.   A collection of stories including some North American big game hunting.   Scarce.

Rae, Thomas
Profitable Game Bird Management.   Cayuga, 1945, Beacon Milling. Fifth edition.   71 pp., photographic plates.   8vo.   Paper wrappers.

Rae, William, editor
A Treasury of Outdoor Life.   New York, 1975, Harper & Row, Publishers, Inc. / Outdoor Life Books.   394 pp., illustrations in color and black and white.   4to; dust jacket.   (Revised and reprinted several times, same format and publisher)   An anthology of stories published in the first 75 years of *Outdoor Life* magazine.

Race, C. N. and H. H. Smith
Two Weeks Wild.   Caro, Michigan, 1926, Privately printed.   25 pp., photographic plates, drawings.   4to.   Paper wrappers.   An account of a group of businessmen's two week hunting trip in northern Michigan.

Ragland, Samuel Evan
Menasha.   Memphis, Tennessee, 1945, Privately printed. 16 pp., illustrations.   8vo.   Paper wrappers.   A description of St. Francis Valley Club on Lake Menasha, near Memphis with some hunting.

Raihala, Michael
Six Months in the Wilderness; the adventures of a young trapper in northern Minnesota.   New York, 1955, Exposition Press.   162 pp., photographic plates.   8vo; dust jacket.

The Ralston-Purina Co.
The Purina Gun Dog Book; tips on training pointers, setters, spaniels, retrievers, by leading handlers of these breeds.   St. Louis, 1951, The Ralston-Purina Co.   83 pp., illustrations.   16mo.   Paper wrappers.
The Purina Hound Book.   St. Louis, 1950, The Ralston-Purina Co.   61 pp., drawings.   16mo.   Paper wrappers.

Rand, Austin L.   b. 1905

American Water and Game Birds.   New York, 1956, E. P. Dutton & Co., Inc.   239 pp., color and black and white illustrations.   4to; dust jacket.

Mammals of Yukon.   Ottawa, 1945, National Museum of Canada.   93 pp., drawings, maps.   8vo.   Paper wrappers.

Mr. Rand was an ornithologist of considerable repute who also wrote several items regarding mammals and furbearers of Canada.

Rand, William M.

Just Fishin' and Huntin.'   New York, 1972, Vantage Press.   160 pp., photographic plates.   8vo; dust jacket.   Contains some North American big and small game hunting.

Randall, K. C.

Wild Hunter.   New York, 1951, Franklin Watts.   235 pp., drawings. 8vo; dust jacket.   An older juvenile about pheasant hunting in Michigan.

Randall, Willet

Wilderness Patchwork.   Bradford, Pennsylvania, 1968, Hounds and Hunting Magazine.   147 pp., photographic plates, drawings.   8vo.   Paper wrappers.   Hunting with beagles in Pennsylvania.

Randolph, John W.

The World of "Wood, Field and Stream;" an outdoorsman's collection from the columns of *The New York Times.* New York, 1962, Holt, Rinehart & Winston.   177 pp., drawings by John Groth.   8vo; dust jacket.

Randolph, Vance

The Camp of Wildcat Creek.   New York, 1934, Alfred A. Knopf, Inc. 211 pp., drawings by Howard Simon.   A title in Knopf's Borzoi Books For Boys series.   12mo; dust jacket.   An older juvenile with camping, fishing and hunting.

Randolph, Vance and Guy W. Von Schriltz

Ozark Outdoors.   New York, 1934, Vanguard Press.   299 pp., illustrations. 8vo; dust jacket.   Hunting and angling stories in the Ozark Mountains.

Ransom, Elmer

Fishing's Just Luck.   New York, 1945, Howell.   160 pp.   8vo; dust jacket.   Mostly fishing tales, but some turkey and quail hunting.

Rau, Margaret

Musk Oxen; bearded ones of the Arctic.   New York, 1976, Thomas Y. Crowell Company.   41 pp., illustrations from etchings by Patricia Collins.   8vo; dust jacket.

Rau, Ron

    Sage Lake Road. Oshkosh, Wisconsin, 1983,Willow Creek Press. 97 pp. 8vo. Some deer hunting with bow and arrow.

Raup, Hugh M.

    Range Conditions in the Wood Buffalo Park of Western Canada With Notes on the History of the Wood Bison. 1933, International Wildlife Federation / National Museum of Canada. 52 pp., fold-out map, bibliography. 8vo. Paper wrappers.

Rawley, Edwin V. and William J. Bailey

    Utah Upland Game Birds. No place, 1964, Utah State Department of Fish and Game. 31 pp., illustrations. 8vo. Paper wrappers.

Rawlings, Marjorie K.   **1896-1953**

    South Moon Under. New York, 1933, Charles Scribner's Sons. 334 pp. 8vo; dust jacket. The author's first novel; set in the Florida Big Scrub, with much hunting.

    The Yearling. New York, 1938, Charles Scribner's Sons. 428 pp., decorations by Edward Shenton. 8vo; dust jacket. (Reprinted many times, various formats) A Pulitzer prize-winning novel of a boy and his relationship with a fawn.

Rawstorne, Lawrence   **1774-1850**

    Gamonia; or the art of preserving game and improved method of making plantations and covers, explained and illustrated. Philadelphia, 1930, David McKay Co. 255 pp., color illustrations. With a new introduction by Eric Parker. 4to; dust jacket. (A reproduction of the 1837 first edition)

Reader, H. J.

    Newfoundland Wit, Humor and Folklore. Corner Brook, No date (ca. 1955), Privately printed. 57 pp. 8vo. Paper wrappers. With much on hunting and fishing in the region.

Rechnitzer, F. E.

    Raff; the story of an English setter. Philadelphia, 1948, John C. Winston Co. 240 pp., color and black and white illustrations by Marguerite Kirmse. 8vo; dust jacket. A well written and illustrated story with much on field trials and hunting. Scarce.

Reece, Maynard

    The Waterfowl Art of Maynard Reece. Venice, Florida, 1984, Mill Pond Press. 157 pp., color illustrations. Elephant folio. (Reprinted 1985, Abrams, slightly smaller format)

Reed, N. P. and D. Drabelle

The United States Fish and Wildlife Service. Boulder, Colorado, 1984, Westview. 164 pp., photographic plates, drawings. 8vo. An account of the history and organization of this agency.

Reed, Henry M.

The A. B. Frost Book. Rutland, Vermont, 1967, Charles E. Tuttle. 149 pp., color and black and white illustrations, bibliography. Forward by Eugene V. Connett, 3rd. Folio; dust jacket; slipcased.

Reed, Walt, editor

The Illustrator in America, 1900-1960. New York, 1966, Reinhold Publishing Corp. 268 pp., illustrations in black and white and in color, bibliography. Folio; dust jacket. Includes the works of A. B. Frost, Lynn Bogue Hunt, John Atherton and Paul Brown as well as other non-sporting illustrators.

Rees, Clair

Be an Expert Shot; with rifle, handgun or shotgun. Piscataway, New Jersey, 1984, Winchester Press. 186 pp., photographic plates. 4to; dust jacket.

Beginner's Guide To Guns and Shooting. Northfield, Illinois, 1978, DBI Books. 224 pp., illustrations. 4to. Paper wrappers.

Matching The Gun To the Game. Tulsa, 1982, Winchester Press. 302 pp., color and black and white illustrations. 8vo; dust jacket

The Sportsman's Handgunning Bible. Garden City, New York, 1985, Doubleday & Co. 138 pp., illustrations. 4to. Paper wrappers.

Rees, Clair and H. Wixom

Penny Pinching, Tight-Fisted, Save-a-Buck Guide To Bigger Fish and Better Hunting. Tulsa, Oklahoma, 1980, Winchester Press. 139 pp., photographic plates. 8vo; dust jacket.

Reeve, J. Stanley   1878-1960

Foxhunting Formalities. New York, 1930, The Derrydale Press. 54 pp., illustrations from drawings by Paul Brown. Limited to 990 copies. 8vo. [Also a large paper edition, specially bound and limited to 99 numbered copies signed by the author] (Much of the text appearing in this work first appeared as a supplement to *The Sportsman* magazine, issued in 1929 with the same title. Also reprinted, 1958, in paper wrappers by the Blue Ridge Hunt)

Foxhunting Recollections; a journal of the Radnor hounds and other packs. Philadelphia, 1928, J. B. Lippincott Co. 320 pp., photographic plates, color frontispiece. Introduction by Henry G. Vaughan. 8vo.

Reeve, J. Stanley, continued

Further Foxhunting Recollections; including The Great Lenape Run, together with other notes and entries from the journal (1928-1935).   New York, 1935, At the Sign of the Gosden Head.   160 pp., illustrations by Robert Ball. Limited to 950 numbered copies.   8vo; dust jacket.

The Golden Days of Foxhunting.   Philadelphia, 1958, Dorrance Publishing Company.   375 pp., illustrations.   Tall 8vo.

Radnor Reminiscences; a foxhunting journal.   Boston, 1921, Houghton Mifflin Company.   204 pp., illustrations.   8vo.

Red Coats in Chester County.   New York, 1940, The Derrydale Press. 390 pp., plates.   Limited to 570 numbered copies.   Tall 8vo.

"Rhubarb;" the diary of a gentleman's hunter.   Philadelphia, 1908, Privately printed by the Lippincott Press.   58 pp., frontispiece.   8vo.

That Reminds Me; a series of sporting incidents in the life of a country gentleman, as told to his grandson.   Philadelphia, 1957, Dorrance Publishing Company.   125 pp., illustrations.   Tall 8vo.

Reeves, Henry M.

A Contribution To An Annotated Bibliography of North American Cranes, Rails, Woodcock, Snipe, Doves and Pigeons.   Springfield, 1975, N.T.I.S. 527 pp.   4to.   Paper wrappers.

Reichenbach, William

Automatic Pistol Marksmanship.   Onslow County, North Carolina, 1937, Small Arms Technical Publishing Company.   140 pp., illustrations from drawings by Richard Kroth and Edwin Bender.   18mo; dust jacket.

The Elusive Ten; a new deal in revolver shooting.   Wantagh, Long Island, New York, 1935, Hathaway Oaks.   84 pp., photographic plates.   24mo. Rare.

Sixguns and Bullseyes.   Onslow County, North Carolina, 1936, Small Arms Technical Publishing Company.   145 pp., illustrations from drawings. 18mo; dust jacket.   (Reprinted 1943, same format and publisher)   This is an expanded edition of his previous work, *The Elusive Ten.*

Reichner, Morgan S. A.

A Wall-To-Wall Tour of the Leash.   New York, 1975, Privately printed. 21 pp., drawings.   Limited to 300 numbered copies.   8vo.   A history of this private New York hunting and angling club.

Reiger, George   b. 1939

Wanderer on My Native Shore.   New York, 1983, Simon & Schuster. 286 pp., drawings by Bob Hines, bibliography.   8vo; dust jacket.   The author's personal conclusions regarding the ecology of America's east coast.

Reiger, George, continued

The Wings of Dawn; the complete book of North American waterfowling. New York, 1980, Stein & Day, Publishers. 320 pp., color and black and white illustrations, bibliography. Tall 8vo; dust jacket.

Reiger, George, editor

Zane Grey, Outdoorsman; Zane Grey's best hunting and fishing tales. Englewood Cliffs, New Jersey, 1972, Prentice-Hall, Inc. 349 pp., photographic plates. 8vo; dust jacket.

Reiger, George and Kenneth Garrett

Floaters and Stick-Ups; a personal survey of wildfowl decoys. Boston, 1986, David R. Godine, Publishers, Inc. 190 pp., color photographs, bibliography. 4to; dust jacket.

Mr. Reiger has also written several angling books.

Reiger, John   b. 1943

American Sportsmen and the Origins of Conservation. New York, 1975, Winchester Press. 316 pp., photographic plates. 8vo; dust jacket. An important work advocating that sportsmen were, in large part, the moving force of the conservation movement in America.

The Passing of the Great West; selected papers of George Bird Grinnell. New York, 1972, Winchester Press. 182 pp., photographic plates. 8vo; dust jacket. (Reprinted 1984, University of Oklahoma Press) A thorough documentation of Grinnell's early writing about the west and conservation.

Reimann, Lewis

The Game Warden and the Poachers. Ann Arbor, Michigan, 1959, Northwoods Publishers. 196 pp., drawings. 8vo; dust jacket.

Reitz, Robert

The Mighty Buck; a practical guide to a successful deer hunt. No place, 1978, Gridiron Publishers. 115 pp., photographic plates. 8vo. Paper wrappers.

Remington, Charles Henry

See **Cooper River Joe**

Render, Lorne E.

An Artist's View of Nature: Carl Rungius. Edmonton, Alberta, 1969, Provincial Museum. 24 pp., color and black and white illustrations. 4to. Paper wrappers. A collection of Rungius' big game paintings, drawings and prints.

Reneau, Jack and Susan Reneau

Colorado's Biggest Bucks and Bulls. Colorado Springs, Colorado, 1983, Colorado Big Game Trophy Records, Inc. 275 pp., photographic plates, charts. 8vo.

Reynal, Eugene S., M.H. 1878-1940

Thoughts Upon the Hunting Kit. York, 1934, Privately printed for the author. Unpaginated; plates. 16mo. Foxhunting.

Rhodes, Cecil E.

Adventures in Deer Hunting. New York, 1979, Carlton Press. 62 pp. 8vo; dust jacket.

Riccuti, Edward R.

Killer Animals. New York, 1976, Walker and Company. 319 pp., illustrations. 8vo; dust jacket.

The Wild Cats. New York, 1979, The Ridge Press. 239 pp., color and black and white illustrations. 4to; dust jacket. Containing descriptions of all species, including North American.

Rice, F. Philip

Outdoor Life Gun Data Book. New York, 1975, Harper & Row, Publishers, Inc. / Outdoor Life Books. 570 pp. 12mo; dust jacket.

Rice, F. Philip and John Dahl

Game Bird Hunting. New York, 1965, Harper & Row, Publishers, Inc. / Outdoor Life Books. 190 pp., illustrations. 8vo; dust jacket. (Reprinted several times to 1981, paper wrappers, same publisher)

Hunting Dogs. New York, 1978, Outdoor Life Books. 200 pp., illustrations. 8vo. Paper wrappers. (Reprinted several times, same format and publisher)

Rich, Louise Dickinson

Start of the Trail; the story of a young Maine guide. Philadelphia, 1949, J. B. Lippincott Co. 216 pp., color frontispiece. A juvenile story. Ms. Rich wrote several other books (including *We Took to the Woods*) about Maine and its wood-lore with incidental mention of hunting.

Richard, Ed

Deer Production vs. Doe Reduction in the Adirondacks. No place, 1951, Privately printed. Unpaginated (15 pp.) Paper wrappers.

Richards, S. H. and R. L. Hine

Wisconsin Fox Populations. Madison, 1953, Wisconsin Department of Game Management. 78 pp., photographic plates, drawings. 8vo. Paper wrappers.

Richardson, Arthur H.

Conservation By the People; the history of the conservation movement in Ontario to 1970. Toronto, 1974, University of Toronto. 154 pp., photographic plates, map. 8vo; dust jacket.

Richardson, Arthur H. and L. E. Petersen

History and Management of South Dakota Deer. Pierre, 1974, South Dakota Department of Game. 113 pp., photographic plates, maps. 8vo. Paper wrappers.

Richardson, Lee

Those Were the Days; bird hunting memoirs. Caldwell, Idaho, 1985, Privately printed by The Caxton Printers. 227 pp., color frontispiece by David Hagerbaumer and other black and white illustrations. Limited to 500 numbered copies. 8vo. The memoirs of a western wildfowler.

Richardson, Robert. H.

Ward Bros. Decoys Working Models; 50 years of progress. Cambridge, Maryland, No date (ca. 1969), Privately printed. 12 pp., photographic plates. Elephant folio (newspaper format). Paper wrappers.

Richardson, Robert. H., et al.

Chesapeake Bay Decoys; the men who made them and used them. Cambridge, Maryland, 1973, Crow Haven Publishers. 192 pp., photographic plates. Limited to 2000 copies. 4to; dust jacket. (Also a 1973 revised and corrected edition, same publisher with Tidewater Publishers) [Also a deluxe first edition, specially bound and limited to 100 numbered copies signed by all seven authors] An important work.

Riddell, John *(pseud. of* **Cory Ford)**
See **Ford, Corey**

Riddle, Maxwell

The New Complete Brittany Spaniel. New York, 1974, Howell Book House. 288 pp., illustrations. 8vo. (Reprinted and revised several times)
The Springer Spaniel. Chicago, 1939, Judy Publishing Co. 158 pp., photographic plates, drawings. 8vo; dust jacket. (Reprinted and revised several times, same format and publisher. Later editions called, *The Springer Spaniel For Show and Field*)

Riddle, Maxwell, continued

The Wild Dogs in Life and Legend. New York, 1979, Howell Book House. (Reprinted, same publisher and format)

Rieffenberger, J. C.

West Virginia Black Bear. Charleston, 1981, West Virginia Department of Natural Resources. 55 pp., photographic plates. 8vo. Paper wrappers.

Rigg, H. K., editor

Tales From the Skipper. Barre, Massachusetts, 1968, Barre Publishers, Ltd. 256 pp. 8vo; dust jacket. An anthology of stories originally published from this nautical magazine, including "The Ledge," a duck hunting story by L. S. Hall and a nautical story by Eugene V. Connett, 3rd.

Rikhoff, Jim   b. 1931

Fair Chase. Clinton, New Jersey, 1984, Amwell Press. 264 pp., drawings by Tom Hennessey. 8vo. [Also a deluxe edition, limited to 1000 numbered copies signed by the author and artist; slipcased] A collection of Rikhoff's hunting stories.

Mixed Bag. Clinton, New Jersey, 1979, Amwell Press. 248 pp., drawings by Gordon Allen. Limited to 1000 numbered and signed copies; slipcased. 8vo; slipcased. (Also a 1984 trade edition, same format and publisher)

Rikhoff, Jim, editor

The Compact Book of Hunting. New York, 1964, Pratt. 93 pp., photographic plates. 8vo. Paper wrappers.

Hunting the Big Cats; an anthology. Clinton, New Jersey, 1981, Amwell Press. Two volumes containing a total of 900 pp., color and black and white illustrations by Bob Kuhn. Limited to 1000 numbered and signed sets. 8vo; slipcased.

Hunting the World's Mountains; an anthology. Clinton, New Jersey, 1984, Amwell Press. Two volumes containing a total of 937 pp., color and black and white illustrations by Gordon Allen and Peter Skirka. Limited to 1000 numbered and signed sets. 8vo; slipcased.

Mr. Rikhoff worked for Winchester Western and was involved in the founding of Winchester Press. For many years he also wrote a monthly column appearing in *The American Rifleman* magazine titled "Mixed Bag." In 1976 he founded The National Sporting Fraternity, which used the Amwell Press imprint to publish many sporting books.

Riley, Perry G.

Bowhunting the Fake Scrape. Kingman, Indiana, 1985, Privately printed. 54 pp. Paper wrappers.

Outwitting the Whitetail. Kingman, Indiana, 1981, Privately printed. 85 pp., illustrations. Paper wrappers.

Riling, Raymond L. J.   1896-1974

Guns and Shooting; a selected chronological bibliography.   New York, 1951, Greenberg: Publishers.   Unpaginated, 2769 entries, plates.   Limited to 1500 copies.   8vo; dust jacket.   (Also a 1984 edition limited to 500 numbered copies, Ray Riling Arms Books)   A standard reference work devoted mostly to firearms titles, but also with some hunting titles. It is arranged by year of publication and is cross-indexed by author and title.

The Powder Flask Book.   New Hope, Pennsylvania, 1953, River House. 495 pp., photographic plates, map, introduction by Harold Peterson.   Thick 4to; dust jacket.   (Reprinted, Bonanza)   Still a definitive work.

Ripley, A. Lassell   1896-1969

Aiden Lassell Ripley, 1896-1969. Watercolors.   New York, 1982, Coe Kerr Gallery.   38 pp., black and white reproductions of paintings.   8vo.   Paper wrappers.

Gunning in America; The Field & Stream portfolio.   New York, no date (1947), Field & Stream Magazine.   A portfolio 16" X 13" containing 6 Ripley paintings.   Issued with a volume of text.   Elephant folio.

Paintings.   Barre, Massachusetts, 1972, Barre Publishing Co., Inc. / Boston Guild of Artists.   Unpaginated, 50 plates in color and black and white, text by Edward Weeks.   Limited to 1500 copies.   Oblong 4to; dust jacket.   [Also a deluxe edition, specially bound and limited to 500 numbered and signed copies; slipcased]   More scarce in either edition than the limitation would suggest.

Sporting Etchings.   Barre, Massachusetts, 1970, Barre Publishing Co., Inc.   91 pp., with 40 reproductions of etchings, Commentary by Dana Lamb. Oblong 4to; dust jacket.   [Also a deluxe edition, limited to 500 numbered copies with a special frontispiece; slipcased]

Mr. Ripley illustrated many hunting and angling books and articles from the 1920's to the 1960's.

Ripley, Ozark (*pseud.* of **Thompson, John Baptiste de Macklot**)   **b. 1872**

Bird Dog Training Made Easy.   Cincinnati, Ohio, 1926, Sportsman's Digest Publishing Company.   82 pp.   12mo.   (Reprinted 1936, in paper wrappers, Hunter-Trader-Trapper)

Sport in Field and Forest.   New York, 1926, D. Appleton & Co.   180 pp., illustrations.   8vo; dust jacket.

Quail and the Quail Dog.   Columbus, Ohio, 1939, Hunter-Trader-Trapper.   110 pp.   16mo.   Paper wrappers.   (Reprinted 1941, The Outdoorsman Handbook Series.   Originally published, 1924, Sportsman's Digest Publishing Company)

Upland Game Bird Hunting.   No place, 1934, Sears, Roebuck & Co. 32 pp., photographic plates.   18mo.   Paper wrappers.

Ripley, Sidney Dillon   b. 1913

    A Paddling of Ducks.   New York, 1957, Harcourt, Brace & Co., Inc. 256 pp., illustrations by Francis Lee Jaques.   8vo; dust jacket.   (Reprinted in a slightly smaller format, 1969, Smithsonian Institute)

    Rails of the World; a monograph of the family Rallidae.   Boston, 1977, David R. Godine, Publishers, Inc.   430 pp., color illustrations.   Limited to 400 numbered and signed copies.   Folio; slipcased.   (Also published, 1977, Feheley)

Ripley, Sidney Dillon and Lynette L. Scribner

    Ornithological Books in The Yale University; including the Library of William Robertson Coe.   New Haven, 1961, Yale University Press.   338 pp., frontispiece, bibliography.   4to; dust jacket.

Ripley, Thomas H.

    The Bobwhite in Massachusetts.   Boston, 1957, Massachusetts Fish and Game Commission.   20 pp., photographic plates, drawings, map, bibliography. 8vo.   Paper wrappers.

Riviere, Bill

    Pole, Paddle and Portage.   New York, 1969, D. Van Nostrand Company, Inc.   259 pp., illustrations.   8vo; dust jacket.   A canoeing guide with some hunting and angling.

Rivinus, Marion W. M.

    Purely Personal.   No place, No date (ca. 1970), Privately printed.   87 pp.   8vo.   Memoirs of angling and bird shooting.   Rare.

Roberts, Jack

    The Amazing Adventures of Lord Gore.   Colorado, 1977, Sundance Publishing.   220 pp.   Limited to 2000 numbered and signed copies.   8vo.   The story of an Irish lord's hunting experiences in America between the years 1854 and 1856.

Roberts, Jessie David

    Bears, Bibles and a Boy.   New York, 1961, W. W. Norton & Co., Inc. 256 pp., drawings by Gil Walker.   8vo; dust jacket.   The autobiography of a man who grew up in the Adirondacks.

Roberts, Maj. Ned Henry   1866-1948

    The Muzzle-Loading Cap Lock Rifle.   Manchester, New Hampshire, 1940, The Granite Press.   432 pp., frontispiece plus other illustrations from photographs and drawings.   8vo.   (Also a 1944 new edition, including the supplement, The Clarke Press.   Also a 1947 edition, The Military Service Publishing Company.   This edition published by Military Service was reprinted several times.   Also reprinted, Bonanza)   An important history of America's early firearms.

Roberts, Maj. Ned Henry, continued
 Supplement to the Muzzle-Loading Cap Lock Rifle. Manchester, New Hampshire, 1940, The Clarke Press. Paged as a continuation of the first edition, from 433-528 pp., illustrations. 8vo.
 Big Game Hunting; white-tailed deer and black bear. Chicago, 1947, Paul, Richmond & Company. 160 pp., illustrations. 18mo; dust jacket.

Roberts, Maj. Ned Henry and Ken Waters
 The Breech Loading Single-Shot Match Rifle. Princeton, New Jersey, 1967, D. Van Nostrand Company, Inc. 293 pp., photographic plates. A Van Nostrand Sporting Book. 4to; dust jacket.

Robertson, Anthony
 Above Tide; reflections on Roderick Haig-Brown. Madiera Park, British Columbia, 1984, Harbour Publishing Company. 136 pp., illustrations. 8vo. Paper wrappers. A most thorough interpretation and bibliography of Haig-Brown's works.

Robertson, William B.
 Investigations of Ring-Necked Pheasant in Illinois. Springfield, 1958, Illinois Department of Conservation. 138 pp., photographic plates, maps, drawings. 8vo. Paper wrappers.

Robinson, Alan James
 Game Animals; ten etchings hand water-colored by Alan James Robinson. Easthampton, Massachusetts, 1981, Cheloniidae Press. A portfolio of hand-colored prints limited to 100 copies. 4to. [The first 26 copies of the edition are specially bound and are lettered A through Z, and are housed in a clam-shell box]

Robinson, Ben C.
 Woodland, Field and Waterfowl Hunting. Philadelphia, 1946, David McKay Co. 333 pp., photographic plates. 12mo; dust jacket.

Robinson, Bradley, editor
 World's Greatest Stories of Hunting and Adventure. New York, 1947, National Travel Club. 384 pp. 8vo; dust jacket. An anthology of mostly big game hunting stories by Selous, Clark, Morden and others containing some North American episodes.

Robinson, Jerome B.
 Hunt Close! a realistic guide to training close working gun dogs for today's tight cover conditions. New York, 1978, Winchester Press. 221 pp., photographic plates. 8vo; dust jacket.

Robinson, Jimmy   b. 1897

The Best of Jimmy Robinson; the best stories of over seventy years of hunting of Jimmy Robinson and his friends.   Detroit Lakes, Minnesota, 1980, John Meyer.   334 pp., color illustrations from paintings by Kouba, Maass, Scott and others.   8vo; dust jacket.

Forty Years of Hunting. Minneapolis, 1947, Privately printed.   160 pp., photographic plates.   8vo.   Much on wildfowling with a section on Fred Kimball, inventor of the modern shotgun choke.

Hits ands Misses of the Trap Shooting and Skeet World - Hunting Tips. Minneapolis, 1942, Privately printed.   224 pp., photographic plates.   8vo.

Hunting Adventures With Jimmy Robinson; highlights of hunting experiences over a span of 50 years.   Minneapolis, Minnesota, 1958, T. S. Denison & Co., Inc.   264 pp., color and black and white illustrations by Roger Preuss and Les Kouba.   8vo.

The Life and Times of Jimmy Robinson.   Minneapolis, 1973, Privately printed.   128 pp., photographic plates.   4to.   The scarce autobiography of this popular hunting and shooting author.

Trap Shooting and Skeet, Hunting. Minneapolis, 1942, Privately printed. 224 pp., photographic plates.   8vo.

Wild Duck Calling.   Minneapolis, No date (ca. 1945), Privately printed. 31 pp. Paper wrappers.   (Also reported co-authored with Walt Bush in an edition of 44 pp.)   A scarce Robinson title.

Wing Shooting, Trap and Skeet; Volume II   Minneapolis, 1955, Privately printed.   223 pp., color and black and white illustrations.   8vo.

Mr. Robinson was an associate editor of *Sports Afield* magazine.

Robinson, Jimmy and Jim Nichols

The Grand....75 Years. A history of trapshooting.   Dayton, Ohio, 1974, United Color.   400 pp., photographic plates, illustrations from paintings by Les Kouba.   8vo.   A history of the Grand American Trapshooting Tournament held annually at Vandalia, Ohio.

Robinson, Rollo S.

Shots At Mule Deer.   No place, 1970, Privately printed.   209 pp., photographic plates.   4to.   Spiral bound paper wrappers.   (Reprinted several times, cloth bound, Winchester Press)

Robinson, Rowland E.   1833-1900

Danvis Folks and *A Hero of Ticonderoga.*   Rutland, Vermont, 1934, Tuttle.   287 pp., illustrations. 8vo; dust jacket.

In New England Fields and *Woods With Sketches and Stories.*   Rutland, Vermont, 1937, Tuttle.   256 pp., bibliography of the author's works. Foreword by Sinclair Lewis.   8vo; dust jacket.

Out of Bondage; and other stories.   Rutland, Vermont, 1933, Tuttle. 248 pp., illustrations. 8vo; dust jacket.

Robinson, Rowland E., continued

Uncle Lisha's Outing, The Buttles Gals and *Along Three Rivers*. Rutland, Vermont, 1934, Tuttle. 258 pp., illustrations. Introduction by Henry W. Lanier. 8vo; dust jacket.

Uncle Lisha's Workshop and *A Danvis Pioneer*. Rutland, Vermont, 1933, Tuttle. 248 pp., illustrations. 8vo; dust jacket.

Sam Lovell's Boy and *Stream Fables*. Rutland, Vermont, 1936, Tuttle. 255 pp., illustrations. 8vo; dust jacket.

Sam Lovel's Camp; and other stories. Rutland, Vermont, 1934, Tuttle. 264 pp., illustrations. 8vo; dust jacket.

Mr. Robinson was a popular outdoor writer of the late nineteenth and early twentieth centuries. All of these titles were originally published then, but these seven volumes were issued as a set between 1933 and 1937 in a "Centennial edition." He wrote mostly of country life in Vermont and New England and most of his works contained some hunting or angling. See Phillips.

Robinson, William L.

Ruffed Grouse Management; state of the art in the early 1980's; proceedings from a symposium. No place, 1984, Privately printed. 181 pp., illustrations. 8vo. Paper wrappers.

Fool Hen; the spruce grouse on the yellow dog plains. Madison, 1980, University of Wisconsin Press. 221 pp., photographic plates, bibliography. 8vo; dust jacket. The first book devoted entirely to the subject; a thorough work.

Rockwell, Robert H.

My Way of Becoming a Hunter. New York, 1955, W. W. Norton & Co., Inc. 285 pp., photographic plates. 8vo; dust jacket. (Reprinted several times, same format and publisher. Also a 1956 British edition) Mr. Rockwell was the taxidermist for the American Museum of Natural History, and this is an account of his hunting experiences, many of which were in North America.

Rodgers, Frank Howell

Breaking a Gun Shy Dog. Jackson, Mississippi, 1924, Torgerson. 16 pp.

Rodgers, Walter R.

Huntin' Gun; men, gun feel, game. Washington, D. C., 1949, Infantry Journal Press. An N. R. A. Library Book. 179 pp., illustrations from drawing by Jim Berryman and Gib Crockett. 8vo; dust jacket. Containing a good deal of deer hunting.

Roe, Frank G.

The North American Buffalo; a critical study of the species in its wild state. Toronto, 1951, University of Toronto Press. 957 pp., illustrations. Thick 8vo. (Reprinted several times in paper wrappers, same publisher. Also a 1972 British edition) A definitive study.

Roebuck, Kenneth

    Gun-Dog Training; Pointing Dogs. Harrisburg, 1983, Stackpole Books. 183 pp., illustrations. 8vo; dust jacket.

    Gun-Dog Training; Spaniels and Retrievers. Harrisburg, 1982, Stackpole Books. 192 pp., illustrations. 8vo; dust jacket.

Rofkar, Franklin V.

    The Hunting Game. New York, 1950, Exposition Press. 51 pp., illustrations from drawings by Julia Rofkar. 8vo; dust jacket.

Rogers, Glenn

    The Blue Grouse in Colorado. No place, 1968, Colorado Fish and Game Department. 63 pp., photographic plates, maps. 8vo. Paper wrappers.

    Sage Grouse Investigations in Colorado. No place, 1964, Colorado Game, Fish and Parks. 132 pp., color and black and white illustrations, bibliography. 8vo. Paper wrappers.

Rogers, John L.

    See **Strickland, Roy W.**

Rogers, Robert

    Big Rack; Texas all time largest white-tails from 1892-1975. Corpus Christi, Texas, 1976, Outdoor Worlds of Texas, Inc. 167 pp., photographic plates. 8vo; dust jacket. (Also a 1980 second edition) [Also a deluxe first edition, specially bound, numbered and signed by the author] A record of Texas whitetail trophies.

    Great Whitetails of North America. Corpus Christi, Texas, 1981, Texas Hunting Service. 223 pp., photographic plates. 8vo; dust jacket.

    Great Whitetails of North America, Volume II. Corpus Christi, Texas, 1981, Privately printed. 256 pp., photographic plates. 8vo; dust jacket.

    The Professional's Guide To Whitetail. Corpus Christi, Texas, 1984, Privately printed. 170 pp., photographic plates. 8vo.

Rogers, Robert and John Small

    Big Rack. Dallas, 1975, Privately printed. 151 pp., illustrations. 8vo. Records of typical and non-typical deer taken in Texas.

Rogers, Robert

    Also see **Garza, L. R.**

Rohan, Jack

    Yankee Arms Maker; the incredible career of Samuel Colt. New York and London, 1935, Harper & Brothers. 301 pp., photographic plates. 8vo; dust jacket. (Also a 1948 revised edition, same publisher)

Rollins, Philip Ashton

Ephraim Ursus. American Pioneer; the biography of a grizzly bear. New York, No date, Privately printed. 16 pp. 8vo.

Romashko, Sandra

Wild Ducks and Geese of North America. Miami, 1978, Windward. 64 pp., color illustrations by Russ Smiley. 8vo. Paper wrappers.

Romer, F.

Makers of History; a story of the development of the history of our country and the part played in it by Colt. Hartford, Connecticut, 1926, Colt Patent Firearms Manufacturing Company. 64 pp., illustrations from drawings. 16mo. Paper wrappers.

Romero, Pablo Bush

Mexico and Africa; from the sight of my rifle. No place (Mexico), No date (ca. 1960), Privately printed. 322 pp., color and black and white illustrations. Limited to 1000 signed copies. 8vo; dust jacket. A big game hunting title describing hunts in Mexico, India and Africa.

Rood, Ronald

Animals Nobody Loves. Brattleboro, Vermont, 1971, Stephen Greene Press. 215 pp. drawings. 8vo; dust jacket. A general discussion of species such as coyote, wolf, rat, octopus, snakes, eels, etc.

Roosevelt, Anna Eleanor, editor

Hunting Big Game in the Eighties; letters of Elliot Roosevelt, sportsman. New York, 1932, Charles Scribner's Sons. 182 pp. A deluxe numbered edition. 8vo. (Also a 1933 trade edition, same format and publisher) Elliot was the brother of Theodore Roosevelt.

Roosevelt, Theodore   1858-1919

American Bears; selections from the writings of Theodore Roosevelt. Boulder, 1983, University of Colorado Press. Edited by Paul Schullery. 193 pp., photographic plates. 8vo; dust jacket.

Hunting Adventures in the West. New York, 1927, G. P. Putnam's Sons. 247 pp. plus 372 pp., illustrations by A. B. Frost, Frederick Remington and others. Thick 8vo; dust jacket. This is a reissue in one volume of *Hunting Trips of a Ranchman* and *Wilderness Hunter,* both published previous to 1925.

Memories of The American Frontier. Charleston, West Virginia, 1977, Westvaco Paper Company. The company's 1977 presentation book. 187 pp., illustrations by Frederick Remington. 8vo; slipcased.

Ranch Life and the Hunting-Trail. Austin, Texas, 1966, Pemberton. 186 pp., drawings by Frederick Remington 8vo; dust jacket. (Also reprinted, 1969, Winchester Press. Originally published, 1888, The Century Company)

Roosevelt, Theodore, continued

Ranch Life in the Far West. Flagstaff, Arizona, 1985, Northlands. 89 pp., drawings by Frederick Remington. 4to; dust jacket. (These six articles originally appeared in *Century* magazine in 1888 and were also contained in *Ranch Life and the Hunting Trail*)

Who Should Go West. New York, 1927, Privately printed. 9 pp. Limited to 73 copies. 8vo.

As president of the United States, founder of The Boone & Crockett Club, and dedicated conservationist, Roosevelt did more for enacting modern conservation practices than anyone in history. He was a prolific writer on natural history, American history, politics and nature and co-edited the first several Books of The Boone and Crockett Club. See Phillips.

Roosevelt, Theodore

Also see **Cutright, Paul Russell**
Also see **Day, Donald, editor**
Also see **Lorant, Stefan**
Also see **McCreight, M. I.**
Also see **Morris, Edmund**
Also see **Willis, Jack**

Roosevelt, Theodore, Jr.

All in the Family. New York, 1929, G. P. Putnam's Sons. 189 pp., photographic plates. 8vo; dust jacket. (Reprinted, same format and publisher)

Mostly family life, but a chapter on duck shooting at Oyster Bay, Long Island.

Roosevelt, Mrs. Theodore, et al.

Cleared For Strange Ports. New York, 1927, Charles Scribner's Sons. 254 pp., photographic plates. 8vo; dust jacket. Containing some Alaska bear hunting.

Roper, Walter F.   1881-1954

Pistol and Revolver Shooting. New York, 1945, The Macmillan Company. 256 pp., photographic plates. Tall 8vo; dust jacket. (Reprinted several times, same format and publisher)

Experiments of a Handgunner. New York and Harrisburg, 1949, Stackpole and Heck, Inc. 202 pp., illustrations from drawings and photographs. An N. R. A. Library Book. 8vo; dust jacket.

Rorabacher, J. Albert

The American Buffalo in Transition. St. Cloud, Minnesota, 1970, North Star Press. 146 pp. 8vo; dust jacket. A conservation success story that presents a historical overview of the buffalo from the early 1900's, when the species was nearly extinct, to the present, when its survival is certain.

Rosa, Joseph C.

Colonel Colt, London; the history of Colt's London firearms, 1851-1857. Ontario, 1976, Fortress Publishing Co. 215 pp., photographic plates. 4to; dust jacket. (Also a 1976 British edition)

Rosa, Joseph C., et al.

An Illustrated History of Guns and Small Arms. New Jersey, 1974, Castle Books. 96 pp., illustrations. 8vo; dust jacket.

Rose, Stuart

There's a Fox in the Spinney; memories of foxhunting, racing and publishing. Garden City, New York, 1967, Doubleday & Co., Inc. 328 pp. 8vo; dust jacket. Mr. Rose was a senior editor of *The Saturday Evening Post* as well as an accomplished horseman.

Rosenbauer, Tom, editor

The Orvis Anthology; the C. F. Orvis outdoor writing awards. Brattleboro, Vermont, 1984, Riverwood Press. 210 pp., drawings by Ernest Lussier. Foreword by John Merwin. 8vo. [Also a deluxe edition, limited to 300 numbered and signed copies.; slipcased]

Rosenberg, Frantz

Big Game Shooting in British Columbia and Norway. London, 1928, Martin Hopkinson & Co. 261 pp., photographic plates. 8vo. A scarce work with sheep, caribou, goat, bear and moose hunting as well as salmon fishing.

Rosenberry, Marvin B., editor

A History of Deerfoot Lodge; memories of happy hunting. Wisconsin, 1941, Privately printed. 70 pp., photographic plates, maps. An account of this Wisconsin deer camp.

Rosenblum, Edwin E.

How To Raise and Train a Brittany Spaniel. Jersey City, New Jersey, 1965, TFH Publications. 64 pp., illustrations. 8vo. Paper wrappers.

Rosene, Walter

The Bobwhite Quail; its life and management. New Brunswick, New Jersey, 1969, Rutgers University Press. 418 pp., color and black and white illustrations by Richard Parks. 4to; dust jacket. (Reprinted 1984, Sun Press) [Also a deluxe first edition, specially bound with special illustrations laid in, and limited to 250 numbered and signed copies; slipcased] A most thorough and detailed work.

Ross, Lillian
   Portrait of Hemingway.   New York, 1961, Simon & Schuster.   65
pp., frontispiece.   8vo; dust jacket.   (Originally appeared in *New Yorker*
magazine, 1950)

Ross, M. I.
   Wilderness River; adventures in the fur trapping country.   New York,
1952, Harper & Brothers.   214 pp.   8vo; dust jacket.

Ross, Robert E.
   Wings Over the Marshes; shooting sketches from an old log book.
London, 1948, Batchworth.   152 pp., photographic plates.   8vo; dust jacket.
Some European shooting, but mostly bird and wildfowl shooting on the west coast of North America.

Rossell, Leonard
   Tracks and Trails.   New York, 1928, Boy Scouts of America.   138 pp.,
illustrations.   12mo; dust jacket.

Rossman, George
   The Loon; Minnesota's state bird.   Grand Rapids, Minnesota, 1967,
Herald Review.   16 pp., color and black and white illustrations.   8vo. Paper
wrappers.
   Bald Eagles of the Chippewa Forest.   Grand Rapids, Minnesota, 1967,
Herald Review.   32 pp., photographic plates.   8vo.   Paper wrappers.
   The Ruffed Grouse in Minnesota.   Grand Rapids, Minnesota, 1965,
Herald Review.   22 pp., color and black and white photographic plates.   8vo.
Paper wrappers.

Rost, Tom
   Sportoons. Harrisburg, 1952, The Stackpole Company.   Unpaginated
(64 pp.), illustrated with cartoons.   Oblong 4to. Paper wrappers.   Humorous
cartoons of hunting and angling.

Roth, Charles B.
   The Sportsman's Outdoor Guide.   Englewood Cliffs, New Jersey, 1953,
Prentice-Hall, Inc.   170 pp., illustrations.   8vo; dust jacket.

Rothhaar, Roger
   In Pursuit of Trophy Whitetails.   Indiana, 1982, Blue-J Inc.   112 pp.

Roush, Sigel
   The Swamps.   Strasburg, Virginia, 1929, Privately printed.   321 pp.
12mo.   A rare work depicting lowland hunting incidents in the mid-west.

Rowan, John J.

The Emigrant and Sportsman in Canada. Toronto, 1972, Coles. 440 pp., fold-out maps. 8vo. Paper wrappers. (A facsimile reproduction of the 1876 edition) Much on early angling and hunting in the eastern provinces.

Rowlands, John T.

Cache Lake Country; life in the North Woods. New York, 1947, W. W. Norton & Co., Inc. 272 pp., drawings by Henry B. Kane. 8vo; dust jacket. (Reprinted 1959, same publisher in a "Wilderness Edition") A wonderfully written book dealing mostly with woodcraft.

Ruark, Robert Chester   1915-1965

I Didn't Know It Was Loaded. New York, 1948, Doubleday & Co., Inc. 255 pp., drawings by R. Taylor. 8vo; dust jacket.

The Old Man and The Boy. New York, 1957, Holt, Rinehart & Winston. 303 pp., drawings by Walter Dower. 8vo; dust jacket. (Reprinted many times, same format and publisher) A series of stories about a boy growing up in North Carolina, with much hunting and angling. Most originally appeared in *Field & Stream,* when the author was an associate editor for that magazine.

The Old Man's Boy Grows Older. New York, 1961, Holt, Rinehart & Winston. 302 pp., drawings by Walter Dower. 8vo; dust jacket. (Reprinted many times, same format and publisher) A continuation and companion volume to *The Old Man and the Boy.*

Mr. Ruark was a gifted author who also wrote a syndicated newspaper column for many years. In addition to the above, he also wrote extensively about Africa, two regarding big game hunting (*Horn of the Hunter, Use Enough Gun*) and two insightful perspectives of the pre-independent cultures of several African nations (*Something of Value,* and *Uhuru*). See Foster.

Rue, Leonard Lee, III   b. 1926

Complete Guide To Game Animals; a field book of North American species. New York, 1981, D. Van Nostrand Company / Outdoor Life Books. 638 pp., photographic plates. 12mo; dust jacket. (Also a 1981 revised edition, same format and publisher)

Cottontail. New York, 1965, Thomas Y. Crowell Company. 112 pp., photographic plates, bibliography. 8vo; dust jacket.

The Deer of North America. New York, 1978, Crown Publishers, Inc. / Outdoor Life Books. 463 pp., illustrations. 8vo; dust jacket. (Reprinted several times, same format and publisher)

Furbearing Animals of North America. New York, 1981, Crown Publishers, Inc. 343 pp., illustrations. 8vo; dust jacket.

Game Birds of North America. New York, 1973, Outdoor Life Books. 490 pp., color plates by Douglas Allen, photographic plates, maps. 8vo; dust jacket. (Reprinted 1976, same format and publisher)

How I Photograph Wildlife and Nature. New York, 1984, W. W. Norton & Co., Inc. 287 pp., color and black and white photographic plates. 8vo; dust jacket. (Reprinted several times, various publishers)

Rue, Leonard Lee, III, continued

Meet the Moose. New York, 1985, Dodd Mead & Co. 78 pp., illustrations. 8vo; dust jacket.

Meet the Opossum. New York, 1983, Dodd Mead & Co. 62 pp., illustrations. 8vo; dust jacket.

Sportsman's Guide To Game Animals. New York, 1968, Outdoor Life Books. 655 pp., illustrations. 12mo; dust jacket. (Reprinted many times, same format and publisher)

The World of the Beaver. Philadelphia, 1964, J. B. Lippincott Co. 155 pp., photographic plates, bibliography. A title in the Living World series. 4to; dust jacket. (Reprinted 1964, same format and publisher)

The World of the Raccoon. Philadelphia, 1964, J. B. Lippincott Co. 145 pp., photographic plates, bibliography. A title in the Living World series. 4to; dust jacket.

The World of the Red Fox. Philadelphia, 1969, J. B. Lippincott Co. 204 pp., photographic plates, bibliography. A title in the Living World series. 4to; dust jacket.

The World of the Ruffed Grouse. Philadelphia, 1973, J. B. Lippincott Co. 204 pp., photographic plates, bibliography. A title in the Living World series. 4to; dust jacket.

The World of the White-Tailed Deer. Philadelphia, 1962, J. B. Lippincott Co. 134 pp., photographic plates. A title in the Living World series. 4to; dust jacket. (Reprinted 1962, same format and publisher)

Rue, Leonard Lee, III

Also see **Fischl, Josef**

Ruediger, George J.

German Shorthaired Pointer Activities. Minneapolis, 1953. 320 pp., illustrations. 8vo. Paper wrappers.

Ruffer, J. E. M.

The Art of Good Shooting. New York, 1972, Drake. 25 pp., photographic plates, drawings. 8vo; dust jacket.

Rule, Roger C.

The Rifleman's Rifle. Northridge, California, 1982, Alliance Books. 369 pp., photographic plates, drawings. Limited to 500 numbered copies. 4to; slipcased. A detailed work giving the history of the Winchester Model 70 rifle.

Rungius, Carl   1869-1959
See **Render, Lorne E.**
See **New York Zoological Society**
See **Schaldach, William J.,** *Carl Rungius, Big Game Painter*
See **Whyte, Jon and E. J. Hart**

Rush, William M.
Northern Yellowstone Elk Study.   Helena, 1932, Montana Fish and Game.   131 pp., photographic plates, charts, map.   8vo.   Paper wrappers.
Wild Animals of the Rockies; adventures of a forest ranger.   New York, 1942, Harper & Brothers.   296 pp., photographic plates. 8vo; dust jacket. (Reprinted 1947, Halcyon House)
Wildlife of Idaho.   Boise, 1942, Idaho Fish and Game Department.   299 pp., color and black and white illustrations.   8vo.

Russell, Andy   b. 1915
Adventures With Wild Animals.   Edmonton, Alberta, 1977, Hurtig. 183 pp., drawings by Harry Savage.   8vo; dust jacket.   (Also reprinted, 1978, Alfred A. Knopf, Inc.)
Grizzly Country.   New York, 1967, Alfred A. Knopf, Inc.   302 pp., photographic plates.   8vo; dust jacket.   (Reprinted several times, same format and publisher.   Also a 1969 British edition)
The High West. New York, 1974, Viking Press. 141 pp., photographs by Les Blacklock.   4to; dust jacket.
Horns in the High Country.   New York, 1973, Alfred A. Knopf, Inc. 259 pp., photographic plates.   8vo; dust jacket.   (Reprinted 1973, smaller format, same publisher)   Sheep and goat hunting in the Rockies.
Memoirs of a Mountain Man.   New York, 1984, The Macmillan Company.   305 pp., illustrations. 8vo; dust jacket.   (Also a 1984 Canadian edition)
Trails of a Wilderness Wanderer.   New York, 1971, Alfred A. Knopf, Inc.   298 pp., photographic plates.   8vo; dust jacket.   (Reprinted several times, same format and publisher)

Russell, Carl P.
Firearms, Traps and Tools of Mountain Men.   New York, 1967, Alfred A. Knopf, Inc.   448 pp., illustrations, bibliography.   8vo; dust jacket.
The Guns of the Early Frontiers; a history of firearms from colonial times through the years of the western fur trade.   Berkeley, 1962, University of California Press.   395 pp., illustrations, bibliography.   Paper wrappers.

Russell, Dan
Woodcock.   Frankfort, 1957, Kentucky Department of Fish and Wildlife Resources.   19 pp.   Paper wrappers.

Russell, Dan M.

The Dove Shooter's Handbook. New York, 1974, Winchester Press. 256 pp., photographic plates, bibliography. 8vo; dust jacket. (Reprinted, same format and publisher)

Russell, Franklin

The Hunting Animal. New York, 1983, Harper & Row, Publishers, Inc. 211 pp. 8vo; dust jacket. A philosophic and enlightening discussion of man and his hunting activities.

Russell, Keith C. (b. 1920), et al.

The Duck Huntingest Gentleman; a collection of waterfowling stories. Pepper Pike, Ohio, 1977, Dairypail Press. 285 pp., illustrations. Limited to 1000 numbered copies, signed by Mr. Russell. Tall 8vo;slipcased. (Also a 1980 trade edition, Winchester Press)

For Whom the Ducks Toll; a select gathering of memorable waterfowl tales. New York, 1984, Winchester Press. 292 pp., drawings by Joseph Fornelli. 8vo; dust jacket. [Also a deluxe edition, specially bound and limited to 1500 numbered copies signed by Mr. Russell]

Mr. Russell also edited and contributed to *The Fly Fishingest Gentleman* and *Sex and the Flyfisherman.* Despite his use of tongue-in-cheek titles and use of authors who are primarily sportsmen but not professional writers, these works are highly regarded anthologies.

Russell, Osborne

Journal of a Trapper (1834-1843). Lincoln, 1965, University of Nebraska Press. 191 pp. (Originally published, 1914, Syms-York Co.)

Russell, Phillips

Red Tiger; adventures in Yucatan and Mexico. New York, 1929, Brentano's Publishers. Drawings in color and black and white by Leon Underwood. 8vo. [Also a deluxe edition, limited to 250 numbered and signed copies; slipcased] Contains some jaguar hunting. Scarce.

Russell, William F.

Falconry; a handbook for hunters. New York, 1940, Charles Scribner's Sons. 180 pp., photographic plates, drawings by W. D. Sargent. 8vo; dust jacket.

Russo, John P.

The Desert Bighorn Sheep in Arizona. Phoenix, 1956. 153 pp., illustrations. 8vo. Paper wrappers. (Reprinted several times, same format)

Rutherford, W. H.

The Canada Geese of Southeastern Colorado. 1970, Colorado Division of Game and Fish. 65 pp. Paper wrappers.

Ruthven, John A. and William Zimmerman
    Top Flight: Speed Index To Waterfowl of North America. Milwaukee, 1965, Moebius.   112 pp., illustrated in color. Introduction by Erwin Bauer. Narrow 4to. Paper wrappers.   (Reprinted many times, same format, various publishers)

Rutledge, Archibald   1883-1973
    An American Hunter. New York, 1937, Frederick A. Stokes Co.   461 pp., illustrations by Lynn Bogue Hunt.   8vo; dust jacket. (Reprinted several times, same format and publisher) Stories about hunting deer, turkey and wildfowl.
    Bolio; and other dogs. New York, 1930, Frederick A. Stokes Co.   249 pp. 8vo; dust jacket. Stories about hunting dogs.
    Days Off in Dixie. New York, 1924, Doubleday, Page & Co., Inc.   298 pp., photographic plates. 8vo; dust jacket. A scarce title with much on turkey and grouse hunting.
    Fireworks in the Peafield Corner; a treasury of the best of the sage of Hampton Plantation and the first poet laureate of South Carolina.   Clinton, New Jersey, 1986, Amwell Press.   357 pp., drawings. Edited and foreword by Irvine H. Rutledge. 8vo; slipcased.   [Also a deluxe edition limited to 1000 numbered and signed copies; slipcased]
    From the Hills To the Sea; facts and legend of the Carolinas. Indianapolis, 1958, The Bobbs-Merrill Company.   201 pp. 4to; dust jacket. Mostly folklore, but some mention of hunting.
    God's Children; my Negro friends at Hampton.   Indianapolis, 1947, The Bobbs-Merrill Company.   159 pp., photographic plates. 8vo; dust jacket. [Also a "Hampton edition," with a special illustrated page signed by the author] An interesting account of Rutledge's attitude toward the black men and women in and around his Hampton Plantation. Containing accounts of turkey and deer hunting.
    Heart of the South.   Columbia, South Carolina, 1924, The State Company.   391 pp. 8vo.   A scarce Rutledge title containing some deer hunting.
    Home By the River. Indianapolis, Indiana, 1941, The Bobbs-Merrill Company.   167 pp., photographic plates. 8vo; dust jacket. (Reprinted several times, same format and publisher. Also reprinted, 1983, Sandlapper Press) [Also a few copies of the first edition were issued by the publisher with a special bound-in sheet signed by the author.   Also a "South Carolina" edition limited to 500 numbered and signed copies.] Hunting at Rutledge's Hampton Plantation in South Carolina.
    Hunter's Choice. West Hartford, Vermont, 1946, The Countryman Press. 210 pp., line drawings and color illustrations by Paul Bransom. Limited to 5000 copies. 4to; dust jacket.   [Also a deluxe first edition limited to 475 numbered copies signed by the author and the artist; slipcased]
    A Monarch of the Sky.   New York, 1926, The Purdey Press.   12 pp. 12mo. Rare.

Rutledge, Archibald, continued

    Old Plantation Days. New York, 1921, Frederick A. Stokes Co. 344 pp., illustrations. 8vo; dust jacket. (Also an edition published in Cumberland, Maryland by Eddy Press Corp. This edition has some of the stories contained in the Stokes edition, but also several others)

    Peace in the Heart. Garden City, New York, 1930, Doubleday, Doran & Co., Inc. 316 pp. 8vo; dust jacket. (Reprinted several times, same format and publisher) Containing some turkey hunting.

    Plantation Game Trails. Boston, 1921, Houghton Mifflin Company. 300 pp., illustrations. 8vo; dust jacket. (Also a British edition) A scarce and desirable Rutledge title.

    Rain on the Marsh. Columbia, 1940, Bostick & Thornley. 236 pp. 8vo; dust jacket. A collection of poetry on the outdoors, including some on hunting.

    Santee Paradise. Indianapolis, Indiana, 1956, The Bobbs-Merrill Company. 232 pp., plus a 24 pp. section of wildlife photographs. 8vo; dust jacket. (Reprinted, same format and publisher)

    Those Were the Days. Richmond, Virginia, 1955, The Dietz Press. 426 pp. 8vo; dust jacket. An anthology of the author's best hunting stories.

    Tom and I on the Old Plantation. New York, 1918, Frederick A. Stokes Co. 214 pp., illustrations. 8vo; dust jacket.

    Wild Life of the South. New York, 1935, Frederick A. Stokes Co. 253 pp., drawings by C. E. Pont. 12mo; dust jacket. (Reprinted twice, same format and publisher)

    A Wildwood Tale; a drama of the open. New York, 1950, Fleming H. Revell. 48 pp. 12mo; dust jacket. A scarce Rutledge deer hunting title.

    Willie Was A Lady. Columbia, South Carolina, 1966, Wing Publications. 123 pp., illustrations by Gerald Harvey. 8vo; dust jacket.

    The Woods and Wild Things I Remember. Columbia, South Carolina, 1970, R. L. Bryan Co. 260 pp., illustrations. 8vo.

    In addition to Rutledge's beautifully written hunting stories, he also wrote many other works of prose and poetry. He was South Carolina's *poet laureat* from 1934 until his death in 1973. Following is a list of all the author's non-sporting works:

The Angel Standing; or faith alone gives poise.	1958, Fleming H. Revell
The Ballad of the Howling Hound; and other poems.	1965, The Dietz Press
The Banners of the Coast.	1908, The State Co.
Beauty in the Heart.	1953, Fleming H. Revell
The Beauty of the Night.	1947, Fleming H. Revell
Bright Angel; and other poems.	1955, R. L. Bryan Co.
Brimming Chalice.	1936, H. Harrison.
Brimming Tide; and other poems.	1954, Fleming H. Revell
Children of Swamp and Wood.	1927, Doubleday, Page
Christ is God.	1941, Fleming H. Revell
Collected Poems.	1925, The State Co.
Deep River; the complete poems of Archibald Rutledge.	1960, R. L. Bryan Co.
The Everlasting Light and Other Poems.	1949, University of Georgia
The Flower of Hope.	1930, Fleming H. Revell
The Heart's Citadel; and other poems.	1953, The Dietz Press
I Hear America Singing.	1970, R. L. Bryan Co.

Rutledge, Archibald, continued

How Wild Was My Village.	1969, Wing Publications
It Will Be Daybreak Soon.	1938, Fleming H. Revell
Life's Extras.	1928, Fleming H. Revell
Love's Meaning.	1943, Fleming H. Revell
My Colonel and His Lady.	1937, The Bobbs-Merrill Co.
A Plantation Boyhood.	1932
Sanctuary.	1920
Songs From a Valley.	unknown
The Sonnets.	1938, Privately printed
South of Richmond.	1923
Under the Pines; and other poems.	1906, Privately printed
Veiled Eros.	1933, H. Harrison
Voices of Long Ago; Bible stories retold.	1973, R. L. Bryan Co.
When Boys go Off To School.	1935, Fleming H. Revell
The World Around Hampton.	1960, The Bobbs-Merrill Co.

Rutledge, Archibald

Also see **Rutledge, Irvine H.**
Also see **Bodie, Idella**

Rutledge, Archibald, et al.

Carolina Low Country.   New York, 1931, The Macmillan Company. 326 pp., color and black and white illustrations.   4to; dust jacket.   A selection of stories outlining life in the Low Country, including one on plantation life by Rutledge.

Rutledge, Frederick

Fair Fields of Memory. Asheville, North Carolina, 1958, Privately printed.   63 pp.   8vo.   Stories of hunting in North and South Carolina originally appearing in the *Asheville Citizen*.

Rutledge, Irvine H.

We Called Him Flintlock; a picture story of Archibald Rutledge. Columbia, South Carolina, 1974, R. L. Bryan Co..   68 pp., photographic plates.

Rutstrum, Calvin

Chips From a Wilderness Log. New York, 1978, Stein and Day, Publishers. 243 pp., illustrations. 8vo; dust jacket.

The New Way of the Wilderness. New York, 1958, The Macmillan Company.   276 pp., drawings by Les Kouba. 8vo; dust jacket. (Reprinted 1960, same format and publisher)   Incidental hunting, mostly camping lore and woodcraft.

Once Upon a Wilderness.   New York, 1973, The Macmillan Company. 181 pp., photographic plates.   8vo; dust jacket.   Mostly wilderness lore.

The Wilderness Cabin. New York, 1961, The Macmillan Company. 169 pp., drawings by Les Kouba.   8vo; dust jacket.   (Reprinted 1970, same format and publisher)

Rutter, Russell and Douglas Pimlott

The World of the Wolf. Philadelphia, 1968, J. B. Lippincott Co. 202 pp., photographic plates, diagrams. A title in Lippincott's Living World series. 4to; dust jacket.

Ruxton, George

See **Porter, Clyde and Mae Reed**

Ryan, Clendenin J.

The Entire Library of the Late Clendenin J. Ryan. New York, 1940, Parke-Bernet Galleries, Inc. 46 pp. 8vo. Paper wrappers. An auction catalog containing many sporting books, including a complete run of *The American Turf Register.*

Ryan, Pat

Deer Hunting; current evidence and advanced techniques. New York, 1982, Privately printed. 52 pp. Paper wrappers.

Ryden, Hope

Bobcat Year. New York, 1981, Viking Press. 211 pp., photographic plates. 8vo; dust jacket. A fictional account based on actual observation, of the life of a bobcat.

God's Dog. New York, 1975, Coward, McCann and Geoghegan, Inc. 288 pp., color and black and white photographic plates. 8vo; dust jacket. A study of the coyote.

The Little Deer of the Florida Keys. New York, 1978, G. P. Putnam's Sons. 62 pp., illustrations. An anti-hunting juvenile.

Ryman, D. P.

Better Bowhunting. Ohio, 1982, SBHA, Inc. 72 pp. Paper wrappers.

Rywell, Martin   1905-1971

American Antique Guns and Their Current Prices, 1950-51. Harriman, Tennessee, 1951, Pioneer Press. 95 pp., photographic plates. 8vo. Paper wrappers. (Also several other yearly editions to 1959, same format and publisher)

American Antique Rifles and Their Current Prices, 1956-57. Harriman, Tennessee, 1957, Pioneer Press. 72 pp., photographic plates. 8vo. Paper wrappers. (Also a 1960-61 edition)

Colt Guns. Harriman, Tennessee, 1953, Pioneer Press. 134 pp., illustrations, ads. 8vo. Paper wrappers. (Also a 1957 edition, same format and publisher)

Samuel Colt; a man and an epoch. Harriman, Tennessee, 1952, Pioneer Press. 200 pp., illustrations. 8vo. (Also a 1955 second edition, same format and publisher)

Rywell, Martin, continued

Confederate Guns and Their Prices. Harriman, Tennessee, 1952, Pioneer Press. 54 pp., illustrations. 8vo.

Fell's Collector Guide to American Antique Firearms. New York, 1963, Frederick Fell. 215 pp., illustrations. 8vo.

Gun Collector's Guide. Harriman, Tennessee, 1954, Pioneer Press. 128 pp., illustrations. 8vo. Paper wrappers. (Reprinted and revised several times, same format and publisher)

The Gun That Shaped American Destiny. Harriman, Tennessee, 1957, Pioneer Press. 156 pp., illustrations. 8vo.

The Powder Flask; the complete guide for the collector of the principle accessory to the firearm. Harriman, Tennessee, 1959, Pioneer Press. 81 pp., illustrations. 8vo.

The Sharps Rifle; the gun that shaped American destiny. Harriman, Tennessee, 1957, Pioneer Press. 156 pp., illustrations. 8vo. Paper wrappers.

Smith & Wesson; the story of the revolver. Harriman, Tennessee, 1953, Pioneer Press. 136 pp., photographic plates. 8vo.

The Trial of Samuel Colt. Harriman, Tennessee, 1953, Pioneer Press. 327 pp. Limited to 1000 numbered copies. 8vo; dust jacket. A detailed account of a case tried in 1851, that has much information on the history and development of Colt's firearms.

U. S. Military Muskets, Rifles Carbines and Their Current Prices. Harriman, Tennessee, 1951, Pioneer Press. 47 pp., photographic plates. 8vo. Paper wrappers. (Also a 1957 and a 1959 edition, same format and publisher)

Safari Club International

The Safari Club International Record Book of Trophy Animals; a book of Safari Club International Awards Program containing tabulations of outstanding big game trophies in Africa, Asia, Europe, North and South America, Australia and New Zealand. Tucson, Arizona, 1978, Safari Club International. 217 pp., photographic plates. Limited to 1000 numbered copies. 4to. (At least four editions following; 1980, 1981, 1982, and 1984, same format and publisher)

Salisbury, Howard M.

Duck Guns, Shooting and Decoying. Chicago, 1947, Paul, Richmond & Company. 168 pp., illustrations. 18mo; dust jacket. (Reprinted 1957, same format and publisher)

Salley, A. S., Jr.

The Happy Hunting Ground; personal experiences in the Low Country of South Carolina. Columbia, South Carolina, 1926, Privately printed by The State Company. 83 pp., photographic plates. 8vo; dust jacket. Deer, turkey and wildcat hunting. Rare.

Salter, Ben

Portsmouth Island, Shore Stories and History. No place, 1972, Privately printed. 62 pp., illustrations. 8vo. Paper wrappers. A description of the hunting and fishing on the island.

Samson, John G. "Jack"   **b. 1922**

Falconry Today. New York, 1976, Walck. 112 pp., illustrations, bibliography. 4to; dust jacket.

Modern Falconry; your illustrated guide to the art and sport of hunting with North American hawks. Harrisburg, 1984, Stackpole Books. 160 pp., photographic plates. 8vo. Paper wrappers.

The Sportsman's World. New York, 1976, Holt, Rinehart & Winston. 252 pp., color and black and white photographic plates. 4to; dust jacket. A general discussion of hunting and angling for various species around the world.

Samson, John G. "Jack," editor

The Bear Book. Clinton, New Jersey, 1979, Amwell Press. 250 pp., drawings by Al Barker. Limited to 1000 numbered and signed copies. 8vo; slipcased. (Also a 1982 trade edition, titled *Man and Bear;* adventures in the wild; issued with the editor's *The Grizzly Book* as a set, same publisher; dust jackets) An anthology of stories written by Roosevelt, Annabel, Keith, O'Connor and others.

Samson, John G. "Jack," editor, continued
   The Grizzly Book. Clinton, New Jersey, 1981, Amwell Press. 304 pp., color and black and white illustrations by Al Barker. Foreword by Gene Hill. Limited to 1000 numbered and signed copies. 8vo; slipcased. (Also a 1982 trade edition, issued with the editor's *The Bear Book* as a set, same publisher. Also a 1982 trade edition, Outdoor Life Book Club)
   Hunting the Southwest. Clinton, New Jersey, 1985, Amwell Press. 172 pp., drawings by Victoria Blanchard. Limited to 1000 numbered and signed copies. 8vo; slipcased. (Also a 1985 trade edition, same content and publisher; slipcased)

Samson, John G. "Jack", editor
   The Worlds of Ernest Thompson Seton. New York, 1976, Alfred A. Knopf, Inc. 204 pp., color and black and white illustrations by Seton. Oblong 4to; dust jacket.

Sandberg, Walt
   The Turn in the Trail; Northwoods tales of the upper Great Lakes. Clinton, New Jersey, 1980, Amwell Press. 215 pp., drawings by Gordon Allen. Limited to 1000 numbered and signed copies. 8vo; slipcased.

Sanderson, Glen C., editor
   Management of Migratory Shore and Upland Game Birds in North America. Washington, D. C., 1977, International Association of Fish and Wildlife. 358 pp., photographic plates, maps, diagrams. 8vo; dust jacket. (Also a 1980 edition in paper wrappers)

Sanderson, Glen C. and Helen C. Schultz
   Wild Turkey Management; current problems and programs. Columbia, 1973, University of Missouri Press. 355 pp., photographic plates, maps, bibliography. Tall 8vo; dust jacket. An important work.

Sanderson, Ivan
   Animal Tales; an anthology of animal literature of all countries.. New York, 1946, Alfred A. Knopf, Inc. 511 pp., two color illustrations by the author. Thick 8vo; dust jacket.

Sanderson, Wilford E.
   Trapping With Havahart Traps. New York, 1965. Revised edition. 48 pp., illustrations. 8vo. Paper wrappers.

Sandler, Martin

As New England Played. Chester, Connecticut, 1979, Globe Pequot Press. 96 pp., many illustrations. 4to. Paper wrappers. A description of turn-of-the-century outdoor pastimes, including some hunting and fishing.

Sandoz, Mari

The Buffalo Hunters; the story of the hide men. New York, 1954, Hastings House. 372 pp., illustrations. 8vo; dust jacket. (Reprinted, same format and publisher)

Sands, Ledyard   b. 1887

The Bird, the Gun and the Dog. New York, 1939, Carlyle House. 494 pp., illustrations in color and duotone from paintings by Courtenay Brandreth. 4to; dust jacket. [Also a deluxe edition, specially bound with an original signed etching by Anthony La Paglie and limited to 100 numbered copies, signed by the author]

Sands, Oliver Jackson

A Story of Sport and The Deep Run Hunt Club. Richmond, Virginia, 1977, Privately printed. 235 pp., color and black and white illustrations. Limited to 750 numbered and signed copies. 8vo. A history of this Virginia foxhunting club.

Satterlee, Leroy De Forest, editor   b. 1891

A Catalog of Firearms For the Collector. Detroit, 1927, Privately printed by the author. 242 pp., photographic plates. 8vo. Limited to 500 copies. (Also a 1939 second edition, published for the subscribers and limited to 200 copies)

Ten Old Gun Catalogs For the Collector. Detroit, 1940, Printed for the subscribers. Unpaginated, a facsimile reproduction. Limited to 100 copies. Tall 8vo. (Revised and reprinted several times, various publishers)

Fourteen Old Gun Catalogs. Detroit, 1941, Printed for the subscribers Unpaginated, a facsimile reproduction. Tall 8vo. (Revised and reprinted several times, various publishers)

Satterlee, Leroy De Forest

Also see **Gluckman, Col. Arcadi**

Sawyer, Charles Winthrop   1868-1943

Firearms in American History: Volume II, The Revolver. San Leandro, California, 1939, Privately printed. 219 pp., photographic plates. Limited to 1000 numbered copies. 8vo. (Originally published, 1911. A Volume I was titled *Firearms in American History*, published in 1910 and a Volume III was titled *Our Rifles*, published in 1920) See Riling.

Sawyer, Charles Winthrop, continued

Our Rifles. Boston, 1941, Williams Bookstore. 412 pp., illustrations. 8vo. (Also reprinted, 1944, 1946, same format and contents. Originally published, 1920, Cornhill) See Riling.

Scammell, Robert

The Outside Story. Edmonton, Alberta, 1982, Reidmore. 206 pp., drawings by Jack Cowin. 8vo; dust jacket. (Reprinted 1982, Toronto, Fleet Press) Stories of angling and hunting.

Schaldach, William J.   1896-1982

Coverts and Casts; field sports and angling in words and pictures. West Hartford, Vermont, 1943, The Countryman Press. 138 pp., black and white and color illustrations by the author. 4to; dust jacket. (Reprinted 1946, same format and publisher) [Also a deluxe first edition, specially bound and limited to 160 numbered copies signed by the author; dust jacket; slipcased]

Currents and Eddys; chips from the log of an angler-artist. West Hartford, Vermont, 1944, The Countryman Press. 138 pp., black and white and color illustrations by the author. Limited to 5000 copies. 4to; dust jacket. [Also a deluxe edition, specially bound and limited to 250 numbered copies, signed by the author; dust jacket; slipcased] (Both *Coverts and Casts* and *Currents and Eddys* were reprinted in 1970 by Freshet Press and issued as a slipcased set)

Fish by Schaldach; collected etchings, drawings, and water colors of trout, salmon and other game fish. Philadelphia, 1937, J. B. Lippincott Co.. Unpaginated (approx. 150 pp.), color and black and white plates. Limited to 1560 numbered copies. Folio; boxed. [Also a deluxe edition, specially bound and illustrated and limited to 157 numbered and signed copies; boxed]

Fisherman's Fancy; a portfolio of fresh-water favorites. No place, 1950, Harrison & Smith. Unpaginated (16 pp.), 6 black and white drawings plus text. 8vo. Paper wrappers. A scarce Schaldach item.

Path To Enchantment; an artist in the Sonoran desert. New York, 1963, The Macmillan Company. 225 pp., drawings by the author. 4to; dust jacket.

Carl Rungius, Big Game Painter. West Hartford, Vermont, 1945, The Countryman Press. 117 pp., illustrations in black and white and in color by Rungius. Limited to 1275 numbered copies. 4to; slipcased. [Also a deluxe edition of 160 numbered copies, specially bound with a signed Rungius etching as a frontispiece and also signed by Schaldach and Rungius; slipcased]

Upland Gunning; collected etchings, drawings and watercolors of the sport. West Hartford, Vermont, 1946, The Countryman Press. Unpaginated, illustrations in black and white and in color by the author. 4to; dust jacket. [Also a deluxe edition, specially bound with a signed Schaldach etching as a frontispiece and limited to 160 numbered copies signed by the author; slipcased]

Schaldach, William J., continued
  The Wind on Your Cheek; or more chips from the log of an artist sportsman. Rockville Center, New York, 1972, Freshet Press. 159 pp., color and black and white illustrations by the author. 4to; dust jacket. [Also a deluxe edition, specially bound with a signed Schaldach etching as a frontispiece and limited to 200 copies; slipcased]
   Mr. Schaldach's literary and book design abilities were considerable. He was one of the most popular wildlife illustrators of the mid-twentieth century; all of his published works are listed here. In addition to writing and illustrating these works, many of his paintings graced the covers of periodicals like *Sports Afield.* His illustrations were also commissioned for many other sporting books written by Claflin, Connett, Arms and others.

Schaldach, William J.
  Also see **Ordeman, John T.**

Scharff, Robert
  The Collier Quick and Easy Guide To Hunting. New York, 1963, Collier Books. 157 pp., drawings. 4to. Paper wrappers.
  Complete Duck Shooter's Handbook. New York, 1957, G. P. Putnam's Sons. 250 pp., illustrations. 8vo; dust jacket.

Scharnberg, James Fagin
  Beagling and Basseting; a primer for the filed, with a roster of the packs of the United States and Canada. Richmond, 1973, Old Dominion. 104 pp., photographic plates, drawings. 8vo. Paper wrappers.

Schaul, H. Edwin
  The Golden Retriever. No place, 1954, Springs Press. 119 pp., photographic plates. 8vo; dust jacket.

Scheffer, Victor B.
  A Voice For Wildlife. New York, 1974, Charles Scribner's Sons. 245 pp., illustrations, bibliography. 8vo; dust jacket.

Scheid, Dan W.
  Raising Game Birds. Ft. Atkinson, Wisconsin, 1970, Highsmith. 111 pp., illustrations. 8vo. Paper wrappers.

Schemnitz, Sanford D., editor
  Wildlife Management Techniques Manual; Fourth Edition, Revised. Washington, D. C., 1980, The Wildlife Society. 686 pp., photographic plates, drawings, bibliography. 4to. A textbook with a large and useful bibliography.

Scherman, Kathrine
   Spring On an Arctic Island.   Boston, 1956, Little, Brown & Company.
331 pp., photographic plates.   8vo; dust jacket.   Seal hunting with Eskimos.

Schick, Alice
   The Peregrine Falcons.   New York, 1975, Dial Press.   83 pp., drawings
by Peter Parnell.   8vo; dust jacket.   (Reprinted 1976, same format and publisher)

Schilbred, Maj. Corn.
   Irish Setter History; translated from *Pointer of Setter* (Oslo, 1927) by
William G. Thompson and Olav Wallo.   Silver Spring, Maryland, 1949,
Denlinger's.   44 pp., illustrations.

Schlegelmilch, Charles W.
   Memories of a Hunter.   Lancaster, Pennsylvania, 1967, Privately
printed.   189 pp., photographic plates.   8vo.   Big game hunting in North America,
India and Africa.

Schley, Frank
   American Partridge and Pheasant Shooting. New York, 1967,
Abercrombie & Fitch, Inc. 220 pp., plates from old engravings. 8vo; dust jacket.
(A facsimile reproduction of the 1877 first edition)

Schmidt, J. L. and Douglas L. Gilbert
   Big Game of North America; ecology and management.   Harrisburg /
Washington D. C., 1980, Stackpole Books / Wildlife Management Institute.   494
pp., color and black and white illustrations.   Thick 8vo; ; dust jacket.

Schmitt, Victoria Sandwick
   Four Centuries of Sporting Art; selections from the John L. Wehle
collection.   Mumford, 1984, Genesee Country Museum.   165 pp., color and
black and white illustrations, biographies of the artists.   Oblong 4to.   Paper
wrappers.   Containing British and European artists as well as American.

Schneider, Bill
   Where the Grizzly Walks.   Missoula, Montana, 1977, Mountain Press.
191 pp., photographic plates, maps, bibliography.   8vo; dust jacket.   A discussion of
grizzly bear habitat needs compared to population pressures and government policies that are
contrary to these needs.

Schneider, Norris F.   b. 1898
   Zane Grey; the man whose books made the West famous.   Zanesville,
Ohio, 1967, Privately printed.   32 pp., photographic plates.   8vo.   Paper
wrappers.   A scarce biography of Grey with a good bibliography of his works.

Schoenfeld, Clay   b. 1918

Canada Goose Management; current continental problems and programs. Madison, Wisconsin, 1966, Dembar Education Research Services. 195 pp., illustrations. 4to.

Down Wisconsin Sideroads. Wisconsin, 1979, Tamarack Press.   201 pp. 8vo.

Wisconsin Sideroads To Somewhere.   Madison, Wisconsin, 1966, Dembar Education Research Services.   246 pp.   8vo.   Both of these works are essays on Wisconsin's outdoors with some hunting.

Schoonmaker, W. J.

The World of the Grizzly Bear. Philadelphia, 1968, J. B. Lippincott Co. 190 pp., photographic plates, bibliography.   A title in Lippincott's Living World series.   4to; dust jacket. (Reprinted several times, same format and publisher)

The World of the Woodchuck. Philadelphia, 1966, J. B. Lippincott Co. 146 pp., photographic plates.   A title in Lippincott's Living World series.   4to; dust jacket.

Schorger, A. W.   1884-1972

The Passenger Pigeon; its natural history and extinction. Madison, 1955, University of Wisconsin.   424 pp., frontispiece in color, photographic plates, bibliography. 8vo; dust jacket. (Reprinted 1973, University of Oklahoma)

The Wild Turkey; its history and domestication. Norman,   1966, University of Oklahoma Press.   625 pp., plates, color frontispiece.   8vo; dust jacket.   An authoritative work containing an excellent 114 pp. bibliography.

Schroeder, Joseph, editor

Rare Selections From Old Gun Catalogs, 1880 - 1920.   Northfield, Illinois, 1977, DBI Books. 96 pp., illustrations.   8vo.   Paper wrappers.   Including manufacturer's illustrations from the catalogs of Remington, Ithaca, Winchester, Fisher and others.

Schroeder, Roger

How to Carve Waterfowl; 9 North American masters reveal the carving and painting techniques that win them international blue ribbons.   Harrsiburg, 1984, Stackpole Books.   255 pp., color and black and white illustrations.   4to; dust jacket.

Schroeder, Roger and James D. Sprankle

Waterfowl Carving With J. D. Sprankle; the fully illustrated reference to carving and painting 25 decorative ducks.   Harrsiburg, 1985, Stackpole Books. 224 pp., color and black and white illustrations.   4to; dust jacket.

Schubert, Ray

Hunting - Fishing - Trapping; a collection of interesting facts, methods and tricks used by the Indians of the Americas for taking wild game from field and wood. Rhinecliff, No date, Privately printed. Unpaginated (approx. 30 pp.). 4to. Paper wrappers.

Schueren, Arnold C.

Foxy's Lion Tales. Chicago, 1943, Privately printed. 158 pp., photographic plates. Limited to 990 numbered copies. 8vo; dust jacket. Hunting mountain lion, mostly in Utah.

Schuh, Dwight

Bowhunting For Mule Deer. Stevensville, Montana, 1985, Stonydale Press. 175 pp., photographic plates. 8vo; dust jacket.

Bugling For Elk; a complete guide for early-season elk hunting. Stevensville, Montana,, 1983, Stonydale Press. 162 pp., photographic plates. 8vo; dust jacket. (Also produced in paper wrappers)

Hunting Open Country Mule Deer; a guide to taking Western bucks with rifle and bow. 1985, Sage Books. 179 pp., photographic plates. 8vo.

Schullery, Paul   b. 1948

The Bears of Yellowstone. Yellowstone Library and Museum Association, 1980, Yellowstone National Park. 176 pp., color and black and white illustrations. 8vo. Paper wrappers.

Mountain Time. New York, 1984, Nick Lyons Books. 221 pp., map. 8vo; dust jacket. A perspective of Yellowstone National Park.

Schullery, Paul, editor

Old Yellowstone Days. Boulder, Colorado, 1979, Colorado Association. 250 pp., illustrations. 8vo. A collection of stories by Remington, Roosevelt, Muir and others recounting their experiences in the region and its game.

Schullery, Paul, editor

Also see **Roosevelt, Theodore**, *American Bears*

Schult, M. J. and A. O. Haugen

Where Buffalo Roam. South Dakota, 1979, Badlands Natural History Association. 30 pp., drawings. 8vo. Paper wrappers.

Schultz, Roy A., editor

A Portrait of Sheep and Sheep Hunting. St. Paul, 1980, Foundation For North American Wild Sheep. 167 pp., black and white illustrations. 4to; dust jacket. Intended for both the promotion of the sport and for its game management.

Schuyler, Keith C.   b. 1919

Archery; from golds to big game.   Cranberry, New Jersey, 1970, A. S. Barnes and Company, Inc.   569 pp., photographic plates.   8vo; dust jacket. (Also printed, 1970, Castle)

Bow Hunting For Big Game.   Harrisburg, 1974, The Stackpole Company.   224 pp., photographic plates.   8vo; dust jacket.

Schwartz, Charles W.

The Prairie Chicken in Missouri.   No place, 1944, Missouri State Conservation Department.   Unpaginated (178 pp.), color and black and white illustrations.   Folio; dust jacket.

Schwartz, Elizabeth and Charles W. Schwartz

Bobwhite; from egg to chick to egg.   New York, 1959, Holiday House. 48 pp., illustrations by the author.   8vo.   A juvenile.

Schwarzkopf, Chet

Fur, Fin and Feather.   New York, 1954, Thomas Y. Crowell Co.   149 pp., illustrations by Dimitri Alexandroff.   8vo; dust jacket. Anthropomorphic stories of several species of animals found in the giant redwood country of California.

Heart of the Wild.   Garden City, New York, 1962, Doubleday & Co., Inc.   234 pp., illustrations by Wayne Trimm.   8vo; dust jacket.   More animal stories of the redwood forest.

Schwerdt, C. F. G. R.   1862-1939

Hunting, Hawking, Shooting; illustrated in a catalog of books, manuscripts, prints, drawings.   London, 1928-1937, Privately printed for the author by Waterlow & Sons, Ltd.   Four volumes.   Volume I, 325 pp., 1928. Volume II, 359 pp., 1928.   Volume III, 257 pp., 1928.   Volume IV, 261 pp., 1937.   Each lavishly illustrated in color and black and white.   Limited to 300 numbered and signed sets.   Folio. (Reprinted 1985, The Netherlands, same format but with all plates in black and white)   Mr. Schwerdt amassed an impressive sporting book library and had this bibliographic reference prepared from it.   It records works published in all languages with some regarding North American game animals and foxhunting. It is especially useful for early hawking titles. A scarce, beautiful and important work.

Scott, Jack Denton

All Outdoors.   Harrisburg, 1956, The Stackpole Company.   268 pp., illustrations.   8vo; dust jacket.

Scott, Jack Denton, continued

Speaking Wildly.   New York, 1966, William Morrow & Co., Inc.   289 pp.   8vo; dust jacket.   Animal observations of various land and sea animals.

Scott, Jack Denton and Ozzie Sweet

Moose. New York, 1981, G. P. Putnam's Sons. 64 pp., illustrations. 4to; dust jacket. A juvenile.

Scott, Martha B.

The Artist and the Sportsman. New York, 1968, Renaissance. 95 pp., color and black and white illustrations. 4to; dust jacket. Containing illustrations of shooting, angling, cockfighting, racing, etc., with brief biographies of the artists.

Scott, Sir Peter Markham   1909-1989

A Coloured Key To the Wildfowl of the World. London, 1957, Wildfowl Trust. 71 pp., illustrations by the author. 8vo. Paper wrappers. (Reprinted and revised many times, various dates and publishers)

A Field & Stream Portfolio. New York, 1953, Field & Stream. A portfolio of six paintings of waterfowl by Scott. Introduction and text by Robert Ruark. Oblong Folio. Paper wrappers. Scarce.

The Eye of the Wind; an autobiography. Boston, 1961, Houghton Mifflin Company. 679 pp., color and black and white illustrations. 8vo; dust jacket. (Simultaneously published, London, Hodder & Stoughton, Ltd.; also reprinted by them several times)

Morning Flight; a book of wildfowl. London / New York, 1935, Country Life Press / Charles Scribner's Sons. 138 pp., illustrations from the author's paintings. Limited to 750 numbered and signed copies. 4to; dust jacket. (Also a 1936 trade edition. This edition reprinted several times, same format and publisher)

Observations of Wildlife. Ithaca, New York, 1980, Cornell University Press. 112 pp., color and black and white illustrations. 4to; dust jacket. [Also a deluxe edition published in Great Britain, specially bound and limited to 200 numbered and signed copies; slipcased] Mostly wildfowl.

The Swans. London, 1972, Michael Joseph, Ltd. 242 pp., color and black and white illustrations by the author, bibliography. 4to; dust jacket. (Also printed, 1972, Houghton Mifflin Company, on British sheets)

Wild Geese and Eskimos; a journal of the Perry River expedition of 1949. London / New York, 1951, Country Life Press / Charles Scribner's Sons. 254 pp., color and black and white illustrations. 8vo; dust jacket. An account of Scott's expedition to the Canadian Arctic and his study of the Ross Goose.

Wild Chorus. London, 1938, Country Life Press. 122 pp., color and black and white illustrations by the author. Limited to 1250 numbered and signed copies. 4to; dust jacket; slipcased. (Also a 1939 trade edition. This edition reprinted several times, same format and publisher)

Scott, Sir Peter Markham and James Fisher

A Thousand Geese. Boston, 1954, Houghton Mifflin Company. 240 pp., color frontispiece by Scott, photographic plates. 8vo; dust jacket. (Printed from British sheets. Simultaneously published in London, Collins) Banding Pink Footed Geese in Iceland.

Most of Scott's books were co-published in the U. S. He also wrote *The Battle of the Narrow Seas;* a history of the light coastal forces in the channel and North Seas, 1939-1945, and *Animals of Africa.*

Scott, Sir Peter Markham

Also see **Delacour, Jean**

Scott, Thomas G.

Bobwhite Thesaurus. Edgefield, South Carolina, 1985, International Quail Foundation. 306 pp., color frontispiece by Bob Carey. 8vo; dust jacket. An extensive bibliography of titles relating to this game bird.

Scott, Walter E., editor

Silent Wings; a memorial to the passenger pigeon. Madison, 1947, Wisconsin Society For Ornithology. 42 pp., color and black and white illustrations. 8vo. Paper wrappers. A scarce passenger pigeon item with articles by Leopold, Jackson and others.

Scoville, Samuel

Wild Honey. Boston, 1929, Little, Brown & Company. 203 pp., illustrations from plates by Emerson Tuttle. 8vo. Essays on various wild creatures, including owls and peregrine falcons.

Seagears, Clayton B.

The Fox in New York; an educational bulletin. Albany, 1945, New York State Conservation. 85 pp., photographic plates, drawings by the author. 8vo. Paper wrappers.

Sears, George Washington

See **Nessmuk**

Seavey, Elizabeth and James Seavey

Lord and Lady Baranof. Eugene, Oregon, 1947, Privately printed. Unpaginated (17 pp.). 8vo. Includes a description of a grizzly bear hunt and the capture of two grizzly cubs, while the authors were on a cruise to Alaska.

Sedlack, Pat

The School-Boy Trapper; the standard guide for young, sub-teen and teenage trappers. Belle Vernon, 1967, Privately printed. 164 pp., photographic plates, drawings. 8vo. Paper wrappers.

Seegmiller, Rick F. and Robert D. Ohmart

Ecological Relationships of Feral Burros and Desert Bighorn Sheep. Washington, D. C., 1981, The Wildlife Society. 58 pp., photographic plates, bibliography. 8vo. Paper wrappers. The effects of grazing by burros on big horn sheep.

Seibert, J. Donald, et al.

Nesting Ecology of Golden Eagles in Elko County, Nevada. Denver, 1976, United States Department of the Interior, Bureau of Land Management. 17 pp., photographic plates, bibliography. 4to. Paper wrappers.

Seiger, H. F. and F. von Dewitz-Colpin

The Complete German Short-Haired Pointer. Silver Spring, Maryland, 1950, Denlinger's. 304 pp., illustrations. 8vo. (Also a 1951 revised and expanded edition, same format and publisher) [Also a deluxe revised and expanded edition, specially bound and limited to 100 numbered and signed copies]

Seigne, J. W. and E. C. Keith

Woodcock and Snipe. New York, 1936, Charles Scribner's Sons. 254 pp., photographic plates. 12mo; dust jacket. A British work co-published in the U. S. that includes natural history as well as hunting. Scarce.

Sell, DeWitt

Collector's Guide To American Cartridge Handguns. Harrisburg, 1963, The Stackpole Company. 244 pp., photographic plates, bibliography. 8vo; dust jacket.

Sell, Francis E.   b. 1902

Advanced Hunting On Deer and Elk Trails. Harrisburg, 1954, The Stackpole Company. 156 pp., photographic plates. 8vo; dust jacket.

The American Deer Hunter. Harrisburg, 1950, Stackpole and Heck, Inc. 174 pp., illustrations. Edited by Ellis Christian Lenz. 8vo; dust jacket. (Reprinted, year unknown, same format, with a slightly different colored cloth binding and different dust jacket, same publisher) A very thorough treatment of deer hunting.

The American Shotgunner. Harrisburg, 1962, The Stackpole Company. 301 pp., photographic plates. 8vo; dust jacket.

The Deer Hunter's Guide. Harrisburg, 1964, The Stackpole Company. 192 pp., photographic plates. 8vo; dust jacket. (Reprinted several times, various publishers, some with the title *Art of Successful Deer Hunting*)

Hunting With Camera and Binoculars. New York, 1961, Chilton Book Company. 128 pp., photographic plates. 8vo; dust jacket.

Sell, Francis E., continued

Small Game Hunting. Harrisburg, 1955, The Stackpole Company. 158 pp., photographic plates. 8vo; dust jacket. (Reprinted 1957, same format and publisher)

Sure-Hit Shotgun Ways. Harrisburg, 1967, The Stackpole Company. 160 pp., illustrations. 8vo; dust jacket.

Mr. Sell's books were widely distributed, and his *American Deer Hunter* remains one of the best deer hunting books produced this century. He also wrote several angling titles. See Bruns.

Seminatore, Mike

Your Bird Dog and You. New York, 1977, A. S. Barnes and Company, Inc. 160 pp., photographic plates. 8vo; dust jacket.

Serven, James Edsall   b. 1899

The Collecting of Guns. Harrisburg, 1964, The Stackpole Company. 272 pp., illustrations. 4to; dust jacket. (Reprinted, Bonanza)

Colt Dragoon Pistols; a saga of the six-shooter, and the trails it blazed. Dallas, Texas, 1946, Carl Metzger. 56 pp., illustrations from photographs and drawings. 4to. Paper wrappers.

Colt Firearms; from 1836. Santa Anna, California, 1960, Privately printed. 394 pp., photographic plates, drawings. 4to. (Reprinted may times, various publishers)

Colt Firearms, 1836 - 1954. Santa Anna, California, 1954, Privately printed. 385 pp., photographic plates, drawings. Limited to 100 numbered and signed copies. Folio; slipcased.

Colt Percussion Pistols; a pictorial review of model variations, facts about their manufacture and use. Dallas, Texas, 1947, Carl Metzger. 59 pp., illustrations from photographs and drawings. 4to. Paper wrappers.

Coltiana. Dallas, Texas, 1946, 1947 Carl Metzger. This work contained *Colt Firearms;* from 1836, *Colt Firearms, 1836 - 1954* and *Colt Percussion Pistols*; a pictorial review of model variations, facts about their manufacture and use; bound together in blue cloth in an edition of less than 200 copies. 4to.

Conquering the Frontiers; stories of American pioneers and the guns which helped them establish a new life. LaHabre, California, 1974, Foundation Press. 256 pp., photographic plates, drawings, color illustrations. 4to; dust jacket.

Guns of the World; the complete collector's guide. Los Angeles, 1972, Peterson Publishing Company. 400 pp., illustrations. 4to. Paper wrappers.

Paterson Pistols; first of the famous repeating firearms patented and promoted by Samuel Colt. Dallas, Texas, 1946, Carl Metzger. 31 pp., illustrations from photographs and drawings. 4to. Paper wrappers.

The Rare and Valuable Antique Arms. St. Paul, Minnesota, 1976, Pioneer Press. 106 pp., illustrations. 8vo.

Serven, James Edsall, continued

200 Years of American Firearms. Chicago, 1975, Follett Publishing Co. 224 pp., photographic plates. 4to. Paper wrappers.

Serven, James Edsall and James B. Trefethen

Americans and Their Guns; the story of the National Rifle Association. Harrsiburg, 1967, Stackpole Books. 320 pp., illustrations. 4to; dust jacket.

Seth, J. B. and M. S. Seth

Recollections of a Long Life on the Eastern Shore. Easton, Maryland, 1926, Star-Democrat. 82 pp., photographic plates. 8vo. Some wildfowl hunting and foxhunting in a scarce title.

Seton, Ernest Thompson   1860-1946

Animal Tracks and Hunter Signs. New York, 1958, Doubleday & Co., Inc. 160 pp., drawings by the author. 8vo; dust jacket. (Also a 1959 British edition)

The Arctic Prairies; a canoe-journey of 2000 miles in search of the caribou. New York, 1943, International University Press. 308 pp. Illustrations. 8vo; dust jacket. (Also reprinted, 1981, in paper wrappers, Harper & Row, Publishers, Inc. Originally published, 1911, Charles Scribner's Sons)

Art Anatomy of Animals. Philadelphia, 1977. 96 pp., illustrations. Folio. Paper wrappers. (A facsimile reproduction of the 1896 first edition)

The Biography of an Arctic Fox. New York, 1937, D. Appleton-Century Company. 126 pp., illustrations. 8vo; dust jacket.

Great Historic Animals; mainly about wolves. New York, 1937, Charles Scribner's Sons. 319 pp., illustrations. 8vo; dust jacket. A scarce Seton title.

THE LIBRARY OF PIONEERING AND WOODCRAFT. Six volumes, *Rolf in the Woods, Wild Animal Ways, Two Little Savages, Book of Woodcraft, Woodland Tales,* and *Wild Animals at Home.* New York, 1926, Doubleday, Page & Co. With 436 pp., 243 pp., 552 pp., 590 pp., 235 pp., and 229 pp. respectively, all illustrated by the author. 8vo; dust jackets. (This set published several times. All titles were previously published)

Life Histories of Northern Animals; an account of the mammals of Manitoba. New York, 1974, Arno Press. 560 pp., illustrations by the author. 8vo; cloth. (A reproduction of the 1909 first edition)

Lives of Game Animals; an account of those land animals in America, north of the Mexican border, which are considered "game," either because they have held the attentions of sportsmen or received the protection of the law. Garden city, New York, 1925, 1926, 1927, 1928, Doubleday, Page & Co., Inc. Four volumes with a total of 3115 pp., many illustrations by the author, maps, bibliography. 4to; dust jackets. (Also reprinted, 1929, in eight volumes, same publisher) [Also a deluxe first edition, specially bound and limited to 177 numbered and signed sets]

Seton, Ernest Thompson, continued

Ernest Thompson Seton's America; selections from the writings of the artist-naturalist. New York, 1954, The Devin-Adair Company. Edited and with an introduction by Farida A. Wiley. 412 pp., photographic frontispiece of Seton, drawings by Seton. 8vo; dust jacket.

Ernest Thompson Seton's Trail and Campfire Stories. New York, 1940, D. Appleton-Century Company. 156 pp., illustrations. 12mo; dust jacket. (Reprinted 1968, Seton Village Press)

Trail of an Artist Naturalist; the autobiography of Ernest Thompson Seton. New York, 1940, Charles Scribner's Sons. 320 pp., photographic frontispiece, other drawings by the author. 8vo; dust jacket. (Reprinted 1948, same format and publisher. Also a 1951 British edition)

Ernest Thompson Seton was a British-born naturalist who had most of his works published between 1890 and 1920. In addition to the titles listed above, many of his pre-1925 published works were also reprinted in the 1930's through the 1970's. He played an important role in conservation by popularizing the values of wild game and the outdoors. Mr. Seton wrote and illustrated many scholarly works on large North American animals and birds as well as juveniles dealing with the same subjects and with woodcraft. See Phillips.

Seton, Julia M.

By a Thousand Fires; nature notes and extracts from the life and unpublished journals of Ernest Thompson Seton. Garden City, 1967, Doubleday & Co., Inc. 271 pp., photographic plates, drawings by Ernest Thompson Seton. 8vo; dust jacket.

Severinson, Keith

Hunter Climb High. Wellington, New Zealand, 1963, A. H. & A. W. Reed. 228 pp., photographic plates. 8vo; dust jacket. (Also a British edition, 1963) Hunting big game around the world including Dall ram, moose, bear and Rocky Mountain goat in the U. S.

Seybolt, Paul S.

The First Editions of Henry William Herbert "Frank Forester" 1807-1858. Boston, 1932, Privately printed. 16 pp. Limited to 60 copies. 12mo. Paper wrappers.

Seymour, George

Furbearers of California. Sacramento, 1960. 55 pp., illustrations. 12mo. Paper wrappers.

Shaffer, William C.

Greed and Carelessness; an analysis of the hunting accident problem. Harrisburg, 1946, The Telegraph Press. 238 pp., illustrations. 8vo; dust jacket. Ironically, a rare title on a subject in which all hunters should have an interest.

Sharp, Hal
   Sportsman's Digest of Hunting. New York, 1952, Sterling. 250 pp., illustrations. 8vo; dust jacket. (Reprinted several times, various publishers)

Sharpe, Philip B.   1903-1961
   Complete Guide To Handloading; a treatise on handloading for pleasure, economy and utility. New York, 1937, Funk & Wagnalls Company. 465 pp., copiously illustrated with photographs, tables and charts.   4to; dust jacket. (Supplement published, 1942, same size and publisher, 72 pp., photographic plates. Also a 1941 second edition and a 1949 third edition. Both the second and third editions included the 72 pp. supplement and were reprinted several times, same publisher)
   The Rifle in America. New York, 1938, William Morrow & Co., Inc. 641 pp., photographic plates. tables and charts. Introduction by Julian S. Hatcher. 4to; dust jacket. (Reprinted several times, same format and publisher.   Also a revised and expanded 1947 second edition, Funk & Wagnalls Company) [First edition also observed bound in full leather; probably issued in this state as presentation copies by the author]
   This Handloading Game.   Chicago, 1936, Outdoors Publishing Company. 48 pp., photographic plates. 4to. Paper wrappers.

Shaughnessy, Dick and Tap Goodenough
   Skeet and Trapshooting. New York, 1950, A. S. Barnes and Company, Inc.   180 pp., photographic plates.   A title in The Sportsman's Library series. 8vo; dust jacket.

Shaughnessy, Patrick and Diane Swingle
   Hard Hunting.   New York, 1978, Winchester Press.   182 pp., photographic plates. 8vo; dust jacket.

Shaul, H. Edwin
   The Golden Retriever; history, conformation, true type, breeding, training, feeding, care of the "Gentleman Sportsman" of the world of dogs. Boston, 1954, Indian Springs.   119 pp., photographic plates, drawings, fold-out chart. 8vo; dust jacket. A scarce work on this popular breed. Not in Jones.

Shaw, Harley G.
   Mountain Lion Field Guide.   Phoenix, 1983, Arizona Fish and Game Commission.   Second edition.   37 pp., color and black and white illustrations. 8vo. Paper wrappers. (Reprinted several times, same format and publisher)

Sheldon, Charles   1867-1928

The Wilderness of Denali; explorations of a hunter-naturalist in northern Alaska.   New York, 1930, Charles Scribner's Sons.   412 pp., photographic plates, fold-out map.   8vo; dust jacket.   (Reprinted 1960, same format and publisher)   Mr. Sheldon's account of this hunting expedition for sheep, caribou and grizzly in what is now Mt. McKinley National Park is an important and much collected big game title.

The Wilderness of Desert Bighorns and Seri Indians. A historical classic of the southwest.   The southwestern journals of Charles Sheldon.   Phoenix, Arizona, 1979, Arizona Desert Bighorn Sheep Society.   177 pp., photographic plates, drawings, maps.   Limited to 1000 numbered copies, signed by William Sheldon, the author's son.   8vo. [Also a deluxe edition of 100 numbered and signed copies; slipcased] The first publication of Sheldon's manuscripts of the southwest written between 1912 and 1922.

Wilderness of the Upper Yukon, The Wilderness of Denali, The Wilderness of the North Pacific Coast Islands. Three volumes.   Clinton, New Jersey, 1983, Amwell Press.   Limited to 1000 numbered copies signed by William G. Sheldon, the author's son.   8vo; slipcased together.   (Facsimile reproductions of the first editions)

Charles Sheldon's contribution to our knowledge about North American big game animals is significant. He kept meticulous journals of his experiences and would never go to sleep in camp until he had recorded his day's activities and the habits of the game he had seen. His two works published prior to 1925, *The Wilderness of the North Pacific Coast Islands,* 1911, and *The Wilderness of the Upper Yukon,* 1912, were also very important big game books. Mr. Sheldon's library was in large part the source of John C. Phillips' bibliography, *American Game Mammals and Birds.* Mr. Sheldon also co-edited *Hunting and Conservation* with George Bird Grinnell. See Phillips.

Sheldon, H. H.

The Deer of California. Santa Barbara, 1933, Museum of Natural History.   71 pp. photographic plates, fold-out map, bibliography.   8vo.   Paper wrappers.

Sheldon, Col. Harold P.   1887-1951

Tranquillity. New York, 1936, The Derrydale Press.   216 pp., illustrations from drawings by Ralph Boyer. Limited to 950 numbered copies. Tall 8vo.

Tranquillity Revisited. New York, 1940, The Derrydale Press.   130 pp., illustrations in color (tipped in) from paintings by A. L. Ripley.   Limited to 485 numbered copies.   4to.

A Private Affair. New York, 1941, Privately printed for Col. Woods King by The Derrydale Press.   19 pp.   12mo; boxed.   (This story originally appeared in *Tranquillity Revisited*)

Sheldon, Col. Harold P., continued

Tranquillity, Tranquillity Revisited, Tranquillity Regained. West Hartford, Vermont, 1945, The Countryman Press. Three volumes. 194 pp., 186 pp., and 160 pp. respectively, all with line drawings by Arthur Fuller. Limited to 5000 sets. 8vo; dust jackets; slipcased together. [Also a deluxe edition, specially bound and limited to 475 sets, *Tranquillity Regained* being numbered and signed by the author and artist; slipcased together] (Reprinted, three volumes in one, 1974, Winchester Press)

Col. Sheldon's lyrical stories of hunting are among those that represent the epitome of sporting literature.

Sheldon, Col. Harold P. and Frederick C. Lincoln

Sportsman's Guide to Wild Ducks. Washington,, 1946, The Wildlife Management Institute. 35 pp., illustrations in color from paintings by Fred Everett. 8vo. Paper wrappers. (Also published, 1946, same format, Outdoor Life Books)

Sheldon, William G.

The Book of the American Woodcock. Amherst, 1967, University of Massachusetts Press. 227 pp., color frontispiece by A. Lassell Ripley, photographic plates, bibliography. 4to; dust jacket. (Reprinted 1971, same format and publisher) A scholarly and complete work based on a study conducted over many years.

Exploring For Wild Sheep in British Columbia in 1931 and 1932. Clinton, New Jersey, 1981, Amwell Press. 246 pp., color frontispiece by Carl Rungius, photographic plates. Foreword by John Batten. Limited to 1000 numbered and signed copies. 8vo; slipcased. The account of William Sheldon and Richard Borden's expeditions undertaken when both were young men.

William Sheldon was the son of Charles Sheldon and was a competent naturalist in his own right. He also wrote *The Wilderness Home of the Giant Panda,* an important work.

Shelley, Er M.

Bird Dog Training Today and Tomorrow. New York, 1947, G. P. Putnam's Sons. 140 pp., photographic plates. Foreword by Nash Buckingham. 8vo; dust jacket. (Reprinted several times, same format and publisher) The author also wrote *Twentieth Century Bird Dog Training and Kennel Management,* published by A F. Hockwalt in 1921 and reprinted many times thereafter. Many feel his methods form the foundation of modern bird dog training.

Shelton, Lawrence P.

California Gunsmiths, 1846 - 1900. Fair Oaks, 1977, Privately printed. 289 pp., illustrations. Edited by Cindy Sovenski. 4to. (Also an edition by George Shumway)

Shepard, Paul

Man in the Landscape. New York, 1967, Alfred A. Knopf, Inc. 290 pp., illustrations. 8vo; dust jacket. Presents a classic essay of the benefits and reason man hunts.

The Tender Carnivore and the Sacred Game. New York, 1973, Charles Scribner's Sons. 302 pp., drawings by Fons Van Woerkorn. 8vo; dust jacket. A provocative advocacy of man's abandonment of agriculture to return to a hunter-gatherer state.

Shepard, Paul and Barry Shepard

The Sacred Paw; the bear in nature, myth and literature. New York, 1985, Viking Press. 244 pp., illustrations. 8vo; dust jacket.

Shepperd, Tad

Pack & Paddock. New York, 1938, The Derrydale Press. 144 pp., illustrations from drawings by Paul Brown. Limited to 950 numbered copies. 12mo; two-piece box. Foxhunting.

Sherlock, Herb

Black Powder Snapshots. Huntington, West Virginia, 1946, Standard Publications, Inc. Unpaginated (approx. 60 pp.), plates from drawings by the author. Folio; slipcased. A collections of drawings depicting scenes in early American history in which the use of firearms were prominent. Scarce.

Sherrill, Robert

The Saturday Night Special; and other guns with which Americans won the West, protected bootleg franchises, slew wildlife, bobbed countless banks, shot husbands profusely and by mistake, and killed presidents, together with the debate on continuing same. New York, 1973, Charterhouse. 338 pp., illustrations. 8vo; dust jacket. Scarce.

Sherwood, Morgan

Big Game In Alaska; a history of wildlife and people. New Haven, Connecticut, 1981, Yale University Press. 200 pp., photographic plates, bibliography. 8vo; dust jacket. Much on hunting as well as a history of Alaskan wildlife management.

Shick, Charles

A Study of Pheasants on the 9,000 Acre Farm in Saginaw County, Michigan. Lansing, 1952, Michigan Department of Conservation. 134 pp., photographic plates, charts. 8vo. Paper wrappers.

Shiras, George

Hunting Wildlife With Camera and Flashlight. Washington, D. C., 1935, National Geographic Society. Two volumes; Volume I: Lake Superior Region; Volume II: Wild Life of Coasts, Islands and Mountains. 450 pp. and 454 pp., respectively, photographic plates. 8vo. (Reprinted 1936, same format and publisher)

Shoemaker, Carl D.

The Stories Behind the Organization of the National Wildlife Federation and Its Early Struggles For Survival. Washington, D. C., 1960, National Wildlife Federation. 49 pp., illustrations. 8vo.

Shoemaker, Paul E.

Training Retrievers; for field trials and hunting. Seattle, 1970, Superior Publishing Co. 144 pp., photographic plates, drawings. 4to.

Shoemaker, Henry W. and Joseph S. Illick

In Penn's Woods; a handy and helpful pocket manual of the natural wonders and recreational facilities in the State Forests of Pennsylvania. Harrisburg, 1925, Department of Forests and Waters. 86 pp., illustrations. 8vo. Paper wrappers. A scarce Pennsylvania item. Not in Phillips.

Shoenberger, J. H.

From the Great Lakes to the Pacific; pioneering the wilderness in 1875. San Antonio, Texas, 1934, The Naylor Company. 211 pp., illustrations. 8vo. With some buffalo and wolf hunting. Scarce.

Shore, Evelyn Berglund

Born on Snowshoes. Boston, 1954, Houghton Mifflin Company. 209 pp., photographic plates. 8vo; dust jacket. An account of this family's life in the Alaska-Yukon Territory with much hunting and trapping.

Short, Wayne

The Cheechakoes. New York, 1964, Random House, Inc. 254 pp., drawings by Peter Parnall. 8vo; dust jacket. An account of an Alaskan pioneering family's adventures beginning about 1946. With some bear hunting.

This Raw Land. New York, 1968, Random House, Inc. 203 pp., map. 8vo; dust jacket. More adventures of an Alaskan pioneer family.

Shortt, Angela

The Hunting If. New York, 1932, Privately printed by The Derrydale Press. Unpaginated; vignette sketches. 16mo. Limited to 100 copies. Foxhunting.

Shortt, Angus H, and   B. W. Cartwright
> *Sports Afield Collection of Know Your Ducks and Geese.* Minneapolis, 1948, Sports Afield. Unpaginated (80 pp.), 36 color plates with text. Elephant Folio. (Reprinted and revised several times, various formats and publishers)   A collection of illustrations originally appearing, one at a time, in issues of *Sports Afield* magazine from 1946 through 1948.

Shourds, Harry V. and Anthony Hillman
> *Carving Duck Decoys.* New York, 1981, Dover. 64 pp., color and black and white illustrations. Folio. Paper wrappers.
> *Carving Shorebirds;* with full size patterns.   New York, 1982, Dover. 70 pp., drawings, color plates. Folio. Paper wrappers.
> *Exotic Duck Decoys For the Woodcarver;* with full size templates. New York, 1984, Dover. 4pp. text, 16 full size templates. Folio. Paper wrappers.

Shumaker, P. L.
> *Colt's Variation of the Old Model Pocket Pistol 1848 - 1872.*   New York, 1957, Fadco.   150 pp., photographic plates.   8vo; dust jacket.

Shumway, George
> *Pennsylvania Longrifles of Note.*   York, Pennsylvania, 1968, George Shumway.   63 pp., photographic plates.   8vo.   Paper wrappers.
> *Rifles of Colonial America.*   No place, 1980, George Shumway. Two volumes containing approximately 655 pp., photographic plates, maps. Limited to 2800 sets.   4to; dust jackets. [Also a deluxe edition of 200 numbered sets]

Siedensticker, John C., et al.
> *Mountain Lion Social Organization in the Idaho Primitive Area.* Washington, D. C., 1973, The Wildlife Society.   59 pp., photographic plates. 4to. Paper wrappers.

Siegel, Col. Henry A. (1914-1997), Harry C. Marschalk, Jr. and Isaac Oelgart
> *The Derrydale Press;* a bibliography.   Goshen, Connecticut, 1981, The Angler's And Shooter's Press.   266 pp., photographic plates. Limited to 1250 numbered copies.   8vo; slipcased. [Also a deluxe edition, specially bound and limited to 26 lettered copies; boxed]   A scholarly and thorough bibliography of this sporting book publisher with a biography of its founder, Eugene V. Connett, 3rd .

Siegler, Hilbert R., editor
> *The White-Tailed Deer of New Hampshire.*   Concord, 1968, New Hampshire Fish and Game Department.   256 pp., photographic plates, bibliography. 8vo.

Sigler, William F.
    Wildlife Law Enforcement. Dubuque, Iowa, 1956, Brown. 318 pp., photographic plates, bibliography. 8vo. A textbook for wildlife conservation officers.

Silver, Helenette
    A History of New Hampshire Game and Furbearers. Concord, 1957, New Hampshire Fish and Game Commission. 457 pp., photographic plates, maps, bibliography. 8vo. (Also a 1974 second edition, paper wrappers, same publisher)

Silver, Helenette and Walter T. Silver
    Growth and Behavior of the Coyote Like Canids of Northern New England With Observations on Canid Hybrids. Washington, D. C., 1969, The Wildlife Society. Monograph # 17. 41 pp., photographic plates, maps, bibliography. 4to. Paper wrappers.

Simkin, D. W.
    A Preliminary Report of the Woodland Caribou Study in Ontario. 1965, Ontario Department of Lands and Forests. 76 pp., photographic plates, bibliography. 8vo. Paper wrappers.

Simmons, Albert Dixon
    Flight; a selection of twelve sporting photographs sincere in their realism, tense with arrested action and...unique. Boston, ca. 1930, National Sportsman. A portfolio of 12 B&W photographic plates, each about 10" X 15," with a facsimile of the author's signature.
    Photography For Sportsmen. New York, 1951, D. Van Nostrand Company, Inc. 172 pp., plates. A Van Nostrand Sporting Book. 8vo; dust jacket.
    Wing Shots; a series of camera studies of American game birds and other birds of field and stream on the wing. New York, 1936, The Derrydale Press. Unpaginated; 83 photographic plates by the author. Limited to 950 numbered copies. 4to; dust jacket.

Simmons, Richard F.
    Custom Built Rifles. New York and Harrisburg, 1949, Stackpole and Heck, Inc. 202 pp., photographic plates. An N. R. A. Library Book. 8vo; dust jacket. (Reprinted, Bonanza. Also a 1955 revised second edition, same format, The Stackpole Company)
    Wildcat Cartridges. New York, 1947, William Morrow and Co., Inc. 333 pp., photographic plates. 8vo; dust jacket. A rather technical work explaining conversion of factory made ammunition into custom calibers.

Simms, Jeptha Root   1807-1883

Trappers of New York; or, a biography of Nicholas Stoner and Nathaniel Foster. Anecdotes of other celebrated hunters, and some account of Sir William Johnson, and his style of living. Harrison, New York, 1980, Harbor Hill Books. 308 pp., illustrations. 8vo; dust jacket. (Originally published, 1850)

Simon, Noel and Paul Geroudet

Last Survivors; the natural history of animals in danger of extinction. New York, 1970, World Publishing Company.   275 pp., color and black and white illustrations, bibliography.   4to; dust jacket.

Simpson, Gene M.

Pheasant Farming.   Eugene, Oregon, 1927.   96 pp., photographic plates.   8vo.   Paper wrappers.

Sines, Harley, et al.

Profitable Outdoor Pursuits. Columbus, Ohio, 1922, A. R. Harding. 79 pp., illustrations. Paper wrappers.

Singer, Frank L.

Singer's Trapper's Guide.   Peekskill, New York, No date, Privately printed. 34 pp., photographic plates.   8vo.   Paper wrappers.

Sirotek, Robert L.

The Wayne-DuPage Hunt; a chronicle of events, 1928-1980 with historical data from 1835. Broadview, Illinois, 1980, Privately printed.   153 pp., illustrations.   A history of this foxhunting club.

Sisley, Nick

All About Varmint Hunting. Washington, D. C., 1982, Stone Wall Press. 182 pp., photographic plates.   8vo.   Paper wrappers.

Grouse and Woodcock; an upland hunter's book.   Harrisburg, 1980, Stackpole Books.   159 pp., photographic plates.   8vo; dust jacket. (Reprinted 1981, same format and publisher)

Grouse Magic. Apollo, Pennsylvania, 1981, Privately printed.   240 pp., drawings by Earl Martz.   Limited to 1500 numbered and signed copies.   8vo; slipcased.

Hunting the Ruffed Grouse. Apollo, Pennsylvania, 1970, Privately printed.   136 pp., photographic plates.   8vo. Spiral bound paper wrappers.

Sisley, Nick, editor

Deer Hunting Across North America.   Rockville Center, New York, 1975, Freshet Press. 281 pp., photographic plates.   8vo; dust jacket.

Sitton, Thad and James H. Conrad, editors
Every Sun That Rises; Wyatt Moore of Caddo Lake. Austin, Texas, 1985, University of Texas Press. 167 pp., photographic plates, drawings. 8vo; dust jacket. The biography of Wyatt Moore, including much hunting and fishing.

Sitwell, Sacheverell
The Hunters and the Hunted. New York, 1948, The Macmillan Company. 314 pp., photographic plates. 8vo; dust jacket.

Skiff, Frederick Woodward
Adventures in Americana; recollections of forty years collecting books, furniture, china, guns and glass. Portland, 1935, Metropolitan Press Publishers. 365 pp., illustrations. Limited to 800 numbered and signed copies. 8vo. Mr. Skiff amassed a huge book collection of over 20,000 volumes. He was an ardent angler and gun collector. Scarce.

Skinner, Frederick Gustavus
See **Smith, Harry Worcester,** *A Sporting Family of the Old South.*

Slater, Kitty
The Hunt Country of America. South Brunswick, New Jersey, 1967, A. S. Barnes and Company, Inc. 247 pp., illustrations. 8vo; dust jacket. (Reprinted several times, various publishers) A survey of foxhunting in America.

Small, Anne
Masters of Bird Carving. New York, 1981, Winchester Press. 256 pp., color and black and white photographic plates. 4to; dust jacket.
Masters of Decorative Bird Carving. Tulsa, 1981, Winchester Press. 147 pp., color and black and white photographic plates. 4to; dust jacket.

Smeeton, Miles
Completely Foxed. Toronto, 1980, D. Van Nostrand Company, Inc. 148 pp., photographic plates. 8vo; dust jacket.
Moose Magic. Toronto, 1974, William Collins. 191 pp., photographic plates. 8vo; dust jacket. (Also a 1974 British edition) Both of these titles are accounts of the author's game farm in Alberta.

Smith, Allen G.
Ecological Factors Affecting Waterfowl Production in the Alberta Parklands. Washington, D. C., 1971, United States Department of the Interior. 49 pp., photographic plates, bibliography. 4to. Paper wrappers.

Smith, Art

Pavement's End; a collection of his hunting and fishing columns from the *New York Herald Tribune.* Clinton, New Jersey, 1985, Amwell Press.   213 pp., drawings by Tom Hennessey. Limited to 1000 numbered and signed copies. 8vo; slipcased.

Smith, Arthur D. and D. M. Beale

Pronghorn Antelope in Utah; some research and observations.   No place, No date (ca. 1972), Utah Division of Wildlife. 88 pp., photographic plates, maps. 8vo. Paper wrappers.

Smith, Carl

Training the Rabbit Hound: a book on Bassets and Beagles. Columbus, Ohio, 1926, Hunter-Trader-Trapper. 185 pp., illustrations. 12mo. (Reprinted several times, same format and publisher)

Smith, Dick and Robert Easton

California Condor; vanishing American. A study of an ancient and symbolic giant of the sky. Charlotte, 1964, McNally. 111 pp., photographic plates, drawings. 4to; dust jacket.

Smith, Donald B.

The Great Trapline. Franklin, North Carolina, 1980, Macon. 199 pp., photographic plates. 8vo; dust jacket. Trapping in northern Ontario.

Smith, Dwight R.

The Bighorn Sheep in Idaho; its status, life history and management. Boise, No date (ca. 1954), Idaho Department of Fish and Game.   154 pp., photographic plates, drawings, maps, bibliography. 8vo. Paper wrappers.   Also includes a survey of winter ranges along the middle fork of the Salmon River and adjacent areas.

Smith, Edmund Ware   b. 1900

For Maine Only. New York, 1959, Frederick Fell Publishers, Inc. 295 pp., illustrated. 8vo; dust jacket.

The Further Adventures of the One-Eyed Poacher. New York, 1947, Crown Publishers, Inc. 219 pp., drawings by A. Lassell. Ripley. 8vo; dust jacket [Also a limited edition of 750 numbered and signed copies; slipcased]

The One-Eyed Poacher and the Maine Woods.   New York, 1955, Frederick Fell Publishers, Inc. 269 pp.   8vo; dust jacket. (Reprinted, ca. 1980 in paper wrappers, Down East Publishers)

The One-Eyed Poacher of Privilege. New York, 1941, The Derrydale Press. 187 pp., drawings by A. Lassell Ripley. Limited to 750 numbered copies. Tall 8vo.

Smith, Edmund Ware, continued

Tall Tales and Short. New York, 1938, The Derrydale Press. 187 pp., drawings by Milton C. Weiler. Limited to 950 numbered copies. Tall 8vo.

A Tomato Can Chronicle; and other stories of fishing and shooting. New York, 1937, The Derrydale Press. 189 pp., drawings by Ralph Boyer. Limited to 950 numbered copies. Tall 8vo.

A Treasury of the Maine Woods. New York, 1958, Frederick Fell Publishers, Inc. 295 pp., drawings by Maurice Day. Introduction by John Gould. 8vo; dust jacket. (Reprinted, ca. 1980 in paper wrappers, Down East Publishers)

Up River and Down; stories from the Maine woods. New York, 1965, Holt, Rinehart and Winston. 240 pp., drawings by Maurice Day. 8vo; dust jacket. (Reprinted twice, same format and publisher)

Mr. Smith's fictionalized accounts of Jeff Coongate's hunting and angling escapades in the Maine woods are among the most popular sporting fiction of the twentieth century.

Smith, Elmer H.

Klu-E-Lae Camp Log. No place, no date (1950), Privately printed. 81 pp., photographic plates, map. 8vo. Spiral bound paper wrappers. An account of a big game hunting trip in British Columbia.

Smith, Elmer L.

American Wildfowl Decoys; from folk art to factory. Lebanaon, 1974, Applied Arts. 32 pp., photographic plates. 4to. Paper wrappers.

Smith, George C., Jr.

Sporting and Colored Plate Books .....Collected by the Late George C. Smith, Jr., New York, New York. New York, 1937, American Art Association. 192 pp. 8vo. Paper wrappers. An auction catalog with 583 lots, some of which were sporting books.

Smith, Harry Worcester   1865-1945

The Library of the Late Harry Worcester Smith, Worcester, Massachusetts, comprising sporting books and prints. New York, 1948, Parke-Bernet Galleries, Inc. 47 pp. 8vo. Paper wrappers. The sale catalog of this famous sportsman, which was heavily weighted toward the equestrian sports.

Life and Sport in Aiken; and those who made it. New York, 1935, The Derrydale Press. 237 pp., plates. Limited to 950 copies. Tall 8vo; dust jacket. An account of this South Carolina community and the lives of Mr. And Mrs. Thomas Hitchcock, who did much to promote the sport of foxhunting in the U. S.

A Sporting Family of the Old South; including *Reminiscences of an Old Sportsman* by Frederick Gustavus Skinner. Albany, New York, 1936, Lyon. 477 pp., photographic plates, reproductions of old plates. 8vo; dust jacket. Much on foxhunting and horse racing, but also hunting quail, grouse, turkey, deer, etc., as well as a section on old sporting books. F. G. Skinner was the founder and publisher of the *American Turf Register,* the first sporting periodical published in America.

Smith, Harry Worcester, continued

A Sporting Tour Through Ireland, England, Wales and France. Columbia, South Carolina, 1925, The State Co. Two volumes containing 437 total pp., photographic plates, maps. Limited to 350 numbered and signed sets. 8vo. Mr. Smith was a colorful and outspoken proponent of the American thoroughbred for use in foxhunting. This book describes his exploits in competition against horses bred on the continent, but also contains sections on sporting art and sporting books.

Smith, James A. and Elmer Swanson

The Antique Pistol Book. Hoboken, New Jersey, 1948, Speedwell Publishing Company. 336 pp., line drawings by James A. Smith. A numbered, limited edition of unspecified quantity. 8vo. (Later issued with **Swanson, Elmer**, *Automatic Firearm Pistols*, which see)

Smith, Lawrence B.   1889-1971

American Game Preserve Shooting. New York, 1933, Windward House. 175 pp., photographic plates, drawings. 4to; dust jacket. (Reprinted 1937, Garden City Publishing Company)

Better Trapshooting; with a section on skeet. New York, 1931, E. P. Dutton & Co., Inc. 301 pp., photographic plates, drawings. 8vo; dust jacket.

Fur or Feather; days with dog and gun. New York, 1946, Charles Scribner's Sons. 144 pp., drawings by Paul Brown. 8vo; dust jacket.

Modern Gun Dogs. New York, 1936, Charles Scribner's Sons. 173 pp., photographic plates. 8vo; dust jacket.

Modern Shotgun Shooting. New York, 1935, Charles Scribner's Sons. 171 pp., illustrations. 8vo; dust jacket.

Shotgun Psychology. New York, 1938, Charles Scribner's Sons. 295 pp., illustrations. 8vo; dust jacket. (Reprinted 1950, same format and publisher)

Smith, Myron J., Jr.

Equestrian Studies. Metuchen, New Jersey, 1981, Scarecrow Press. 361 pp. 8vo. A bibliography of equestrian books, including those on American foxhunting.

Smith, Ned

Field & Stream's Portfolio of Game Birds. New York, no date, Field & Stream. Portfolio of eight color plates inserted in envelope. Folio. Quail, turkey and other upland species.

Gone For the Day. Harrisburg, 1971, The Pennsylvania Game Commission. An anthology of the author's stories and essays originally published in the *Pennsylvania Game News*.

Smith, Otis "Toad"

Toad's Tricks To Taking Whitetails in the Corn....And Everywhere Else. Minnesota, No date, Privately printed. 113 pp.

Smith, Ray M.

The Story of Pope's Barrels. Harrisburg, 1960, The Stackpole Company. 211 pp., illustrations. 4to; dust jacket. Harry H. Pope (1861-1950) was the premier rifle barrel maker in the U. S. from about 1890 to 1920. A scarce title.

Smith, Red

View of Sport. New York, 1954, Alfred A. Knopf, Inc. 293 pp., drawings by Marc Simont. 8vo; dust jacket. Some commentary on hunting.

Smith, Richard P.

Animal Tracks and Signs of North America. Harrisburg, 1982, Stackpole Books. 271 pp., photographic plates. Paper wrappers.

The Book of the Black Bear. Piscataway, New Jersey, 1985, Winchester Press. 224 pp., photographic plates. 8vo; dust jacket.

Deer Hunting. Harrisburg, 1978, Stackpole Books. 256 pp., photographic plates, bibliography. 8vo; dust jacket.

Smith, Russell D.

The Indian Canoe. New York, 1925, The Century Company. 319 pp., illustrations. 8vo; dust jacket. An older juvenile with much hunting and fishing in Maine. Not in Phillips.

Smith, Stan

Manual For the Hunter. New York, 1950. 64 pp., photographic plates, drawings. 8vo. Paper wrappers.

Smith, Steve

Hunting Ducks and Geese. Harrisburg, 1984, Stackpole Books. 150 pp., photographic plates. 8vo; dust jacket.

Smith, Walter Harold Black   1901-1959

Basic Manual of Military Small Arms. Harrisburg, 1943, Military Service Publishing Company. 213 pp., many illustrations. 4to. Paper wrappers. (Reprinted and revised many times, all successive issues were cloth bound, most were titled *Small Arms of the World*, same publisher)

Gas, Air and Spring Guns. Harrisburg, 1957, The Military Service Publishing Company. 279 pp., photographic plates. 4to; dust jacket.

Mannlicher Rifles and Pistols; famous sporting and military weapons. Harrisburg and Washington, D. C., 1947, The Military Service Publishing Company. 239 pp., with illustrations from original manufacturers drawings. An N. R. A. Library Book. 8vo; dust jacket.

Mauser Rifles and Pistols. Harrisburg, 1946, Military Service Publishing Company. 234 pp., many illustrations. 8vo; dust jacket. (Revised and reprinted several times, various publishers)

Smith, Walter Harold Black, continued

Pistols & Revolvers. Volume One of the N. R. A. Book of Small Arms. Washington / Harrisburg, 1946, The National Rifle Association of America / The Military Service Publishing Company. 638 pp., many illustrations, tables and charts. 8vo; dust jacket. (Revised and reprinted several times, with later editions titled, *The Book of Pistols and Revolvers*)

Rifles. Volume Two of the N. R. A. Book of Small Arms. Washington, D. C., and Harrisburg, 1948, The National Rifle Association of America / The Military Service Publishing Company. 546 pp., glossary, appendices and photographic plates. 8vo; dust jacket. (Revised and reprinted several times, with later editions titled, *The Book of Rifles*)

Walther Pistols. Harrisburg, 1946, The Military Service Publishing Company. 94 pp., illustrations. 8vo; dust jacket. (Also a 1962 revised edition titled *Walther Pistols and Rifles*, The Stackpole Company)

Smith, William N.

Marsh Tales; market hunting, duck trapping and gunning. Centerville, Maryland, 1985, Tidewater Publishers. 228 pp., photographic plates. 8vo; dust jacket.

Smith, Winston O.

The Sharps Rifle. New York, 1943, William Morrow and Co., Inc. 138 pp., illustrations from photographic plates and line drawings. Tall 8vo; dust jacket. (Reprinted twice, same format and publisher)

Snyder, Col. Harry M.   b. 1882

Snyder's Book of Big Game Hunting. New York, 1950, Greenberg: Publishers. 312 pp., photographic plates. Tall 8vo; dust jacket. [Also a deluxe edition, specially bound and illustrated with a two page color frontispiece by Carl Rungius and limited to 99 numbered and signed copies; slipcased]   Hunting big game around the world with emphasis on North American species.

Somerville, Edith Oe.   1861-1949

The States Through Irish Eyes. Boston, 1930, Houghton Mifflin Company. 200 pp., drawings by the author. 8vo; dust jacket.

Ms. Somerville wrote extensively about life and foxhunting in her native Ireland; many of her books were co-authored by her cousin, Violet Martin, who used the pen name, Martin Ross. Most of her works describing Irish life and its foxhunting were co-published or reprinted in America by Scribner's, The Derrydale Press and others. See Siegel or Frazier.

Somerville, William, Esq.

The Chace.   Garden City, New York, 1929, Doubleday, Doran & Co., Inc.   118 pp., engravings by Thomas Bewick.   Introduction by A. Henry Higginson.   Limited to 375 numbered copies.   Folio. (A reproduction of the 1735 edition)   A classic foxhunting work originally published in England.

Soothill, Eric and Peter Whitehead
Wildfowl of the World. Poole, 1978, Blandford. 297 pp., color and black and white illustrations. 8vo; dust jacket.

Soper, J. Dewey
The Blue Goose; an account of its breeding ground, migration, eggs, nests and general habits. Ottawa, 1930, Department of the Interior, North West Territories. 64 pp., color frontispiece by Allan Brooks, photographic plates, fold-out map, bibliography. 8vo. Paper wrappers.
Life History of the Blue Goose; Chen caerulescens. Boston, 1942, Boston Society of Natural History. 97 pp., photographic plates, drawings, bibliography. 8vo. Paper wrappers. Scarce.

Sorenson, Harold D.
Decoy Collector's Guide, 1963-64-65. Burlington, Iowa, 1971, Privately printed. 384 pp., photographic plates. 8vo. This is a reprint of all twelve of the original guides that were issued quarterly.

Sorenson, Harold D., continued
Decoy Collector's Guide Burlington, Iowa, 1963, Privately printed. 128 pp., photographic plates. 8vo. Spiral bound paper wrappers. (Also annual revised editions in 1964, 1965, 1966-67, 1968 and in 1977, same format and publisher)

Soskin, Mark
The Blazed Trail / Outdoor Diary. New York, 1974, Abercrombie & Fitch. 191 pp., photographic plates. 8vo. A collection of hunting and angling tips with travel suggestions; also a blank section for a diary; leather bound.

South, Zary
Southwest Hunting and Fishing. Tucson, Arizona, 1950, Tucson Chamber of Commerce. 24 pp., maps. 8vo. Paper wrappers.

Southesek, The Earl of
Saskatchewan and the Rocky Mountains; a diary and narrative of travel, sport and adventure during a journey through the Hudson's Bay Company's territories in 1959 and 1860. Rutland, Vermont / Edmonton, Alberta, 1969, Charles E. Tuttle Co., Inc. / Hurtig. 448 pp., fold-out maps in color. 12mo; dust jacket. (A reproduction of the 1875 edition)

Sowls, Lyle K.

Prairie Ducks; a study of their behavior, ecology and management. Harrisburg / Washington D. C. / 1955, The Stackpole Company / The Wildlife Management Institute. 193 pp., photographic plates, color frontispiece from a painting by Sir Peter Scott. Tall 8vo; dust jacket.

Sparano, Vin T., editor

Complete Outdoor Encyclopedia. New York, 1972, Harper & Row, Publishers, Inc. / Outdoor Life Books. 622 pp., illustrations. 4to; dust jacket.

The Greatest Hunting Stories Ever Told. New York, 1983, Beaufort Books. 263 pp. 8vo; dust jacket. An anthology of stories by Buckingham, Ruark, MacQuarrie and others.

Sparks, John and Tony Soper

Owls; their natural and unnatural history. New York, 1970, Taplinger. 206 pp., color and black and white illustrations, bibliography. 8vo; dust jacket.

Spaulding, Edward S.   b. 1891

Deer! No place (Santa Barbara, California), No date (ca. 1968), Privately printed. 133 pp., drawings by David Hagerbaumer. Folio. Paper wrappers.

The Quails. New York, 1949, The Macmillan Company. 123 pp., color plates from paintings by Francis Lee Jaques. 4to; dust jacket. Natural history plus hunting all the North American species.

Venison and a Breath of Sage; tales of the San Juan ranch. Santa Barbara, California, 1967, W. T. Genns. 312 pp., illustrations by Ric Johnson. 8vo.

Speare, E. Ray

Hollywood Club Memoirs. No place, 1952, Privately printed. 69 pp., photographic plates. Tall 8vo. A history of this Adirondack hunting and fishing club.

Spears, Borden, editor

Wilderness Canada. Toronto, 1970. 174 pp., color and black and white illustrations. Folio; dust jacket.

Speltz, Merlin G.

Camp 17. Minnesota, No date, Privately printed. 27 pp. An account of setting up a Minnesota deer camp.

Supplement #1 to the Camp 17 History. Minnesota, 1984, Privately printed. 13 pp.

Spencer, Howard E.

The Black Bear and Its Status in Maine. Augusta, 1955, Maine Fish and Game Commission. 55 pp., photographic plates, bibliography. 8vo. Paper wrappers. (Reprinted 1966, same format and publisher)

Spencer, James B.

Retriever Training Tests. New York, 1983, Arco. 165 pp., photographic plates. 8vo; dust jacket.

Sperry, Charles C.

Food Habits of the Coyote. Washington, D. C., 1941, United States Fish and Wildlife Commission. 70 pp., color frontispiece, photographic plates, bibliography. 8vo. Paper wrappers.

Food Habits of a Group of Shorebirds: Woodcock, Snipe, Knot and Dowitcher). Washington, D. C., 1940, United States Department of the Interior. 37 pp., color plates, bibliography. 8vo. Paper wrappers.

Spielman, Patrick

How To Make Recurve Bows and Matched Arrows. Milwaukee, Wisconsin, 1964. 63 pp., photographic plates. 8vo. Paper wrappers.

Making Wood Decoys. New York, 1982, Sterling. 160 pp., color and black and white illustrations. 4to. Paper wrappers. (Reprinted 1982, same format and publisher)

Spiller, Burton L.   1886-1973

Drummer in the Woods. New York, 1962, D. Van Nostrand Company, Inc. 239 pp., frontispiece. 8vo; dust jacket. (Reprinted 1980, same contents, Stackpole Books) Tales of grouse hunting.

Firelight. New York, 1937, The Derrydale Press. 197 pp., illustrations from drawings by Lynn Bogue Hunt. Limited to 950 numbered copies. 4to. (Reprinted 1985, same contents, Premier Press)

Fishin' Around. New York, 1974, Winchester Press. 245 pp., drawings by Milton C. Weiler. Foreword by Tap Tapply. 8vo; dust jacket. [Also a deluxe edition co-published with Amwell Press, limited to 1000 numbered and signed copies; slipcased] Hunting and fishing in Maine.

Grouse Feathers. New York, 1935, The Derrydale Press. 207 pp., illustrations from drawings by Lynn Bogue Hunt. Limited to 950 numbered copies. 4to. (Reprinted 1947, same format and contents, The Macmillan Company. Also reprinted, 1972, Crown Publishers, Inc.) [Also a deluxe edition of the Crown Publishers, Inc. edition, limited to 750 numbered copies signed by the author; dust jacket]

Spiller, Burton L., continued

More Grouse Feathers. New York, 1938, The Derrydale Press. 238 pp., illustrations from drawings by Lynn Bogue Hunt. Limited to 950 numbered copies. 4to. (Reprinted 1972, Crown Publishers, Inc.) [Also a deluxe edition of the Crown Publishers, Inc. edition, limited to 750 numbered copies signed by the author; dust jacket]

Northland Castaways. Indianapolis, 1957, The Bobbs-Merrill Company. 228 pp., drawings. 8vo; dust jacket. An older juvenile novel with much hunting and fishing in Quebec. A scarce Spiller title.

Thoroughbred. New York, 1936, The Derrydale Press. 200 pp., illustrations from drawings by Lynn Bogue Hunt. Limited to 950 numbered copies. 4to.

Mr. Spiller's stories of grouse hunting and the outdoors are entertaining as well as knowledgeable accounts of this game bird and its habits.

Spirer, Louise and Herbert Spirer

This is the German Pointer, Shorthaired and Wirehaired. Jersey City, New Jersey, 1970, TFH Publications. 240 pp., photographic plates. 8vo.

Sporting Arms and Ammunition Institute

Handbook on Shotgun Shooting. New York, 1939, Sporting Arms and Ammunition Institute. 100 pp., photographic plates. 8vo. Paper wrappers. (Reprinted many times, same format and publisher)

Sports Afield

Sports Afield Hunting Annual. Minneapolis, 1948, Sports Afield. 64 pp., illustrations. Folio. Paper wrappers. (Several editions produced yearly up to at least 1968)

Sports Illustrated

Book of Dog Training. Philadelphia, 1959, J. B. Lippincott Co. 88 pp., photographic plates. 8vo; dust jacket. With emphasis on gun dogs.

Book of the Shotgun Sports. Philadelphia, 1967, J. B. Lippincott Co. 90 pp., illustrations. 8vo; dust jacket. Intended for the novice.

The Sportsman's Bookshelf

Guide To American Waterfowl. Harrisburg, 1950, Stackpole & Heck, Inc. 128 pp., illustrations. Volume III of The Sportsman's Bookshelf series. 8vo. Paper wrappers.

Pheasants Afield. Harrisburg, 1953, The Stackpole Company. 128 pp., illustrations. Text by Durwood Allen. Volume XVI of The Sportsman's Bookshelf series. 8vo. Paper wrappers.

Rifle Shooting. Harrisburg, 1950, Stackpole & Heck, Inc. 128 pp., illustrations. Text by Frank Dufresne. Volume V in The Sportsman's Bookshelf series. 8vo. Paper wrappers.

The Sportsman's Bookshelf, continued

Rifles Past and Present. Harrisburg, 1950, Stackpole & Heck, Inc. 128 pp., illustrations. Volume IV in The Sportsman's Bookshelf series. 8vo. Paper wrappers.

Shotguns and Shotgun Shooting. Harrisburg, 1950, Stackpole & Heck, Inc. 128 pp., illustrations. Volume I in The Sportsman's Bookshelf series. 8vo. Paper wrappers.

Upland Game and Gunning. Harrisburg, 1950, Stackpole and Heck, Inc. 128 pp., photographic plates. Volume VI in the Sportsman's Bookshelf series. 8vo. Paper wrappers.

Springs, R. A.

Wildfowling Log. New York, 1954, Sports Logs. Unpaginated (approx. 100 pp.) Oblong 8vo. A log book for waterfowling.

Sprungman, Ormal

Photography Afield. Harrisburg, 1951, The Stackpole Company. 449 pp., photographic plates in color and black and white. 4to; dust jacket.

Sprunt, Alexander

North American Birds of Prey. New York, 1955, Harper & Brothers. 227 pp., color and black and white illustrations by Brooks, Fuertes, Peterson and Weber. 8vo; dust jacket. (Reprinted, Bonanza)

Gamebirds; a guide to North American species and their habits. New York, 1961, Golden Press. 160 pp., color illustrations. 16mo. Paper wrappers.

Squire, Emma Lindsay

On Autumn Trails; and adventures in captivity. New York, 1923, Cosmopolitan Book Company. 239 pp., illustrations by Paul Bransom. 12mo; dust jacket. Fictional stories about the wild game of Nova Scotia. Not in Phillips.

The Wild Heart. New York, 1922, Cosmopolitan. 220 pp., illustrations by Paul Bransom. 12o; dust jacket. Containing mostly wildlife stories from the Northwest. Not in Phillips.

Squire, Lorene

Wildfowling With a Camera. Philadelphia, 1938, J. B. Lippincott Co. Unpaginated (approx. 250 pp.), photographic plates. 4to; dust jacket.

Stadt, Ronald W.

Winchester Shotguns and Shotshells; from the hammer double to the Model 59. Tacoma, Washington, 1984, Armory Publishing. 184 pp., illustrations. 4to; dust jacket.

Stadtfeld, Curtis K.
Whitetail Deer; a year's cycle. New York, 1975, The Dial Press. 163 pp., drawings, bibliography. 8vo; dust jacket.

Staender, Vivian
Adventures With Arctic Wildlife. Caldwell, Idaho, 1970, Caxton Printers, Ltd. 260 pp., photographic plates. 8vo; dust jacket.

Stalker, Tracy
How To Make Modern Archery Tackle. New York, 1948, Casein Company. 34 pp., photographic plates, drawings, diagrams. 8vo. Paper wrappers. (Also a 1954 second edition, same format and publisher)

Stanger, Margaret A.
That Quail, Robert. Philadelphia, 1966, J. B. Lippincott Co. 127 pp., illustrations by Kathy Baldwin. 8vo; dust jacket. (Reprinted many times, same format and publisher) The story of a pet quail.

Stanton, Don C.
A History of the White-Tailed Deer in Maine. Bangor, 1963, Department of Inland Fisheries and Game. 75 pp., photographic plates, bibliography. 8vo. Paper wrappers.

Stanwell-Fletcher, Theodore C.
Driftwood Valley. Boston, 1946, Little Brown & Company. 384 pp., photographic plates, map. 8vo; dust jacket. (Reprinted several times, same format and publisher) Living in British Columbia with much hunting, angling and trapping.

Stark, Loren D.
Big Game Hunting on Three Continents. Houston, 1970, Privately printed. 82 pp., illustrations by the author. Limited to 500 numbered copies. 4to. Paper wrappers. (Also a 1971 revised and expanded edition, cloth bound in dust jacket, same publisher) A scarce work with brown bear and Dall sheep in Alaska.

Starkloff, Gene B., M. D.
"Make it Happen, Captain;" field trial tales and thoughts on judging. Olathe, Kansas, 1983, Privately printed. 120 pp., photographic plates, drawings. 4to; dust jacket.

Starr, George Ross
Decoys of the Atlantic Flyway. New York, 1974, Winchester Press. 308 pp., color and black and white illustrations. 4to; dust jacket. (Reprinted, same format and publisher, Tulsa) [Also a deluxe first edition, specially bound and limited to 375 numbered and signed copies; slipcased]

417

Starr, George Ross, continued

How To Make Working Decoys. Piscataway, New Jersey, 1978, Winchester Press. 164 pp., color and black and white photographic plates. 4to; dust jacket.

Starr, V. M.

The Muzzle Loading Shotgun; its care and its use. Eden, South Dakota, No date, Privately printed. 11 pp. 8vo. Paper wrappers.

Stearns, Jean Pride

A Catalog of the Duck Stamp Prints; with biographies of the artists. Revised by Russell A. Fink. No place (Lorton, Virginia), 1973, Privately printed. 109 pp., photographic plates in two volumes. Limited to 1500 numbered copies. 4to. Loose leaf, in a three ring binder.

A Catalog of the Maryland State Duck and Trout Stamp Prints; with biographies of the artists. Stevensville, 1979, Privately printed. 28 pp., with color reproductions of the paintings. Limited to 500 numbered and signed copies. 4to. Loose leaf, in a three ring binder. [Also a deluxe edition, on heavier stock with special end-papers, limited to 200 numbered and signed copies]

Stearns, Marshall

Along the Trail. No place, 1936, Privately printed. 152 pp., illustrations by Donald Gardner. 8vo. Salmon fishing and grouse hunting.

Just Memories. No place, 1932, Privately printed. 202 pp. 8vo. Upland hunting and trout fishing.

Memories and Reflections. No place, 1935, Privately printed. 158 pp., photographic plates. 8vo. Contains some grouse shooting.

Stebbins, Henry M.

How To Select and Use Your Big Game Rifle. Washington, D. C., 1952, Combat Forces Press. 237 pp., photographic plates. 8vo; dust jacket.

Pistols; a modern encyclopedia. Harrisburg, 1961, The Stackpole Company. 380 pp., photographic plates. 4to; dust jacket.

Rifles; a modern encyclopedia. Harrisburg, 1958, The Stackpole Company. 376 pp., photographic plates. 4to; dust jacket. (Reprinted, Castle Books)

Small Game and Varmint Rifles. New York, 1947, A. S. Barnes, Inc. 234 pp., photographic plates. A title in The Sportsman's Library series. 8vo; dust jacket.

Steele, W. O.

The Lone Hunt. New York, 1956, Harcourt, Brace & Co., Inc. 176 pp., illustrations. 8vo; dust jacket. A juvenile with buffalo hunting in Tennessee.

Stehsel, D. L.
   Hunting the California Black Bear.   1965, Privately printed.   194 pp.,
photographic plates.   8vo.   Paper wrappers.

Stein, Arthur Henry, Jr.
   Of a Hunter, Now! and other poems.   Albany, New York, 1944, Argus
Press.   Unpaginated, drawings by Arthur H. Stein.   8vo.

Steindler, R. A.
   The Firearms Dictionary.   Harrisburg, 1970, The Stackpole Company.
288 pp., photographic plates.   8vo; dust jacket.   (Also a revised and expanded
1985 edition titled, *Steindler's New Firearms Dictionary*, same publisher)
   Home Gunsmithing Digest.   Northfield, Illinois, 1975, DBI Books.   288
pp., illustrations.   4to.   Paper wrappers.   (Revised and reprinted several times,
same format and publisher)
   The Modern ABC's of Guns.   Harrisburg, 1965, The Stackpole Company.
191 pp., photographic plates.   8vo; dust jacket.
   Rifle Guide.   South Hackensack, New Jersey, 1978, Stoeger Publishing
Company.   304 pp., illustrations.   4to.   Paper wrappers.
   Reloader's Guide.   South Hackensack, New Jersey, 1975, Stoeger
Publishing Company.   223 pp., illustrations.   4to.   Paper wrappers. (Revised
and reprinted several times, same format and publisher)
   Shooting the Muzzle Loader.   Paramus, New Jersey, 1975, Jolex.   256
pp., color and black and white illustrations.   4to.

Stelfox, John G.
   Range Ecology of Rocky Mountain Bighorn Sheep.   Ottawa, 1976,
Canadian Wildlife Service.   49 pp., photographic plates, maps, bibliography.
4to.   Paper wrappers.

Stelle, J. P. and W. B. Harrison
   The Gunsmith's Manual; a complete handbook for the amateur
gunsmith, being a practical guide to all branches of the trade. Plantersville, South
Carolina, 1945, Small Arms Technical Publishing Company.   376 pp., color
frontispiece, drawings.   12mo; dust jacket.   (A facsimile reproduction of the
1883 first edition)

Stemple, David
   High Ridge Gobbler; a story of the American wild turkey.   New York,
1979, Collins.   47 pp., drawings by Ted Lewin.   8vo; dust jacket.   A juvenile.

Stenlund, Milt
>*Popple Leaves and Boot Oil;* a wildlife biologist in northern Minnesota. Grand Rapids, Minnesota, 1985, Heritage North Publishers. 126 pp., illustrations by Harvey Sandstrom. 8vo.

Stephen, David
>*Six Pointer Buck.* Philadelphia, 1957, J. B. Lippincott Co. 254 pp. 8vo; dust jacket.
>*String Lug the Fox.* Boston, 1952, Little, Brown & Company. 174 pp., illustrations. 8vo; dust jacket. Foxhunting.

Stephens, Chester H.
>*Reeve's Pheasant Investigations in Kentucky.* Frankfort, 1966, Kentucky Department of Fish and Game. 32 pp., photographic plates. 4to. Paper wrappers. A study of the survival rate of pen-raised Reeve's pheasants.

Stephens, Dan V.
>*Cottonwood Yarns;* being mostly stories told to children about some more or less wild animals that live at "The Cottonwoods" on the Elkhorn River in Nebraska. Fremont, 1935, Hammond and Stephens. 109 pp., photographic plates, drawings. 4to. Rare.

Stephens, Martin
>*Fair Game;* the open air of four continents. London, 1936, Murray. 274 pp., photographic plates. 8vo. Big game hunting around the world with sheep hunting in British Columbia.
>*Novice's Luck;* or some sporting sprints. New York, 1936, Charles Scribner's Sons. 225 pp., drawings by Tulling. 8vo. (Printed from British sheets) Containing some North American big game hunting.

Stephens, William L., Jr.
>*Rifle Marksmanship.* New York, 1941, A. S. Barnes and Company, Inc. 88pp., line drawings. 8vo; dust jacket.

Stetson, Joe
>*The Hunter's Handbook of Gundogs.* Jersey City, New Jersey, 1965, TFH Publishers. 64 pp., photographic plates. Paper wrappers.
>*Hunting With Flushing Dogs.* Jersey City, New Jersey, 1965, TFH Publishers. 64 pp., photographic plates, bibliography. Paper wrappers.
>*Hunting With Pointing Dogs.* Jersey City, New Jersey, 1965, TFH Publishers. 64 pp., photographic plates, bibliography. Paper wrappers.
>*Hunting With Retrievers.* Jersey City, New Jersey, 1965, TFH Publishers. 64 pp., photographic plates. Paper wrappers.

Stevens, Montague

Meet Mr. Grizzly; a saga on the passing of the grizzly. Albuquerque, 1943, University of New Mexico. 281 pp., frontispiece by Frederick Remington, photographic plates. 8vo; dust jacket. (Reprinted 1944, same format and publisher. Also a 1950 British edition)

Stevens, Ross O.

Talks About Wildlife; for hunters, fishermen and nature lovers. Raleigh, 1944, Privately printed. 229 pp., photographic plates, drawings. 8vo.

Stevens, W. E.

The Northwest Muskrat of the Mackenzie Delta, Northwest Territories, 1947-1948. Ottawa, 1953, Canadian Wildlife Service. 40 pp., photographic plates, maps. 4to. Paper wrappers.

Stewart, P. M.

Round the World With Rod and Rifle. London, 1924, Thornton Butterworth, Ltd. 294 pp., photographic plates, maps. 8vo. (Reprinted 1936, same format and publisher) Contains some North American hunting and angling. Not in Phillips.

Tales of Travel and Sport. London, 1938, Thornton Butterworth, Ltd. 319 pp., photographic plates. 8vo. (Reprinted 1940, same format and publisher) Contains bear and moose hunting in western Canada.

Travel and Sport in Many Lands. Garden City, New York, 1928, Doubleday, Doran & Co. 320 pp., photographic plates. 8vo. Containing grizzly bear, sheep, goat and caribou hunting in North America.

Stillman, Don

The Outdoor Trail of Don Stillman. Harrisburg, 1952, The Stackpole Company. 182 pp. 8vo; dust jacket. A collection of the author's columns originally appearing in the *New York Herald Tribune*.

Stilwell, Hart   1902-1975

Hunting and Fishing in Texas. New York, 1946, Alfred A. Knopf, Inc. 255 pp., color and black and white photographic plates. A Borzoi Book For Sportsmen. 8vo; dust jacket.

Stimson, Henry L.

My Vacations. No place, 1949, Privately printed. 180 pp., photographic plates. 8vo. The hunting, fishing and wilderness memoirs of this former Secretary of State. A scarce title describing hunting trips in the area that became Glacier National Park.

Stirling, Ian, et al.
The Ecology of the Polar Bear (Ursus maritimus) Along the Western Coast of Hudson Bay. Ottawa, 1977, Canadian Wildlife Service.   64 pp., maps, bibliography.   8vo.   Paper wrappers.

Stockbridge, V. D.
Digest of Patents Relating To Breech Loading and Magazine Small Arms (Except revolvers) Granted in the United States From 1836 to 1873.   New Milford, Connecticut, 1973, Flayderman.   176 pp., illustrations.   8vo; dust jacket.   (A reproduction of the 1874 edition)

Stockton, M. L., Jr.
Duck Hunter's Determinant.   Harrisburg, 1940.   36 pp., illustrations. 16mo.   Paper wrappers.   Scarce.

Stoddard, Gordon
Go North, Young Man; modern homesteading in Alaska.   Portland, Oregon, 1957, Binsford and Mort.   239 pp., photographic plates.   8vo; dust jacket.   A guide with much on hunting and fishing in the area.

Stoddard, Herbert L.   b. 1889
The Bobwhite Quail; its habits, preservation and increase.   New York, 1931, Charles Scribner's Sons.   559 pp., photographic plates, color plates from paintings by E. R. Kalmbach.   4to; dust jacket.   (Reprinted several times, same format and publisher)   [Also a deluxe first edition, specially bound with an original signed etching by Frank Benson and limited to 260 numbered and signed copies; slipcased] An impressive and important work covering species, habitat development, natural predators, management, etc.
Maintenance and Increase of the Eastern Wild Turkey on Private Lands of the Coastal Plain of the Deep Southeast.   Tallahassee, Florida, 1963, Tall Timbers Plantation.   49 pp., frontispiece.   8vo.   Paper wrappers.
Memoirs of a Naturalist.   Norman, 1969, University of Oklahoma Press.   303 pp., photographic plates, plates in color by G. M. Sutton, bibliography. 8vo; dust jacket.   The author's autobiography.
Progress on Cooperative Quail Investigation.   No place, 1925, U. S. Biological Survey / Quail Study Fund For South Georgia and North Florida.   22 pp., illustrations.   8vo.   Paper wrappers.
Report on Cooperative Quail Investigation, 1925-1926. No place, 1926, U. S. Biological Survey / Quail Study Fund For South Georgia and North Florida. 62 pp., illustrations.   8vo.   Paper wrappers.

Stoddard, Herbert L., et al.
    The Cooperative Quail Study Association; May 1, 1931 - May 1, 1943. Tallahassee, Florida, 1961, Tall Timbers Plantation.   500 pp., bibliographies throughout.   8vo. Paper wrappers. A reprint of 42 of the reports of this commission.

Stokes, Bill
    Hi-Ho Silver, Anyway.   Milwaukee, 1979, The Milwaukee Journal. 227 pp.   A compilation of stories by this outdoor writer.

Stokes, G. V.
    Sporting Dogs. London / New York, 1938, Country Life Press / Charles Scribner's Sons. 167 pp., color frontispiece, drawings.   4to; dust jacket.

Stone, George Cameron
    A Glossary of the Construction, Decoration and Use of Arms and Armor in All Countries and In All Times. Portland, Maine, 1934, The Southworth Press. 694 pp., illustrations.   Limited to 400 copies. Folio. (Reprinted several times, various publishers) [Also a deluxe first edition, specially bound and limited to 35 copies]

Stone, George W.
    The Winchester 1873 Handbook.   Arvada, Colorado, 1973, Frontier Press.   234 pp., photographic plates, drawings.   4to. A collector's guide to this legendary rifle.

Stone, Walton Edgar
    Walton Stone; a Bunyan, Boone, Crockett, a Robinson Crusoe.   New York, 1931, Privately printed. 345 pp., frontispiece. 8vo. (Also a revised edition, 1937) Bear hunting, trapping and wildfowling in North Carolina.

Storer, Tracy I. and L. P. Tevis, Jr.
    California Grizzly. Berkeley, 1955, University of California Press.   335 pp., color and black and white illustrations. 8vo; dust jacket. (Reprinted 1978, University of Nebraska Press)

Storm, Barry
    Practical Pistoleering; a manual of practical revolver shooting techniques. Aguila, Arizona, 1943, Southwestern Press. 41 pp., photographic plates. 18mo. Paper wrappers.

Storm, Hugo
    Seven Lead Hounds. Los Angeles, 1940, Harper and Davis.   76 pp., drawings. 8vo; dust jacket. Poetry on hunting with coon hounds.

Stout, Gardner D., et al., editors
 The Shorebirds of North America. New York, 1967, Viking Press. 270 pp., color and black and white illustrations by Robert V. Clem, bibliography. Text by Peter Matthiessen and Robert S. Palmer. Folio; dust jacket. (Reprinted 1968, same format and publisher) [Also a deluxe first edition, specially bound and limited to 350 numbered copies signed by the editor, authors and artist; slipcased]

Stowe, Leland
 Crusoe of Lonesome Lake. New York, 1957, Random House, Inc. 234 pp. 8vo; dust jacket. (Reprinted, same format and publisher) The story of Ralph Edwards homesteading in British Columbia, with some hunting.

Straight, Lee
 How To Hunt Deer and Other Game. Vancouver, British Columbia, 1974, Saltaire. 160 pp.

Street, Alfred B.
 Woods and Waters; or the Saranacs and racket, with map of the route and nine illustrations on wood. Harrison, New York, 1976, Harbor Hill Books. 345 pp., illustrations. 8vo. (A facsimile reproduction of the 1860 first edition) Early big and small game hunting in the Adirondacks.

Street, James
 The Biscuit Eater. New York, 1941, The Dial Press. 88 pp., drawings by Arthur Fuller. 8vo; dust jacket. An older juvenile about farm life in the old South with a boy and his English pointer.

Streeter, Thomas Winthrop 1883-1965
 The Thomas Winthrop Streeter Collection of Americana. New York, 1966, 1967, Parke-Bernet Galleries, Inc. Seven volumes with 3002 total pp., plus an index volume of 352 pp., all with photographic plates. 8vo. An auction catalog of this most comprehensive collection of Americana. It includes several hundred North American hunting titles.

Streever, Fred
 The American Trail Hound. New York, 1948, A. S. Barnes and Company, Inc. 202 pp., plates. A title in The Sportsman's Library series. 8vo; dust jacket.

Strickland, Roy W. (as told to **John L. Rodgers**)
 Common Sense Grouse and Woodcock Dog Training. Grand Rapids, Michigan, 1981, Privately printed. 82 pp., photographic plates. 8vo. Paper wrappers.

Stringfellow, Robert B.
    The Standard Book of Hunting and Shooting. New York, 1950, Greystone Press. 567 pp., photographic plates, line drawings, color frontispiece. 4to; dust jacket. (This, an abridged edition of *The Hunter's Encyclopedia,* edited by **Raymond C. Camp**, which see)

Strong, Gen. William E.
    Canadian River Hunt. Norman, 1960, University of Oklahoma Press. 47 pp., illustrations, folding map. Limited to 1050 copies. 8vo; slipcased. This is a reproduction of an 1878 journal of a hunt in the Oklahoma Indian Territory.

Strong, Gen. William E., continued
    A Trip to the Yellowstone National Park in July, August and September, 1875. Norman, 1968, University of Oklahoma Press. 165 pp., illustrations. 8vo; dust jacket. (Originally published, 1876) Includes some deer and elk hunting inside the park.

Strong, Karl F.
    Evaluative Review of Deer Yard Management in New Hampshire and Maine. Concord, 1977, New Hampshire Fish and Game Commission. Illustrated. 4to. Spiral bound paper wrappers.

Stroudt, Jerome
    Ecological Factors Affecting Waterfowl Production in the Saskatchewan Parklands. Washington, D. C., 1971, United States Department of the Interior. 58 pp., photographic plates, maps, bibliography. 4to. Paper wrappers.

Strung, Norman
    The Art of Hunting. Minneapolis, 1984, Cy DeCosse, Inc. 160 pp., color illustrations. 4to. (Also a 1984 edition, Hunting and Fishing Library)
    The Complete Hunter's Catalog. Philadelphia, 1977, J. B. Lippincott Co. 438 pp., illustrations. 4to; dust jacket.
    Deer Hunting; tactics and guns for hunting all North American deer. Philadelphia, 1973, J. B. Lippincott Co. 239 pp., illustrations. 8vo; dust jacket. (Reprinted, same format and publisher)
    The Hunter's Almanac. New York, 1971, The Macmillan Company. 240 pp., illustrations. 12mo.
    Misty Mornings and Moonless Nights. New York, 1974, The Macmillan Company. 251 pp., photographic plates, maps. 8vo; dust jacket. An entertaining guide to waterfowling, including blinds, decoys, etc.

Stuart, Jack
    Bird Dogs and Upland Game Birds. Fairfax, Virginia, 1983, Denlinger's, Inc. 111 pp., photographic plates, drawings. 4to. Paper wrappers.

Stuart, Frank S.
    Wild Wings; chronicles of the annual migration of a flock of ducks. New York, 1952, McGraw-Hill Publishing Company. 222 pp. 8vo; dust jacket.

Sullivan, C. John
    A Chronicle of Letters; Robert F. McGaw. Jr., decoy maker, 1879-1958. Fallston, 1985, Maplehurst. 170 pp., photographic plates. Limited to 1000 numbered and signed copies. 8vo; dust jacket. (Also produced in a limited edition of 400 numbered and signed copies in paper wrappers, same publisher and year)
    Waterfowling; the upper Chesapeake's legacy. Fallston, 1983, Maplehurst. 170 pp., photographic plates. Limited to 1000 numbered and signed copies. 8vo; dust jacket. An informal history of the area and its gunning clubs.

Sutherland, Robert Q. and Robert Lawrence Wilson
    The Book of Colt Firearms. Kansas City, 1971, Privately printed. 604 pp., many color and black and white illustrations. Folio; dust jacket. (Reprinted several times, same format) The most desirable reference work for colt firearms collectors.

Sutton, George Miksch   1898-1982
    Eskimo Year; a naturalist's adventures in the far north. New York, 1934, The Macmillan Company. 321 pp., illustrations. 8vo; dust jacket. (Reprinted and revised several times, various publishers)
    High Arctic; an expedition to the unspoiled north. New York, 1971, P. S. Eriksson. 119 pp., color and black and white illustrations. 4to; dust jacket. (Reprinted 1975, same format and publisher)
    To a Young Bird Artist; letters from L. A. Fuertes to George M. Sutton. Norman, 1979, University of Oklahoma Press. 147 pp., color and black and white illustrations by Sutton and Fuertes. 8vo; dust jacket.
    Mr. Sutton was an acclaimed ornithologist and bird illustrator. Most of the books were non-sporting, but many of his illustrations were used in hunting related titles.

Sutton, George W. and Marvin Briggs
    Camping By the Highway. New York, 1925, Field & Stream. 160 pp., illustrations by Lynn Bogue Hunt. 8vo. Canvas wrappers. Volume I in the Field & Stream Outdoorsman's Library. Not in Phillips. A scarce Lynn Bogue Hunt item.

Sutton, Dr. Richard Lightburn
    An Arctic Safari. St. Louis, 1932, C. V. Mosby Company. 199 pp., illustrations, map. 8vo; dust jacket. Hunting for seal, walrus and polar bear. Scarce.

Sutton, Dr. Richard Lightburn, continued

Silver Kings of Arkansas Pass; and other stories.　Kansas City, 1937, Brown-White. 352 pp., frontispiece. 8vo; dust jacket. Mostly angling, but some quail and turkey hunting. Scarce.

Suydam, Charles R.

The American Cartridge; an illustrated study of the rimfire cartridge in the United States.　Santa Anna, California, 1960, G. Robert Lawrence.　185 pp., photographic plates, bibliography.　8vo; dust jacket. A monograph of the .22 caliber rimfire cartridge.

Swank, Wendell G.

The Mule Deer in Arizona Chaparral; and an analysis of other important deer herds - A Research and Management Study.　Phoenix, 1958, Arizona Game and Fish Department.　109 pp., illustrations.　8vo.　Paper wrappers. (Reprinted twice to 1965, same format and publisher)

Swanson, Anton

M is For Moose; monarch of the forest.　New York, 1954, Vantage Press.　64 pp., illustrations.　8vo; dust jacket.

Swanson, Elmer

Automatic Firearm Pistols.　Weehawken, New Jersey, 1955, Wesmore Book Co.　210 pp., illustrations.　8vo.　(This title was often issued with **Smith, James A.**, *Antique Pistol Book*, together in a slip case, which see) [Also a numbered, limited edition]

Swanson, Gustav A., editor

The Mitigation Symposium; a national workshop on mitigating losses of fish and wildlife habitat.　Fort Collins, Colorado, 1979, United States Forest Service.　684 pp., photographic plates, maps.　4to.　Paper wrappers.

Swantner, David, editor

Texas Hunter's Directory. 1983, Outdoor Worlds of Texas.　160 pp.

Swayne, Sam and Zoa Swayne

Great-Grandfather in the Honey Tree.　New York, 1949, Viking Press. 53 pp., line drawings by Zoa Swayne. 8vo. Humorous account of a mighty hunter.

Swayze, Nathan L.

'51 Colt Navies.　1967, Privately printed.　243 pp., photographic plates, drawings.　4to. Scarce.

Swendsen, David

Badge in the Wilderness; my 30 dangerous years combating wildlife violators. Harrisburg, 1985, Stackpole Books. 191 pp., illustrations. 8vo; dust jacket.

Swenson, G. W. P.

Pictorial History of the Rifle. New York, 1972, Drake Publishers. 184 pp., illustrations, bibliography. 8vo; dust jacket. (Reprinted several times, various publishers)

Swift, Ernest

A History of Wisconsin Deer. Madison, 1946, Department of Conservation. 96 pp.

Swiggert, Hal, editor

Hal Swiggert on North American Deer. Oakland, New Jersey, 1980, Jolex. 272 pp., photographic plates, drawings. 4to. Paper wrappers.

Swinehart, Bob

Sagittarius. Covina, California, 1970, The Gallant Publishing Co. 240 pp., color and black and white illustrations. 4to; dust jacket. Many considered Swinehart the greatest archer in history. A privately printed title with sections on hunting big game in America and Africa as well as a section on Howard Hill, another great archer-hunter. Scarce.

Tabor, Richard and Raymond F. Dassmann

The Balcktailed Deer of the Chaparral; its life history and management in the North Coast Range of California. Sacramento, 1958, California Department of Fish and Game. 8vo. Paper wrappers.

Tabor, F. Wallace

High Adventure Odyssey; with rod, rifle and camera, bow and boat into Alaska, Canada, Africa, South America and the U. S. A. El Paso, Texas, 1981, Privately printed. 100 pp., illustrations. Paper wrappers.

North to Adventure; with rod, rifle and camera, bow and boat into Alaska, Canada and Norway. Dallas, 1964, Privately printed. 96 pp., photographic plates. 4to. Paper wrappers. With much big game hunting.

Road to Romance; up the famed Alaskan Highway and beyond with rifle, rod and camera. Denver, 1958, Privately printed. 96 pp., photographic plates. 4to. Paper wrappers.

Tiger By the Tail; with rod, rifle and camera, bow and boat in Mexico, Hawaii and India. Dallas, 1964, Privately printed. 95 pp., photographic plates. Paper wrappers.

Mr. Tabor was a renowned big game hunter who also wrote and published *Assignment Safari* and *Rifleman in Africa.*

Tait, R. H.

Newfoundland. New York, 1939, Privately printed. 260 pp., illustrations. Mostly history of the area, but some hunting.

Talbot, Nelson S.

The Cabin. No place (Dayton, Ohio), 1946, Privately printed. 124 pp., photographic plates. 4to. The author built and decorated a room in his home that duplicated a Canadian hunting cabin. In this work he recounts episodes of camp life and his various hunting adventures while at the cabin. A scarce and curious hunting title.

Tappe, Donald T.

The Status of Beavers in California. California, 1942. 59 pp., photographic plates. 8vo. Paper wrappers.

Tapply, H. G. "Tap"

The Sportsman's Notebook and Tap's Tips. New York, 1964, Holt, Rinehart and Winston. 333 pp., drawings by Walter Dower. 8vo; dust jacket. An anthology of hunting and angling stories originally published in *Field & Stream* magazine. Mr. Tapply's chief contribution to sporting literature was as an angling writer. See Bruns.

Tarrant, Bill

Best Way To Train Your Gun Dog; The Delmar Smith Method. New York, 1977, David McKay Co. 186 pp., photographic plates. 8vo; dust jacket. (Reprinted many times, same format and publisher)

Tarrant, Bill, continued

Bill Tarrant's Gun Dog Book; a treasury of happy tails. Scottsdale, Arizona, 1980, Sun Trails Publishing Company. 177 pp., drawings. 8vo; dust jacket.

Tawes, William

Creative Bird Carving. Cambridge, Maryland, 1969, Tidewater Publishers. 207 pp., photographic plates, drawings. 4to; dust jacket. (Reprinted twice, same format and publisher). The contents are heavily skewed toward waterfowl carving.

Taylerson, A. W. F., et al.

The Revolver, 1818-1865. New York, 1966, Crown Publishers, Inc. 360 pp., photographic plates. 8vo; dust jacket. (Reprinted 1968, same format and publisher)

Taylersen, A. W. F.

The Revolver, 1865-1888. New York, 1966, Crown Publishers, Inc. 292 pp., illustrations, bibliography. 8vo; dust jacket.

The Revolver, 1889-1914. New York, 1971, Crown Publishers, Inc. 324 pp., illustrations. 8vo; dust jacket.

Revolving Arms. New York, 1967, Walker. 123 pp., illustrations. 8vo; dust jacket.

All of these titles written by Taylerson were British works co-published in New York.

Taylor, Paul

Regarding Stories. Lake Worth, 1971, Privately printed. 83 pp. 8vo. Some angling and moose hunting in these reminiscences.

Taylor, Walter P.   b. 1888

The Deer of North America. Harrisburg, 1956, The Stackpole Company / The Wildlife Management Institute. 668 pp., photographic plates, diagrams, two color illustrations from paintings by Walter A. Weber. Thick 8vo; dust jacket. (Reprinted three times to 1969; same format and publishers) [Also a deluxe first edition, specially bound, but with no specified limitation, same publisher] The first thorough, scientific work on the subject and still an important book.

Taylor, Zack

Successful Waterfowling. New York, 1974, Crown Publishers, Inc. 276 pp., illustrations. 4to; dust jacket. (Reprinted 1975, same format and publisher. Reprinted 1981, paper wrappers, Stackpole Books)

Teague, R. D., editor
  A Manual of Wildlife Conservation. Washington, D. C., 1973, The Wildlife Society. 206 pp., photographic plates, drawings by F. L. Jaques and others. 4to. Paper wrappers.

Teer, James G., et al.
  Ecology and Management of White Tailed Deer in the Llano Basin of Texas. Washington, 1965, The Wildlife Society. Monograph # 15. 62 pp., illustrations. 4to. Paper wrappers.

Tener, J. S.
  Muskoxen in Canada; a biological and taxonomic review. Ottawa, 1965, Canadian Wildlife Survey. 166 pp., photographic plates, bibliography. 8vo.

Tenney, Horace Kent
  Vert and Venison. Chicago, 1924, Privately printed by the Lakeside Press. 155 pp. 8vo. Hunting and angling stories. Not in Phillips.
  The Quick-As-Scat Book. No place, 1931, Privately printed. 53 pp., photographic plate. 8vo. Children's stories about animals with a setting of the Huron Mountain Club.
  Selected Writings. Chicago, 1937, Privately printed. 202 pp. 8vo. This was published posthumously by the Tenny family as a memorial to the author.

Tennyson, Jon R.
  A Singleness of Purpose; the story of Ducks Unlimited. Chicago, 1977, Ducks Unlimited. 127 pp., color and black and white illustrations. 4to; dust jacket.

Tetso, John
  Trapping is My Life. Toronto, 1970, Peter Martin Associates. Revised edition. 116 pp., illustrations. 8vo; dust jacket. (Reprinted 1976, same format and publisher)

Texas Game, Fish and Oyster Commission
  Principal Game Birds and Mammals of Texas; their distribution and management. Austin, 1945, Texas Game, Fish and Oyster Commission. 149 pp., illustrations, fold out maps. 8vo.

Thalheimer, Roland
  Percussion Revolvers of the United States. St. Louis, 1970, Privately printed. 224 pp., photographic plates, glossary, bibliography. 8vo; dust jacket.

Thomas, Jack Ward and Dale E. Toweill, editors
Elk of North America; ecology and management.   Harrisburg /
Washington D. C., 1982, The Stackpole Company / Wildlife Management
Institute.   698 pp., extensively illustrated with photographic plates, drawings,
maps, charts.   4to; dust jacket. An extensive and authoritative work.

Thomas, Gough   (*pseud.* of **G. T. Garwood**)   **1900-1987**
Gough Thomas's Gun Book; shotgun lore for the sportsman.   New York,
1970, Winchester Press.   227 pp., photographic plates, drawings.   8vo; dust
jacket.   (Reprinted 1972, same format and publisher.   Originally published,
1969, Great Britain)
Gough Thomas's Second Gun Book; more shotgun lore for the
sportsman.   New York, 1972, Winchester Press.   227 pp., photographic plates,
diagrams. 8vo; dust jacket. (Originally published, 1971, Great Britain)
Shotgun Shooting Facts and Fancies.   New York, 1978, Winchester
Press.   280pp., photographic plates, drawings.   Tall 8vo; dust jacket. (Reprinted
1979, same format and publisher.   Also a 1978 British edition) This is essentially a
revised edition of *Gough Thomas' Second Gun Book.*

Thomas, H. H.
The Story of Allen and Wheelock Firearms.   Lexington, 1965, Privately
printed.   125 pp., photographic plates.   8vo.   A history of this early New England
arms manufacturer.

Thomas, Joseph B., M. F. H.   **1879-1955**
Hounds and Hunting Through the Ages.   New York, 1928, The
Derrydale Press. 272 pp., photographic plates.   Limited to 750 copies. Folio;
dust jacket.   (Reprinted 1929, same format and publisher; limited to 250 copies.
Also reprinted, 1933, smaller format, Windward House.   Also reprinted, 1937,
smaller format, Garden City publishing Co.) [Also a deluxe first edition, specially
bound and limited to 50 numbered copies signed by the author]
How To Ride To Hounds. New York, 1927, Privately printed for Donald
Perkins, M. F. H.   27 pp.   8vo.   Paper wrappers.
Observation on Borzoi; called in America Russian Wolfhounds.
Campbell, 1976, Dehack.   123 pp., color frontispiece, photographic plates. 8vo.
(Originally published, 1912, Houghton Mifflin Company)

Thomas, Lowell   **1892-1981**
Rolling Stone; the life and adventures of Arthur Radcliffe Dugmore.
New York, 1934, Doubleday, Doran & Co., Inc. 311 pp., illustrations.   8vo;
dust jacket.   Arthur Dugmore was a talented wildlife painter and the author of *Romance of the
Newfoundland Caribou,* 1913, and several other books.

Thomas, Lowell, continued

Tall Stories; the rise and triumph of the Great American Whopper. New York, 1945, Harvest. 186 pp., drawings. 8vo; dust jacket. Includes many angling and hunting tales too fantastic to be true.

Thompson, Donald R. and J. C. Moulton

An Evaluation of Wisconsin Ruffed Grouse Surveys. Madison, 1981, Wisconsin Department of Natural Resources. 12 pp., illustrations. 4to. Paper wrappers.

Thompson, J. Maurice

The Witchery of Archery. Revised edition. Pinehusrt, North Carolina, 1928, The Archer's Company. 259 pp., frontispiece. Edited by Robert Elmer. 12mo. (Originally published, 1877, Charles Scribner's Sons) Maurice Thompson and his brother Will, two of the founders of The National Archery Association, did much to popularize archery. This title has much on hunting with the bow and arrow.

Thompson, John Baptiste de Macklot
    See, **Ripley, Ozark**

Thompson, Lewis S.

The Long Point Company. New York, 1932, Privately printed by the Scribner Press. 85 pp., illustrations by Frank Benson and Louis Agassiz Fuertes. 4to. A history of this Ontario shooting club noted for its immense waterfowl populations.

Thompson, Raymond

The Wilderness Trapper. Columbus, Ohio, 1924, Hunter-Trader-Trapper. 226 pp., illustrations. 12mo. (Reprinted many times, various publishers)

Thompson, William C.

The Irish Setter in Word and Pictures. Richmond, Virginia, 1954, Denlinger's. 544 pp., illustrations. 8vo.

The New Irish Setter. New York, 1968, Howell Book House. 272 pp., photographic plates. 8vo. (Reprinted many times, same format and publisher)

Thornberry, Russell

Trophy Deer of Alberta. Alberta, 1982, Green Horn Publishing. 299 pp., photographic plates, drawings. 8vo; dust jacket. An account of some 600 trophy mule and white tail deer taken in Alberta from about 1900 to 1980.

Thorne, Tom

The Status, Mortality & Response To Management of the Bighorn Sheep of Whiskey Mountain. Cheyenne, 1979, Wyoming Fish and game Commission. 213 pp., color and black and white illustrations. 4to. Paper wrappers.

Thorp, Raymond W.
 Doc W. F. Carver; spirit gun of the west. California, 1957, Arthur H. Clarke Co. 266 pp., illustrations. 8vo; dust jacket. The biography of Doc Carver, legendary trapper, buffalo hunter, marksman and originator of "Wild West shows."

Tillett, Paul
 Doe Day; the antler-less deer controversy in New Jersey. New Brunswick, 1963, Rutgers University Press. 126 pp., tables. 8vo; dust jacket. A discussion of the pros and cons of harvesting antler-less deer.

Timmer, Dan
 Eastern Wild Turkey in Louisiana. Baton Rouge, No date (ca. 1985), Louisiana Department of Wildlife. 24 pp., photographic plates. 8vo. Paper wrappers.

Tinker, Ben
 Mexican Wilderness and Wildlife. Austin, 1978, University of Texas Press. 131 pp., drawings. Foreword by A. Starker Leopold. 8vo; dust jacket. An excellent overview with much on desert big horn sheep.

Tinkle, Lon
 An American Original; the life of J. Frank Dobie. Boston, 1978, Little, Brown and Company. 264 pp., photographic plates, bibliography. 8vo; dust jacket. The biography of this popular southwestern America writer.

Tinsley, Russell
 Bow Hunter's Guide. South Hackensack, New Jersey, 1975, Stoeger Publishing Company. 191 pp., illustrations. 4to. Paper wrappers.
 Hunting the Whitetail Deer. New York, 1965, Outdoor Life Books. 144 pp., photographic plates. 8vo. Paper wrappers. (Reprinted many times, same format and publisher)
 Taxidermy Guide. South Hackensack, New Jersey, 1967, Stoeger Publishing Company. 191 pp., photographic plates, drawings. 4to. Paper wrappers. (Also a 1977 revised edition, same format and publisher)

Tinsley, Russell, editor
 All About Small Game Hunting in America. New York, 1976, Winchester Press. 308 pp., photographic plates. 8vo; dust jacket. With contributions by Bauer, Dalrymple, Duffey and others.

Todd, Frank S.
 Waterfowl; ducks, geese and swans of the world. New York, 1979, Harcourt, Brace and Jovanovich, Inc. 399 pp., color photographic plates. Square 4to; dust jacket. (Also printed, 1979, Seaworld Press)

Todd, John

    Long Lake. Harrison, New York, 1983, Harbor Hill Books. 100 pp., illustrations plus a new 28 pp. introduction by W. H. Cadbury. 12mo; dust jacket. (A facsimile reproduction of the 1845 first edition) Described as the earliest Adirondack book, with much hunting and suggestions for settlers.

Tolman, F. Harold

    A Disciple of John Peel; being the reminiscences and confessions of an interested member of the Millwood Hunt. Brookline, Massachusetts, 1932, Privately printed. 18 pp., drawings by Charles Wales Holmes. Limited to 500 copies. 8vo; slipcase. Memoirs of foxhunting.

Tolman, Newton F.

    North of Monadnock. Boston, 1961, Little, Brown & Company. 236 pp. 8vo; dust jacket. Life in the Monadnock region of New Hampshire. Containing some grouse shooting.

Tome, Philip   1782-1855

    Pioneer Life; or thirty years a hunter, being scenes and adventures in the life of Philip Tome, 15 years interpreter for Corn-planter and Governor Blacksnake, chiefs on the Allegheny River. Harrisburg, 1928, Privately printed by the Aurand Press. 173 pp., frontispiece. Limited to 500 numbered copies, signed by the publisher. 8vo. (A reproduction of the 1854 first edition) Instances of bear, elk and panther hunting in early Pennsylvania.

Tooker, Jack

    Hunting Technic. Denver, 1944, Privately printed. 71 pp., photographic plates, drawings by Paul de Gaston. 12mo. Paper wrappers. The author's views regarding hunting technique on small and large game.

Topperwein, Ad

    Snap Shooting. New Haven, Connecticut, 1939, Winchester Repeating Arms Company. 15 pp., illustrations. 8vo. Paper wrappers. For many years the author was a spokesman for Winchester who toured the country performing trick shooting exhibitions.

Tose, Frank

    Trapping, Tanning, Taxidermy. Columbus, Ohio, 1928, Hunter-Trader-Trapper. 174 pp., illustrations. 12mo.

Totten, M. G.

    A Pocket Guide of Ducks and Decoys. Dedham, No date (ca. 1950), Privately printed. 32 pp., drawings. 16mo.

Townsend, E. Jane
　　Gunner's Paradise; wildfowling and decoys on Long Island.　Stoney Brook, New York, 1979, The Museum at Stoney Brook.　152 pp., color and black and white illustrations, bibliography.　Oblong 8vo.　Paper wrappers.

Townsend, M. T. and M. W. Smith
　　The White-Tailed Deer of the Adirondacks.　Syracuse, New York, 1933, Bulletin of the Roosevelt Wild Life Experiment Station.　385 pp., illustrations, fold-out maps, bibliography.　8vo.　Paper wrappers.

Traister, John
　　Learn Gunsmithing; the troubleshooting method.　Tulsa, Oklahoma, 1980, Winchester Press.　202 pp., photographic plates.　8vo; dust jacket.

Traff, Cliff and John Lindgren
　　Last of the Prairie Carvers; decoys by John Tax.　No place (Minneapolis), 1970, Privately printed.　32 pp., photographic plates.　8vo. Paper wrappers.

Trausch, William D.
　　The Grab Bag.　New York, 1939, Pegasus Publishing Company.　156 pp.　8vo.　A collection of stories, some of which include fly fishing, deer and small game hunting.

Traver, Robert (*pseud.* of **John Voelker**)　　**1903-1991**
　　Danny and the Boys; being some legends of Hungry Hollow.　New York, 1951, World Publishing Company.　254 pp.　8vo; dust jacket.　(Reprinted several times, same format and publisher)　A fictionalized account of a lumberjack's adventures with some hunting and angling.
　　Mr. Voelker was a successful Michigan　attorney who also became a popular author. Beside writing *Anatomy of a Murder,* which was a bestseller and later became a motion picture, he also wrote several angling titles (*Anatomy of a Fisherman, Trout Madness, Trout Magic*) He also wrote several non-sporting novels.

Trefethen, James B.　　1916-1976
　　An American Crusade For Wildlife.　New York, 1975, Winchester Press / Boone and Crockett Club.　409 pp., plates.　8vo; dust jacket.　(Reprinted 1985, same format and publisher)　[Also a specially bound, limited first edition of 200 numbered copies; slipcased]　A revised edition of the author's *Crusade For Wildlife.*
　　Crusade For Wildlife; highlights in conservation progress.　Harrisburg, 1961, The Stackpole Company / Boone and Crockett Club.　377 pp., black and white and color illustrations from paintings and drawings by Bob Hines and Carl Rungius. 8vo; dust jacket.　[Also a deluxe edition, specially bound, but with no specified limitation]

Trefethen, James B., continued
Wildlife Management And Conservation. Boston, 1964, D. C. Heath. 120 pp., illustrations., map. 8vo.

Trefethen, James B., editor
The American Landscape, 1776-1976; two centuries of change. Washington, D. C., 1976, Wildlife Management Institute. 91 pp., color and black and white illustrations. 4to.

The Wild Sheep in Modern North America; the proceedings of the workshop on the management biology of North American wild sheep at the University of Montana in 1974. New York, 1975, Winchester Press / Boone and Crockett Club. 302 pp., plates. Tall 8vo; dust jacket. (Reprinted 1981, in paper wrappers, same publisher) [Also a specially bound, limited first edition of 100 numbered copies; slipcased]

Trefethen, James B.
Also see **Cottam, Clarence**

Trefzger, Hardy
My Fifty Years; of hunting, fishing, prospecting, guiding, trading and trapping in Alaska. New York, 1963, Exposition Press. 118 pp., photographic plates., maps. 8vo; dust jacket.

Trego, Keith and Ted Upgren
Hungarian Partridge Bibliography. Bismarck, 1975, North Dakota Game and Fish Department. 115 pp. 4to. Paper wrappers.

Trembly, Ray
Trails of an Alaskan Game Warden. Anchorage, 1985, Alaska Northwest Publishing Company. 176 pp., illustrations. 8vo. Paper wrappers.

Trails of an Alaskan Trapper; from the Midwest to the Far North, a trap line diary. Anchorage, 1983, Alaska Northwest Publishing Company. 169 pp., drawings, map. Foreword by Calvin Rutstrum. 8vo; dust jacket. (Reprinted in paper wrappers, same publisher)

Trench, Charles C.
A History of Marksmanship. Chicago, 1972, Follett Publishing Company. 319 pp., color and black and white illustrations. 4to; dust jacket. (Reprinted 1980, Exeter) Concerning both firearms and archery.

Trigg, Haiden C.
The American Fox Hound. No place, No date, Privately printed. 67 pp., illustrations. 8vo. Paper wrappers. (A reproduction of the 1890 edition) Outlining the history of the Trigg, Birdsong and Maupin strains of fox hounds.

Trinity College

    Ornithology Books In the Library of Trinity College, Hartford. Hartford, Connecticut, 1983, Trinity College. 270 pp., photographic plates. A numbered edition of unspecified limitation. 4to; dust jacket. This library contains the collection of the late Ostram Enders, whose main area of interest was game birds. A useful reference that had a supplement published in 1991.

Trippensee, R. E.

    Wild Life Management; upland game and general principles. Volume I. New York, 1948, McGraw-Hill Publishing Company. 479 pp., bibliography. 8vo. (Reprinted several times, same format and publisher)

    Wild Life Management; furbearers, waterfowl and fish. New York, 1952, McGraw-Hill Publishing Company. Volume II. 479 pp., bibliography. 8vo. (Reprinted several times, same format and publisher) Both are college-level textbooks.

Trolard, Tom

    Winchester Commemoratives. Dallas, 1985, Privately printed. 183 pp., photographic plates. Oblong 8vo. A description of the various models of commemorative firearms produced by Winchester.

Troy, John

    Ben; the adventures of a hunting retriever. Oshkosh, Wisconsin, 1984, Willow Creek Press. 96 pp., cartoon drawings. 8vo. (Reprinted 1985, same format and publisher)

True, Dan.

    A Family of Eagles. New York, 1980, Everest. 159 pp., color illustrations. 8vo; dust jacket. Observations of a bald eagle family in Texas.

Trueblood, Ted

    The Hunter's Handbook. New York, 1954, Thomas Y. Crowell Company. 247 pp., photographic plates. 8vo; dust jacket.

    The Ted Trueblood Hunting Treasury. New York, 1978, David McKay Co. 348 pp., photographic plates. Foreword by Ed Zern. 8vo; dust jacket.

    Ted Trueblood on Hunting. New York, 1953, Arco. 143 pp., illustrations. 4to. (Also reprinted, 1953, in paper wrappers, Fawcett Books)

Truesdell, Stephen R.

    The Rifle. Harrisburg, 1947, The Military Service Publishing Company. 274 pp., photographic plates, tables, bibliography. 8vo; dust jacket. An important work detailing the development of the modern big-bore hunting rifle with actual hunters identified, the specific rifles they used and the number of species taken by them.

Trzoniec, Stanley W.
Modern American Centerfire Handguns. Tulsa, Oklahoma, 1981, Winchester Press. 260 pp., color and black and white illustrations. 8vo; dust jacket.

Tsukamoto, George K.
Hunting the Desert Ram. Reno, 1983, Nevada Department of Wildlife. 28 pp., illustrations. 8vo. Paper wrappers. Desert big horn sheep hunting in Nevada.

Tuck, Davis H.
The Complete English Setter. Silver Springs, Maryland, 1951, Denlinger's. 368 pp., photographic plates. 8vo.
The New Complete English Setter; a compilation of interesting facts, data and observations on breeding, raising, training and showing and hunting English Setters. New York, 1964, Howell Book House. 352 pp., illustrations. Revised by Ellsworth S. Howell. 8vo. (Reprinted several times, same format and publisher)

Tuck, Leslie M.
The Snipes; a study of the genus *Capella.* Ottawa, 1972, Canadian Wildlife Service. 429 pp., photographic plates, maps, large bibliography. 8vo. A thorough monograph with a section on early hunting, including an account by Pringle.

Tudor, J.
The Golden Retriever. New York, 1972, Howell Book House. 241 pp., illustrations. 8vo; dust jacket. (First published, 1966, London)

Tully, Babette
A Field Guide to the Eagles, Hawks and Falcons of Colorado. Grand Junction, Colorado, 1980, Precision Printing Co. 59 pp., color and black and white illustrations. 8vo. Paper wrappers.

Turner, David B.
Professional Opportunities in the Wildlife Field. Washington, D. C., 1948, Wildlife Management Institute / American Nature Association. 208 pp. Tall 8vo; dust jacket. Scarce.

Turner, Florence Hayes
Days of Elk and Buffalo. London, 1955, Arco. 214 pp., frontispiece. 8vo. One chapter describing elk and buffalo hunting on her family's 9000 acre game reserve in Colorado.

Turner-Turner, J.

Three Years Hunting and Trapping in America and the Great Northwest. New York, 1967, Abercrombie & Fitch, Inc. 182 pp., plates from old engravings, map. 4to; dust jacket. (A facsimile reproduction of the 1888 first edition)

Turpin, Tom

Hunting the Wild Turkey; the first reprint with a new introduction by Roger Latham. Delmont, Pennsylvania, 1966, Penn's Woods Call. 54 pp., photographic plates. 8vo. Paper wrappers. (A facsimile reproduction of the first edition)

Turrell, George B.

How to Hunt; a guide for beginners. New York, 1953, Greenberg: Publishers. 64 pp., illustrated. 4to; dust jacket. Scarce.

Tuttle, Emerson   1890-1946

Fifty Prints. New Haven, 1948, Yale University Press. Unpaginated, (approx. 140 pp.), 50 full page reproductions of Tuttle prints. Introduction by Chauncey Brewster Tinker. Critique by Lewis E. York. 4to; dust jacket. [Also a deluxe edition, specially illustrated, in an edition of 100 numbered copies] An important outline of this wildlife artist.

Tuxedo Club

Officers, Members, Constitution, Rules and History of the Tuxedo Club, 1886-1936. No place, 1937, Privately printed. 62 pp., photographic plates. 8vo. (Also a 1938 edition, same format and publisher) An account of this club with much hunting and fishing.

Tweedsmuir, Lord

Hudson's Bay Trader. New York, 1951, W. W. Norton & Co., Inc. 195 pp., photographic plates. 8vo; dust jacket.

Tyler, Homer C.

Browning .22 Caliber Rifles, 1914 - 1984. 1985, Privately printed. 304 pp., photographic plates. Limited to 1000 numbered copies. 4to.

Udall, Stewart L.

The Quiet Crisis. New York, 1963, Holt, Rinehart and Winston. 209 pp., color and black and white illustrations. Introduction by John F. Kennedy. 8vo; dust jacket. Secretary of the Interior Udall stresses the need for conservation, with much on the works of early conservationists.

Underwood, Lamar, editor

The Bobwhite Quail Book. Clinton, New Jersey, 1980, Amwell Press. 442 pp., illustrations by Donald Shoffstall. Limited to 1000 numbered and signed copies. 8vo; slipcased. (Also a 1981 trade edition, same publisher)

The Deer Book. Clinton, New Jersey, 1980, Amwell Press. 460pp., illustrations by Al Barker. Limited to 1000 numbered and signed copies. 8vo; slipcased. (Also a 1982 trade edition, same publisher)

The Duck Hunter's Book. Clinton, New Jersey, 1982, Amwell Press. 607 pp., color and black and white illustrations by Tom Hennessey. Limited to 1000 numbered and signed copies. 8vo; slipcased. (Also a 1983 trade edition, same publisher)

Hunting the North Country. Clinton, New Jersey, 1982, Amwell Press. Two volumes of 1102 total pages; color and black and white illustrations. Limited to 1000 numbered and signed copies. 8vo; slipcased together.

Underwood, William

Wilderness Adventures. Boston, 1927, Ginn and Company. 244 pp., photographic plates. 8vo.

United States Department of the Interior

Alaska's Fish and Wildlife. Washington, D. C., 1953, United States Department of the Interior. 60 pp., illustrations. Paper wrappers.

Brown Bears of Alaska; hearing before the Special Committee on Conservation of Wildlife Resources, U. S. Senate on protection and preservation of brown and grizzly bears of Alaska. Washington, D. C., 1932, Government Printing Office. 108 pp. 8vo. Paper wrappers.

Duck Stamp Data; information for stamp collectors and conservationists. Washington, D. C., United States Department of the Interior. Illustrations. 8vo. Paper wrappers. (Revised several times, same format and publisher)

Rare and Endangered Fish and Wildlife of the United States. Washington, D. C., 1966, United States Government Printing Office. Unpaginated (158 pp.). 4to. Paper wrappers, punched for three-ring binder.

The Restoration of Breeding Canada Goose Populations on National Wildlife Refuges. Washington, D. C., 1958, United States Fish and Wildlife Service. 21 pp.

United States Department of the Interior, continued

Wildlife Restoration and Conservation; proceedings of the North American Wildlife Conference called by President Franklin D. Roosevelt. Washington, D. C., 1936, United States Government Printing Office. 675 pp., photographic plates. 8vo. A compilation of papers given by Gabrielson, Darling, McAtee, Bump and many others. Scarce.

Woodcock Ecology and Management. Washington, D. C., 1982, United States Fish and Wildlife Service. 191 pp. 8vo. Paper wrappers.

Unkelbach, Kurt

Murphy. Englewood Cliffs, New Jersey, 1959, Prentice-Hall, Inc. 186 pp. 8vo; dust jacket. An older juvenile about a beagle.

Those Loveable Retrievers. New York, 1973, McGraw-Hill Publishing Company. 204 pp., plates. 8vo; dust jacket.

Vacher, Andre

Summer of the Grizzly. Saskatoon, Saskatchewan, 1985, Western. First English edition. 137 pp., photographic plates. 8vo. Paper wrappers. An account of the grizzly attacks at Banff in 1980.

Valdez, Raul

Lords of the Pinnacles; wild goats of the world. Mesilla, New Mexico, 1985, Wild Sheep and Goat International. 212 pp., color and black and white illustrations, maps, bibliography. Limited to 1000 numbered and signed copies. 4to; dust jacket.

The Wild Sheep of the World; with a chapter on hunting by John Batten. Mesilla, New Mexico, 1982, Wild Sheep and Goat International. 186 pp., color and black and white illustrations, maps, bibliography. 4to; dust jacket. A comprehensive survey.

Vale, Robert B.   b. 1872

Wings, Fur & Shot; a grass-roots guide to American hunting, wherein is included a practical study of wild life habits, conservation and other sensible matters designed to make hunting a greater sport. New York and Harrisburg, 1936, Stackpole Sons. 199 pp., frontispiece in color, other drawings by George M. Sutton. 8vo; dust jacket. (Second edition, same size and contents in four printings up to 1956, The Military Service Publishing Company, but with the title *How To Hunt American Game*)

Tuscarora Tales; 22 rare stories. No place (Chester, Pennsylvania), 1957, Privately printed. 158 pp. A limited edition of an unspecified number. 8vo. Tales from the Alleghenies, including one angling and two hunting stories.

Van Camp, Laurel F. and Charles J. Henry

The Screech Owl; its life history and population ecology in northern Ohio. Washington, D. C., 1975, United States Department of the Interior. 65 pp., photographic plates. 8vo. Paper wrappers.

Vance, Joel

Confessions of an Outdoor Maladroit. Clinton, New Jersey, 1983, Amwell Press. 210 pp., color and black and white illustrations by Anthony Hillman. Foreword by Michael McIntosh. 8vo; dust jacket. [Also a limited edition of 1000 numbered and signed copies; slipcased] A collection of humorous hunting and angling mishaps.

Grandma and the Buck Deer; and other tales of youthful disaster. Tulsa, 1980, Winchester Press. 173 pp., drawings. 8vo; dust jacket.

Upland Bird Hunting. New York, 1981, E. P. Dutton & Co. / Outdoor Life Books. 311 pp., illustrations by Tom Beecham. 8vo; dust jacket.

Vanderweide, Harry

Grouse Foolish and Other Stories. Yarmouth, Maine, 1979, Delmore Publishing Co. 137 pp., illustrations by John Holub. 8vo; dust jacket. A collection of hunting and angling tales originally published in *Maine Sportsman* magazine.

Van Doren, Mark

The Mayfield Deer. New York, 1941, Henry Holt and Company, Inc. 272 pp., illustrations. 8vo; dust jacket. (Reprinted 1959, Hill and Wang) An epic poem recalling the legend of a boy who shoots the pet deer of a lonesome hunter.

Van Dyke, Theodore S.   b. 1842

The Still Hunter. New York, 1932, The Macmillan Company. 390 pp., illustrations by Carl Rungius. 8vo; dust jacket. (A reprint of the 1882 first edition. Also reprinted many other times) The author believed that by knowing the habits and habitat of deer, the hunter would not only be more successful, but also realize more enjoyment from the sport. A very important deer hunting book.

Van Rensselaer, Stephen

American Firearms; an histology of American gunsmiths, arms manufacturers & patentees with detailed descriptions of their arms. Watkins Glen, New York, 1948, Century House. 288 pp., photographic plates. Tall 8vo. Limited to about 2000 unnumbered copies bound in red cloth. [Also a deluxe edition limited to 50 numbered copies, same year and publisher]

American Firearms; the Colt supplement. Watkins Glen, New York, 1948, Century House. 95 pp., photographic plates. Tall 8vo. (Issued as a supplement to the above work and bound similarly in a trade edition of about 2000 unnumbered copies and 500 numbered copies of a limited edition)

Van Sinderen, Adrian

Canter, Please! Random memories of Glenholme Farm and of our other playmates and playgrounds. New York, 1935, Privately printed by the Derrydale Press. 93 pp., photographic plates. 8vo; slipcased. Miscellaneous equestrian memoirs including riding and competition, western U. S. trail riding and a chapter on sporting books. Scarce.

van Urk, J. Blan   b. 1902

The Horse, The Valley and the Chagrin Valley Hunt. New York, 1947, Richard Ellis. 266 pp., color frontispiece of Windsor T. White, plus photographic plates. Limited to 700 copies. 4to; slipcased. The Club commissioned van Urk to write this history of their Gates Mills, Ohio foxhunting club. In 1992, the clubhouse burned to the ground; destroyed with it were several hundred new, undistributed copies of this work.

The Story of American Foxhunting. New York, 1940 and 1941, The Derrydale Press. Two volumes of 283 pp. and 435 pp. respectively, photographic plates, illustrations from drawings and maps. Limited to 950 sets. Folio. An authoritative and beautiful history of the sport.

van Urk, J. Blan, continued
The Story of Rolling Rock. New York, 1950, Charles Scribner's Sons. 298 pp., color frontispiece of Richard B. Mellon, photographic plates, folding map. 4to. A history of this western Pennsylvania sporting club.

Van Winkle, William M.   b. 1885
Henry William Herbert (Frank Forester); a bibliography of his writings, 1832-1858. Portland, Maine, 1936, Southworth-Anthoensen Press. 189 pp., photographic plates. 8vo. (Also reprinted, 1971, Burt Franklin) Although no limitation is stated, it is generally believed 300 copies were produced.
The Renowned Library on American Sport Collected by William Mitchell Van Winkle. New York, 1940, Parke-Bernet Galleries, Inc. 137 pp. illustrations. 8vo. Paper wrappers. The auction catalog of Van Winkle's important sporting book collection which included many first editions of Frank Forester.

Van Wormer, Joe   b. 1913
The Black Bear Book. Caldwell, Idaho, 1974, Caxton Printers, Ltd. Unpaginated (approx. 70 pp.), photographic plates. 4to; dust jacket.
Eagles. New York, 1985, E. P. Dutton & Co., Inc.   56 pp., illustrations. Square 8vo; dust jacket.
How To Be a Wildlife Photographer. New York, 1982, Lodestar Books. 153 pp., photographic plates. 8vo.
Squirrels. New York, 1978, E. P. Dutton & Co. 58 pp., photographic plates. 8vo; dust jacket.
There's a Marmot on the Telephone. Caldwell, Idaho, 1974, Caxton Printers, Ltd. 116 pp., illustrations. 4to; dust jacket.
The Wildlife Photography of Joseph Van Wormer. Sandy, Oregon, 1980, Blue Mountain Services. 66 pp., chiefly illustrations. 4to.
The World of the American Elk. Philadelphia, 1969, J. B. Lippincott Co. 159 pp., photographic plates, bibliography. A title in Lippincott's Living World series. 4to; dust jacket.
The World of the Black Bear. Philadelphia, 1966, J. B. Lippincott Co. 163 pp., photographic plates, bibliography. A title in Lippincott's Living World series. 4to; dust jacket.
The World of the Bobcat. Philadelphia, 1964, J. B. Lippincott Co.   128 pp., photographic plates. A title in Lippincott's Living World series.   4to; dust jacket. (Reprinted several times, same format and publisher)
The World of the Canada Goose. Philadelphia, 1968, J. B. Lippincott Co. 192 pp., photographic plates, bibliography. A title in Lippincott's Living World series. 4to; dust jacket.
The World of the Coyote. Philadelphia, 1964, J. B. Lippincott Co.   150 pp., photographic plates, bibliography. A title in Lippincott's Living World series. 4to; dust jacket.

Van Wormer, Joe, continued

    The World of the Moose. Philadelphia, 1972, J. B. Lippincott Co. 160 pp., photographic plates, bibliography. A title in Lippincott's Living World series. 4to; dust jacket.

    The World of the Pronghorn Antelope. Philadelphia, 1968, J. B. Lippincott Co. 190 pp., photographic plates, bibliography. A title in Lippincott's Living World series. 4to; dust jacket. (Reprinted 1969, same format and publisher)

    The World of the Swan. Philadelphia, 1972, J. B. Lippincott Co. 156 pp., photographic plates, bibliography. A title in Lippincott's Living World series. 4to; dust jacket.

Vassos, John

    Dogs Are Like That. New York, 1941, E. P. Dutton & Co. 108 pp., photographic plates. 8vo; dust jacket. With some bird hunting over setters.

Vaughan, Henry G.

    Roster of the Hunts of America, 1934 - 1935. Reprinted and presented to the members of The Masters of Foxhounds Association of America by Henry G. Vaughan, President. Folio. Paper wrappers. This originally appeared in *The Sportsman* magazine, Volume XVI, No. 3.

Vaught, R. W. and L. M. Kirsch

    Canada Geese of the Eastern Prairie Population; with special reference to the Swan Lake flock. No place, 1966, Missouri Department of Conservation. 91 pp., photographic plates, maps, drawings. 4to. Paper wrapper.

Veasey, William and Cary Schuler Hull

    Waterfowl Carving; blue ribbon techniques. Exton, Pennsylvania, 1982, Schiffer Publishing Company. 272 pp., color and black and white illustrations. 4to; dust jacket.

Veasey, William

    Blue Ribbon Pattern Series. Exton, Pennsylvania, 1982, Schiffer Publishing Company. Unpaged, drawings. Oblong 4to. Paper wrappers. (Done in three volumes as Book I, Book II, and Book III)

    Burning and Texturing Methods; blue ribbon techniques. West Chester, Pennsylvania, 1984, Schiffer Publishing Company. 64 pp., photographic plates. Oblong 8vo. Paper wrappers.

    Waterfowl Painting; blue ribbon techniques. Exton, Pennsylvania, 1983, Schiffer Publishing Company. 224 pp., color and black and white illustrations. 8vo; dust jacket.

Vecchiarelli, C. E.

U. S. Duck Stamps. Hayward, 1979, L. A. Meyer. 104 pp., illustrations. 4to; dust jacket.

Venable, Sam

An Island Unto Itself. No place, 1981, Little Pecan Properties. 96 pp., color photographic plates. 4to. Hunting and fishing in southern Louisiana. Scarce.

Vermes, Jean C.

Enjoying Life as a Sportsman's Wife. Harrisburg, 1965, The Stackpole Company. 192 pp. 8vo; dust jacket. Advice to women on how to enjoy the outdoors with their husbands.

Vermont Department of Fish and Game

Vermont Hunting and Fishing. Montpelier, 1933, Vermont Department of Fish and Game. Unpaginated (25 pp.), photographic plates, maps. 8vo. Paper wrappers. (Published in several editions up to about 1942)

Vest, George Graham

Old Drum; being an account of George Graham Vest and his now famous "Eulogy to the Dog." Kirkwood, 1970, Privately printed. 35 pp. Limited to 100 copies. 8vo. The story of the trial of a man accused of killing a hunting dog.

Vickery, Wayne F.

Advanced Gunsmithing; a manual of instruction in the manufacture, alteration and repair of firearms in-so-far as the necessary metal work with hand and machine tools is concerned, with chapters on the boring, rifling and chambering of rifles, for amateur and professional gunsmiths. Onslow County, North Carolina, 1940, Small Arms Technical Publishing Company. 429 pp., photographic frontispiece, drawings by Oliver B. Hamilton. 16mo; dust jacket. (Reprinted several times, same publisher and format. Also reprinted in a slightly larger format, The Stackpole Company)

Voelker, John

See **Traver, Robert**

Vosburgh, John R.

Texas Lion Hunter. San Antonio, Texas, 1949, The Naylor Company. 112 pp., photographic plates, maps, drawings by Clifford Mantooth. 8vo; dust jacket. The story of John Hearn.

Wadsworth, W. Austin
The Hunting Diaries of W. Austin Wadsworth M.F.H., Genesee Valley Hunt Club. Genesco, New York, 1984, Privately printed by the club. Limited to 950 copies. 8vo.

Wadsworth, William H., editor
Bowhunting Deer. No place, 1978, New York State Department of Environmental Conservation. 78 pp., illustrations. Paper wrappers.

Wadsworth, William P.
Riding to Hounds in America; an introduction for foxhunters. Berryville, Virginia, 1962, Chronicle of the Horse. 44 pp., illustrations by H. Stewart Treviranus. 8vo. Paper wrappers.

Wagstaff, Blanche Shoemaker
Bob: The Spaniel; the true story of a Springer. New York, 1927, G. Howard Watt. 115 pp., photographic frontispiece. 12mo; dust jacket. The author was the sister of David Wagstaff, the noted sporting book collector.

Wagstaff, David   1883-1951
XVII-XX Century Sporting Books - Angling, Hunting, Racing, Birds, Dogs, Horses, Etc. Collected by the Late David Wagstaff, Tuxedo Park, New York. New York, 1957, Parke-Bernet Galleries, Inc. 106 pp. 8vo. Paper wrappers. The auction catalog of this significant sporting book library.

Wagstaff, Henry
Wiley Buck and other Stories of the Concord Community. Chapel Hill, 1953, University of North Carolina Press. 118 pp. 8vo; dust jacket. Containing hunting and fishing memories from turn of the century Person County, North Carolina. Scarce.

Wahl, Paul
Arms Trade; Yearbook 1955. Bogota, New Jersey, 1955, Privately printed. 78 pp. 8vo. Spiral bound. A listing of firearms dealers specializing in collectible firearms.
The Gun Trader's Guide. New York, 1953, Greenberg: Publishers. 225 pp., photographic plates. 8vo; dust jacket. (Also a 1957 second edition, same format and publisher. Also many other editions after 1957, mostly annually, by various publishers in paper wrappers)

Waingrow, Jeff
American Wildfowl Decoys; a history and collector's guide. New York, 1985, E. P. Dutton & Co. / Weathervane Books. 117 pp., color illustrations. 4to; dust jacket.

Walker, Ralph T.
　　Black Powder Gunsmithing.　Northfield, Illinois,　1978, DBI Books. 288 pp., illustrations.　4to.　Paper wrappers.

Wallace, Dillon　　1863-1939
　　With Dog and Canoe; a story of the big north woods.　New York, 1928, Fleming H. Revell.　269 pp., illustrations.　12mo.　An older juvenile with much hunting and fishing.
　　The Fur Traders Of Kettle Harbor.　New York, 1931, Fleming H. Revell Company.　269 pp., frontispiece, illustrations.　8vo.
　　Mr. Wallace wrote extensively on the North; many of his works were older juveniles and most pre-dated 1925.　See Phillips.

Wallace, David Raines
　　The Dark Range; a naturalist's night notebook.　San Francisco, 1978, Sierra Club.　131 pp., color and black and white illustrations by Roger Bayless. 4to; dust jacket.

Wallack, Louis Robert　　b. 1919
　　American Pistol and Revolver Design and Performance.　New York, 1978, Winchester Press.　234 pp., photographic plates.　4to; dust jacket.
　　American Rifle Design and Performance.　New York, 1977, Winchester Press.　213 pp., illustrations.　4to; dust jacket.
　　American Shotgun Design and Performance.　New York, 1977, Winchester Press.　213 pp., illustrations.　4to; dust jacket.
　　The Anatomy of Firearms.　New York, 1965, Simon & Schuster.　320 pp., illustrations.　8vo; dust jacket.
　　The Deer Rifle. New York, 1978, Winchester Press.　244 pp., illustrations.　8vo; dust jacket.
　　Encyclopedia of Gun Design and Performance.　New York, 1983, Winchester Press.　630 total pages, illustrations.　4to; dust jacket. (This is essentially the author's three earlier works of similar title, in one volume)
　　Modern Accuracy; in bench rest shooting. New York, 1951, Greenberg: Publishers.　151 pp., photographic plates, diagrams.　4to; dust jacket.

Wallmo, Olof C., editor
　　Mule and Black-Tailed Deer of North America.　Lincoln, 1981, University of Nebraska Press.　605 pp., color and black and white illustrations, charts, maps.　Thick 4to; dust jacket.　A definitive treatment of the subject.

Wallmo, Olof C. and J. W. Schoen, editors
　　Sitka Blacktailed Deer: Proceedings of a Conference in Juneau, Alaska. Washington, D. C., No date (1978), United States Department of Agriculture, Forest Service.　231 pp., charts, maps.　4to.　Paper wrappers.

Walpole, Stewart J.
    Scrapbook Selections. Chicago, No date (ca. 1940), American Field Publishing Company. 64 pp., illustrations. 12mo.
    Scrapbook Selections, Book II. Chicago, No date (ca. 1942), American Field Publishing Company. 86 pp., illustrations. 12mo.
    Scrapbook Selections, Book III. Chicago, No date (ca. 1944), American Field Publishing Company. 104 pp., illustrations. 8vo. All three of these works contain reminiscences of hunting and angling around the world.

Walrod, Dennis
    Grouse Hunter's Guide; solid facts, insights and observations on how to hunt the ruffed grouse. Harrisburg, 1985, Stackpole Books. 192 pp., photographic plates. 8vo; dust jacket.
    More Than a Trophy. Harrisburg, 1983, Stackpole Books. 267 pp., illustrations. 8vo; dust jacket. An account of what to do with the deer after the kill.

Walsh, Clune and Lowell G. Jackson
    Waterfowl Decoys of Michigan and The Lake St. Clair Region. Detroit, 1983, Gale Graphics. 175 pp., color and black and white illustrations. Oblong 8vo; dust jacket.

Walsh, Harry
    The Outlaw Gunner. Cambridge, Maryland, 1971, Tidewater Publishers. 192 pp., photographic plates. Tall 8vo; dust jacket. Market gunning for wildfowl.

Walsh, Roy E.
    Gunning the Chesapeake; duck and goose shooting on the Eastern shore. Cambridge, Maryland, 1960, Tidewater Publishers. 118 pp., illustrations including an identification guide by Angus Shortt. 4to; dust jacket.
    Sanctuary Pond; a conservation piece. Barre, Massachusetts, 1967, Barre Publishing Co., Inc. 94 pp., photographic plates. 8vo; dust jacket. Waterfowl conservation on this eastern shore wildlife sanctuary.

Walters, D. L. and Ann Walters
    Training Retrievers To Handle. La Cygne, 1979, Privately printed. 133 pp., photographic plates. 4to; dust jacket.

Wambold, H. R. "Dutch"
    Bowhunting For Deer; a fresh approach to archery deer hunting. Harrisburg, 1964, The Stackpole Company 160 pp., illustrations. Foreword by Fred Bear. 8vo; dust jacket. (Reprinted 1964, same format and publisher. Also a 1965 revised edition, same format and publisher. Also a 1978 revised and enlarged edition, by Doug Kitteredge, Stackpole Books)

Ward, Rowland   1848-1912

Records of Big Game. Ninth edition. London, 1928, Rowland Ward. 523 pp., photographic plates, drawings, charts. 8vo; dust jacket. This was the last of the Rowland Ward record books to include both African and North American big game records. See Phillips for the first eight editions.

Ward, Mary Alice and Sara M. Barbaresi

How To Raise and Train a Beagle. Jersey City, New Jersey, 1958, TFH Publications. 64 pp., illustrations. 8vo. Paper wrappers.

Ward, Peter and Bruce Batt

Propagation of Captive Waterfowl; the Delta Waterfowl Research Station system. Edited by James B. Trefethen.   Washington, D. C., 1973, Wildlife Management Institute / Delta Waterfowl Research Station.   64 pp., photographic plates, drawings. 8vo. Paper wrappers.

Warner, James A. and Margaret J. White

The Decoy as Art; waterfowl in a wooden soul. Wilmington, Delaware, 1985, Middle Atlantic Press. Unpaginated (90 pp.), color photographic plates. Square folio; dust jacket.

Warre, Capt. H.

Sketches in North America and The Oregon Territory. Barre, Massachusetts, 1970, Imprint Society.   26 pp. text plus 71 plates in color and black and white. Limited to 1950 numbered copies.   4to; slipcased. An account of an 1845 journey across North America by two British officers, with some mention of hunting and fishing.

Warren, Donald R.

My Bongo / A Week of Arctic Daylight.   Los Angeles, No date (ca. 1964), Privately printed.   33 pp., photographic plates. 8vo. The story of two hunting trips made by the author - one to Africa for bongo and one to the far North for sheep.

Warren, Edward R.   1860-1942

The Beaver; its work and its ways.   Baltimore, 1927, Williams & Wilkins Co. 177 pp., illustrations. 8vo; dust jacket. An important and scarce monograph produced by The American Society of Mammalogists.

A Study of the Beaver; in the Yancey region of Yellowstone National Park and notes on the beaver colonies in the Longs Peak Region of Estes Park, Colorado.   Syracuse, New York, 1926, Roosevelt Wildlife Foundation.   234 pp., photographic plates, drawings, fold-out maps, fold-out panoramic photographs. 4to. Paper wrappers. A scarce and extensive report on the beaver in this region.

Warren, George G., Jr. and H. J. Burlington, editors
   The Outdoor Heritage of New Jersey. Camden, New Jersey, 1937, New Jersey Game and Fish Commission. 82 pp., color plates. 8vo.

Warwick, Helen
   The Complete Labrador Retriever. New York, 1964, Howell Book House. 304 pp., illustrations. (Reprinted and revised several times, same format and publisher)

Washburn, O. A.
   General Red; the story of the hound who led the pack against bear and cougar. New York, 1962, Exposition Press. 160 pp. 8vo; dust jacket. This is the author's tribute to a hound he owned and used as rancher, hunter and guide in the southern Rockies. Scarce.

Waterman, Charles F.   b. 1913
   The Hunter's World. New York, 1976, The Ridge Press, Inc. / Random House, Inc. 250 pp., color and black and white illustrations. 4to; dust jacket. (Reprinted 1983, Winchester Press)
   Hunting in America. New York, 1973, Holt, Rinehart & Winston / The Ridge Press, Inc. 250 pp., color and black and white illustrations. 8vo; dust jacket.
   Hunting Rabbits and Squirrels. New Jersey, 1970, Athletic Activities Publishing Company. 64 pp., illustrations. 8vo. Paper wrappers.
   Hunting Upland Birds. New York, 1972, Winchester Press. 311 pp., photographic plates. 8vo; dust jacket.
   The Part I Remember. New York, 1974, Winchester Press. 199 pp., illustrations. 8vo; dust jacket. Humorous hunting and angling stories.
   Ridge Runners and Swamp Rats. Clinton, New Jersey, 1983, Amwell Press. 347 pp., color and black and white illustrations by Shepard H. Foley. Limited to 1000 numbered and signed copies. 8vo; slipcased. (Also a 1984 trade edition, same publisher)
   The Treasury of Sporting Guns. New York, 1979, The Ridge Press / Random House. 240 pp., color illustrations. 4to; dust jacket.
   Mr. Waterman is a popular hunting and fishing author who also has been published extensively in outdoor periodicals.

Waters, Frank
   The Man Who Killed the Deer. New York, 1942, Farrar & Rinehart. 311 pp. 8vo. (Reprinted 1942, University of Denver Press. Also reprinted, 1971, Pocket Books) A novel of the Hopi Indians, with some hunting.

Waters, Robert S., et al., editors

    North American Big Game. Pittsburgh, Pennsylvania, 1971, Boone and Crockett Club. 403 pp., photographic plates, frontispiece in color. (Reprinted 1973, same format and publisher) Tall 8vo; dust jacket. The sixth Boone and Crockett Club record book.

    Records of North American Big Game. New York, 1964, Holt, Rinehart and Winston. 398 pp., photographic plates, frontispiece in color. (Reprinted twice, same format and publisher) 8vo; dust jacket. The fifth Boone and Crockett Club record book.

Watrous, George R.

    Winchester Rifles and Shotguns. New Haven, Connecticut, 1966, Winchester Western Press. 159 pp., illustrations. Edited by T. E. Hall and Pete Kuhloff. 4to; slipcased. (Revised and reprinted, same format and publisher. Also a third and fourth editions with the title *The History of Winchester Firearms, 1866-1966.*) [Also a 1976 deluxe edition, co-authored with Jim Rikhoff and Thomas Hall, limited to 1000 numbered and signed copies, Amwell Press]

Watson, F.

    Winslow Homer. New York, 1942, Crown Publishers, Inc. 112 pp., color and black and white illustrations from paintings by Winslow Homer. 4to; dust jacket. A biography of this famous American artist, who produced some sporting art.

Watson, Frederick   b. 1885

    Hunting Pie; the whole art and craft of foxhunting. New York, 1931, The Derrydale Press. 64 pp., illustrations from drawings by Paul Brown. Tall 8vo. Limited to 750 copies. (Also a British edition)

Watson, L. M. and A. D. Holcombe

    The Yellow Creek Story. Bucklin, Missouri, 1954, Tri-State Printers. 89 pp., photographic plates. 8vo. Paper wrappers. The history of the development of the Yellow Creek strain of hounds.

Watson, J. N. P.

    The Book of Foxhunting. London, 1977, Batsfort. 240 pp., illustrations., maps. 8vo. (Reprinted 1978, Arco) With chapters on hunting in the U. S. as well as other countries.

Waugh, Hal and C. J. Keim

    Fair Chase With Alaskan Guides. Anchorage, 1981, Alaska Northwest Publishing Company. 205 pp., photographic plates. 8vo. Paper wrappers. Hunting various species of Alaskan big game.

Weatherhead, Albert J., Jr.

    Hunter's Paradise. Cleveland, Ohio, 1947, Privately printed. 35 pp., drawings. 8vo. The author's adventures hunting wildfowl and upland birds in Cuba.

Weaver, John

    The Wolves of Yellowstone. Washington, D. C., 1978, United States Department of the Interior. 38 pp., photographic plates, map, bibliography. 4to. Paper wrappers.

Webb, David and John Stevens, editors

    Early Bounty Hunters of Butler County, Pennsylvania. Chillicothe, Ohio, 1934, Privately printed. 27 pp. Limited to 300 copies. 12mo. Paper wrappers. A listing of over 1200 wolves, panthers, foxes, etc. taken in the first half of the nineteenth century.

Webb, R.

    Alberta's Big Game Resources. Edmonton, 1958, Department of Lands and Forests. 31 pp., maps. 8vo. Paper wrappers.

Webb, Samuel, et al., editors

    Records of North American Big Game. New York, 1952, Charles Scribner's Sons. 178 pp., photographic plates, color frontispiece. 8vo. The third Boone and Crockett Club record book.

    Records of North American Big Game. New York, 1958, Henry Holt and Company. 264 pp., photographic plates, frontispiece in color. (Reprinted twice, same format and publisher) 8vo. The fourth Boone and Crockett Club record book.

Webb, Sherman

    Practical Pointer Training; hints on training the pointing breeds of bird dogs. New York, 1974, Winchester Press. 178 pp., photographic plates. 12mo; dust jacket.

Webster, David and William Kehoe

    Decoys at the Shelbourne Museum. Shelbourne, Vermont, 1961, Shelbourne Museum. 129 pp., color and black and white illustrations, some by Browne and Pleissner. 8vo. (Also a 1971 revised edition, same publisher)

Webster, Donald B.

    Suicide Specials. Harrisburg, 1958, The Stackpole Company. 192 pp., illustrations. 8vo; dust jacket. A scarce book detailing inexpensive handguns.

Weeden, Robert B.

    Grouse and Ptarmigan in Alaska; their ecology and management. Juneau, 1965, Alaska Department of Fish and Game. 110 pp., maps, bibliography. 4to. Spiral bound paper wrappers.

    Wildlife Management and Alaska Land Use Decisions. Fairbanks, 1973, Institute of Social, Economic and Government Research. 51 pp. 8vo.

Weeden, Robert B. and Laurence N. Ellison

    The Upland Gamebirds of Forest and Tundra. Juneau, Alaska, 1968, Alaska Division of Game. 44 pp., drawings by R. T. Wallen. Paper wrappers.

Weeks, Edward

    The Miramichi Fish and Game Club; a history. Frederickton, New Brunswick, 1984, Privately printed by The Brunswick Press. 80 pp., photographic plates. 8vo. Mr. Weeks was editor of *The Atlantic Monthly* for many years. He also wrote and edited several other angling books. See Bruns.

Wegner, Robert

    Deer and Deer Hunting; the serious hunter's guide. Harrisburg, 1984, Stackpole Books. 316 pp., photographic plates, large bibliography. 8vo; dust jacket. Mr. Wegner later wrote two revised editions to this title, as well as *Wegner's Bibliography on Deer and Deer Hunting*, published in 1992.

Wehle, Robert G.

    Wing and Shot; gun dog training. Scottsville, 1964, Country Press. 190 pp., color and black and white illustrations. 8vo; dust jacket; slipcased. A deluxe edition of unspecified limitation. (Reprinted once in the deluxe edition format and four times in a trade edition format)

Weigand, John and Janson Reuel

    Montana's Ring-Necked Pheasant; history, ecology and management. No place, 1976, Montana Fish and Game Commission. 178 pp., color and black and white illustrations, maps. 8vo. Paper wrappers.

Weiler, Milton C.   **1910-1974**

    The Classic Decoy Series; a portfolio of paintings. New York, 1969, Winchester Press. Text by Ed Zern. Foreword by William J. Mackey. 24 loose plates in color in a portfolio; text bound in. Limited to 1000 numbered and signed copies. Folio; slipcased.

    Classic Shorebird Decoys; a portfolio of paintings. New York, 1971, Winchester Press. Text by William J. Mackey. 24 loose plates in color in a portfolio; 28 pp. text with illustrations, bound in. Limited to 975 numbered and signed copies. Elephant folio; slipcased. Both of these portfolios are elegant productions.

Weiss, John   b. 1944

Hunting Gear You Can Make. New York, 1978, Outdoor Life Books. 163 pp., photographic plates. 8vo. Paper wrappers. (Reprinted several times, same contents and publisher)

Venison; from field to table. New York, 1984, Outdoor Life Books. 365 pp., photographic plates, drawings. 8vo; dust jacket.

The Whitetail Deer Hunter's Handbook. New York, 1979, Winchester Press. 265 pp., illustrations. 8vo; dust jacket.

Weiss, Norman D.

All About Grizzly Bears. Middleburg, Virginia, 1966, Denlinger. 32 pp., illustrations. 4to. Paper wrappers.

Weitz, Chauncey

A Game Warden's Diary. Oshkosh, Wisconsin, 1983, Willow Creek Press. 134 pp. 8vo. Memoirs of a Wisconsin game warden spanning the years 1932 to 1965.

Welch, Fay, editor

The Old Guide's Story of the Northern Adirondacks; reminiscences of Charles E. Merrill. No place, 1973, Privately printed. 224 pp., photographic plates, drawings. 4to; dust jacket. Hunting bear, dear and wildcat in the Adirondacks.

Welch, Marie Louise

Your Friend and Mine. Baltimore, 1934, Privately printed. 71 pp., photographic plates. 8vo. Relating to Irish setters, with breeding, kennels, etc.

Weller, Milton W.

Freshwater Marshes; ecology and wildlife management. Minneapolis, 1981, University of Minnesota Press. 146 pp., color and black and white illustrations. 8vo. (Reprinted several times, various publishers)

Growth, Weights and Plumages of the Redhead, Aythya americana. The Wilson Bulletin, 1957. 38 pp., photographic plates, drawings, bibliography. 8vo. Paper wrappers.

The Island Waterfowl. Ames, 1980, Iowa State University. 121 pp., photographic plates, bibliography. 8vo. An interesting study of isolated island dwelling wildfowl species and their adaptations to their surroundings.

Welles, Ralph E.

The Bighorn of Death Valley. Washington, D. C., 1961, United States Department of the Interior. 242 pp., photographic plates, fold-out map, bibliography. 8vo. Paper wrappers.

Wells, Hunter   1947-1983

They Call Me Hunter. Prescott, Arizona, 1984, Ralph Tanner Associates. 241 pp., illustrations.   Tall 8vo.   The personal recollections of a western hunting guide.

Wells-Gosling, Nancy

Flying Squirrels; gliders in the dark.   Washington, D. C., 1985, Smithsonian Institute.   128 pp., photographic plates, maps, bibliography.   8vo; dust jacket.

Wels, Byron G.

Fell's Guide To Guns and How To Use Them Safely-Legally-Responsibly. New York, 1969.   173 pp., photographic plates, drawings.   8vo.

Wensel, Gene

Bowhunting Rutting Whitetails.   Hamilton, Montana, 1981, Privately printed. 152 pp.   8vo. (Also a 1982 revised edition, same format and publisher)

Werber, Bill

Hunting is For the Birds. Naples, Florida, 1981, Privately printed. 326 pp., photographic plates.   8vo; dust jacket. (Also an edition in paper wrappers) Hunting upland birds and waterfowl throughout the western hemisphere.

Westminster Kennel Club

Westminster Kennel Club. New York, 1929, The Derrydale Press. 34 pp., illustrated from old plates.   Limited to 100 numbered copies.   12mo. (Originally published, 1886)

Weston, Dr. Frederick H.

Hunting the White-Tailed Deer in Texas. San Antonio, 1954, Western Outdoor Publications. 148 pp., photographic plates. 8vo; dust jacket.

Weston, Capt. Paul B.

The Handbook of Handgunning. New York, 1968, Crown Publishers, Inc. 138 pp., illustrations. Tall 8vo; dust jacket. (Reprinted 1972, same format and publisher)

Target Shooting Today. New York, 1950, Greenberg: Publishers. 81 pp., photographic plates. 12mo; dust jacket.

Captain Weston also wrote several handgun related books for use in police departments.

Wheatley, Harriet

Lady Angler; fishing, hunting and camping in wilderness areas of North America.   San Antonio, Texas, 1952, The Naylor Company.   192 pp., illustrations.   8vo; dust jacket.

Wheeler, Guy

The Year 'Round; a perennial miscellany for foxhunters.   Washington, D. C., 1968, Robert B. Luce, Inc.   112 pp., illustrations by Peter Biegel.   8vo; slipcased.   Memoirs of a foxhunter.

Wheeler, Robert J.

The Wild Turkey in Alabama. Montgomery, 1948, Alabama Department of Conservation.   92 pp., photographic plates, fold-out map, bibliography.   8vo. Paper wrappers.

Wheeler, Sessions

Gentleman in the Outdoors; a portrait of Max C. Fleischmann.   Reno, 1985, University of Nevada Press.   158 pp., photographic plates.   8vo; dust jacket.   A biographical sketch of Fleischmann (of Fleischmann's yeast) including much salmon and trout fishing and some hunting.

Whelen, Lt. Col. Townsend   1877-1961

Amateur Gunsmithing.   Washington, D. C., 1924, The National Rifle Association of America.   173 pp., photographic plates.   8vo. A scarce Whelen title. It is interesting to note that this book was proposed and edited by a young Thomas G. Samworth, then an N. R. A. staff member who wanted that organization to publish a series of books about firearms and their technical aspects. A few years later, when the N. R. A. refused to commission more titles, Samworth went on to found The Small Arms Technical Publishing Company, which specialized in firearms titles from 1926 to 1952. See Smith, Brian.

American Big Game Hunting.   East Alton, Illinois, 1925, Western Cartridge Company.   48 pp., photographic plates.   12mo.   Paper wrappers. (Reprinted many times, same format and publisher; later printings with the title *American Big Game Shooting*)

The American Rifle; a treatise, a textbook and a book of practical instruction in the use of the rifle. New York, 1918, The Century Company. 637 pp., illustrations.   8vo. The first comprehensive book covering all breech-loading long arms.

The Best of Col. Townsend Whelen. Clinton, New Jersey, 1983, Amwell Press.   404 pp., photographic plates.   Edited and with a foreword by Bradford Angier. Limited to 1000 numbered and signed copies.   Tall 8vo; slipcased. A collection of Whelen's best articles.

Big Game Hunting; for the novice and expert. No place, 1923, Outers Book Company / Recreation Library.   93 pp., photographic plates, drawings by the author. 8vo. Paper wrappers. (Also a 1923 edition reported, Outdoor Life Publishing Company)

Fundamentals of Scope Sights.   Washington, D. C., 1952.   74 pp., photographic plates. 8vo. Paper wrappers.

Whelen, Lt. Col. Townsend, continued

The Hunting Rifle; design, selection, ballistics, marksmanship. New York and Harrisburg, 1940, Stackpole Sons. 463 pp., photographic plates and drawings by the author. 8vo. (Also a 1948 revised and enlarged edition, which was reprinted in 1950, same format, Stackpole and Heck, Inc. Also reprinted, 1984, Wolfe Publishing Company in an edition limited to 1500 numbered copies)

Small Arms Design and Ballistics. Two volumes. Plantersville, South Carolina, 1945, 1946, Small Arms Technical Publishing Company. Volume I: Design, 352 pp., photographic plates and drawings by Roger Marsh. Volume II: Ballistics, 314 pp., photographic plates, drawings. 8vo; dust jackets. Volume II contains 10 loose folding charts of ballistic data prepared by DuPont ballistic experts. (Reprinted, The Stackpole Company) Still a valuable reference.

Small Bore Rifle Handbook. New York, 1928, Sporting Arms and Ammunition Manufacturers' Institute. 38 pp., illustrations. 8vo. Paper wrappers. (Revised and reprinted many times, with later printings titled *Handbook on Small Bore Rifle Shooting*)

Telescopic Rifle Sights. Onslow County, North Carolina, 1936, Small Arms Technical Publishing Company. 132 pp., photographic plates and drawings. 18mo. (Also a 1944 second revised edition, same publisher)

Tips To Shooters of Shotguns, Rifles and Pistols. 1945, Outer's Laboratories. 20 pp., illustrations. 16mo. Paper wrappers. This was written as an advertisement for the publisher.

Why Not Load Your Own? Basic handloading for everyone. Washington, D. C., 1949, Infantry Journal Press. 215 pp., photographic plates, drawings, charts. 8vo; dust jacket. (Also a revised and enlarged edition which was reprinted several times, Combat Forces Press)

Wilderness Hunting and Wildcraft; with notes on the habits and life histories of big game animals. Marshallton, Delaware, 1927, Small Arms Technical Publishing Company. 338 pp., photographic plates, drawings, charts. 8vo. Covers all the major big game species in America.

Whelen, Lt. Col. Townsend, editor

Hunting Big Game. Two Volumes. Harrisburg, 1946, The Military Service Publishing Company. Volume I: Asia and Africa., 282 pp., illustrations. Volume II: The Americas. 339 pp., illustrations. 8vo; dust jackets. (Reprinted 1947, same format and publisher) An anthology of hunting stories covering big game around the world.

The Ultimate in Rifle Precision. Washington, D. C., 1951, Sportsman's Digest Publishing Company. 346 pp., photographic plates, drawings, plus ads. 8vo. (Also revised editions in 1954 and 1958 with dust jackets, The Stackpole Company) The first two editions of this yearbook of The Benchrest Shooters' Annual were edited by **Donaldson, Harvey A.,** which see.

Whelen, Lt. Col. Townsend and Bradford Angier

Mister Rifleman. Los Angeles, 1965, Peterson Publishing Company. 377 pp., photographic plates, drawings, charts. 4to; dust jacket. [Also published specially bound as part of a two volume set with Elmer Keith's *Guns and Ammo For Hunting Big Game*] This was published posthumously and is a discussion of Whelen's contribution to the shooting sports as well as a discourse on his favorite rifles.

On Your Own in the Wilderness. Harrisburg, 1958, The Stackpole Company. 330 pp., illustrations. 8vo; dust jacket. (Reprinted many times, various publishers. Some of the later printings only list Angier as the author) Lt. Col. Townsend Whelen was called "Mr. Rifleman" because he used his knowledge of ballistics to teach American competitive shooters and hunters. His two volume set, *Small Arms Design and Ballistics* is a much-valued work by ballisticians as well as precision shooters.

Whisker, James

The Right To Hunt. No place (New York), 1981, North River Press. 173 pp., bibliography. 8vo; dust jacket. A general discussion of the legal, historic and conservation aspects of the sport.

Whisker, Vaughn and James B. Whisker

The Bedford County Gunsmiths and Gunmakers. Bedford, Pennsylvania, 1979, Privately printed. 35 pp., illustrations. 8vo. Paper wrappers.

White, Fred Z., M.D.

The Brittany in America. Chillicothe, Ohio, 1965, Privately printed. Second revised edition. 228 pp., photographic plates, drawings. 8vo. A scarce work detailing the history of the breed in America.

White, Henry P. and Burton D. Munhall

Centerfire Metric Pistol and Revolver Cartridges; Volume I of "Cartridge Identification" Washington, D. C., 1948, Infantry Journal Press. 97 pp., many illustrations. 4to; dust jacket.

Centerfire American and British Pistol and Revolver Cartridges. Volume II of "Cartridge Identification." Washington, D. C., 1950, Infantry Journal Press.. 143 pp., many illustrations. 4to; dust jacket.

White, John G.

A Souvenir of Wyoming; being a diary of a fishing trip in Jackson Hole and Yellowstone Park, with remarks on early history and historical geography. Cleveland, Ohio, 1926, Privately printed. Three volumes with a total of 455 pp. and with over 125 mounted photographs, fold out maps and photographic panoramas. Limited to eight typewritten copies. Folio. There is only incidental mention of hunting in this work, but its importance as a historical record for the area can not be ignored. John G. White was a Cleveland industrialist who amassed an incredible collection of books in many areas of interest. He bequeathed this collection (which includes many hunting books as well as every book to bear The Derrydale Press imprint) to the Cleveland Public Library, where it resides today in its Special Collections.

White, Luke
    Henry William Herbert and The American Publishing Scene, 1831-1858. Newark, New Jersey, 1943, Carteret Book Club.   71 pp., illustrations from old wood-cuts, facsimile letter in rear pocket.   Limited to 200 copies. (Reprinted 1970, University Microfilms) A scholarly examination of Frank Forester's contributions and impact on publishing.

White, Stewart Edward   1873-1946
    Dog Days; other times, other dogs. The autobiography of a man and his dog friends through four decades of changing America.   Garden City, 1930, Doubleday, Doran & Co., Inc. 285 pp., drawings by Will Crawford. 8vo; dust jacket.
    The Long Rifle. New York, 1932, Doubleday, Doran & Co., Inc. 536 pp. 8vo; dust jacket. A novel of pioneer life.
    Speaking For Myself. Garden City, New York, 1943, Doubleday, Doran & Co. 245 pp., illustrations by David Hendrickson. 8vo; dust jacket. (Reprinted several times, various publishers) Mr. White's discussion of how his personal experiences inspired his books.
    Wild Geese Calling. New York, 1940, Doubleday, Doran & Co., Inc. pp., illustrations by 8vo; dust jacket. A novel of pioneer life in Alaska.
    Stewart Edward White was a popular writer the first four decades of the twentieth century. Subjects of his works included pioneering, general outdoors, logging, African adventure, and general adventure, and most had incidental mention of hunting or angling. See Phillips.

White, T. H.
    The Goshawk. New York, 1951, G. P. Putnam's Sons.   215 pp., drawings. 8vo; dust jacket. Training the goshawk for falconry.

Whitehead, G. Kenneth
    Deer of the World. London, 1972, Constable   194 pp., color and black and white illustrations.   Tall 8vo; dust jacket.
    The Game Trophies of the World. Hamburg, Germany, 1981, Parey. 216 pp., drawings. Text in German, French and English. 8vo. Paper wrappers. A system of trophy evaluation proposed by the author.
    Hunting and Stalking Deer Throughout the World. London / New York, 1982, Batsford / St. Martin's Press.   336 pp., photographic plates, drawings, maps. 8vo; dust jacket.

Whitford, C. B.
    Training the Bird Dog. New York, 1928, The Macmillan Company. 258pp., photographic plates. Revised by Edward Cave. (Originally published 1908, Outing Publishing Company)

Whitington, Charles S.

Tall Timber Gabriels; the gobblings of a turkey hunter. No place, 1971, privately printed. 104 pp., color and black and white illustrations. Tall 8vo.

Whitney, George D.

This is the Beagle. Jersey City, New Jersey, 1955, T. F. H. Publications, Inc. 252 pp., illustrations by Ernest H. Hart. 8vo; dust jacket.

Whitney, Leon F.   b. 1894

Bloodhounds and How To Train Them. New York, 1947, Orange-Judd Publishing Co. 142 pp., illustrations. 8vo; dust jacket. (Reprinted 1955, same format and publisher)

The Raccoon. Orange, Connecticut, 1952, Practical Science Publishing Co. 177 pp., illustrations. 8vo; dust jacket.

This is the Cocker Spaniel. Orange, Connecticut, 1956, Practical Science Publishing Co. 253 pp., illustrations. 8vo; dust jacket.

Whitney, Leon F. and A. B. Underwood

The Coon Hunter's Handbook. New York, 1952, Henry Holt and Company, Inc. / Field & Stream. 210 pp., drawings. 12mo; dust jacket. (Reprinted 1964, same format and publisher)

Whittington, Lt. Col. Robert, III

The Colt Whitneyville-Walker Pistol; a study of the pistol and associated characters. Hooks, Texas, 1984, Brownlee Books. 95 pp., illustrations. Limited to 1000 numbered copies. 8vo; dust jacket.

Whyte, Jon and E. J. Hart

Carl Rungius; painter of the western wilderness. Salem, New Hampshire, 1985, Salem House. 184 pp., color and black and white illustrations. Square 4to; dust jacket. A biography of Rungius showcasing some of his finest works.

Widener, Peter A. B. and Joseph E. Widener

The Renowned Collections of Sporting and Colored Plate Books Belonging to the Estates of P. A. B. and Joseph Widener. New York, 1944, Parke-Bernet Galleries, Inc. 147 pp. 8vo. Paper wrappers. The auction catalog of early sporting works from these two libraries.

Wilbur, Edward Russell

Snap Shots of Many Years. New York, 1929, Privately printed. 63 pp., illustrations. 8vo. A rare book on hunting woodcock, grouse and geese with some trout fishing.

Wilbur, Sanford R.
The California Condor, 1966-1976; a look at its past and future. Washington, D. C., 1978, United States Department of the Interior. 136 pp., photographic plates, maps, bibliography. 8vo. Paper wrappers.

Wilcox, Sidney W.
Deer Production in the United States, 1969-1973; data relating to deer and deer hunters. Tempe, 1976, Arizona State University. 77 pp. Oblong 8vo.

Wilder, F. L.
Sporting Prints. New York, 1974, Viking Press. 224 pp., color illustrations. 4to; dust jacket. With many from the collection of Paul Mellon.

Wildlife Management Institute
Wood Duck Management and Research; a symposium. Washington, D. C., 1966, Wildlife Management Institute. 212 pp. 8vo. Paper wrappers.

Wildlife Management Institute
Also see **Haskell, William S.**

The Wildlife Society
Grouse Management Symposium. Washington, D. C., 1963, The Wildlife Society. 369 pp., illustrations. 4to. Paper wrappers.

Wileden, Arthur F.
A Lifetime of Hunting and Fishing Experiences. Wisconsin, 1982, Privately printed. 211 pp.
The Buckshot Story, 1928-1972. Wisconsin, No date, Privately printed. 20 pp. The history of a Wisconsin deer camp.

Wilkerson, Don
The Post War Colt Single Action Revolver. Apple Valley, Minnesota, 1978, Privately printed. 151 pp., color and black and white illustrations. Limited to 3000 copies signed by the author. 4to. (Reprinted, Taylor Publishing Co)

Wilkinson, Frederick
Antique Firearms. Garden City, New York, 1969, Doubleday & Company. 276 pp., illustrations in color and black and white. 4to. (Reprinted 1977, Presidio Press)
Flintlock Pistols. Harrisburg, 1968, The Stackpole Company. 75 pp., photographic plates. 8vo. Paper wrappers.

Will, Paul, editor

Improve Your Instinctive Shooting; guide to better archery.   Waverly, 1958, AMADA.   21 pp., photographic plates.   8vo.   Paper wrappers.

Willett, Roderick Fraser

The Good Shot. South Brunswick, New Jersey, 1979, A. S. Barnes and Company, Inc.   155 pp., illustrations.   8vo; dust jacket.   (Originally published, Great Britain)   A general instructional on shotgun shooting.

Williams, Alfred

Newhouse Bear Traps.   Salem, 1985, Privately printed.   44 pp., illustrations.   4to.

Williams, A. Bryan

Fish and Game in British Columbia. Vancouver, 1935, Sun Directories, Ltd.   206 pp., illustrations.   8vo.

Williams, Ben Ames   1889-1953

Fraternity Village. Boston, 1949, Houghton Mifflin Company.   336 pp. 8vo; dust jacket.   (Reprinted 1949, same format and publisher)   Hunting and angling in Maine.

The Happy End. New York, 1939, The Derrydale Press.   240 pp., illustrations from drawings by Churchill Ettinger. Limited to 1250 numbered copies.   Tall 8vo. (Also encountered with the title page marked "Clove Valley Rod & Gun Club Edition, 1942")

Mr. Williams was a best-selling author of many other novels, some having incidental mention of hunting or angling.

Williams, Ben Ames

Also see **McCorrison, Albert L.**

Williams, C. S.

Honker; a discussion of the habits and needs of the largest of our Canada geese.   Princeton, New Jersey, 1967, D. Van Nostrand Company, Inc.   197 pp., photographic plates, maps, drawings, bibliography.   4to; dust jacket.

Williams, Clarence Tucker

Essays and Poems of Hunting and Fishing.   Piedmont, 1974, Privately printed by Lawton and Alfred Kennedy.   Unpaginated (approx. 40 pp.), illustrations.   8vo.   Paper wrappers.

Williams, Clark

The Story of a Grateful Citizen; an autobiography.   New York, 1934, Privately printed.   Two volumes of 294 pp. and 313 pp. respectively, illustrations. 8vo.   Containing some hunting experiences in South Carolina and angling reminiscences in Maine, Quebec and Alaska.

Williams, Donald R.

Oliver H. Whitman; Adirondack guide.   New York, 1979, Privately printed.   186 pp.

Williams, Edward Huntington

Pine Flat Camp Fire Tales.   New York, 1924, The Goodhue Co.   169 pp., photographic plates, drawings.   12mo.   Tales of hunting and fishing in California's Sierra Nevada Mountains. Not in Phillips.

Williams, Gaar

Hunting and Fishing.   Chicago, No date.   A portfolio of 19 plates. 4to.   This collection of 19 cartoons originally appeared in *The Chicago Tribune* in the 1930's.

Williams Gun Sight Company

How To Convert Military Rifles.   Michigan,   Williams Gun Sight Company.   77 pp., photographic plates.   4to.   Paper wrappers.   (Reprinted several times, same format and publisher)   A discussion of methods used to convert military rifles to sporting use.

Williams, Jay P.   d. 1954

Alaskan Adventure. Harrisburg, 1952, The Stackpole Company.   299 pp., photographic plates.   Preface by Lt. Col. Townsend Whelen.   8vo; dust jacket. Hunting and trapping in Alaska.

Williams, Lovett E., Jr.

The Book of the Wild Turkey.   Tulsa, 1981, Winchester Press.   181 pp., color and black and white illustrations.   4to; dust jacket.   (Reprinted, same format and publisher)

The Voice and Vocabulary of the Wild Turkey.   Gainesville, 1984, Real Turkeys.   185 pp., photographic plates, drawings.   8vo; dust jacket.

Williams, M. B.

Jasper Trails.   No place, No date (ca. 1950), Canadian Department of the Interior.   43 pp., photographic plates.   12mo.   Paper wrappers.   A guide to hunting and fishing in the area.

Williams, Marjorie, and Glenn H. Williams, editors
The Buck's Camp Log, 1916-1928. Oshkosh, Wisconsin, 1974, Wisconsin Sportsman Publications. 111 pp., illustrations. 8vo; dust jacket. An account of an early Wisconsin deer hunting camp.

Williams, Mason
The Sporting Use of the Handgun. No place, 1979, Thomas Publishers. 272 pp., photographic plates. 8vo; dust jacket.

Williams, Russell
See **Bishop, Richard,** *The Ways of Wildfowl*

Williamson, F. Phillips, editor
The Waterfowl Gunner's Book; an anthology. Clinton, New Jersey, 1979, Amwell Press. 282 pp., color and black and white illustrations by Donald Shoffstall. Limited to 1000 numbered and signed copies. 8vo; slipcased. (Also a 1986 trade edition, same format and publisher)

Williamson, Harold
Winchester, The Gun That Won the West. Washington, D. C., 1952, Combat Forces Press. 494 pp., many photographic plates. Tall 8v; dust jacket. (Reprinted in 1961 and 1967, A. S. Barnes and Company, Inc.)

Williamson, Henry
The Phasian Bird. Boston, 1950, Little, Brown & Company. 276 pp., illustrations. 8vo; dust jacket. The story of a hybrid pheasant. (Originally published 1948, London)

Willis, Charles E.
The Three Must Get Theirs. No place, No date (ca. 1943), Privately printed. 26 pp. 12mo. The narrative of a canoe trip down the Cain River in New Brunswick, with much hunting and fishing.

Willis, Jack
Roosevelt in the Rough. New York, 1931, Washburn. 246 pp., photographic plates. 8vo. Hunting with Roosevelt for many species of big game in the American west.

Willoughby, V. E.
The Cream of Pointerdom; 1900-1945. Norman, Oklahoma, 1946, Privately printed. 382 pp. 8vo. A history of English pointers.
The Cream of Setterdom, 1900-1945. Norman, Oklahoma, 1946, Privately printed. 354 pp. 8vo.

Wilmore, Sylvia Bruce

Swans of the World. New York, 1974, Taplinger's. 229 pp., photographic plates. 8vo. (Also a 1974 British edition. Reprinted 1979, various formats and publishers)

Wilson, Bill

Ol' Hunters Never Lie; and other hunting and fishing stories. Kansas City, 1985, Ashcraft. 227 pp., drawings. 8vo; dust jacket.

Wilson, Clifford

North of 55; Canada from the 55th parallel to the Pole. Toronto, 1954, The Ryerson Press. 192 pp., photographic plates, drawings, maps. 8vo; dust jacket. Contains some hunting and trapping.

Wilson, Eugene E.

A North Woods Rendezvous. Hartford, Connecticut, 1953, Privately printed. 232 pp., drawings by Clifford Jones, map. Limited to 1200 numbered and signed copies. 8vo; slipcased. A narrative of the author's hunting and angling experiences. The author also wrote *A Pilgrimage of Anglers,* 1952. See Bruns.

Wilson, Kenneth A. and Ernest A. Vaughn

The Bobwhite Quail in Eastern Maryland. Baltimore, 1944, Maryland Game and Fish Commission. 138 pp., photographic plates, maps, drawings. 8vo. Paper wrappers.

Wilson, Loring D.

The Handy Sportsman. New York, 1976, Winchester Press. 218 pp., photographic plates, drawings. Tall 8vo; dust jacket. Instructions on how to make tackle boxes, gun cabinets, loading benches, etc.

Wilson, R. K.

Textbook of Automatic Pistols; being a treatise on the history, development and functioning of the modern military self-loading pistol - its special ammunition - and their evolvement into the sub-machine gun - together with a supplementing chapter on the light machine gun. Plantersville, South Carolina, 1943, Small Arms Technical Publishing Company. 349 pp., photographic plates. 8vo; dust jacket.

Wilson, Robert Lawrence   b. 1939

The Arms Collection of Colonel Colt. Bullville, New York, 1964, Herb Glass. 131 pp., illustrations. 8vo.

The Book of Colt Engraving. Los Angeles, 1974, Beinfeld Publishing Co. 422 pp., color and black and white illustrations. Folio; dust jacket. (Also a 1982 revised edition titled, *Colt Engraving,* same publisher)

Wilson, Robert Lawrence, continued

 The Book of Winchester Engraving. Los Angeles, 1975, Beinfeld Publishing Co. 402 pp., color and black and white illustrations. Folio; dust jacket.

 Colt: The American Legend; Sesquicentennial Edition. The Official History of Colt Firearms From 1836 to the present. New York, No date (ca. 1985), Abbeville Press. 406 pp., color and black and white illustrations. 4to; dust jacket.

 Colt Commemorative Firearms; from the G. M. Bartelmay collection. Illinois, 1973, Privately printed by Robert Cherry. 126 pp., color illustrations. 8vo. (Also a 1973 revised edition, in paper wrappers, same publisher)

 The Colt Heritage; the official history of Colt firearms from 1836 to the present. New York, 1979, Simon & Schuster. 358 pp., many color illustrations. Limited to 3850 copies. Oblong 4to; dust jacket. [Also a deluxe edition, specially bound and limited to the first 1850 numbered copies of this printing; slipcased]

 Samuel Colt Presents; a loan exhibition of presentation percussion Colt firearms. Hartford, Connecticut, 1961, Atheneum. 295 pp., illustrations. 4to; slipcased. (Reprinted 1962, same format and publisher)

 The Evolution of the Colt; firearms from the Robert Q. Sutherland collection. No place, 1967, privately printed. 54 pp., photographic plates, bibliography of Colt references. 8vo. Paper wrappers.

 L. D. Nimschke, Firearms Engraver. Teaneck, New Jersey, 1965, John J. Mallory. 158 pp., photographic plates. Folio; dust jacket.

 The Rampart Colt; the story of a trademark. Spencer, Indiana, 1969, T. Haas. 107 pp., color and black and white illustrations. 4to; dust jacket.

 Theodore Roosevelt: Outdoorsman. New York, 1971, Winchester Press. 278 pp., illustrations. 4to; dust jacket.

 Winchester; the Golden Age of American gunsmithing and the Winchester 1 of 1000. Cody, Wyoming, 1983, Winchester Arms Museum. 144 pp., many color illustrations. Oblong 4to; dust jacket.

Wilson, Robert Lawrence and R. E. Hable

 Colt Pistols, 1836-1976. Dallas, Texas, 1976, Privately printed. 381 pp., color and black and white photographic plates, drawings. Limited to 300 numbered and signed copies. 8vo; slipcased.

Wilson, Robert Lawrence

 Also see **Phillips, Philip R.**
 Also see **Sutherland, Robert Q.**

Winans, Clarence

    C. A. Johnson on Here, Whoa, Dead Bird. No place, 1985, Privately printed. 74 pp., photographic plates. 8vo. Paper wrappers. A successful breeder and trainer gives his views on the English setter.

Winant, Lewis

    Early Percussion Firearms; the history of firearms ignition from Forsyth To Winchester 44-40. New York, 1959, William Morrow & Co., Inc. 292 pp., illustrations. 8vo; dust jacket. (Reprinted, Bonanza)

    Firearms Curiosa. New York, 1955, Greenberg: Publishers. 281 pp., photographic plates, bibliography. Limited to 1000 numbered copies. Tall 8vo; dust jacket. (Reprinted, Bonanza. Also reprinted, 1961, St. Martin's Press / Ray Riling Arms Books)

    Pepperbox Firearms. New York, 1952, Greenberg: Publishers. 188 pp., photographic plates. Tall 8vo; dust jacket. (Reprinted several times, various publishers with the title *American, British and Continental Pepperbox Firearms*)

Winchester-Western Company

    Ammunition Handbook For Shooters and Hunters. New York, 1964, Winchester Western Company. 185 pp., photographic plates. 32mo. Paper wrappers.

    The Fundamentals of Claybird Shooting. No place, 1965, Winchester Arms Co. 44 pp., illustrations. 12mo. Paper wrappers.

    Rifle and Pistol Ammunition Handbook; a handy reference work on the development and use of metallic cartridges. East Alton, Illinois, 1927, Western Cartridge Company. 64 pp., photographic plates. 12mo. Paper wrappers.

    Upland Game Restoration. East Alton, Illinois, 1936, Western Cartridge Corporation. 67 pp., photographic plates, drawings. 8vo. Paper wrappers. (Reprinted 1938 and 1940, same format and publisher) Basic game conservation for the landowner.

Wing, Leonard W.

    Practice of Wildlife Conservation. New York, 1951, John Wiley & Sons, Inc. 412 pp., illustrations. 8vo; dust jacket.

Winge, Ojvind

    Inheritance in Dogs; with special reference to hunting breeds. Ithaca, New York, 1950, Comstock Press / Cornell University Press. 153 pp., color plates, bibliography. 8vo; dust jacket.

Winterhelt, Sigbot and Edward D. Bailey

    The Training and Care of the Versatile Hunting Dog. Puslinch, 1973, Privately printed. Third edition. 105 pp., photographic plates. 8vo.

Wisner, Chuck

The Weston Gun Club, 1933-1983. No place, No date (ca. 1984), Privately printed. Unpaginated (approx. 70 pp.), photographic plates, drawings. 8vo. A history of this Connecticut shooting club.

Witter, George

A Funny Thing Happened and A Hunt in the Yukon. Jericho, New York, 1974, Exposition Press. 92 pp., photographic plates. 8vo. A scarce big game hunting title.

Wolf, Bill

Reveries of an Outdoor Man; tales of field and stream. New York, 1946, G. P. Putnam's Sons. 181 pp., drawings by Luis Henderson. 8vo; dust jacket. [Also a specially bound and illustrated limited edition of 350 numbered and signed copies]

Wolfe, David R.

Yours Truly, Harvey Donaldson. Prescott, Arizona and Clinton, New Jersey, 1980, Wolfe Publishing Company and Amwell Press. 271 pp., photographic plates. Foreword by John T. Amber. Limited to 150 numbered and signed copies. 8vo; slipcased.

Wolff, Ed

Elk Hunting in the Northern Rockies. Stevensville, Montana, 1984, Stoneydale Press. 162 pp., illustrations. 8vo; dust jacket.

Wolff, Eldon G.

Ballard Rifles in the Henry J. Nunnemacher Collection. Milwaukee, Wisconsin, 1945, Privately printed. 77 pp., photographic plates, fold-out chart. 4to. Paper wrappers.

Wolontis, Margaret, editor

The German Wirehaired Pointer in America, 1959 - 1969. Rumson, 1969, German Wirehaired Pointer Club of America. 80 pp., photographic plates. 8vo. Paper wrappers. (Reprinted 1973, same format and publisher)

Wolters, Richard A. b. 1920

Beau; from both ends of his leash. New York, 1966, E. P. Dutton & Co., Inc. 190 pp. 8vo; dust jacket. A dog story and a tribute to Jack Randolph, sporting editor of the *New York Times.*

Family Dog. New York, 1963, E. P. Dutton & Co., Inc. 150 pp., photographic plates. 8vo; dust jacket. (Reprinted many times, same format and publisher)

471

Wolters, Richard A., continued

Game Dog; the hunter's retriever for upland birds and waterfowl   New York, 1983, E. P. Dutton & Co., Inc.   203 pp., photographic plates.   Foreword by Dave Meissner.   Epilogue by Gene Hill.   8vo; dust jacket.   (Reprinted many times, same format and publisher) [Also a deluxe first edition of 100 numbered copies, 1985, Amwell Press / E. P. Dutton & Co., Inc.] Training retrievers.

Gun Dog; revolutionary rapid training method.   New York, 1961, E. P. Dutton & Co., Inc.   150 pp., photographic plates.   8vo; dust jacket.   (Reprinted many times, same format and publisher)

The Labrador Retriever; the history, the people.   Los Angeles, 1981, Peterson Publishing Company.   200 pp., color illustrations by Reece, Pleissner and others.   4to; dust jacket.   [Also a deluxe edition of 200 numbered copies, Amwell Press / Peterson Publishing Company]

Water Dog; a revolutionary rapid training method.   New York, 1964, E. P. Dutton & Co., Inc.   179 pp., photographic plates.   8vo; dust jacket.   (Reprinted many times, same publisher and format)

Wong, Herbert W.

Ducks, Geese and Swans.   Menlo Park, California, 1960, Lane Book Co.   65 pp., color and black and white illustrations.   8vo.

Wood, Carl P.

The Gun Digest Book of Hunting Dogs.   Northfield, Illinois, 1985, DBI Books.   256 pp., illustrations.   4to.   Paper wrappers.

Wood, Casey A. and F. Marjorie Fyfe, editor and translator

The Art of Falconry; being the *De Arte Venandi Cum Avibus* of Frederick II of Hohenstaufen.   Stanford, California, 1943, Stanford University Press.   637 pp.   Folio.   (Reprinted, C. T. Branford)

Wood, Gene W. and R. W. Barrett

Status of Wild Pigs in the United States.   Washington, D. C., 1979, The Wildlife Society.   10 pp., bibliography.   4to.   Paper wrappers.

Wood, Peter

Thoughts on Beagling.   London and New York, 1938.   55 pp., illustrations by T. Ivestor Lloyd.   4to.

Woodcock, E. N.

Fifty Years a Hunter and Trapper; experiences and observations of E. N. Woodcock, noted hunter and trapper, as written by himself.   Columbus, Ohio, 1941, A. R. Harding.   318 pp., illustrations.   16mo.   (Originally published, 1908, same format and publisher)

Woodford, Michael
> *A Manual of Falconry;* with chapters on rook hawking and game hawking by J. G. Mavrogordato and E. E. Allen.   Newton, Massachusetts, 1960, Charles Branford.   192 pp., illustrations.   8vo; dust jacket.   (Originally published, 1960, Great Britain)

Woods, Shirley E.
> *Gunning For Upland Birds and Wildfowl.* New York, 1976, Winchester Press.   194 pp., illustrations by Tom Hennessey.   Foreword by Dana Lamb.   8vo; dust jacket.   (Reprinted several times, same format and publisher)
> *The Squirrels of Canada.*   Ottawa, 1980, National Museum.   199 pp., color and black and white illustrations.   4to; dust jacket.

Woodstream Corporation
> *Trapping and Wildlife Management.*   Lititz, 1974, Woodstream Corporation.   8vo.   Paper wrappers.   A general discussion from the manufacturers of Victor and Conibear traps.

Woodworth, Jim
> *The Kodiak Bear.*   Harrisburg, 1958, The Stackpole Company.   204 pp., photographic plates.   8vo; dust jacket.   An insightful look at the species with valuable information on hunting.

Woolner, Frank   b. 1916
> *Grouse and Grouse Hunting.*   New York, 1970, Crown Publishers, Inc.   192 pp., photographic plates.   4to; dust jacket.   (Reprinted several times, various publishers)
> *My New England.*   Lexington, Massachusetts, 1972, Stone Wall Press.   166 pp., drawings.   8vo; dust jacket.   Containing some hunting stories.
> *Timberdoodle;* a thorough practical guide to the American woodcock and woodcock hunting.   New York, 1974, Crown Publishers, Inc.   168 pp., photographic plates.   4to; dust jacket.   (Reprinted, Nick Lyons Books)
> *Upland Game Hunting.*   New Jersey, 1970, Athletic Activities Publishing Company.   64 pp., illustrations.   8vo.   Paper wrappers.

Wooters, John
> *Hunting Trophy Deer.*   New York, 1977, Winchester Press.   251 pp., photographic plates.   8vo; dust jacket.

Worcester, Hugh
> *Hunting the Lawless.*   Berkeley, California, 1955, American Wildlife Associates.   297 pp.   8vo; dust jacket.   The author recounts his experiences as a federal game warden.   Scarce.

Worker's Project Administration
Maine; a guide 'Down East.' Boston, 1937, Houghton Mifflin
Company. 476 pp., photographic plates, maps, drawings. A title in the
American Guide Series. 8vo; dust jacket. With much on hunting and fishing in the
area.

Worsham, James J.
The Gun Hunter's Guide. Santa Monica, California, 1950, Seward and
Flood Printing Company. 32 pp. 18mo. Paper wrappers.

Wright, A. F.
G. W. Wright and the Early Settlers. New York, 1963, Calton Press.
73 pp. 8vo. Settling Nebraska with some prairie chicken, grouse and duck hunting.

Wright, Bruce S.   1912-1975
Black Duck Spring. New York, 1966, E. P. Dutton & Co., Inc. 191
pp., drawings. 8vo; dust jacket. (Reprinted 1966, same format and publisher.
Also a 1966 Canadian edition) An explanation of the life cycle and migration patters of the
black dusk.
The Eastern Panther; a question of survival. Toronto, 1972, Clarke,
Irwin. 180 pp., illustrations. 8vo; dust jacket.
The Ghost of North America; the story of the eastern panther. New
York, 1959, Vantage Press. 140 pp., photographic plates. 8vo; dust jacket.
High Tide and East Wind; the story of the black duck. Harrisburg /
Washington D. C., 1954, The Stackpole Company / Wildlife Management
Institute. 162 pp., illustrations, maps. 8vo; dust jacket.
The Monarch of Mularchy Mountain. Frederickton, New Brunswick,
1963, Brunswick Press. 149 pp. 8vo. The story of a buck white-tailed deer.
The Moose of New Brunswick; a report to the Minister of Lands and
Mines. Frederickton, 1956, University of New Brunswick. 63 pp., photographic
plates, maps, bibliography. 4to. Paper wrappers.
Wildlife Sketches Near and Far. Frederickton, New Brunswick, 1962,
Brunswick Press. 288 pp., photographic plates, bibliography. 8vo; dust
jacket.

Wright, H. and S. Rapport, editors
Great Adventures With Wild Animals. New York, 1967, Harper and
Row, Inc. 308 pp. 8vo; dust jacket.

Wright, Lyle H.
Sporting Books in the Huntington Library. San Marino, California,
1937, Huntington Library Lists. 132 pp. 8vo. Paper wrappers. A scarce
bibliography of this extensive sporting book collection.

Wright, Solomon Alexander

My Rambles; as East Texas cowboy, hunter, fisherman, tie-cutter. Austin, Texas, 1942, Texas Folklore Society. 159 pp., illustrations. Introduction by J. Frank Dobie. 8vo; dust jacket.

Wright, William H.   b. 1856

The Grizzly Bear; the narrative of a hunter-naturalist.   Lincoln, 1977, University of Nebraska Press. 274 pp., frontispiece. 8vo. (Originally published, 1909, Charles Scribner's Sons) An important work.

Wulff, Lee   1905-1991

Sports Photography. New York, 1942, A. S. Barnes, Inc. A title in The Sportsman's Library series. 184 pp., photographic plates. 8vo; dust jacket.

The Ancient Age Sportsman Book. Frankfort, Kentucky, 1955, Ancient Age Distilling Co. 32 pp., color and black and white illustrations. 16mo. Paper wrappers. With hints on hunting, fishing and woodcraft.

Wulff, Lee, editor

The Sportsman's Companion. New York, 1968, Harper & Row, Publishers, Inc. 413 pp., illustrations. 4to; dust jacket. Advise on hunting and angling by Janes, Lyman and Woolner.

Wylie, Stephen and S. S. Furlong

Key to North American Waterfowl. Wynnewood, 1972, Livingston. 32 pp., color illustrations. 8vo. Paper wrappers. A handy field guide printed on waterproof paper.

Wyman, Frank

The ABC of Pistol Shooting. Washington, D. C., 1940, The National Rifle Association of America. 30 pp., photographic plates. 8vo. Paper wrappers.

Wyman, Frank, et al.

Pistol Marksmanship. Washington, D. C., 1950, The National Rifle Association of America. 60 pp., photographic plates. 12mo. Paper wrappers.

Wyman, Walker D.   b. 1907

Mythical Creatures of the North Country; including a reprint of William T. Cox's "Fearsome Creatures of the Lumberwoods". River Falls, Wisconsin, 1969, River Falls State University Press. 65 pp., drawings. An account of such mythical creatures as a slide rock bolter, whirling whimpus, fur-bearing small mouth bass and others.

Wyshinski, Nick

    Muskrats; the trappers meal ticket.　No place, 1964, Privately printed. 46 pp., illustrations.　12mo.　Paper wrappers.　(Reprinted, same format and publisher)

Yarnell, Duane

    Through Forest and Stream. Cleveland, 1940, World Publishing Company. 245 pp. 8vo; dust jacket. A juvenile with hunting and fishing.

Yeager, Dorr G.

    Chita. Philadelphia, 1939, Penn Publishing Company. 227 pp. illustrations by Lynn Bogue Hunt. 8vo; dust jacket. (Reprinted several times, slightly smaller format, Alfred A. Knopf, Inc.) A story about a mountain lion.

    Gray Dawn, the Wolf Dog. New York, 1942, The William Penn Publishing Company. 222 pp., frontispiece. 8vo; dust jacket.

    Our Wilderness Neighbors; a sympathetic description of the most interesting animals in Yellowstone National Park. Chicago, 1931, A. C. McClurg & Co. 160 pp., photographic plates. 12mo.

    Scarface; the story of a grizzly. Philadelphia, 1935, Penn Publishing Company. 254 pp., color frontispiece. 8vo; dust jacket.

    All of these titles by Yeager were older juveniles.

Yeatter, Ralph E.

    Bird Dogs in Sport and Conservation. Urbana, Illinois, 1948, Illinois Natural History Service. 64 pp., illustrations, bibliography. 8vo. Paper wrappers.

    The Hungarian Partridge in the Great Lakes Region. Ann Arbor, 1934, University of Michigan Press. 92 pp., photographic plates, bibliography. 8vo. Paper wrappers.

Yoakum, J. D. and D. E. Spalinger

    American Pronghorn Antelope; articles published in *Journal of Wildlife Management*, 1937-1977. Washington, D. C., 1979, The Wildlife Society. 244 pp., photographic plates. 4to. Paper wrappers.

Young, F. M. and Coralie Beyer

    Man Meets Grizzly; encounters in the wild from Lewis & Clark to modern times. Boston, 1980, Houghton Mifflin Company. 298 pp. 8vo; dust jacket.

Young, George Orville   b. 1873

    Alaskan Trophies Won and Lost. Boston, 1928, Christopher Publishing House. 251 pp., photographic plates, fold-out map. 8vo.

    Alaskan-Yukon Trophies Won and Lost. Huntington, West Virginia, 1947, Standard Publications, Inc. 273 pp., photographic plates. 4to; dust jacket. (Reprinted 1985, Wolfe Publishing Company) West Virginia State Senator Young was disappointed in the book produced by Christopher. Herman Dean, owner of Standard Publications, Inc., proposed this new volume with more photographs and text than the first edition. It has proven to be an important account of big game hunting in the area.

Young, Howard C.

Outdoorsman's Odyssey; a trek down memory trail. Lyme Center, 1985, Privately printed. 142 pp., photographic plates. 8vo. Paper wrappers. Memoirs of hunting and fishing with some trapping, mostly in New Hampshire.

Young, Ralph W.

Grizzlies Don't Come Easy; my life as an Alaskan bear hunter. Tulsa, 1981, Winchester Press. 168 pp., illustrations. 8vo; dust jacket. (Reprinted, same format and publisher)

My Lost Wilderness; adventures of an Alaskan hunter and guide. Piscataway, New Jersey, 1983, Winchester Press. 191 pp., illustrations. Foreword by Bob Good. 8vo; dust jacket.

Young, Stanley P.   b. 1889

The Bobcat of North America; its history, life habits, economic status and control, with a list of currently recognized subspecies. Harrisburg / Washington D. C., 1958, The Stackpole Company / The Wildlife Management Institute. 193 pp., photographic plates, color frontispiece form a painting by Harold Cramer Smith, bibliography. Tall 8vo; dust jacket. An important work.

Deer Hunting as a Means of Coyote Control. Washington, D. C., 1937, United States Government Printing Office. 8 pp., illustrations. 8vo. Paper wrappers.

Hints on Mountain Bobcat Trapping. Washington, D. C., 1931, United States Government Printing Office. 6 pp., illustrations. 8vo. Paper wrappers.

Hints on Mountain Lion Trapping. Washington, D. C., 1933, United States Government Printing Office. 8 pp., illustrations. 8vo. Paper wrappers.

The Last of the Loners. New York, 1970, The Macmillan Company. 316 pp., photographic plates. 8vo; dust jacket. (Reprinted 1970, same format and publisher) American wolves.

Sketches of American Wildlife. Baltimore, 1946, Monumental Press. 143 pp., photographic plates. 8vo; dust jacket.

The Wolf in North American History. Caldwell, Idaho, 1946, Caxton Printers, Ltd. 149 pp., photographic plates. 8vo; dust jacket.

Young, Stanley P. and Edward A. Goldman

The Puma; mysterious American cat. Washington, D. C., 1946, The American Wildlife Institute. 358 pp., photographic plates, maps, color frontispiece from a painting by Walter A. Weber. 8vo; dust jacket.

The Wolves of North America. Washington, D. C., 1944, The American Wildlife Institute. 636 pp., photographic plates, maps, six color illustrations from paintings by Walter A. Weber. Thick 8vo; dust jacket. An important work regarding this much maligned predator.

Young, Stanley P. and Hartley H. T. Jackson

The Clever Coyote; its life history, life habits, economic status and control with classification of the races by H. T. Jackson. Harrisburg / Washington, D. C., 1951, The Stackpole Company / The Wildlife Management Institute. 411 pp., photographic plates, color frontispiece from a painting by Walter A. Weber. Tall 8vo; dust jacket.

Young, Stanley P.

Also see **Carhart, Arthur H.**

Zeigler, Don L.

The Okanogan Mule Deer. Olympia, 1978, Washington Department of Game. 106 pp., illustrations. 4to. Paper wrappers.

Zern, Edward Geary 1910-1994

Hunting and Fishing From A to Zern. New York, 1985, Nick Lyons Books / Winchester Press. 312 pp., illustrations by the author. 8vo; dust jacket.

To Hell With Hunting. New York, 1946, D. Appleton-Century Company, Inc. 99 pp., drawings by the author. 8vo. (Reprinted several times, same format and publisher) Both of these books are humorous looks at the sport.

Zimmerman, William

Waterfowl of North America. Louisville, Kentucky, 1974, Frame House Gallery. Unpaginated (approx. 50 pp.), color illustrations by the author. Limited to 1000 numbered and signed copies. Elephant folio; cased. More scarce than the limitation would suggest.

Zumbo, Jim

Hunt Elk. Piscataway, New Jersey, 1985, Winchester Press. 200 pp., photographic plates, maps, scoring charts. 8vo; dust jacket. (Reprinted, same format and publisher)

Zumbo, Jim and Robert Elman

All American Deer Hunter's Guide. New York, 1983, Winchester Press. 320 pp., illustrations. 4to; dust jacket. (Reprinted 1984, same format and publisher)

Hunting America's Mule Deer. Tulsa, 1981, Winchester Press. 358 pp., photographic plates. 8vo; dust jacket.

Zurcher, Marvin

Trapping the Red Fox; how to professionally out fox the fox, Lear sets, methods and most important basics, how where, equipment and precautions. No place, 1985, Privately printed. 74 pp., photographic plates, drawings. 8vo. Paper wrappers.

Zurhorst, Charles

The Conservation Fraud. New York, 1970, Cowles. 164 pp. 8vo; dust jacket. A plea for close examination of our conservation policies.

Zutz, Don

The Double Shotgun. New York, 1978, Winchester Press. 265 pp., photographic plates. 8vo; dust jacket. (Reprinted several times, same format and publisher. Also a 1985 revised edition, same publisher)

Zutz, Don, continued

Handloading For Hunters.   New York, 1977, Winchester Press.   318 pp., photographic plates.   8vo; dust jacket.   (Reprinted 1978, same format and publisher)

Modern Waterfowl Guns and Gunning.   South Hackensack, New Jersey, 1985, Stoeger Publishing Company.   288 pp., illustrations.   4to.   Paper wrappers.

Index

Alaska Hunting and Fishing Tales
    The Alaskan Sportsman
Alaska Journal, 1979
    Adams, Patricia
Alaska Nellie
    Lawing, Nellie Neal
Alaska Sourdough
    Morenus, Richard
Alaska Trail Dogs
    Caldwell, Elsie Noble
Alaska-Yukon Caribou
    Murie, Olaus J.
Alaskan Adventure
    Williams, Jay P.
Alaskan Bear Adventures
    Finton, Walter L.
Alaskan Bear Tales
    Kanuit, Larry
The Alaskan Bird Sketches of Olaus Murie
    Murie, Margaret
Alaskan Hunter
    Chandler, Roy F.
Alaskan Tales
    Annabel, Russell
Alaskan Trophies Won and Lost
    Young, G. O.
Alaskan-Yukon Trophies Won and Lost
    Young, G. O.
Alaska's Animals and Fishes
    Dufresne, Frank
Alaska's Fish and Wildlife
    United States Department of the Interior
Alaska's Kodiak Island
    Ameigh, G. C.
Alaska's Mammoth Brown Bears
    Chase, Will H.
Alberta's Big Game Resources
    Webb, R.
Algonquin
    Henderson, Dion
The Alien Animals
    Laycock, George
Alive in the Wild
    Cahalane, Victor H.
All About Deer Hunting in America
    Elman, Robert
All About Grizzly Bears
    Weiss, Norman D.
All About Rifle Hunting and Shooting in America
    Ferber, Steve
All About Small Game Hunting in America
    Tinsley, Russell
All About Varmint Hunting
    Sisley, Nick

All About Wildfowling in America
    Knap, Jerome J.
All American Deer Hunter's Guide
    Zumbo, Jim
All in the Family
    Roosevelt, Theodore, Jr.
All Outdoors
    Scott, Jack Denton
All Season Hunting
    Gilsvik, Bob
All Seasons Afield
    Camp, Raymond R.
All Setters
    Lloyd, Freeman
All Spaniels
    Lloyd, Freeman
All the Answers To All Your Questions About Training Pointing Dogs
    Long, Paul
The Allagash
    Deitz, Lew
Ward Allen - Savannah River Market Hunter
    Cay, John Eugene, Jr.
Bob Allen's Shooter's Digest
    Allen, Bob
Allison's Fishing Birds
    Haig-Brown, Roderick
Along the Trail
    Stearns, Marshall
The Amateur Guncraftsman
    Howe, James Virgil
Amateur Gunsmithing
    Whelen, Lt. Col. Townsend
The Amateur Taxidermist
    LaBrie, Jean
The Amazing Adventures of Lord Gore
    Roberts, Jack
The Amazing Bob Davis
    Mathias, Fred S.
America; the men and their guns...
    Boddington, Craig
American Ammunition and Ballistics
    Matunas, Edward
American Antique Guns and Their Current Prices
    Rywell, Martin
American Antique Rifles and Their Current Prices
    Rywell, Martin
American Arms and Arms Makers
    Gardner, Robert Edward
American Beagling
    Old Kickapoo
American Bears
    Beebe, B. F.

American Bears
Roosevelt, Theodore
The American Beaver and His Work
Morgan, Lewis
American Big Game and How To Hunt Them
McGinn, O. T.
American Big Game Hunting
Whelen, Lt. Col. Townsend
American Big Game Shooting
Whelen, Lt. Col. Townsend
American Bird Decoys
Mackey, William J. Jr.
The American Bison
Garretson, Martin S.
American Boy's Rifles
Perkins, Jim
American, British and Continental Pepperbox Firearms
Dunlap, Jack
The American Buffalo in Transition
Rorabacher, J. Albert
The American Cartridge
Suydam, Charles R.
American Conservation in Picture and Story
Butler, Ovid M.
American Decorative Bird Carving
Basile, Kenneth
American Decoys
Colio, Quintina
The American Deer Hunter
Sell, Francis
American Duck, Goose and Brant Shooting
Bruette, Dr. William A.
The American Eagle
Herrick, Francis Hobart
American Engraved Powder Horns
DuMont, John S.
American Engraved Powder Horns
Grancsay, Stephen V.
American Etchers
Benson, Frank W.
American Factory Decoys
Fleckenstein, Henry A.
American Firearms
Van Rensselaer, Stephen
American Firearms Makers
Carey, A. Merwyn
American Fisherman and Hunter's Annual
Anonymous
The American Foxhound
Trigg, Haiden C.
The American Foxhound, 1747 - 1967
Mackay - Smith, Alexander
American Foxhunting
Mackay - Smith, Alexander

American Game Birds
Edminster, Frank C.
American Game Mammals and Birds
Phillips, John C.
American Game Preserve Shooting
Smith, Lawrence B.
The American Game Protective and Propagation Association
Haskell, William S.
American Game Shooting
Curtis, Capt. Paul A.
The American Goldeneye in Central New Brunswick
Carter, Brian C.
American Gun Makers
Gluckman, Col. Arcadi
American Hawking
Peeters, Hans J.
The American Hunting Dog
Miller, Warren H.
The American Hunting Myth
Baker, Ron
The American Landscape
Trefethen, James B.
American Lions and Cats
Beebe, B. F.
American Partridge and Pheasant Shooting
Schley, Frank
American Pistol and Revolver Design and Performance
Wallack, Louis Robert
American Pistol Shooting
Frazer, Maj. William D.
American Pronghorn Antelope
Yoakum, J. D.
The American Rifle
Hagie, C. E.
The American Rifle
Whelen, Lt. Col. Townsend
American Rifle Design and Performance
Wallack, Louis Robert
The American Shooter's Manual
Kester, Jesse Y.
The American Shotgun
Askins, Charles, Sr.
The American Shotgun
Butler, David F.
American Shotgun Design and Performance
Wallack, Louis Robert
The American Shotgunner
Sell, Francis E.
American Sighting Scopes
Ness, Fred C.
The American Spaniel Club Year Book
Brown, Paul

Arizona Wetlands and Waterfowl
  Brown, David E.
Arizona Wildlife Trophies
  Arizona Wildlife Federation
Arms and Armor Annual
  Held, Robert
Arms and Armor in Colonial America
  Peterson, Harold L.
The Arms Collection of Colonel Colt
  Wilson, Robert L.
Arms Fabricators Ancient and Modern
  Gardner, Robert Edward
Arms Makers of Maryland
  Hartzler, Daniel
Arms Trade
  Wahl, Paul
Armsmear
  Barnard, Henry
Art Anatomy of Animals
  Seton, Ernest Thompson
The Art and Appreciation of Trophy Bowhunting
  Kirschner, Bob
The Art and Science of Taking To the Woods
  Colby, C. B.
The Art and Sport of Falconry
  Kotsiopoulos, George
Art For Conservation
  Gilmore, Jene C.
The Art of Bird Carving
  Gilley, Wendell
The Art of the Decoy
  Earnest, Adele
The Art of Deer and Bear Hunting
  Goodwin, Fred
The Art of Falconry
  Wood, Casey A.
The Art of Good Shooting
  Ruffer, J. E. M.
The Art of the Gunmaker
  Hayward, J. F.
The Art of Handgun Shooting
  Askins, Charles, Jr.
The Art of Hunting
  Strung, Norman
The Art of Hunting Big Game in North America
  O'Connor, Jack
The Art of Ogden Pleissner
  Bergh, Peter
The Art of Shooting
  Chapel, Charles Edward
The Art of Successful Deer Hunting
  Sell, Francis E.
The Art of Wing Shooting
  Leffingwell, W. Bruce

The Artist and the Sportsman
  Scott, Martha B.
As the Falcon Her Bells
  Glasier, Phillip
As Far As the Yukon
  Jaques, Florence Page
As Hounds Ran
  Higginson, A. Henry
As New England Played
  Sandler, Martin
Askins on Pistols and Revolvers
  Askins, Charles, Jr.
Assignment Down East
  Buxton, Henry
At Home in the Wilderness
  Bear, Sun
At Home With the High Ones
  Crawford, John S.
At The Top of Their Game
  Boyle, Robert H.
The Atlantic Flyway
  Elman, Robert
The Atlantic Flyway Waterfowl Management Guide
  Atlantic Waterfowl Council
Atwater's Prairie Chicken
  Lehman, Valgene W.
John James Audubon
  Ford, Alice
John James Audubon
  Cahalane, Victor H.
Audubon Game Animals
  Audubon, John James
Audubon's America
  Peattie, Donald C.
Audubon's Animals
  Ford, Alice
Automatic and Repeating Shotguns
  Arnold, Richard
Automatic Firearm Pistols
  Swanson, Elmer
Automatic Pistol Marksmanship
  Reichenbach, William
Autumn Hawk Flights
  Heintzelman, Donald S.
Autumn of the Eagle
  Laycock, George
Away From It All
  Kidney, Dorothy Boone

495

496

504

506

508

514

A Golden Cross on Trails From the Valdez
Glacier
    Cooper River Joe
The Golden Days of Foxhunting
    Reeve, J. Stanley
The Golden Eagle
    Arnold, Lee W.
The Golden Eagle
    Murphy, Robert
Golden Eagle Country
    Olendorff, Richard R.
A Golden Guide To Guns
    Koller, Larry
The Golden Plover and Other Birds
    Allen, Arthur A.
The Golden Retriever
    Golden Retriever Club of America
The Golden Retriever
    Schaul, H. Edwin
The Golden Retriever
    Tudor, J.
Golden Retrievers
    Charlesworth, W. M.
Gone Away
    Houghland, Mason
Gone Away With the Fort Leavenworth Hunt
    Davison, Paul
Gone Away With O'Malley
    Knott, M. O'Malley
Gone For the Day
    Smith, Ned
Gone Huntin'
    Elliott, Charles
The Good Chance
    Fosburg, Hugh
Good Hunting
    Clark, James Lippitt
Good Shooting!
    Mackay, John W.
Good Shot!
    Holland, Bob
The Good Shot
    Willett, Roderick Fraser
The Good Trail
    Geagan, Bill
Goodbye To A River
    Graves, Robert
Goose and Duck Shooting
    Haynes, William Barber
Goose Hunting
    Cadieux, Charles L.
The Goshawk
    White, T. H.
The Grab Bag
    Trausch, William D.

Grandma and the Buck Deer
    Vance, Joel
Grandpa Recalls Deer Hunting Stories
    Michmerhuizen, Lewey
Gran'pappy's Pistol
    McConnell, Duncan
The Grand...75 Years
    Robinson, Jimmy
The Grand Spring Hunt
    Jacob, Bart
The Grand Slam of North American Wild Sheep
    Householder, Bob
The Grasshopper Trap
    McMannus, Patrick F.
Gray and Fox Squirrels
    Madson, John
Gray Dawn, the Wolf Dog
    Yeager, Dorr G.
Gray Squirrel Management in Alabama
    Davis, James R.
Gray's Journal
    Gray, Ed
Great Adventures With Wild Animals
    Wright, H.
The Great American Shooting Prints
    Elman, Robert
The Great Arc of the Wild Sheep
    Clark, James Lippitt
The Great Buffalo Hunt
    Gard, Wayne
Great Camps of the Adirondacks
    Kaiser, Harvey H.
The Great Gallery of Ducks and Other
Waterfowl
    LeMaster, Richard
Great Game Animals of the World
    Aitken, Russell Burnett
Great-Grandfather in the Honey Tree
    Swayne, Sam
The Great Gray Owl
    Nero, Robert W.
The Great Guns
    Peterson, Harold L.
Great Historic Animals
    Seton, Ernest Thompson
Great Hunting and Fishing Stories
    Brown, J. Hammond
Great Moments in Action
    Hall, G. Harper
Great Outdoor Adventures
    Outdoor Life Books
The Great Outdoors
    Godfrey, Joe, Jr.
Great Shooting Stories
    Ludlum, Stuart D.

516

Hints on Mountain Bobcat Trapping
   Young, Stanley P.
Hints on Mountain Lion Trapping
   Young, Stanley P.
Hints To Riflemen
   Cleveland, H. W. S.
History and Management of Meriam's Wild Turkey
   Ligon, J. Stokley
History and Management of South Dakota Deer
   Richardson, Arthur H.
History and Management of the Wild Turkey in West Virginia
   Bailey, R. W.
The History and Status of the Black Bear in Massachusetts and Adjacent New England States
   Cardoza, James
A History of Browning Guns From 1831
   Browning, John M.
A History of the Chesapeake Bay Retrievers
   Heller, Louise
A History of the Colt Revolver
   Haven, Charles T.
A History of Deerfoot Lodge
   Rosenberry, Marvin B.
A History of the Elk Ridge Foxhunting Club, The Elk Ridge Hounds, ...
   McIntosh, J. Rieman
A History of Firearms
   Pollard, Hugh B. C.
A History of Firearms From the Earliest Times
   Carman, W. Y.
History of the Forest Lake Club, 1882-1932
   Calhoun, William Caldwell
The History of Foxhunting
   Longrigg, Roger
History of Game Strains
   Johnson, W. T.
History of the Hollenbeck Club, 1900-1978
   Poole, J. Lawrence
A History of Hunting in Perry County
   Chandler, Roy F.
History of Hunting Trip in Sierra Madres, Northern Mexico, August 21 to October 1, 1922
   Carlton, L. A.
History of the League of Kentucky Sportsmen, 1935 - 1957
   Gooch, Dennie
A History of Marksmanship
   Trench, Charles C.
The History of the Montreal Hunt
   Cooper, John Irwin

A History of New Hampshire Game and Furbearers
   Silver, Helenette
A History of the Packs of Harriers, Beagles and Bassets of New Jersey
   Jones, James S.
History of Smith & Wesson
   Jinks, Roy G.
A History of the White-Tailed Deer in Maine
   Stanton, Don C.
History of Wild Turkey Restocking in Alabama
   Davis, James R.
The History of Wildlife in America
   Borland, Hal
The History of Winchester Firearms, 1866 - 1980
   Barnes, Duncan
The History of Winchester Firearms, 1866 - 1966
   Watrous, George R.
A History of Wisconsin Deer
   Swift, Ernest
History, Tradition and Adventure in the Chippewa Valley
   Bartlett, William W.
Hits and Misses of the Trap Shooting and Skeet World
   Robinson, Jimmy
Hitting the Bullseye
   Askins, Charles, Jr.
Hobby Gunsmithing
   Lewis, J.
Albert Frederick Hochwalt
   Brown, William F.
Hodge Podge
   Phibbs, Harry C.
Hodgman's Handy Book of Sportsman's Secrets
   Burlingame, Mark W.
Roy Hoff Tells It As It Was
   Hoff, Roy
Hold That Tiger
   Bond, James
Hollica Snooze
   Cook, Earnshaw
Hollywood Club Memoirs
   Speare, E. Ray
Home Book of Taxidermy and Tanning
   Grantz, Gerald J.
Home by the River
   Rutledge, Archibald
Home Grown Honkers
   Dill, Herbert H.
The Home Guide To Cartridge Conversions
   Nonte, George C.

523

532

Narrow Escapes and Wilderness Adventures
East, Ben
National Directory of Decoy Collectors
Kangas, Gene
National Field Trial Champions
Brown, William F.
The National Rifle Association Guide To Firearms Assembly
The National Rifle Assoc. of America
National Retriever Field Trial Club
Labrador Retriever Club
The National Retriever Field Trial Club, 1941 - 1960
Fraser, John
A Nationwide Survey on the Wild Turkey
Boyer, Samuel P.
Natural History in America
Hanley, Wayne
A Natural History of the Ducks
Phillips, John C.
Natural History of the King Rail
Meanly, Brooke
A Naturalist in Alaska
Murie, Adolph
A Naturalist in Canada
McCowand, Dan
The Nature of Heritible Wildness in Turkeys
Leopold, A. Starker
Nature Photography at Night
Gregory, Tappan
Nature's Silent Call
Deason, Wilborn J.
Neighbors Have My Ducks
Pickering, Harold G.
Nesting Biology of Black Ducks and Mallards in Northern New England
Coulter, Malcolm W.
Nesting, Distribution and Mortality Studies of Canada Geese
Ballou, R. M.
Nesting Ecology of the Bobwhite in Southern Illinois
Klimstra, W. D.
Nesting Ecology of the Golden Eagle in Elko County, Nevada
Seibert, J. Donald
Nesting Habits and Surveying Techniques For Common Western Raptors
Call, Mayo W.
Never Cry Wolf
Mowat, Farley
Never Stiff a Gift Fish
McMannus, Patrick F.
The New Archery
Butler, David F.

The New Complete Brittany Spaniel
Riddle, Maxwell
The New Complete English Setter
Tuck, Davis H.
The New Complete English Springer Spaniel
Goodall, Charles S.
New England Game Conference
Phillips, John C.
New England Grouse Shooting
Foster, William Harnden
The New England Gun
Lindsay, Merrill
The New German Shorthaired Pointer
Maxwell, C. Bede
New Guide To Better Archery
Forbes, Thomas
The New Irish Setter
Thompson, William C.
New Jersey Decoys
Fleckenstein, Henry A.
New Methods in Exterior Ballistics
Moulton, Forest Ray
New York State Big Buck Club Record Book
Dam, Brian
New York State Big Buck Club Record Book
Alsheimer, Charles J.
New York Waterfowl Identification Guide
Atlantic Waterfowl Council
The New Way of the Wilderness
Rutstrum, Calvin
Newfoundland
Tait, R. H.
Newfoundland and Its Untrodden Ways
Millais, J. G.
Newfoundland Wit, Humor and Folklore
Reader, H. J.
Newhouse Bear Traps
Williams, Alfred
Night of the Grizzlies
Olsen, Jack
The Night Watchers
Cameron, Angus
L. D. Nimschke, Firearms Engraver
Wilson, Robert L.
Nine Mile Bridge
Hamlin, Helen
The 1982 Derrydale Price Guide
Oelgart, Isaac J.
1975 Official National Pictorial of the Irish Setter Club of America
Bacon, Bernard
The 1935 International Wild Duck Census
More Game Birds in America Foundation
The Ninety-Nine
Murray, Douglas

Our American Game Birds
  Heilner, Van Campen
Our Friend the Cocker Spaniel
  Johns, Rowland
Our Friend the Springer Spaniel
  Johns, Rowland
Our Natural World
  Borland, Hal
Our Rifles
  Sawyer, Charles Winthrop
Our Southern Highlanders
  Kephart, Horace
Our Summer With the Eskimos
  Helmericks, Constance
Our Wilderness Neighbors
  Yeager, Dorr G.
Our Wildlife Neighbors
  Barber, Lunette
Our Wildlife Legacy
  Allen, Durward L.
Our Winged Heritage
  Ducks Unlimited
Out of Bondage
  Robinson, Rowland E.
The Out-of-Doors
  Floing, William O.
Out of the Woods
  Crump, Irving
The Outdoor Encyclopedia
  Kesting, Ted
The Outdoor Guide
  Henderson, Luis M.
The Outdoor Heritage of New Jersey
  Warren, George G.
Outdoor Horizons
  Brings, Lawrence M.
The Outdoor Life Bear Book
  Fish, Chet
Outdoor Life Cyclopedia
  Outdoor Life Books
The Outdoor Life Deer Hunter's Encyclopedia
  Madson, John
Outdoor Life Deer Hunter's Yearbook
  Outdoor Life Books
Outdoor Life Gun Data Book
  Rice, F. Philip
Outdoor Life Shooting Book
  O'Connor, Jack
Outdoor Life's Anthology of Hunting
Adventures
  Outdoor Life Books
Outdoor Life's Deer Hunting Book
  Outdoor Life Books

Outdoor Life's Gallery of North American
Game
  Outdoor Life Books
Outdoor Life's Shooting and Hunting Annual
  Outdoor Life Books
Outdoor Life's Sportsman's Encyclopedia
  O'Connor, Jack
Outdoor Observations
  Anderson, Mabry I.
The Outdoor Paintings of Robert K. Abbett
  Abbett, Robert K.
The Outdoor Photographer's Handbook
  Oberrecht, Kenn
Outdoor Photography
  Bauer, Erwin A.
Outdoor Photography
  Dimock, Julian
Outdoor Reference Guide
  Long, Amelia Reynolds
Outdoor Sports the Year Round
  Popular Mechanics Press
The Outdoor Trail of Dan Stillman
  Stillman, Dan
Outdoor Writers Instruction Manual
  Outdoor Writers Association of America
Outdoor Yarns and Outright Lies
  Hill, Gene
Outdoors
  McGillen, Pete
Outdoors - New Brunswick
  New Brunswick Travel Bureau
Outdoors Unlimited
  Brown, J. Hammond
Outdoors With "Dad" Lammon
  Lammon, L. D.
Outdoors With Gregory Clark
  Clark, Gregory
The Outdoorsman
  Foss, Joe
The Outdoorsman's Emergency Manual
  Acerrano, Anthony
The Outdoorsman's Handbook
  Ormond, Clyde
Outdoorsman's Odyssey
  Young, Howard C.
The Outdoorsman's Workshop
  Burch, Monte
Outlaw
  Long, Jeff
The Outlaw Gunner
  Walsh, Harry
The Outside Story
  Scammell, Robert
Outwitting the Whitetail
  Riley, Perry G.

Timberline Tales
  Montgomery, Rutherford G.
The Time of the Buffalo
  McHugh, Tom
Tips To Shooters of Shotguns, Rifles and Pistols
  Whelen, Lt. Col. Townsend
Tips to Trappers, 1930-31
  Muskrat, Johnny and His Trapper Friends
Tirrell Pond
  Abbott, Henry
To A Young Bird Artist
  Sutton, George Miksch
To All Sportsmen and Particularly To Farmers and Gamekeepers
  Hanger, George
To Far Western Alaska For Big Game
  Hubback, Theodore Rathbone
To Hell With Hunting
  Zern, Edward Geary
To Keep a Tryst With Dawn
  Ordeman, John T.
To Ride the Wind
  Hochbaum, H. Albert
To Win the Hunt
  McIlvaine, Jane
Toad's Tricks to Taking Whitetails in Corn....and Everywhere Else
  Smith, Otis "Toad"
John Tobias, Sportsman
  Cox, Charles E., Jr.
Told Around the Campfire
  DeSormo, Maitland
Told at the Explorers Club
  Blossom, F. A.
Tom Tells Tall Turkey Tales
  Gaskins, Tom
Tom and I and the Old Plantation
  Rutledge, Archibald
A Tomato Can Chronicle
  Smith, Edmund Ware
Top Flight: Speed Index to Waterfowl of North America
  Ruthven, John A.
Touch of Wilderness
  Dietz, Lew
A Tour of the Prairies
  Irving, Washington
The Track of the Grizzly
  Craighead, Frank C.
Track of the Kodiak
  Clark, Marvin H.
The Tracker
  Brown, Tom., Jr.
Tracker
  Paulsen, Gary

Tracking the Big Cats
  Hert, Carl
Tracks and Tracking
  Brunner, Josef
Tracks and Trailcraft
  Jaeger, Ellsworth
Tracks and Trails
  Rossell, Leonard
Traditions of Hartwood
  Campbell, Charles A.
The Trail of the Buffalo
  Montgomery, Rutherford G.
Trails of an Alaskan Game Warden
  Trembly, Ray
Trails of an Alaskan Trapper
  Trembly, Ray
Trails of An Artist Naturalist
  Seton, Ernest Thompson
Trails of Enchantment
  Brandreth, Paul
Trails of the Hunted
  Clark, James Lippitt
Trails of a Wilderness Wanderer
  Russell, Andy
Trails To Successful Trapping
  Lynch, V. E.
Trails, Trout and Tigers
  Kelly, Robert G.
The Training and Care of the Versatile Hunting Dog
  Winterhelt, Sigbot
Training and Hunting the Brittany Spaniel
  Hammond, Ralph B.
The Training and Hunting of Hounds in the Field
  American Foxhound Club
Training Grouse and Woodcock Dogs
  Bennett, Logan J.
Training Gun Dogs To Retrieve
  Elliot, David D.
Training Pointers and Setters
  Maurice, J. B.
Training Pointing Dogs
  Long, Paul
Training Retrievers
  Shoemaker, Paul E.
Training Retrievers To Handle
  Walters, D. L.
Training Setters and Pointers For Trials
  Beazley, John
Training the Bird Dog
  Whitford, C. B.
Training the Hunting Retriever
  Cofield, Thomas R.

The Winchester Book
    Madis, George
Winchester Commemoratives
    Trolard, Tom
The Winchester 1873 Handbook
    Stone, George W.
The Winchester Era
    Madis, George
The Winchester Handbook
    Madis, George
Winchester Hunter's Handbook, 1972 - 1973
    Kozicky, Edward
The Winchester Model 12
    Madis, George
Winchester Rifles and Shotguns
    Watrous, George R.
Winchester '73, '76
    Butler, David F.
Winchester Shotguns and Shotshells
    Stadt, Ronald W.
Winchester, The Gun That Won the West
    Williamson, Harold
The Wind and the Caribou
    Munsterhjelm, Erik
The Wind Birds
    Matthiessen, Peter
The Wind on Your Cheek
    Schaldach, William J.
Wing and Shot
    Wehle, Robert G.
Wing and Trap Shooting
    Askins, Charles, Sr.
Wing and Trap Shooting
    Askins, Charles, Jr.
Wing Shooting
    Askins, Charles, Sr.
Wing Shooting and Angling
    Connett, Eugene V., 3rd
Wing Shooting, Trap and Skeet
    Robinson, Jimmy
Wing Shots
    Simmons, Albert Dixon
The Wingless Crow
    Fergus, Charles
Wings at Dusk
    Murphey, Eugene Edmund
Wings, Fur and Shot
    Vale, Robert B.
Wings in the Blue
    Boardman, Edwin A.
Wings in the Wilderness
    Cruickshank, Allan
The Wings of Dawn
    Reiger, George

Wings Over the Marshes
    Ross, Robert E.
Wings, Water and Dogs
    Pidcock, Jane Rainaud
The Winter of the Fisher
    Langford, Cameron
Wisconsin Fox Populations
    Richards, S. H.
Wisconsin Grouse Problems
    Grange, Wallace B.
Wisconsin Pheasant Populations
    Buss, Irven O.
Wisconsin Sideroads To Somewhere
    Schoenfeld, Clay
The Witchery of Archery
    Thompson, J. Maurice
With Both Eyes Open
    Bonner, Paul Hyde
With Dog and Canoe
    Wallace, Dillon
The Wolf
    Mech, L. David
Wolf and Coyote Trapping
    Harding, A. R.
Wolf and Man
    Hall, Roberta A.
Wolf Control Operations: Wood Buffalo
National Park, 1951 - 1952
    Fuller, William A.
Wolf Country
    Clarkson, Ewan
Wolf Depredation on Livestock in Minnesota
    Fritts, Steven H.
Wolf Ecology and Prey Relationships on Isle
Royale
    Peterson, Rolf Olin
The Wolf in North American History
    Young, Stanley P.
The Wolf in the Southwest
    Brown, David E.
Wolf Predation in the North Country
    Callison, I. P.
The Wolves at Cooking Lake
    McClintock, Gray
Wolves, Bears and Bighorns
    Crawford, John S.
Wolves in Canada and Alaska
    Carbyn, Ludwig N.
The Wolves of Isle Royale
    Mech, L. David
Wolves of Minong
    Allen, Durward L.
The Wolves of Mt. McKinley
    Murie, Adolph

The Wolves of North America
 Young, Stanley P.
The Wolves of Yellowstone
 Weaver, John
The Women's Guide To Handguns
 Carmichael, Jim
The Wonderful World of Gunning Waterfowl
 Eley, Howard Clifton
Wonders of Geese and Swans
 Fegely, Thomas D.
Wonders of the Pronghorn
 Chace, Earl G.
Wonders of Wild Ducks
 Fegely, Thomas D.
The Wood Duck in Louisiana
 Bateman, Hugh
The Wood Duck in Massachusetts
 Grice, David
Wood Duck Management and Research
 Wildlife Management Institute
Wood Duck Research in Massachusetts, 1970 - 1980
 Heusmann, H. W.
Wood Ducks in Alabama
 Beshears, W. Walter
The Woodchuck Hunter
 Estey, Paul C.
Woodchucks and Woodchuck Rifles
 Landis, Charles S.
Woodcock
 Knight, John Alden
Woodcock
 Russell, Dan
Woodcock and Snipe
 Seigne, J. W.
The Woodcock Book
 Evans, George Bird
Woodcock Ecology and Management
 United States Department of the Interior
Woodcock Status Report
 Clark, Eldon R.
Woodcock Ways
 Hall, Henry Marion
Woodland, Field and Waterfowl Hunting
 Robinson, Ben C.
Woodland Tales
 Seton, Ernest Thompson
The Woodmont Story
 Bridges, Harry P.
Woods and Lakes of Maine
 Hubbard, Lucius L.
Woods and River Tales
 Haig-Brown, Roderick
The Woods and the Sea
 Lunt, Dudley C.

Woods and Waters
 Street, Alfred B.
The Woods and Wild Things I Remember
 Rutledge, Archibald
Woods With Sketches and Stories
 Robinson, Rowland E.
Woodsmoke
 Jaeger, Ellsworth
Uncle Dick Wooten
 Conrad, Howard Louis
The Workers in the Wilds
 Dugmore, A. Radclyffe
Working Bibliography of the Owls of the World
 Clark, Richard J.
Working Decoy Plans
 Murphy, Charles F.
Working Decoy Plans For Working Decoys
 Murphy, Charles F.
The Working Retriever
 Quinn, Tom
The World of Guns
 Akehurst, Richard
The World of Guns
 Mann, E. B.
The World of the American Elk
 Van Wormer, Joe
The World of the Beaver
 Rue, Leonard, Lee, III
The World of the Bison
 Park, Ed
The World of the Black Bear
 Van Wormer, Joe
The World of the Bobcat
 Van Wormer, Joe
The World of the Canada Goose
 Van Wormer, Joe
The World of the Coyote
 Van Wormer, Joe
The World of the Gray Squirrel
 Barkalow, F. S.
The World of the Great Horned Owl
 Austing, G. Ronald
The World of the Grizzly Bear
 Schoonmaker, W. J.
The World of the Moose
 Van Wormer, Joe
The World of the Opossum
 Keefe, James F.
The World of the Otter
 Park, Ed
The World of the Polar Bear
 Larsen, Thor
The World of the Polar Bear
 Perry, Richard

References Cited

The following out-of-print sporting book dealer catalogs have been used as sources of information for this compilation: Adams Angling Books; Kenneth Anderson; Angler's and Shooter's Bookshelf; Armchair Angler; Gary Backman; Matthew Biscotti & Company; Robin Bledsoe; Judith Bowman Books; Callahan & Co.; Classic Arms Books; James Cummins Books; Dale's Decoy Den; Dutchman Books; Gary Estabrook; Fair Chase, Inc.; Fin n' Feather Gallery; David Foley; Gunnerman Books; Jim Hodgson Books; Theodore Holsten; The Inquisitive Sportsman; Just Good Books; Melvin Marcher; Frank Mikesh; W. R. Olmsted Sporting Books; Pisces and Capricorn Books; Kathleen Rais & Company; L. & T. Respess Books; Seven Gables Bookshop; John Valle.

Books used:

Abbott, Henry
   The Birch Bark Books of Henry Abbott.   Harrison, NY, 1980, Harbor Hill Books.

Berra, Tim M.
   William Beebe; an annotated bibliography.   Hamden, Connecticut, 1977, Archon Books.

Biscotti, M. L.
   The Borzoi Books For Sportsmen.   Madison, Ohio, 1992, Sunrise Publishing Company.
   American Sporting Book Series.   Austinburg, Ohio, 1994, Sunrise Publishing Company.

Bruns, Henry P.
   Angling Books of the Americas.   Atlanta, 1975, Anglers Press.

Callahan, J. Kenneth
   A Dictionary of Sporting Pen Names.   Peterborough, New Hampshire, 1995, Callahan & Company, Booksellers.

Crouch, Donald
   Carl Rungius; the complete prints.   Missoula, Montana, 1989, Mountain Press Publishing Co.

Farley, G. M.
   An Annotated Zane Grey Checklist.   Mattituck, New York, 1988, Ameron House.

Foster, Hugh
　　Someone of Value: A Biography of Robert Ruark.　Agoura, California, 1992, Trophy Room Books.

Frazier, Don
　　Recognizing Derrydale Books.　Morristown, New Jersey, 1983, Privately printed.

Hand, Richard A.
　　A Bookman's Guide To Hunting, Shooting, Angling, and Related Subjects.　Metuchen, New Jersey, 1991, Scarecrow Press.

Heller, Morris
　　American Hunting and Fishing Books.　Mesilla, New Mexico, 1997, Wild Sheep and Goat International.

Higginson, A. Henry
　　British and American Sporting Authors; their writings and biographies. Berryville, Virginia, 1949, Blue Ridge Press.

Jones, E. Gwynne
　　A Bibliography of the Dog; books published in the English language, 1570 - 1965.　London, 1971, The Library Association.

Lake, Fred and Hal Wright
　　A Bibliography of Archery.　Manchester, England, 1974, The Simon Archery Foundation.

Lippincott, Bill and Nancy Lippincott
　　Arthur R. MacDougall, Jr., Maine Author; a bibliography. Farmington, Maine, 1983, University of Maine.

Oelgart, Isaac J.
　　Falconry and Hawking Treatises Printed in the English Language. Newburryport, Massachusetts, 1976, New Mews Press.

Olendorff, Richard R. and Sharon E. Olendorff
　　An Extensive Bibliography of Falconry, Eagles, Hawks, Falcons, and Other Diurnal Birds of Prey.　Fort Collins, Colorado, 1968, Privately printed.

Phillips, John C.
　　American Game Mammals and Birds.　Boston, 1930, Houghton Mifflin Company.

Podeschi, John B.
Books on the Horse and Horsemanship; riding, hunting, breeding and racing, 1400 - 1941. New Haven, Connecticut, 1981, The Tate Gallery For the Yale Center For British Art.

Reiger, John F.
American Sportsmen and the Origins of Conservation. New York, 1975, Winchester Press.

Riling, Raymond L. J.
Guns and Shooting; a selected chronological bibliography. New York, 1951, Greenberg: Publishers.

Siegel, Col. Henry A., et al.
The Derrydale Press; a bibliography. Goshen, Connecticut, 1981, The Angler's And Shooter's Press.

Smith, Brian R.
Samworth Books; a descriptive bibliography. Luke, Maryland, 1990, The Marksman's Bookshelf.

Wegner, Robert
Wegner's Bibliography on Deer and Deer Hunting. DeForest, Wisconsin, 1992, St. Hubert's Press.

Wetzel, Charles M.
American Fishing Books. Newark, 1950, Privately printed in an edition limited to 200 numbered copies.

Zemple, Edward N. and Linda A. Verkler, editors
First Editions; a guide to identifications. Third edition. Peoria, Illinois, 1995, Spoon River Press.